Psychotherapy and Counseling

Techniques in Intervention

Second Edition

Edited by

William S. Sahakian
Suffolk University

Houghton Mifflin Company/Boston
Dallas   Geneva, Ill.   Hopewell, N.J.   Palo Alto   London

*Dedicated to
DR. JOSEPH SAHAKIAN,
brother, friend, and interesting
companion*

Contents

Preface/xv

Acknowledgments/xvii

PART ONE

DYNAMIC AND PSYCHOANALYTIC APPROACHES

1   Psychoanalysis/2
SIGMUND FREUD
The First Axiom of Psychoanalytic Therapy. *The Unconscious as the Cause of Symptoms.* Catharsis and Abreaction. Free Association, Resistance, and Repression. *Free Association and Resistance. Repression. Symptom-Formation.* Etiological Factors in Neurosis. *Fixation. Regression and Repression. Frustration and Symptom Formation. Frustration and Sublimation.* Psychoanalytic Therapy and Transference. *The Dynamics of Therapy. Transference. Psychoanalysis and Hypnosis. The Libido and Symptom Dissolution.* Dream Analysis and Interpretation. Personality Theory and Mental Illness. *Personality Development and the Oedipus Complex. Id, Primary Process, and Instincts (Eros and Thanatos). Ego and Reality Principle. Superego and Conscience. A Theory of Neurosis and Psychosis.*

2   Individual Psychology Therapy/43
ALFRED ADLER
Fundamental Principles for the Practive of Individual Psychology. Individual Psychology: Its Psychotherapeutic Technique. *Foundations of Individual Psychology's Therapy. The Counseling Session.* Life-Plan, Goal, and Finalism. Neurotic Striving for Superiority and Fictional Finalism. Organ Inferiority and the Neurotic Disposition. Neurotic Overcompensation and Lust for Superiority. The Nature and Cause of Neurosis. *The Arrangement of the Neurosis.* Psychotherapy of the Neurosis. *Psychotherapy of Compulsion-Neurosis.* Therapeutic Value of Early Memories and Dreams. Therapy as a Maternal Function. *Therapy Through Social Usefulness. Therapy Through Understanding.* Child Therapy. *Style of Life and the Law of Movement.* Questionnaire of Individual Psychology. *Adult Therapy. Questionnaire for Adults.*

3   Analytical Psychotherapy/80
CARL GUSTAV JUNG
Personality Theory. Fundamental Principles of Treatment. *Unsuccessful Attempts to Free Individuality from the Collective Psyche. Successful Method of Treatment.* The Transcendent Function in the Treatment of Neurosis. The Psychogenesis of Schizophrenia and Its Distinction from Neurosis. The Psychotherapeutic Value of Dreams. *The Compensatory Nature of Dreams. The Form of Dreams.* The Four Stages of Treatment. Transference. The Therapeutic Value of Abreaction. Word Association Method. Dialectical Method of Psychotherapy. *Individuation.* Periods of Consultation.

4   Will Therapy/115
OTTO RANK
Will Therapy: The Therapeutic Experience. The Basis of Will Therapy. *Will-to-Health.* Understanding, Denial, and Verbalizing. Love and Self-Acceptance. Will, Fate, and Self-Determination. The Therapist and Neurotic as Complementary Types. End Phase and Therapeutic Agent.

5   The Washington School: The Interpersonal Theory of Psychotherapy/123
HARRY STACK SULLIVAN
The Interpersonal Theory of Psychiatry. *A Psychiatry of Peoples.* The Psychiatric Interview. *Definition of the Psychiatric Interview.* Basic Concepts in the Psychiatric Interview. The Psychiatrist as a Participant Observer. Parataxic Distortion. Stages of the Psychiatric Interview. Theorem of Reciprocal Emotion. Patterns of Outcome of Interpersonal Situations.

6   Character Analysis Therapy/141
KAREN HORNEY
Horney's Theory of Neurosis. *The Cultural Basis of Neurosis: Intrapsychic Processes and Human Relations. Self-Idealization: The Pride System. The Real Self and the Idealized Self (Pride System). Character Analysis Compared with Psychoanalysis. Self-Actualization and Neurotic Self-Idealization.* Character Analysis Therapy. *The Therapeutic Process from the Patient's Standpoint. Defensiveness, Resistance, and the Status Quo. Obstructive Forces During Analysis: Neurotic Needs and Anxiety. Therapy through Self-Knowledge and Self-Realization. Intellectual Understanding and Emotional Experience. Reorientation in Reference to the Pride System, Values, and Goals.* Analysis and Synthesis: The Therapeutic Value of Constructive Forces. *Alienation of the Self.* Self-Idealization and Self-Realization: The Pride System and the Real Self.

PART TWO

LEARNING THEORY APPROACHES

7   Learning Theory Psychotherapy/168
JOHN DOLLARD, NEAL E. MILLER
Learning Theory and Neurosis. *Neurotic Conflict as the Cause of Misery and*

Stupidity. The Neurotic's Reduction of Conflict through Symptoms. Fundamentals of Learning Theory. *Extinction. Rate of Extinction. Spontaneous Recovery. Gradient of Generalization. Discrimination. Gradient in the Effects of Reinforcement. Anticipatory Response.* Fear as a Learned Drive and Fear Reduction as a Reinforcement. *Functional Definitions of Stimulus and Response. Innate Factors in Fear. Reinforcement of Fear. Extinction of Fear. Responses Inhibiting Fear. Fear as a Cue and Learned Generalization. How Fear Functions.* Higher Mental Processes. *Cue-Producing Responses. Role of Cue-Producing Responses in Higher Mental Processes. Social Training and the Higher Mental Processes.* Neurosis as Learned. *Social Conditions for the Learning of Neurosis.* Symptoms as Learned. *Phobias. Hysterical Symptoms. Regression. Displacement. Rationalization. Hallucinations. Projection.* Repression as Learned. Main Factors in Therapy. Selecting Patients Who Can Learn. Free Association. Transference as a Generalized Response. Labeling. *Three Methods by Which Patients Learn New Verbal Responses.* Teaching the Patient New Discriminations. Gains from Restoring the Higher Mental Processes. Eradicating Symptoms. *Eliminating Symptoms by Eliciting Strong Incompatible Responses. Increased Repression and Inhibition. Effects of Supportive Therapy. Removal of Inhibition and Repression.* Techniques of Therapeutic Intervention. *Reward and Punishment: Approval and Disapproval. Permissiveness: Failing to Criticize or Show Alarm as a Powerful Intervention. Sympathetic Interest and Understanding. Reassurance.* Motivating the Patient to Continue Therapy. Prerequisites of a Psychotherapist. *Mental Freedom. Empathy. Restraint. Positive Outlook.* Confronting Failure in Psychotherapy.

8   Psychotherapy as Modeling and Vicarious Processes/206
ALBERT BANDURA
Behavior Modification through Modeling and Vicarious Processes. *Three Effects of Modeling Influences.* No Trial Learning Therapy. *Attentional Processes.* Retention Processes and Rehearsal Operations. Symbolic Representations of Modeled Patterns. *Incentive and Motivational Processes. Establishment of New Response Patterns through Modeling.* Treatment of Autism through Modeling. Vicarious Extinction. Vicarious Learning.

9   Psychotherapy by Reciprocal Inhibition/213
JOSEPH WOLPE
Learning Theory as the Basis of Behavior Therapy. *Positive Reconditioning. Experimental Extinction.* Assertive Training. *Preliminary Measures. Instigating Assertive Behavior. Behavior Rehearsal.* Systematic Desensitization. *The Formal Basis of Systematic Desensitization. General Statement of Desensitization Paradigm. The Technique of Systematic Desensitization.* Aversion Therapy. *Description of Techniques.*

10   Interference Theory: Assertion-Structured Therapy/234
E. LAKIN PHILLIPS
The Nature of Assertion-Structured Psychotherapy. Interference Theory of Psychotherapy. *A Case Study. Characteristics of Assertion-Structured Therapy.* Precepts of Assertion-Structured Therapy. Learning Theory in Assertion-Structured Therapy. Writing Therapy.

PART THREE

COGNITIVE APPROACHES TO PSYCHOTHERAPY

11   Logotherapy/250
VIKTOR E. FRANKL
The Meaning of Logotherapy. *The Existential Vacuum. Logotherapy and Noology. Self-Transcendence and Noodynamics.* Will-to-Meaning. Existential Frustration. Noetic Therapy. Logotherapy. *Dereflection, Hyperintention, and Hyperreflection. Paradoxical Intention and Anticipatory Anxiety. Self-Detachment.* Paradoxical Intention as a Principal Logotherapeutic Technique. *Counterindications.*

12   Rational-Emotive Psychotherapy/272
ALBERT ELLIS
Rational-Emotive Psychotherapy Defined. The Rational-Emotive Orientation. The Cognitive Aspect of the Theory. Behavioristic Techniques of Rational-EmotiveTherapy. *Emotive Release.* RET as the Application of Logic and Scientific Method. Validation of Rational-Emotive Psychotherapy. Applications of Rational-Emotive Psychotherapy. Characteristics of RET.

13   Philosophical Psychotherapy/286
WILLIAM S. SAHAKIAN
Philosophical Background of the Theory. Philosophical Psychotherapy Defined. The Character of Philosophical Psychotherapy. *The Effectiveness of Philosophical Psychotherapy.* Technique of Philosophical Psychotherapy. Case Studies. *Case One. Case Two.* Conclusion. Philosophical Psychotherapy: An Existential Approach. *The Nature of Existential Psychotherapy. Objective of Existential Psychotherapy. Characteristics of Existential Psychotherapy.* Case Studies. *Case One (Illustrating Being-of-the Future). Case Two (Illustrating Choice, Decision, and Authenticity).* Summary.

14   Morita Therapy:
Zen Buddhism Applied to Psychotherapy/303
SHOMA MORITA
The Origin and Development of Morita Therapy. Morita's Theory of "Nervosity," Classification and Statistics of Nervosity. *Ordinary Nervosity (So-called Neurasthenia). Paroxysmal Neurosis (Anxiety Neurosis). Obsession (Phobia).* Principles of Morita Therapy. *Contradiction of Thought. Realization and Understanding. Obedience to Nature.* Practice of Morita Therapy. *Four Stages of Treatment in the Hospital.* Recovery by Morita Therapy. Criticism of Morita Therapy.

15   Reality Therapy/324
WILLIAM GLASSER
Facing Reality. The Need to be Cared for. Two Basic Needs: To Love and be Loved. Responsibility. Procedures of Reality Therapy. Characteristics of Reality Therapy. Synopsis of Reality Therapy.

16   Gestalt Psychotherapy/330
FREDERICK S. PERLS, RALPH F. HEFFERLINE, PAUL GOODMAN
Gestalt Personality Development. *Interaction of Organism and Environment. The Subject Matter of Psychology. Definition of Psychology and Abnormal Psychology. The Figure of Contact against the Ground of the Organism/Environment Field. Therapy as Gestalt-Analysis. Destroying as Part of Figure/Background Formation. Contact is "Finding and Making" the Coming Solution.* Fundamental Principles of Gestalt Therapy. *Gestalt Therapy and Psychoanalysis. Gestalt Therapy and Gestalt Psychology. Psychology of the "Conscious" and "Unconscious." Reintegration of the Psychologies of the "Conscious" and the "Unconscious." Fundamental Gestalt Concepts. The Contextual Method of Argument. The Contextual Method Applied to Theories of Psychotherapy. Creative Adjustment: The Structure of Art-Working and Children's Play. Creative Adjustment: In General. Creative Adjustment: "Organismic Self-Regulation. Creative Adjustment: The Function of "Self."* Some Differences in General Therapeutic Attitude. The Self: Ego, Id, and Personality. *Self as the System of Present Contacts and the Agent of Growth. Self as Actualization of the Potential.* Neurosis as the Loss of Ego-Functions. *The Figure/Background of Neurosis. Analysis of Neurosis: Loss of Ego-Functions.* Gestalt Therapy of the Neurosis. *Stratagem of Therapy of "Neurotic Characters." Mechanisms and "Characters" as Stages of Interruption of Creativity. The Moments of Interruption. Schematic Moments of Interruption. The Above Is Not a Typology of Neurotic Persons. Example of Reversing the Sequence of Fixations. Sense of Boundaries. Therapy of Boundaries. The Criterion.*

17   Constructive Alternativism Psychotherapy: Personal Construct Psychology/364
GEORGE A. KELLY
Psychology of Personal Constructs. *Fundamental Postulate and Corollaries. Formal Aspects of Constructs. Constructs Classified According to the Nature of Their Control Over Their Elements. General Diagnostic Constructs. Constructs Relating to Transition.* Constructive Alternativism Psychotherapy. *Psychotherapy as an Aid to Reconstruction. Personal Construct Psychotherapy as Experimental. Diagnostic Constructs and Control.* Fixed-Role Sketch Therapy.

PART FOUR

PHENOMENOLOGICAL AND EXISTENTIAL APPROACHES

18   Nondirective Counseling: Client-Centered Therapy/382
CARL R. ROGERS
Synopsis of Client-Centered Therapy. *Conditions of the Therapeutic Process. The Process of Therapy. Outcomes in Personality and Behavior. Comments on the Theory of Therapy. The Nature of Man.* Perfect Adjustment: The Fully Functioning Person. Nondirective Therapy. *The Character of Client-Centered Therapy. Characteristic Steps in Nondirective Counseling.* When Counseling is Indicated. The Therapeutic Relationship. *Limits to the Therapeutic Relationship. The Uniqueness of the Therapeutic Relationship.* The Superiority of Nondirective

over Directive Therapy. Releasing Expression. *The Free Release of Feeling.* The Achievement of Insight. The Closing Phases of Therapy. Personality Theory. *Postulated Characteristics of the Human Infant. The Development of the Self. The Need for Positive Regard. The Development of the Need for Self-Regard. The Development of Conditions of Worth. The Development of Incongruence Between Self and Experience. The Development of Discrepancies in Behavior. The Experience of Threat and the Process of Defense. The Process of Breakdown and Disorganization. The Process of Reintegration.*

19   Existential Psychotherapy and Dasein Analysis/423
ROLLO MAY, LUDWIG BINSWANGER, HENRI F. ELLENBERGER
Existential Analysis. *Existential Philosophy. Existential Psychotherapy. Binswanger's Existential Analysis.* Existential Psychotherapy. *Implications of Existential Analysis for Psychotherapy.* Binswanger's Existential Psychotherapy. *The Patient's Life History as a Being-in-the-World. The Experience of the Fullness of One's Humanity. The Plane of Common Existence. Dreams as a Specific Way of Existing. Existential Therapy as the Understanding of the Structure of Human Existence.* Rollo May's Existential Psychotherapy. *Presence. The Aim of Therapy: The Patient's Experience of his Existence* (Dasein) *as Real. Commitment.*

20   Experiential or Nonrational Psychotherapy/449
CARL A. WHITAKER, THOMAS P. MALONE
Experiential/Nonrational Psychotherapy. Explicit Psychotherapy. Nongenetic Psychotherapy. The Process of Psychotherapy. *The Symbolic and the Real in Psychotherapy. The Loci of the Process. Disequilibrium Dynamics. Stages of the Interview Segment. Termination of Therapy. The Post-Interview. The Function of Re-repression.* Definition of Psychotherapeutic Technique.

PART FIVE

GROUP PSYCHOTHERAPY

21   Transactional Analysis Psychotherapy/472
ERIC BERNE
Synopsis of Transactional Analysis Psychotherapy. *Procedure. Introduction. Complete Diagnosis.* Analysis of Transactions. *Transactional Analysis.* Analysis of Games. *Pastimes. Games People Play.* Analysis of Scripts.

22   Group Psychotherapy and Psychodrama/486
J. L. MORENO
Spontaneity-Creativity. *Spontaneity, Anxiety, and the Moment. Spontaneity and Libido Theory Contrasted. Spontaneity-Creativity as the Essence of Personality.* Psychodrama. Sociodrama. Role Test and Role-Playing. Group Psychotherapy. Construction of the Sociometric Test. Directions for Sociometric Testing. The Sociometrist. Psychodrama versus Psychoanalysis. *Model. Objectivity and Neutrality of the Therapist. The Auxiliary Ego. Psychodrama à Deux. Ferenczi and Freud. The Problem of Control.* Glossary of Technical Terms.

23   **Analytic Group Psychotherapy/513**
      S. R. SLAVSON
      Group Psychotherapy. Activity Group Psychotherapy. Transitional Groups. Play
      Group Psychotherapy. Activity-Interview Group Psychotherapy. Analytic Group
      Psychotherapy. Para-Analytic Group Psychotherapy.

24   **Milieu Therapy: The Therapeutic Community/530**
      MAXWELL JONES, ROBERT N. RAPOPORT
      The Community as Doctor. The Formation of a Treatment Ideology. The Organi-
      zation of Staff Roles. The Organization of Patient Activities. The Involvement of
      Individuals Outside the Hospital in Treatment. The Conceptualization of Treat-
      ment and Rehabilitation. The Therapeutic Community.

25   **The Encounter Group/568**
      CARL R. ROGERS
      The Group Process. *Milling Around. Resistance to Personal Expression or Explo-
      ration. Description of Past Feelings. Expression of Negative Feelings. Expression
      and Exploration of Personally Meaningful Material. The Expression of Immediate
      Interpersonal Feelings in the Group. The Development of a Healing Capacity in
      the Group. Self-Acceptance and the Beginning of Change. The Cracking of
      Facades. The Individual Receives Feedback. Confrontation. The Helping Rela-
      tionship outside the Group Sessions. The Basic Encounter. The Expression of
      Positive Feelings and Closeness. Behavior Changes in the Group.*

26   **Conjoint Family Therapy/583**
      VIRGINIA SATIR
      Family Theory. Theory and Practice of Conjoint Family Therapy.

PART SIX

COUNSELING PSYCHOLOGY: EDUCATIONAL AND GUIDANCE COUNSELING

27   **Counseling Psychology/598**
      C. H. PATTERSON
      Counseling Psychology Defined. Characteristics of Counseling. The Counseling
      Relationship. The Counselor's Function. Vocational Counseling. Testing in Voca-
      tional Counseling. *Uses of Tests.* The Purpose of Tests in Guidance Counseling.
      Group Counseling and Individual Counseling.

28   **Counseling Psychology and the Counseling Relationship/609**
      EDWARD S. BORDIN
      The Counseling Relationship in Counseling Psychology. *Counseling Defined.* The
      Goal of Psychological Counseling. The Counselor's Initial Orientation. Clarifying

the Goal. Clarifying the Task. Meeting the Client's Initial Needs. The Diagnostic Potentialities of Initial Interviews. Process Issues in the Developmental Model. *Exploration and Contract Setting.*

PART SEVEN

HYNOPTIC TECHNIQUE IN PSYCHOTHERAPY

29   Hypnotherapy/624
LEWIS R. WOLBERG
The Technic of Hypnosis. *Susceptibility to Hypnosis. Suggestibility Tests. The Depth of Trance.* The First Hypnotic Session. The Second Hypnotic Session. *Trance Management in Resistive Patients. Increasing Trance Depth. Awakening the Patient.* Subsequent Hypnotic Sessions. *Continued Training in Trance Depth. Conditioning the Trance to a Given Signal. Administration of Therapeutic Suggestions. Hypnoanalytic Procedures.* Self-Hypnosis and Group Hypnosis. Hypnosis in Anxiety Neurosis. Hypnosis in Conversion Hysteria. Hypnosis in Anxiety Hysteria. Hypnosis in Compulsion Neurosis. Hypnosis in Traumatic Neurosis. Hypnosis in Psychosomatic Conditions. Hypnosis in Character Disorders. Hypnosis in Alcoholism. Hypnosis in Psychosis. Hypnosis in Miscellaneous Conditions.

Name Index/645

Subject Index/649

Preface

The *raison d'être* of this book is to make accessible in a single volume the salient portions of the major works of the principal contributors to the development of psychotherapy. The book possesses a dual value: that of introducing the novice to the wealth of contributions of those psychotherapists who have distinguished themselves in this field, and that of providing the professional with the opportunity of a comparative and evaluative study of the foremost systems of psychotherapy. This volume affords the opportunity to examine a variety of psychotherapeutic systems in the light of their similar accentuations, variant inflections, issues of disagreement and contradiction, and diverse fundamental approaches. One has only to consider the students freshly introduced to and stimulated by the wealth of information at their fingertips here, to envision the contagion of their enthusiasm captivating the seasoned professional as well.

The study of psychotherapy has passed beyond the stage of treating a single system in a course of study—whether that system be psychoanalysis or client-centered therapy. Today, in order to face the issue squarely and responsibly, one cannot avoid the careful examination and consideration of numerous contending systems.

Furthermore, in the area of psychotherapy, the value of a text lies not in its substitution for primary sources, but as a complement to a careful reading or perusal of such sources. Merely to expose the reader to secondary source material, as is often done in courses and classroom presentations, is to shortchange the student. With primary source material readily available in a convenient single volume, there is neither a satisfactory alternative to, nor a justification for not, allowing the student to experience a face-to-face encounter with Freud, Jung, Rogers, Frankl, Wolpe, and many others, speaking for themselves.

I would like to express my appreciation for the generous assistance favored me by the staff of reference librarians at the Francis A. Countway Library of Medicine (of the Harvard Medical School and Boston Medical Library), and also to my assistants at Suffolk University who devotedly worked on this project.

WILLIAM S. SAHAKIAN

Beacon Hill
Boston, Massachusetts

Acknowledgments

The editor wishes to credit the original publishers of the selections in this book and to express his gratitude to them, to the authors, and to the many other individuals and institutions who hold the copyrights, for their generosity and cooperation in making the source materials available to him.

Reprinted from *A General Introduction to Psychoanalysis* by Sigmund Freud, translated by Joan Riviere. By permission of Liveright Publishing Corp., New York, and George Allen & Unwin Ltd., London. Copyright renewed © 1963 by Joan Riviere.

Reprinted from *Studies on Hysteria* by Josef Breuer and Sigmund Freud, volume 11, in Standard Edition of THE COMPLETE PSYCHOLOGICAL WORKS OF SIGMUND FREUD, translated and edited by James Strachey, 1957. By permission of Basic Books, Inc., New York, and The Hogarth Press Ltd., London, Sigmund Freud Copyrights Ltd., the Institute of Psychoanalysis, and Mrs. Alix Strachey.

Reprinted from *An Outline of Psychoanalysis* by Sigmund Freud, volume 23, in Standard Edition of THE COMPLETE PSYCHOLOGICAL WORKS OF SIGMUND FREUD. Translated and newly edited by James Strachey. Copyright 1949 by W. W. Norton & Company, Inc. Copyright © 1969 by the Institute of Psychoanalysis and Alix Strachey. By permission of W. W. Norton & Company, Inc., New York, and The Hogarth Press Ltd., London.

Reprinted from *The Practice and Theory of Individual Psychology* by Alfred Adler, translated by P. Radin, 1929. By permission of Humanities Press Inc., New York, and Routledge & Kegan Paul Ltd., London.

Reprinted from *Social Interest: A Challenge to Mankind* by Alfred Adler, translated by John Linton and Richard Vaughn, 1938. Reprinted by permission of Sanford Jerome Greenburger, New York, and David Higham Associates, Ltd., London.

Reprinted from *What Life Should Mean to You* by Alfred Adler, 1931. By permission of Sanford Jerome Greenburger, New York.

Reprinted from *Problems of Neurosis: A Book of Case Histories* by Alfred Adler, 1929. By permission of the publisher, Routledge & Kegan Paul Ltd., London.

Reprinted from *Two Essays on Analytical Psychology,* volume 7, in THE COLLECTED WORKS OF C. G. JUNG, Bollingen Series XX, translated by R. F. C. Hull and edited by G. Adler, M. Fordham, and H. Read, copyright 1953 and © 1966 by Bollingen Foundation. Reprinted by permission of Princeton University Press, and Routledge & Kegan Paul Ltd., London.

Reprinted from *The Structure and Dynamics of the Psyche,* volume 8, in THE COLLECTED WORKS OF C. G. JUNG, Bollingen Series XX, translated by R. F. C. Hull and edited by G. Adler, M. Fordham, and H. Read, copyright © 1960 by Bollingen Foundation and copyright © 1969 by Princeton University Press. Reprinted by permission of Princeton University Press, and Routledge & Kegan Paul Ltd., London.

Reprinted from *The Psychogenesis of Mental Disease,* volume 3, in THE COLLECTED WORKS OF C. G. JUNG, Bollingen Series XX, translated by R. F. C. Hull and edited by G. Adler, M. Fordham, and H. Read, copyright © 1960 by Bollingen Foundation. Reprinted by permission of Princeton University Press, and Routledge & Kegan Paul Ltd., London.

Reprinted from *The Practice of Psychotherapy,* volume 16, in THE COLLECTED WORKS OF C. G. JUNG, Bollingen Series XX, translated by R. F. C. Hull and edited by G. Adler, M. Fordham, and H. Read, copyright 1954 and © 1966 by Bollingen Foundation. Reprinted by permission of Princeton University Press and Routledge & Kegan Paul Ltd., London.

Reprinted from *Will Therapy and Truth and Reality* by Otto Rank, translated by Jessie Taft. Copyright 1936 and renewed 1964 by Alfred A. Knopf, Inc., New York. Reprinted by permission of the publisher.

Reprinted from *Psychiatry* (1948) and from *The Fusion of Psychiatry and Social Science* by Harry Stack Sullivan, M.D., with introduction and commentaries by Helen Swick Perry. Copyright © 1964 by The William Alanson White Psychiatric Foundation. Reprinted by permission of W. W. Norton & Company, Inc., New York.

Reprinted from *The Interpersonal Theory of Psychiatry* by Harry Stack Sullivan, M.D., edited by Helen Swick Perry and Mary Ladd Gawel, with an introduction by Mabel Blake Cohen, M.D. Copyright 1953 by The William Alanson White Psychiatric Foundation. Reprinted by permission of W. W. Norton & Company, Inc., New York.

Reprinted from *The Psychiatric Interview* by Harry Stack Sullivan, M.D., edited by Helen Swick Perry and Mary Ladd Gawel, with an introduction by Otto Allen Will, M.D. Copyright 1954 by The William Alanson White Psychiatric Foundation. Reprinted by permission of W. W. Norton & Company, Inc., New York.

Reprinted from *Neurosis and Human Growth* by Karen Horney, M.D. Copyright 1950 by W. W. Norton & Company, Inc. By permission of W. W. Norton & Company, Inc., New York, and Routledge & Kegan Paul Ltd., London.

Reprinted from *Personality and Psychotherapy* by John Dollard and Neal E. Miller. Copyright 1950 by McGraw-Hill Book Company, New York. Used by permission of the publisher.

Reprinted from *Principles of Behavior Modification* by Albert Bandura, 1969. By permission of the publisher, Holt, Rinehart and Winston.

Reprinted from *The Practice of Behavior Therapy* by Joseph Wolpe, 1974. By permission of Pergamon Press, Inc. and Joseph Wolpe, M.D.

Reprinted from E. Lakin Phillips, *Psychotherapy: A Modern Theory and Practice* © 1956. Reprinted by permission of Prentice-Hall, Inc., Englewood Cliffs, N.J.

Reprinted from *Short-Term Psychotherapy and Structured Behavior Change* by E. Lakin Phillips and Daniel W. Wiener. Copyright 1966 by McGraw-Hill Book Company, New York. Used with permission of McGraw-Hill Book Company, New York.

Reprinted from "Psychiatry and Man's Quest for Meaning" by Viktor E. Frankl, in *Journal of Religion and Health* (1962). By permission of the Academy of Religion and Mental Health, New York.

Reprinted from "The Spiritual Dimension in Existential Analysis and Logotherapy" by Viktor E. Frankl, in *Journal of Individual Psychology* (1959). By permission of the publisher, University of Vermont, Burlington.

Reprinted from "Logotherapy and Existential Analysis—A Review" by Viktor E. Frankl, in *American Journal of Psychotherapy* (1966). By permission of the Association for the Advancement of Psychotherapy, Lancaster, Pa.

Reprinted from "Paradoxical Intention: A Logotherapeutic Technique" by Viktor E. Frankl, in *American Journal of Psychotherapy* (1960). By permission of the Association for the Advancement of Psychotherapy, Lancaster, Pa.

Reprinted from "Philosophical Psychotherapy" by William S. Sahakian, in *Psychologia* (1974). By permission of the Psychologia Society.

Reprinted from "Stoic Philosophical Psychotherapy" by William S. Sahakian, in *Journal of Individual Psychology* (1969). By permission of the Journal of Individual Psychology.

Reprinted from "A Psychotherapy of Neurosis" by Momoshige Miura and Shinichi Usa, in *Psychologia*, 3 (1970). By permission of the Psychologia Society. Originally reprinted from *Yonago Acta Medica* 14 (1970), organ of the School of Medicine, Tottori University, Yonago City, Tottori Prefecture.

Abridged from pp. 6, 7, 9, 13, 21, 27–28, 45–46 in *Reality Therapy: A New Approach to Psychiatry* by William Glasser. Copyright © 1965 by William Glasser. By permission of Harper & Row, Publishers, Inc.

Reprinted from "Reality Therapy" by William Glasser and Leonard Zunin, in *Current Psychotherapies*, edited by Raymond Corsini, 1973. Reproduced by permission of the publisher, F. E. Peacock Publishers, Inc., Itasca, Illinois.

Reprinted from *Gestalt Therapy* by Frederick Perls, Ralph Hefferline, and Paul Goodman, 1951. By permission of The Julian Press, Inc., New York.

Reprinted from *The Psychology of Personal Costructs*, volumes 1 and 2, by George A. Kelly, Ph.D. Copyright 1955 by George A. Kelly. Reprinted by permission of the publisher, W. W. Norton & Company, Inc., New York.

Reprinted from "A Theory of Therapy, Personality, and Interpersonal Relationships as Developed in the Client-Centered Framework" by Carl R. Rogers, in *Psychology: A Study of a Science*, volume 3, edited by Sigmund Koch. Copyright 1959 by McGraw-Hill Book Company, New York. Used by permission of McGraw-Hill Book Company.

Reprinted from *Counseling and Psychotherapy* by Carl R. Rogers. Copyright 1942 by Carl R. Rogers. Reprinted by permission of the publisher, Houghton Mifflin Company, Boston.

Reprinted from *Existence: A New Dimension in Psychiatry and Psychology*, edited by Rollo May, Ernest Angel, and Henri F. Ellenberger, © 1958 by Basic Books, Inc., Publishers, New York.

Reprinted from "Existential Analysis and Psychotherapy" by Ludwig Binswanger, in *Progress in Psychotherapy*, volume 1, edited by Frieda Fromm-Reichmann and J. L. Moreno, 1956. By permission of Grune & Stratton, Inc., New York.

Reprinted from "Rational and Nonrational Psychotherapy" by Thomas P. Malone, Carl A. Whitaker, John Warkentin, and Richard E. Felder, in *American Journal of Psychotherapy* (1961). By permission of the editor, New York.

Reprinted from *The Roots of Psychotherapy* by Carl A. Whitaker and Thomas P. Malone. Copyright 1953 by The Blakiston Company. Used with permission of McGraw-Hill Book Company.

Reprinted from *Transactional Analysis in Psychotherapy*, by Eric Berne, 1961. By permission of Grove Press, Inc., New York. Copyright © 1961 by Eric Berne, and Souvenir Press, Ltd., London.

Reprinted from *Who Shall Survive: Foundations of Sociometry, Group Psychotherapy and Sociodrama* by J. L. Moreno, 1953. By permission of Beacon House, Inc., Beacon, N.Y., and the author.

Reprinted from *Psychodrama: Foundations of Psychotherapy*, volume 2, 1959, by J. L. Moreno. By permission of Beacon House, Inc., Beacon, N.Y., and the author.

Reprinted from *Child Psychotherapy* by S. R. Slavson, 1952. By permission of Columbia University Press, New York.

Reprinted from *A Textbook in Analytic Group Psychotherapy* by S. R. Slavson, 1964. By permission of International Universities Press, Inc., New York, and the author; permission covers pages 473–81 of this volume.

Reprinted from *Community as Doctor: New Perspectives on a Therapeutic Community* by Robert N. Rapoport, 1960. By permission of the author.

Reprinted from *The Therapeutic Community: A New Treatment Method in Psychiatry* by Maxwell Jones and associates, © 1953 by Basic Books, Inc., Publishers, New York. By permission of Basic Books, Inc. and Routledge & Kegan Paul Ltd., London.

Reprinted from "The Process of the Basic Encounter Group" by Carl R. Rogers, in *Challenges of Humanistic Psychology*, edited by James F. Bugental. Copyright © 1967 by McGraw-Hill Inc. Used with permission of McGraw-Hill Book Company.

Reprinted by permission of the author and the publisher from Virginia Satir. *Conjoint Family Therapy*. Rev. ed. Palo Alto, California: Science and Behavior Books, 1967.

Reprinted from *An Introduction to Counseling in the School* by C. H. Patterson. Copyright © 1971 by C. H. Patterson. By permission of Harper & Row, Publishers, Inc.

Reprinted from *Psychological Counseling*, 2nd ed. by Edward S. Bordin. © 1968, pp. 10, 11, 12, 221–31, 429–32. By permission of Prentice-Hall, Inc., Englewood Cliffs, New Jersey.

Reprinted from *The Principles of Hypnotherapy*, volume I in MEDICAL HYPNOSIS, by Lewis R. Wolberg, 1948. By permission of Grune & Stratton, Inc., New York, and the author.

PART ONE

Dynamic and Psychoanalytic Approaches

PSYCHOANALYSIS

Sigmund Freud

Sigmund Freud (1856–1939) was born of Jewish parentage in Moravia. At the age of seventeen he entered the University of Vienna, where he planned for a career in medicine, specializing in physiology. His publications began to appear when he was only twenty-one years old. From 1876 to 1882 he worked under Brücke at the latter's physiological laboratory. He earned an M.D. degree in 1881. In 1882 Freud, for financial reasons, left Brücke's physiological laboratory and entered General Hospital, Vienna's principal hospital, where he became an "aspirant" and later a junior resident physician, enjoying direction under the reputed Meynert.

Freud's clinical publications earned him an appointment as lecturer in neuropathology in 1885, and shortly afterward he was awarded a traveling fellowship which enabled him to visit Paris. During Freud's student days at Salpêtrière he had established an acquaintance with Charcot, from whom he learned of the validity of hysterical phenomena. From Joseph Breuer, whom Freud had met at Brücke's Institute of Physiology in the 1870s, he learned of the "talking cure," abreaction, and catharsis.

In 1886, Freud, then thirty, married and settled down in Vienna. He set up a medical practice, specializing in nervous diseases. From 1886 to 1891 he engaged in little scientific study or publication as he sought to establish his private practice, seemingly a fruitless endeavor. As late as 1900 he had no new cases for eight months.

Freud's academic career had begun in 1883 at the University of Vienna, where he was docent. In 1902 he was promoted to the rank of associate professor through the intercession of an influential female patient. But it was not until 1920 that he achieved full professorship, a rank that he held until 1938.

The Freudian movement gained momentum after 1906, when the Swiss, Jung and Bleuler, took an interest in psychoanalysis. In 1908 the first congress of the Vienna Psychoanalytical Society took place in Salzburg, and the First International Psychoanalytical Congress was held in Nuremberg in 1910. The movement gained international stature when Jung was appointed the first president of the International Psychoanalytic Society, and Freud was invited to deliver a series of lectures at Clark University. These lectures were subsequently published as "The Origin and Development of Psychoanalysis" in the *American Journal of Psychology* 21 (1910) : 181–218. During the years 1911–13, both Jung and Adler dissociated themselves from Freudianism and founded their own schools of psychotherapy, named analytical psychology and individual psychology, respectively.

After the Nazi book burnings of 1933, which included Freud's books, he emigrated from Vienna to England, where he sought British citizenship. His death in London at the age of eighty-three was caused by cancer of the jaw.

Freudian psychotherapy, or psychoanalysis as Freud termed it, theorizes that neuroses are the result of unsatisfactory libidinal or sexual development, stemming from a polymorphous perverse childhood. The neurotic, owing to social taboos placed upon incest, represses his guilt-ridden, incestual experiences or fantasies transpiring during childhood, thus developing an Oedipus complex. Through *free association,* the neurotic must break down every resistance by recalling *(anamnesis)* every repressed thought and experience that is buried deep in the unconscious mind. As the patient audibly recites repressed experiences, intense emotional feelings *(abreactions)* are unleashed, indicative of the original emotional experience that was initially repressed. Thus an emotional cleansing or catharsis of the unconscious conflict is brought about.

During the process of psychoanalysis the patient establishes a rapport *(transference)* with the psychoanalyst that resembles an attachment of love for his therapist. This love transference is interpreted as the original love of the patient, as a child, for his mother *(object-cathexis).* The therapist, to whom this love is presently being transferred, now has the responsibility of dissolving the relationship by having the patient make suitable adjustments to life. Negative transferences (hostile relationships of patient to therapist) are indicative of narcissistic neuroses (paranoic and other psychoses). Transference neuroses (those that can be successfully treated by psychoanalysis) are phobias, hysteria, anxiety, and obsessive-compulsive neuroses.

The method of analysis is aided by dream interpretation; the understanding of the structure of personality of id, ego, and superego (conscience) in conflict; the stages of successful personality development or its periods of maladjustment of fixation and regression; the suppression and sublimation of instincts of life and death (eros and thanatos); and the manner in which the ego defends itself (mechanisms of defense).

Freud applied psychoanalysis to numerous fields including art, religion, humor, myth, literature, and history. His more influential books are: *Studies on Hysteria* (1895), *The Interpretation of Dreams* (1900), *Psychopathology of Everyday Life* (1904), *A General Introduction to Psychoanalysis* (1911–13), *Totem and Taboo* (1913), *Beyond the Pleasure Principle* (1920), *The Ego and the Id* (1923), *Inhibitions, Symptoms, and Anxiety* (1926), *Civilization and Its Discontents* (1930), *New*

Introductory Lectures on Psychoanalysis (1933), *An Autobiographical Study* (1935), *An Outline of Psychoanalysis* (1938), and *Moses and Monotheism* (1939). Freud's works have been collected and published as *The Standard Edition of the Complete Psychological Works of Sigmund Freud.*

The First Axiom of Psychoanalytic Therapy

The Unconscious as the Cause of Symptoms

Consider now, in addition, that the facts established . . . are confirmed in every symptom of every neurotic disease; that always and everywhere the meaning of the symptoms is unknown to the sufferer; that analysis invariably shows that these symptoms are derived from unconscious mental processes which can, however, under various favorable conditions, become conscious. You will then understand that we cannot dispense with the unconscious part of the mind in psychoanalysis, and that we are accustomed to deal with it as with something actual and tangible. Perhaps you will also be able to realize how unfitted all those who only know the unconscious as a phrase, who have never analysed, never interpreted dreams, or translated neurotic symptoms into their meaning and intention, are to form an opinion on this matter. I will repeat the substance of it again in order to impress it upon you: The fact that it is possible to find meaning in neurotic symptoms by means of analytic interpretation is an irrefutable proof of the existence—or, if you prefer it, of the necessity for assuming the existence—of unconscious mental processes.

But that is not all. Thanks to a second discovery of Breuer's, for which he alone deserves credit and which seems to me even more far-reaching in its significance than the first, more still has been learnt about the relation between the unconscious and the symptoms of neurotics. Not merely is the meaning of the symptom invariably unconscious; there exists also a connection of a substitutive nature between the two; the existence of the symptom is only possible by reason of this unconscious activity. You will soon understand what I mean. With Breuer, I maintain the following: Everytime we meet with a symptom we may conclude that definite unconscious activities which contain the meaning of the symptom are present in the patient's mind. Conversely, this meaning must be unconscious before a symptom can arise from it. Symptoms are not produced by conscious processes; as soon as the unconscious processes

The First Axiom of Psychoanalytic Therapy, from Sigmund Freud, *A General Introduction to Psychoanalysis,* trans. Joan Riviere (New York: Liveright, 1935), pp. 246–47.

involved are made conscious the symptom must vanish. You will perceive at once that here is an opening for therapy, a way by which symptoms can be made to disappear. It was by this means that Breuer actually achieved the recovery of his patient, that is, freed her from her symptoms; he found a method of bringing into her consciousness the unconscious processes which contained the meaning of her symptoms and the symptoms vanished. . . .

The symptom is formed as a substitute for something else which remains submerged. Certain mental processes would, under normal conditions, develop until the person became aware of them consciously. This has not happened; and, instead, the symptom has arisen out of these processes which have been interrupted and interfered with in some way and have had to remain unconscious. Thus something in the nature of an exchange has occurred; if we can succeed in reversing this process by our therapy we shall have performed our task of dispersing the symptom.

Breuer's discovery still remains the foundation of psychoanalytic therapy. The proposition that symptoms vanish when their unconscious antecedents have been made conscious has been borne out by all subsequent research, although the most extraordinary and unexpected complications are met with in attempting to carry this proposition out in practice. Our therapy does its work by transforming something unconscious into something conscious, and only succeeds in its work in so far as it is able to effect this transformation. . . .

Catharsis and Abreaction

A chance observation has led us, over a number of years, to investigate a great variety of different forms and symptoms of hysteria, with a view to discovering their precipitating cause—the event which provoked the first occurrence, often many years earlier, of the phenomenon in question. In the great majority of cases it is not possible to establish the point of origin by a simple interrogation of the patient, however thoroughly it may be carried out. This is in part because what is in question is often some experience which the patient dislikes discussing; but principally because he is genuinely unable to recollect it and often has no suspicion of the causal connection between the precipitating event and the pathological phenomenon. As a rule it is necessary to hypnotize the

Catharsis and Abreaction, from Joseph Breuer and Sigmund Freud, *Studies on Hysteria,* trans. James Strachey, in Standard Edition of THE COMPLETE PSYCHOLOGICAL WORKS OF SIGMUND FREUD, vol. 11, ed. James Strachey (London: Hogarth, 1955; New York: Basic Books, 1957), pp. 3, 6–11, 17.

patient and to arouse his memories under hypnosis of the time at which the symptom made its first appearance; when this has been done, it becomes possible to demonstrate the connection in the clearest and most convincing fashion. . . .

For we found, to our great surprise at first, that *each individual hysterical symptom immediately and permanently disappeared when we had succeeded in bringing clearly to light the memory of the event by which it was provoked and in arousing its accompanying affect, and when the patient had described that event in the greatest possible detail and had put the affect into words.* Recollection without affect almost invariably produces no result. The psychical process which originally took place must be repeated as vividly as possible; it must be brought back to its *status nascendi* and then given verbal utterance. Where what we are dealing with are phenomena involving stimuli (spasms, neuralgias and hallucinations) these reappear once again with the fullest intensity and then vanish forever. Failures of function, such as paralyses and anaesthesias, vanish in the same way, though, of course, without the temporary intensification being discernible. . . .

Hysterics suffer mainly from reminiscences. . . .

At first sight it seems extraordinary that events experienced so long ago should continue to operate so intensely—that their recollection should not be liable to the wearing away process to which, after all, we see all our memories succumb. The following considerations may perhaps make this a little more intelligible.

The fading of a memory or the losing of its affect depends on various factors. The most important of these is *whether there has been an energetic reaction to the event that provokes an affect.* By "reaction" we here understand the whole class of voluntary and involuntary reflexes—from tears to acts of revenge—in which, as experience shows us, the affects are discharged. If this reaction takes place to a sufficient amount a large part of the affect disappears as a result. Linguistic usage bears witness to this fact of daily observation by such phrases as "to cry oneself out" [*"sich ausweinen"*], and to "blow off steam" [*"sich austoben,"* literally "to rage oneself out"]. If the reaction is suppressed, the affect remains attached to the memory. An injury that has been repaid, even if only in words, is recollected quite differently from one that has had to be accepted. Language recognizes this distinction, too, in its mental and physical consequences; it very characteristically describes an injury that has been suffered in silence as "a mortification" [*"Kränkung,"* lit. "making ill"]. The injured person's reaction to the trauma only exercises a completely "cathartic" effect if it is an *adequate* reaction—as, for instance, revenge. But language serves as a substitute for action; by its help, an affect can be "abreacted" almost as effectively. In other cases, speaking is itself the adequate reflex, when, for instance, it is a lamentation or giving utterance to a tormenting secret, e.g., a confession. If there is no such reaction, whether in deeds or words, or in the mildest cases in tears, any recollection of the event retains its affective tone to begin with.

"Abreaction," however, is not the only method of dealing with the situation that is open to a normal person who has experienced a psychical trauma. A memory of such a trauma, even if it has not been abreacted, enters the great complex of associations, it comes alongside other experiences, which may contradict it, and is subjected to rectification by other ideas. After an accident, for instance, the memory of the danger and the (mitigated) repetition of the fright becomes associated with the memory of what happened afterwards—rescue and the consciousness of present safety. Again, a person's memory of a humiliation is corrected by his putting the facts right, by considering his own worth, etc. In this way a normal person is able to bring about the disappearance of the accompanying affect through the process of association.

To this we must add the general effacement of impressions, the fading of memories which we name "forgetting" and which wears away those ideas in particular that are no longer affectively operative.

Our observations have shown, on the other hand, that the memories which have become the determinants of hysterical phenomena persist for a long time with astonishing freshness and with the whole of their affective coloring. We must, however, mention another remarkable fact, which we shall later be able to turn to account, namely, that these memories, unlike other memories of their past lives, are not at the patients' disposal. On the contrary, *these experiences are completely absent from the patients' memory when they are in a normal psychical state, or are only present in a highly summary form.* Not until they have been questioned under hypnosis do these memories emerge with the undiminished vividness of a recent event. . . .

This can only be explained on the view that these memories constitute an exception in their relation to all the wearing-away processes which we have discussed above. *It appears, that is to say, that these memories correspond to traumas that have not been sufficiently abreacted;* and if we enter more closely into the reasons which have prevented this, we find at least two sets of conditions under which the reaction to the trauma fails to occur. . . .

It may therefore be said that the ideas which have become pathological have persisted with such freshness and affective strength because they have been denied the normal wearing-away processes by means of abreaction and reproduction in states of uninhibited association. . . .

It will now be understood how it is that the psychotherapeutic procedure which we have described in these pages has a curative effect. *It brings to an end the operative force of the idea which was not abreacted in the first instance, by allowing its strangulated affect to find a way out through speech; and it subjects it to associative correction by introducing it into normal consciousness (under light hypnosis) or by removing it through the physician's suggestion, as is done in somnambulism accompanied by amnesia.* . . .

Free Association, Resistance, and Repression

Free Association and Resistance

First: when we undertake to cure a patient of his symptoms he opposes against us a vigorous and tenacious *resistance* throughout the entire course of the treatment. . . .

The resistance shown by patients is highly varied and exceedingly subtle, often hard to recognize and protean in the manifold forms it takes; the analyst needs to be continually suspicious and on his guard against it. In psychoanalytic therapy we employ the technique which is already familiar to you through dream interpretation: we require the patient to put himself into a condition of calm self-observation, without trying to think of anything, and then to communicate everything which he becomes inwardly aware of, feelings, thoughts, remembrances, in the order in which they arise in his mind. We expressly warn him against giving way to any kind of motive which would cause him to select from or to exclude any of the ideas (associations), whether because they are too "disagreeable," or too "indiscreet" to be mentioned, or too "unimportant" or "irrelevant" or "nonsensical" to be worth saying. We impress upon him that he has only to attend to what is on the surface consciously in his mind, and to abandon all objections to whatever he finds, no matter what form they take; and we inform him that the success of the treatment, and, above all, its duration, will depend upon his conscientious adherence to this fundamental technical rule. We know from the technique of dream interpretation that it is precisely those associations against which innumerable doubts and objections are raised that invariably contain the material leading to the discovery of the unconscious.

The first thing that happens as a result of instituting this technical rule is that it becomes the first point of attack for the resistance. The patient attempts to escape from it by every possible means. First he says nothing comes into his head, then that so much comes into his head that he can't grasp any of it. Then we observe with displeasure and astonishment that he is giving in to his critical objections, first to this, then to that; he betrays it by the long pauses which occur in his talk. At last he admits that he really cannot say something, he is ashamed to, and he lets this feeling get the better of his promise. Or else, he has thought of something but it concerns someone else and not himself, and is therefore to be made an exception to the rule. Or else, what he has just thought of is really too unimportant, too stupid and too absurd, I could never have meant that he should take account of such thoughts. So it goes on, with untold variations, to which one continually replies that telling everything really means telling everything.

Free Association, Resistance, and Repression, from Freud, *A General Introduction to Psychoanalysis,* pp. 253–64.

One hardly ever meets with a patient who does not attempt to make a reservation in some department of his thoughts, in order to guard them against intrusion by the analysis. One patient, who in the ordinary way was remarkably intelligent, concealed a most intimate love affair from me for weeks in this way; when accused of this violation of the sacred rule he defended himself with the argument that he considered this particular story his private affair. Naturally analytic treatment cannot countenance a right of sanctuary like this. . . .

Obsessional patients are exceedingly clever at making the technical rule almost useless by bringing their overconscientiousness and doubt to bear upon it. Patients with anxiety-hysteria sometimes succeed in reducing it to absurdity by only producing associations which are so far removed from what is wanted that they yield nothing for analysis. However, I do not intend to introduce you to these technical difficulties of the treatment. It is enough to know that finally, with resolution and perseverance, we do succeed in extracting from the patient a certain amount of obedience for the rule of the technique; and then the resistance takes another line altogether. It appears as intellectual opposition, employs arguments as weapons, and turns to its own use all the difficulties and improbabilities which normal but uninstructed reasoning finds in analytical doctrines. We then have to hear from the mouth of the individual patient all the criticisms and objections which thunder about us in chorus in scientific literature. What the critics outside shout at us is nothing new, therefore. It is indeed a storm in a teacup. Still, the patient can be argued with; he is very glad to get us to instruct him, teach him, defeat him, point out the literature to him so that he can learn more; he is perfectly ready to become a supporter of psychoanalysis on the condition that analysis shall spare him personally. We recognize resistance in this desire for knowledge, however; it is a digression from the particular task in hand and we refuse to allow it. In the obsessional neurosis the resistance makes use of special tactics which we are prepared for. It permits the analysis to proceed uninterruptedly along its course, so that more and more light is thrown upon the problems of the case, until we begin to wonder at last why these explanations have no practical effect and entail no corresponding improvement in the symptoms. Then we discover that the resistance has fallen back upon the doubt characteristic of the obsessional neurosis and is holding us successfully at bay from this vantage point. The patient has said to himself something of this kind: "This is all very pretty and very interesting. I should like to go on with it. I am sure it would do me a lot of good if it were true. But I don't believe it in the least, and as long as I don't believe it, it doesn't affect my illness." So it goes on for a long time, until at last this reservation itself is reached and then the decisive battle begins.

The intellectual resistances are not the worst; one can always get the better of them. But the patient knows how to set up resistances within the boundaries of analysis proper, and the defeat of these is one of the most difficult tasks of the technique. Instead of remembering certain of the feelings and states of mind of his previous life, he reproduces them, lives through again such of them as, by means of what is called the "transference," may be made effective in opposition against the physician and the treatment. If the patient is a man, he usually takes this material from his relationship with his father, in whose place he has now put the physician; and in so doing he erects resistances out of his struggles to attain to personal independence and independence of judgment, out of his ambition, the earliest aim of which was to equal or to excel the father, out of his disinclination to take the burden of gratitude upon himself for the second time in his life. There are periods in which one feels that the patient's desire to put the analyst in the wrong, to make him feel his impotence, to triumph over him, has completely ousted the worthier desire to bring the illness to an end. Women have a genius for exploiting in the interests of resistance a tender erotically tinged transference to the analyst; when this attraction reaches a certain intensity all interest in the actual situation of treatment fades away, together with every obligation incurred upon undertaking it. The inevitable jealousy and the embitterment consequent upon the unavoidable rejection, however considerately it is handled, is bound to injure the personal relationship with the physician, and so to put out of action one of the most powerful propelling forces in the analysis.

Resistances of this kind must not be narrowly condemned. They contain so much of the most important material from the patient's past life and bring it back in so convincing a fashion that they come to be of the greatest assistance to the analysis, if a skillful technique is employed correctly to turn them to the best use. What is noteworthy is that this material always serves at first as a resistance and comes forward in a guise which is inimical to the treatment. Again it may be said that they are character traits, individual attitudes of the ego, which are thus mobilized to oppose the attempted alterations. One learns then how these character traits have been developed in connection with the conditions of the neurosis and in reaction against its demands, and observes features in this character which would not otherwise have appeared, at least, not so clearly: that is, which may be designated latent. Also you must not carry away the impression that we look upon the appearance of these resistances as an unforeseen danger threatening our analytic influence. No, we know that these resistances are bound to appear; we are dissatisfied only if we cannot rouse them definitely enough and make the patient perceive them as such. Indeed, we understand at last that the overcoming of these resistances is the essential work of the analysis, that part of the work which alone assures us that we have achieved something for the patient.

Besides this, you must take into account that all accidental occurrences arising during the treatment are made use of by the patient to interfere with it, anything which could distract him or deter him from it, every hostile expression of opinion from anyone in his circle whom he can regard as an authority, any chance organic illness or one complicating the neurosis; indeed, he even converts every improvement in his condition into a motive for slackening his efforts. Then you will have obtained an approximate, though still incomplete, picture of the forms and the measures taken by the resistances which must be met and overcome in the course of every analysis. I have given such a detailed consideration to this point because I am about to inform you that our dynamic conception of the neuroses is founded upon this experience of ours of the resistances that neurotic patients set up against the cure of their symptoms. Breuer and I both originally practiced psychotherapy by the hypnotic method. Breuer's first patient was treated throughout in a state of hypnotic suggestibility; at first I followed his example. I admit that at that time my work went forward more easily and agreeably and also took much less time: but the results were capricious and not permanent; therefore I finally gave up hypnotism. And then I understood that no comprehension of the dynamics of these affections was possible as long as hypnosis was employed. In this condition the very existence of resistances is concealed from the physician's observation. Hypnosis drives back the resistances and frees a certain field for the work of the analyis, but dams them up at the boundaries of this field so that they are insurmountable; it is similar in effect to the doubt of the obsessional neurosis. Therefore I may say that true psychoanalysis only began when the help of hypnosis was discarded. . . .

In the course of the treatment the resistance varies in intensity continually; it always increases as a new topic is approached, it is at its height during the work upon it, and dies down again when this theme has been dealt with. Unless certain technical errors have been committed we never have to meet the full measure of resistance, of which any patient is capable, at once. Thus we could definitely ascertain that the same man would take up and then abandon his critical objections over and over again in the course of the analysis. Whenever we are on the point of bringing to his consciousness some piece of unconscious material which is particularly painful to him, then he is critical in the extreme; even though he may have previously understood and accepted a great deal, yet now all these gains seem to be obliterated; in his struggles to oppose at all costs he can behave just as though he were mentally deficient, a form of "emotional stupidity." If he can be successfully helped to overcome this new resistance he regains his insight and comprehension. His critical faculty is not functioning independently, and therefore is not to be respected as if it were; it is merely a maid-of-all-work for his affective attitudes and is directed by his resistance. When he dislikes anything, he can defend himself against it most ingeniously; but when anything suits his book he can be credulous enough. We are perhaps all much the same; a person being analyzed shows this dependence of the intellect upon the affective life so clearly because in the analysis he is so hard pressed.

In what way can we now account for this fact observed, that the patient struggles so energetically against the relief of his symptoms and the restoration of his mental processes to normal functioning? We say that we have come upon the traces of powerful forces at work here opposing any change in the condition; they must be the same forces that originally induced the condition. In the formation of symptoms some process must have been gone through, which our experience in dispersing them makes us able to reconstruct. As we already know from Breuer's observations, it follows from the existence of a symptom that some mental process has not been carried through to an end in a normal manner so that it could become conscious; the symptom is a substitute for that which has not come through. Now we know where to place the forces which we suspect to be at work. A vehement effort must have been exercised to prevent the mental process in question from penetrating into consciousness and as a result it has remained unconscious; being unconscious it had the power to construct a symptom. The same vehement effort is again at work during analytic treatment, opposing the attempt to bring the unconscious into consciousness. This we perceive in the form of resistances. The pathogenic process which is demonstrated by the resistances we call *repression*.

Repression

It will now be necessary to make our conception of this process of *repression* more precise. It is the essential preliminary condition for the development of symptoms, but it is also something else, a thing to which we have no parallel. Let us take as a model an impulse, a mental process seeking to convert itself into action: we know that it can suffer rejection, by virtue of what we call *repudiation* or *condemnation;* whereupon the energy at its disposal is withdrawn, it becomes powerless, but it can continue to exist as a memory. The whole process of decision on the point takes place with the full cognizance of the ego. It is very different when we imagine the same impulse subject to *repression:* it would then retain its energy and no memory of it would be left behind; the process of repression, too, would be accomplished without the cognizance of the ego. This comparison therefore brings us no nearer to the nature of repression.

I will expound to you those theoretical conceptions which alone have proved useful in giving greater definiteness to the term *repression*. For this purpose it is first necessary that we should proceed from the purely descriptive meaning of the word *unconscious* to its systematic meaning; that is, we resolve to think of the consciousness or unconsciousness of a mental process as merely one of its qualities and not necessarily definitive. Suppose that a process of this kind has remained unconscious, its being withheld from consciousness may be merely a sign of the fate it has undergone, not necessarily the fate itself. Let us suppose, in order to gain a more concrete notion of this fate, that every mental process—there is one exception, which I will go into later—first exists in an unconscious state or phase, and only develops out of this into a conscious phase, much as a photograph is first a negative and then becomes a picture through the printing of the positive. But not every negative is made into a positive, and it is just as little necessary that every unconscious mental process should convert itself into a conscious one. It may be best expressed as follows: Each single process belongs in the first place to the unconscious psychical system; from this system it can under certain conditions proceed further into the conscious system.

The crudest conception of these systems is the one we shall find most convenient, a spatial one. The unconscious system may therefore be compared to a large anteroom, in which the various mental excitations are crowding upon one another, like individual beings. Adjoining this is a second, smaller apartment, a sort of reception room, in which consciousness resides. But on the threshold between the two there stands a personage with the office of doorkeeper, who examines the various mental excitations, censors them, and denies them admittance to the reception room when he disapproves of them. You will see at once that it does not make much difference whether the doorkeeper turns any one impulse back at the threshold, or drives it out again once it has entered the reception room; that is merely a matter of the degree of his vigilance and promptness in recognition. Now this metaphor may be employed to widen our terminology. The excitations in the unconscious, in the antechamber, are not visible to consciousness, which is of course in the other room, so to begin with they remain unconscious. When they have pressed forward to the threshold and been turned back by the doorkeeper, they are *"incapable of becoming conscious"*; we call them then *repressed*. But even those excitations which are allowed over the threshold do not necessarily become conscious; they can only become so if they succeed in attracting the eye of consciousness. This second chamber therefore may be suitably called *the preconscious system*. In this way the process of becoming conscious retains its purely descriptive sense. Being repressed, when applied to any single impulse, means being unable to pass out of the unconscious system because of the doorkeeper's refusal of admittance into the preconscious. The doorkeeper is what we have learned to know as resistance in our attempts in analytic treatment to loosen the repressions. . . .

Still, I should like to assure you that these crude hypotheses, the two chambers, the doorkeeper on the threshold between the two, and consciousness as a spectator at the end of the second room, must indicate an extensive approximation to the actual reality. I should also like to hear you admit that our designations, unconscious, preconscious, and conscious, are less prejudicial and more easily defensible than some others which have been suggested or have come into use, e.g., subconscious, interconscious, coconscious, etc. . . .

Do you realize, moreover, what it is that supports these conceptions of the two systems and the relationship between them and consciousness? The doorkeeper between the unconscious and the preconscious is nothing else than the *censorship* to which we found the form of the manifest dream subjected.

The residue of the day's experience, which we found to be the stimuli exciting the dream, was preconscious material which at night during sleep had been influenced by unconscious and repressed wishes and excitations and had thus by association with them been able to form the latent dream, by means of their energy. Under the dominion of the unconscious system this material had been elaborated (worked over)—by condensation and displacement—in a way which in normal mental life, i.e., in the preconscious system, is unknown or admissible very rarely. This difference in their manner of functioning is what distinguishes the two systems for us; the relationship to consciousness, which is a permanent feature of the preconscious, indicates to which of the two systems any given process belongs. Neither is dreaming a pathological phenomenon; every healthy person may dream while asleep. Every inference concerning the constitution of the mental apparatus which comprises an understanding of both dreams and neurotic symptoms has an irrefutable claim to be regarded as applying also to normal mental life. . . .

Symptom-Formation

This is as much as we will say about repression for the present. Moreover, it is but a necessary preliminary condition, a prerequisite, a symptom-formation. We know that the symptom is a substitute for some other process which was held back by repression; but even given repression we have still a long way to go before we can obtain comprehension of this substitute formation. There are other sides to the problem of repression itself which present questions to be answered: What kind of mental excitations suffer repression? What forces effect it? And from what motives? On one point only, so far, have we gained any knowledge relevant to these questions. While investigating the problem of resistance we learned that the forces behind it proceed from the ego, from character traits, recognizable or latent: it is these forces therefore which have also effected the repression, or at least they have taken a part in it. We know nothing more than this at present. . . .

Every time we should be led by analysis to the sexual experiences and desires of the patient, and every time we should have to affirm that the symptom served the same purpose. This purpose shows itself to be the gratification of sexual wishes; the symptoms serve the purpose of sexual gratification for the patient; they are a substitute for satisfactions which he does not obtain in reality. . . .

I wish to avoid making reservations later on about the universal applicability of these statements, and therefore I will ask you to notice that all I have just been saying about repression, symptom-formation and symptom-interpretation has been obtained from the study of three types of neurosis, and for the present is only applicable to these three types—namely, *anxiety-hysteria, conversion-hysteria,* and *the obsessional neurosis.* These three disorders, which we are accustomed to combine together in a group as the *transference neuroses,* constitute the field open to psychoanalytic therapy. . . .

Everything that has been said, then, applies only to the three transference neuroses and I will now add another piece of information which throws further light upon the significance of the symptoms. A comparative examination of the situations out of which the disease arose yields the following result, which may be reduced to a formula—namely, that these persons have fallen ill from the *privation* (*frustration*) which they suffer when reality withholds from them gratification of their sexual wishes. You will perceive how beautifully these two conclusions supplement one another. The symptoms are now explicable as substitute-gratifications for desires which are unsatisfied in life. . . .

But we have long ago learned from psychoanalysis that opposites do not constitute a contradiction. We might extend our proposition and say that the purpose of the symptom is either a sexual gratification or a defense against it; in hysteria the positive, wish-fulfilling character predominates on the whole, and in the obsessional neurosis the negative ascetic character. The symptoms can serve the purpose both of sexual gratification and of its opposite. . . .

Etiological Factors in Neurosis

Fixation

. . . Let me simply say that we consider it possible that single portions of every separate sexual impulse may remain in an early stage of development, although at the same time other portions of it may have reached their final goal. You will see from this that we conceive each such impulse as a current continuously flowing from the beginning of life, and that we have divided its flow to some extent artificially into separate, successive, forward movements. Your impression that these conceptions require further elucidation is correct, but the attempt would lead us too far afield. We will, however, decide at this point to call this *arrest* in a component impulse at an early stage a *fixation* (of the impulse).

The second danger in a development by stages such as this we call *regression;* it also happens that those portions which have proceeded further may easily revert in a backward direction to these earlier stages. The impulse will find occasion to *regress* in this way when the exercise of its function in a later and more developed form meets with powerful external obstacles, which thus prevent it from attaining the goal of satisfaction. It is a short step to assume

---

Etiological Factors in Neurosis, from Freud, *A General Introduction to Psychoanalysis,* pp. 298–303.

that fixation and regression are not independent of each other; the stronger the fixations in the path of development the more easily will the function yield before the external obstacles, by regressing on to those fixations; that is, the less capable of resistance against the external difficulties in its path will the developed function be. If you think of a migrating people who have left large numbers at the stopping places on their way, you will see that the foremost will naturally fall back upon these positions when they are defeated or when they meet with an enemy too strong for them. And again, the more of their number they leave behind in their progress, the sooner will they be in danger of defeat.

It is important for comprehension of the neuroses that you should keep in mind this relation between fixation and regression. You will thus acquire a secure foothold from which to investigate the causation of the neuroses—their etiology—which we shall soon consider.

Regression and Repression

For the present we will keep to the question of regression. After what you have heard about the development of the libido you may anticipate two kinds of regression; a return to the first objects invested with libido, which we know to be incestuous in character, and a return of the whole sexual organization to earlier stages. Both kinds occur in the transference neuroses, and play a great part in their mechanism. In particular, the return to the first incestuous objects of the libido is a feature found with quite fatiguing regularity in neurotics. There is much more to be said about the regressions of libido if another group of neuroses, called the narcissistic, is taken into account; but this is not our intention at the moment. These affections yield conclusions about other developmental processes of the libido function, not yet mentioned, and also show us new types of regression corresponding with them. I think, however, that I had better warn you now above all not to confound *regression* with *repression* and that I must assist you to clear your minds about the relation between the two processes. *Repression,* as you will remember, is the process by which a mental act capable of becoming conscious (that is, one which belongs to the preconscious system) is made unconscious and forced back into the unconscious system. And we also call it *repression* when the unconscious mental act is not permitted to enter the adjacent preconscious system at all, but is turned back upon the threshold by the censorship. There is therefore no connection with sexuality in the concept of *repression;* please mark this very carefully. It denotes a purely psychological process; and would be even better described as *topographical,* by which we mean that it has to do with the spatial relationships we assume within the mind, or if we again abandon these crude aids to the formulation of theory, with the structure of the mental apparatus out of separate psychical systems.

The comparisons just now instituted showed us that hitherto we have not been using the word *regression* in its general sense but in a quite specific one. If you give it its general sense, that of a reversion from a higher to a lower stage of development in general, then repression also ranges itself under regression; for repression can also be described as reversion to an earlier and lower stage in the development of a mental act. Only, in repression this retrogressive direction is not a point of any moment to us; for we also call it repression in a dynamic sense when a mental process is arrested before it leaves the lower stage of the unconscious. Repression is thus a topographic-dynamic conception, while regression is a purely descriptive one. But what we have hitherto called *regression* and considered in its relation to fixation signified exclusively the return of the *libido* to its former halting places in development, that is, something which is essentially quite different from repression and quite independent of it. Nor can we call regression of the libido a purely psychical process; neither do we know where to localize it in the mental apparatus; for though it may exert the most powerful influence upon mental life, the organic factor in it is nevertheless the most prominent.

Discussions of this sort tend to be rather dry; therefore let us turn to clinical illustrations of them in order to get a more vivid impression of them. You know that the group of the transference neuroses consists principally of hysteria and the obsessional neurosis. Now in hysteria, a regression of the libido to the primary incestuous sexual objects is without doubt quite regular, but there is little or no regression to an earlier stage of sexual organization. Consequently the principal part in the mechanism of hysteria is played by repression. If I may be allowed to supplement by a construction the certain knowledge of this neurosis acquired up to the present I might describe the situation as follows: The fusion of the component-impulses under the primacy of the genital zone has been accomplished; but the results of this union meet with resistance from the direction of the preconscious system with which consciousness is connected. The genital organization therefore holds good for the unconscious, but not also for the preconscious, and this rejection on the part of the preconscious results in a picture which has a certain likeness to the state prior to the primacy of the genital zone. It is nevertheless actually quite different. Of the two kinds of regression of the libido, that on to an earlier phase of sexual organization is much the more striking. Since it is absent in hysteria and our whole conception of the neuroses is still far too much dominated by the study of hysteria which came first in point of time, the significance of libido-regression was recognized much later than that of repression. We may be sure that our points of view will undergo still further extensions and alterations when we include consideration of still other neuroses (the narcissistic) in addition to hysteria and the obsessional neurosis.

In the obsessional neurosis, on the other hand, regression of the libido to the antecedent stage of the sadistic-anal organization is the most conspicuous factor and determines the form taken by the symptoms. The impulse to love must then mask itself under the sadistic impulse. The obsessive thought, "I should like to murder you," means (when it has been detached from certain superimposed elements that are not, however, accidental but indispensable to it) nothing else but "I should like to enjoy love of you." When you consider in addition that regression to the primary objects has also set in at the same time, so that this impulse concerns only the nearest and most beloved persons, you can gain some idea of the horror roused in the patient by these obsessive ideas and at the same time how unaccountable they appear to his conscious perception. But repression also has its share, a great one, in the mechanism of this neurosis, and one which is not easy to expound in a rapid survey such as this. Regression of libido without repression would never give rise to a neurosis, but would result in a perversion. You will see from this that repression is the process which distinguishes the neuroses particularly and by which they are best characterized.

Frustration and Symptom-Formation

I think that you will be soonest reconciled to this exposition of fixation and regression of the libido if you will regard it as preparatory to a study of the *etiology* of the neuroses. So far I have only given you one piece of information on this subject, namely, that people fall ill of a neurosis when the possibility of satisfaction for the libido is removed from them—they fall ill in consequence of a "frustration," as I called it, therefore—and that their symptoms are actually substitutes for the missing satisfaction. This of course does not mean that every frustration in regard to libidinal satisfaction makes everyone who meets with it neurotic, but merely that in all cases of neurosis investigated the factor of frustration was demonstrable. The statement therefore cannot be reversed. You will no doubt have understood that this statement was not intended to reveal the whole secret of the etiology of the neuroses, but that it merely emphasized an important and indispensable condition.

Frustration and Sublimation

Now in order to consider this proposition further we do not know whether to begin upon the nature of the frustration or the particular character of the person affected by it. The frustration is very rarely a comprehensive and absolute one; in order to have a pathogenic effect it would probably have to strike at the only form of satisfaction which that person desires, the only form of which he is capable. In general, there are very many ways by which it is possible to endure lack of libidinal satisfaction without falling ill. Above all we know of people who are able to take such abstinence upon themselves without injury; they are then not happy, they suffer from unsatisfied longing, but they do not become ill. We therefore have to conclude that the sexual impulse-excitations are exceptionally "plastic," if I may use the word. One of them can step in in place of another; if satisfaction of one is denied in reality, satisfaction of another can offer full recompense. They are related to one another like a network of communicating canals filled with fluid, and this in spite of their subordination to the genital primacy, a condition which is not at all easily reduced to an image. Further, the component-instincts of sexuality, as well as the united sexual impulse which comprises them, show a great capacity to change their object, to exchange it for another—i.e. for one more easily attainable; this capacity for displacement and readiness to accept surrogates must produce a powerful counter effect to the effect of a frustration. One amongst these processes serving as protection against illness arising from want has reached a particular significance in the development of culture. It consists in the abandonment, on the part of the sexual impulse, of an aim previously found either in the gratification of a component-impulse or in the gratification incidental to reproduction, and the adoption of a new aim—which new aim, though genetically related to the first, can no longer be regarded as sexual, but must be called social in character. We call this process *sublimation,* by which we subscribe to the general standard which estimates social aims above sexual (ultimately selfish) aims. Incidentally sublimation is merely a special case of the connections existing between sexual impulses and other, asexual ones. . . .

Your impression now will be that we have reduced want of satisfaction to a factor of negligible proportions by the recognition of so many means of enduring it. But no; this is not so: it retains its pathogenic power. The means of dealing with it are not always sufficient. The measure of unsatisfied libido that the average human being can take upon himself is limited. The plasticity and free mobility of the libido are not by any means retained to the full in all of us; and sublimation can never discharge more than a certain proportion of libido, apart from the fact that many people possess the capacity for sublimation only in a slight degree. The most important of these limitations is clearly that referring to the mobility of the libido, since it confines the individual to the attaining of aims and objects which are very few in number. Just remember that incomplete development of the libido leaves behind it very extensive (and sometimes also numerous) libido-fixations upon earlier phases of organization and types of object-choice, mostly incapable of satisfaction in reality; you will then recognize fixation of libido as the second powerful factor working together with frustration in the causation of illness. We may condense this schematically and say that libido-fixation represents the internal, predisposing factor, while frustration represents the external, accidental factor, in the etiology of the neuroses.

I will take this opportunity to warn you against taking sides in a quite superfluous dispute. It is a popular habit in scientific matters to seize upon one side of the truth and set it up as the whole truth, and then in favor of that element in truth to dispute all the rest which is equally true. More than one faction has already split off in this way from the psychoanalytic movement; one of them recognizes only the egoistic impulses and denies the sexual; another perceives only the influence of real tasks in life but overlooks that of the individual's past life, and so on. Now here is occasion for another of these antitheses and moot points: Are the neuroses exogenous or endogenous diseases—the inevitable result of a certain type of constitution or the product of certain injurious (traumatic) events in the person's life? In particular, are they brought about by the fixation of libido and the rest of the sexual constitution, or by the pressure of frustration? This dilemma seems to me about as sensible as another I could point to: Is the child created by the father's act of generation or by the conception in the mother? You will properly reply: Both conditions are alike indispensable. The conditions underlying the neuroses are very similar, if not exactly the same. . . .

Psychoanalytic Therapy and Transference

The Dynamics of Therapy

First of all there is the hereditary disposition—we do not often mention it because it is so strongly emphasized in other quarters and we have nothing new to say about it. But do not suppose that we underestimate it; as practitioners we are well aware of its power. In any event we can do nothing to change it; for us also it is a fixed datum in the problem, which sets a limit to our efforts. Next, there is the influence of the experiences of early childhood, which we are accustomed in analysis to rank as very important; they belong to the past, we cannot undo them. Then there is all that unhappiness in life which we have included under "frustration in reality," from which all the absence of love in life proceeds—namely, poverty, family strife, mistaken choice in marriage, unfavorable social conditions, and the severity of the demands by which moral convention oppresses the individual. . . .

Health is to be won by "free living," then. There would be this blot upon analysis, to be sure, that it would not be serving general morality; what it gave to the individual it would take from the rest of the world.

But now, who has given you such a false impression of analysis? It is out of the question that part of the analytic treatment should consist of advice to "live freely"—if for no other reason because we ourselves tell you that a stubborn conflict is going on in the patient between libidinal desires and sexual

Psychoanalytic Therapy and Transference, from Freud, *A General Introduction to Psychoanalysis*, pp. 374–88, 392–98.

repression, between sensual and ascetic tendencies. This conflict is not resolved by helping one side to win a victory over the other. It is true we see that in neurotics asceticism has gained the day; the result of which is that the suppressed sexual impulses have found a vent for themselves in the symptoms. If we were to make victory possible to the sensual side instead, the disregarded forces repressing sexuality would have to indemnify themselves by symptoms. Neither of these measures will succeed in ending the inner conflict; one side in either event will remain unsatisfied. . . .

In considering this question people usually overlook the essential point of the whole difficulty—namely, that the pathogenic conflict in a neurotic must not be confounded with a normal struggle between conflicting impulses all of which are in the same mental field. It is a battle between two forces of which one has succeeded in coming to the level of the preconscious and conscious part of the mind, while the other has been confined on the unconscious level. That is why the conflict can never have a final outcome one way or the other; the antagonists meet each other as little as the whale and the polar bear in the well-known story. An effective decision can be reached only when they confront each other on the same ground. And, in my opinion, to accomplish this is the sole task of the treatment.

Besides this, I can assure you that you are quite misinformed if you imagine that advice and guidance concerning conduct in life forms an integral part of the analytic method. On the contrary, so far as possible we refrain from playing the part of mentor; we want nothing better than that the patient should find his own solutions for himself. To this end we expect him to postpone all vital decisions affecting his life, such as choice of career, business enterprises, marriage or divorce, during treatment to execute them only after it has been completed. Now confess that you had imagined something very different. Only with certain very young or quite helpless and defenseless persons is it impossible to keep within such strict limitations as we should wish. With them we have to combine the positions of physician and educator; we are then well aware of our responsibility and act with the necessary caution.

You must not be led away by my eagerness to defend myself against the accusation that in analytic treatment neurotics are encouraged to "live a free life" and conclude from it that we influence them in favor of conventional morality. That is at least as far removed from our purpose as the other. We are not reformers, it is true; we are merely observers; but we cannot avoid observing with critical eyes, and we have found it impossible to give our support to conventional sexual morality or to approve highly of the means by which society attempts to arrange the practical problems of sexuality in life. We can demonstrate with ease that what the world calls its code of morals demands more sacrifices than it is worth, and that its behavior is neither dictated by honesty nor instituted with wisdom. We do not absolve our patients from listening to these criticisms; we accustom them to an unprejudiced consideration of sexual matters like all other matters; and if after they have become independent by the effect of the treatment they choose some intermediate course between unrestrained sexual license and unconditional asceticism, our conscience is not burdened whatever the outcome. We say to ourselves that anyone who has successfully undergone the training of learning and recognizing the truth about himself is henceforth strengthened against the dangers of immorality, even if his standard of morality should in some respect deviate from the common one. Incidentally, we must beware of overestimating the importance of abstinence in affecting neurosis; only a minority of pathogenic situations due to frustration and the subsequent accumulation of libido thereby induced can be relieved by the kind of sexual intercourse that is procurable without any difficulty.

So you cannot explain the therapeutic effect of psychoanalysis by supposing that it permits patients free sexual indulgence; you must look round for something else. I think that one of the remarks I made while I was disposing of this conjecture on your part will have put you on the right track. Probably it is the substitution of something conscious for something unconscious, the transformation of the unconscious thoughts into conscious thoughts, that makes our work effective. You are right; that is exactly what it is. By extending the unconscious into consciousness the repressions are raised, the conditions of symptom-formation are abolished, and the pathogenic conflict exchanged for a normal one which must be decided one way or the other. We do nothing for our patients but enable this one mental change to take place in them; the extent to which it is achieved is the extent of the benefit we do them. Where there is no repression or mental process analogous to it to be undone there is nothing for our therapy to do.

The aim of our efforts may be expressed in various formulas—making conscious the unconscious, removing the repressions, filling in the gaps in memory; they all amount to the same thing. . . .

What then have we to do in order to bring what is unconscious in the patient into consciousness? At one time we thought that would be very simple; all we need do would be to identify this unconscious matter and then tell the patient what it was. However, we know already that that was a short-sighted mistake. Our knowledge of what is unconscious in him is not equivalent to his knowledge of it; when we tell him what we know he does not assimilate it *in place of* his own unconscious thoughts, but *alongside* of them, and very little has been changed. We have rather to regard this unconscious material topographically; we have to look for it in his memory at the actual spot where the repression of it originally ensued. This repression must be removed, and then the substitution of conscious thought for unconscious thought can be effected straightaway. How is a repression such as this to be removed? Our work enters upon a second phase here; first, the discovery of the repression, and then the removal of the resistance which maintains this repression.

How can this resistance be got rid of? In the same way: by finding it out and telling the patient about it. The resistance too arises in a repression, either from the very one which we are endeavoring to dispel, or in one that occurred earlier. It is set up by the countercharge which rose up to repress the repellent impulse. So that we now do just the same as we were trying to do before; we interpret, identify, and inform the patient; but this time we are doing it at the right spot. The countercharge or the resistance is not part of the unconscious, but of the ego which cooperates with us, and this is so, even if it is not actually conscious. We know that a difficulty arises here in the ambiguity of the word "unconscious," on the one hand, as a phenomenon, on the other hand, as a system. That sounds very obscure and difficult; but after all it is only a repetition of what we have said before, is it not? We have come to this point already long ago.—Well then, we expect that this resistance will be abandoned, and the countercharge withdrawn, when we have made the recognition of them possible by our work of interpretation. What are the instinctive propelling forces at our disposal to make this possible? First, the patient's desire for recovery, which impelled him to submit himself to the work in cooperation with us, and secondly, the aid of his intelligence which we reinforce by our interpretation. There is no doubt that it is easier for the patient to recognize the resistance with his intelligence, and to identify the idea in his unconscious which corresponds to it, if we have first given him an idea which rouses his expectations in regard to it. . . .

And now for the fact! In quite a number of the various forms of nervous illness, in the hysterias, anxiety-conditions, obsessional neuroses, our hypothesis proves sound. By seeking out the repression in this way, discovering the resistances, indicating the repressed, it is actually possible to accomplish the task, to overcome the resistances, to break down the repression, and to change something unconscious into something conscious. As we do this we get a vivid impression of how, as each individual resistance is being mastered, a violent battle goes on in the soul of the patient—a normal mental struggle between two tendencies on the same ground, between the motives striving to maintain the countercharge and those which are ready to abolish it. The first of these are the old motives which originally erected the repression; among the second are found new ones more recently acquired which it is hoped will decide the conflict in our favor. We have succeeded in revivifying the old battle of the repression again, in bringing the issue, so long ago decided, up for revision again. The new contribution we make to it lies, first of all, in demonstrating that the original solution led to illness and in promising that a different one would pave the way to health, and secondly, in pointing out that the circumstances have all changed immensely since the time of that original repudiation of these impulses. Then, the ego was weak, infantile, and perhaps had reason to shrink with horror from the claims of the libido as being dangerous to it. Today it is strong and experienced and moreover has a helper at hand in the physician. So we may expect to lead the revived conflict through a better outcome than repression; and, as has been said, in hysteria, anxiety-neurosis, and the obsessional neurosis success in the main justifies our claims. . . .

Transference

When we keep to consideration of hysterical and obsessional neurotics we are very soon confronted with a second fact, for which we were quite unprepared. After the treatment has proceeded for a while we notice that these patients behave in a quite peculiar manner towards ourselves. . . .

We observe then that the patient, who ought to be thinking of nothing but the solution of his own distressing conflicts, begins to develop a particular interest in the person of the physician. Everything connected with this person seems to him more important than his own affairs and to distract him from his illness. Relations with the patient then become for a time very agreeable; he is particularly docile, endeavors to show his gratitude wherever he can, exhibits a fineness of character and other good qualities which we had perhaps not anticipated in him. The analyst thus forms a very good opinion of the patient and values his luck in being able to render assistance to such an admirable personality. If the physician has occasion to see the patient's relatives he hears with satisfaction that this esteem is mutual. The patient at home is never tired of praising the analyst and attributing new virtues to him. . . .

The analysis too makes splendid progress under these conditions, the patient understands the suggestions offered to him, concentrates upon the tasks appointed by the treatment, the material needed—his recollections and associations—is abundantly available; he astonishes the analyst by the sureness and accuracy of his interpretations, and the latter has only to observe with satisfaction how readily and willingly a sick man will accept all the new psychological ideas that are so hotly contested by the healthy in the world outside. A general improvement in the patient's condition, objectively confirmed on all sides, also accompanies this harmonious relationship in the analysis.

But such fair weather cannot last forever. There comes a day when it clouds over. There begins to be difficulties in the analysis; the patient says he cannot think of anything more to say. One has an unmistakable impression that he is no longer interested in the work, and that he is casually ignoring the injunction given him to say everything that comes into his mind and to yield to none of the critical objections that occur to him. His behavior is not dictated by the situation of the treatment; it is as if he had not made an agreement to that effect with the physician; he is obviously preoccupied with something which at the same time he wishes to reserve to himself. This is a situation in which the treatment is in danger. Plainly a very powerful resistance has risen up. What can have happened?

If it is possible to clear up this state of things, the cause of the disturbance is found to consist in certain intense feelings of affection which the patient has transferred on to the physician, not accounted for by the latter's behavior nor by the relationship involved by the treatment. The form in which this affectionate feeling is expressed and the goal it seeks naturally depend upon the circumstances of the situation between the two persons. If one of them is a young girl and the other still a fairly young man, the impression received is that of normal love; it seems natural that a girl should fall in love with a man with whom she is much alone and can speak of very intimate things, and who is in the position of an adviser with authority—we shall probably overlook the fact that in a neurotic girl some disturbance of the capacity for love is rather to be expected. The farther removed the situation between the two persons is from this supposed example, the more unaccountable it is to find that nevertheless the same kind of feeling comes to light in other cases. It may be still comprehensible when a young woman who is unhappily married seems to be overwhelmed by a serious passion for her physician, if he is still unattached, and that she should be ready to seek a divorce and give herself to him, or, where circumstances would prevent this, to enter into a secret love affair with him. That sort of thing, indeed, is known to occur outside psychoanalysis. But in this situation girls and women make the most astonishing confessions which reveal a quite peculiar attitude on their part to the therapeutic problem: they had always known that nothing but love would cure them, and from the beginning of the treatment they had expected that this relationship would at last yield them what life had so far denied them. It was only with this hope that they had taken such pains over the analysis and had conquered all their difficulties in disclosing their thoughts. We ourselves can add: "and had understood so easily all that is usually so hard to accept." But a confession of this kind astounds us; all our calculations are blown to the winds. Could it be that we have omitted the most important element in the whole problem?

And actually it is so; the more experience we gain the less possible does it become for us to contest this new factor, which alters the whole problem and puts our scientific calculations to shame. The first few times one might think that the analytic treatment had stumbled upon an obstruction in the shape of an accidental occurrence, extraneous to its purpose and unconnected wth it in origin. But when it happens that this kind of attachment to the physician regularly evinces itself in every fresh case, under the most unfavorable conditions, and always appears, even in circumstances of a positively grotesque incongruity—in elderly women, in relation to gray-bearded men, even on occasions when our judgement assures us that no temptations exist—then we are compelled to give up the idea of a disturbing accident and to admit that we have to deal with a phenomenon in itself essentially bound up with the nature of the disease.

The new fact which we are thus unwillingly compelled to recognize we call *transference*. By this we mean a transference of feelings on to the person of the physician, because we do not believe that the situation in the treatment can account for the origin of such feelings. We are much more disposed to suspect that the whole of this readiness to develop feeling originates in another source; that it was previously formed in the patient, and has seized the opportunity provided by the treatment to transfer itself on to the person of the physician. The transference can express itself as a passionate petitioning for love, or it can take less extreme forms; where a young girl and an elderly man are concerned, instead of the wish to be wife or mistress, a wish to be adopted as a favorite daughter may come to light, the libidinous desire can modify itself and propose itself as a wish for an everlasting, but ideally platonic friendship. Many women understand how to sublimate the transference and to mold it until it acquires a sort of justification for its existence; others have to express it in its crude, original, almost impossible form. But at bottom it is always the same, and its origin in the same source can never be mistaken.

Before we enquire where we are to range this new fact, we will amplify the description of it a little. How is it with our male patients? There at least we might hope to be spared the troublesome element of sex difference and sex attraction. Well, the answer is very much the same as with women. The same attachment to the physician, the same overestimation of his qualities, the same adoption of his interests, the same jealousy against all those connected with him. The sublimated kinds of transference are the forms more frequently met with between man and man, and the directly sexual declaration more rarely, in the same degree to which the manifest homosexuality of the patient is subordinated to the other ways by which this component-instinct can express itself. Also, it is in male patients that the analyst more frequently observes a manifestation of the transference which at the first glance seems to controvert the description of it just given—that is, the hostile or *negative* transference.

First of all, let us realize at once that the transference exists in the patient from the beginning of the treatment, and is for a time the strongest impetus in the work. Nothing is seen of it and one does not need to trouble about it as long as its effect is favorable to the work in which the two persons are cooperating. When it becomes transformed into a resistance, attention must be paid to it; and then it appears that two different and contrasting states of mind have supervened in it and have altered its attitude to the treatment: first, when the affectionate attraction has become so strong and betrays signs of its origin in sexual desire so clearly that it was bound to arouse an inner opposition against itself; and secondly, when it consists in antagonistic instead of affectionate feeling. The hostile feelings as a rule appear later than the affectionate and under cover of them; when both occur simultaneously they provide a very good exemplification of that ambivalence in feeling which governs most of our intimate relationships with other human beings. The hostile feelings therefore, indicate an attachment of feeling quite similar to the affectionate, just as defiance indicates a similar dependence upon the other person to that belonging to obedience, though with a reversed prefix. There can be no doubt that the hostile feelings against the analyst deserve the name of *transference,* for the situation in the treatment certainly gives no adequate occasion for them; the necessity for regarding the negative transference in this light is a confirmation of our previous similar view of the positive or affectionate variety.

Where the transference springs from, what difficulties it provides for us, how we can overcome them, and what advantage we can finally derive from it, are questions which can only be adequately dealt with in a technical exposition of the analytic method; I can merely touch upon them here. It is out of the question that we should yield to the demands made by the patient under the influence of his transference; it would be nonsensical to reject them unkindly, and still more so, indignantly. The transference is overcome by showing the patient that his feelings do not originate in the current situation, and do not really concern the person of the physician, but that he is reproducing something that had happened to him long ago. In this way we require him to transform his *repetition* into *recollection.* Then the transference which, whether affectionate or hostile, every time seemed the greatest menace to the cure becomes its best instrument, so that with its help we can unlock the closed doors in the soul. I should like, however, to say a few words to dispel the unpleasant effects of the shock that this unexpected phenomenon must have been to you. After all, we must not forget that this illness of the patient's which we undertake to analyze is not a finally accomplished, and as it were, consolidated thing; but that it is growing and continuing its development all the time like a living thing. The beginning of the treatment puts no stop to this development; but, as soon as the treatment has taken a hold upon the patient, it appears that the entire productivity of the illness henceforward becomes concentrated in one direction—namely, upon the relationship to the physician. The transference then becomes comparable to the cambium layer between the wood and the bark of a tree, from which proceeds the formation of new tissue and the growth of the trunk in diameter. As soon as the transference has taken on this significance the work upon the patient's recollections recedes far into the background. It is then not incorrect to say that we no longer have to do with the previous illness, but with a newly created and transformed neurosis which has replaced the earlier one. This new edition of the old disease has been followed from its inception, one sees it come to light and grow, and is particularly familiar with it since one is oneself its central object. All the patient's symptoms have abandoned their original significance and have adapted themselves to a new meaning, which is contained in their relationship to the transference; or else only those symptoms remain which were capable of being adapted in this way. The conquest of this new artificially acquired neurosis coincides with the removal of the illness which existed prior to the treatment, that is, with accomplishing the therapeutic task. The person who has become normal and free from the influence of repressed instinctive tendencies in his relationship to the physician remains so in his own life when the physician has again been removed from it.

The transference has this all important, absolutely central significance for the cure in hysteria, anxiety-hysteria, and the obsessional neurosis, which are in consequence rightly grouped together as the *transference neuroses.* Anyone who has grasped from analytic experience a true impression of the fact of transference can never again doubt the nature of the suppressed impulses which have manufactured an outlet for themselves in the symptoms; and he will require no stronger proof of their libidinal character. We may say that our conviction of the significance of the symptoms as a substitutive gratification of the libido was only finally and definitely established by evaluating the phenomenon of transference.

Now, however, we are called upon to correct our former dynamic conception of the process of cure and to bring it into agreement with the new discovery. When the patient has to fight out the normal conflict with the resistances which we have discovered in him by analysis, he requires a powerful propelling force to influence him towards the decision we aim at, leading to recovery. Otherwise it might happen that he would decide for a repetition of the previous outcome, and allow that which had been raised into consciousness to slip back again under repression. The outcome in this struggle is not decided by his intellectual insight—it is neither strong enough nor free enough to accomplish such a thing—but solely by his relationship to the physician. In so far as his transference bears the positive sign, it clothes the physician with authority, transforms itself into faith in his findings and in his views. Without this kind of transference or with a negative one, the physician and his arguments would never even be listened to. Faith repeats the history of its own origin; it is a derivative of love and at first it needed no arguments. Not until later does it admit them so far as to take them into critical consideration if they have been offered by someone who is loved. Without this support arguments have no weight with the patient, never do have any with most people in life. A human being is therefore on the whole only accessible to influence, even on the intellectual side, in so far as he is capable of investing objects with libido; and we have good cause to recognize, and to fear, in the measure of his narcissism a barrier to his susceptibility to influence, even by the best analytic technique.

The capacity for the radiation of libido towards other persons in object-investment must, of course, be ascribed to all normal people; the tendency to transference in neurotics, so called, is only an exceptional intensification of a universal characteristic. Now it would be very remarkable if a human character trait of this importance and universality had never been observed and made use of. And this has really been done. Bernheim, with unerring perspicacity, based the theory of hypnotic manifestations upon the proposition that all human beings are more or less open to suggestion, are "suggestible." What he called suggestibility is nothing else but the tendency to transference, rather too narrowly circumscribed so that the negative transference did not come within its scope. But Bernheim could never say what suggestion actually was nor how it arises; it was an axiomatic fact to him and he could give no explanation of its origin. He did not recognize the dependence of "suggestibility" on sexuality, on the functioning of the libido. And we have to admit that we have only abandoned hypnosis in our methods in order to discover suggestion again in the shape of transference. . . .

Psychoanalysis and Hypnosis

In the light of the knowledge we have obtained through psychoanalysis, the difference between hypnotic and psychoanalytic suggestion may be described as follows: The hypnotic therapy endeavors to cover up and as it were to whitewash something going on in the mind, the analytic to lay bare and to remove something. The first works cosmetically, the second surgically. The first employs suggestion to interdict the symptoms; it reinforces the repressions, but otherwise it leaves unchanged all the processes that have led to symptom-formation. Analytic therapy takes hold deeper down nearer the roots of the disease, among the conflicts from which the symptoms proceed; it employs suggestion to change the outcome of these conflicts. Hypnotic therapy allows the patient to remain inactive and unchanged, consequently also helpless in the face of every new incitement to illness. Analytic treatment makes as great demands for efforts on the part of the patient as on the physician, efforts to abolish the inner resistances. The patient's mental life is permanently changed by overcoming these resistances, is lifted to a higher level of development, and remains proof against fresh possibilities of illness. The labor of overcoming the resistances is the essential achievement of the analytic treatment; the patient has to accomplish it and the physician makes it possible for him to do this by suggestions which are in the nature of an *education*. It has been truly said therefore, that psychoanalytic treatment is a kind of *reeducation*. . . .

The Libido and Symptom Dissolution

We now need to complete our description of the process of recovery by expressing it in terms of the libido theory. The neurotic is incapable of enjoyment or of achievement—the first because his libido is attached to no real object, the last because so much of the energy which would otherwise be at his disposal is expended in maintaining the libido under repression, and in warding off its attempts to assert itself. He would be well if the conflict between his ego and his libido came to an end, and if his ego again had the libido at its disposal. The task of the treatment, therefore, consists in the task of loosening the libido from its previous attachments, which are beyond the reach of the ego, and in making it again serviceable to the ego. Now where is the libido of a neurotic? Easily found: it is attached to the symptoms, which offer it the substitutive satisfaction that is all it can obtain as things are. We must master the symptoms then, dissolve them—just what the patient asks of us. In order to dissolve the symptoms it is necessary to go back to the point at which they originated, to review the conflict from which they proceeded, and with the help of propelling forces which at that time were not available to guide it toward a new solution. This revision of the process of repression can only partially be effected by means of the memory-traces of the processes which led up to repression. The decisive part of the work is carried through by creating—in the relationship to the physician, in "the transference"—new editions of those early conflicts, in which the patient strives to behave as he originally behaved, while one calls upon all the available forces in his soul to bring him to another decision. The transference is thus the battlefield where all the contending forces must meet.

All the libido and the full strength of the opposition against it are concentrated upon the one thing, upon the relationship to the physician; thus it becomes inevitable that the symptoms should be deprived of their libido; in place of the patient's original illness appears the artificially acquired transference, the transference-disorder; in place of a variety of unreal objects of his libido appears the one object, also "fantastic," of the person of the physician. This new struggle which arises concerning this object is by means of the analyst's suggestions lifted to the surface, to the higher mental levels, and is there worked out as a normal mental conflict. Since a new repression is thus avoided, the opposition between the ego and the libido comes to an end; unity is restored within the patient's mind. When the libido has been detached from its temporary object of the person of the physician it cannot return to its earlier objects, but is now at the disposal of the ego. The forces opposing us in this struggle during the therapeutic treatment are on the one hand the ego's aversion against certain tendencies on the part of the libido, which has expressed itself in repressing tendencies; and on the other hand the tenacity or "adhesiveness" of the libido, which does not readily detach itself from objects it has once invested.

The therapeutic work thus falls into two phases; in the first all the libido is forced away from the symptoms into the transference and there concentrated, in the second the battle rages round this new object and the libido is made free from it. The change that is decisive for a successful outcome of this renewed conflict lies in the preclusion of repression, so that the libido cannot again withdraw itself from the ego by a flight into the unconscious. It is made possible by changes in the ego ensuing as a consequence of the analyst's suggestions. At the expense of the unconscious the ego becomes wider by the work of interpretation which brings the unconscious material into consciousness; through education it becomes reconciled to the libido and is made willing to grant it a certain degree of satisfaction; and its horror of the claims of its libido is lessened by the new capacity it acquires to expend a certain amount of the libido in sublimation. The more nearly the course of the treatment corresponds with this ideal description the greater will be the success of the psychoanalytic therapy. Its barriers are found in the lack of mobility in the libido, which resists being released from its objects, and in the rigidity of the patient's narcissism, which will not allow more than a certain degree of object-transference to develop. Perhaps the dynamics of the process of recovery will become still clearer if we describe it by saying that, in attracting a part of it to ourselves through transference, we gather in the whole amount of the libido which has been withdrawn from the ego's control.

It is as well here to make clear that the distributions of the libido which ensue during and by means of the analysis afford no direct inference of the nature of its disposition during the previous illness. Given that a case can be successfully cured by establishing and then resolving a powerful father-transference to the person of the physician, it would not follow that the patient had previously suffered in this way from an unconscious attachment of the libido to his father. The father-transference is only the battlefield on which we conquer and take the libido prisoner; the patient's libido has been drawn hither away from other "positions." The battlefield does not necessarily constitute one of the enemy's most important strongholds; the defense of the enemy's capital city need not be conducted immediately before its gates. Not until after the transference has been again resolved can one begin to reconstruct in imagination the dispositions of the libido that were represented by the illness.

In the light of the libido theory there is a final word to be said about dreams. The dreams of a neurotic, like his "errors" and his free associations, enable us to find the meaning of the symptoms and to discover the dispositions of the libido. The forms taken by the wish-fulfillment in them show us what are the wish-impulses that have undergone repression, and what are the objects to which the libido has attached itself after withdrawal from the ego. The interpretation of dreams therefore plays a great part in psychoanalytic treatment, and in many cases it is for lengthy periods the most important instrument at work. We already know that the condition of sleep in itself produces a certain relaxation of the repressions. By this diminution in the heavy pressure upon it the repressed desire is able to create for itself a far clearer expression in a dream than can be permitted to it by day in the symptoms. Hence the study of dreams becomes the easiest approach to a knowledge of the repressed unconscious, which is where the libido which has withdrawn from the ego belongs.

The dreams of neurotics, however, differ in no essential from those of normal people; they are indeed perhaps not in any way distinguishable from them. It would be illogical to account for the dreams of neurotics in a way that would not also hold good of the dreams of normal people. We have to conclude therefore that the difference between neurosis and health prevails only by day; it is not sustained in dream-life. It thus becomes necessary to transfer to healthy persons a number of conclusions arrived at as a result of the connections between the dreams and the symptoms of neurotics. We have to recognize that the healthy man as well possesses those factors in mental life which alone can bring about the formation of a dream or of a symptom, and we must conclude further that the healthy also have instituted repressions and have to expend a certain amount of energy to maintain them; that their unconscious minds too harbor repressed impulses which are still suffused with energy, and that *a part of the libido is in them also withdrawn from the disposal of the ego.* The healthy man too is therefore virtually a neurotic, but the only symptom that he *seems* capable of developing is a dream. To be sure when you subject his waking life also to a critical investigation you discover something that contradicts this specious conclusion; for this apparently healthy life is pervaded by innumerable trivial and practically unimportant symptom-formations.

The difference between nervous health and nervous illness (neurosis) is narrowed down therefore to a practical distinction, and is determined by the practical result—how far the person concerned remains capable of a sufficient degree of capacity for enjoyment and active achievement in life. The difference can probably be traced back to the proportion of the energy which has remained free relative to that of the energy which has been bound by repression, i.e., it is a quantitative and not a qualitative difference. I do not need to remind you that this view provides a theoretical basis for our conviction that the neuroses are essentially amenable to cure, in spite of their being based on a constitutional disposition. . . .

Dream Analysis and Interpretation

Dreams, as everyone knows, may be confused, unintelligible or positively nonsensical, what they say may contradict all that we know of reality, and we behave in them like insane people, since, so long as we are dreaming, we attribute objective reality to the contents of the dream.

Dream Analysis and Interpretation, from Sigmund Freud, *An Outline of Psychoanalysis,* trans. James Strachey, in Standard Edition of THE COMPLETE PSYCHOLOGICAL WORKS OF SIGMUND FREUD, vol. 23 (London: Hogarth, 1964), pp. 165–68. An earlier version is found in Sigmund Freud, *An Outline of Psychoanalysis* (New York: W. W. Norton, 1949), pp. 47–52. In the last paragraph internal references have been deleted.

We find our way to the understanding ("interpretation") of a dream by assuming that what we recollect as the dream after we have woken up is not the true dream-process but only a *façade* behind which that process lies concealed. Here we have our distinction between the *manifest* content of a dream and the *latent* dream-thoughts. The process which produces the former out of the latter is described as the *dream-work.* The study of the dream-work teaches us by an excellent example the way in which unconscious material from the id (originally unconscious and repressed unconscious alike) forces its way into the ego, becomes preconscious and, as a result of the ego's opposition, undergoes the changes which we know as *dream-distortion.* There are no features of a dream which cannot be explained in this way.

It is best to begin by pointing out that the formation of a dream can be provoked in two different ways. Either, on the one hand, an instinctual impulse which is ordinarily suppressed (an unconscious wish) finds enough strength during sleep to make itself felt by the ego, or, on the other hand, an urge left over from waking life, a preconscious train of thought with all the conflicting impulses attached to it, finds reinforcement during sleep from an unconscious element. In short, dreams may arise either from the id or from the ego. The mechanism of dream formation is in both cases the same and so also is the necessary dynamic precondition. The ego gives evidence of its original derivation from the id by occasionally ceasing its functions and allowing a reversion to an earlier state of things. This is logically brought about by its breaking off its relations with the external world and withdrawing its cathexes from the sense organs. We are justified in saying that there arises at birth an instinct to return to the intrauterine life that has been abandoned—an instinct to sleep. Sleep is a return of this kind to the womb. Since the waking ego governs motility, that function is paralyzed in sleep, and accordingly a good part of the inhibitions imposed on the unconscious id become superfluous. The withdrawal or reduction of these "anticathexes" thus allows the id what is now a harmless amount of liberty.

The evidence of the share taken by the unconscious id in the formation of dreams is abundant and convincing. (1) Memory is far more comprehensive in dreams than in waking life. Dreams bring up recollections which the dreamer has forgotten, which are inaccessible to him when he is awake. (2) Dreams make an unrestricted use of linguistic symbols, the meaning of which is for the most part unknown to the dreamer. Our experience, however, enables us to confirm their sense. They probably originate from earlier phases in the development of speech. (3) Memory very often reproduces in dreams impressions from the dreamer's early childhood of which we can definitely assert not only that they had been forgotten but that they had become unconscious owing to repression. That explains the help—usually indispensable—given us by dreams in the attempts we make during the analytic treatment of neuroses to reconstruct the dreamer's early life. (4) Furthermore, dreams bring to light material which cannot have originated either from the dreamer's adult life or from his forgotten childhood. We are obliged to regard it as part of the *archaic heritage* which a child brings with him into the world, before any experience of his own, influenced by the experiences of his ancestors. We find the counterpart of this phylogenetic material in the earliest human legends and in surviving customs. Thus dreams constitute a source of human prehistory which is not to be despised.

But what makes dreams so invaluable in giving us insight is the circumstance that, when the unconscious material makes its way into the ego, it brings its own modes of working along with it. This means that the preconscious thoughts in which the unconscious material has found its expression are handled in the course of the dream-work as though they were unconscious portions of the id; and, in the case of the alternative method of dream formation, the preconscious thoughts which have obtained reinforcement from an unconscious instinctual impulse are brought down to the unconscious state. It is only in this way that we learn the laws which govern the passage of events in the unconscious and the respects in which they differ from the rules that are familiar to us in waking thought. Thus the dream-work is essentially an instance of the unconscious working-over of preconscious throught processes. To take an analogy from history: invading conquerors govern a conquered country, not according to the judicial system which they find in force there, but according to their own. It is, however, an unmistakable fact that the outcome of the dream-work is a compromise. The ego-organization is not yet paralyzed, and its influence is to be seen in the distortion imposed on the unconscious material and in what are often very ineffective attempts at giving the total result a form not too unacceptable to the ego (*secondary revision*). In our analogy this would be an expression of the continued resistance of the defeated people.

The laws that govern the passage of events in the unconscious, which come to light in this manner, are remarkable enough and suffice to explain most of what seems strange to us about dreams. Above all there is a striking tendency to *condensation,* an inclination to form fresh unities out of elements which in our waking thought we should certainly have kept separate. As a consequence of this, a single element of the manifest dream often stands for a whole number of latent dream-thoughts as though it were a combined allusion to all of them; and in general the compass of the manifest dream is extraordinarily small in comparison with the wealth of material from which it has sprung. Another peculiarity of the dream-work, not entirely independent of the former one, is the case with which psychical intensities (cathexes) are *displaced* from one element to another, so that it often happens that an element which was of little importance in the dream-thoughts appears as the clearest and accordingly most important feature of the manifest dream, and vice versa, that essential elements of the dream-thoughts are represented in the manifest dream only by slight allusions. Moreover, as a rule the existence of quite insignificant points in common between two elements is enough to allow the dream-work to replace one by the other in all further operations. It will easily be imagined how greatly these mechanisms of condensation and displacement can increase the difficulty of interpreting a dream and of revealing the relations between the manifest dream and the latent dream-thoughts. From the evidence of the existence of these two tendencies to condensation and displacement our theory infers that in the unconscious id the energy is in a freely mobile state and that the id sets more store by the possibility of discharging quantities of excitation than by any other consideration; and our theory makes use of these two peculiarities in defining the character of the primary process we have attributed to the id.

Personality Theory and Mental Illness

Personality Development and the Oedipus Complex

The first organ to emerge as an erotogenic zone and to make libidinal demands on the mind is, from the time of birth onwards, the mouth. To begin with, all psychical activity is concentrated on providing satisfaction for the needs of that zone. Primarily, of course, this satisfaction serves the purpose of self-preservation by means of nourishment; but physiology should not be confused with psychology. The baby's obstinate persistence in sucking gives evidence at an early stage of a need for satisfaction which, though it originates from and is instigated by the taking of nourishment, nevertheless strives to obtain pleasure independently of nourishment and for that reason may and should be termed *sexual.*

During this oral phase sadistic impulses already occur sporadically along with the appearance of the teeth. Their extent is far greater in the second phase, which we describe as the sadistic-anal one, because satisfaction is then sought in aggression and in the excretory function. Our justification for including aggressive urges under the libido is based on the view that sadism is an instinctual fusion of purely libidinal and purely destructive urges, a fusion which thenceforward persists uninterruptedly.

The third phase is that known as the phallic one, which is, as it were, a forerunner of the final form taken by sexual life and already much resembles it. It is to be noted that it is not the genitals of both sexes that play a part at

Personality Development and the Oedipus Complex, from Freud, *An Outline of Psychoanalysis,* pp. 153–55 (pp. 28–31 in the Norton edition).

this stage, but only the male ones (the phallus.) The female genitals long remain unknown: in children's attempts to understand the sexual processes they pay homage to the venerable cloacal theory—a theory which has a genetic justification.

With the phallic phase and in the course of it the sexuality of early childhood reaches its height and approaches its dissolution. Thereafter boys and girls have different histories. Both have begun to put their intellectual activity at the service of sexual researches; both start off from the premise of the universal presence of the penis. But now the paths of the sexes diverge. The boy enters the Oedipus phase; he begins to manipulate his penis and simultaneously has fantasies of carrying out some sort of activity with it in relation to his mother, till, owing to the combined effect of a threat of castration and the sight of the absence of a penis in females, he experiences the greatest trauma of his life and this introduces the period of latency with all its consequences. The girl, after vainly attempting to do the same as the boy, comes to recognize her lack of a penis or rather the inferiority of her clitoris, with permanent effects on the development of her character; as a result of this first disappointment in rivalry, she often begins by turning away altogether from sexual life.

It would be a mistake to suppose that these three phases succeed one another in a clear-cut fashion. One may appear in addition to another; they may overlap one another, may be present alongside of one another. In the early phases the different component instincts set about their pursuit of pleasure independently of one another; in the phallic phase there are the beginnings of an organization which subordinates the other urges to the primacy of the genitals and signifies the start of a coordination of the general urge towards pleasure into the sexual function. The complete organization is only achieved at puberty, in a fourth, genital phase. A state of things is then established in which (1) some earlier libidinal cathexes are retained, (2) others are taken into the sexual function as preparatory, auxiliary acts, the satisfaction of which produces what is known as fore-pleasure, and (3) other urges are excluded from the organization, and are either suppressed altogether (repressed) or are employed in the ego in another way, forming character traits or undergoing sublimation with a displacement of their aims.

Id, Primary Process, and Instincts (Eros and Thanatos)

The core of our being . . . is formed by the obscure *id,* which has no direct communication with the external world and is accessible even to our own

---

Id, Primary Process, and Instincts (Eros and Thanatos), from Freud, *An Outline of Psychoanalysis,* pp. 197–98 (pp. 108–9 in the Norton edition).

knowledge only through the medium of another agency. Within this id the organic *instincts* operate, which are themselves compounded of fusions of two primal forces (Eros and destructiveness) in varying proportions and are differentiated from one another by their relation to organs or systems of organs. The one and only urge of these instincts is towards satisfaction, which is expected to arise from certain changes in the organs with the help of objects in the external world. But immediate and unheeding satisfaction of the instincts, such as the id demands, would often lead to perilous conflicts with the external world and to extinction. The id knows no solicitude about ensuring survival and no anxiety; or it would perhaps be more correct to say that, though it can generate the sensory elements of anxiety, it cannot make use of them. The processes which are possible in and between the assumed psychical elements in the id (*the primary process*) differ widely from those which are familiar to us through conscious perception in our intellectual and emotional life; nor are they subject to the critical restrictions of logic, which repudiates some of these processes as invalid and seeks to undo them.

The id, cut off from the external world, has a world of perception of its own. It detects with extraordinary acuteness certain changes in its interior, especially oscillations in the tension of its instinctual needs, and these changes become conscious as feelings in the pleasure-unpleasure series. It is hard to say, to be sure, by what means and with the help of what sensory terminal organs these perceptions come about. But it is an established fact that self-perceptions —coenaesthetic feelings and feelings of pleasure-unpleasure—govern the passage of events in the id with despotic force. The id obeys the inexorable pleasure principle. But not the id alone. It seems that the activity of the other psychical agencies too is able only to modify the pleasure principle but not to nullify it; and it remains a question of the highest theoretical importance, and one that has not yet been answered, when and how it is ever possible for the pleasure principle to be overcome. The consideration that the pleasure principle demands a reduction, at bottom the extinction perhaps, of the tensions of instinctual needs (that is, *Nirvana*) leads to the still unassessed relations between the pleasure principle and the two primal forces, Eros and the death instinct.

Ego and Reality Principle

The other agency of the mind, which we believe we know best and in which we recognize ourselves most easily—what is known as the *ego*—has been developed out of the id's cortical layer, which, through being adapted to the

---

Ego and Reality Principle, from Freud, *An Outline of Psychoanalysis,* pp. 198–200 (pp. 109–12 in the Norton edition).

reception and exclusion of stimuli, is in direct contact with the external world (*reality*). Starting from conscious perception it has subjected to its influence ever larger regions and deeper strata of the id, and, in the persistence with which it maintains its dependence on the external world, it bears the indelible stamp of its origin (as it might be "Made in Germany"). Its psychological function consists in raising the passage [of events] in the id to a higher dynamic level (perhaps by transforming freely mobile energy into bound energy, such as corresponds to the preconscious state); its constructive function consists in interpolating, between the demand made by an instinct and the action that satisfies it, the activity of thought which, after taking its bearings in the present and assessing earlier experiences, endeavors by means of experimental actions to calculate the consequences of the course of action proposed. In this way the ego comes to a decision on whether the attempt to obtain satisfaction is to be carried out or postponed or whether it may not be necessary for the demand by the instinct to be suppressed altogether as being dangerous. (Here we have the *reality principle.*) Just as the id is directed exclusively to obtaining pleasure, so the ego is governed by considerations of safety. The ego has set itself the task of self-preservation, which the id appears to neglect. It [the ego] makes use of the sensations of anxiety as a signal to give a warning of dangers that threaten its integrity. Since memory-traces can become conscious just as perceptions do, especially through their association with residues of speech, the possibility arises of a confusion which would lead to a mistaking of reality. The ego guards itself against this possibility by the institution of *reality-testing,* which is allowed to fall into abeyance in dreams on account of the conditions prevailing in the state of sleep. The ego, which seeks to maintain itself in an environment of overwhelming mechanical forces, is threatened by dangers which come in the first instance from external reality; but dangers do not threaten it from there alone. Its own id is a source of similar dangers, and that for two different reasons. In the first place, an excessive strength of instinct can damage the ego in a similar way to an excessive "stimulus" from the external world. It is true that the former cannot destroy it; but it can destroy its characteristic dynamic organization and change the ego back into a portion of the id. In the second place, experience may have taught the ego that the satisfaction of some instinctual demand which is not in itself intolerable would involve dangers in the external world, so that an instinctual demand of that kind itself becomes a danger. Thus the ego is fighting on two fronts; it has to defend its existence against an external world which threatens it with annihilation as well as against an internal world that makes excessive demands. It adopts the same methods of defense against both, but its defense against the internal enemy is particularly inadequate. As a result of having originally been identical with this latter enemy and of having lived with it since on the most intimate terms, it has great difficulty in escaping from the internal dangers. They persist as threats, even if they can be temporarily held down.

Superego and Conscience

We have no way of conveying knowledge of a complicated set of simultaneous events except by describing them successively; and thus it happens that all our accounts are at fault to begin with owing to one-sided simplification and must wait till they can be supplemented, built on to, and so set right.

The picture of an ego which mediates between the id and the external world, which takes over the instinctual demands of the former in order to lead them to satisfaction, which derives perceptions from the latter and uses them as memories, which, intent on its self-preservation, puts itself in defense against excessively strong claims from both sides and which, at the same time, is guided in all its decisions by the injunctions of a modified pleasure principle —this picture in fact applies to the ego only up to the end of the first period of childhood, till about the age of five. At about that time an important change has taken place. A portion of the external world has, at least partially, been abandoned as an object and has instead, by identification, been taken into the ego and thus become an integral part of the internal world. This new psychical agency continues to carry on the functions which have hitherto been performed by the people [the abandoned objects] in the external world: it observes the ego, gives it orders, judges it and threatens it with punishments, exactly like the parents whose place it has taken. We call this agency the *superego* and are aware of it in its judicial functions as our *conscience*. It is a remarkable thing that the superego often displays a severity for which no model has been provided by the real parents, and moreover that it calls the ego to account not only for its deeds but equally for its thoughts and unexecuted intentions, of which the superego seems to have knowledge. This reminds us that the hero of the Oedipus legend too felt guilty for his deeds and submitted himself to self-punishment, although the coercive power of the oracle should have acquitted him of guilt in our judgment and his own. The superego is in fact the heir to the Oedipus complex and is only established after that complex has been disposed of. For that reason its excessive severity does not follow a real model but corresponds to the strength of the defense used against the temptation of the Oedipus complex. Some suspicion of this state of things lies, no doubt, at the bottom of the assertion made by philosophers and believers that the moral sense is not instilled into men by education or acquired by them in their social life but is implanted in them from a higher source.

So long as the ego works in full harmony with the superego it is not easy to distinguish between their manifestations; but tensions and estrangements between them make themselves very plainly visible. The torments caused by the reproaches of conscience correspond precisely to a child's fear of loss of love, a fear the place of which has been taken by the moral agency. On the

---

Superego and Conscience, from Freud, *An Outline of Psychoanalysis,* pp. 205–6 (pp. 120–23 in the Norton edition).

other hand, if the ego has successfully resisted a temptation to do something which would be objectionable to the superego, it feels raised in its self-esteem and strengthened in its pride, as though it has made some precious acquisition. In this way the superego continues to play the part of an external world of the ego, although it has become a portion of the internal world. Throughout later life it represents the influence of a person's childhood, of the care and education given him by his parents and of his dependence on them—a childhood which is prolonged so greatly in human beings by a family life in common. And in all this it is not only the personal qualities of these parents that are making themselves felt, but also everything that had a determining effect on them themselves, the tastes and standards of the social class in which they lived and the innate dispositions and traditions of the race from which they sprang. Those who have a liking for generalizations and sharp distinctions may say that the external world, in which the individual finds himself exposed after being detached from his parents, represents the power of the present; that his id, with its inherited trends, represents the organic past; and that the superego, which comes to join them later, represents more than anything the cultural past, which a child has, as it were, to repeat as an after-experience during the few years of his early life.

A Theory of Neurosis and Psychosis

We have heard how the weak and immature ego of the first period of childhood is permanently damaged by the stresses put upon it in its efforts to fend off the dangers that are peculiar to that period of life. Children are protected against the dangers that threaten them from the external world by the solicitude of their parents; they pay for this security by a fear of *loss of love* which would deliver them over helpless to the dangers of the external world. This factor exerts a decisive influence on the outcome of the conflict when a boy finds himself in the situation of the Oedipus complex, in which the threat to his narcissism by the danger of castration, reinforced from primeval sources, takes possession of him. Driven by the combined operation of these two influences, the contemporary real danger and the remembered one with its phylogenetic basis, the child embarks on his attempts at defense—repressions—which are effective for the moment but nevertheless turn out to be psychologically inadequate when the later reanimation of sexual life brings a reinforcement to the instinctual demands which have been repudiated in the past. If this is so, it would have to be said from a biological standpoint that the ego comes to grief over the task of mastering the excitations of the early sexual period, at a time when its immaturity makes it incompetent to do so. It is in this lagging of ego

---

A Theory of Neurosis and Psychosis, from Freud, *An Outline of Psychoanalysis,* pp. 200–202 (pp. 112–16 in the Norton edition).

development behind libidinal development that we see the essential precondition of neurosis; and we cannot escape the conclusion that neuroses could be
avoided if the childish ego were spared this task—if, that is to say, the child's
sexual life were allowed free play, as happens among many primitive peoples.
It may be that the etiology of neurotic illnesses is more complicated than we
have here described it; if so, we have at least brought out one essential part
of the etiological complex. Nor should we forget the phylogenetic influences,
which are represented in some way in the id in forms that we are not yet able
to grasp, and which must certainly act upon the ego more powerfully in that
early period than later. On the other hand, the realization dawns on us that
such an early attempt at damming up the sexual instinct, so decided a partisan-
ship by the young ego in favor of the external as opposed to the internal world,
brought about by the prohibition of infantile sexuality, cannot be without its
effect on the individual's later readiness for culture. The instinctual demands
forced away from direct satisfaction are compelled to enter on new paths
leading to substitutive satisfaction, and in the course of these *détours* they may
become desexualized and their connection with their original instinctual aims
may become looser. And at this point we may anticipate the thesis that many
of the highly valued assets of our civilization were acquired at the cost of
sexuality and by the restriction of sexual motive forces.

We have repeatedly had to insist on the fact that the ego owes its origin
as well as the most important of its acquired characteristics to its relation to
the real external world. We are thus prepared to assume that the ego's pathological states, in which it most approximates once again to the id, are founded
on a cessation or slackening of that relation to the external world. This tallies
very well with what we learn from clinical experience—namely, that the
precipitating cause of the outbreak of a psychosis is either that reality has
become intolerably painful or that the instincts have become extraordinarily
intensified—both of which, in view of the rival claims made on the ego by the
id and the external world, must lead to the same result. The problem of
psychoses would be simple and perspicuous if the ego's detachment from
reality could be carried through completely. But that seems to happen only
rarely or perhaps never. Even in a state so far removed from the reality of the
external world as one of hallucinatory confusion, one learns from patients after
their recovery that at the time in some corner of their mind (as they put it)
there was a normal person hidden, who, like a detached spectator, watched the
hubbub of illness go past him. I do not know if we may assume that this is
so in general, but I can report the same of other psychoses with a less tempestu-
ous course. I call to mind a case of chronic paranoia in which after each attack
of jealousy a dream conveyed to the analyst a correct picture of the precipitating cause, free from any delusion. An interesting contrast was thus brought
to light: while we are accustomed to discover from the dreams of neurotics
jealousies which are alien to their waking lives, in this psychotic case the

delusion which dominated the patient in the daytime was corrected by his dream. We may probably take it as being generally true that what occurs in all these cases is a psychical *split*. Two psychical attitudes have been formed instead of a single one—one, the normal one, which takes account of reality, and another which under the influence of the instincts detaches the ego from reality. The two exist alongside of each other. The issue depends on their relative strength. If the second is or becomes the stronger, the necessary precondition for a psychosis is present. If the relation is reversed, then there is an apparent cure of the delusional disorder. Actually it has only retreated into the unconscious—just as numerous observations lead us to believe that the delusion existed ready-made for a long time before its manifest irruption.

2

INDIVIDUAL PSYCHOLOGY THERAPY

Alfred Adler

Alfred Adler (1870–1937), an Austrian psychiatrist of Jewish parentage, was born and educated in Vienna. In 1926 he left Vienna for New York, where he accepted a visiting professorship at Columbia University. Thereafter Adler spent the major portion of each year in the United States. From 1932 until his death he was professor of medical psychology at what is today named the State University of New York, Downstate Medical Center.

Freud, impressed by Adler's favorable review of his *The Interpretation of Dreams* (1900), invited Adler to join the weekly psychoanalytic discussion group in 1902. It was not long before it became apparent that Adler's views were not consonant with Freud's. The breach widened until Adler was obliged to resign from the society in 1911 and also to forego his post of coeditor of the *Zentralblatt.* In 1912 Adler founded his own group, the Society for Individual Psychology.

The same year Adler established the *Journal for Individual Psychology,* whose publication was interrupted during World War I when Adler assumed duties as a military physician. In 1922 the organ changed its name to the *International Journal for Individual Psychology.* Its publication was interrupted again during World War II and its demise came in 1948. The English counterpart of this publication appeared in America in 1935 (with Adler as its editor) and since 1957 has been entitled *Journal of Individual Psychology.*

With the rise of nazism in Europe, Adler's followers were compelled to disperse, and the guidance clinics that he had founded were forced to close in 1934. Adler was obliged to move his family to the United States.

Adler's Russian wife, Raissa, was a close friend of Trotsky, which accounts for the fact that many of his followers were socialists and for his psychology of *social interest.* His children, Kurt and Alexandra, both psychiatrists, are practicing the principles of individual psychology enunciated by their father.

Just as many psychologists account for psychoanalysis, in a number of respects, as the outgrowth of Freud's childhood and neurotic experiences, so can one view individual psychology as the result of Adler's early life, in certain respects. Adler's childhood was marked by illness, accident-proneness, and failure in academic studies. Instead of being overcome by a feeling of inferiority for his childhood weaknesses and failures, Adler tried to compensate for them by striving for success. In compensation for illness, Adler determined to become a physician. And like Demosthenes, he turned failure into success, moving from a failing rank in mathematics to the top of the class.

Adler's death occurred in Scotland, where he was delivering a series of lectures at the University of Aberdeen. He collapsed in the street and died of a heart attack on May 28, 1937.

Adler's psychotherapeutic system is contingent upon his theory of the difference between a neurotic and a wholesome personality. Adler views a person as an individual, a unity that is not divided against itself by those internal conflicting forces comprising the personality structure. The personality is neither a battleground of conscious and unconscious minds nor a rebellion of id, ego, and superego, as Freud presumed. Personality is a dynamic unity pursuing a goal as a whole. Personality has numerous cooperating parts subserving a dominant, fundamental goal or life-plan.

The personality strives for superiority or success with an inherent freedom. This freedom for choices and decisions creates the condition of conflict that intimidates neurotics, causing responses of hesitation which enable them to gain time. Neurotics in their "godlikeness" (impossible idealism) pursue unrealistic goals far beyond human reach, and consequently never escape from a sense of failure and inferiority. They strive vainly to attain impossible goals. Accordingly, mental disturbance, particularly neurosis, is not illness, but an erroneous way of living, a faulty life-style, while mental health is a less faulty style of living. Consequently, individual psychology seeks, by reeducation, to replace grossly erroneous ways of living with less severe mistakes.

The establishment of mental health is to provide an absolute answer to the meaning of life, but since there is no absolute answer, the therapist must provide the most feasible one. Adler believed in the life of social usefulness, for healthy individuals live socially useful lives, while psychotics and others are antisocial or social indigents. Whereas the former are self-transcending, seeking to attain a socially useful goal as their mark of superiority, the latter are self-centered, exerting their superiority by causing harm to others. Thus mental illness is a mistaken striving for an invalid goal, while mental health is the pursuit of superiority or success, a goal that is to the common benefit of all. Therapy consists, therefore, in widening and intensifying the patient's social interest and diminishing inferiority feelings that motivate egoistic and socially useless endeavors.

Psychotherapy is inextricably connected to sincere interpersonal relationships, whereby the therapist confers an enlightened social feeling to the patient. Thus transference is simply social feeling. The psychoanalytic couch is dispensed with and the therapist assumes a vis-à-vis position with the patient. Early memories of childhood, which the patient recalls, are profoundly significant owing to the present motivational power they possess.

The patient's egoistic interests and avoidance of responsibility must be transmuted into a life of socially useful activity. Individual psychology psychotherapy is social therapy or milieu therapy, requiring more than mere insight into one's problems; it is a renewal of one's role and position in society as well as the heightening of one's interest in others.

Some of Adler's books are comprised of lectures, which students have reconstructed; others are composed of papers. His books in English, with the year of English publication following the date of the original (where applicable), are: *Study of Organ Inferiority and Its Psychical Compensation* (1907, 1917); *The Neurotic Constitution* (1912, 1926); *The Practice and Theory of Individual Psychology* (1920, 1927); *Understanding Human Nature* (1927); *The Case of Miss R.: The Interpretation of a Life Story* (1928, 1929); *Problems of Neurosis: A Book of Case Histories* (1929); *The Science of Living* (1929); *The Education of Children* (1930); *The Pattern of Life* (1930); *What Life Should Mean to You* (1931); *Social Interest: A Challenge to Mankind* (1933, 1938); *The Problem Child* (1930, 1963); and *Superiority and Social Interest* (H.L. Ansbacher, ed., 1964).

Fundamental Principles for the Practice of Individual Psychology

I. Every neurosis can be understood as an attempt to free oneself from a feeling of inferiority in order to gain a feeling of superiority.

II. The path of the neurosis does not lead in the direction of social functioning, nor does it aim at solving given life-problems but finds an outlet for itself in the small family circle, thus achieving the isolation of the patient.

III. The larger unit of the social group is either completely or very extensively pushed aside by a mechanism consisting of hyper-sensitiveness and intolerance. Only a small group is left over for the manoeuvres aiming at the various types of superiority to expend themselves upon. At the same time protection and the withdrawal from the demands of the community and the decisions of life are made possible.

IV. Thus estranged from reality, the neurotic man lives a life of imagination and fantasy and employs a number of devices for enabling him to sidestep the demands of reality and for reaching out toward an ideal situation which would free him from any service for the community and absolve him from responsibility.

Fundamental Principles for the Practice of Individual Psychology, from Alfred Adler, *The Practice and Theory of Individual Psychology,* trans. P. Radin, 2nd ed. (London: Routledge & Kegan Paul; New York: Humanities Press, 1929), pp. 23–26.

V. These exemptions and the privileges of illness and suffering give him a substitute for his original hazardous goal of superiority.

VI. Thus the neurosis and the psyche represent an attempt to free oneself from all the constraints of the community by establishing a counter-compulsion. This latter is so constituted that it effectively faces the peculiar nature of the surroundings and their demands. Both of these convincing inferences can be drawn from the manner in which this counter-compulsion manifests itself and from the neuroses selected.

VII. The counter-compulsion takes on the nature of a revolt, gathers its material either from favorable affective experiences or from observations. It permits thoughts and affects to become preoccupied either with the above-mentioned stirrings or with unimportant details, as long as they at least serve the purpose of directing the eye and the attention of the patient away from his life-problems. In this manner, depending upon the needs of the situation, he prepares anxiety- and compulsion-situations, sleeplessness, swooning, perversions, hallucinations, slightly pathological affects, neurasthenic and hypochondriacal complexes and psychotic pictures of his actual condition, all of which are to serve him as excuses.

VIII. Even logic falls under the domination of the counter-compulsion. As in psychosis this process may go as far as the actual nullification of logic.

IX. Logic, the will to live, love, human sympathy, cooperation and language, all arise out of the needs of human communal life. Against the latter are directed automatically all the plans of the neurotic individual striving for isolation and lusting for power.

X. To cure a neurosis and a psychosis it is necessary to change completely the whole upbringing of the patient and turn him definitely and unconditionally back upon human society.

XI. All the volition and all the strivings of the neurotic are dictated by his prestige-seeking policy, which is continually looking for excuses which will enable him to leave the problems of life unsolved. He consequently automatically turns against allowing any community feeling to develop.

XII. If therefore we may regard the demand for a complete and unified understanding of man and for a comprehension of his (undivided) individuality as justified—a view to which we are forced both by the nature of reason and the individual-psychological knowledge of the urge toward an integration of the personality—then the method of *comparison,* the main tool of our method, enables us to arrive at some conception of the powerlines along which an individual strives to attain superiority. The following will serve as the two contrasting poles for comparison:

1. Our own attitude in a situation similar to that of a patient hardpressed by some demand. In such a case it is essential for the practitioner to possess, in a considerable degree, the gift of *putting himself in the other person's place.*

2. The patient's attitudes and anomalies dating from early childhood. These can always be shown as dominated by the relation of the child to his environment, by his erroneous and in the main generalized evaluation (of himself), by his obstinate and deep-rooted feeling of inferiority and by his striving after power.

3. Other types of individuals, particularly those specifically neurotic. In these cases we shall come upon the patent discovery that what one type attains by means of neurasthenic troubles, another endeavors to obtain by means of fear, hysteria, neurotic-compulsion, or psychosis. Traits of character, affects, principles and nervous symptoms, pointing toward the same goal and, when torn from their context, frequently giving a contrary significance, all these serve as a protection against the shock caused by the demands of the community.

4. Those very demands of the community which the nervous individual, in varying degrees, sidesteps, such as cooperation, fellow-feeling, love, social adaptation and the responsibilities of the community.

By means of this individual-psychological investigation we realize that the neurotic individual, far more than the ordinary normal man, arranges his psychic life in accordance with the desire for power over his fellow men. His longing for superiority enables him continually and extensively to reject all outside compulsion, the demands made upon him by others and the responsibilities imposed by society. The realization of this basic fact in the psychic life of the neurotic so lightens the task of obtaining an insight into psychic interconnections that it is bound to become the most useful working hypothesis in the investigation and curing of neurotic diseases, until a more profound understanding of the individual enables us to disentangle and grasp, in their full significance, the real factors involved in each case. ...

Individual Psychology: Its Psychotherapeutic Technique

We are concerned at present to establish convincing proofs of the unity of the personality on evidence which will leave no room for doubt. We also succeed more quickly in tracing the strangest aberrations of the human mind to the sense of some personal peculiarity which gives rise to a failure to cope with reality. The *unconscious* of the textbooks, in which current attempts to elucidate its meaning have already distinguished several levels, each able to serve

---

Individual Psychology: Its Psychotherapeutic Technique, from Adler, *Practice and Theory,* pp. v–vi.

as an *asylum ignorantiae*, resolves itself for us chiefly into the patient's failure to understand his impulses in relation to his social environment. In consonance with our earliest conclusions, dreams are seen with increasing clearness to be a preparation for confronting some problem which has presented itself in accordance with the desire for superiority and by means of an analogy. As one of the most important safeguards we have the *elimination* of the customary modes of life, whereby neurotic or perverse behavior is rendered possible. This shows the worthlessness of pleasure and pain as causes and justification for unsocial behavior. They can always be modified and take the form of further safeguards when once a wrong course is to be adopted. The effects of suggestion and auto-suggestion are revealed ever more clearly as partial phenomena which can never be rationally explained except in relation to a total setting.

Our contention, too, that all forms of neurosis and developmental failure are expressions of inferiority and disappointment rests on a firm basis. And if success in treating these maladies—even in their gravest forms—is a criterion, then its practical application has shown that Individual Psychology comes well out of the test. To encourage the student I would further add that we Individual Psychologists are in a position, if a proper procedure is observed, to get a clear conception of the fundamental psychic error of the patient at the first consultation. And the way to a cure is thus opened. . . .

Foundations of Individual Psychology's Therapy

The sense of inferiority, the struggle to overcome, and social feeling—the foundations upon which the researches of Individual Psychology are based— are therefore essential in considering either the individual or the mass. The truth they represent may be evaded or put into different words; they may be misunderstood and attempts may be made to split hairs about them, but they can never be obliterated. In the right estimate of any personality these facts must be taken into account, and the state of the feeling of inferiority, of the struggle to overcome, and of the social feeling must be ascertained.

But just as other civilizations under the pressure of evolution drew different conclusions and followed wrong courses, so does every single individual. It is the child's work to create, in the stream of development, the mental structure of a style of life and the appropriate emotions associated with it. The child's emotional, and as yet barely grasped, capacity of action, serves him as a standard of his creative power in an environment that is by no means neutral, and provides a very indifferent preparatory school for life. Building on a subjective impression, and guided often by successes or defeats that supply insufficient criteria, the child forms for himself a path, a goal, and a vision of

Foundations of Individual Psychology's Therapy, from Alfred Adler, *Social Interest: A Challenge to Mankind,* trans. John Linton and Richard Vaughan (London: Faber & Faber; New York: Capricorn Books, 1938), pp. 38–41.

a height lying in the future. All the methods of Individual Psychology that are meant to lead to an understanding of the personality take into account the meaning of the individual about his goal of superiority, the strength of his feeling of inferiority, and the degree of his social feeling. A closer scrutiny of the relation of these factors to one another will make it clear that they all contribute to the nature and extent of the social feeling. The examination proceeds in a way similar to that of experimental psychology, or to that of functional tests in medical cases. The only difference is that it is life itself that sets the test, and this shows how strong the bond is between the individual and the problems of life. That is to say, the individual as a complete being cannot be dragged out of his connection with life—perhaps it would be better to say, with the community. His attitude to the community is first revealed by his style of life. For that reason experimental tests, which at the best deal only with partial aspects of the individual's life, can tell us nothing about his character or even about his future achievements in the community. And even the *Gestalt-psychologie* needs to be supplemented by Individual Psychology in order to be able to form any conclusion regarding the attitude of the individual in the life-process.

The technique of Individual Psychology employed for the discovery of the style of life must therefore in the first place presuppose a knowledge of the problems of life and their demands on the individual. It will be evident that their solution presumes a certain degree of social feeling, a close union with life as a whole, and an ability to cooperate and mix with other persons. If this ability is lacking there can be noticed an acute feeling of inferiority in its innumerable variations together with its consequences. This in the main will take the form of evasiveness and the "hesitant attitude." The interrelated bodily and mental phenomena that make their appearance with it I have called an "inferiority complex." The unresting struggle for superiority endeavors to mask this complex by a "superiority complex," which, ignoring social feeling, always aims at the glitter of personal conquest. Once all the phenomena occurring in a case of failure are clearly understood, the reasons for the inadequate preparation are to be sought for in early childhood. By this means we succeed in obtaining a faithful picture of the homogeneous style of life, and at the same time in estimating the extent of the divergence from social feeling in the case of a failure. This is always seen to be a lack of ability to get into contact with other people. It follows from this that the task of the educationist, the teacher, the physician, the pastor is to increase the social feeling and thereby strengthen the courage of the individual. He does this by convincing him of the real causes of his failure, by disclosing his wrong meaning—the mistaken significance he has foisted on life—and thus giving him a clearer view of the meaning that life has ordained for humanity.

This task can only be accomplished if a thoroughgoing knowledge of the problems of life is available, and if the too slight tincture of social feeling both in the inferiority and superiority complexes, as well as in all kinds of human errors, is understood. There is likewise required in the consultant a wide experience regarding those circumstances and situations which are likely to hinder the development of social feeling in childhood. Up till now my own experience has taught me that the most trustworthy approaches to the exploration of the personality are to be found in a comprehensive understanding of the earliest childhood memories; of the place of the child in the family sequence; of any childish errors; of day and night dreams; and of the nature of the exogenous factor that causes the illness. All the results of such an investigation—and along with these the attitude to the doctor has also to be included —have to be assessed with great caution, and the conclusion drawn from them has constantly to be tested for its harmony with other facts that have been established. . . .

The Counseling Session

Our fundamental principle of the unity of the style of life fashioned in the earliest childhood was already known to me when I began my labors, although I did not understand it, and it enabled me to assume at once that the person who comes for advice reveals his personality the moment he appears, without knowing very much about it. For the patient the consultation is a social problem. Every encounter of one person with another is a problem of that kind. Everyone will introduce himself according to his law of movement. The expert can often tell something of the patient's social feeling at the first glance. Dissimulation is of little use with an experienced Individual Psychologist. The patient expects a good deal of social feeling from his adviser. Since experience has taught us not to expect much social interest from the patient, one will not demand very much. There are two considerations that give us essential help in this connection. The first is that as a rule the general level of social feeling is not high; the second is that we have usually to deal with people who have been pampered as children, and who in their later years cannot free themselves from their unreal world. It would not be very surprising if many of my readers have accepted without a shock the fact that people ask: "Why should I love my neighbor?" After all Cain put a similar question.

The glance, the gait, the vigor or weakness of the patient's approach can reveal a great deal. Much may be missed if one makes it a rule to indicate, say, a particular seat—a sofa—or to keep strictly to a special hour. The first interview should be a test by its being entirely unconstrained. Even the way of shaking hands may suggest a definite problem. One often sees pampered persons leaning against something and children clinging to their mother. But, just as with everything that constitutes a problem for the consultant's ability to guess, so in these cases also one should avoid rigorous rules and make a close

The Counseling Session, from Adler, *Social Interest,* pp. 286–98.

examination. It is preferable to keep one's views to oneself, so that later on, after the case has been understood, they may be used in a suitable way without injuring the patient's hypersensitiveness, which is always in evidence. Occasionally one should tell the patient to sit anywhere he likes, without indicating any particular seat. The distance from the doctor or the consultant reveals—precisely as it does in the case of school children—a good deal about the patient's nature. Further, it is important that the "popular" psychology that is the rage in such consultations, and even in social gatherings, should be rigorously forbidden, and that at the beginning of the treatment strictly technical answers to the questions of the patient or his relatives should be avoided. The Individual Psychologist should not forget that, leaving out of account his own trained ability to guess, he has also to bring proof to others who have not had his experience. To the parents and relatives of the patient the consultant should never appear to be taking up an attitude of doubt. He should rather describe the case as worth consideration and not hopeless, even when he is not inclined to undertake it himself, unless weighty reasons in an absolutely hopeless case demand the telling of the truth. I see an advantage in not interrupting the patient's movements. Let him get up, come and go, or smoke as he likes. I have even occasionally given my patients the opportunity of going to sleep in my presence—a suggestion on their part made for the purpose of making my task more difficult. Such an attitude was just as significant a language for me as if they had expressed themselves in words that showed their opposition. A patient's sidelong glance clearly indicates his slight inclination to take part in the common task that links the patient to the doctor. This disinclination to cooperation can be strikingly shown in another way, when the patient says little or nothing, when he beats about the bush, or when he prevents the doctor from speaking by his incessant talking. The Individual Psychologist, unlike other psychotherapeutists, will avoid being sleepy, or going to sleep or yawning, showing a want of interest in the patient, using harsh words, giving premature advice, letting himself be looked upon as the last resort, being unpunctual, getting into a dispute, or declaring that there is no prospect of a cure. In the latter case, when the difficulties are too great, the course recommended is to explain that one is unable to deal with the case and to refer the patient to others who may be more capable. Any attempt at assuming an authoritative manner prepares the way for a failure, and all boasting is an obstacle to the cure. From the very beginning of the treatment the consultant must try to impress on the patient that the responsibility for his cure rests in his own hands. For as the English proverb very rightly says: "You can take a horse to the water, but you can't make him drink."

It should be a strict rule to consider the success of the treatment and the cure as due not to the consultant but to the patient. The adviser can only point out the mistakes, it is the patient who must make the truth living. Since, as we have seen, all cases of failure are due to a want of cooperation, advantage should be taken from the start of every means by which the patient's cooperation with the consultant can be increased. Obviously this is only possible when the patient can trust his adviser. Consequently this work in common is of supreme importance as the first serious attempt made in a scientific spirit to lift the social feeling to a higher level. Among other things the consultant must strictly avoid calling into existence—especially by insisting on suppressed sexual components—that psychic current which Freud has called the positive transference. This is frankly demanded in the psychoanalytic cure, and it is also used by other consultants when there is a permanent feeling of inferiority and when the patient has very little faith in his adviser, but it only adds a new problem to the treatment. This artificially created condition has, at the best, to be made to disappear. If the patient, who is almost always a spoiled child or an adult craving to be pampered, has learned to take full responsibility for his behavior, the consultant will easily avoid leading him into that snare which seems to promise an easy and immediate satisfaction of his unfulfilled desires. Since on the whole every unfulfilled wish appears to be a repression to spoiled persons, I should like to say once more here that Individual Psychology demands the repression of neither justifiable nor unjustifiable wishes. It does teach, however, that unjustifiable wishes must be recognized as being opposed to social feeling, and that they can be made to disappear not by suppression but by an addition to social interest. . . .

The patient must in any case get the conviction that he is absolutely free with regard to the treatment. He can do or leave undone anything he likes. One should only avoid giving the impression that the patient will begin to get rid of his symptoms even at the very beginning of the treatment. . . .

I will make another recommendation. The doctor should bind himself not to speak to anyone else of his conversations with the patient—and he should keep his word. On the other hand the patient should be left absolutely free to tell anything he thinks fit. Certainly one runs the risk here of a patient's using the doctor's explanations to slip into the "popular" psychology in company. ("What they've learned yesterday they want to teach today. What a swift evacuation they must surely have!") But a friendly talk can take the edge off that. Or there may follow complaints about the patient's family. These must also be anticipated in order to make it plain to the patient beforehand that his relatives are to blame only so long as he makes them blameworthy by his conduct, and that they will immediately be blameless as soon as he feels himself well. Further, it must be pointed out to him that one cannot expect more knowledge from the patient's relatives than he himself possesses and that he has on his own responsibility used the influences of his environment as material for constructing his own style of life. It is also as well to remind him that his parents, in the event of their being at fault, can appeal to the mistakes of their parents, and so on through the generations; so that for this reason there can be no blame in his sense of the word.

It seems to me important that the patient should not get the idea that the work of an Individual Psychologist is meant to add to his own gain and glory. Keenness to secure patients can only cause harm. This is true also of depreciatory or perhaps spiteful remarks about other consultants. . . .

If the patient at the first interview is in doubt as to whether he will undergo the treatment, leave the decision over until the next few days. The usual question about the duration of the treatment is not easy to answer. I consider this question quite justified, because a large number of those who visit me have heard of treatments that have lasted eight years and have been unsuccessful. Treatment by Individual Psychology, if properly carried out, must show at least a perceptible partial success in three months, in most cases even earlier. Since, however, success depends on the cooperation of the patient the correct procedure is to keep a door open for social feeling from the start by emphasizing the fact that the duration of the cooperation depends on the patient, that the physician, if he is well-grounded in Individual Psychology, can find his bearings after half an hour, but that he has to wait until the patient as well has recognized his style of life and its mistakes. Still one can add: "If you are not convinced after one or two weeks that we are on the right path, I will stop the treatment."

The unavoidable question of the fee causes difficulties. I have often received patients who have lost a not inconsiderable fortune in previous treatments. The consultant must bring himself into line with the fees customary in his district. He may also take into consideration any extra trouble and expenditure of time the case requires. He should, however, abstain from making unusually large demands, especially when these would be harmful to the patient. Gratuitous treatment should be carried through in such a tactful manner that poor patients will not feel that the consultant shows in any way a lack of interest in their case. In most cases they never fail to notice this. The payment of a lump sum, even when that seems acceptable, or a promise to pay after a successful cure, should be declined, not because the latter is uncertain, but because it artificially introduces a new motive into the relationship between the doctor and his patient, and this makes successful treatment difficult. Payment should be made weekly or monthly, and always at the end of the period. Demands or expectations of any kind always do harm to the treatment. Even trivial kindly services which the patient quite often himself offers to give must be refused. Gifts should be declined in a friendly manner, or their acceptance postponed until after the cure has been completed. There should be no mutual invitations or joint visits during the treatment. The treatment of relatives or of persons known to the consultant is of a rather more difficult complexion, because in the nature of things any feeling of inferiority becomes more oppressive in the presence of an acquaintance. The person who has to deal with the case, too, is also averse to tracing his patient's feeling of inferiority, and he has to do his very utmost to make the patient feel at his ease. Any tension is greatly relieved when one has the good fortune, as in Individual Psychology, to be able in the treatment always to draw attention only to errors and never to innate defects, always to show that there is the possibility of a cure and make the patient feel that he is just as important as anyone else, and always to the point to the universally low level of social feeling. This helps us also to understand why Individual Psychology has never seen traces of the great "resistance" that other systems have found. It is easy to see that the treatment in Individual Psychology never comes to a crisis. ... I have always considered it a great advantage to keep the level of tension in the treatment as low as possible, and I have frankly developed a method of saying to almost every patient that there are jocular situations that are almost completely similar in structure to his particular neurosis, and therefore that he can take his trouble more lightly than he is doing. As for those critics who are rather dense, at the risk of being redundant I must take the word from their lips and add that, of course, such jocular allusions will not lead to the revival of the feeling of inferiority (which Freud at present finds so extraordinarily enlightening). References to fables and historical personages, and quotations from the poets and philosophers, help to strengthen the belief in Individual Psychology and in its conceptions.

At every interview it ought to be noted whether or not the patient is on the way to cooperation. Every gesture, every expression, the material for discussion he brings with him or has not brought with him will supply proof of this. A thorough understanding of dreams gives at the same time the opportunity of taking account of success or failure and of the amount of cooperation. But special caution must be exercised in spurring the patient on towards any particular line of action. If there should be any talk about this the doctor should not say anything for or against, but, ruling out as a matter of course all undertakings that are generally considered dangerous, he should tell the patient that, while he was convinced that he would be successful, he was not quite able to judge precisely whether he was really ready for the venture. Any incitement given before the patient has acquired a greater social feeling revenges itself as a rule by a strengthening or a recurrence of the symptoms.

Stronger measures may be taken when it comes to the question of a vocation. This does not in any way mean that the patient should be ordered to take up a profession, but simply that the consultant should point out to him that he is best prepared for a particular calling, and that he will most likely be successful in following it. As on the whole at every stage of the treatment, here also we must keep strictly to the method of encouraging the patient. We must act on the conviction of Individual Psychology—which has made so many unstable and vain people feel that their toes have been trodden on—viz. "that" (apart from outstanding, special achievements about whose structure we can say very little) "everyone can do anything." ...

Life-Plan, Goal, and Finalism

Let me observe that if I know the goal of a person I know in a general way what will happen. I am in a position to bring into their proper order each of the successive movements made, to view them in their connections, to correct them and to make, where necessary, the required adaptations for my approximate psychological knowledge of these associations. If I am acquainted only with the causes, know only the reflexes, the reaction times, the ability to repeat and such facts, I am aware of nothing that actually takes place in the soul of the man.

We must remember that the person under observation would not know what to do with himself were he not oriented toward some goal. As long as we are not acquainted with the objective which determines his "life-line," the whole system of his recognized reflexes, together with all their causal conditions, can give us no certainty as to his next series of movements. They might be brought into harmony with practically any psychic resultant. This deficiency is most clearly felt in association tests. I would never expect a man suffering from some great disappointment to associate "tree" with "rope." The moment I knew his objective, however, namely suicide, then I might very well expect that particular sequence of thoughts—expect it with such certainty that I would remove knives, poison, and weapons from his immediate vicinity.

If we look at the matter more closely, we shall find the following law holding in the development of all psychic happenings: *we cannot think, feel, will, or act without the perception of some goal.* For all the causalities in the world would not suffice to conquer the chaos of the future nor obviate the planlessness to which we would be bound to fall a victim. All activity would persist in the stage of uncontrolled gropings; the economy visible in our psychic life unattained; we should be unintegrated and in every aspect of our physiognomy, in every personal touch, similar to organisms of the rank of the amoeba.

No one will deny that by assuming an objective for our psychic life we accommodate ourselves better to reality. This can be easily demonstrated. For its truth in individual examples, where phenomena are torn from their proper connections, no doubt exists. Only watch, from this point of view, the attempts at walking made by a small child or a woman recovering from a confinement. Naturally he who approaches this whole matter without any theory is likely to find its deeper significance escape him. Yet it is a fact that before the first step has been taken the objective of the person's movement has already been determined.

Life-Plan, Goal, and Finalism, from Adler, *Practice and Theory,* pp. 3–7.

In the same way it can be demonstrated that all psychic activities are given a direction by means of a previously determined goal. All the temporary and partially visible objectives, after the short period of psychic development of childhood, are under the domination of an imagined terminal goal, of a final point felt and conceived of as definitely fixed. In other words the psychic life of man is made to fit into the fifth act like a character drawn by a good dramatist.

The conclusion thus to be drawn from the unbiased study of any personality viewed from the standpoint of Individual Psychology leads us to the following important proposition: *Every psychic phenomenon, if it is to give us any understanding of a person, can only be grasped and understood if regarded as a preparation for some goal.*

To what an extent this conception promotes our psychological understanding is clearly apparent as soon as we become aware of the *multiplicity of meaning of those psychical processes that have been torn from their proper context. . . .*

Our science demands a markedly individualizing procedure and is consequently not much given to generalizations. For general guidance, I would like to propound the following rule: *As soon as the goal of a psychic movement or its life-plan has been recognized, then we are to assume that all the movements of its constituent parts will coincide with both the goal and the life-plan.*

This formulation, with some minor provisos, is to be maintained in the widest sense. It retains its value even if inverted: *the properly understood part-movements must, when combined, give the picture of an integrated life-plan and final goal.* Consequently we insist that, without worrying about the *tendencies, milieu and experiences,* all psychical powers are under the control of a directive idea and all expressions of emotion, feeling, thinking, willing, acting, dreaming, as well as psychopathological phenomena, are permeated by one unified life-plan. Let me, by a slight suggestion, prove and yet soften down these heretical propositions: more important than tendencies, objective experience and milieu is *the subjective evaluation,* an evaluation which stands furthermore in a certain, often strange, relation to realities. Out of this evaluation however, which generally results in the development of a permanent mood *of the nature of a feeling of inferiority* there arises, depending upon the unconscious technique of our thought-apparatus, an imagined goal, an attempt at a planned final compensation and a life-plan.

I have so far spoken a good deal of men who have "grasped the situation." My discussion has been as irritating as that of the theorists of the "psychology of understanding" or of the psychology of personality, who always break off just when they are about to show us what exactly it is they understood, as for instance, Jaspers. The danger of discussing briefly this aspect of our investigations namely, *the results of Individual Psychology,* is sufficiently great. To do so we should be compelled to force the dynamics of life into static words and pictures, overlook differences in order to obtain unified formulas, and have, in short, in our description to make that very mistake that in practice is strictly prohibited: of approaching the psychic life of the individual with a dry formula, as the Freudian school attempts.

This then being my assumption, I shall in the following present to you the most important results of our study of psychic life. Let me emphasize the fact that the dynamics of psychic life that I am about to describe hold equally for healthy and diseased. What distinguishes the nervous from the healthy individual is the stronger safeguarding tendency with which the former's life-plan is filled. With regard to the "positing of a goal" and the life-plan adjusted to it there are no fundamental differences.

Neurotic Striving for Superiority and Fictional Finalism

I shall consequently speak of a general goal of man. A thorough-going study has taught us that we can best understand the manifold and diverse movements of the psyche as soon as our *most general presupposition,* that the psyche has as its objective the *goal of superiority,* is recognized. Great thinkers have given expression to much of this; in part everyone knows it, but in the main it is hidden in mysterious darkness and comes definitely to the front only in insanity or in ecstatic conditions. Whether a person desires to be an artist, the first in his profession, or a tyrant in his home, to hold converse with God or humiliate other people; whether he regards his suffering as the most important thing in the world to which everyone must show obeisance, whether he is chasing after unattainable ideals or old deities, overstepping all limits and norms, at every part of his way he is guided and spurred on by his longing for superiority, the thought of his godlikeness, the belief in his special magical power. . . .

This goal of complete superiority, with its strange appearance at times, does not come from the world of reality. Inherently we must place it under "fictions" and "imaginations." Of these Vaihinger (*The Philosophy of "As If"*) rightly says that their importance lies in the fact that whereas in themselves without meaning, they nevertheless possess in practice the greatest importance. For our case this coincides to such an extent that we may say *that this fiction of a goal of superiority, so ridiculous from the viewpoint of reality, has become the principal conditioning factor of our life as hitherto known.* It is this that teaches us to differentiate, gives us poise and security, molds and guides our deeds and activities, and forces our spirit to look ahead

Neurotic Striving for Superiority and Fictional Finalism, from Adler, *Practice and Theory,* pp. 7–15.

and to perfect itself. There is of course also an obverse side, for *this goal introduces into our life a hostile and fighting tendency,* robs us of the simplicity of our feelings, and is always the cause for an estrangement from reality since it puts near to our hearts the idea of attempting to overpower reality. Whoever takes this goal of godlikeness seriously or literally will soon be compelled to flee from real life and compromise, by seeking a life within life; if fortunate in art, but more generally in pietism, neurosis, or crime.

I cannot give you particulars here. A clear indication of this supermundane goal is to be found in every individual. Sometimes this is to be gathered from a man's carriage, sometimes it is disclosed only in his demands and expectations. Occasionally one comes upon its track in obscure memories, fantasies, and dreams. If purposely sought it is rarely obtained. However, every bodily or mental attitude indicates clearly its origin in a striving for power and carries within itself the ideal of a kind of perfection and infallibility. In those cases that lie on the confines of neurosis there is always to be discovered a reinforced pitting of oneself against the environment, against the dead or heroes of the past.

A test of the correctness of our interpretation can be easily made. If everyone possesses within himself an ideal of superiority, such as we find to an exaggerated degree among the nervous, then we ought to encounter phenomena whose purpose is the oppression, the minimizing, and undervaluation of others. Traits of character such as intolerance, dogmatism, envy, pleasure at the misfortune of others, conceit, boastfulness, mistrust, avarice,—in short, of all those attitudes that are the substitutes for a struggle—force their way through to a far greater extent, in fact, than self-preservation demands. . . .

The whole weight of the personal striving for power and superiority passes, at a very early age in the case of the child, into the form and the content of its striving, its thought being able to absorb for the time being only so much as the eternal, real, and physiologically rooted *community feeling* permits. Out of the latter are developed tenderness, love of neighbor, friendship, and love, the desire for power unfolding itself in a veiled manner and seeking secretly to push its way along the path of group consciousness. . . .

From the method of presentation of the present work it is to be inferred that as in the case of psychotherapeutic cure, our analysis proceeds backwards; examining first the *superiority-goal,* explaining by means of it the type of *conflict-attitude* adopted particularly by nervous patients and only then attempting to investigate the sources of the vital psychic mechanism. One of the bases of the psychical dynamics we have already mentioned, the presumably unavoidable artistic trait of the psychical apparatus which, by means of the *artistic artifice of the creation of a fiction and the setting of a goal,* adjusts itself to and extends itself into the world of possible reality. I shall now proceed to explain briefly how the goal of godlikeness transforms the relation of the individual to his environment into hostility and how the struggle drives an individual towards a goal either along a direct path such as aggressiveness or along byways suggested by precaution. If we trace the history of this aggressive attitude back to childhood we always come upon the outstanding fact that *throughout the whole period of development, the child possesses a feeling of inferiority in its relations both to parents and the world at large.* Because of the immaturity of his organs, his uncertainty and lack of independence, because of his need for dependence upon stronger natures and his frequent and painful feeling of subordination to others, a sensation of inadequacy develops that betrays itself throughout life. This feeling of inferiority is the cause of his continual restlessness as a child, his craving for action, his playing of roles, the pitting of his strength against that of others, his anticipatory pictures of the future and his physical as well as mental preparations. The whole potential educability of the child depends upon this feeling of insufficiency. In this way the future becomes transformed into the land that will bring him compensations. His conflict-attitude is again reflected in his feeling of inferiority; and only conflict does he regard as a compensation which will do away permanently with his present inadequate condition and will enable him to picture himself as elevated above others. Thus the child arrives at the positing of a goal, an imagined goal of superiority, whereby his poverty is transformed into wealth, his subordination into domination, his suffering into happiness and pleasure, his ignorance into omniscience, and his incapacity into artistic creation. The longer and more definitely the child feels his insecurity, the more he suffers either from physical or marked mental weakness, the more he is aware of life's neglect, the higher will this goal be placed and the more faithfully will it be adhered to. He who wishes to recognize the nature of this goal should watch a child at play, at optionally selected occupations or when fantasying about his future profession. The apparent change in these phenomena is purely external, for in every new goal the child imagines a predetermined triumph. A variant of this weaving of plans, one frequently found among weakly aggressive children, among girls and sickly individuals, might be mentioned here. This consists of so misusing their frailties that they compel others to become subordinate to them. They will later on pursue the same method until their life-plan and life-falsehood have been clearly unmasked.

The attentive observer will find the nature of the *compensatory dynamics* presenting a quite extraordinary aspect as soon as he permits the sexual role to be relegated to one of minor importance and realizes that it is the former that is impelling the individual toward superhuman goals. In our present civilization both the girl and the youth will feel themselves forced to extraordinary exertions and manoeuvres. A large number of these are admittedly of a distinctively progressive nature. To preserve this progressive nature but to ferret out those by-paths that lead us astray and cause illness, to make these harmless, that is our object and one that takes us far beyond the limits of medical art. It is to this aspect of our subject that society, child education and folk education may look for germs of a far-reaching kind. *For the aim of this point of view is to gain a reinforced sense of reality, the development of a feeling of responsibility and a substitution for latent hatred of a feeling of mutual goodwill, all of which can be gained only by the conscious evolution of a feeling for the common weal and the conscious destruction of the will-to-power. ...*

Organ Inferiority and the Neurotic Disposition

As the basic principle for the practice of the individual psychological method I would like to emphasize the following: *the retracing of all the nervous symptoms occurring in an individual case back to their "lowest common denominator."* That this reduction, made with the aid of the patient, is correct is proved by the fact that the psychical picture gained in each case coincides with a real psychical situation that can be traced back to the patient's earliest childhood. In other words the psychic foundations of neurotic disease and its symptoms have been taken over unchanged from childhood. Upon this foundation, however, has been erected in the course of years a widely ramifying superstructure, the individual neurosis, which is not amenable to treatment unless the basis itself is changed. Into this superstructure have been absorbed all the developmental tendencies, character traits and personal experiences. Among these I would particularly like to emphasize the mood-residues which go back to a single or a repeated failure along the main line of human endeavor. This is the actual cause for the appearance of the neurotic disease. From that moment on, all the thoughts of the patient are centered upon the idea of making good his failure, of running greedily after useless triumphs, and, above all, of protecting himself against new failures and the trials of fortune. His manifesting neurosis, assuming the nature of a means of support, makes this possible. Nervous anxiety, pains, paralyses, and nervous doubts prevent him from participating actively in life. In exchange the nervous compulsion bestows upon him, in his compulsion-thinking and his compulsion-acting, the semblance of his lost activity, giving him thus, as his excuse for remaining passive, a legitimate disease.

I found myself compelled in the exercise of the Individual Psychological method to break up still further this infantile situation of pretending to be ill. In so doing I came upon sources arising out of the injurious influences of family life. Beyond that, however, a cause cropped up that helped in part to form this

Organ Inferiority and the Neurotic Disposition, from Adler, *Practice and Theory*, pp. 17–20.

detrimental milieu, namely the *familial organic constitution.* Regularly and inexorably was it forced upon my attention that the possession of inherited inferior organs, organic systems and glands with internal secretions created a situation, in the early stages of a child's development, *whereby a normal feeling of weakness and helplessness had been enormously intensified and had grown into a deeply felt sense of inferiority.*[1] On account of the delayed and defective as well as inadequate constitution of organic inferiority, conditions of the following nature were initially visible: weakness, sickliness, awkwardness, ugliness, (often caused by external degenerative symptoms), clumsiness, and a large number of infantile defects, such as twitching of the eyes, cross-eyedness, left-handedness, deaf-and-dumbness, stuttering, speech defects, vomiting, bedwetting, and stool-anomalies for which the child was frequently subjected to humiliation, or made the object of ridicule, for which he was often punished and which rendered him socially unfit. The infantile psychic picture often shows striking intensification of traits otherwise normal, such as infantile helplessness, the need for cuddling, for tenderness; and these then develop into anxiety, fear of being alone, timidity, shyness, fear of strangers and unknown people, hypersensitiveness to pain, prudishness, permanent fear of punishment and fear of the consequences of every act—in short into characteristics that impart *unmistakable feminine traits* to the boy.

It is not long before this *feeling of being pushed aside* comes to the front, markedly so in those children disposed to neurosis. Together with it there develops a *hypersensitiveness* which repeatedly disturbs the peaceful and even flow of the psyche. . . .

The following is the final conclusion to be drawn from direct observations of the child's life: The infantile traits of submissiveness, lack of independence, and obedience, in short, the passivity of the child, are very soon and, in the case of individuals with neurotic dispositions, very abruptly displaced by hidden traits of defiance and rebellion, i.e. by signs of resentment. An accurate insight discloses *a mixture of passive and active characteristics although there is always present likewise a tendency for a girlish kind of obedience to change into a boyish kind of defiance.* There are indeed sufficient reasons for coming to the belief that these traits of defiance are to be interpreted as a reaction, a protest against the synchronous stirrings of obedience or against an enforced submission; that furthermore their purpose consists in obtaining for the child a more speedy gratification of his instincts, importance, attention, and privileges. When the child has reached this fatal point in his development he feels himself threatened by an enforced submission and consequently obstructs all the arrangements of its everyday life—eating, drinking, falling asleep, washing, stool and urinary functions. The demands for the community feeling are strangled. The craving

---

[1]A. Adler, *Studie über Minderwertigkeit der Organe* (1907), and its continuation: Adler, "Ueber neurotisch Disposition," in *Heilen und Bilden.*

for power expresses itself, in the main, in an arid inadequate sham-fight and an imaginary prestige.

Another, perhaps the most dangerous type of neurotically disposed child, exhibits these contrasting tendencies of submissiveness and active protest wrought together into a closer union resembling that subsisting between means and end. These children have apparently guessed at a little of the dialectic of life and *wish to gratify their unlimited desires by the most complete kind of submission (masochism).* They are just the people who can least stand undervaluation, lack of success, compulsion, waiting, the delay in victory and they, just as those with different dispositions, are thoroughly frightened by actions, decisions, anything strange or new. They develop an alibi for the fatal weakness of which they are conscious, in order thereafter to avoid the demands of the community and to isolate themselves. . . .

Neurotic Overcompensation and Lust for Superiority

In 1907 I proved in my book on Organ Inferiority (Vienna) that the inherited constitutional anomalies are not to be regarded as manifesting themselves merely in degenerative processes, but as causing the appearance likewise of compensatory and hypercompensatory activities and significant correlation-phenomena to which the reinforced psychic activity essentially contributed. This compensatory psychic exertion, in order to conquer the psychic tensions, frequently strikes out along new and different lines. To the observer this compensatory activity appears to be of a well-tested nature, thus fulfilling its purpose of covering up some imagined deficiency in a most wonderful manner. The most widely distributed method adopted by the *feeling of inferiority,* appearing during childhood, to prevent its being unmasked is the creation of a compensatory psychic superstructure, *the neurotic modus vivendi.* This seeks to regain, by means of fully tested preparations and defenses, a point of vantage and superiority in life. Any departure from the normal can subsequently be explained either by a greater ambition or by a more marked degree of precaution. All the devices and arrangements, including therein the neurotic character, traits and symptoms, derive their value from previous attempts, experiences, identifications, and imitations that are not entirely unknown even to a healthy individual. The language they speak, rightly understood, makes it evident that an individual is here struggling for recognition, actually attempting to force it; that he is aspiring ceaselessly to a godlike domination over

---

Neurotic Overcompensation and Lust for Superiority, from Adler, *Practice and Theory,* 32–35.

his environment from out the region of his insecurity and his sense of inferiority.

Placing on one side this, the root of neurotic behavior, we find the latter to consist of a variegated assortment of incitements and potentialities for incitement, which do not represent *the cause,* but rather the consequences of the neurosis. In a short treatise: "Aggressionsbetrieb im Leben u. in der Neurose" (*Heilen und Bilden,* 1914), I have tried to present this frequently intensified "affective activity" and to show how, in order either to achieve some purpose or escape some danger, it is often converted into an apparent "aggression-check." What is customarily known as "disposition to neurosis" *(neurotic disposition)* is a real neurosis already, the more suitable neurotic symptoms appearing more definitely and as proofs of disease only on those actual occasions when *an inward need demands the calling forth of strengthened devices.* This demonstration of illness and the "arrangements" associated with it are specifically needed for the following purposes:

1. To serve as excuses if life denies the longed-for triumphs.
2. So that all *decisions may be postponed.*
3. To permit those goals already attained to appear in an intenser light, since they have been gained *in spite of suffering.* These and other devices clearly exhibit the striving of the neurotic *for the semblance of things....*

In reality, however, the same struggle takes place within the sexual domain that we have found within our entire psychic life; the original inferiority feeling forces itself forward along by-paths (in sexual life along the road of masturbation, homosexuality, fetichism, algolagny, over-evaluation of sexuality, etc.), so as not to lose its orientation toward the goal of superiority. The schematic formula, "I wish to be a complete man," then serves as the abstract and concretistic goal of the neurotic. It is a compensating termination for the basic feeling of an inferiority interpreted as feminine. The scheme that has been apperceived in this manner and upon which the individual has proceeded is antithetic throughout and it has, in conscious falsification, been interpreted as containing within itself *hostile elements.* We can consequently always recognize as the unconscious premises of the neurotic goal-striving the following two facts:

1. *Human relations in all circumstances represent a struggle.*
2. *The feminine sex is inferior and by its reaction serves as the measure of masculine strength.*

These two unconscious presuppositions that both masculine and feminine patients reveal in equal degree are at the bottom of the distortion and poisoning of all human relationships, of the appearance of affect-disturbances and strengthenings, and the occurrence of permanent dissatisfaction instead of frankness. Dissatisfaction generally becomes lightened after intensification of the symptoms and after a successful demonstration of the existence of a disease. *The symptom is a substitute, in a way, for the neurotic lust for superiority with its associated affect.* In the patient's emotional life it leads more certainly to a sham-victory over the environment than would be true in the case of a straightforward battle, a definite trait of character, or resistance. *For me the understanding of the symptom-language has become the main condition for the success of the psychotherapeutic cure. . . .*

The Nature and Cause of Neurosis

The practical importance of Individual Psychology is to be sought in the degree of certainty with which an individual's life-plan and life-lines can be determined from his attitude toward life, *toward society, toward the normal and necessary problems of communal life,* his plans of obtaining prestige, and the nature of his group consciousness. Assuming the acceptance of many of my conclusions, let me direct your attention to the fundamental and, at the same time, the determining factor in the psychic life of both healthy and nervous people—"*the feeling of inferiority.*" Similar in nature must be reckoned the "*urge toward the positing of a goal,* toward the heightening of ego consciousness," a "*compensatory*" *function* as well as the "life-plan" obtruding itself upon the individual for the attainment of his goal through the employment of various "aggressions" and "deviations," along the line of the "masculine protest" or the "fear of taking a decision." I shall further assume a knowledge of the neurotic and psychotic psychic life, the fixation upon a "guiding fiction" in contrast to its absence in the healthy man, who regards his ideal "guiding principle" as giving only an "approximate orientation" and to be used as a means only. Finally, I assume the acceptance of the fact that, regarded as a whole, neurosis and psychosis are to be interpreted as a "*safety mechanism*" of the ego consciousness. . . .

The Arrangement of the Neurosis

The feeling of inferiority, afterwards purposely adhered to and emphasized, developing from the impressions of reality, incites the patient continuously in his childhood, to fix some goal for his striving, a goal extending beyond human

---

The Nature and Cause of Neurosis, from Adler, *Practice and Theory,* pp. 37–41, with the exception of the first paragraph which is from p. 100; in the latter an internal reference has been deleted.

limits, one which approaches a deification and which coerces an individual to march along lines rigidly determined. The neurotic system, *the life-plan of the nervous man,* lies between these two points—his feeling of inferiority and his striving for superiority. This compensatory psychical structure, this nervous "willing," utilizes all of one's own and foreign experience, purposefully distorting them, it is true, and falsifying their value at times, yet, on the other hand, employing their correct content whenever it suffices for the neurotic objective.

On closer inspection we find a perfectly explicable phenomenon, namely that all these lines of direction are provided, on numerous sides, with warning signs and encouragement, with reminders and summons to action, so that it is really possible to speak of the existence of a widely ramifying safety net. Everywhere we encounter the neurotic psychic life forming a superstructure built over a threatening infantile situation, a superstructure, changing in the course of years and adapting itself to reality more than would have been the case in the child's ordinary evolution. It is not to be wondered at then, if every psychic phenomenon of the neurotic is permeated by this rigid system and appears *like an analogy* in which the lines of direction always stand out in relief. Such phenomena are: the neurotic character, the nervous symptom, the demeanor, every device used in life, the evasions and deviations that occur as soon as decisions are about to threaten the godlike state of the neurotic, and finally his view of the world, his attitude to men and women, and his dreams. I presented my interpretation of the last named phenomenon in 1911. Bringing my views upon dreams into harmony with those on neuroses, I found their *main function to consist of simplified early trials, and of warnings and encouragements favorable to the life-plan; and to have as their object the solution of some future problem. . . .*

In order to present an intelligible, but admittedly schematic picture of the peculiar orientation of neurotics and psychotics, I suggest that we present the common attitude towards nervousness in a formula and then compare that formula with another representing the above views and corresponding better with reality. The first formula would appear as follows:

Individual+experience+environment+demands of life=a neurosis.

In this formula the individual is regarded as weakened either by a feeling of inferiority, by heredity, by "sexual constitution," by emotionality, or by his character. Furthermore his experiences, the environment and the external demands weigh upon the patient so heavily that they induce him to "take refuge in sickness." This interpretation is manifestly wrong and gains no support from the secondary hypothesis that the deficiency in wish-fulfillments or the "libido" that exists, in reality, is corrected by the neurosis.

A better formula would read as follows:

Evaluation (I + E + M) + arrangement (experiences + character + emotionality + symptoms) = personality-ideal.

In other words the only *definite and fixed point conceived of is the person-ality-ideal.* In order to approximate more nearly to his godlikeness, the neurotic makes a tendentious evaluation of his individuality, his experiences, and his environment. But since this does not by any means suffice to bring him to his life-line or nearer to his goal, he *provokes experiences* which his previously determined favorable applications make easier—of feeling setback, deceived, suffering—all of which give him the trusted and desired basis of aggression. That he constructs so much from real experiences and from possibilities and builds just the type of *character traits and affect-preparations* that fit into his personality-ideal, follows from the above description and has been discussed by me in detail. In a similar fashion the patient identifies himself with his symptoms, all his experiences taking the form that appears necessary and useful for the heightening of his feeling of personality. Not the slightest trace of a predetermined autochthonous teleology is to be found in this modus vivendi, projected and tenaciously adhered to by means of a self-suggested principal goal. The neurotic life-plan is maintained and teleologically arranged only by the urge toward superiority, by the careful evasion of dangerous-looking decisions, by previously tested wanderings along a few clearly determined lines of direction and the enormously increased safety net. In consequence, the questions relating to the conservation or loss of psychic energy lose all their meaning. The patient will create just so much psychic energy as will enable him to remain on his path of superiority and express his masculine protest and godlikeness.

Psychotherapy of the Neurosis

The most important element in the therapeutics is the disclosure of the neurotic system or life-plan. In its entirety this can only be conserved if the patient succeeds in keeping it away from his own self-criticism. The partially unconscious course of the neurosis, working in opposition with reality, is explained first and foremost by the definite tendency of the patient to arrive at his goal. Its opposition to reality, *i.e.* to the logical demands of the community, is in this system connected with the limited experiences and differences in the type of the relations which were efficacious at the time of the construction of the life-plan, *i.e.* in earliest childhood. An insight into the meaning of this plan is best obtained through artistic and intuitive self-identification with the patient's personality. A person will then realize for himself how unconsciously

Psychotherapy of the Neurosis, from Adler, *Practice and Theory,* pp. 41–47.

comparisons are made between himself and the patient, between different attitudes of the latter or similar actions of other patients. In order to bring order into the material apperceived, into the patient's symptoms, experiences, manner of life and development, I make use of two prejudices of my own gained from experience. The first deals with the *origin of the life-plan under aggravated conditions*—(organ-inferiorities, pressure in the family, a neurotic family tradition)—and centers my attention upon identical or similar reaction types in childhood. The second lies in the *assumption of the above empirically obtained and fictitious identification* according to which I estimate my apperceptions. . . .

From my remarks it is apparent that I always expect from my patient the same attitude that he has shown, in conformity with his life-plan, toward the persons of his early entourage, and at a still earlier period, toward his own family. At the time of his meeting with the physician and frequently earlier, the same connection of feelings is found as that which exists in persons of greater ability. That the transference of such feelings or the opposition to them seems to begin later must be based on some mistake. The physician probably recognizes them in these cases later. Often too late, especially in those instances where the patient, in the consciousness of his hidden superiority, brings his treatment to an end or where through an aggravation of the symptoms, an unbearable condition has been created. That the patient is under no circumstances to be offended I need not inform psychologically trained doctors. But this may occur without the knowledge of the physician and harmless remarks may be purposely revaluated if the latter does not clearly understand the nature of the patient. It is therefore essential, particularly at the beginning, to proceed with caution and to fathom as quickly as possible the neurotic system of an individual. As a rule, with any experience, this is discovered on the first day.

Even more significant is the necessity of *obviating the possibility of positive aggressive preparation for an attack.* At this place I can only give a few hints, designed to prevent the physician *from falling into the position of being treated by the patient.* First of all, not even in the safest cases, should a *successful issue of the cure* be promised; it should never be made more than a possibility. One of the most important devices in psychotherapeutics is to *ascribe the work and the success of the cure to the patient,* who is to be employed as a fellow worker and treated like a friend. The custom of having *payments* depend upon the success of the treatment creates enormous difficulties. It is best, at every point, to keep to the assumption that the patient, *craving for superiority as we know him to be, is going to use every promise of the physician—that which he makes with respect to the duration of the cure as well*—to secure the discomfiture of the doctor. Consequently all the necessary questions—the visiting time, a friendly and open welcome, the question of payments, free treatment, the physician's pledge to secrecy, etc.—should be regulated immediately and strictly adhered to. It is under all circumstances a tremendous advantage if the patient goes to the physician. *To prophesy, where it is certain, an aggravation of the disease as in cases* of fainting-spells, pains or agoraphobia, saves an enormous amount of work at the beginning, because the attacks, as a rule, do not then take place, a fact that corroborates our view about the marked negativism of neurotics. *To clearly show pleasure at a partial success or to boast about it would be a great mistake.* The situation would soon take a turn for the worse. It is therefore best to center all interest upon the difficulties patiently, without annoyance, and in a calm scientific manner.

In complete agreement with the above is the basic principle never to allow the patient, except under great protestations and explanations, to force upon anyone a superior role such as that of teacher, father, savior, etc. Such attempts represent the beginning of a movement on the part of the patient to pull down, in a manner to which he has been previously accustomed, *all persons standing above him and by thus administering a defeat, to disavow the physician.* To insist upon any superior rank or right is always disadvantageous with nervous patients. The best thing is to be open and to avoid, bearing in mind the danger of a mistake in technique, being dragged into any undertakings by him. It would be even more dangerous to take him into your own service, put requests to him, expect anything from him, etc. To expect secrecy from a patient indicates a complete absence of an elementary knowledge of the psychic life of a neurotic.

While these and similar measures dictated by the same attitude bring about the best adapted relationship of equality, *the uncovering of the neurotic life-plan* proceeds apace in friendly and free conversation, it being always the *better tactic to let the patient take the initiative.* I found it the safest course to search for and merely unmask the neurotic line of operation as shown in expressions and in the train of thought, and at the same time unobtrusively educate the patient for the same kind of work. The physician must be so convinced of the *uniqueness and exclusiveness of the neurotic direction-line* that he is able to call up the true content (of the patient's mind), always telling him beforehand his disturbing "arrangements" and constructions, and trying to discover and explain until the patient, completely upset, gives them up in order to place new and better hidden ones in their place. How often this will occur it is impossible to say beforehand. Finally, however, the patient will give in, all the more easily, if his relation to the physician has not permitted the feeling of a (possible) defeat to develop.

Just as there are these "arrangements" lying along the path of the feeling of superiority, so there are also definite subjective sources of error utilized and conserved merely because they possibly deepen the feeling of inferiority and thus furnish irritations and stimulations for further constructions. *Such errors and their tendencies* must be brought within the vision of the patient.

The patient's primitive apperception scheme, which *definitely and distinctly evaluates all impressions* and then groups them in a purposeful manner (above-below, victor-vanquished, masculine-feminine, nothing-everything, etc.), is always to be indicated, unmasked, and shown to be immature, untenable, and with a purpose in view; namely, that of continued hostility. It is this scheme likewise that shows us, in the psychic life of the neurotics, traits similar to those found in the beginnings of culture, where necessity has forced people to such types of safety. It would savor of the fantastic to suspect in such analogies anything more than mimicry, possibly a repetition of phylogenesis. What impresses us in primitive man and in the genius is the overbubbling power, the Titan-like defiance, the raising of one's self from nothing to the godhead, constructing out of nothing a world-dominating sanctuary. In the neurotic as in dreams, this can easily be seen to be a "bluff" even though it is the cause of great suffering. The fictitious triumph that the nervous patient gains by his manoeuvres exists only in his imagination. We must show him the view point of others, who generally feel their superiority demonstrated in a fashion similar to the love-relation of the neurotic or his perversions. At the same time there takes place, step by step, the *uncovering of his unattainable goal of superiority, the demonstration of the purposive veiling of the same,* of his all-dominating, direction-determining power and of the patient's lack of freedom and hostility toward mankind conditioned by the goal. In a similarly simple fashion we find, as soon as sufficient material is at hand, the proof that all neurotic character traits, neurotic affects and symptoms, serve as means partly to continue along the prescribed path, partly to make that path secure. It is important to understand the nature of the genesis of the affect and the symptom, which, as we have shown above, owes its efficiency to a frequently meaningless "junktim" also operating according to plan. The patient often discloses the "junktim" quite innocently. At other times it has to be extracted from his analogizing explanations, his previous history, or his dreams.

The same tendency of the life-line is disclosed in the world-view and the life-view of the patient, as well as in his outlook upon and his grouping of experiences. Falsifications and conscious additions, purposive special applications markedly one-sided, unbounded fears and expectations clearly impossible of fulfillment are encountered at every step and they always serve the patient's life-plan with its glorious last act. Many derailments and checks will have to be unearthed and this only succeeds after a careful, ever-increasing understanding of the unified tendency (of the life-plan) has been attained.

Since the physician obstructs the neurotic strivings of the patient he is regarded as an obstacle in the way, as an obstruction preventing the attainment of the superiority-ideal along the path of the neurosis. *For that reason every patient will attempt to disqualify the physician,* deprive him of his influence, conceal from him the true state of affairs and he will always find some new turn of affairs to hold against the practitioner. Particular attention is to be paid to these, for in a well-planned treatment they disclose most clearly the tendency of the sick person, by means of a neurosis, to maintain his superiority. And especially is it to be borne in mind that the further the improvement has progressed—(when there is a standstill there exists almost always a hearty friendship and peace except that the attacks continue)—the more energetic will be the patient's attempts, by means of unpunctuality, waste of time or nonattendance, to jeopardize the success of the treatment. At times a marked hostility arises which, like all the phenomena of resistance possessing the same tendency, is only to be neutralized if the patient's attention is drawn again and again to the realization that his behavior is quite natural. *I always find the hostile relation of the patient's relatives to the physician of advantage and I sometimes have carefully attempted to stir it up.* Since generally, the tradition of the entire family of the sick person is neurotic, it is possible by uncovering and explaining it, to greatly benefit the patient. *The bringing about of a change in the nature of the patient can emanate from him alone.* I always found it most profitable ostentatiously, to sit with my hands in my lap, fully convinced that the patient, no matter what I might be able to say on the point, as soon as he has recognized his life-line, can obtain nothing from me that he, as the sufferer, does not understand better. . . .

Psychotherapy of Compulsion-Neurosis

The explanation of compulsion-neurosis according to the individual psychological method discloses the unconscious purpose of the patient *to unburden and free himself by means of a diseased compulsion from the compulsion due to* the necessary demands made by society: to construct a subsidiary field of action in order to be able to flee from the main battlefield of life and fritter away time that might otherwise compel him to fulfill his individual tasks.

The only test for the correctness of the psychological demonstration of our views must be a proof that the patient has been planning to withdraw himself from the demands of life or at least to obtain some mitigation of the responsibility for his decisions or his actions, by the use of means other than those of the compulsion-neurosis, i.e., quite independently of pathological manifestations, and by the employment of excuses, evasions, and pretexts.

The treatment should consist in clearing up the nature of the facts, in removing of erroneous notions dating from childhood, in frank discussion and treatment of the exaggerated ambition, and lastly, in isolating the patient's self-love and hyperanxiety tendencies. . . .

Psychotherapy of Compulsion-Neurosis, from Adler, *Practice and Theory,* p. 207.

Therapeutic Value of Early Memories and Dreams

Among all psychic expressions, some of the most revealing are the individual's memories. His memories are the reminders he carries about with him of his own limits and of the meaning of circumstances. There are no "chance memories": out of the incalculable number of impressions which meet an individual, he chooses to remember only those which he feels, however darkly, to have a bearing on his situation. Thus his memories represent his "Story of My Life"; a story he repeats to himself to warn him or comfort him, to keep him concentrated on his goal, to prepare him, by means of past experiences, to meet the future with an already tested style of action. The use of memories to stabilize a mood can be plainly seen in everyday behavior. If a man suffers a defeat and is discouraged by it, he recalls previous instances of defeat. If he is melancholy, all his memories are melancholy. When he is cheerful and courageous, he selects quite other memories; the incidents he recalls are pleasant, they confirm his optimism. In the same way, if he feels himself confronted with a problem, he will summon up memories which help to prepare the mood in which he will meet it. Memories thus serve much the same purpose as dreams. Many men, when they have decisions to make, will dream of examinations which they have successfully passed. They see their decision as a test, and try to re-create the mood in which they succeeded before. What holds true of the variations of mood within an individual style of life holds true also of the structure and balance of his moods in general. A melancholiac could not remain melancholiac if he remembered his good moments and his successes. He must say to himself, "All my life I was unfortunate"; and select only those events which he can interpret as instances of his unhappy fate. Memories can never run counter to the style of life. If an individual's goal of superiority demands that he should feel, "Other people always humiliate me," he will choose for remembrance incidents which he can interpret as humiliations. In so far as his style of life alters, his memories also will alter; he will remember different incidents, or he will put a different interpretation on the incidents he remembers.

Early recollections have especial significance. To begin with, they show the style of life in its origins and in its simplest expressions. We can judge from them whether the child was pampered or neglected; how far he was training for cooperation with others; with whom he preferred to cooperate; what problems confronted him, and how he struggled against them. In the early recollections of a child who suffered from difficulties in seeing and who trained himself to look more closely, we shall find impressions of a visual nature. His recollections will begin, "I looked around me . . . ," or he will describe colors and

---

Therapeutic Value of Early Memories and Dreams, from Alfred Adler, *What Life Should Mean to You* (Boston: Little, Brown, 1931), pp. 73–75.

shapes. A child who had difficulties of movement, who wanted to walk or run or jump, will show these interests in his recollections. Events remembered from childhood must be very near to the main interest of the individual; and if we know his main interest we know his goal and his style of life. It is this fact which makes early recollections of such value in vocational guidance. We can find, moreover, the child's relations towards his mother, his father and the other members of the family. It is comparatively indifferent whether the memories are accurate or inaccurate; what is of most value about them is that they represent the individual's judgment, "Even in childhood, I was such and such a person," or "Even in childhood, I found the world like this."

Most illuminating of all is the way he begins his story, the earliest incident he can recall. The first memory will show the individual's fundamental view of life; his first satisfactory crystallization of his attitude. It offers us an opportunity to see at one glance what he has taken as the starting point for his development. I would never investigate a personality without asking for the first memory. Sometimes people do not answer, or profess that they do not know which event came first; but this itself is revealing. We can gather that they do not wish to discuss their fundamental meaning, and that they are not prepared for cooperation. In the main people are perfectly willing to discuss their first memories. They take them as mere facts, and do not realize the meaning hidden in them. Scarcely any one understands a first memory; and most people are therefore able to confess their purpose in life, their relationship to others and their view of the environment in a perfectly neutral and unembarrassed manner through their first memories.

Another point of interest in first memories is that their compression and simplicity allow us to use them for mass investigations. We can ask a school class to write their earliest recollections; and, if we know how to interpret them, we have an extremely valuable picture of each child. . . .

Therapy as a Maternal Function

It is well for the practitioner to realise at the outset that nothing can be done by force. The patient must be appealed to in a friendly way, coaxed into a receptive frame of mind. Indeed, the task of the physician or psychologist is to give the patient the experience of contact with a fellow man, and then to enable him to transfer this awakened social feeling to others.

Therapy as a Maternal Function, from Alfred Adler, *Problems of Neurosis: A Book of Case Histories* (London: Kegan Paul, Trench, Trubner, 1929; New York: Harper & Row, 1964), pp. 20–21.

This method, of winning the patient's good will, and then transferring it to his environment, is strictly analogous to the maternal function. The social duty of motherhood is to interpret society to the individual, and if the mother fails in this duty, the duty is likely to devolve much later upon the physician who is heavily handicapped for the task. The mother has the enormous advantage of the physical and psychic relation; she is the greatest experience of love and fellowship that the child will ever have. Her duty is mentally to relate the growing child to herself as it was formerly related to her physically, nourishing the child's growing consciousness with true and normal conceptions of society, of work, and of love. In this way she gradually transforms the child's love for her and dependence upon her into a benevolent, confident, and responsible attitude towards society and the whole environment. This is the two-fold function of motherhood, to give the child the completest possible experience of human fellowship, and then to widen it into a life-attitude towards others. . . .

Therapy Through Social Usefulness

The psychotherapist must lose all thought of himself and all sensitiveness about his ascendancy and must never demand anything of the patient. His is a belated assumption of the maternal function, and he must work with a corresponding devotion to the patient's needs. What the Freudians call transference (so far as we can discuss it apart from sexual implications) is merely social feeling. The patient's social feeling, which is always present in some degree, finds its best possible expression in the relation with the psychologist. The so-called "resistance" is only lack of courage to return to the useful side of life, which causes the patient to put up a defense against treatment for fear that his relation with the psychologist should force him into some useful activity in which he will be defeated. For this reason we must never force a patient, but guide him very gently towards his easiest approach to usefulness. If we apply force he is certain to escape. My own practice, also, is never to advise marriage or free relations. I find it always leads to bad results. A person who is told that he should marry or seek sexual experience is quite likely to develop impotence. The first rule in treatment is to win the patient; the second is for the psychologist never to worry about his own success: if he does so he forfeits it.

Therapy Through Understanding

The elimination of all constraint, the freest possible relationship—these are the indispensable conditions between patient and physician. For a cure depends

Therapy Through Social Usefulness, from Adler, *Problems of Neurosis,* pp. 73–74.

upon their unity in understanding the patient's goal which has been hitherto a heavily guarded secret. I have already alluded to this necessity for the truth underlying the individual life-style in reference to the treatment of drunkenness, morphia taking, and similar habits. Merely to take away the poison and say some encouraging words is useless. The patient must realize *why* he took to drink. Insufficient also would be his recognition of the general principles of Individual Psychology, that those who turn inebriate have lost social courage and interest, or succumbed to fear of an imminent defeat. It is easy for the physician to say, and even for the patient to believe, that he turned to drink because of a sense of inferiority which originated in childhood, but nothing will come out of the mere phraseology. The physician must grasp the special structure and development of that individual life with such accuracy, and express it with such lucidity, that the patient knows he is plainly understood and recognizes his own mistake. When patients or practitioners come to me and say: "We have explained everything," or "We quite understand and yet we cannot succeed," I consider their statements ridiculous. Always if I go into such a case of failure I find that neither physician nor patient have understood the matter nor explained anything. Sometimes the patient has felt inferior and suppressed by the physician, and resisted all true explanation. Occasionally the tables have been turned and the patient has been treating the doctor! Not infrequently an inexperienced practitioner teaches the patient the theories of Individual Psychology, in such phrases as "You lack social courage, you are not interested in others, you feel inferior," and so forth, which may be worse than useless. A real explanation must be so clear that the patient knows and feels his own experience in it instantly. . . .

Child Therapy

Style of Life and the Law of Movement

Once the child has found his law of movement in which there must be noted the rhythm, the temperament, the activity, and above all the degree of social feeling—phenomena that can often be recognized even in the second year and without fail in the fifth—then all his other capacities with their particular trends are also linked with these to this law of movement. This work will deal chiefly with the apperception connected with this law of movement—the way in which man looks at himself and the external world. In other words we shall

---

Style of Life and the Law of Movement, from Adler, *Social Interest,* pp. 15–17.

deal with the conception which the child, and later, on the same lines, the adult, has acquired of himself and the world. Further, this meaning cannot be gathered from the words and thoughts of the person under examination. These are all far too strongly under the spell of the law of movement, which aims at conquest, and therefore even in the case of self-condemnation still casts longing glances toward the heights. Of greater importance is the fact that life in its wholeness, named concretely by me, "style of life," is built up by the child at a time when he has neither language nor ideas adequate to give it expression. If he develops further in his intelligence he does so in a movement that has never been comprehended in words and is therefore not open to the assaults of criticism; it is even withdrawn from the criticism of experience. There can be no question here of anything like a repressed unconscious; it is rather a question of something not understood, of something withheld from the understanding. But man speaks to the adept with his style of living and with his reaction to the problems of life, which demand social feeling for their solution.

So far then as man's meaning about himself and about the external world is concerned, this can be best discovered from the significance he finds in life and from the significance he gives to his own life. It is obvious that here possible discord with an ideal social feeling, with social life, cooperation, and the sense of fellowship can be distinctly heard.

We are now prepared to understand how important it is to get to know something of the meaning of life and also to discover the conceptions different people have of this meaning. If there exists, at least to some extent, a reliable knowledge of that meaning of life which lies beyond the scope of our own experience, then it is clear that this puts those persons in the wrong who flagrantly contradict it. . . .

Questionnaire of Individual Psychology

With regard to the examination of a child who is on his first visit to the consultant, I consider the questionnaire which I and my collaborators have outlined, to be the best among all I have seen up till now. I append it here. Certainly only those will be able to handle it correctly who are possessed of adequate experience, who have an accurate knowledge of the views of Individual Psychology in their iron framework, and who have had sufficient practice in the art of guessing. In its use they will once again perceive that the whole art of understanding human characteristics consists in comprehending the individual's style of life that has been completed in childhood, in grasping the influences that were at work when the child was forming it, and in seeing how this style of life unfolds itself in grappling with the social problems of

---

Questionnaire of Individual Psychology, from Adler, *Social Interest,* pp. 298–306.

humanity. To the questionnaire, which was framed some years ago, it should be added that the degree of aggression—the activity—has to be noted; and it ought not to be forgotten that the vast majority of childish mistakes are due to the pampering that continuously intensifies the child's emotional struggle and thus leads him constantly into temptation. He is in this way so allured by enticements of the more varied kinds that he finds it difficult to resist, especially when he is in bad company. . . .

For the understanding and treatment of difficult children. Compiled and annotated by the International Society for Individual Psychology.

1. How long have the troubles lasted? In what situation was the child, materially and mentally, when the failings became noticeable?

(The following are important: changes in surroundings, starting school, change of school, change of teacher, birth of younger members of the family, setbacks at school, new friendships, illnesses of the child or of the parents, etc.)

2. Was there anything unusual about the child previously? Due to bodily or mental weakness? Cowardice? Carelessness? Desire to be alone? Clumsiness? Jealousy? Dependence on others at meals, in dressing, washing, going to bed? Is he afraid of being left alone? Afraid of darkness? Has he a clear idea of his sex? Any primary, secondary, and tertiary sexual characteristics? How does he regard the other sex? How far has his instruction in sexual questions proceeded? Step-child? Illegitimate? Boarded out? What were his foster-parents like? Is he still in touch with them? Has he learned to walk and speak at the normal time? Does he do this without mistakes? Was the teething normal? Had he any noticeable difficulties in learning to write, calculate, draw, sing, swim? Has he had any special attachment to any one—mother, father, grandparents, nurse?

(Care should be taken to discover the establishment of a hostile attitude to life, anything that might rouse feelings of inferiority, tendencies to exclude difficulties and persons, traits of egotism, irritability, impatience, heightened emotion, activity, eagerness, caution.)

3. Has the child caused much trouble? What things or persons does he fear most? Does he cry out at night? Does he wet his bed? Does he want to domineer? Over strong, or only over weak persons? Has he shown a particular fondness for lying in the bed of one of his parents? Is he awkward? Intelligent? Was he much teased and laughed at? Does he show excessive vanity about his hair, clothing, shoes? Does he pick his nose? Bite his nails? Is he greedy at table? Has he stolen anything? Has he difficulties at the stool?

(This will show clearly whether he has given evidence of more or less activity in striving for preeminence. Further, whether obstinacy has prevented the cultivation of his instinctive activity.)

4. Did he make friends easily, or was he unsociable, and did he torment people and animals? Does he attach himself to younger persons

(older), girls (boys)? Is he inclined to take the lead? Or does he stand aside? Does he collect things? Is he niggardly? Fond of money?

(This will show his ability to make contact with other persons, and the extent to which he is discouraged.)

5. How does the child conduct himself at present in all these relationships? How does he behave at school? Does he attend willingly? Does he arrive too late? Is he agitated before going to school; does he hurry? Does he lose his books, satchel, and papers? Does he get excited about school tasks and examinations? Does he forget or refuse to do his home-lessons? Does he waste his time? Is he grubby? Indolent? Has he much or little concentration? Does he disturb the lessons? Attitude to his teacher? Critical? Arrogant? Indifferent? Does he seek help from others in his work, or does he always wait for them to make the offer? Is he keen about gymnastics and sports? Does he consider himself partly or entirely devoid of talent? Does he read a great deal? What sort of reading does he prefer? Is he backward in every subject?

(These questions will give an insight into the child's preparation for school life and into the results of experiments at school on the child. They will also show his attitude towards difficulties.)

6. Correct information regarding his home conditions, illnesses in the family, alcoholism, criminal tendencies, neurosis, debility, syphilis, epilepsy, standard of living? What deaths have there been? How old at the time? Is the child orphaned? Who rules in the family? Is the upbringing strict, faultfinding, pampering? Are the children frightened at life? How are they looked after? Stepfather or mother?

(This gives a view of the child in his position in the family and enables an estimate to be made of the influences that have helped to form the child.)

7. What is the place of the child in the family succession? Is he the oldest, second, youngest, or an only child? Any rivalries? Frequent crying? A spiteful laugh? Tendency to depreciate other persons without cause?

(Important for characterology; throws light on the child's attitude to other persons.)

8. What kind of ideas has the child at present about his future calling? What does he think about marriage? What are the professions of the other members of the family? What are the marital relations of his parents?

(From the answers it is possible to draw conclusions about the child's courage and his hope for the future.)

9. Favorite games? Favorite stories? Favorite characters in history and poetry? Is he fond of interrupting the games of other children? Does he become lost in fantasies? Daydreams?

(This indicates his prototypes in his striving for superiority.)

10. Earliest recollections? Impressive or frequently recurring dreams? (Of flying, falling, being hindered, arriving too late for a train, running a race, being imprisoned, anxiety dreams.)

(One often finds in these a tendency to isolation; warning voices that lead the child to take excessive caution; ambitious impulses and the preference for certain persons, for passivity, etc.)

11. In what respect is the child discouraged? Does he feel himself slighted? Does he react favorably to appreciation and praise? Has he superstitious notions? Does he retreat from difficulties? Does he begin to do various things and then soon leave them alone? Is he uncertain about his future? Does he believe in the injurious effects of heredity? Was he systematically discouraged by those around him? Has he a pessimistic outlook on life?

(This will give important viewpoints for discovering whether the child has lost confidence in himself and is seeking his path in a wrong direction.)

12. Additional faults: Does he make grimaces? Does he behave himself stupidly, childishly, comically?

(Rather uncourageous attempts to draw attention to himself.)

13. Has he defects in speech? Is he ugly? Ungainly? Club-footed? Rickets? Knock-kneed or bow-legged? Badly developed? Abnormally stout, tall, small? Defects in the eyes or the ears? Is he mentally arrested? Left-handed? Does he snore at night? Is he strikingly good-looking?

(Here we are dealing with difficulties in life which the child as a rule exaggerates. These may lead to a chronic state of discouragement. A similar mistaken development often occurs in the case of very handsome children. They get the idea that everything must be given them to be retained without effort and in this way they neglect to make the right preparation for living.)

14. Does the child speak openly of his lack of ability, of his "not being gifted enough" for school, for work, for life? Has he thoughts of suicide? Is there any connection in point of time between his want of success and his mistakes? (Neglect, forming gangs.) Does he place too great value on material success? Is he servile? Hypocritical? Rebellious?

(These are expressive forms of a deep-seated discouragement. They often occur after vain attempts to excel which have come to grief not only on account of their inherent aimlessness, but also as the result of want of understanding on the part of those round the child. After the failure there comes the search for a substitutive gratification in another field of struggle.)

15. The child's positive achievements? Type? Visual, acoustic, kinaesthetic?

(An important finger-post, since possibly the interest, inclination and preparation of the child point in another direction than that formerly taken.)

On the basis of these questions, which should not be put point by point, but conversationally, never mechanically, but always naturally and progressively, there is always formed a picture of the child's personality. By this the child's errors, though they are certainly not justified, will be made quite intelligible. When mistakes are discovered they should always be explained in a friendly manner, patiently and without threats.

Adult Therapy

Questionnaire for Adults

In connection with the mistakes of adults I have found the following model of examination to be of some value. By adhering to it the expert will gain well within half an hour a penetrating insight into the individual's style of life.

Certainly my own inquiries do not always keep to the rule of the following sequence. The expert will not fail to notice its agreement with a medical questionnaire. By following it the Individual Psychologist, on account of the system by which he works, will gain from the answers many a hint that would otherwise have remained unnoticed. The following is approximately the sequence:

1. What are your complaints?
2. How were you situated when you noticed your symptoms?
3. How are you situated now?
4. What is the nature of your calling?
5. Describe your parents in relation to their character, health, the illness of which they died, if they are not alive; what was their relation to yourself?
6. How many brothers and sisters have you? How are you placed among them? What is their attitude towards you? How are the others placed in life? Do they also have any illness?
7. Who was your father's or your mother's favorite?
8. Look for signs of pampering in childhood (timidity, shyness, difficulties in forming friendships, disorderliness, etc.).
9. Illnesses and attitude to illnesses in childhood?
10. Earliest recollections of childhood?
11. What do you fear, or what did you fear the most?
12. What are your ideas about the other sex, in childhood or in later years?
13. What calling would have most interested you, and in the event of your not having adopted it, why did you not do so?
14. Ambitious, sensitive, inclined to angry outbursts, pedantic, domineering, shy, impatient?
15. What sort of persons are around you at present? Impatient? Bad-tempered? Affectionate?
16. How do you sleep?
17. Dreams? (Of falling, flying, recurrent dreams, prophetic, about examinations, missing a train, etc.)
18. Illnesses in the family tree?

3

ANALYTICAL PSYCHOTHERAPY

Carl Gustav Jung

Carl Gustav Jung (1875–1961) founded the school of analytical psychology. Born near Lake Constance in Kesswil, Switzerland, Jung was the only son of a Protestant minister. When he was four years old, his family moved to Basel. His grandfather had founded the first mental hospital in Basel and was dean of the University of Basel's School of Medicine. At the University of Basel, Jung studied medicine, earning his M.D. in 1902. His dissertation was entitled "On the Psychology and Pathology of So-Called Occult Phenomena." The same year took him to Paris, where he continued his psychological studies under Pierre Janet. The following year he married Emma Rauschenbach. Jung was connected with the University of Zurich from 1900 to 1913—up to 1909 as physician in the psychiatric clinic, Burghölzli, and from 1905 to 1913 as lecturer in psychology.

Jung's brief association with Freud lasted from 1907 to 1913. It culminated with Jung's resignation from the International Psychoanalytic Society and the founding of his own school in Zurich, later to be known as analytical psychology. In 1909 he accompanied Freud to Clark University in Worcester, Massachusetts. His break with psychoanalysis terminated his position as editor of a journal founded by Bleuler and Freud, *Yearbook for Psychological and Psychopathological Research*.

Jung journeyed extensively throughout the world in pursuit of research. Unlike Freud, he made a number of visits to the United States. In 1933 he accepted the post of professor of psychology at the Federal Polytechnical College in Zurich, which he held until 1942. During the years 1933 to 1939, he edited the *Central Journal for Psychotherapy and Related Fields*. In 1944 he was appointed professor of medical psychology at the University of Basel. His death, on June 6, 1961, was in Küsnacht, on Lake Zurich.

Jung's psychotherapeutic technique stresses a dialectical procedure and the individuation process, the process whereby individual parts of an organism gain wholeness. A person's psyche must be regarded as a totality, a unity in which the individual parts are coordinated in an integrated system. The inability to integrate the conscious and the unconscious minds, so that they complement each other, causes mental illness. The unconscious overwhelming the conscious is disastrous, but so is the state where the personality does not utilize the profound archetypes of the unconscious. What is called for is a *transcendent function,* a mutual compensation or complement of conscious and unconscious mind—not two separate parts—but as integral portions of a single unity.

Neurosis is lack of maturation, requiring a broadening of the consciousness so that the impaired psychic development may attain self-realization or wholeness. By the individuation process a person reaches his full development or maturity.

Religious development is an integral factor in the individuation process. Lack of religion or improper religious function may engender mental disturbance.

To attain this normal or wholesome state of development, the psychotherapist must utilize the archetypes of the collective unconscious for suitable modes of motivation. Archetypes in a patient may be reached through dream analysis and interpretation.

Jungian therapy differs from Freudian in several respects: it minimizes the role of sex and it emphasizes the place of the social unconscious (collective) and its numerous archetypes. The Jungian therapist is not content with remaining passive; he is often active. In place of free association he employs *amplification,* the practice of directing association by utilizing the symbols and motifs of the unconscious in order to understand the significance of dreams and in turn the problems of the patient.

The works of Jung, comprising eighteen volumes, have been collected and published by the Bollingen Foundation in New York under the editorship of Herbert Read, Michael Fordham, and Gerhard Adler. His more important writings are the following:

Symbols of Transformation (1912): He detects symbolic meanings of the contents of the unconscious and develops his libido theory.

Studies in Word Association (1918): He offers a method of detecting "feeling-toned" psychic contents of the unconscious, which he identified by the term *complex.*

Psychological Types (1921): He presents the principles of analytical psychology and discloses two fundamental types of personality—introvert and extrovert. Also included is his treatment of the four functions (thinking, feeling, sensation, and intuition), and when the functions are combined with the two types of personality, they produce eight different types of personality.

Two Essays on Analytical Psychology, consisting of the books, *The Psychology of the Unconscious* (rev. ed., 1943) and *The Relations between the Ego and the Unconscious* (rev. ed., 1945): These two essays treat the concepts of the personal and collective unconscious, archetypes, persona, anima, and therapy.

Archetypes and the Collective Unconscious (published in English in 1958): This contains his theory of personality, treating such concepts as the ego, shadow, syzygy (anima and animus), self, individuation process, archetypes, and the conscious and the unconscious mind.

The Psychogenesis of Mental Disease (volume 3 of the *Collected Works,* 1960):
This volume comprises his papers on the cause and nature of mental illness.
The Practice of Psychotherapy (volume 16 of the *Collected Works,* 1954): This
volume is devoted to his therapeutic technique, papers, talks, etc., covering
topics from abreaction, dream analysis, and transference, to practical aspects
and philosophy in therapy.
The Structure and Dynamics of the Psyche (volume 8 of the *Collected Works,*
1960): This volume deals with such important concepts as the transcendent
function, complexes, psyche, dreams, instinct, unconscious, and stages of
life.

Personality Theory

A. It is considered advisable to subdivide the psychological processes into
conscious contents and *unconscious* contents.

1. The *conscious contents* are in part *personal* inasmuch as their universal
validity is not recognized, and in part *impersonal,* that is, *collective,* inasmuch
as their universal validity is recognized.

2. The *unconscious* contents are in part *personal,* in so far as we have to
deal with components of a personal nature which were once relatively conscious and were then simply repressed; their universal validity is in consequence wholly unrecognized when they become unconscious again. They are
in part *impersonal,* in so far as we have to do with components that are
recognized as impersonal, as having quite general value, and of which it is
impossible to prove any anterior or even relative consciousness.

B. The Constitution of the Persona.

1. The conscious personal components constitute the conscious personality, the *conscious* ego.

2. The unconscious personal components constitute the "self," the *unconscious* or subconscious ego.

3. The conscious and unconscious components of a personal nature constitute the persona.

C. Constitution of the Collective Psyche.

1. The conscious and unconscious components of an *impersonal,* i.e.,
collective, nature constitute the psychological *nonego,* the image of the objective world (the *object-imago*). These components may appear in analysis as
projections of either feeling or judgment, but they are *a priori* collective, and
identical with the object-imago; that is, they appear to be qualities of the object,

Personality Theory, from Carl Gustav Jung, *Two Essays on Analytical Psychology.* vol. 7 of
THE COLLECTED WORKS OF C. G. JUNG, 2nd ed., Bollingen Series XX, ed. G. Adler, M.
Fordham, and H. Read, trans. R. F. C. Hull (New York: Bollingen Foundation, 1966), pp. 290–92.

and it is only *a posteriori* that they are recognized as subjective psychological qualities.

2. The persona is the grouping of conscious and unconscious components that are opposed to the nonego and constitute the ego. A general comparison of the personal elements belonging to different individuals shows the great resemblance between these components, which may even amount to identity, and largely cancels out the *individual* nature of the personal components and of the persona at the same time. To the degree that it does so, the persona must be considered as a segment of the collective psyche and, to that same degree, the persona is a component of the collective psyche.

3. The collective psyche, then, is composed of the object-imago and of the persona.

D. Individuality.

1. Individuality manifests itself partly as the principle which selects, and sets limits to, the components adopted as personal.

2. Individuality is the principle which makes possible, and if need be compels, a progressive differentiation of the collective psyche.

3. Individuality manifests itself partly as an obstacle to collective productivity and partly as resistance to collective thinking and feeling.

4. Individuality is that which is peculiar and unique in combinations of general (collective) psychological components.

E. The conscious and unconscious contents are subdivided into *individual* components and *collective* components.

1. A component whose developmental tendency is towards differentiation from the collective is individual.

2. A component whose developmental tendency is towards a general value is collective.

3. We lack adequate criteria to characterize a given component as purely individual or purely collective, for the characteristic of individuality is very difficult to determine, although always and everywhere present. . . .

Fundamental Principles of Treatment

Unsuccessful Attempts to Free Individuality from the Collective Psyche

The Regressive Restoration of the Persona.   The unbearable feeling of identity with the collective psyche drives the patient, as we have just said, to some radical solution.

Fundamental Principles of Treatment, from Jung, *Two Essays,* pp. 278, 280, 282–88.

Two ways are open to him. The first possibility is to try to reestablish regressively the primitive persona, seeking to control the unconscious by the application of a reductive theory—by, for example, declaring that it is "nothing but" a manifestation of the repressed sexual tendencies of early infancy, for which normal sexual activity would be an advantageous substitute. This explanation is based on the undeniably sexual symbolism of the language of the unconscious and on its concretistic interpretation. Alternatively the theory of the will-to-power may be invoked and, relying upon the equally undeniable power-tendencies of the unconscious, the feeling of "godlikeness" may be interpreted as a masculine protest, the infantile desire for omnipotence and need for security. Lastly, the unconscious may be regarded as it manifests itself in the collective-archaic psychology of the primitive, which would explain not only the sexual symbolism and the godlike will-to-power, but also the religious, philosophical, and mythological aspects and tendencies inherent in the unconscious contents.

In each case the conclusion will be the same, for what it amounts to is a repudiation of the unconscious as something useless, infantile, and devoid of sense, impossible and obsolete. . . .

Identification with the Collective Psyche.   The second way leads to identification with the collective psyche. This is equivalent to the symptoms of deification, but erected into a system; that is to say, one believes oneself to be the happy possessor of the great truth which was only waiting to be discovered, of that final knowledge which spells the salvation of all people. This attitude is not necessarily megalomania in its common form, but in the mitigated and well-known form of *prophetic inspiration.* . . .

Successful Method of Treatment

To find a practical method of treatment which leads to success through assimilation of the collective psyche, it is first of all necessary to take account of the error of the two procedures we have just described. We have seen that neither the one nor the other can lead to good results.

The first, by abandoning the vital values contained in the collective psyche, simply leads back again to the point of departure. The second penetrates directly into the collective psyche, but at the price of losing that separate human existence which alone can render life supportable and satisfying. Yet each of these ways proffers benefits that are indubitably precious, of which the individual ought never to be deprived.

The mischief, then, lies neither with the collective psyche nor with the individual psyche, but in the fact that we permit the one to exclude the other. . . .

The fundamental error of the two procedures we have examined consists in identifying the subject collectively with one side or the other of his psychology. His psychology is as much individual as collective, but not in the sense that the individual ought to merge himself in the collective, nor the collective in the individual. We must rigorously separate the concept of the individual from that of the persona, for the persona itself *can* be entirely dissolved in the collective. But the *individual* is precisely that which can never be absorbed into the collective and which moreover is never identical with it. That is why both the identification with the collective and the will to segregate oneself from it are alike synonymous with disease.

As I have already pointed out, the individual reveals himself primarily in the selection of the particular elements of the collective psyche which serve to constitute his persona. The component elements, as we have seen, are not individual but collective: their combination, however, or the selection of a certain group already combined in an exemplary pattern is individual. Thus we have the individual kernel dissimulated by the personal mask. It is in the particular differentiation of his persona that the individual exhibits his resistance to the collective psyche. By analyzing the persona, we confer a greater value upon the individuality and thus accentuate its conflict with collectivity. This conflict naturally consists in a psychological opposition within the subject. The dissolution of the compromise between the two halves of a pair of opposites renders their activity more intense. In ordinary, purely conscious life, this conflict does not take place, although the purely psychological life has to satisfy individual and collective requirements equally. The natural and unconscious adjustment is harmonious. The body, its faculties, and its needs furnish naturally the rules and the limitations that place any excess or disproportion out of the question. Because of its exclusive character, a differentiated psychological function always tends to disequilibrium which reasonable conscious intentions nevertheless manage to regulate. For the "mental individuality," too, is an expression of the corporeal individuality and is, so to speak, identical with it. (This is no less true from the spiritual standpoint from which one sees no reason to doubt the psychological fact that the individuality and the physical body are intimately related.) At the same time, it is in the body that the subject is in the highest degree similar to other individuals, although each individual body is distinguishable from other bodies. Every mental or moral individuality is different from all the others, and yet is so constituted as to render every man similar to all other men. The living being therefore who, free from all constraint, is able to develop himself quite individually, will best realize, by the very perfection of his own individuality, the ideal type of his species, and by the same token will achieve a collective value.

The persona is always identical with a *typical* attitude dominated by a single psychological function, for example, by feeling, thinking, or intuition. Consequently its exclusive character causes the relative repression of the other

functions. For this reason the persona is harmful to the individual's development. The dissolution of the persona is therefore absolutely necessary for
individuation. Hence it is impossible to lead individuation towards its true goal
by conscious intention, for conscious intention leads infallibly to a conscious
attitude, which excludes whatever does not fit in with it. The assimilation of
the content of the unconscious produces, on the contrary, a state of mind from
which conscious intention is excluded, having been displaced by a development
that appears to be irrational. Such a procedure in itself constitutes individuation, and the result of it is individuality as we have previously defined it:
particular and universal at once. So long as the persona persists, individuality
is repressed, and hardly betrays its existence except in the choice of its personal
accessories—by its actors' wardrobe, one might say. It is only through the
assimilation of the unconscious that the individuality can manifest itself more
clearly, together with that psychological phenomenon which links the ego with
the nonego and is designated by the word *attitude*. But this time we have to
do with an attitude that is not typical but individual.

What is it, at this moment and in this individual, that represents the
natural urge of life? That is the question.

That question neither science, nor wisdom, nor religion, nor the best of
advice can resolve for him. The resolution will be attained only by absolutely
impartial observation of those germs of psychological life which are born on
the one hand from the natural collaboration of the conscious and the unconscious and on the other from that of the individual elements and the collective
elements. Where do we find those germs of life? One man seeks them in the
conscious mind, another in the unconscious. But the conscious mind only
represents one side of man's psychology, and the unconscious is only the
reverse of it. We must never forget that dreams are the compensators of the
conscious mind. . . .

It is the creation of *fantasies* that we find the unitive function we are
seeking. All the elements engaged by the active tendencies flow into the imagination. The imagination has, it is true, a poor reputation among psychologists,
and up to the present psychoanalytic theories have treated it accordingly. For
Freud as for Adler it is only a so-called "symbolic" veil disguising the tendencies or the primitive desires presupposed by those two investigators. But one
can set against this opinion—not upon theoretical principle, but essentially for
practical reasons—the fact that, though it is possible to explain and to depreciate imagination in respect of its causality, imagination is nevertheless the
creative source of all that has made progress possible to human life. Imagination holds in itself an irreducible value, for it is the psychic function whose
roots ramify at the same time in the contents of the conscious mind and of the
unconscious, in the collective as in the individual.

But whence has the imagination acquired its bad reputation? Above all,
from the circumstance that its manifestations cannot be taken at their face

value. If one takes them concretely they are of no value: if, like Freud, one attributes *semantic* significance to them, they are interesting from the scientific point of view; but if we regard them, according to the *hermeneutic* conception, as authentic symbols, then they provide the directive signs we need in order to carry on our lives in harmony with ourselves.

The symbol is not a sign that veils something everybody knows. Such is not its significance; on the contrary, it represents an attempt to elucidate, by means of analogy, something that still belongs entirely to the domain of the unknown or something that is yet to be. Imagination reveals to us, in the form of a more or less striking analogy, what is in process of becoming. If we reduce this by analysis to something else universally known, we destroy the authentic value of the symbol; but to attribute hermeneutic significance to it conforms to its value and its meaning.

The essential character of hermeneutics, a science which was widely practiced in former times, consists in making successive additions of other analogies to the analogy given in the symbol: in the first place of subjective analogies produced at random by the patient, and then of objective analogies found by the analyst in the course of erudite research. This procedure widens and enriches the initial symbol, and the final outcome is an infinitely complex and varied picture, in which certain "lines" of psychological development stand out as possibilities that are at once individual and collective. There is no science on earth by which these lines could be proved "right": on the contrary, rationalism could very easily prove that they are not right. Their validity is proved by their intense value for life. And that is what matters from the point of view of practical treatment. The important thing is that men should have life, not that the principles by which they live should be demonstrable rationally as "right."

Faithful to the spirit of scientific superstition, someone may now begin to talk about *suggestion*. But we ought to have realized long ago that a suggestion is not accepted unless it is agreeable to the person receiving it. Unless it is acceptable, all suggestion is futile; otherwise the treatment of the neuroses would be an extremely simple affair: one would merely have to suggest the state of health. These pseudoscientific assertions about suggestion are based upon the unconscious superstition that suggestion is possessed of some self-generated magical power. But in the case of anyone who is disinclined in the depths of his own being to acquiesce in it, all suggestion is powerless.

Hermeneutic treatment of imaginative ideas leads to the synthesis of the individual and the collective psyche. This is true enough in theory but in practice another indispensable condition must be fulfilled. One characteristic of the essentially regressive nature of the neurotic (which moreover is partly acquired in the course of his illness) is his refusal to take either himself or the world seriously: he seeks to be cured first by one doctor and then by another, now by such and such a method, or in such and such circumstances, irrespective of any serious cooperation on his own part. Now, no one can be washed without getting wet. Without the most perfect goodwill and the absolutely serious intentions of the patient, no recovery is possible. As soon as ever we begin to map out the lines of advance that are symbolically indicated, the patient must begin to proceed along them. If he remains hypocritically inert, his own inaction precludes any cure. He is in truth obliged to take the way of individual life which is revealed to him, and to persist in it until and unless an unmistakable reaction from his unconscious warns him that he is on the wrong track.

Whoever is incapable of this moral resolution, of this loyalty to himself, will never be relieved of his neurosis. On the other hand, whoever is capable of it will certainly find the way to cure himself.

Neither the doctor nor the patient, therefore, ought to let himself slip into a belief that "analysis" is by itself sufficient to dispel a neurosis. That would be a mistake and a self-deception. Infallibly, in the last resort, it is the *moral factor* which is decisive for health or for disease.

The elaboration of the "life-lines" reveals to consciousness the true direction of the currents of the libido. These life-lines are by no means identical with the "guiding fictions" discovered by Adler; the latter are only arbitrary efforts to separate the persona from the collective psyche and lend it an independent existence. One might rather say that the "guiding fiction" is nothing but an unsuccessful attempt to constitute a life-line. Moreover—and this shows the uselessness of a fiction—such a line as it does produce persists far too long; it has the tenacity of a cramp. . . .

The Transcendent Function in the Treatment of Neurosis

There is nothing mysterious or metaphysical about the term *transcendent function.* It means a psychological function comparable in its way to a mathematical function of the same name, which is a function of real and imaginary numbers. The psychological *transcendent function* arises from the union of conscious and unconscious contents.

Experience in analytical psychology has amply shown that the conscious and the unconscious seldom agree as to their contents and their tendencies. This lack of parallelism is not just accidental or purposeless, but is due to the fact that the unconscious behaves in a compensatory or complementary manner towards the conscious. We can also put it the other way round and say

The Transcendent Function in the Treatment of Neurosis, from Carl Gustav Jung, "The Transcendent Function," *The Structure and Dynamics of the Psyche,* vol. 8 of THE COLLECTED WORKS OF C. G. JUNG (New York: Bollingen Foundation, 1960; Princeton, N.J.: Princeton University Press, 1969), pp. 69, 72–75.

that the conscious behaves in a complementary manner towards the unconscious. The reasons for this relationship are:

1. Consciousness possesses a threshold intensity which its contents must have attained, so that all elements that are too weak remain in the unconscious.

2. Consciousness, because of its directed functions, exercises an inhibition (which Freud calls censorship) on all incompatible material, with the result that it sinks into the unconscious.

3. Consciousness constitutes the momentary process of adaptation, whereas the unconscious contains not only all the forgotten material of the individual's own past, but all the inherited behavior traces constituting the structure of the mind.

4. The unconscious contains all the fantasy combinations which have not yet attained the threshold intensity, but which in the course of time and under suitable conditions will enter the light of consciousness.

This readily explains the complementary attitude of the unconscious towards the conscious.

The definiteness and directedness of the conscious mind are qualities that have been acquired relatively late in the history of the human race, and are for instance largely lacking among primitives today. These qualities are often impaired in the neurotic patient, who differs from the normal person in that his threshold of consciousness gets shifted more easily; in other words, the partition between conscious and unconscious is much more permeable. The psychotic, on the other hand, is under the direct influence of the unconscious. . . .

There is a widespread prejudice that analysis is something like a "cure," to which one submits for a time and is then discharged healed. That is a layman's error left over from the early days of psychoanalysis. Analytical treatment could be described as a readjustment of psychological attitude achieved with the help of the doctor. Naturally this newly won attitude, which is better suited to the inner and outer conditions, can last a considerable time, but there are very few cases where a single "cure" is permanently successful. It is true that medical optimism has never stinted itself of publicity and has always been able to report definitive cures. We must, however, not let ourselves be deceived by the all-too-human attitude of the practitioner, but should always remember that the life of the unconscious goes on and continually produces problematical situations. There is no need for pessimism; we have seen too many excellent results achieved with good luck and honest work for that. But this need not prevent us from recognizing that analysis is no once-and-for-all "cure"; it is no more, at first, than a more or less thorough readjustment. There is no change that is unconditionally valid over a long period of time. Life has always to be tackled anew. There are, of course, extremely durable collective attitudes which permit the solution of typical conflicts. A collective attitude enables the individual to fit into society without friction, since it acts upon him like any other condition of life. But the patient's difficulty consists precisely in the fact that his individual problem cannot be fitted without friction into a collective norm; it requires the solution of an individual conflict if the whole of his personality is to remain viable. No rational solution can do justice to this task, and there is absolutely no collective norm that could replace an individual solution without loss.

The new attitude gained in the course of analysis tends sooner or later to become inadequate in one way or another, and necessarily so, because the constant flow of life again and again demands fresh adaptation. Adaptation is never achieved once and for all. One might certainly demand of analysis that it should enable the patient to gain new orientations in later life, too, without undue difficulty. And experience shows that this is true up to a point. We often find that patients who have gone through a thorough analysis have considerably less difficulty with new adjustments later on. Nevertheless, these difficulties prove to be fairly frequent and may at times be really troublesome. That is why even patients who have had a thorough analysis often turn to their old analyst for help at some later period. In the light of medical practice in general there is nothing very unusual about this, but it does contradict a certain misplaced enthusiasm on the part of the therapist as well as the view that analysis constitutes a unique "cure." In the last resort it is highly improbable that there could ever be a therapy that got rid of all difficulties. Man needs difficulties; they are necessary for health. What concerns us here is only an excessive amount of them.

The basic question for the therapist is not how to get rid of the momentary difficulty, but how future difficulties may be successfully countered. The question is: What kind of mental and moral attitude is it necessary to have towards the disturbing influences of the unconscious, and how can it be conveyed to the patient?

The answer obviously consists in getting rid of the separation between conscious and unconscious. This cannot be done by condemning the contents of the unconscious in a one-sided way, but rather by recognizing their significance in compensating the one-sidedness of consciousness and by taking this significance into account. The tendencies of the conscious and the unconscious are the two factors that together make up the transcendent function. It is called "transcendent" because it makes the transition from one attitude to another organically possible, without loss of the unconscious. The constructive or synthetic method of treatment presupposes insights which are at least potentially present in the patient and can therefore be made conscious. If the analyst knows nothing of these potentialities he cannot help the patient to develop them either, unless analyst and patient together devote proper scientific study to this problem, which as a rule is out of the question.

In actual practice, therefore, the suitably trained analyst mediates the transcendent function for the patient, i.e., helps him to bring conscious and unconscious together and so arrive at a new attitude. In this function of the analyst lies one of the many important meanings of the *transference*. The patient clings by means of the transference to the person who seems to promise him a renewal of attitude; through it he seeks this change, which is vital to him, even though he may not be conscious of doing so. For the patient, therefore, the analyst has the character of an indispensable figure absolutely necessary for life. However infantile this dependence may appear to be, it expresses an extremely important demand which, if disappointed, often turns to bitter hatred of the analyst. It is therefore important to know what this demand concealed in the transference is really aiming at; there is a tendency to understand it in the reductive sense only, as an erotic infantile fantasy. But that would mean taking this fantasy, which is usually concerned with the parents, literally, as though the patient, or rather his unconscious, still had the expectations the child once had towards the parents. Outwardly it still is the same expectation of the child for the help and protection of the parents, but in the meantime the child has become an adult, and what was normal for a child is improper in an adult. It has become a metaphorical expression of the not consciously realized need for help in a crisis. Historically it is correct to explain the erotic character of the transference in terms of the infantile *eros.* But in that way the meaning and purpose of the transference are not understood, and its interpretation as an infantile sexual fantasy leads away from the real problem. The understanding of the transference is to be sought not in its historical antecedents but in its purpose. The one-sided, reductive explanation becomes in the end nonsensical, especially when absolutely nothing new comes out of it except the increased resistances of the patient. The sense of boredom which then appears in the analysis is simply an expression of the monotony and poverty of ideas—not of the unconscious, as is sometimes supposed, but of the analyst, who does not understand that these fantasies should not be taken merely in a concretistic-reductive sense, but rather in a constructive one. When this is realized, the standstill is often overcome at a single stroke.

Constructive treatment of the unconscious, that is, the question of meaning and purpose, paves the way for the patient's insight into that process which I call the transcendent function. . . .

The Psychogenesis of Schizophrenia and Its Distinction from Neurosis

I fully agree with Bleuler that the great majority of symptoms [of schizophrenia] are of a secondary nature and are due chiefly to psychic causes. For the

The Psychogenesis of Schizophrenia and its Distinction from Neurosis, from Carl Gustav Jung, *The Psychogenesis of Mental Disease,* vol. 3 of THE COLLECTED WORKS OF C. G. JUNG (New York: Bollingen Foundation, 1960), pp. 234–38.

primary symptoms, however, Bleuler assumes the existence of an organic cause. As *the* primary symptom he points to a peculiar disturbance of the association-process. According to his description, some kind of disintegration is involved, inasmuch as the associations seem to be peculiarly mutilated and disjointed. He refuses to accept Wernicke's concept of "sejunction" because of its anatomical implications. He prefers the term *schizophrenia*, obviously understanding by this a *functional* disturbance. Such disturbances, or at least very similar ones, can be observed in delirious states of various kinds. Bleuler himself points out the remarkable similarity between schizophrenic associations and the association-phenomena in dreams and half-waking states. From his description it is sufficiently clear that the primary symptom coincides with the condition which Pierre Janet termed *abaissement du niveau mental.* It is caused by a peculiar *faiblesse de la volonté.* If the main guiding and controlling force of our mental life is willpower, then we can agree that Janet's concept of *abaissement* explains a psychic condition in which a train of thought is not carried through to its logical conclusion, or is interrupted by strange contents that are insufficiently inhibited. Though Bleuler does not mention Janet, I think that Janet's *abaissement* aptly formulates Bleuler's views on the primary symptoms.

It is true that Janet uses his hypothesis chiefly to explain the symptomatology of hysteria and other neuroses, which are indubitably psychogenic and quite different from schizophrenia. Yet there are certain noteworthy analogies between the neurotic and the schizophrenic mental condition. If you study the association tests of neurotics, you will find that their normal associations are disturbed by the spontaneous intervention of complex contents typical of an *abaissement.* The dissociation can even go so far as to create one or more secondary personalities, each, apparently, with a separate consciousness of its own. But the fundamental difference between neurosis and schizophrenia lies in the maintenance of the potential unity of the personality. Despite the fact that consciousness can be split up into several personal consciousnesses, the unity of all the dissociated fragments is not only visible to the professional eye but can be reestablished by means of hypnosis. This is not the case with schizophrenia. The general picture of an association test of a schizophrenic may be very similar to that of a neurotic, but closer examination shows that in a schizophrenic patient the connection between the ego and some of the complexes is more or less completely lost. The split is not relative, it is absolute. An hysterical patient might suffer from a persecution-mania very similar to real paranoia, but the difference is that in the former case one can bring the delusion back under the control of consciousness, whereas it is virtually impossible to do this in paranoia. A neurosis, it is true, is characterized by the relative autonomy of its complexes, but in schizophrenia the complexes have become disconnected and autonomous fragments, which either do not reintegrate back to the psychic totality, or, in the case of a remission, are unexpectedly joined together again as if nothing had happened.

The dissociation in schizophrenia is not only far more serious, but very often it is irreversible. The dissociation is no longer fluid and changeable as it is in a neurosis, it is more like a mirror broken up into splinters. The unity of personality which, in a case of hysteria, lends a humanly understandable character to its own secondary personalities is definitely shattered into fragments. In hysterical multiple personality there is a fairly smooth, even tactful, cooperation between the different persons, who keep to their respective roles and, if possible, do not bother each other. One feels the presence of an invisible *spiritus rector,* a central manager who arranges the stage for the different figures in an almost rational way, often in the form of a more or less sentimental drama. Each figure has a suggestive name and an admissible character, and they are just as nicely hysterical and just as sentimentally biased as the patient's own consciousness.

The picture of a personality dissociation in schizophrenia is quite different. The split-off figures assume banal, grotesque, or highly exaggerated names and characters, and are often objectionable in many other ways. They do not, moreover, cooperate with the patient's consciousness. They are not tactful and they have no respect for sentimental values. On the contrary, they break in and make a disturbance at any time, they torment the ego in a hundred ways; all are objectionable and shocking, either in their noisy and impertinent behavior or in their grotesque cruelty and obscenity. There is an apparent chaos of incoherent visions, voices, and characters, all of an overwhelmingly strange and incomprehensible nature. If there is a drama at all, it is certainly far beyond the patient's understanding. In most cases it transcends even the physician's comprehension, so much so that he is inclined to suspect the mental sanity of anybody who sees more than plain madness in the ravings of a lunatic.

The autonomous figures have broken away from the control of the ego so thoroughly that their original participation in the patient's mental makeup has vanished. The *abaissement* has reached a degree unheard of in the sphere of neurosis. An hysterial dissociation is bridged over by a unity of personality which still functions, whereas in schizophrenia the very foundations of the personality are impaired.

The *abaissement*

1. Causes the loss of whole regions of normally controlled contents.

2. Produces split-off fragments of the personality.

3. Hinders normal trains of thought from being consistently carried through and completed.

4. Decreases the responsibility and the adequate reaction of the ego.

5. Causes incomplete realizations and thus gives rise to insufficient and inadequate emotional reactions.

6. Lowers the threshold of consciousness, thereby allowing normally inhibited contents of the unconscious to enter consciousness in the form of autonomous invasions.

We find all these effects of *abaissement* in neurosis as well as in schizophrenia. But in neurosis the unity of personality is at least potentially preserved, whereas in schizophrenia it is almost irreparably damaged. Because of this fundamental injury the cleavage between dissociated psychic elements amounts to a real destruction of their former connections.

The psychogenesis of schizophrenia therefore prompts us to ask, first of all: Can the primary symptom, the extreme *abaissement,* be considered an effect of psychological conflicts and other disorders of an emotional nature, or not? I do not think it necessary to discuss in detail whether or not the *secondary symptoms,* as described by Bleuler, owe their existence and their specific form to psychological determination. Bleuler himself is fully convinced that their form and content, i.e., their individual phenomenology, are derived entirely from emotional complexes. I agree with Bleuler, whose experience of the psychogenesis of secondary symptoms coincides with my own, for we were collaborating in the years which preceded his famous book on dementia praecox. As a matter of fact, I began as early as 1903 to analyse cases of schizophrenia for therapeutic purposes. There can, indeed, be no doubt about the psychological determination of secondary symptoms. Their structure and origin are in no way different from those of neurotic symptoms, with, of course, the important exception that they exhibit all the characteristics of mental contents no longer subordinated to the supreme control of a complete personality. There is, as a matter of fact, hardly one secondary symptom which does not show some signs of a typical *abaissement.* This characteristic, however, does not depend upon psychogenesis but derives entirely from the primary symptom. Psychological causes, in other words, produce secondary symptoms exclusively on the basis of the primary condition.

In dealing with the question of psychogenesis in schizophrenia, therefore, we can dismiss the secondary symptoms altogether. There is only one problem, and that is the psychogenesis of the primary condition, i.e., the extreme *abaissement,* which is, from the psychological point of view, the root of the schizophrenic disorder. We therefore ask: Is there any reason to believe that the *abaissement* can be due to causes which are strictly psychological? An *abaissement* can be produced—as we well know—by many causes: by fatigue, normal sleep, intoxication, fever, anaemia, intense affects, shocks, organic diseases of the central nervous system; likewise it can be induced by mass-psychology or a primitive mentality, or by religious and political fanaticism, etc. It can also be caused by constitutional and hereditary factors.

The more common form of *abaissement* does not affect the unity of the personality, at least not seriously. Thus all dissociations and other psychic phenomena derived from this general form of *abaissement* bear the stamp of the integral personality.

Neuroses are specific consequences of an *abaissement;* as a rule they arise from a habitual or chronic form of it. Where they appear to be the effect of an acute form, a more or less latent psychological disposition always existed prior to the *abaissement,* so that the latter is no more than a conditional cause.

Now there is no doubt that an *abaissement* which leads to a neurosis is produced either by exclusively psychological factors or by these in conjunction with other, perhaps more physical, conditions. Any *abaissement,* particularly one that leads to a neurosis, means in itself that there is a weakening of the supreme control. A neurosis is a relative dissociation, a conflict between the ego and a resistant force based upon unconscious contents. These contents have more or less lost their connection with the psychic totality. They form themselves into fragments, and the loss of them means a depotentiation of the conscious personality. The intense conflict, on the other hand, expresses an equally intense desire to reestablish the severed connection. There is no cooperation, but at least there is a violent conflict, which functions instead of a positive connection. Every neurotic fights for the maintenance and supremacy of his ego-consciousness and for the subjugation of the resistant unconscious forces. But a patient who allows himself to be swayed by the intrusion of strange contents from the unconscious, a patient who does not fight, who even identifies with the morbid elements, immediately exposes himself to the suspicion of schizophrenia. His *abaissement* has reached the fatal, extreme degree, when the ego loses all power to resist the onslaught of an apparently more powerful unconscious.

Neurosis lies on this side of the critical point, schizophrenia on the other. We do not doubt that psychological motives can bring about an *abaissement* which eventually results in a neurosis. A neurosis approaches the danger line, yet somehow it manages to remain on the hither side. If it should transgress the line it would cease to be a neurosis. Yet are we quite certain that a neurosis never steps beyond the danger line? You know that there are such cases, neuroses to all appearances for many years, and then it suddenly happens that the patient steps beyond the line and clearly transforms himself into a real psychotic.

Now, what do we say in such a case? We say that it has always been a psychosis, a "latent" one. . . .

The Psychotherapeutic Value of Dreams

The Compensatory Nature of Dreams

Although in the great majority of cases compensation aims at establishing a normal psychological balance and thus appears as a kind of self-regulation of

---

The Psychotherapeutic Value of Dreams, from Jung, "On the Nature of Dreams," *The Structure and Dynamics of the Psyche,* pp. 288–96.

the psychic system, one must not forget that under certain circumstances and in certain cases (for instance, in latent psychoses) compensation may lead to a fatal outcome owing to the preponderance of destructive tendencies. The result is suicide or some other abnormal action, apparently preordained in the life-pattern of certain hereditarily tainted individuals.

In the treatment of neurosis, the task before us is to reestablish an approximate harmony between conscious and unconscious. This, as we know, can be achieved in a variety of ways: from "living a natural life," persuasive reasoning, strengthening the will, to analysis of the unconscious.

Because the simpler methods so often fail and the doctor does not know how to go on treating the patient, the compensatory function of dreams offers welcome assistance. I do not mean that the dreams of modern people indicate the appropriate method of healing, as was reported of the incubation-dreams dreamt in the temples of Aesculapius. They do, however, illuminate the patient's situation in a way that can be exceedingly beneficial to health. They bring him memories, insights, experiences, awaken dormant qualities in the personality, and reveal the unconscious element in his relationships. So it seldom happens that anyone who has taken the trouble to work over his dreams with qualified assistance for a longer period of time remains without enrichment and a broadening of his mental horizon. Just because of their compensatory behavior, a methodical analysis of dreams discloses new points of view and new ways of getting over the dreaded impasse.

The term *compensation* naturally gives us only a very general idea of the function of dreams. But if, as happens in long and difficult treatments, the analyst observes a series of dreams often running into hundreds, there gradually forces itself upon him a phenomenon which, in an isolated dream, would remain hidden behind the compensation of the moment. This phenomenon is a kind of developmental process in the personality itself. At first it seems that each compensation is a momentary adjustment of one-sidedness or an equalization of disturbed balance. But with deeper insight and experience, these apparently separate acts of compensation arrange themselves into a kind of plan. They seem to hang together and in the deepest sense to be subordinated to a common goal, so that a long dream-series no longer appears as a senseless string of incoherent and isolated happenings, but resembles the successive steps in a planned and orderly process of development. I have called this unconscious process spontaneously expressing itself in the symbolism of a long dream-series the individuation process. . . .

The question whether a long series of dreams recorded outside the analytical procedure would likewise reveal a development aiming at individuation is one that cannot be answered at present for lack of the necessary material. The analytical procedure, especially when it includes a systematic dream-analysis, is a "process of quickened maturation," as Stanley Hall once aptly remarked. It is therefore possible that the motifs accompanying the individuation process appear chiefly and predominantly in dream-series recorded under analysis, whereas in "extra-analytical" dream-series they occur only at much greater intervals of time.

I have mentioned before that dream interpretation requires, among other things, specialized knowledge. While I am quite ready to believe that an intelligent layman with some psychological knowledge and experience of life could, with practice, diagnose dream compensation correctly, I consider it impossible for anyone without knowledge of mythology and folklore and without some understanding of the psychology of primitives and of comparative religion to grasp the essence of the individuation process, which, according to all we know, lies at the base of psychological compensation.

Not all dreams are of equal importance. Even primitives distinguish between "little" and "big" dreams, or, as we might say, "insignificant" and "significant" dreams. Looked at more closely, "little" dreams are the nightly fragments of fantasy coming from the subjective and personal sphere, and their meaning is limited to the affairs of everyday. That is why such dreams are easily forgotten, just because their validity is restricted to the day-to-day fluctuations of the psychic balance. Significant dreams, on the other hand, are often remembered for a lifetime, and not infrequently prove to be the richest jewel in the treasure house of psychic experience. How many people have I encountered who at the first meeting could not refrain from saying: "I once had a dream!" Sometimes it was the first dream they could ever remember, and one that occurred between the ages of three and five. I have examined many such dreams, and often found in them a peculiarity which distinguishes them from other dreams: they contain symbolical images which we also come across in the mental history of mankind. It is worth noting that the dreamer does not need to have any inkling of the existence of such parallels. This peculiarity is characteristic of dreams of the individuation process, where we find the mythological motifs or mythologems I have designated as archetypes. These are to be understood as specific forms and groups of images which occur not only at all times and in all places but also in individual dreams, fantasies, visions, and delusional ideas. Their frequent appearance in individual case material, as well as their universal distribution, prove that the human psyche is unique and subjective or personal only in part, and for the rest is collective and objective.

Thus we speak on the one hand of a *personal* and on the other of a *collective* unconscious, which lies at a deeper level and is further removed from consciousness than the personal unconscious. The "big" or "meaningful" dreams come from this deeper level. They reveal their significance—quite apart from the subjective impression they make—by their plastic form, which often has a poetic force and beauty. Such dreams occur mostly during the critical phases of life, in early youth, puberty, at the onset of middle age (thirty-six to forty), and within sight of death. Their interpretation often involves considerable difficulties, because the material which the dreamer is able to contribute is too meager. For these archetypal products are no longer concerned with personal experiences but with general ideas, whose chief significance lies in their intrinsic meaning and not in any personal experience and its associations. For example, a young man dreamed of *a great snake that guarded a golden bowl in an underground vault.* To be sure, he had once seen a huge snake in a zoo, but otherwise he could suggest nothing that might have prompted such a dream, except perhaps the reminiscence of fairytales. Judging by this unsatisfactory context the dream, which actually produced a very powerful effect, would have hardly any meaning. But that would not explain its decided emotionality. In such a case we have to go back to mythology, where the combination of snake or dragon with treasure and cave represents an ordeal in the life of the hero. Then it becomes clear that we are dealing with a collective emotion, a typical situation full of affect, which is not primarily a personal experience but becomes one only secondarily. Primarily it is a universally human problem which, because it has been overlooked subjectively, forces itself objectively upon the dreamer's consciousness.

A man in middle life still feels young, and age and death lie far ahead of him. At about thirty-six he passes the zenith of life, without being conscious of the meaning of this fact. If he is a man whose whole makeup and nature do not tolerate excessive unconsciousness, then the import of this moment will be forced upon him, perhaps in the form of an archetypal dream. It would be in vain for him to try to understand the dream with the help of a carefully worked out context, for it expresses itself in strange mythological forms that are not familiar to him. The dream uses collective figures because it has to express an eternal human problem that repeats itself endlessly, and not just a disturbance of personal balance.

All these moments in the individual's life, when the universal laws of human fate break in upon the purposes, expectations, and opinions of the personal consciousness, are stations along the road of the individuation process. This process is, in effect, the spontaneous realization of the whole man. The ego-conscious personality is only a part of the whole man, and its life does not yet represent his total life. The more he is merely "I," the more he splits himself off from the collective man, of whom he is also a part, and may even find himself in opposition to him. But since everything living strives for wholeness, the inevitable one-sidedness of our conscious life is continually being corrected and compensated by the universal human being in us, whose goal is the ultimate integration of conscious and unconscious, or better, the assimilation of the ego to a wider personality.

Such reflections are unavoidable if one wants to understand the meaning of "big" dreams. They employ numerous mythological motifs that characterize the life of the hero, of that greater man who is semidivine by nature. Here we find the dangerous adventures and ordeals such as occur in initiations. We meet dragons, helpful animals, and demons; also the Wise Old Man, the animal man, the wishing tree, the hidden treasure, the well, the cave, the walled garden, the transformative processes and substances of alchemy, and so forth —all things which in no way touch the banalities of everyday. The reason for this is that they have to do with the realization of a part of the personality which has not yet come into existence but is still in the process of becoming. . . .

But if dreams produce such essential compensations, why are they not understandable? I have often been asked this question. The answer must be that the dream is a natural occurrence, and that nature shows no inclination to offer her fruits gratis or according to human expectations. It is often objected that the compensation must be ineffective unless the dream is understood. This is not so certain, however, for many things can be effective without being understood. But there is no doubt that we can enhance its effect considerably by understanding the dream, and this is often necessary because the voice of the unconscious so easily goes unheard. "What nature leaves imperfect is perfected by the art," says an alchemical dictum.

The Form of Dreams

Coming now to the form of dreams, we find everything from lightning impressions to endlessly spun-out dream narrative. Nevertheless there are a great many "average" dreams in which a definite structure can be perceived, not unlike that of a drama. For instance, the dream begins with a STATEMENT OF PLACE, such as, "*I was in a street, it was an avenue*" (1), or, "*I was in a large building like a hotel*" (2). Next comes a statement about the PROTAGONISTS, for instance, "*I was walking with my friend X in a city park. At a crossing we suddenly ran into Mrs. Y*" (3), or, "*I was sitting with Father and Mother in a train compartment*" (4), or, "*I was in uniform with many of my comrades*" (5). Statements of time are rarer. I call this phase of the dream the EXPOSITION. It indicates the scene of action, the people involved, and often the initial situation of the dreamer.

In the second phase comes the DEVELOPMENT of the plot. For instance: "*I was in a street, it was an avenue. In the distance a car appeared, which approached rapidly. It was being driven very unsteadily, and I thought the driver must be drunk*" (1). Or: "*Mrs. Y seemed to be very excited and wanted to whisper something to me hurriedly, which my friend X was obviously not intended to hear*" (3). The situation is somehow becoming complicated, and a definite tension develops because one does not know what will happen.

The third phase brings the CULMINATION or *peripeteia*. Here something decisive happens or something changes completely: "*Suddenly I was in the car and seemed to be myself this drunken driver. Only I was not drunk, but strangely insecure and as if without a steering-wheel. I could no longer control the fast moving car, and crashed into a wall"* (1). Or: *"Suddenly Mrs. Y turned deathly pale and fell to the ground"* (3).

The fourth and last phase is the *lysis*, the SOLUTION or RESULT produced by the dream work. (There are certain dreams in which the fourth phase is lacking, and this can present a special problem, not to be discussed here.) Examples: *"I saw that the front part of the car was smashed. It was a strange car that I did not know. I myself was unhurt. I thought with some uneasiness of my responsibility"* (1). *"We thought Mrs. Y was dead, but it was evidently only a faint. My friend X cried out: 'I must fetch a doctor'"* (3). The last phase shows the final situation, which is at the same time the solution "sought" by the dreamer. In dream 1 a new reflectiveness has supervened after a kind of rudderless confusion, or rather, should supervene, since the dream is compensatory. The upshot of dream 3 is the thought that the help of a competent third person is indicated.

The first dreamer was a man who had rather lost his head in difficult family circumstances and did not want to let matters go to extremes. The other dreamer wondered whether he ought to obtain the help of a psychiatrist for his neurosis. Naturally these statements are not an interpretation of the dream, they merely outline the initial situation. This division into four phases can be applied without much difficulty to the majority of dreams met with in practice —an indication that dreams generally have a "dramatic" structure.

The essential content of the dream action, as I have shown above, is a sort of finely attuned compensation of the one-sidedness, errors, deviations, or other shortcomings of the conscious attitude. An hysterical patient of mine, an aristocratic lady who seemed to herself no end distinguished, met in her dreams a whole series of dirty fishwives and drunken prostitutes. In extreme cases the compensation becomes so menacing that the fear of it results in sleeplessness.

Thus the dream may either repudiate the dreamer in a most painful way, or bolster him up morally. The first is likely to happen to people who, like the last-mentioned patient, have too good an opinion of themselves; the second to those whose self-valuation is too low. Occasionally, however, the arrogant person is not simply humiliated in the dream, but is raised to an altogether improbable and absurd eminence, while the all-too-humble individual is just as improbably degraded, in order to "rub it in," as the English say.

Many people who know something, but not enough, about dreams and their meaning, and who are impressed by their subtle and apparently intentional compensation, are liable to succumb to the prejudice that the dream actually has a moral purpose, that it warns, rebukes, comforts, foretells the future, etc. If one believes that the unconscious always knows best, one can easily be betrayed into leaving the dreams to take the necessary decisions, and is then disappointed when the dreams become more and more trivial and meaningless. Experience has shown me that a slight knowledge of dream psychology is apt to lead to an overrating of the unconscious which impairs the power of conscious decision. The unconscious functions satisfactorily only when the conscious mind fulfills its tasks to the very limit. A dream may perhaps supply what is then lacking, or it may help us forward where our best efforts have failed. If the unconscious really were superior to consciousness it would be difficult to see wherein the advantage of consciousness lay, or why it should ever have come into being as a necessary element in the scheme of evolution. If it were nothing but a *lusus naturae,* the fact of our conscious awareness of the world and of our own existence would be without meaning. The idea that consciousness is a freak of nature is somehow difficult to digest, and for psychological reasons we should avoid emphasizing it, even if it were correct—which, by the way, we shall luckily never be in a position to prove (any more than we can prove the contrary). . . .

The Four Stages of Treatment

Each stage in the development of our psychology has something curiously final about it. Catharsis, with its heart-felt outpourings, makes one feel: "Now we are there, everything has come out, everything is known, the last terror lived through and the last tear shed; now everything will be all right." Elucidation says with equal conviction: "Now we know where the neurosis came from, the earliest memories have been unearthed, the last roots dug up, and the transference was nothing but the wish-fulfilling fantasy of a childhood paradise or a relapse into the family romance; the road to a normally disillusioned life is now open." Finally comes education, pointing out that no amount of confession and no amount of explaining can make the crooked plant grow straight, but that it must be trained upon the trellis of the norm by the gardener's art. Only then will normal adaptation be reached. . . .

All life is living history. Even the reptile still lives in us *par sous-entendu.* In the same way, the three stages of analytical psychology so far dealt with are by no means truths of such a nature that the last of them has gobbled up and replaced the other two. On the contrary, all three are salient aspects of one and the same problem, and they no more invalidate one another than do confession and absolution.

The Four Stages of Treatment, from Carl Gustav Jung, "Problems of Modern Psychotherapy," *The Practice of Psychotherapy,* vol. 16 of THE COLLECTED WORKS OF C. G. JUNG, 2nd ed. (New York: Bollingen Foundation, 1966), pp. 68–75.

The same is true of the fourth stage, transformation. It too should not claim to be the finally attained and only valid truth. ...

By no device can the treatment be anything but the product of mutual influence, in which the whole being of the doctor as well as that of his patient plays its part. In the treatment there is an encounter between two irrational factors, that is to say, between two persons who are not fixed and determinable quantities but who bring with them, besides their more or less clearly defined fields of consciousness, an indefinitely extended sphere of nonconsciousness. Hence the personalities of doctor and patient are often infinitely more important for the outcome of the treatment than what the doctor says and thinks (although what he says and thinks may be a disturbing or a healing factor not to be underestimated). For two personalities to meet is like mixing two different chemical substances: if there is any combination at all, both are transformed. In any effective psychological treatment the doctor is bound to influence the patient; but this influence can only take place if the patient has a reciprocal influence on the doctor. You can exert no influence if you are not susceptible to influence. It is futile for the doctor to shield himself from the influence of the patient and to surround himself with a smoke screen of fatherly and professional authority. By so doing he only denies himself the use of a highly important organ of information. The patient influences him unconsciously none the less, and brings about changes in the doctor's unconscious which are well known to many psychotherapists: psychic disturbances or even injuries peculiar to the profession, a striking illustration of the patient's almost "chemical" action. One of the best known symptoms of this kind is the countertransference evoked by the transference. But the effects are often much more subtle, and their nature can best be conveyed by the old idea of the demon of sickness. According to this, a sufferer can transmit his disease to a healthy person whose powers then subdue the demon—but not without impairing the well-being of the subduer.

Between doctor and patient, therefore, there are imponderable factors which bring about a mutual transformation. In the process, the stronger and more stable personality will decide the final issue. I have seen many cases where the patient assimilated the doctor in defiance of all theory and of the latter's professional intentions—generally, though not always, to the disadvantage of the doctor.

The stage of transformation is grounded on these facts, but it took more than twenty-five years of wide practical experience for them to be clearly recognized. Freud himself has admitted their importance and has therefore seconded my demand for the analysis of the analyst.

What does this demand mean? Nothing less than that the doctor is as much "in the analysis" as the patient. He is equally a part of the psychic process of treatment and therefore equally exposed to the transforming influences. Indeed, to the extent that the doctor shows himself impervious to this influence, he forfeits influence over the patient; and if he is influenced only unconsciously, there is a gap in his field of consciousness which makes it impossible for him to see the patient in true perspective. In either case the result of the treatment is compromised.

The doctor is therefore faced with the same task which he wants his patient to face—that is, he must become socially adapted or, in the reverse case, appropriately nonadapted. This therapeutic demand can of course be clothed in a thousand different formulae, according to the doctor's beliefs. One doctor believes in overcoming infantilism—therefore he must first overcome his own infantilism. Another believes in abreacting all affects—therefore he must first abreact all his own affects. A third believes in complete consciousness—threfore he must first reach consciousness of himself. The doctor must consistently strive to meet his own therapeutic demand if he wishes to ensure the right sort of influence over his patients. All these guiding principles of therapy make so many ethical demands, which can be summed up in the single truth: be the man through whom you wish to influence others. . . .

The step from education to self-education is a logical advance that completes the earlier stages. The demand made by the stage of transformation, namely that the doctor must change himself if he is to become capable of changing his patient, is, as may well be imagined, a rather unpopular one, and for three reasons. First, because it seems unpractical; second, because of the unpleasant prejudice against being preoccupied with oneself; and third, because it is sometimes exceedingly painful to live up to everything one expects of one's patient. . . .

I would like to emphasize once again that the newest developments in analytical psychology confront us with the imponderable elements in the human personality; that we have learned to place in the foreground the personality of the doctor himself as a curative or harmful factor; and that what is now demanded is his own transformation—the self-education of the educator. Consequently, everything that occurred on the objective level in the history of our psychology—confession, elucidation, education—passes to the subjective level; in other words, what happened to the patient must now happen to the doctor so that his personality shall not react unfavorably on the patient. The doctor can no longer evade his own difficulty by treating the difficulties of others: the man who suffers from a running abscess is not fit to perform a surgical operation.

Just as the momentous discovery of the unconscious shadow-side in man suddenly forced the Freudian school to deal even with questions of religion, so this latest advance makes an unavoidable problem of the doctor's ethical attitude. The self-criticism and self-examination that are indissolubly bound up with it necessitates a view of the psyche radically different from the merely biological one which has prevailed hitherto; for the human psyche is far more than a mere object of scientific interest. It is not only the sufferer but the doctor as well, not only the object but also the subject, not only a cerebral function but the absolute condition of consciousness itself.

What was formerly a method of medical treatment now becomes a method of self-education, and with this the horizon of our psychology is immeasurably widened. The crucial thing is no longer the medical diploma, but the human quality. This is a significant turn of events, for it places all the implements of the psychotherapeutic art that were developed in clinical practice, and then refined and systematized, at the service of our self-education and self-perfection, with the result that analytical psychology has burst the bonds which till then had bound it to the consulting room of the doctor. . . .

Transference

Practical analysis has shown that unconscious contents are invariably projected at first upon concrete persons and situations. Many projections can ultimately be integrated back into the individual once he has recognized their subjective origin; others resist integration, and although they may be detached from their original objects, they thereupon transfer themselves to the doctor. Among these contents the relation to the parent of opposite sex plays a particularly important part, i.e., the relation of son to mother, daughter to father, and also that of brother to sister. As a rule this complex cannot be integrated completely, since the doctor is nearly always put in the place of the father, the brother, and even (though naturally more rarely) the mother. Experience has shown that this projection persists with all its original intensity (which Freud regarded as etiological), thus creating a bond that corresponds in every respect to the initial infantile relationship, with a tendency to recapitulate all the experiences of childhood on the doctor. In other words, the neurotic maladjustment of the patient is now *transferred* to him. Freud, who was the first to recognize and describe this phenomenon, coined the term *transference neurosis.*

This bond is often of such intensity that we could almost speak of a "combination." When two chemical substances combine, both are altered. This is precisely what happens in the transference. Freud rightly recognized that this bond is of the greatest therapeutic importance in that it gives rise to a *mixtum compositum* of the doctor's own mental health and the patient's maladjustment. In Freudian technique the doctor tries to ward off the transference as much as possible—which is understandable enough from the human point of view, though in certain cases it may considerably impair the therapeutic effect. It is inevitable that the doctor should be influenced to a certain extent

---

Transference, from Jung, "Psychology of the Transference," *The Practice of Psychotherapy,* pp. 170–73.

and even that his nervous health should suffer.[1] He quite literally "takes over" the sufferings of his patient and shares them with him. For this reason he runs a risk—and must run it in the nature of things.[2] The enormous importance that Freud attached to the transference phenomenon became clear to me at our first personal meeting in 1907. After a conversation lasting many hours there came a pause. Suddenly he asked me out of the blue, "And what do you think about the transference?" I replied with the deepest conviction that it was the alpha and omega of the analytical method, whereupon he said, "Then you have grasped the main thing."

The great importance of the transference has often led to the mistaken idea that it is absolutely indispensable for a cure, that it must be demanded from the patient, so to speak. But a thing like that can no more be demanded than faith, which is only valuable when it is spontaneous. Enforced faith is nothing but spiritual cramp. Anyone who thinks that he must "demand" a transference is forgetting that this is only one of the therapeutic factors, and that the very word *transference* is closely akin to *projection*—a phenomenon that cannot possibly be demanded. I personally am always glad when there is only a mild transference or when it is practically unnoticeable. Far less claim is then made upon one as a person, and one can be satisfied with other effective therapeutic factors. Among these the patient's own insight plays an important part, also his goodwill, the doctor's authority, suggestion, good advice, understanding, sympathy, encouragement, etc. Naturally the more serious cases do not come into this category. . . .

The Therapeutic Value of Abreaction

If the curative effect depended solely upon the rehearsal of experience, abreaction could be performed by the patient alone, as an isolated exercise, and there

---

[1]Freud had already discovered the phenomenon of the "countertransference." Those acquainted with his technique will be aware of its marked tendency to keep the person of the doctor as far as possible beyond the reach of this effect. Hence the doctor's preference for sitting behind the patient, also his pretense that the transference is a product of his technique, whereas in reality it is a perfectly natural phenomenon that can happen to him just as it can happen to the teacher, the clergyman, the general practitioner, and—last but not least—the husband. Freud also uses the expression *transference-neurosis* as a collective term for hysteria, hysterical fears, and compulsion neuroses. . . .

[2]The effects of this on the doctor or nurse can be very far-reaching. I know of cases where, in dealing with borderline schizophrenics, short psychotic attacks were actually "taken over," and during these moments it happened that the patients were feeling more than ordinarily well. I have even met a case of induced paranoia in a doctor who was analyzing a woman patient in the early stages of latent persecution mania. This is not so astonishing since certain psychic disturbances can be extremely infectious if the doctor himself has a latent predisposition in that direction.

The Therapeutic Value of Abreaction, from Jung, "The Therapeutic Value of Abreaction," *The Practice of Psychotherapy,* pp. 132–33.

would be no need of any human object upon whom to discharge the affect. But the intervention of the doctor is absolutely necessary. One can easily see what it means to the patient when he can confide his experience to an understanding and sympathetic doctor. His conscious mind finds in the doctor a moral support against the unmanageable affect of his traumatic complex. No longer does he stand alone in his battle with these elemental powers but someone whom he trusts reaches out a hand, lending him moral strength to combat the tyranny of uncontrolled emotion. In this way the integrative powers of his conscious mind are reinforced until he is able once more to bring the rebellious affect under control. This influence on the part of the doctor, which is absolutely essential, may, if you like, be called suggestion.

For myself, I would rather call it his human interest and personal devotion. These are the property of no method, nor can they ever become one; they are moral qualities which are of the greatest importance in all methods of psychotherapy, and not in the case of abreaction alone. The rehearsal of the traumatic moment is able to reintegrate the neurotic dissociation only when the conscious personality of the patient is so far reinforced by his relationship to the doctor that he can consciously bring the autonomous complex under the control of his will.

Only under these conditions has abreaction a curative value. But this does not depend solely on the discharge of affective tension; it depends, as McDougall shows, far more on whether or not the dissociation is successfully resolved. Hence the cases where abreaction has a negative result appear in a different light.

In the absence of the conditions just mentioned, abreaction by itself is not sufficient to resolve the dissociation. If the rehearsal of the trauma fails to reintegrate the autonomous complex, then the relationship to the doctor can so raise the level of the patient's consciousness as to enable him to overcome the complex and assimilate it. But it may easily happen that the patient has a particularly obstinate resistance to the doctor, or that the doctor does not have the right kind of attitude to the patient. In either case the abreactive method breaks down.

It stands to reason that when dealing with neuroses which are traumatically determined only to a minor degree, the cathartic method of abreaction will meet with poor success. It has nothing to do with the nature of the neurosis, and its rigid application is quite ludicrous here. Even when a partial success is obtained, it can have no more significance than the success of any other method which admittedly had nothing to do with the nature of the neurosis.

Success in these cases is due to suggestion; it is usually of very limited duration and clearly a matter of chance. The prime cause is always the transference to the doctor, and this is established without too much difficulty provided that the doctor evinces an earnest belief in his method. Precisely because it has as little to do with the nature of neurosis as, shall we say, hypnosis and other such cures, the cathartic method has, with few exceptions, long been abandoned in favor of analysis.

Now it happens that the analytical method is most unassailable just where the cathartic method is most shaky: that is, in the relationship between doctor and patient. . . .

Word Association Method

The history of the association method in vogue in psychology, as well as the method itself, is, of course, so familiar to you that there is no need to enlarge upon it. For practical purposes I make use of the following formula:

1. head	26. blue	51. frog	76. to wash
2. green	27. lamp	52. to part	77. cow
3. water	28. to sin	53. hunger	78. friend
4. to sing	29. bread	54. white	79. luck
5. dead	30. rich	55. child	80. lie
6. long	31. tree	56. to take care	81. deportment
7. ship	32. to prick	57. lead pencil	82. narrow
8. to pay	33. pity	58. sad	83. brother
9. window	34. yellow	59. plum	84. to fear
10. friendly	35. mountain	60. to marry	85. stork
11. to cook	36. to die	61. house	86. false
12. to ask	37. salt	62. dear	87. anxiety
13. cold	38. new	63. glass	88. to kiss
14. stem	39. custom	64. to quarrel	89. bride
15. to dance	40. to pray	65. fur	90. pure
16. village	41. money	66. big	91. door
17. lake	42. foolish	67. carrot	92. to choose
18. sick	43. pamphlet	68. to paint	93. hay
19. pride	44. despise	69. part	94. contented
20. to cook	45. finger	70. old	95. ridicule
21. ink	46. expensive	71. flower	96. to sleep
22. angry	47. bird	72. to beat	97. month
23. needle	48. to fall	73. box	98. nice
24. to swim	49. book	74. wild	99. woman
25. voyage	50. unjust	75. family	100. to abuse

This formula has been constructed after many years of experience. The words are chosen and partially arranged in such a manner as to strike easily almost all complexes which occur in practice. As shown above, there is a regulated mixing of the grammatical qualities of the words. For this there are definite reasons.

Word Association Method, from Carl Gustav Jung, "The Association Method," *American Journal of Psychology* 21 (1910): 219–40. Graphs and charts have been omitted without the use of intervening signs to indicate the break.

Before the experiment begins the test-person receives the following instruction: "Answer as quickly as possible with the first word that occurs to your mind." This instruction is so simple that it can easily be followed. The work itself, moreover, appears extremely easy, so that it might be expected anyone could accomplish it with the greatest facility and promptitude. But, contrary to expectation, the behavior is quite otherwise.

The first thing that strikes us is the fact that many test-persons show a marked prolongation of the reaction time. This would seem to be suggestive of intellectual difficulties—wrongly, however, for we are often dealing with very intelligent persons of fluent speech. The explanation lies rather in the emotions. In order to understand the matter, comprehensively, we must bear in mind that the association experiments cannot deal with a separated psychic function, for any psychic occurrence is never a thing in itself, but is always the resultant of the entire psychological past. The association experiment, too, is not merely a method for the reproduction of separated word couplets, but it is a kind of pastime, a conversation between experimenter and test-person. In a certain sense it is still more than that. Words really represent condensed actions, situations, and things. When I give a stimulus word to the test-person, which denotes an action, it is as if I represented to him the action itself, and asked him, "How do you behave towards it? What do you think of it? What would you do in this situation?" If I were a magician, I should cause the situation corresponding to the stimulus word to appear in reality, and placing the test-person in its midst, I should then study his manner of reaction. The result of my stimulus words would thus undoubtedly approach infinitely nearer perfection. But as we are not magicians, we must be contented with the linguistic substitutes for reality; at the same time we must not forget that the stimulus word will almost without exception conjure up its corresponding situation. All depends on how the test-person reacts to this situation. The word *bride* or *bridegroom* will not evoke a simple reaction in a young lady; but the reaction will be deeply influenced by the strong feeling tones evoked, the more so if the experimenter be a man. It thus happens that the test-person is often unable to react quickly and smoothly to all stimulus words. There are certain stimulus words which denote actions, situations, or things, about which the test-person cannot think quickly and surely, and this fact is demonstrated in the association experiments. The examples which I have just given show an abundance of long reaction times and other disturbances. In this case the reaction to the stimulus word is disturbed. The stimulus words therefore act upon us just as reality acts; indeed, a person who shows such great disturbances to the stimulus words is in a certain sense but imperfectly adapted to reality. Disease itself is an imperfect adaptation; hence in this case we are dealing with something morbid in the psyche—with something which is either temporarily or persistently pathological in character, that is, we are dealing with a psychoneurosis, with a functional disturbance of the mind. This rule, however, as we shall see later, is not without its exceptions.

Let us, in the first place, continue the discussion concerning the prolonged reaction time. It often happens that the test-person actually does *not* know what to answer to the stimulus word. He waives any reaction, and for the moment he totally fails to obey the original instructions, and shows himself incapable of adapting himself to the experimenter. If this phenomenon occurs frequently in an experiment, it signifies a high degree of disturbance in adjustment. I would call attention to the fact that it is quite indifferent what reason the test-person gives for the refusal. Some find that too many ideas suddenly occur to them; others, that they suffer from a deficiency of ideas. In most cases, however, the difficulties first perceived are so deterrent that they actually give up the whole reaction. . . .

Yet another sign of impeded adaptation is the often occurring *repetition of the stimulus words*. The test-persons repeat the stimulus word as if they had not heard or understood it distinctly. They repeat it just as we repeat a difficult question in order to grasp it better before answering. This same tendency is shown in the experiment. The questions are repeated because the stimulus words act on hysterical individuals in much the same way as difficult personal questions. In principle it is the same phenomenon as the subsequent completion of the reaction.

In many experiments we observe that the same reaction constantly reappears to the most varied stimulus words. These words seem to possess a special reproduction tendency, and it is very interesting to examine their relationship to the test-person. For example, I have observed a case in which the patient repeated the word *short* a great many times and often in places where it had no meaning. The test-person could not directly state the reason for the repetition of the word *short*. From experience I knew that such predicates always relate either to the test-person himself or to the person nearest to him. I assumed that in this word *short* he designated himself, and that in this way he helped to express something very painful to him. The test-person is of very small stature. . . .

It has long been thought that the association experiment enables one to distinguish certain *intellectual* types. That is not the case. The experiment does not give us any particular insight into the purely intellectual, but rather into the emotional processes. To be sure we can erect certain types of reaction; they are not, however, based on intellectual peculiarities, but depend entirely on the *proportionate emotional states*. Educated test-persons usually show superficial and linguistically deep-rooted associations, whereas the uneducated form more valuable associations and often of ingenious significance. This behavior would be paradoxical from an intellectual viewpoint. The meaningful associations of the uneducated are not really the product of intellectual thinking, but are simply the results of a special emotional state. The whole thing is more important to the uneducated, his emotion is greater, and for that reason he pays more attention to the experiment than the educated person, and his associations are therefore more significant. Apart from those determined by education, we have to consider three principal individual types:

1. An objective type with undisturbed reactions.
2. A so-called complex-type with many disturbances in the experiment occasioned by the constellation of a complex.
3. A so-called definition-type. The peculiarity of this type consists in the fact that the reaction always gives an explanation or a definition of the content of the stimulus word. . . .

The complex-type shows no particular tendency except the *concealment* of a complex, whereas the definition- and predicate-types betray a positive tendency to exert in some way a *definite* influence on the experimenter. But whereas the definition-type tends to bring to light its intelligence, the predicate-type displays its emotion. I need hardly add of what importance such determinations are for the diagnosis of character.

After finishing an association experiment I usually add another of a different kind, the so-called *reproduction* experiment. I repeat the same stimulus words and ask the test-persons whether they still remember their former reactions. In many instances the memory fails, and as experience shows, these locations are stimulus words which touched an emotionally accentuated complex, or stimulus words immediately following such critical words. . . .

By far the larger number of neurotics show a pronounced tendency to cover up their intimate affairs in impenetrable darkness, even from the doctor, so that he finds it very difficult to form a proper picture of the patient's psychology. In such cases I am greatly assisted by the association experiment. When the experiment is finished, I first look over the general course of the reaction times. I see a great many very prolonged intervals; this means that the patient can only adjust himself with difficulty, that his psychological functions proceed with marked internal friction, with *resistances*. The greater number of neurotics react only under great and very definite resistances; there are, however, others in whom the average reaction times are as short as in the normal, and in whom the other complex indicators are lacking, but, despite that fact, they undoubtedly present neurotic symptoms. These rare cases are especially found among very intelligent and educated persons, chronic patients who, after many years of practice, have learned to control their outward behavior and therefore outwardly display very little if any trace of their neuroses. The superficial observer would take them for normal, yet in some places they show disturbances which betray the repressed complex.

After examining the reaction times I turn my attention to the type of the association to ascertain with what type I am dealing. If it is a predicate-type

I draw the conclusions which I have detailed above; if it is a complex-type I try to ascertain the nature of the complex. With the necessary experience one can readily emancipate one's judgment from the test-person's statements and almost without any previous knowledge of the test-persons it is possible under certain circumstances to read the most intimate complexes from the results of the experiment. I look at first for the reproduction words and put them together, and then I look for the stimulus words which show the greatest disturbances. In many cases merely assorting these words suffices to unearth the complex. In some cases it is necessary to put a question here and there. . . .

Dialectical Method of Psychotherapy

When, as a psychotherapist, I set myself up as a medical authority over my patient and on that account claim to know something about his individuality, or to be able to make valid statements about it, I am only demonstrating my lack of criticism, for I am in no position to judge the whole of the personality before me. I cannot say anything valid about him except in so far as he approximates to the "universal man." But since all life is to be found only in individual form, and I myself can assert of another individuality only what I find in my own, I am in constant danger either of doing violence to the other person or of succumbing to his influence. If I wish to treat another individual psychologically at all, I must for better or worse give up all pretensions to superior knowledge, all authority and desire to influence. I must perforce adopt a dialectical procedure consisting in a comparison of our mutual findings. But this becomes possible only if I give the other person a chance to play his hand to the full, unhampered by my assumptions. In this way his system is geared to mine and acts upon it; my reaction is the only thing with which I as an individual can legitimately confront my patient. . . .

The universal man has the characteristics of a savage and must therefore be treated with technical methods. It is in fact bad practice to treat collective man with anything other than "technically correct" methods, i.e., those collectively recognized and believed to be effective. In this sense the old hypnotism or the still older animal magnetism achieved, in principle, just as much as a technically irreproachable modern analysis, or for that matter the amulets of the primitive medicine man. It all depends on the method the therapist happens to believe in. His belief is what does the trick. If he really believes, then

Dialectical Method of Psychotherapy, from Jung, "Principles of Practical Psychotherapy," *The Practice of Psychotherapy*, pp. 5–10.

he will do his utmost for the sufferer with seriousness and perseverance, and this freely given effort and devotion will have a curative effect—up to the level of collective man's mentality. But the limits are fixed by the "individual-universal" antinomy.

This antinomy constitutes a psychological as well as a philosophical criterion, since there are countless people who are not only collective in all essentials but are fired by a quite popular ambition to be nothing but collective. This accords with all the current trends in education which like to regard individuality and lawlessness as synonymous. On this plane anything individual is rated inferior and is repressed. In the corresponding neuroses individual contents and tendencies appear as psychological poisons. There is also, as we know, an overestimation of individuality based on the rule that "the universal signifies nothing in comparison with the individual." Thus, from the psychological (not the clinical) point of view, we can divide the psychoneuroses into two main groups: the one comprising collective people with underdeveloped individuality, the other individualists with atrophied collective adaptation. The therapeutic attitude differs accordingly, for it is abundantly clear that a neurotic individualist can only be cured by recognizing the collective man in himself—hence the need for collective adaptation. It is therefore right to bring him down to the level of collective truth. On the other hand, psychotherapists are familiar with the collectively adapted person who has everything and does everything that could reasonably be required as a guarantee of health, but yet is ill. It would be a bad mistake, which is nevertheless very often committed, to normalize such a person and try to bring him down to the collective level. In certain cases all possibility of individual development is thereby destroyed.

Since individuality, as we stressed in our introductory argument, is absolutely unique, unpredictable, and uninterpretable, in these cases the therapist must abandon all his preconceptions and techniques and confine himself to a purely dialectical procedure, adopting the attitude that shuns all methods.

You will have noticed that I began by presenting the dialectical procedure as the latest phase of psychotherapeutic development. I must now correct myself and put this procedure in the right perspective: it is not so much an elaboration of previous theories and practices as a complete abandonment of them in favor of the most unbiased attitude possible. In other words, the therapist is no longer the agent of treatment but a fellow participant in a process of individual development.

I would not like it to be supposed that these discoveries dropped straight into our laps. They too have their history. Although I was the first to demand that the analyst should himself be analyzed, we are largely indebted to Freud for the invaluable discovery that analysts too have their complexes and consequently one or two blind spots which act as so many prejudices. The psychotherapist gained this insight in cases where it was no longer possible for him to interpret or to guide the patient from on high or *ex cathedra,* regardless of his own personality, but was forced to admit that his personal idiosyncrasies or special attitude hindered the patient's recovery. When one possesses no very clear idea about something, because one is unwilling to admit it to oneself, one tries to hide it from the patient as well, obviously to his very great disadvantage. The demand that the analyst must be analyzed culminates in the idea of a dialectical procedure, where the therapist enters into relationship with another psychic system both as questioner and answerer. No longer is he the superior wise man, judge, and counsellor; he is a fellow participant who finds himself involved in the dialectical process just as deeply as the so-called patient. . . .

Individuation

It is now perfectly clear that this realization involves a very considerable shift of standpoint compared with the older forms of psychotherapy. In order to avoid misunderstandings, let me say at once that this shift is certainly not meant to condemn the existing methods as incorrect, superfluous, or obsolete. The more deeply we penetrate the nature of the psyche, the more the conviction grows upon us that the diversity, the multi-dimensionality of human nature requires the greatest variety of standpoints and methods in order to satisfy the variety of psychic dispositions. It is therefore pointless to subject a simple soul who lacks nothing but a dose of common sense to a complicated analysis of his impulses, much less expose him to the bewildering subtleties of psychological dialectic. It is equally obvious that with complex and highly intelligent people we shall get nowhere by employing well-intentioned advice, suggestions, and other efforts to convert them to some kind of system. In such cases the best thing the doctor can do is lay aside his whole apparatus of methods and theories and trust to luck that his personality will be steadfast enough to act as a signpost for the patient. At the same time he must give serious consideration to the possibility that in intelligence, sensibility, range, and depth the patient's personality is superior to his own. But in all circumstances the prime rule of dialectical procedure is that the individuality of the sufferer has the same value, the same right to exist, as that of the doctor, and consequently that every development in the patient is to be regarded as valid, unless of course it corrects itself of its own accord. Inasmuch as a man is merely collective, he can be changed by suggestion to the point of becoming —or seeming to become—different from what he was before. But inasmuch as he is an individual he can only become what he is and always was. To the extent that "cure" means turning a sick man into a healthy one, cure is change. Wherever this is possible, where it does not demand too great a sacrifice of personality, we should change the sick man therapeutically. But when a patient realizes that cure through change would mean too great a sacrifice, then the doctor can, indeed he should, give up any wish to change or cure. He must either refuse to treat the patient or risk the dialectical procedure. This is of more frequent occurrence than one might think. In my own practice I always have a fair number of highly cultivated and intelligent people of marked individuality who, on ethical grounds, would vehemently resist any serious attempt to change them. In all such cases the doctor must leave the individual way to healing open, and then the cure will bring about no alteration of personality but will be the process we call "individuation," in which the patient becomes what he really is. If the worst comes to the worst, he will even put up with his neurosis, once he has understood the meanings of his illness. More than one patient has admitted to me that he has learned to accept his neurotic symptoms with gratitude, because, like a barometer, they invariably told him when and where he was straying from his individual path, and also whether he had let important things remain unconscious. . . .

Periods of Consultation

All methods of influence, including the analytical, require that the patient be seen as often as possible. I content myself with a maximum of four consultations a week. With the beginning of synthetic treatment it is of advantage to spread out the consultations. I then generally reduce them to one or two hours a week, for the patient must learn to go his own way. This consists in his trying to understand his dreams himself, so that the contents of the unconscious may be progressively articulated with the conscious mind; for the cause of neurosis is the discrepancy between the conscious attitude and the trend of the unconscious. This dissociation is bridged by the assimilation of unconscious contents. Hence the interval between consultations does not go unused. In this way one saves oneself and the patient a good deal of time, which is so much money to him; and at the same time he learns to stand on his own feet instead of clinging to the doctor.

The work done by the patient through the progressive assimilation of unconscious contents leads ultimately to the integration of his personality and hence to the removal of the neurotic dissociation.

Periods of Consultation, from Jung, "Principles of Practical Psychotherapy," *The Practice of Psychotherapy*, p. 20.

4

WILL THERAPY

Otto Rank

Otto Rank (1884–1939), Vienna-born psychotherapist, like Freud and Adler was of Jewish parentage. Although he earned a doctorate at the University of Vienna in 1913, he was to a considerable extent a self-educated scholar, influenced profoundly by Schopenhauer, Nietzsche, and Freud.

In 1905 Freud, deeply impressed with Rank, received him as secretary of the Psychoanalytic Society. He also assisted him in the revision and publication of his first book, *Art and Artist,* published in 1907 (and expanded in an English version in 1932). The work theorizes on the role of the artist and creativity in cultural evolution. From 1912 to 1914 Rank was editor of the first two psychoanalytic journals: *Imago* and *Internationale Zeitschrift für Psychoanalyse.* From 1919 to 1924 he directed Freud's psychoanalytic publishing house, Der Internationale Psychoanalytische Verlag.

Notwithstanding its dedication to Freud, Rank's *The Trauma of Birth* (1924; English, 1929) generated intense controversy on the grounds that its theory deviated from orthodox Freudianism and caused his forced departure from Freud's Psychoanalytic Society. The work theorized birth trauma as having an unconscious significance for the patient, viewing the separation from therapy as the birth process, whereby transference is analogous to the mother-infant relationship. Contrary to Freudianism, Rank held birth (not castration and the Oedipus complex) as the original traumatic experience, and the breast (not the penis) as the initial libidinal object. Rankian theory, however, failed to explain why neurosis is not universal since the trauma of birth is, except to assert that the degree of traumatic fear is the decisive factor in one's becoming neurotic.

In 1926 Rank moved to Paris. The last decade of his life he spent in New York and became an American citizen. Between 1926 and 1931 he produced his three-volume *Technik der Psycho-analyse* (1929, 1931), which was published in English in 1936 under the title of *Will Therapy.* (*Will Therapy* contains only volumes 2 and 3 because volume 1 is Freudian, whereas the others are characteristically Rankian.) Volume 1 treats the ego's biological development, origin of genitality, guilt feelings, and some mechanisms of defense. Volume 2 is concerned with the development of personality, treating a person as a social, ethical, and emotional being. These two volumes were initially lectures in English delivered at the New York School of Social Work. Volume 3, also a lecture, was delivered at the Pennsylvania School of Social Work.

The *Technik* was supplied with supporting theory by his 1929 work, *Outlines of a Genetic Psychology on the Basis of the Psychoanalysis of the Ego Structure* (published in 1936 in English as *Truth and Reality: An Outline of a Philosophy of the Psychic*). *Truth and Reality* is essentially a philosophy of will (its creativity together with its sense of fear and guilt) and of projection and denial (the latter concept being more important to Rank than repression), whereas *Will Therapy* is the process and technique of therapy. These two books were combined in a single volume and republished with editorial notes in 1945.

Rank's originality is most distinctive in his contributions to the process of psychotherapy. Rank's psychotherapy is based on (1) the therapeutic situation being a present experience instead of a mere reliving of the past as in psychoanalysis, (2) the nonsexual nature of the transference relationship which he regarded as a reinstituting of the maternal tie, and (3) the establishment of a therapeutic control by setting a time limit for the termination of treatment. Psychotherapy is the reexperiencing of the "primal libidinal bond to the mother" and severance from the therapeutic relationship, without the patient's fixation and permanent or long-term dependence upon the therapist nor the reproduction of the birth trauma. The setting of a time limit for therapy prepares the patient psychologically for severing the therapeutic relationship. The second aspect of analysis calls for the therapist to place the patient's libido at his own disposal, whereby the patient may form ego-ideals with the aid of the therapist as an educator. Therapy is essentially the work of adaptation or education that originally has been either absent or unsuccessful.

Other of Rank's books include; *The Myth of the Birth of the Hero* (1909; English, 1914) and *The Incest-Motive in Literature and Myth* (1912), which apply psychoanalysis to literature, myth, and art. His *Psychology and Belief in the Soul* (1930; English, 1954) is a critical investigation of depth psychology. His final book, marked by the fact that it is the only one written originally in the English language, *Beyond Psychology* (1941, posthumously), elaborates upon the conclusions found in the previously mentioned work.

Will Therapy: The Therapeutic Experience

The value of the therapeutic experience like that of every real experience lies in its spontaneity and uniqueness, with an important difference to be sure,

---

Will Therapy: The Therapeutic Experience, from Otto Rank, *Will Therapy and Truth and Reality,* trans. Jessie Taft (New York: Knopf, 1945), pp. 5–6.

which constitutes the essence of the whole therapeutic technique. This experience serves primarily only one end, an end which ordinary experience affords only in rare cases, namely assistance in the unfolding and enrichment of the self, the personality. It must, therefore, be intensified consciously and with art into an ego experience in a more far reaching fashion than is usually the case. This value made effectively by the onesidedness of the transference relationship has been, in my opinion, the only spontaneously effective therapeutic element in the analytic situation. However, it has not been utilized constructively, nor has the origin of the guilt feeling necessarily following from the ego enrichment in the experience been understood.

The reason for this failure is that in the classical analytic situation, in spite of the famed passivity of the analyst, the person of the therapist stood in the center, while I unmask all the reactions of the patient, even if they apparently refer to the analyst, as projections of his own inner conflict and bring them back to his own ego. Apparently the narcissism of the analyst has compensated for his passivity, so that he has related all reactions of the patient as far as they do not permit of being put back on an infantile pattern to his own person. My technique, on the contrary, sees the reactions as arising immediately from the therapeutic experience and explains them as projections and attempts at solution of the particular ego conflicts of the patient, which puts the patient himself as chief actor in the center of the situation set up by the analyst, a situation which he creates and re-creates according to his own psychic needs. The so-called transference, which for Freud represents nothing but a reproduction of the infantile, becomes a creative expression of the growth and development of the personality in the therapeutic experience, while the critical phases, labeled resistance by Freud and masculine protest by Adler, I value and utilize constructively as a proof, however negative, of the strength of will on which therapeutic success ultimately depends.

The Basis of Will Therapy

Transference not only contains something passive, temporary, derived, but actually represents that aspect of the relationship to the analyst. But passivity, dependence, or weakness of will in any form is just the difficulty on account of which the neurotic comes for treatment, therefore transference cannot be the therapy to which we attach the idea of something positive.

What is naturally and spontaneously effective in the transference situation and, rightly understood and handled, is also effective therapeutically is the same thing that is potent in every relationship between two human beings,

The Basis of Will Therapy, from Rank, *Will Therapy*, pp. 7, 19.

namely the will. Two wills clash, either the one overthrows the other or both struggle with and against one another for supremacy. . . .

Will-to-Health

This conception of the will conflict and its therapeutic value in the analytic experience throws a light also upon one of the most important of its manifestations, which, without reference to the will psychology, remains unintelligible. It is the problem of the so-called will-to-health. Evidently the patient must have in addition to his neurosis something like a will-to-health also, when he gives himself over to treatment. It seems to me equally certain that this will-to-health becomes less as soon as the treatment has begun and continues to decrease, the further it advances, if one does not understand how to comprehend it psychologically and use it therapeutically. For the first thing the patient does when he begins treatment is to project his will-to-health onto the analyst who represents it as it were, just by virtue of his profession. That is, the patient himself no longer needs to will to become well, as the analyst must and will make him sound. This is an example of the tendency of the patient just described to make the therapist represent positive will, and to keep for himself the negative role, a tendency on whose correct understanding the whole psychotherapeutic process stands or falls. Its success depends on just this, the ability to allow this will-to-health to be preserved and strengthened in the patient himself, instead of permitting it to be projected upon the analyst. This is possible only when the whole therapeutic situation in all its manifestations is evaluated constructively in terms of the will problem. The positive strengthening of the will-to-health to the level of an actual becoming well and remaining well depends completely and entirely upon the will of the patient which even for the period of this treatment must take over the capacity for becoming well and later for remaining well.

Understanding, Denial, and Verbalizing

We might say the seeker for help suffers only temporarily or apparently from weakness of will, in reality from a too strong will which he must constantly deny, rationalize, project and even occasionally break as is the case in the neurosis. The means of cure, we said, is the therapist, that is, the counter-will on which the positive will of the patient is strengthened and in relation to which the positive will of the patient is strengthened and in relation to which he may again will. How does this happen, or how is it effected in spite of the opposing difficulties, or is to be effected therapeutically at all?

Understanding, Denial, and Verbalizing, from Rank, *Will Therapy.* pp. 20–23.

Psychoanalysis, as far as it has been able to discuss the what and how of therapy as such, has answered that psychotherapy is at bottom a love therapy, that is, that it works on the basis of the transference relationship, which is a revival of the parental relationship. . . .

The adult cannot be brought up or reeducated anymore, but must be understood, that is, accepted. In the love therapy, it is only the wish to be understood (corresponding to the wish to be loved) that makes the situation "infantile." The perfect understanding of the analyst is like an all-pardoning of the parents; constructive understanding on the contrary is a self-accusation in Ibsen's meaning, a "holding court" over one's own ego. The understanding by the other rests on a love identification: therefore in the understanding of the analyst we have a phenomenon of identification, a proof of love as the patient seeks it from the other. He may arrive finally at self-understanding, which is the true therapeutic goal only by identification with the analyst who understands him. . . .

The therapeutic factor lies in the verbalizing of the conscious emotions, while the so-called "making conscious of the unconscious" always remains an interpretation of very doubtful value, a substitution of one rationalization for another if it does not actually deteriorate into a duel of wills with the analyst. The verbalizing is important because it represents first of all a self-guidance of the individual, an act of will, in which will and consciousness, these two fundamental factors of our psychic life, come together. It is different from confession, which means avowal or submission to another, just as it is different from making conscious through another, which usually means compulsion. It is a kind of confession to one's self, a voluntary subjection of one's own will under the compulsion of emotion, and is accordingly less in danger of leading to misunderstanding of one's self than the intellectual interpretation which is always based on the denial of emotion, whether it manifests itself as rationalization or as interpretation.

Love and Self-Acceptance

A constructive therapy should not wish to alter the individual but only to develop him so that he can accept himself as he is, at the same time the love claim has to be transformed into his own ethical ideal formation which self-acceptance makes possible. This, then, is the New, which the patient has never experienced before either in the moral-pedagogical parent relations nor in the ethical self-justifying love relations; namely, that he does not need to change himself in terms of any kind of universal or alien ideal so that others may

---

Love and Self-acceptance, from Rank, *Will Therapy,* p. 65.

accept him, but that he alone can and must do both, that is, develop in terms of his own ideal and at the same time on the basis of this ideal also accept himself ethically.

Will, Fate, and Self-Determination

In the therapy of the individual neurotic we deal therefore not with knowledge or ignorance, nor with the need for an "other" or "better" knowing, but with willing, to which knowing in the beginning serves as rationalization and only later opposes itself inhibitingly. The freedom of the will, to which the individual must attain, relates first of all to the self, the individuality; so to will this, as it is, forms the goal of constructive therapy while all forms of educational therapy wish to alter the individual in terms of a given ideology as he ought to be. From the latter viewpoint the individual must accept this ideology as authoritative, that is—believe; from the former, he must first believe in himself instead of being measured by the yardstick of any ideology in terms of which he perceives himself as bad and inferior. This feeling of rejection in relation to an unattainable ideal designates the individual as neurotic, while the creative man who perceives the rejection of the contemporary ideology first in terms of people affirms himself as an individual, as different, and then creates a new ideology for himself which, corresponding to the level of consciousness attained, always works constructively for a definite phase, whether it be in heroic, artistic, or philosophic terms. For all constructiveness is temporary and limited, yes, it consists just in working out and affirming the new aspect of consciousness as immediately manifested in the eternal will-guilt conflict. The earlier this new aspect can be recognized and the more intensively it can be affirmed, the more it can be utilized constructively. This is valid for the therapeutic situation as well as for experience in general, which it represents psychically.

The Therapist and Neurotic as Complementary Types

This evaluation of illness as an expression of the individual creative force leads to a wholly different conception of the neurotic, yes, almost to an apology for

Will, Fate, and Self-Determination, from Rank, *Will Therapy,* pp. 95–96.
The Therapist and Neurotic as Complementary Types, from Rank, *Will Therapy,* pp. 160–61.

the neurotic type who not only unites in himself potentially the possibilities of destructiveness as well as of creativeness, but also demonstrates them factually. The neurotic, although he is not successful in displacing these two basic tendencies ideologically from his own ego to objective work, nevertheless corresponds much more to a miscarried artist (productive person) than to an average man who has not achieved normal development. The attitude of scorn which the therapist type has for the neurotic, in spite of all his understanding, arises in the last analysis from the fact that he sees in him his own destructive self, just as the patient seeks to find in the therapist his own creative ego, by means of identification. In this sense therapist and neurotic form two complementary types, whereby the therapist uses the patient in psychic terms exactly as the patient uses the therapist. The misunderstanding of this situation has led to the misunderstanding already pointed out, that psychoanalytic theory, which represents a psychology of the therapist type, was maintained as a psychology of the neurotic while it is really only his therapy; in other words, that while psychoanalytic theory is therapeutically oriented, the therapy is ideological. The recognition of this fact leads necessarily to my conception that the healing factor of psychotherapy consists not in psychological self-knowledge and its ideological formulation, but in the therapist type itself, whom the neurotic seeks and wants to use as the ideal completion of his own ego.

End Phase and Therapeutic Agent

If the question of his cure becomes for the patient a symbol of his will conflict, the therapist ought to know and share his knowledge with the patient, that there is no criterion for "cure" in psychotherapy, yes, perhaps no "cure" in the medical sense in terms of the removal of a disturbing cause. What is given, however, in dynamic therapy, is a criterion for the ending of the treatment, whose timely and correct conclusion is the most essential therapeutic instrument. For the really therapeutic agent is the freeing of the creative tendency in the individual, and allowing its utilization in the creating, transforming, and endless destroying of the therapeutic relationship, which represents the self, and finally even more the sick (neurotic) part of the ego. This is only possible, however, if from the beginning the role of the active creative ego is relinquished to, shared with, or permitted the patient so that at the end he cannot react in any other way than the right one. In what special form he does it, that is, what individual content and dynamics he utilizes, is of subordinate importance compared to the right general attitude. The self-creating of his role is a truly

---

End Phase and Therapeutic Agent, from Rank, *Will Therapy,* pp. 190–91.

therapeutic experience, as every experience is creative, but the patient can never foresee this because he has been incapable of experiencing; besides most patients come with the more or less clear idea of releasing an earlier, unhappy experience of life, which ideological therapy as a rule also has in view. Dynamic therapy gives them a new experience instead of releasing the old, and insofar as the latter is ultimately "released" therapeutically, it is because the new experience makes it possible. In general the therapist should guard himself against the ideology of "wishing to release," for nothing can be released once and for all, least of all the therapeutic process, especially if it is a dynamic one. Like birth, it represents much more the beginning of something new than the end of the old, and can also be borne thus by the individual much better because it is not final.

5

THE WASHINGTON SCHOOL: THE INTERPERSONAL THEORY OF PSYCHOTHERAPY

Harry Stack Sullivan

Harry Stack Sullivan (1892–1949) was born in Norwich, New York, of Irish ancestry. He was an only child and spent his childhood days on a farm. Though he had little contact with other children, his life was enriched by books and nature study. His was the only Roman Catholic family in a community of Protestants. He remained a bachelor throughout his life. It wasn't until Sullivan had been a physician for twelve years that he and his father became well acquainted with each other's views.

Sullivan's curiosity about personalities and interpersonal relationships was a propelling factor in his decision to enter the field of medicine and psychiatry. He worked his way through the Chicago College of Medicine and Surgery and was granted a medical diploma in 1917. In order to repay the educational debts he had incurred, he was obliged to practice industrial surgery. As a student physician he had served in the National Guard; with the outbreak of World War I he found himself again in military service, this time with the rank of first lieutenant, serving on the Board of Examiners for the Medical Corps. After his discharge, he became assistant medical officer for the Rehabilitation Division of the Federal Board for Vocational Education; then he became executive medical officer, a post which took him to Washington. His next appointment was that of United States Veterans' Liaison Officer, a responsibility which was connected with St. Elizabeth's Hospital, the federal government's hospital for mental illness. It was in this capacity that Sullivan launched his long aspired career of psychiatrist. It was here also that he became acquainted with William Alanson White, a teacher with a profound interest in psychiatric research, who later appointed Sullivan as the president of what is today called the William Alanson White Psychiatric Foundation.

From Washington, Sullivan went to Baltimore to serve as director of clinical research at the Sheppard and Enoch Pratt Hospital, a private hospital for the mentally ill. His intensive studies there resulted in twelve papers, most of which were published in the *American Journal of Psychiatry* and the *Psychoanalytical Review.*

Sullivan's academic career was as associate professor of psychiatry at the University of Maryland Medical School from 1923 to 1930, lecturer at Yale University during 1932–33, and professor and chairman of the department of psychiatry at Georgetown University from 1939. His professional duties also included the coeditorship of *Psychiatry: Journal for the Study of Interpersonal Processes,* the publication of which was subsidized by the William Alanson White Psychiatric Foundation.

From his research efforts, Sullivan concluded that social factors were decisive in the question of mental illness. Respecting the definition of psychiatry, he writes: "In defining it [psychiatry] as the study of interpersonal relations, I sought to segregate from everything else a disciplinary field in which operational methods could be applied with great practical benefits. This made psychiatry the probable locus of another evolving discipline, one of the social sciences, namely, *social psychology.*"[1] Through his efforts, a committee linking psychiatry with the social sciences was established in the American Psychiatric Association.

Sullivan's interpersonal theory of psychiatry views psychotherapy as a specific instance of an interpersonal relationship or one of many interpersonal situations. Psychiatry, as an interpersonal process, is the study of relationships transpiring between people. As the key issue of psychotherapy, the alleviation of anxiety or absolute tension is accomplished by the psychiatrist's functioning as a participant observer in an interpersonal relationship with a patient. Successful therapy engenders euphoria, a pleasant sense of security or total equilibrium. In addition to the pursuit of security as a prime goal of human behavior is the pursuit of satisfactions, resulting from the fulfillment of such biological needs as sleep, food, and sex. These satisfactions, which are essentially those of becoming a person, are derived through the processes of socialization. Emotional contagion, possible in interpersonal therapy as well as in other interpersonal processes, he termed *empathy,* a form of emotional communication. "The tension of anxiety, when present in the mothering one, induces anxiety in the infant" also holds true in the psychiatric interview.[2] Anxiety is the consequence of an interpersonal situation; and satisfaction is the concomitant of the relaxation of tensions, the fulfillment of needs.

With the exception of *Conceptions of Modern Psychiatry* (1940), all of Sullivan's books were published posthumously. They include *The Interpersonal Theory of Psychiatry* (1953), *The Psychiatric Interview* (1954), *Schizophrenia as a Human Process* (1962), *The Fusion of Psychiatry and Social Science* (1964), and *Personal Psychopathology: Earlier Formulation* (1972).

---

[1]Harry Stack Sullivan, *Conceptions of Modern Psychiatry* (New York: Norton, 1940), p. xi.
[2]Harry Stack Sullivan, *The Interpersonal Theory of Psychiatry* (New York: Norton, 1953), p. 41.

The Interpersonal Theory of Psychiatry

In extreme abstract, the theory holds that we come into being as persons as a consequence of unnumbered interpersonal fields of force, and that we manifest intelligible human processes only in such interpersonal fields. Like any mammalian creature, man is endowed with the potentialities for undergoing *fear*, but in almost complete contradistinction to infrahuman creatures, man in the process of becoming a person always develops a great variety of processes directly related to the undergoing of *anxiety*.

As felt experience, marked fear and uncomplicated anxiety are identical, that is, there is nothing in one's awareness of the discomfort which distinguishes the one from the other. Fear, as a significant factor in any situation, is often unequivocal. Anxiety, on the other hand, in anything like the accustomed circumstances of one's life, is seldom clearly represented as such in awareness. Instances of fear in the course of accustomed peacetime living are not numerous while instances of—generally unrecognized—anxiety are very frequent in the waking life of a great many people.

The significant pattern of situations characterized by the tension of fear is not recondite and is roughly the same for all people, excepting for the effects of habituation. The significant pattern of situations which arouse anxiety is generally obscure; can be almost infinitely varied among people, and shows much less, and very much less obvious, effects of habituation.

Habituation is a function of observation and analysis, of information and understanding, of recall and foresight. While fear may impede these processes, anxiety invariably interferes with their effective application to the current situation. The felt component of any "emotion," if sufficiently intense, will interfere with the application of these abilities to the immediate situation, and action in discharge of the tension will become correspondingly undifferentiated and imprecise. Up to the point at which this interference appears, the tension is attended by increasing alertness to factors in the situation which are immediately relevant to the relief of the tension, however great the inattention to other factors may become. In the case of anxiety, the diametrically opposite is the case. Anxiety from its mildest to its most extreme manifestation interferes with effective alertness to the factors in the current situation that are immediately relevant to its occurrence, and thus with the refinement and precision of action related to its relief or reduction.

In the case of every other tension the relief of which is sought by overt and covert activity, excepting only the tension of anxiety and its complex

The Interpersonal Theory of Psychiatry, from Harry Stack Sullivan, "The Meaning of Anxiety in Psychiatry and in Life," *Psychiatry* 11 (1948):1–13; also found in *The Fusion of Psychiatry and Social Science* (New York: W. W. Norton, 1964).

derivatives, energy is transformed in ways that can be said to achieve, approach, compromise, or suppress action towards the objective. Thus the tension of fear is commonly manifested in activity which removes (destroys) the provocative situational factors, escapes them, neutralizes their importance, or defers being afraid to the near future. The tension of anxiety and its congeries, on the other hand, does not ensue in energy transformations directed to its relief by the removal of the situational factors obviously concerned in its provocation. Actions towards avoiding or minimizing anxiety certainly occur, but anxiety combines with other tensions only in opposition. In vector terms the tension of anxiety is always at 180° to any other tension with which it coincides. Moreover, other tensions cannot suppress or defer activity resulting from anxiety.

This series of contrasts should suffice to indicate that anxiety cannot be conceptualized in the terms which cover many other "gross human motivations." Let me now show in summary form some of the conceptual structure which has been constructed to account for anxiety and its many obscure manifestations. (See table 5.1.)

The next table carries us somewhat further. The term *euphoria* refers to a polar construct, an abstract ideal, in which there is *no* tension, therefore no action—tantamount in fact perhaps to something like an empty state of bliss. The level of euphoria and the level of tension are inversely related. There is no zero or utter degree of either. Terror is perhaps the most extreme degree of tension ordinarily observable; the deepest levels of sleep, perhaps the nearest approach to euphoria. (See table 5.2.)

I shall go on, in table 5.3 to show the basic formulation of personality to which this particular theory has come.

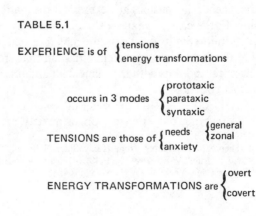

TABLE 5.1

EXPERIENCE is of { tensions / energy transformations

occurs in 3 modes { prototaxic / parataxic / syntaxic

TENSIONS are those of { needs { general / zonal / anxiety

ENERGY TRANSFORMATIONS are { overt / covert

TABLE 5.2

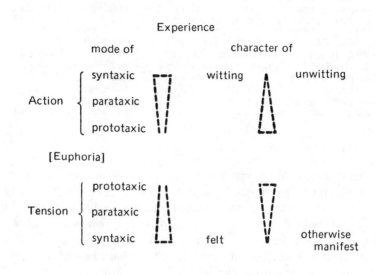

The next table reflects the developmental framework on which our further consideration of anxiety will be spread. (See table 5.4.)

Anxiety as a factor in behavior is first manifested early in infancy. . . .

Very young infants show grossly identical patterns of behavior when they are subjected to "frightening" situations and when they are in contact with the person who mothers them *and that person is anxious, angry, or otherwise disquieted.* Something which develops without a break into the tension state which we have discriminated on the basis of its specific differences from fear can be *induced* in the infant by *interpersonal influence,* in contrast to the evocation of primitive fear by sundry violent influences from "outside" or "inside" the infant's body.

This *interpersonal induction* of anxiety, and the exclusively interpersonal origin of every instance of its manifestations, is the unique characteristic of anxiety and of the congeries of more complex tensions in later life to which it contributes.

TABLE 5.3

Personality	Pattern
The relatively enduring pattern of recurring interpersonal situations which characterize human life.	The envelope of all insignificant differences.

TABLE 5.4

Stages in the development of potentialities which may be manifested in interpersonal fields [from mostly West European data]

1. INFANCY to the maturation of the capacity for language behavior
2. CHILDHOOD to the maturation of the capacity for living with compeers
3. JUVENILE ERA to the maturation of the capacity for isophillic intimacy
4. PREADOLESCENCE to the maturation of the genital lust dynamism
5. EARLY ADOLESCENCE to the patterning of lustful behavior
6. LATE ADOLESCENCE to maturity

A Psychiatry of Peoples

The general science of psychiatry seems to me to cover much the same field
as that which is studied by social psychology, because scientific psychiatry has
to be defined as the study of interpersonal relations, and this in the end calls
for the use of the kind of conceptual framework that we now call *field theory*.
From such a standpoint, personality is taken to be hypothetical. That which
can be studied is the pattern of processes which characterize the interaction
of personalities in particular recurrent situations or fields which "include" the
observer. Since any one participant observer can study but a finite number of
these situations or fields, which, in turn, will be anything but representative
of the whole variegated world of human life, not all of the personality of the
observer will be revealed and "what he comes to know about himself" will
always be somewhat incomplete and variously contingent on poorly defined or
actually unnoticed factors. Generalizations which he can make about "the
other fellow" cannot but be even more incomplete and contingent. . . .

Bear with me now in an attempt to outline a position in general psychiatry
from which I shall presently undertake to make some temporarily valid generalizations of world scope. What anyone can observe and analyze becomes
ultimately a matter of *tensions* and *energy transformations,* many of the latter
being obvious *actions,* but many others of which are obscure activities that go
on, as we say, in the mind.

What anyone can discover by investigating his past is that the *patterns* of
tensions and energy transformations which make up his living are, to a truly
astonishing extent, matters of his education for living in a particular expected
society. If he is clever, he can also notice inadequacies in his educators'
expectations; he finds that he is not any too well-prepared for living in the
groups in which he has come to be involved.

If he is philosophically inclined and historic minded, he is apt to conclude
that this very element of being ill-prepared has characterized people in every
period of expanding world contacts and ensuing accelerated social change.

A Psychiatry of Peoples, from Sullivan, *The Interpersonal Theory of Psychiatry,* pp. 367–81;
also found in "Towards a Psychiatry of Peoples," *Psychiatry* 11(1948):105–16. One internal
reference has been deleted.

If he is interested in psychiatry, he is almost certain to come to consider the role of *foresight* in determining the adequacy and appropriateness of the energy transformations, his overt and covert activity, with respect to the actual demands of the situations in which he finds himself involved with significant others.

I touch here on what I believe is the most remarkable of human characteristics, the importance exercised by often but vaguely formulated aspirations, anticipations, and expectations which can be summed up in the term, *foresight,* the manifest influence of which makes the near future a thoroughly real factor in explaining human events. I hope that you will resist the idea that something clearly teleological is being introduced here: I am saying that, *circumstances not interfering,* man the person lives with his past, the present, and the neighboring future all clearly relevant in explaining his thought and action; and the near future is influential to a degree nowhere else remotely approached among the species of the living.

Note that I have said "circumstances not interfering." It is from study of the interferences which reduce, or otherwise modify, the functional activity of foresight that a great deal of light has been thrown on the nature of man as revealed in his doings with others.

We assume that all biological tensions arise from the course of events "inside" and/or "outside" the gross spatial limits of the organism. Human tensions are no exception to this, but one of their congeries—one very important kind of tension—ensues from a kind of events the experiencing of which is almost unique to the human being.

With this single important exception, tensions can be regarded as needs for particular energy transformations which will dissipate the tension, often with an accompanying change of "mental state," a change of awareness, to which we can apply the general term *satisfaction.*

Thus the particular tension the felt component of which we call *hunger* is pleasantly satisfied by activity which includes the taking of food. Our hunger is *not* the tension, the tension is not merely a "mental state," a phenomenon within awareness, nor is it entirely "within" us in any simple space-time sense. But for practical purposes, I may usually trust this particular once-familiar "mental state" to coincide perfectly with my need for food, and "make up my mind to eat," or "decide to go to dinner," or entertain within awareness some other "thought" which sounds as if something quite powerful named "I" is directing something else, "myself," to do something about "my being hungry" with reasonable certainty that I shall feel more comfortable when the performance has been finished.

Whatever pomp and circumstance may go on "in one's head," the need for food reaches into the past in which it has arisen, and on the basis of which its felt component can be said to have "meaning," and it reaches into the future in which its tension can be foreseen to have been relieved by appropriate action in proper circumstances.

We share most, if not all, of this large congeries of recurrent needs with a good many other species of the living—even including our recurrent need for contact with others, often felt as *loneliness,* which is paralleled in the gregarious animals.

The single other great congeries of recurrent tensions, some grasp on the nature of which is simply fundamental to understanding human life, is probably restricted to man and some of the creatures which he has domesticated. It arises not from the impact of physiochemical and biological events directly connected with keeping alive and reproducing the species, but from the impact of people. The felt component of any of this congeries of tensions includes the experience of *anxiety;* action which *avoids* or *relieves* any of these tensions is experienced as continued or enhanced *self-respect* or *self-esteem,* significantly different from what is ordinarily meant by self-satisfaction. All the factors entering into the vicissitudes of self-esteem, excepting only man's innate capacity for being anxious, are wholly a matter of past experience with people, the given interpersonal situation, and foresight of what will happen.

There is nothing I can conceive in the way of interpersonal action about which one could not be trained to be anxious, so that if such an action is foreseen one feels anxious, and if it occurs one's self-esteem is reduced. The realm of this congeries of tensions is the area of one's *training for life* at the hands of significant others, and of how much or little one has been able to synthesize out of these training experiences.

One cannot be trained by others in advance of certain biological events; namely, the maturation of appropriate capabilities of man the underlying animal. Training efforts exerted before this time are undergone as something very different from what was "intended" and, if they have any effect, exert thoroughly unfortunate influence on the future development of the victim.[3] This biologically ordained serial maturation of capabilities underlies the currently entertained scheme of stages in human development (infancy, childhood, the juvenile era, preadolescence, early adolescence, and late adolescence to maturity). . . . Let me discuss the implication of the idea of developmental stages. When, and only when, maturation of capacities has occurred, experience of a valuable kind can occur. *If it does not occur,* if experience is definitely unsuited to providing competence for living with others, at this particular level of development, the probabilities of future adequate and appropriate interpersonal relations are definitely *and specifically* reduced. The reduction of probability is specifically related to the forms of competence which are customarily developed under favorable circumstances in the course of this particular stage.

Seen from this viewpoint, not the earlier stages only, but each and every stage is equally important, in its own right, in the unfolding of possibilities for

---

[3]They generally contribute to the not-me component of personality, the source of the tension in interpersonal fields elsewhere described as the experience of uncanny emotions—awe, dread, loathing, and horror—felt components of the most strongly disjunctive force of which we have knowledge.

interpersonal relations, in the progression from birth toward mature compe-tence for life in a fully human world. It is often true that severe warp incurred, say, in childhood interferes so seriously with the course of events in the succeeding juvenile era that the constructive effects of living with compeers, and under school and other nonfamily authorities, are meager. It also happens, and not infrequently, that quite serious warp from childhood is all but cor-rected by good fortune early in the juvenile era, so that its residual traces are observable only under circumstances of "intense emotion," severe "fatigue," anoxemia, hypoglycemia, or alcoholic and related "decerebration."

In the course of intensive, guided psychotherapy one may observe, in many instances, a condensed, relatively vicarious, remedying of deficiencies in developmental experience, and this seems to be a successful way of consolidat-ing favorable change in the patient's interpersonal relations. . . .

The often great difficulty encountered in achieving improved ability to live with significant others is considered to arise, then, not from a deficiency of tendency but from something else; something which manifests itself as an equilibrating factor in living, whether the living be fortunate or unfortunate; namely, the extensive organization of experience within personality which I have called the *self-system*.

I think it will suffice for my present purpose to say that anything which would seriously disturb the equilibrium, any event which tends to bring about a basic change in an *established pattern* of dealing with others, sets up the tension of anxiety and calls out activities for its relief. This tension and the activities required for its reduction or relief—which we call *security operations* because they can be said to be addressed to maintaining a feeling of safety in the esteem reflected to one from the other person concerned—always interfere with whatever other tensions and energy transformations they happen to coincide with. . . .

I can perhaps now proceed to the thesis of this paper; namely, that while no one can now be adequately equipped for a greatly significant inquiry into the fundamental "facts of life" of everyone, everywhere, there are many possi-bilities of greatly constructive efforts in this direction—if, and only if, instead of plunging into the field recklessly "hoping for the best," one prefaces one's attempt with a careful survey of one's assets and liabilities for participant observation.

Every constructive effort of the psychiatrist, today, is a strategy of inter-personal field operations which (1) seeks to map the areas of disjunctive force that block the efficient collaboration of the patient and others, and (2) seeks to expand the patient's awareness so that this unnecessary blockage can be brought to an end.

For a psychiatry of peoples, we must follow the selfsame strategy applied to significant groupings of people—families, communities, political entities, regional organizations, world blocs—and seek to map the interventions of disjunctive force which block the integration of the group with other groups in pursuit of the common welfare; and seek out the characteristics of each group's culture or subculture, and the methods used to impose it on the young, which perpetuate the restrictions of freedom for constructive growth.

The master tactics for a psychiatrist's work with a handicapped person consists in (1) elucidating the actual situations in which unfortunate action is currently shown repeatedly, so that the disorder-pattern may become clear; (2) discovering the less obvious ramifications of this inadequate and inappropriate way of life throughout other phases of the present and the near future, including the doctor-patient relationship and the patient's expectations about it; and (3) with the problem of inadequate development now clearly formulated, utilizing his human abilities to explore its origins in his experience with significant people of the past.

It must be noted that an identical distortion of living common to doctor and patient makes this type of inquiry, at the best, very difficult. Neither is able to "see" the troublesome patterns, and both are inclined to relate the difficulties to the unhappy peculiarities of the other people concerned in their less fortunate interpersonal relations. Each respects parallel limitation in the other, and their mutual effort is apt to be concentrated on irrelevant or immaterial problems, until they both become more discouraged or still more firmly deceived about life.

For a psychiatry of peoples, these tactical requirements of good therapy —which is also good research—have to be expanded into (1) a preliminary discovery of the actual major patterns of tensions and energy transformations which characterize more adequate and appropriate living in that group; this is a background for noticing the exceptions—the incidents of mental disorder among these folk—uninformed study of which would be misleading; (2) a parallel development of skill at rectifying the effects of limitations in our own developmental background; in order (3) that it may become possible to observe better the factors that actually resist any tendency to extend the integrations of our subject-persons, so that they would include representatives of other groups relatively alien to them—a pilot test of which is the integration with ourself—and (4) thus to find real problems in the foresight of intergroup living which can be tracked down to their origins in our subject-people's education for life.

There is good reason to believe that all this is not impossible. These world-psychiatric inquiries are not at bottom particularly different from the already mentioned, all too common, instances where doctor and patient suffer approximately *the same* disorders in living. . . .

The theory of interpersonal relations lays great stress on the method of participant observation, and relegates data obtained by other methods to, at most, a secondary importance. This in turn implies that skill in the face-to-face, or person-to-person, *psychiatric interview* is of fundamental importance.

While the value of interchange by use of the mediate channels of communication—correspondence, publications, radio, speaking films—may be very great, especially if the people concerned have already become fairly well acquainted with each other as a result of previous face-to-face exchange, it must be remembered that communication in the psychiatric interview is by no means solely a matter of exchanging verbal contexts, but is rather the development of an exquisitely complex pattern of field processes which *imply* important conclusions about the people concerned.

This is scarcely the place for a discussion of current views about what one can learn about the theory and practice of psychiatric interviewing; I wish chiefly to emphasize the *instrumental* character of the interviewing psychiatrist and the critical importance of his being free to observe—and subsequently analyze—as many as possible of his performances as a dynamic center in the field patterns that make up the interview.

Everything that can be said about good psychiatric interviewing is relevant to the directly interpersonal aspects of any work in the direction of a psychiatry of peoples. Every safeguard useful in avoiding erroneous conclusions about "the other fellow" becomes newly important when the barriers of linguistic and other cultural uncertainties are in the way.

The Psychiatric Interview

Since the field of psychiatry has been defined as the study of interpersonal relations, and since it has been alleged that this is a perfectly valid area for the application of scientific method, we have come to the conclusion that the data of psychiatry arise only in participant observation. In other words, the psychiatrist cannot stand off to one side and apply his sense organs, however they may be refined by the use of apparatus, to noticing what someone else does, without becoming personally implicated in the operation. His principal instrument of observation is his self—his personality, *him* as a person. The processes and the changes in processes that make up the data which can be subjected to scientific study occur, not in the subject person nor in the observer, but in the situation which is created between the observer and his subject.

We say that the data of psychiatry arise in participant observation of social interaction, if we are inclined toward the social-psychological approach, or of interpersonal relations, if we are inclined toward the psychiatric approach, the two terms meaning, so far as I know, precisely the same thing. There are no purely objective data in psychiatry, and there are no valid subjective data, because the material becomes scientifically usable only in the

The Psychiatric Interview, from Harry Stack Sullivan, *The Psychiatric Interview* (New York: Norton, 1954), pp. 3–4. A considerable portion of the remainder of this chapter may be found in "The Psychiatric Interview," *Psychiatry* 14 (1951): 361–73, and "The Psychiatric Interview: II," *Psychiatry* 15 (1952): 127–41.

shape of a complex resultant—*inference.* The vicissitudes of inference is one of the major problems in the study of psychiatry and in the development of practical psychiatric interviews. ...

Definition of the Psychiatric Interview

As a point of reference for comments often somewhat rambling, it may be useful to attempt a definition of what I have in mind when I speak of the psychiatric interview. As I see it, such an interview is a situation of primarily *vocal* communication in a *two-group,* more or less *voluntarily integrated,* on a progressively unfolding *expert-client* basis for the purpose of elucidating *characteristic patterns of living* of the subject person, the patient or client, which patterns he experiences as particularly troublesome or especially valuable, and in the revealing of which he expects to derive *benefit.*

Basic Concepts in the Psychiatric Interview

The psychiatric interview, as considered here, is primarily a two-group in which there is an expert-client relationship, the expert being defined by the culture. Insofar as there is such an expert-client relationship, the interviewee expects the person who sits behind the desk to show a really expert grasp on the intricacies of interpersonal relations; he expects the interviewer to show skill in conducting the interview. The greater this skill, the other things being equal, the more easily will the purpose of the interview be achieved. The interviewer must discover who the client is—that is, he must review what course of events the client has come through to be who he is, what he has in the way of background and experience. And, on the basis of who the person is, the interviewer must learn what this person conceives of in his living as problematic, and what he feels to be difficult. ...

The interviewer's learning wherein his client encounters headaches in dealing with his fellow man and achieving the purposes of his life, which is of the essence of the psychiatric interview, implies that the other fellow must get something in exchange for what he gives. The *quid pro quo* which leads to the best psychiatric interview—as well as the best interview for employment or for other purposes—is that the person being interviewed realizes, quite early, that he is going to learn something useful about the way he lives. In such circumstances, he may very well become communicative; otherwise, he will show as much caution as his intellect and background permit, giving no information

---

Basic Concepts in the Psychiatric Interview, from Sullivan, *The Psychiatric Interview,* pp. 17–19.

that he conceives might in any way do him harm. To repeat, that the person will leave with some measure of increased clarity about himself and his living with other people is an essential goal of the psychiatric interview.

The Psychiatrist as a Participant Observer

As I said at the beginning, psychiatry is peculiarly the field of participant observation. The fact is that we cannot make any sense of, for example, the motor movements of another person except on the basis of behavior that is meaningful to us—that is, on the basis of what we have experienced, done ourselves, or seen done under circumstances in which its purpose, its motivation, or at least the intentions behind it were communicated to us. Without this past background, the observer cannot deduce, by sheer intellectual operations, the meaning of the staggering array of human acts. As an example of this, almost all the things pertaining to communication form such highly conventionalized patterns and are so fixed within the culture that if my pronunciation of a word deviates from yours, you may wonder what in the world I am talking about. Things having to do with your own past experience and with proscriptions of the culture and so on that were common in your home; activities which are attached to you as the person concerned in their doing, and activities to which you respond as if you were the person primarily, directly, and simply concerned in them—all these are the data of psychiatry. Therefore, the psychiatrist has an inescapable, inextricable involvement in all that goes on in the interview; and to the extent that he is unconscious or unwitting of his participation in the interview, to that extent he does not know what is happening. This is another argument in favor of the position that the psychiatrist has a hard enough job to do without any pursuit of his own pleasure or prestige. He can legitimately expect only the satisfaction of feeling that he did what he was paid for—that will be enough, and probably more than he can do well.

Parataxic Distortion

The characteristics of a person that would be agreed to by a large number of competent observers may not appear to you to be the characteristics of the person toward whom you are making adjustive or maladjustive movements.

The Psychiatrist as a Participant Observer, from Sullivan, *The Psychiatric Interview,* p. 19.
Parataxic Distortion, from Sullivan, *The Psychiatric Interview,* pp. 26–27.

The *real* characteristics of the other fellow at that time may be of negligible importance to the interpersonal situation. This we call *parataxic distortion.*

Parataxic distortion as a term may sound quite unusual; actually the phenomena it describes are anything but unusual. The great complexity of the psychiatric interview is brought about by the interviewee's substituting for the psychiatrist a person or persons strikingly different in most significant respects from the psychiatrist. The interviewee addresses his behavior toward this fictitious person who is temporarily in the ascendancy over the reality of the psychiatrist, and he interprets the psychiatrist's remarks and behavior on the basis of this same fictitious person. There are often clues to the occurrence of these phenomena. Such phenomena are the basis for the really astonishing misunderstandings and misconceptions which characterize all human relations, and certain special precautions must be taken against them in the psychiatric interview after it is well under way. Parataxic distortion is also one way that the personality displays before another some of its gravest problems. In other words, parataxic distortion may actually be an obscure attempt to communicate something that really needs to be grasped by the therapist, and perhaps finally to be grasped by the patient. Needless to say, if such distortions go unnoted, if they are not expected, if the possibility of their existence is ignored, some of the most important things about the psychiatric interview may go by default.

Stages of the Psychiatric Interview

The psychiatric interview may be considered as made up of a series of stages which, while really hypothetical, fictional, abstract, and artificial, can be very useful for the psychiatrist to have in mind in arranging his time with the patient. More important, I believe that they are quite necessary for the achievement of the purpose of an intensive relationship of this kind. These stages are: first, the formal inception; second, the reconnaisance; third, the detailed inquiry; and fourth, the termination.

. . . The *inception* includes the formal reception of the person who comes to be interviewed and an inquiry about, or reference to, the circumstances of his coming. It should also include a brief, but considered, reference by the psychiatrist to any information already at his disposal; this is important not only to promote a feeling of confidence on the part of the patient, in the interviewer's straightforwardness, but also to provide an opportunity for the patient to amend the presumptive data which the psychiatrist may have re-

---

Stages of the Psychiatric Interview, from Sullivan, *The Psychiatric Interview,* pp. 39–41.

ceived from another source, if necessary. Finally, an adequate reason for the conference must be established; that is, the psychiatrist should obtain adequate justification for the use of his skill.

Throughout this stage of the interview, the psychiatrist must remember that the person who consults him is a stranger—even though in other circumstances he may be an old friend. Thus the psychiatrist cannot know what impression anything that he says or does may make on this stranger, for he knows nothing of his background and nothing of the parataxic elements which may be very powerful in influencing his impressions. The psychiatrist must, therefore, be very alert to learn something of the impression that he and certain of his performances give, and at the same time very alert to learn how he himself is affected by certain things that the stranger may do and say. The interviewer should proceed in such a way that no complicating situation develops in this stage, for the inception of the interview may either greatly accelerate the achievement of the result desired or make that result practically unattainable.

The second step in procedure, the *reconnaissance,* which should be initiated as "naturally" as possible, consists in obtaining a rough outline of the social or personal history of the patient. In this stage, the interviewer is concerned with trying to get some notion of the person's identity—who he is and how he happened to get to be the person who has come to the office. Thus the interviewer asks conventional questions about age, order of siblings, date of marriage, and so on; he does not try to develop a psychiatric history, but tries to orient himself as to certain basic probabilities. The skill of the interviewer in obtaining and interpreting this history may often largely determine the ease or difficulty of the succeeding detailed inquiry. Moreover, the time to be spent in achieving the purpose of the interview or series of interviews may depend on the concise accuracy with which this history is obtained.

The next stage, the *detailed inquiry,* depends considerably, although not exclusively, on the ostensible purpose of the interview—a topic which I shall discuss shortly. The larger part of these lectures will deal with the principles and techniques of the detailed inquiry—that is, with some of the particulars that make up the almost unlimited variety of subtleties and complexities of this long stretch of inquiry into another person's life and problems. For the moment, I will say only that while the interviewer is governed in this inquiry by the ostensible purpose of the interview, he never carries out a good interview if he forgets what it is really for—namely, to permit an expert in human relations to contribute something to another person's success in living.

The fourth step of the interview, in this particular abstract scheme, is either the *termination* or the *interruption* of the psychiatric interview. By termination, I mean that the interviewer does not expect to see the person again; he is through. And by interruption, I mean that the interviewer has seen his client as long as he is going to on that particular day, and will see him again on the next day, or at some future date. If the interview is interrupted, the psychiatrist should give the patient a prescription for the interval, as a setting for the next session—for example, he may suggest something that the patient might try to recall. If the interview is terminated, the interviewer should make a final statement. In general, the main purpose to be attained, either in terminating an interview or in interrupting it for any length of time, is the consolidation of what has been achieved in terms of some durable benefit for the interviewee.

Theorem of Reciprocal Emotion

Now let me shift to a somewhat more theoretical consideration of the matters which I have been discussing. As I have already indicated, the interview is a system, or a series of systems, *of interpersonal processes,* arising from participant observation in which the interviewer derives certain conclusions about the interviewee. Under these circumstances, interview situations fall under a general principle which I have organized as the *theorem of reciprocal emotion.* That theorem is as follows: Integration in an interpersonal situation is a process in which (1) complementary needs are resolved (or aggravated); (2) reciprocal patterns of activity are developed (or disintegrated); and (3) foresight of satisfaction (or rebuff) of similar needs is facilitated.

This theorem is an extremely general statement which, thus far in my explorations, has seemed to have no serious defects. I believe that if one studies its full implications, a great many things pertaining to the study of interpersonal relations, and pertaining to the participant observation by which the interviewer gets his data, will be clarified. In this general statement, I use the word *needs* in the broadest sense, in the generic sense. Thus, in discussing the development of personality, we speak of all the important motives, or "motors," of human behavior as *needs for satisfaction.* There is a *need* for satisfaction of various forces such as lust and hunger; and *need* in this particular sense also includes the need for a feeling of personal security in interpersonal relations, which in turn can be called a need to avoid, alleviate, or escape from anxiety, or, again, a need for self-esteem. ...

And finally, to apply the last part of my theorem: In this situation, the interviewee will develop an alert foresight of the rebuff of his implied need for reassurance, and this will make it certain that he will protect his self-esteem. That is, the longer such a situation goes on, the more he is governed by the foresight of any indication that there will be an aggravation of his anxiety. Since his anxieties are always detestably unpleasant and a potent driving force

Theorem of Reciprocal Emotion, from Sullivan, *The Psychiatric Interview,* pp. 128–32.

to get him away from that which causes them, he becomes more and more careful that none of his insecurities are advertised to the security-needing interviewer.

Patterns of Outcome of Interpersonal Situations

The interpersonal processes making up the interview follow the general pattern of all interpersonal processes, which can be illustrated by a diagram (Figure 5.1):

FIGURE 5.1

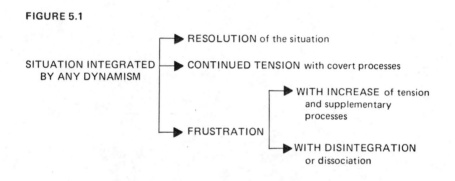

A situation integrated by any dynamism—for example, lust or the pursuit of security—manifests processes which result in one of three subsequent situations: First, there may be a resolution of the situation. For example, the waitress may say, "Do you want cherry or banana pie?" When the customer says, "Banana," that resolves the situation. And in all other situations, the simple, delightful, and final outcome of interpersonal configuration is that it is resolved: all tension connected with it is washed up, and the thing is finished until something provokes a similar situation.

The second possibility is that a situation may be continued with tension and with covert processes. In this case the person goes on doing the same thing, more or less covertly, but he also begins *to think,* whether noted or unnoted. In other words, he begins to look around for what is wrong, to discover what can be done to effect a satisfactory resolution.

The third possibility is that the processes in the situation may lead to what we call *frustration.* There are two possible states subsequent to frustration. One is marked by an *increase of tension,* reflecting the need which was con-

Patterns of Outcome of Interpersonal Situations, from Sullivan, *The Psychiatric Interview,* pp. 132–33.

cerned, and by *supplementary processes*, which may range all the way from circus movements to exceedingly skillful ways of circumventing the obstacles, so that there is a belated resolution of the situation. Sometimes the psychiatrist must deal with situations in which he knows that any frontal attack, any direct approach, would lead to complete frustration. Thus he devises supplementary processes that will weave around the blocking anxiety, so that finally the patient, feeling reasonably secure, will arrive at a point which could never be approached frontally. The other outcome of frustration may be *disintegration of the dynamism* itself and the whole motivational system, or *dissociation*— and processes in interviews involving dissociation are very complex.

6

CHARACTER ANALYSIS THERAPY

Karen Horney

Karen Horney (1885 –1952) was born in Hamburg, Germany. She received her M.D. in 1913 from the University of Berlin. She both studied and taught at the Berlin Institute for Psychoanalysis from 1920 until 1932. In 1932 she left for the United States to assume the associate directorship of the Chicago Institute for Psycho-analysis, a post which she relinquished in 1934. That same year she left Chicago for New York, where she accepted an appointment on the teaching staff of the New York Psychoanalytic Institute. In 1941 she founded the American Institute for Psychoanalysis in New York and served as its dean until her death in 1952.

Credited with being one of the founders of the Association for the Advance-ment of Psychoanalysis, she was honored as a fellow of the American Psychiatric Association and served as editor of the *American Journal of Psychoanalysis*.

Her ideas on personality and psychotherapy as they developed over the years are found in *The Neurotic Personality of Our Time* (1937), *New Ways in Psycho-analysis* (1939), *Self-Analysis* (1942), *Our Inner Conflicts* (1945), *Are You Consid-ering Psychoanalysis?* (1946), and *Neurosis and Human Growth* (1950).

In *The Neurotic Personality of our Time,* Horney elaborates her theory of the cultural basis of neurosis by laying heavy stress upon specific cultural conditions as well as particular individual experiences as the root of neurosis, explaining neurosis on the basis of character structure. Neurosis is propelled by a "basic anxiety," generated by loss of love and respect during childhood. Neurosis is a reaction of hatred by the child who is deprived of filial warmth and affection, with the result that repressed hostility is experienced as anxiety and projected to the outer world.

In *New Ways in Psychoanalysis,* she sees manifest-anxiety as the result of specific safety devices failing to operate. In this work, Horney defines neurosis as a "peculiar kind of struggle for life under difficult conditions."[1] She sees the aim of psychotherapy to be the minimizing of anxiety to a level at which patients may dispense with their neurotic behavior patterns. A second therapeutic goal is "to

---

[1]Karen Horney, *New Ways in Psychoanalysis* (New York: Norton, 1939), p. 11.

restore the individual to himself, to help him regain his spontaneity and find his center of gravity in himself."[2]

In *Our Inner Conflicts,* Horney traces neurosis to a basic conflict in which the neurotic is torn among "moving toward," "moving against," and "moving away from" people. Neurotics' desperate attempts at solving their problems are rooted in their anxiety at being torn apart and the personality's need for a sense of unity. The resolution of basic neurotic conflicts is contingent upon altering the conditions within the personality that caused them. People *can* change and disentangle their own conflicts and can go on changing as long as they live.[3]

Horney's fullest and definitive treatment of the subject of psychotherapy is found in her last book, *Neurosis and Human Growth.* Here, her psychotherapy of character analysis calls for self-actualization to replace the neurotic's self-idealization, i.e., the supplanting of a real self for an idealized self, or *pride system,* as she terms it. Horney maintains that definite constructive forces aiding the therapist's efforts are at work in psychotherapy. Unlike numerous other psychoanalysts, Horney recommends self-analysis in which patients are given an opportunity to exercise their own efforts in general character development for self-realization.

Horney's Theory of Neurosis

The Cultural Basis of Neurosis: Intrapsychic Processes and Human Relations

Together with many others who had discarded Freud's theory of instincts, I first saw the core of neurosis in human relations.[4] Generally, I pointed out, these were brought about by cultural conditions; specifically, through environmental factors which obstructed the child's unhampered psychic growth. Instead of developing a basic confidence in self and others the child developed basic anxiety, which I defined as a feeling of being isolated and helpless toward a world potentially hostile. In order to keep this basic anxiety at a minimum the spontaneous moves toward, against, and away from others became compulsive. While the spontaneous moves were compatible, each with the others, the compulsive ones collided. The conflicts generated in this way, which I called basic conflicts, were therefore the result of conflicting needs and conflicting attitudes with regard to other people. And the first attempts at solution

---

[2]Horney, *New Ways in Psychoanalysis,* p. 11.

[3]Karen Horney, *Our Inner Conflicts* (New York: Norton, 1945), p. 19.

Horney's Theory of Neurosis, from Karen Horney, *Neurosis and Human Growth* (New York: Norton, 1950), pp. 366–78.

[4]Like Erich Fromm, Adolph Meyer, James S. Plant, H. S. Sullivan.

were largely attempts at integration, through giving full rein to some of these needs and attitudes and suppressing others.

This is a somewhat streamlined summary because the intrapsychic processes are too closely interwoven with those going on in interpersonal relations for me to have left them out altogether. They were touched upon at various points. To mention but a few: I could not discuss the neurotic's need for affection, or any equivalent need pertaining to others, without considering the qualities and attitudes which he must cultivate within himself in the service of such a need. Again, among the "neurotic trends" I enumerated in *Self-Analysis* there were some which had an intrapsychic meaning, such as a compulsive need for control through willpower or reason or a compulsive need for perfection. For that matter, in the discussion of Claire's analysis of her morbid dependency (also in *Self-Analysis*) I dealt in condensed form with many intrapsychic factors presented in the same context in the present book. Nevertheless the focus was decidedly on the interpersonal factors. To me neurosis was still essentially a disturbance in human relationships.

Self-Idealization: The Pride System

The first explicit step beyond this definition was the contention that conflicts with regard to others could be solved by self-idealization. When, in *Our Inner Conflicts,* I propounded the concept of the idealized image I did not yet know its full significance. I saw it at that time simply as another attempt to solve inner conflicts. And its very integrating function accounted for the tenacity with which people adhered to it.

But in subsequent years the concept of the idealized image became the central issue from which new insights evolved. It actually was the gateway to the whole area of intrapsychic processes presented in this book. Having grown up scientifically with Freud's concepts, I was aware of the existence of this area. But because Freud's interpretations of it made sense to me only in spots it had remained strange territory.

I now saw gradually that the neurotic's idealized image did not merely constitute a false belief in his value and significance; it was rather like the creation of a Frankenstein monster which in time usurped his best energies. It eventually usurped his drive to grow, to realize his given potentialities. And this meant that he was no longer interested in realistically tackling or outgrowing his difficulties, and in fulfilling his potentials, but was bent on actualizing his idealized self. It entails not only the compulsive drive for worldly glory through success, power, and triumph but also the tyrannical inner system by which he tries to mold himself into a godlike being; it entails neurotic claims and the development of neurotic pride.

With these elaborations of the original concept of the idealized image another problem emerged. While focusing on the attitude toward self, I realized that people hated and despised themselves with the same intensity and the same irrationality with which they idealized themselves. These two opposite extremes remained separate in my mind for a while. But finally I saw that they were not only closely interrelated but were in fact two aspects of one process. This then was, in its original draft, the main thesis of this book: *the godlike being is bound to hate his actual being.* With the recognition of this process as an entity, both extremes become more accessible to therapy. The definition of neurosis too had changed. *Neurosis now became a disturbance in one's relation to self and to others.*

The Real Self and the Idealized Self (Pride System)

Although this thesis remains to some extent the main contention, in recent years it has grown in two directions. The question of the real self, always puzzling to me as to so many others, pushed itself into the foreground of my thought and I came to see the whole inner psychic process, beginning with self-idealization, as a growing alienation from self. More important, I realized that in the last analysis self-hate was directed against the real self. The conflict between the pride system and the real self I called the central inner conflict. This made for an enlargement of the concept of neurotic conflict. I had defined it as a conflict between two incompatible compulsive drives. While retaining this concept, I began to see that it was not the only kind of neurotic conflict. The central inner conflict is one between the constructive forces of the real self and the obstructive forces of the pride system, between healthy growth and the drive to prove in actuality the perfection of the idealized self. Therapy therefore became a help toward self-realization. Through the clinical work of our whole group the general validity of the intrapsychic processes described above became more and more clearly established in our minds.

The body of knowledge also grew as we worked from general to more specific questions. My interest shifted to the variations in different "kinds" of neurosis or of neurotic personalities. At first these appeared as differences in awareness or in accessibility of one or another aspect of the inner processes. Gradually, however, I realized that they resulted from various pseudosolutions of the intrapsychic conflicts. These solutions offered a new—tentative—basis for establishing types of neurotic personalities. . . .

Character Analysis Compared with Psychoanalysis

. . . I am struck with admiration for Freud's power of observation. It is all the more impressive since he did pioneer work in scientifically unexplored territory and did it against the odds of cramping theoretical premises. There are only a few (although relevant) aspects of it, which he either did not see at all or did

not consider important. One of these concerns what I have described as neurotic claims. Freud saw of course the fact that many neurotic patients were
liable to expect an unreasonable amount from others. He also saw that these
expectations could be urgent. But, regarding them as an expression of oral
libido, he did not realize that they could assume the specific character of
"claims," i.e., of demands to the fulfillment of which one feels entitled. Nor
did he consequently realize the key role they play in neurosis. Also, in spite
of using the term *pride* in this or that context, Freud was not cognizant of the
specific properties and implications of neurotic pride. But Freud did observe
belief in magical powers and fantasies of omnipotence; infatuation with oneself
or with one's "ego ideal"—self-aggrandizement, glorification of inhibitions,
etc.; compulsive competitiveness and ambition; the need for power, perfection,
admiration, recognition.

These manifold factors which Freud observed remained for him diverse
and unrelated phenomena. He failed to see that they were expressions of one
powerful current. He did not in other words see the unity in the diversity.

Three main reasons combined to prevent Freud from recognizing the
impact of the drive for glory and its significance for the neurotic process. To
begin with, he was not cognizant of the power of cultural conditions to mold
human character—a lack of knowledge which he shared with most European
scholars of his time.[5] The implication which interests us in this context is, in
simple terms, that Freud mistook the craving for prestige and success, which
he saw all around him, for a universal human propensity. Hence, for instance,
a compulsive drive for supremacy, dominance, or triumph could not and did
not strike him as a problem worth examining, except when such ambition did
not fit into the given pattern of what was considered "normal." Freud considered it problematic only when it reached obviously disturbing proportions or
when, occurring in women, it did not concur with the given code of
"femininity."

Another reason resides in Freud's tendency to explain neurotic drives as
libidinal phenomena. Thus self-glorification was an expression of a libidinal
infatuation with self. (A person overrates himself as he may overrate another
"love-object." An ambitious woman "really" suffers from "penis-envy." A
need for admiration is a need for "narcissistic supplies," etc.) As a result the
inquiry in theory and therapy was directed toward particulars of the love life
past and present (i.e., libidinal relation to self and others) and not toward the
specific qualities, functions, and effects of self-glorification, ambition, etc.

The third reason lies in Freud's evolutionistic-mechanistic thinking. "It
implies that present manifestations not only are conditioned by the past, but

---

[5]Cf. Karen Horney, *New Ways in Psychoanalysis,* chapter 10, "Culture and Neurosis"
(Norton, 1939).

contain nothing but the past; nothing really new is created in the process of development: what we see today is only the old in changed form."[6] . . . On the grounds of this philosophical premise, excessive competitiveness is satisfactorily explained if it is seen as the result of an unresolved Oedipus complex, or of sibling rivalry. Fantasies of omnipotence are regarded as a fixation on, or a retrogression to, the infantile level of "primary narcissism," etc. It is consistent with this viewpoint that only those interpretations are and can be considered "deep" and satisfactory which established a connection with infantile experiences of a libidinal kind.

From my viewpoint the therapeutic effects of interpretations of this kind are limited, if not positively obstructive to important insights. Let us assume, for instance, that a patient has become aware that he tends too easily to feel humiliated by the analyst; he also realizes that in approaching women he is in constant dread of humiliation. He does not feel as virile or as attractive as other men. He may remember scenes when he was humiliated by his father, perhaps in connection with sexual activities. On the grounds of many detailed dates like these from the present and the past, and of dreams, interpretations are given along these lines: that for the patient, the analyst, as well as other authoritative figures, represents the father; that in feeling humiliated, or in his fear thereof, the patient still responds according to the infantile pattern of an unresolved Oedipus complex.

As a result of this work the patient may feel relieved and the feelings of humiliation may be lessened. In part he has in fact benefited from this piece of analysis. He has learned a few things about himself and has realized that his feeling humiliated is irrational. But without his pride being tackled the change cannot possibly be a thorough one. On the contrary it is likely that the surface improvement is largely due to the fact that his pride will not tolerate his being irrational and particularly his being "infantile." The likelihood is that he merely has developed a new set of shoulds. He *should not* be infantile and *should* be mature. He should not feel humiliated because it is infantile to do so; so he does no longer feel humiliated. In this way a seeming progress can in reality be an obstruction to the patient's growth. His feeling of being humiliated is driven underground, and the possibility of his squaring himself with it is considerably lessened. Therapy has thus made use of the patient's pride instead of working against it.

Because of all the theoretical reasons mentioned, Freud could not possibly see the impact of the search for glory. Those factors in the expansive drives which he did observe were not what they seemed to be but were "really" derivatives of infantile libidinal drives. His way of thinking prevented him from appreciating expansive drives as forces carrying their own weight and having their own consequences. . . .

---

[6]Quoted from Karen Horney, *New Ways in Psychoanalysis,* chapter 2, "Some General Premises of Freud's Thinking."

We are struck offhand by much greater similarities between my concept of self-hate and Freud's postulation of a self-destructive instinct, the death instinct. At least here we find the same appreciation of the intensity and significance of self-destructive drives. Also certain details are viewed similarly, such as the self-destructive character of inner taboos, of self-accusations and resultant guilt-feelings. Nevertheless, in this area too there are significant differences. The instinctual character of self-destructive drives, as assumed by Freud, gives them the stamp of finality. When conceived as instinctual they do not arise out of definite psychic conditions and cannot be overcome with changes in these conditions. Their existence and operation then constitute an attribute of human nature. Man has therefore at bottom only the choice of suffering and destroying himself or of making others suffer and destroying them. These drives can be mitigated and controlled but ultimately are unalterable. Moreover, when with Freud we assume an instinctual drive toward self-annihilation, self-destruction, or death, we must consider self-hate, with its many implications, as simply one expression of that drive. The idea of a person hating or despising himself for being as he is is actually alien to Freud's thinking.

Of course, Freud—as well as others sharing his basic premises — observed the occurrence of self-hate, although he was far from recognizing its manifold hidden forms and effects. . . .

Briefly, the depressed consciously hates and accuses himself but in fact *unconsciously* hates and accuses an introjected enemy. ("Hostility toward the frustrating object has turned into hostility toward one's own ego.")[7] Or what *seems* to be self-hate is *"really"* the punitive process of the superego, the latter being an internalized authority. Here again self-hate turns into an interpersonal phenomenon: hate for somebody else or fear of his hate. Or, lastly, self-hate is seen as the sadism of the superego, resulting from a regression to an anal-sadistic phase of infantile libido. Self-hate is thus not only accounted for in ways entirely different from mine but the nature of the phenomenon itself is altogether different. . . .

Another distinct similarity exists between the demands and taboos ascribed to the superego and what I have described as the tyranny of the should. But as soon as we consider their meaning we come to a parting of the ways. To begin with, for Freud the superego is a normal phenomenon representing conscience and morality; it is neurotic if particularly cruel and sadistic. For me the equivalent shoulds and taboos of whatever kind and degree are altogether a neurotic force counterfeiting morality and conscience. According to Freud the superego is partly a derivative of the Oedipus complex, partly a derivative of instinctual forces (destructive and sadistic). According to my views, the inner dictates are an expression of the individual's unconscious drive to make himself over into something he is not (a godlike, perfect being), and

---

[7]Quoted from Otto Fenichel, *The Psychoanalytic Theory of Neurosis,* Norton, 1945.

he hates himself for not being able to do so. Among the many implications entailed in these differences I mention but one. Seeing the shoulds and taboos as corollaries of a special kind of pride allows for a much more accurate understanding of why the same thing is violently demanded in one character structure and forbidden in another. The same possibility for greater exactness applies also to the various attitudes an individual may have toward the superego demands—or inner dictates—some of which are mentioned in Freudian literature:[8] attitudes of appeasement, subordination, bribery, rebellion. These are either generalized as pertaining to all neuroses (Alexander) or are merely related to certain sympathetic pictures such as depression or compulsion neurosis. On the other hand, in the framework of my theory of neurosis their quality is strictly determined by the whole particular character structure. It follows from these differences that the therapeutic aim on this score is different. Freud can aim merely at reducing the severity of the superego while I aim at the individual's being able to dispense with his inner dictates altogether and to assume the direction of his life in accordance with his true wishes and beliefs. This latter possibility does not exist in Freud's thinking.

Summarizing this far, we can say that in the two approaches certain individual phenomena are observed and described in a similar way. But the interpretations of their dynamics and meaning are entirely different. If we now leave the individual aspects and consider the whole complex of their interrelations as it is presented in this book, we see that the possibilities for comparison are exhausted.

The most significant interrelation is that between the search for unlimited perfection and powers, and self-hate. . . .

Freud has not seen it, and we can understand more clearly why he could not see it, when we remember that he did not recognize the search for glory as the compound of inextricably linked drives which I have described and therefore could not realize its power either. He saw the hell of self-destructiveness clearly enough; but, regarding it as the expression of an autonomous drive, he saw it out of context.

Self-Actualization and Neurotic Self-Idealization

Seen from another perspective, the neurotic process presented in this book is a problem of the self. It is a process of abandoning the real self for an idealized one; of trying to actualize this pseudoself instead of our given human potentials; of a destructive warfare between the two selves; of allaying this warfare the best, or at any rate the only, way we can; and finally, through having our constructive forces mobilized by life or by therapy, of finding our real selves. In this sense the problem could hardly have any meaning for Freud. In his

---

[8]Cf. chapter 5, "Self-Hate and Self-Contempt."

concept of the "ego" he depicts the "self" of a neurotic person who is alienated from his spontaneous energies, from his authentic wishes, who does not make any decisions of his own and assume responsibility for them, who merely sees that he does not collide too badly with his environment ("reality-testing"). . . .

The inner psychic process which is the neurotic equivalent to healthy, human striving is tragic. Man under the pressure of inner distress reaches out for the ultimate and the infinite which—though his limits are not fixed—it is not given to him to reach; and in this very process he destroys himself, shifting his very best drive for self-realization to the actualization of his idealized image and thereby wasting the potentialities he actually possesses.

Freud had a pessimistic outlook on human nature and, on the grounds of his premises, was bound to have it. As he saw it, man is doomed to dissatisfaction whichever way he turns. He cannot live out satisfactorily his primitive instinctual drives without wrecking himself and civilization. He cannot be happy alone or with others. He has but the alternative of suffering himself or making others suffer. It is all to Freud's credit that, seeing things this way, he did not compromise with a glib solution. Actually within the framework of his thinking there is no escape from one of these two alternative evils. At best there may be a less unfavorable distribution of forces, better control, and "sublimation."

Freud was pessimistic but he did not see the human tragedy in neurosis. We see tragic waste in human experience only if there are constructive creative strivings and these are wrecked by obstructive or destructive forces. And not only did Freud not have any clear vision of constructive forces in man; he had to deny their authentic character. For in his system of thought there were only destructive and libidinal forces, their derivatives and their combinations. Creativity and love (*eros*) for him were sublimated forms of libidinal drives. In most general terms, what we regard as a healthy striving toward self-realization for Freud was—and could be—only an expression of narcissistic libido.

Albert Schweitzer uses the terms *optimistic* and *pessimistic* in the sense of "world and life affirmation" and "world and life negation." Freud's philosophy, in this deep sense, is a pessimistic one. Ours, with all its cognizance of the tragic element in neurosis, is an optimistic one.

Character Analysis Therapy

Although neurosis may produce acute disturbances or may at times remain fairly static, it implies in its nature neither the one condition nor the other. It

---

Character Analysis Therapy, from Horney, *Neurosis and Human Growth,* pp. 333–64.

is a *process* that grows by its own momentum, that with a ruthless logic of its own envelops more and more areas of personality. It is a process that breeds conflicts and a need for their solution. But, since the solutions the individual finds are only artificial ones, new conflicts arise which again call for new solutions—which may allow him to function in a fairly smooth way. It is a process which drives him farther and farther away from his real self and which thus endangers his personal growth.

We must be clear about the seriousness of the involvement in order to guard against false optimism, envisioning quick and easy cures. In fact the word *cure* is appropriate only as long as we think of a relief of symptoms, like a phobia or an insomnia, and this as we know can be effected in many ways. But we cannot "cure" the wrong course which the development of a person has taken. We can only assist him in gradually outgrowing his difficulties so that this development may assume a more constructive course. We cannot discuss here the many ways in which the aims of psychoanalytic therapy have been defined. Naturally for any analyst the aims evolve from what, according to his convictions, he considers the essentials of neurosis. As long, for instance, as we believed that a disturbance in human relations was the crucial factor in neurosis, we aimed in therapy to help patients to establish good relations with others. Having seen the nature and the importance of intrapsychic processes, we are now inclined to formulate the aim in a more inclusive way. We want to help the patient to find himself, and with that the possibility of working toward his self-realization. His capacity for good human relations is an essential part of his self-realization, but it also includes his faculty for creative work and that of assuming responsibility for himself. The analyst must keep in mind the aim of his work from the very first session to the last, because the aim determines the work to be done and the spirit in which it is done.

The Therapeutic Process from the Patient's Standpoint

In order to arrive at a rough estimate of the difficulties of the therapeutic process we must consider what it involves for the patient. Briefly, he must overcome all those needs, drives, or attitudes which obstruct his growth: only when he begins to relinquish his illusions about himself and his illusory goals has he a chance to find his real potentialities and to develop them. Only to the extent to which he gives up his false pride can he become less hostile to himself and evolve a solid self-confidence. Only as his shoulds lose their coercive power can he discover his real feelings, wishes, beliefs, and ideals. Only when he faces his existing conflicts has he the chance for a real integration—and so forth.

But while this is undeniably true, and clear to the analyst, it is not what the patient feels. He is convinced that his way of life—his solution—is right, and that in this way alone can he find peace and fulfillment. He feels that his pride gives him inner fortitude and worth, that without his shoulds his life would be chaotic, etc. It is easy for the objective outsider to say that all these values are spurious ones. But as long as the patient feels that they are the only ones he has he must cling to them.

Moreover the patient must hold on to his subjective values because not to do so would endanger his whole psychic existence. The solutions he has found for his inner conflicts, briefly characterized by the words *mastery, love,* or *freedom,* not only appear to him as right, wise, and desirable ways but as the only safe ones. They give him a feeling of unity; coming face to face with his conflicts entails for him the terrifying prospect of being split apart. His pride not only gives him a feeling of worth or significance but also safeguards him against the equally terrifying danger of being delivered over to his self-hate and self-contempt.

The particular means by which a patient in analysis wards off the realization of conflicts or of self-hate are those which, in accordance with his whole structure, are available to him. The expansive type steers clear of the realization of having any fears, of feeling helpless, of a need for affection, care, help, or sympathy. The self-effacing type most anxiously averts his eyes from his pride or his being out for his own advantage. The resigned type may present an imperturbable front of polite uninterestedness and inertia in order to prevent his conflicts from being mobilized. In all patients the avoidance of conflicts has a double structure: they do not let conflicting trends come to the surface and they do not let any insight into them sink in. Some will try to escape the comprehension of conflicts by intellectualizing or by compartmentalizing. In others the defense is even more diffuse and shows in an unconscious resistance toward thinking anything through clearly or in holding onto an unconscious cynicism (in the sense of a denial of values). Both the muddled thinking and the cynical attitudes in these cases so befog the issue of conflicts that they are indeed unable to see them.

The central issue in the patient's endeavors to ward off an experience of self-hate or self-contempt is to avoid any realization of unfulfilled shoulds. In analysis he must therefore fight off any real insight into those shortcomings which according to his inner dictates are unpardonable sins. Therefore any suggestion of these shortcomings is felt by him as an unfair accusation and puts him on the defensive. And whether in his defense he becomes militant or appeasing, the effect is the same: it prevents him from a sober examination of the truth.

All these stringent needs of the patient to protect his subjective values and to ward off dangers—or the subjective feeling of anxiety and terror—account for the impairment of his ability to cooperate with an analyst despite good conscious intentions. They account for the necessity of his being on the defensive.

Defensiveness, Resistance, and the Status Quo

His defensive attitude so far aims at maintaining the *status quo*. [9] And for most periods of the analytic work this is its outstanding characteristic. For instance, in the beginning phase of work with a resigned type the patient's need to preserve intact every bit of his detachment, of his "freedom," of his policy of not-wanting or not-fighting entirely determines his attitudes toward analysis. But in the expansive and the self-effacing types there is, particularly at the beginning, still another force obstructing analytic progress. Just as in their lives they are out for the positive goals of attaining the absolute mastery, triumph, or love, they are out for attaining these very goals in and through analysis. Analysis should remove all impediments to their having an undiluted triumph or a never-failing, magic willpower, an irresistible attractiveness, an unruffled saintliness, etc. Hence, here it is not simply a question of the patient's being on the defensive but of patient and analyst pulling actively in opposite directions. Although both may talk in terms of evolution, growth, development, they mean entirely different things. The analyst has in mind the growth of the real self; the patient can think only of perfecting his idealized self.

All these obstructive forces operate already in the patient's motivations for seeking analytic help. People want to be analyzed because of some disturbance like a phobia, a depression, a headache, an inhibition in work, sexual difficulties, repeated failures of some kind or other. They come because they cannot cope with some distressing life situation like the infidelity of the marriage partner or his leaving home. They may also come because in some vague way they feel stuck in their general development. All these disturbances would seem to be sufficient reasons for considering analysis and would not seem to require further examination. But for reasons to be mentioned presently we had better ask: *who* is disturbed? The person himself—with his real wishes for happiness and growth—or his pride?

Certainly we cannot make too neat a distinction, but we must be cognizant that pride plays an overwhelming part in making some existing distress intolerable. A street phobia, for instance, may be unbearable for a person because it hurts his pride in mastering every situation. Being deserted by a husband becomes a catastrophe if it frustrates a neurotic claim for a fair deal. ("I have been such a good wife and hence am entitled to his lasting devotion.") The very sexual difficulty which does not disquiet one person is unbearable to him who must be the utmost of "normality." Being stuck in one's development may be so distressing because the claims for effortless superiority do not seem to be working out. The role of pride also shows in the fact that a person may seek help for a minor disturbance which hurts his pride—like blushing, fear of public speaking, the trembling of his hands—while much more handicap-

---

[9] This was the definition of *resistance* that I propounded in *Self-Analysis,* chapter 10, "Dealing With Resistances" (Norton, 1942).

ping disturbances are passed over lightly and in fact play but a vague part in his resolution to be analyzed.

On the other hand, pride may prevent people from going to an analyst—people who need help and could be helped. Their pride in self-sufficiency and "independence" may render it humiliating to consider the prospect of any help. To do so would be an unpermissible "indulgence"; they should be able to cope with their disturbance by themselves. Or their pride in self-mastery may even prohibit an admission of having any neurotic troubles. They may at best come for a consultation to discuss the neurosis of some friend or relative. And the analyst must in these instances be alert to the possibility that this is the only way for them to talk indirectly about their own difficulties. Pride may thus prevent a realistic appraisal of their difficulties and the attaining of help. Of course it is not necessarily a special pride that prohibits their considering analysis. They may be inhibited by any factor stemming from one of the solutions of the inner conflicts. Their resignation for instance may be so great that they would rather reconcile themselves to their disturbances ("I am made this way"). Or their self-effacement may prohibit them from "selfishly" doing something for themselves.

The obstructive forces also operate in what the patient secretly expects of analysis—which I mentioned when discussing the general difficulties of analytic work. To repeat, he expects in part that analysis should remove some disturbing factors without changing anything in his neurotic structure; in part that it should actualize the infinite powers of his idealized self. Furthermore these expectations concern not only the goal of analysis but also the way in which it should be attained. There is rarely, if ever, a sober appreciation of the work to be done. Several factors are involved here. It is of course difficult for anybody to appraise the work who knows analysis only from reading or from occasional attempts to analyze others or himself. But, just as in any other new work, the patient would in time learn what is entailed if his pride did not interfere. The expansive type underrates his difficulties and overrates his capacity to overcome them. With his master mind, or his omnipotent willpower, he should be able to straighten them out in no time. The resigned type, paralyzed by his lack of initiative and his inertia, instead expects the analyst to supply miraculous clues while he waits patiently, an interested bystander. The more the self-effacing elements prevail in a patient, the more will he expect the analyst to wave a magic wand simply because of his suffering and his pleading for help. All these beliefs and hopes are of course hidden beneath a layer of rational expectations.

The retarding effect of such expectations is fairly obvious. No matter whether the patient expects the analyst's or his own magic powers to bring about the desired results, his own incentive to muster the energies necessary for the work is impaired and analysis becomes a rather mysterious process. Needless to say, rationalized explanations are ineffective because they do not remotely touch the inner necessities determining the shoulds and claims behind them. As long as these tendencies operate, the appeal of short therapies is enormous. Patients overlook the fact that publications about these therapies refer merely to symptomatic changes and they are fascinated by what they mistake for an easy leap into health and perfection.

Obstructive Forces During Analysis:
Neurotic Needs and Anxiety

The forms in which these obstructive forces show during the analytic work vary infinitely. Although a knowledge of them is important for the analyst for the sake of quick recognition, I shall mention only a few of them. . . .

The patient may become argumentative, sarcastic, assaultive; he may take shelter behind a façade of polite compliance; he may be evasive, drop the subject, forget about it; he may talk about it with sterile intelligence as if he did not concern himself; he may respond with spells of self-hate or self-contempt, thus cautioning the analyst not to proceed any further—and so on. All these difficulties may appear in the direct work on the patient's problem or in his relationship with the analyst. Compared with other human relationships, the analytic one is in one regard easier for the patient. The analyst's responses to him come comparatively less into play because he is concentrating on understanding the patient's problems. In other regards it is more difficult, because the patient's conflicts and anxieties are stirred up. Nevertheless it is a *human* relationship, and all the difficulties the patient has with regard to other people operate here too. To mention only a few outstanding ones: his compulsive need for mastery, love, or freedom largely determines the tenor of the relationship and makes him hypersensitive to guidance, rejection, or coercion. Because his pride is bound to be hurt in the process, he tends easily to feel humiliated. Because of his expectations and claims, he often feels frustrated and abused. The mobilization of his self-accusations and his self-contempt makes him feel accused and despised. Or, when under the impact of a self-destructive rage, he will quickly become vituperative and abusive toward the analyst.

Lastly, patients regularly overrate the analyst's significance. He is for them not simply a human being who by dint of his training and his self-knowledge may help them. No matter how sophisticated they are, they secretly do regard him as a medicine man endowed with superhuman faculties for good and evil. . . .

We can appraise the significance of these defenses from several viewpoints. When working with a patient we are impressed with the retarding effect they have on the analytic process. They make it difficult—and sometimes impossible—for the patient to examine himself, to understand himself, and to change. On the other hand—as Freud has recognized, speaking of "resistance" —they are also road signs directing our inquiries. To the extent that we gradually understand the subjective values the patient needs to protect or to enhance, and the danger he is fending off, we learn something about the significant forces operating in him.

Moreover, while the defenses make for manifold perplexities in therapy and—naïvely speaking—the analyst sometimes wishes that there were fewer of them, they also render the procedure much less precarious than it would be without them. The analyst strives to avoid premature interpretations, but since he has no godlike omniscience he cannot prevent the fact that at times more disquieting factors are stirred up in a patient than he is able to cope with. The analyst may make a comment which he considers harmless but the patient will interpret it in an alarmed way. Or, even without such comments, the patient, through his own associations or dreams, may open up vistas which are frightening without as yet being instructive. Hence, no matter how obstructive in effect the defenses are, they also entail positive factors insofar as they are an expression of intuitive self-protective processes, necessary because of the precarious inner condition created by the pride system.

Any anxiety that does arise during analytic therapy is usually alarming to the patient because he tends to regard it as a sign of impairment. But more often than not this is not so. Its significance can be evaluated only in the context in which it appears. It may mean that the patient has come closer to facing his conflicts or his self-hate than he could stand at the given time. In that case his customary ways of allaying anxiety usually will help him to cope with it. The avenue that seemed to open up closes again; he fails to benefit from the experience. On the other hand, an emergent anxiety also may have an eminently positive meaning. For it may indicate that the patient now feels strong enough to take the risk of facing his problems more squarely.

Therapy through Self-Knowledge and Self-Realization

The road of analytic therapy is an old one, advocated time and again throughout human history. In the terms of Socrates and the Hindu philosophy, among others, it is the *road to reorientation through self-knowledge*. What is new and specific about it is the method of gaining self-knowledge, which we owe to the genius of Freud. The analyst helps the patient to become aware of all the forces operating in him, the obstructive and the constructive ones; he helps him to combat the former and to mobilize the latter. Though the undermining of the obstructive forces goes on simultaneously with the eliciting of the constructive ones, we shall discuss them separately. . . .

When similarly we ask here what must the patient become aware of in order to uproot his pride system and all it entails, we can simply say that he must become aware of every single aspect of what we have discussed in this book: his search for glory, his claims, his shoulds, his pride, his self-hate, his alienation from self, his conflicts, his particular solution—and the effect all of these factors have on his human relations and his capacity for creative work.

Moreover the patient must not become aware only of these individual factors but also of their connections and interactions. Most relevant on this score is his recognizing that self-hate is pride's inseparable companion and that he cannot have one without the other. Every single factor must be seen in the context of the whole structure. He must realize, for instance, that his shoulds are determined by his kinds of pride, that their nonfulfillment elicits his self-accusations, and that these in turn account for the need to protect himself from their onslaughts.

Intellectual Understanding and Emotional Experience

Becoming aware of all these factors does not mean having information about them, but having a knowledge of them. . . .

But such a knowledge of self implies two things. It is of no help for the patient to have a general idea of his having quite a lot of false pride, or of his being hypersensitive to criticism and failures, or of his tendency to reproach himself, or of his having conflicts. What counts is his becoming aware of the *specific* ways in which these factors operate within him and how in *concrete detail* they manifest themselves in his *particular* life, past and present. It may seem self-evident that it does not help anybody to know, for instance, about shoulds in general or even about the general fact of their operating in himself, and that instead he must recognize their particular content, the particular factors in him making them necessary, and the particular effects they have on his particular life. But the emphasis on the specific and the particular is necessary because for many reasons (his alienation from self, his need to camouflage unconscious pretenses) the patient tends to be either ambiguous or impersonal.

Furthermore his knowledge of himself must not remain an intellectual knowledge, though it may start this way, but must become an *emotional experience*. Both of these factors are closely interwoven because nobody can experience, for instance, pride in general: he can only experience his particular pride in something definite.[10]

Why, then, is it important that the patient not only think about the forces in himself but feel them? Because the mere intellectual realization is in the strict sense of the word no "realization" at all: it does not become real to him;

---

[10]In the history of psychoanalysis, intellectual knowledge at first seemed to be the curative agent. At that time it meant the emergence of childhood memories. The overrating of intellectual mastery also showed at that time in the expectation that the mere recognition of the irrationality of some trend would suffice to set things right. Then the pendulum swung to the other extreme: the emotional experiencing of a factor became all important and has since been stressed in various ways. As a matter of fact, this shift in emphasis seems to be characteristic of the progress of most analysts. Each one seems to need to rediscover for himself the importance of emotional experience. . . .

it does not become his personal property; it does not take roots in him. What in particular he sees with his intellect may be correct; yet, like a mirror that does not absorb a ray of light but can only reflect it, he may apply such "insights" to others, not to himself. Or his pride in intellect may take over with the speed of lightning in several ways: he becomes proud of having made a discovery which other people shun and shirk; he starts to manipulate the particular problem, to turn and twist it so that in no time his vindictiveness, or his feeling abused, for instance, has become an entirely rational response. Or finally the power of his intellect alone may seem to him sufficient to dispel the problem: seeing *is* solving.

Moreover only when experiencing the full impact in its irrationality of a hitherto unconscious or semiconscious feeling or drive do we gradually come to know the intensity and the compulsiveness of unconscious forces operating within ourselves. It is not enough for a patient to admit the probability that his despair over unrequited love is in reality a feeling of being humiliated because his pride in irresistibility, or in possessing the partner body and soul, is hurt. He must *feel* the humiliation and, later on, the hold which his pride has on him. It is not enough to know vaguely that his anger or self-reproach is probably greater than warranted by the occasion. He must *feel* the full impact of his rage or the very depths of his self-condemnation: only then does the force of some unconscious process (and its irrationality) stare him in the face. Only then may he have an incentive to find out more and more about himself. . . .

Reorientation in Reference to the Pride System, Values, and Goals

Nobody can acquire knowledge of his pride system and his solutions without some reorientation going on within him. He begins to realize that certain ideas he has had about himself were fantastic. He begins to doubt whether his demands upon himself are not perhaps impossible of attainment for any human being, whether his claims on others, besides resting on shaky foundations, are not simply unrealizable.

He begins to see that he was inordinately proud of certain attributes which he does not possess—or at least not to the extent he believed—that, for instance, his independence, of which he was so proud, is rather a sensitivity to coercion than a real inner freedom; that, in fact, he is not so immaculately honest as he saw himself because he is shot through with unconscious pretenses; that with all his pride in mastery he is not even master in his own house; that a good deal of his love for people (which made him so wonderful) results from a compulsive need to be liked or admired.

Finally he begins to question the validity of his set of values and of his goals. Perhaps his self-reproaches are not simply a sign of his moral sensitivity? Perhaps his cynicism is not an indication of his being above common prejudice but merely an expedient escape from squaring himself with his beliefs? Perhaps it is not sheer worldly wisdom to regard everybody else as a crook? Perhaps he loses a great deal through his detachment? Perhaps mastery or love is not the ultimate answer to everything?

All such changes can be described as a gradual work of reality-testing and value-testing. Through these steps the pride system is increasingly undermined. They are all necessary conditions for the reorientation which is the aim of therapy. But so far they are all *disillusioning processes.* And they alone could not and would not have a thorough and lasting liberating effect (if any) if constructive moves did not set in simultaneously.

Analysis and Synthesis: The Therapeutic Value of Constructive Forces

When in the early history of psychoanalysis psychiatrists began to consider analysis as a possible form of psychotherapy, some advocated the point of view that a synthesis would have to follow the analysis. They granted, as it were, the necessity to tear something down. But, after this was done, the therapist must give his patient something positive by which he could live, in which he could believe, or for which he could work. While such suggestions probably arose out of a misunderstanding of analysis and contained many fallacies, they were nevertheless prompted by good intuitive feelings. Actually these suggestions are more pertinent for the analytic thinking of our school than for that of Freud, because he did not see the curative process as we see it: as concerning something obstructive to be relinquished in order to give something constructive the possibility to grow. The main fallacy in the old suggestions was in the role they ascribed to the therapist. Instead of trusting the patient's own constructive forces they felt that the therapist should in a rather artificial way, like a *deus ex machina,* provide for a more positive way of living.

We have come back to the ancient medical wisdom that curative forces are inherent in the mind as they are in the body, and that in cases of disorders of body or mind the physician merely gives a helping hand to remove the harmful and to support the healing forces. *The therapeutic value of the disillusioning process lies in the possibility that, with the weakening of the obstructive forces, the constructive forces of the real self have a chance to grow.*

The task of the analyst in supporting this process is rather different from that in analyzing the pride system. The latter work requires, besides a training in technical skills, an extensive knowledge of possible unconscious complexities and personal ingenuity in discovering, understanding, connecting. To help the patient to find himself the analyst also needs a knowledge, to be gained by experience, of the ways in which—through dreams and other channels—the real self may emerge. . . .

There are healing forces operating in the patient from the very beginning. But at the onset of analysis they are usually deficient in vigor and must be mobilized before they can provide any real help in combating the pride system. Hence, at the beginning the analyst must simply work with the good will or positive interest in analysis that is available. . . .

It would appear most desirable to start mobilizing the real self early in the analytic work. But whether such attempts are feasible and meaningful depends, as does everything, on the patient's interest. As long as his energies are bent on consolidating his self-idealization, and consequently on keeping down his real self, these attempts are liable to be ineffective. However our experience on this score is brief, and there may be many more roads accessible then we now envision. The greatest help at the beginning, as well as later on, comes from the patient's dreams. I cannot develop here our theory of dreams. It must suffice to mention briefly our basic tenets: that in dreams we are closer to the reality of ourselves; that they represent attempts to solve our conflicts, either in a neurotic or in a healthy way; that in them constructive forces can be at work, even at a time when they are hardly visible otherwise.

From dreams with constructive elements the patient can catch a glimpse, even in the initial phase of analysis, of a world operating within him which is peculiarly his own and which is more true to his feelings than the world of his illusions. There are dreams in which the patient expresses in symbolic form the sympathy he feels for himself because of what he is doing to himself. There are dreams which reveal a deep well of sadness, of nostalgia, of longing; dreams in which he is struggling to come alive; dreams in which he realizes that he is imprisoned and wants to get out; dreams in which he tenderly cultivates a growing plant or in which he discovers a room in his house of which he did not know before. The analyst will of course help him to understand the meaning of what is expressed in symbolic language. But in addition he may emphasize the significance of the patient's expressing in his dreams feelings or longings which he does not dare to feel in waking life. And he may raise the question of whether, for instance, the feeling of sadness is not more truly what the patient does feel about himself than the optimism he displays consciously.

In time other approaches are possible. The patient himself may start to wonder about how little he knows about his feelings, his wishes, or his beliefs. The analyst will then encourage such puzzled feelings. In whatever way he does it the much misused word *natural* seems appropriate. For it is indeed natural for man—it is in his nature—to feel his feelings, to know his wishes or beliefs. And there is reason to wonder when these natural capacities do not function. And if the wonder is not volunteered the analyst may initiate such questioning at the proper time. . . .

For a while such occasional comments may be all that is necessary. Only when the patient has become interested in the question "Who am I?" will the analyst more actively try to bring to his awareness how little he does know or care about his real feelings, wishes, or beliefs. As an illustration: a patient is frightened when he sees even a minor conflict in himself. He is afraid of being split apart and of going insane. The problem has been tackled from several angles, such as his feeling safe only when everything is under the control of reason or his fear that any minor conflict will weaken him for his fight against the outside world, which he perceives as hostile. By focusing on the real self, the analyst can point out that a conflict may either be frightening because of its magnitude or because there is as yet too little of the patient's real self operating for him to cope with even a minor conflict. . . .

Besides mobilizing the real self in such indirect ways, the analyst will not lose an opportunity to encourage explicitly any sign the patient gives of greater independence in his thinking or feeling, of assuming responsibility for himself, of being more interested in the truth about himself, of catching on by himself to his pretenses, his shoulds, his externalizations. This would include the encouraging of every attempt at self-analysis in between analytic sessions. Moreover the analyst will show, or underline, the specific influence such steps have upon the patient's human relations: his being less afraid of others, less dependent upon them, and hence being better able to have friendly or sympathetic feelings for them.

Sometimes the patient needs hardly any encouragement because he feels freer and more alive anyway. Sometimes he tends to minimize the importance of the steps taken. The tendency to make light of them must be analyzed because it may indicate a fear concerning the emergence of the real self. In addition the analyst will raise the question as to what made it possible at this point to be more spontaneous, to make a decision, or to be active in his own behalf. For this question may open up an understanding of the factors relevant to the patient's courage to be himself.

Alienation of the Self

As the patient comes to have a little firm ground on which to stand he becomes more capable of *grappling with his conflicts.* This does not mean that the conflicts only now become visible. The analyst has seen them long before, and even the patient has perceived signs of them. The same is true for any other neurotic problem: the process of becoming aware of it, with all the steps it entails, is a gradual one and the work at it goes on throughout analysis. But without a diminution of the alienation from self the patient cannot possibly experience such conflicts as *his* and wrestle with them. As we have seen, many factors contribute to make the realization of conflicts a disruptive experience. But among them the alienation from self is outstanding. The simplest way of understanding this connection is to visualize a conflict in terms of interpersonal relations. . . .

The ways in which patients gradually become aware of their conflicts vary greatly. They may be or become aware of divided feelings with regard to particular situations—such as ambivalent feelings toward a parent or a marriage partner—or of contradictory attitudes with regard to sexual activities, or to schools of thought. A patient may, for instance, become aware of both hating his mother and being devoted to her. It looks as if he were aware of a conflict, even though merely with regard to one particular person. But actually this is the way he visualizes it: on the one hand, he feels sorry for his mother because, being the martyr type, she is always unhappy; on the other hand, he is furious at her on account of her stifling demands for exclusive devotion. Both would be most understandable reactions for the kind of person he is. Next, what he has conceived as love or sympathy becomes clearer. He should be the ideal son and should be able to make her happy and contented. Since this is impossible he feels "guilty" and makes up with redoubled attention. This should (as next appears) is not restricted to this one situation; there is no situation in life where he should not be the *absolute* of perfection. Then the other component of his conflict emerges. He is also quite a detached person, harboring claims to have nobody bother him or expect things of him and hating everybody who does so. *The progress here is from attributing his contradictory feelings to the external situation* (the character of the mother), to *realizing his own conflict* in the particular relationship, *finally to recognizing a major conflict within himself* which, because it is within him, operates in all spheres of his life. . . .

To summarize: conflicts, because of their disrupting nature, are blurred at the beginning of analytic work. Provided they are seen at all, it may be only in relation to specific situations—or they may be visualized in too vague, general forms. They may emerge in flashes, too short-lived to acquire new meaning. They may be compartmentalized. Changes on this score take place in these directions: they come closer home as conflicts and as *their* particular conflicts; and they come down to essentials: instead of seeing only remote manifestations patients start to see exactly what is conflicting in them.

While this work is hard and upsetting, it is also liberating. Instead of a rigid solution there are now conflicts accessible to analytical work. The particular main solution, the value of which has been in the process of deflation all along, finally collapses. Furthermore, unfamiliar or little-developed aspects of the personality have been uncovered and given an opportunity to develop. To be sure, what emerge first are still more neurotic drives. But this is useful, for the self-effacing person must first see his self-seeking egocentricity before he has a chance for healthy assertiveness; he must first experience his neurotic pride before he can approximate a real self-respect. Conversely, the expansive type must first experience his abjectness and his need for people before he can develop genuine humility and tender feelings.

Self-Idealization and Self-Realization: The Pride System and the Real Self

With all this work well under way, the patient now can tackle more directly the most comprehensive conflict of all—that between his pride system and his real self, between his drive to perfect his idealized self and his desire to develop his given potentials as a human being. A gradual line-up of forces occurs, the central inner conflict comes into focus, and it is the foremost task of the analyst in the ensuing time to see to it that it stays in sharp focus because the patient himself is liable to lose sight of it. With this lineup of forces a most profitable but also most turbulent period of analysis sets in, varying in degree and duration. The turbulence is a direct expression of the violence of the inner battle. Its intensity is commensurate with the basic importance of the issue at stake. It is at bottom this question: Does the patient want to keep whatever is left of the grandeur and glamor of his illusions, his claims, and his false pride or can he accept himself as a human being with all the general limitations this implies, and with his special difficulties but also with the possibility of this growth? There is, I gather, no more fundamental crossroad situation in our life than this one.

This period is characterized by ups and downs, often in rapid succession. At times the patient is on the forward move, which may show in a great variety of ways. His feelings are more alive; he can be more spontaneous, more direct; he can think of constructive things to do; he feels more friendly or sympathetic to others. He becomes more alert to the many aspects of his alienation and catches on to them on his own. He may, for instance, quickly recognize when he is not "in" a situation or when, instead of facing something in himself, he is blaming others. He may realize how little he has actually done on his own behalf. He may remember incidents in the past when he has been dishonest or cruel with a more somber judgment and with regret, but without crushing guilt feelings. He begins to see something good in himself, to become aware of certain existing assets. He may give himself due credit for the tenacity of his strivings. . . .

These constructive periods are followed by *repercussions* in which the essential element is a renewed onrush of self-hate and self-contempt. These self-destructive feelings may be experienced as such or they may be externalized through becoming vindictive—feeling abused or having sadistic or masochistic fantasies. Or the patient may but vaguely recognize his self-hate but sharply feel the anxiety with which he responds to the self-destructive impulses. Or finally, not even the anxiety appears as such, but his customary defenses against it—such as drinking, sexual activities, a compulsive need for company, or being grandiose or arrogant—become active again.

All these upsets follow real changes for the better, but in order to evaluate them accurately we must consider the solidity of the improvement and the factors precipitating the "relapses." ...

When in the grip of a repercussion the patient naturally does not know what is going on. He feels simply that he is getting worse. He may feel desperate. Perhaps his improvements were illusory? Perhaps he is too far gone to be helped? He may have fleeting impulses to quit analysis—thoughts which he may never have had before, even in upsetting times. He feels bewildered, disappointed, discouraged.

Actually these are in all instances constructive signs of the patient's grappling with the decision between self-idealization and self-realization. And perhaps nothing else shows so clearly that these two drives are incompatible as the inner struggle going on during the repercussions and the spirit of the constructive moves precipitating them. They do not occur because he sees himself more realistically but because he is willing to accept himself with limitations; not because he can make a decision and do something in his own behalf but because he is willing to heed his real interests and assume responsibility for himself; not because he can assert himself in a matter-of-fact way but because he is willing to assume his place in the world. To put it briefly: *they are growing pains.*

But they yield their full benefits only when the patient becomes aware of the significance of his constructive moves. It is hence all the more important that the analyst does not get bewildered by the seeming relapses but recognizes the swings of the pendulum for what they are and helps the patient to see them. Since the repercussions often set in with predictable regularity, it seems advisable after they have occurred a few times to forewarn the patient when he is on the upward move. This may not forestall the coming repercussions, but the patient may not be quite so helpless before them if he too realizes the predictability of the forces operating at a given time. It helps him to become more objective toward them. It is more relevant than at any other time for the analyst to be an unambiguous ally of the endangered self. If his vision and his stand are clear, then he can give patients the support they so badly need in these trying times. The support consists mostly not of general assurances but of conveying to the patient the fact that he is engaged in a final battle and in showing him the odds against which, and the aims for which, he is fighting.

Each time the meaning of a repercussion is understood by the patient he comes out of it stronger than before. The repercussions gradually become shorter and less intense. Conversely, the good periods become more definitely constructive. The prospect of his changing and growing becomes a tangible possibility, within his reach.

But whatever work is still to be done—and there will always be plenty— the time has come close at hand when the patient can try to do it on his own.

Just as vicious circles were at work to entangle him more and more deeply in his neurosis, now there are circles working in the reverse direction. If, for instance, the patient lessens his standards of absolute perfection, his self-accusations also decrease. Hence he can afford to be more truthful about himself. He can examine himself without becoming frightened. This in turn renders him less dependent upon the analyst and gives him confidence in his own resources. At the same time his need to externalize his self-accusations decreases too. So he feels less threatened by others, or less hostile toward them, and can begin to have friendly feelings for them.

Besides, the patient's courage and confidence in his ability to take charge of his own development gradually increase. In our discussions of the repercussions we focused upon the terror that results from the inner conflicts. This terror diminishes as the patient becomes clear about the direction he wants to take in his life. And his sense of direction alone gives him a greater feeling of unity and strength. Yet there is still another fear attached to his forward moves, one which we have not yet fully appreciated. This is a realistic fear of not being able to cope with life without his neurotic props. The neurotic is after all a magician living by his magic powers. Any step toward self-realization means relinquishing these powers and living by his existing resources. But as he realizes that he can in fact live without such illusions, and even live better without them, he gains faith in himself.

Moreover any move toward being himself gives him a sense of fulfillment which is different from anything he has known before. And while such an experience is at first short-lived, it may in time recur more and more often and for periods of longer duration. Even at first it gives him a greater conviction of being on the right path than anything else he may think or the analyst can say. For it shows him the possibility of feeling in accord with himself and with life. It is probably the greatest incentive for him to work at his own growth, toward a greater self-realization.

The therapeutic process is so fraught with difficulties of manifold kinds that the patient may not attain the stage described. When carried through successfully it will of course bring about observable improvements in his relation to himself, to others, to his work. These improvements, however, are not the criteria for terminating regular analytic work. For they are but the tangible expressions of a deeper change. And only the analyst and the patient himself are aware of this one: a beginning change of values, of direction, of goals. The fictitious values of the patient's neurotic pride and of the phantoms of mastery, surrender, and freedom have lost much of their fascination and he is more strongly bent on realizing his given potentials. He still has ahead of him much work at hidden kinds of pride, of claims, of pretenses, of externalizations, etc. But, being more firmly grounded in himself, he can recognize them for what they are: a hindrance to his growth. Hence he is willing to discover them and to overcome them in time. And this willingness is now not (or, at least, is less) the frantic impatience to remove imperfections by magic. Having begun to accept himself as he is, with his difficulties, he also accepts the work at himself as an integral part of the process of living.

Putting the work to be done in positive terms, it concerns all that is involved in self-realization. With regard to himself, it means striving toward a clearer and deeper experiencing of his feelings, wishes, and beliefs; toward a greater ability to tap his resources and to use them for constructive ends; toward a clearer perception of his direction in life, with the assumption of responsibility for himself and his decisions. With regard to others it means his striving toward relating himself to others with his genuine feelings; toward respecting them as individuals in their own right and with their own peculiarities; toward developing a spirit of mutuality (instead of using them as a means to an end). With regard to work it means that the work itself will become more important to him than the satisfaction of his pride or vanity and that he will aim at realizing and developing his special gifts and at becoming more productive.

PART TWO

Learning Theory Approaches

7

LEARNING THEORY PSYCHOTHERAPY

John Dollard

Neal E. Miller

John Dollard, born in Menasha, Wisconsin, on August 29, 1900, was educated at the University of Wisconsin (A.B., 1922) and at the University of Chicago (A.M., 1930; Ph.D. in sociology, 1931). Yale awarded him an honorary M.A. in 1952. In 1926, after three years with the Union Building Committee at the University of Wisconsin, he was appointed assistant to the president of the University of Chicago, a post that he held until 1929. After spending a few years in Germany, Dollard accepted a research post with Yale University's Institute of Human Relations in 1932, and in 1952 he was elevated to the rank of professor of psychology.

Neal E. Miller, also a native of Wisconsin, was born in 1909 and educated at the University of Washington (B.S., 1931); Stanford (M.A., 1932); and Yale (Ph.D., 1935). After earning his doctorate, Miller went to Vienna, where he did postdoctoral work at the Psychoanalytic Institute. He spent the war years doing psychological research for the Air Force, but prior to that time (from 1936 to 1942) and after the war (from 1946 to 1966) he was with the Institute of Human Relations at Yale. He left Yale in 1966, having achieved the rank of professor of psychology. Currently Miller is professor at Rockefeller University, a post to which he was appointed on July 1, 1966. Among Miller's honors are an honorary D.Sc. degree from the University of Michigan (1965), the National Medal of Science (1965), and the presidency of the American Psychological Association (1960–61).

Dollard and Miller purport to establish human behavior on a scientific basis by synthesizing three psychological schools of thought—the psychoanalysis of Freud; the behaviorism of Pavlov, Thorndike, and Hull; and modern social psychological schools. Emphasis is placed upon the ability of the mind, with its higher mental processes, to solve social and emotional problems. They believe that neurosis is learned and investigation of childhood experiences is important in understanding neurotic development. Therapy is essentially learning (as is neurosis), but it takes place in a social situation because human behavior is the result of social conditions as well as psychological principles.

Dollard and Miller are well known in the field of psychotherapy. In 1941 they published *Social Learning and Imitation*. They are perhaps best known for *Personality and Psychotherapy: An Analysis in Terms of Learning, Thinking, and Culture* (1950). Miller, in addition to publishing a number of articles, in 1952 published *Theoretical Models and Personality*. With others, Dollard published *Steps in Psychotherapy: A Study of a Case in Sex-Fear Conflict* (1953) and *Scoring Human Motives: A Manual* (1959). In 1971 Miller's important papers were published in a work entitled *Selected Papers*.

Learning Theory and Neurosis

If neurotic behavior is learned, it should be unlearned by some combination of the same principles by which it was taught. We believe this to be the case. Psychotherapy establishes a set of conditions by which neurotic habits may be unlearned and nonneurotic habits learned. Therefore, we view the therapist as a kind of teacher and the patient as a learner. In the same way and by the same principles that bad tennis habits can be corrected by a good coach, so bad mental and emotional habits can be corrected by a psychotherapist. There is this difference, however. Whereas only a few people want to play tennis, all the world wants a clear, free, efficient mind. . . .

If a neurosis is functional (i.e., a product of experience rather than of organic damage or instinct), it must be learned. If it is learned, it must be learned according to already known, experimentally verified laws of learning or according to new, and as yet undiscovered, laws of learning. In the former case, such laws, meticulously studied by investigators such as Pavlov, Thorndike, Hull, and their students, should make a material contribution to the understanding of the phenomenon. If new laws are involved, the attempt to study neuroses from the learning standpoint should help to reveal the gaps in our present knowledge and to suggest new principles which could be fruitfully submitted to investigation in the laboratory. It seems likely that not only laws we know but also those we do not know are involved. However, the laws that we *do* know seem sufficient to carry us a long way toward a systematic analysis of psychotherapy.

We have attempted to give a systematic analysis of neurosis and psychotherapy in terms of the psychological principles and social conditions of learning. In order to give the reader a better perspective on this attempt, we shall swiftly list some of its main consequences.

Learning Theory and Neurosis, from John Dollard and Neal E. Miller, *Personality and Psychotherapy* (New York: McGraw-Hill, 1950), pp. 7–16.

1. The principle of reinforcement has been substituted for Freud's pleasure principle. The concept of "pleasure" has proved a difficult and slippery notion in the history of psychology. The same is true of the idea that the behavior that occurs is "adaptive," because it is awkward to have to explain maladaptive behavior on the basis of a principle of adaptiveness. The principle of reinforcement is more exact and rigorous than either the pleasure principle or the adaptiveness principle. Since the effect of immediate reinforcement is greater than that of reinforcement after a delay, the investigator is forced to examine the exact temporal relationships between responses, stimuli, and reinforcement. He is thus provided with a better basis for predicting whether or not adaptive behavior will be learned. Where reinforcement is delayed, some account must be given of the means by which the temporal gap is bridged.

2. The relatively neglected and catchall concept of ego strength has been elaborated in two directions: first is the beginning of a careful account of higher mental processes; second is the description of the culturally valuable learned drives and skills. The importance of the foregoing factors in human behavior can hardly be overemphasized. The functioning of higher mental processes and learned drives is not limited to neuroses or psychotherapy. It is an essential part of the science of human personality.

3. A naturalistic account is given of the immensely important mechanism of repression. Repression is explained as the inhibition of the cue-producing responses which mediate thinking and reasoning. Just what is lost by repression and gained by therapy is much clearer in the light of this account.

4. Transference is seen as a special case of a wider concept, generalization. This explanation draws attention to the fact that many humdrum habits which facilitate therapy are transferred along with those that obstruct it. The analysis shows also why such intense emotional responses should be directed toward the therapist in the transference situation.

5. The dynamics of conflict behavior are systematically deduced from more basic principles. Thus, a fundamental fact of neurosis—that of conflict —is tied in with general learning theory. A clear understanding of the nature of conflict serves to provide a more rational framework for therapeutic practice.

6. We have been obliged to put great stress on the fact that the patient gets well in real life. Only part of the work essential to therapy is done in the therapeutic situation. Reinforcement theory supplies logical reasons why this should be expected.

7. The somewhat vague concept of "reality" is elaborated in terms of the physical and social conditions of learning, especially the conditions provided by the social structure of a society. In order to predict behavior we must know these conditions as well as the psychological principles involved. Psychology supplies the principles while sociology and social anthropology supply the systematic treatment of the crucial social conditions.

8. The concepts of repression and suppression are supplemented by the parallel ones of inhibition and restraint. The idea that it is important to suppress and restrain tendencies to unconventional thoughts and acts is not a novelty with us, but our type of analysis has forced us to reaffirm and expand it.

Neurotic Conflict as the Cause of Misery and Stupidity

Suffering so intense as that shown by neurotics must have powerful causes, and it does. The neurotic is miserable because he is in conflict. As a usual thing two or more strong drives are operating in him and producing incompatible responses. Strongly driven to approach and as strongly to flee, he is not able to act to reduce either of the conflicting drives. These drives therefore remain dammed up, active, and nagging.

Where such a drive conflict is conscious there is no problem in convincing anyone why it should produce misery. If we picture a very hungry man confronting food which he knows to be poisoned, we can understand that he is driven on the one hand by hunger and on the other by fear. He oscillates at some distance from the tempting food, fearing to grasp but unable to leave. Everyone understands immediately the turmoil produced by such a conflict of hunger and fear.

Many people remember from their adolescence the tension of a strong sex conflict. Primary sex responses heightened by imaginative elaboration are met by intense fear. Though usually not allowed to talk about such matters, children sometimes can, and the misery they reveal is one of the most serious prices exacted of adolescents in our culture. . . .

In each of the above cases, however, the individual could eventually solve his conflict. The hungry man could find nourishing food; the sex-tortured adolescent could eventually marry. . . .

With the neurotic this is not the case. He is not able to solve his conflict even with the passage of time. Though obviously intelligent in some ways, he is stupid in-so-far as his neurotic conflict is concerned. This stupidity is not an over-all affair, however. It is really a stupid area in the mind of a person who is quite intelligent in other respects. For some reason he cannot use his head on his neurotic conflicts. . . .

The Neurotic's Reduction of Conflict through Symptoms

Although in many ways superficial, the symptoms of the neurotic are the most obvious aspects of his problems. These are what the patient is familiar with and feels he should be rid of. The phobias, inhibitions, avoidances, compulsions, rationalizations, and psychosomatic symptoms of the neurotic are experienced as a nuisance by him and by all who have to deal with him. The symptoms cannot be integrated into the texture of sensible social relations. The patient, however, believes that the symptoms *are* his disorder. It is these he wishes to be rid of, and not knowing what a serious conflict underlies them, he would like to confine the therapeutic discussion to getting rid of the symptoms.

The symptoms do not solve the basic conflict in which the neurotic person is plunged, but they mitigate it. They are responses which tend to reduce the conflict, and in part they succeed. When a successful symptom occurs it is reinforced because it reduces neurotic misery. The symptom is thus learned as a habit. One very common function of symptoms is to keep the neurotic person away from those stimuli which would activate and intensify his neurotic conflict. . . .

Fundamentals of Learning Theory

The field of human learning covers phenomena which range all the way from the simple, almost reflex, learning of a child to avoid a hot radiator, to the complex processes of insight by which a scientist constructs a theory. Throughout the whole range, however, the same fundamental factors seem to be exceedingly important. These factors are: *drive, response, cue,* and *reinforcement.* They are frequently referred to with other roughly equivalent words—drive as motivation, cue as stimulus, response as act or thought, and reinforcement as reward. . . .

The drive impels responses which are usually channelized by cues from other stimuli not strong enough to act as drives but more specifically distinctive than the drive. If the first response is not rewarded, this creates a dilemma in which the extinction of successive nonreinforced responses leads to so-called random behavior. If some one response is followed by reinforcement, the connection between the stimulus pattern and this response is strengthened, so that the next time the same drive and other cues are present this response is more likely to occur. Since reinforcements presumably produce their effect by reducing the strength of the drive stimulus, events cannot be rewarding in the absence of an appropriate drive. After the drive has been satiated by sufficient reward, the tendency to make the rewarded response is weakened so that other responses occur until the drive reappears. . . .

Fundamentals of Learning Theory, from Dollard and Miller, *Personality and Psychotherapy,* pp. 25–26, 47–58.

Extinction

Reinforcement is essential to the learning of a habit; it is also essential to the maintenance of a habit. When a learned response is repeated without reinforcement, the strength of the tendency to perform that response undergoes a progressive decrease. This decrement is called *experimental extinction,* or, more simply, extinction. . . .

Rate of Extinction

The process of extinction is usually not immediate but extends over a number of trials. The number of trials required for the complete extinction of a response varies with certain conditions.

Stronger habits are more resistant to extinction than weaker habits. Other things equal, any factor which will produce a stronger habit will increase its resistance to extinction. One such factor is a greater number of rewarded training trials. Thus a storekeeper is more likely to give up trying to sell a new line of goods if he fails to make sales to a series of customers near the beginning of his experience with these goods than he is if he has the same streak of bad luck after having made many successful sales. Two additional factors producing a stronger habit and hence a greater resistance to extinction are: a stronger drive during training and a greater amount of reward per trial during training. . . .

Spontaneous Recovery

The effects of extinction tend to disappear with the passage of time. After a series of unsuccessful expeditions, a fisherman may have abandoned the idea of making any further trips to a particular stream. As time goes on, his tendency to try that stream again gradually recovers from the effects of extinction, so that next month or next year he may take another chance. This tendency for an extinguished habit to reappear after an interval of time during which no nonrewarded trials occur is called *spontaneous recovery.* . . .

Gradient of Generalization

The effects of learning in one situation transfer to other situations; the less similar the situation, the less transfer occurs. Stated more exactly, reinforcement for making a specific response to a given pattern of cues strengthens not only the tendency for that pattern of cues to elicit that response but also the tendency for other similar patterns of cues to elicit the same response. The innate tendency for transfer to occur is called innate stimulus generalization.

The less similar the cue or pattern of cues, the less the generalization. This variation in the transfer is referred to as a *gradient of generalization.* . . .

The gradient of generalization refers to the qualitative differences or cue aspect of stimuli. The *distinctiveness* of a cue is measured by its dissimilarity from other cues in the same situation, so that little generalization occurs from one cue to other cues in the situation. Thus the distinctiveness of a cue varies with the other cues that are present. A red book in a row of black books is a more distinctive cue than is the same volume in a row of other red books, because less generalization occurs from red to black than from one shade of red to another. . . .

Discrimination

If a generalized response is not rewarded, the tendency to perform that response is weakened. By the reward of the response to one pattern of cues and the nonreward or punishment of the response to a somewhat different pattern of cues, a discrimination may gradually be established. The process of discrimination tends to correct maladaptive generalizations. It increases the specificity of the cue-response connection. . . .

Gradient in the Effects of Reinforcement

Delayed reinforcements are less effective than immediate ones. In other words, if a number of different responses are made to a cue and the last of these responses is followed by reward, the connection to the last response will be strengthened the most and the connection to each of the preceding responses will be strengthened by a progressively smaller amount. Similarly, in a series of responses to a series of cues—as when a hungry boy takes off his hat in the hall, dashes through the dining room into the kitchen, opens the icebox, and takes a bite to eat—the connections more remote from the reward are strengthened less than those closer to the reward. In this series, the connection between the sight of the hall closet and the response of hanging up the hat will be strengthened less than the connection between the sight of the icebox door and the response of opening it. . . .

The gradient of reinforcement accounts for an increase in tendency to respond, the nearer the goal is approached. Because cue-response connections near the reward are strengthened more than connections remote from the reward, a hungry man on his way to dinner has a tendency to quicken his pace in rounding the last corner on the way home.

The gradient of reinforcement also explains why, after both a longer and a shorter route to the goal have been tried, the shorter route tends to be preferred. A thirsty child learns to secure water from drinking fountains in the park. . . .

In summary, the effects of reinforcement are not limited to the particular cue-response sequence which is immediately associated with reward, but they also strengthen other cue-response connections less immediately associated with reward. This spread of the effects of reinforcement has the function of strengthening the connections to responses comprising the first steps of the sequence leading to reward. It can be greatly facilitated if certain stimuli involved in the sequence acquire a subgoal, or learned rewarding value, by repeated association with the primary reward. Nevertheless, the effects of reward taper off in a gradient so that the connections immediately associated with the reward are strengthened more than remoter connections. This gradient of reinforcement has the function of tending to force the subject to choose the shortest of alternative paths to a goal and to eliminate unnecessary responses from a sequence. . . .

Anticipatory Response

From the principle of the gradient of reinforcement and from that of generalization, an additional principle can be deduced: that responses near the point of reinforcement tend, wherever physically possible, to occur before their original time in the response series, that is, to become anticipatory. . . .

A child touches a hot radiator. The pain elicits an avoidance response, and the escape from pain reinforces this response. Since the sight and the muscular "feel" of the hand approaching the radiator are similar in certain respects to the sight and the musucular "feel" of the hand touching the radiator, the strongly reinforced response of withdrawal will be expected to generalize from the latter situation to the former. After one or more trials, the child will reach out his hand toward the radiator and then withdraw it before touching the radiator. The withdrawal response will become anticipatory; it will occur before that of actually touching the radiator. This is obviously adaptive, since it enables the child to avoid getting burned. . . .

Fear as a Learned Drive and Fear Reduction as a Reinforcement

Fear will be discussed first and in the most detail because it has been studied most thoroughly, provides the clearest examples of basic concepts, and is so important as a learned drive. When the source of fear is vague or obscured by repression, it is often called *anxiety*. . . .

Fear as a Learned Drive and Fear Reduction as a Reinforcement, from Dollard and Miller, *Personality and Psychotherapy*, pp. 63–78.

Functional Definitions of Stimulus and Response

Overt responses can be observed easily and have been fairly well studied. Many of their functional properties are known; they can be learned, generalized to new stimuli, extinguished, inhibited by conflicting responses, facilitated by summation, and so forth. Fear is more difficult to observe, but we are advancing the tentative hypothesis that it has all the functional properties of a response. We have already shown that it has one of these—it can be learned; we shall show that it has others.

Similarly, external sources of stimulation are easy to control so the properties of exterioceptive stimuli are relatively well known: they can vary in distinctiveness and serve as cues; they can vary in strength, and, if strong enough, act as drives. On the basis of the fact that fear has one of the properties of a strong external stimulus (namely, drive), we shall tentatively assume that it has the other property.

In short, we are assuming (1) that fear obeys the same laws as do external responses; and (2) that it has the same drive and cue properties as strong external stimuli. These hypotheses are purely functional; they say nothing about the anatomical location, central or peripheral, of the inferred process. According to them, fear could be a central state that obeys the same laws as an external response and has the same drive and cue properties as a strong external stimulus.

As a short way of expressing the first hypothesis, fear will be called a response; to express the second, one, it will be called stimulus-producing. This is a somewhat unorthodox expansion of the use of these two words. . . .

Innate Factors in Fear

The neurological and physiological basis of fear is, of course, innate. Furthermore, the fear of the painful electric shock was presumably not learned, but was rather an innate response to that stimulus. Finally, there is some evidence suggesting that fear, like other responses, may occupy different positions in the innate hierarchy of responses to different cues so that it is easier to learn to be afraid of some situations than of others. Therefore, in referring to the fear drive per se, it is more exact to describe it as *learnable* than learned. The fear of a previously neutral cue, however, may be described accurately as a learned drive. . . .

Reinforcement of Fear

It is well known that animals or people can be made to fear a neutral stimulus by pairing it with some other stimulus that already elicits strong fear. In this case the stimulus, such as pain, that already elicits the fear is called the reinforcing stimulus, but the exact nature of the reinforcement is still controversial. According to a strict drive-reduction theory, the reinforcement would have to be a reduction in the strength of pain occurring immediately after its sudden onset or as a part of throbbing changes in intensity. According to other hypotheses, contiguity is all that is necessary; pain reinforces the fear by eliciting it in the presence of the neutral stimulus. . . .

Although it is not certain that emotional responses, such as fear, are reinforced by drive reduction, it is known that they obey the same laws (gradient of reinforcement, generalizations, extinction, spontaneous recovery, etc.) as do those instrumental habits that clearly are reinforced by drive reduction. Because the same general laws seem to apply to both situations, we need not take a definite stand on the question of whether or not drive reduction is the sole mechanism of reinforcement. . . .

Extinction of Fear

Like other habits, learned fears seem to be subject to experimental extinction so that they become weaker during a series of trials without primary reinforcements. Many fears, however, are extremely resistant to extinction. . . .

Fear is so resistant to extinction that it is sometimes difficult to determine whether the curve of extinction will eventually reach zero or flatten off at some constant level above zero. Sometimes it is even difficult to be certain that any extinction at all is taking place.

The resistance of fear to extinction seems to be affected by the same factors that apply to other responses. The difficulty of extinguishing fear is increased by anything that makes it stronger: reinforcement by a more painful stimulus, more reinforced trials, more immediate reinforcement, or greater similarity to the originally reinforced stimulus. Furthermore, the procedure of so-called partial reinforcement greatly increases the resistance of fear to extinction. In other words, a painful experience occurring after a number of extinction trials is far more effective in specifically training the subject to remain afraid than the same painful experience would have been as a part of the original learning. This is particularly important in the avoidance of dangerous objects where the person gets hurt only after his fear has extinguished to the point where he begins to be careless. . . .

Responses Inhibiting Fear

Like any other response, fear apparently can be inhibited by responses that are incompatible with it. Apparently eating and the emotional responses that accompany it are at least partially incompatible with fear. If fear is relatively strong with respect to hunger, the eating is inhibited; if hunger is relatively strong with respect to fear, the eating tends to inhibit the fear. . . .

Fear as a Cue and Learned Generalization

If our hypothesis that drives are strong stimuli is correct, we would expect fear to have the other properties of a stimulus and thus be able to function as a cue. That seems to be true. People can be taught to make a specific verbal response, saying the word *afraid* in situations that arouse fear. Once this word is learned as a response to the cue of fear, it will transfer to any new situation that elicits the response producing this cue. This kind of a transfer, mediated by a response-produced cue, is called secondary, or *learned generalization.* . . .

How Fear Functions

Fear is important because it can be learned so quickly and become so strong. Some of its chief effects are:

1. When the fear is learned as a response to a new situation, it brings with it a number of reactions that are either parts of the innate pattern of fear or high in the innate hierarchy of responses to it.

2. When fear is learned as a response to a new situation, it serves as a cue to elicit responses that have previously been learned in other frightening situations.

3. When fear is learned as a response to a new situation, it serves as a drive to motivate trial-and-error behavior. A reduction in the strength of the fear reinforces the learning of any new response that accompanies it. This learning will be influenced by the preceding two factors through their roles in determining which responses are likely to occur.

4. When the responses reducing other drives are punished, fear will be learned and will tend to motivate responses that prevent the reduction of those drives. As we shall show, the conflict between responses motivated by fear and those motivated by other drives, such as aggression and sex, can cause these drives to mount, create misery, and motivate symptoms. . . .

Higher Mental Processes

Cue-Producing Responses

In order to talk about the higher mental processes we need to make the distinction between instrumental and cue-producing responses. . . . An instrumental act is one whose main function is to produce an immediate change in the relationship to the external environment. Opening a door, lifting a box,

Higher Mental Processes, from Dollard and Miller, *Personality and Psychotherapy,* pp. 98–100.

jumping back on the curb are examples of instrumental acts. A cue-producing response is one whose main function is to produce a cue that is part of the stimulus pattern leading to another response. Counting is a cue-producing response. The chief function of counting the money one receives as change is to produce the cue that will lead to the proper instrumental response of putting it in one's pocket, giving some back, or asking for more. . . .

Role of Cue-Producing Responses in Higher Mental Processes

Having made the distinction between instrumental and cue-producing responses, we can improve our description of the distinction between the "lower" and "higher" types of adjustment. In the former, the instrumental response is made directly to the pattern of external cues and internal drives; in the latter, one or more cue-producing responses intervenes.

Our basic assumption is that language and other cue-producing responses play a central role in the higher mental processes. This should be contrasted with the approach of some philosophers who seem to believe that language is a mere means of communicating thoughts which somehow "exist" independently of speech rather than an essential part of most thinking and reasoning. According to our theory, teaching a student the specialized "language" of tensor analysis may enable him to solve problems that for centuries baffled the best minds of the ancients. . . .

Social Training and the Higher Mental Processes

. . . One can see that a number of different conditions have to be met before reasoning and planning can produce adaptive behavior in a given dilemma. First, the direct instrumental responses to the internal drives and external cues must be inhibitied in order to give the cue-producing responses time to occur; the subject must stop and think before rushing precipitately into action. Then, the proper thoughts must occur. These can fail to occur either because they are not in the individual's repertory of learned responses or because they are inhibited by competing thoughts. If the cue-producing responses that have been learned do not parallel objects and events in the environment, the solution or plan will be unrealistic. Finally, it is necessary for the thoughts to be carried over into action. In other words, the instrumental responses elicited indirectly via the cue-producing sequence must be stronger than the direct responses to internal drives and external cues. As we shall see, the likelihood of these conditions being met is enormously increased by specific kinds of training that the child receives in the process of socialization. . . .

The various "levels" of adjustment may now be recapitulated.

Social Training and the Higher Mental Processes, from Dollard and Miller, *Personality and Psychotherapy,* pp. 115, 124–25.

At the lower level are direct responses to cues. These may be innate reflexes (like a blink to a cinder in the eye), responses that are originally learned as direct responses (like the blink to a sudden motion toward the eye), or ones that were originally learned as responses to verbal instructions and later so strongly associated with the external cues that they are out of verbal control (like pressing on the floorboards when a child runs in front of a car in which one is a passenger).

On a higher level are responses mediated by one or more intervening cue-producing responses. Because these responses are not limited by the mechanical and social possibilities of the immediate environment, they can become anticipatory or work backward from the goal step by step. This enables them to mediate adaptive, new combinations of responses that would be unlikely to occur otherwise. Thought is obviously highly creative and vastly superior to instrumental trial and error.

Attaching the same label (or other cue-producing response) to two distinctive stimulus objects increases the generalization of emotional and instrumental responses from one to the other. Attaching different labels (or other distinctive cue-producing responses) to two similar stimulus situations increases the discrimination between the two. If the proper habits have been learned, words can arouse strong learned drives or give powerful reward and reassurance. In this way, verbal responses play an especially important role in mediating the foresightful response to remote rewards or punishments.

Cue-producing responses, such as imagery, that are not socially observable are not subject to direct, intensive social training. The use of these private cue-producing responses thus tends to be relatively unsophisticated. On the other hand, the public cue-producing responses, like words and sentences, that are used in social communication receive an enormous amount of social training. The accumulated cultural heritage of generations of trial and error is represented in the categories, common-sense rules of logic, standards of reasonableness, and sequences of orderly narration of language. This greatly increases the usefulness of verbal responses and their derivatives, such as mathematics, in the solution of social, emotional, and instrumental problems.

In our society, there seems to be much more emphasis on formal training in special techniques for solving problems in the physical environment than on ones for solving emotional problems.

Only a modest and uncertain start has been made toward understanding the marvelous intricacies of language and the higher mental processes. In this extremely important area there is a great need for more detailed observations of patients in therapy and of the socialization of children in the home, for a more rigorous theoretical formulation and a more penetrating experimental analysis.

As we increase our scientific knowledge in this area, we may be able to improve our social training in the use of the higher mental processes. . . .

Neurosis as Learned

Social Conditions for the Learning of Neurosis

An intense emotional conflict is the necessary basis for neurotic behavior. The conflict must further be unconscious. As a usual thing, such conflicts are created only in childhood. How can it be that neurotic conflicts are engendered when there is no deliberate plan to do so? Society must force children to grow up, but it does not idealize neurosis and makes no formal provision in its system of training for the production of neurotic children. Indeed, we deplore the neurotic and recognize him as a burden to himself and to others. How then does it happen? Our answer is that neurotic conflicts are taught by parents and learned by children. . . .

Conflict itself is no novelty. Emotional conflicts are the constant accompaniment of life at every age and social level. Conflicts differ also in strength, some producing strong and some weak stimuli. Where conflicts are strong and unconscious, the individuals afflicted keep on making the same old mistakes and getting punished in the same old way. To the degree that the conflict can be made conscious, the ingenuity and inventiveness of higher mental life can aid in finding new ways out of the conflict situation. This applies to all emotional dilemmas, to those which survive from early childhood and to those which are created in the course of later life.

High drives produced during the nursing period can have disturbing side-effects. The child first faces severe cultural pressure in the cleanliness-training situation. At this time intense anger-anxiety conflicts can arise. Similarly, in the discipline of the masturbation habit and of heterosexual approach tendencies, the sex-anxiety conflict is regularly created in all of us. In some it has traumatic intensity. When the elements of this conflict are unconscious, they can have an abiding effect on life adjustment in the marital sphere. The culture takes a harsh attitude toward the angry and hostile behavior of children and regularly attaches anxiety to it, usually by direct punishment. Anger can be aroused in any of the situations of childhood where frustrating conditions are created. Conflicts centering around social class and mobility are known, especially in families where the parents have different social aspirations for the child.

Not all conflict arises through the pitting of primary drives one against the other, as in the case of hunger vs. pain. It is possible to have severe conflict based on one primary and one strong learned drive. This is exemplified by the sex-anxiety conflict. It is further possible to have severe conflict when two strong learned drives are involved—as in the case of anger-anxiety. In later life

---

Neurosis as Learned, from Dollard and Miller, *Personality and Psychotherapy*, pp. 127, 154–56.

many of the strong learned drives, some quite remote from their primitive sources of reinforcement, can produce painful conflicts. "Ambition" can be pitted against "loyalty." The wish to be truthful can be arrayed against "tact." Wishes for social advancement may be deterred by the fear of appearing vulgar and "pushy." Many of these complex learned drives have never been effectively described in terms of the reinforcing circumstances. We do know, however, that when they compete they can plunge the individual into a painful state.

We must admit that we do not know the exact conditions under which the common conflict-producing circumstances of life generate severe conflicts in some and not-so-severe conflicts in others. We know that the conditions and factors described here *do* occur in those who later turn out to show neurotic behavior. It may be that the circumstances of life are not really "the same for normals and neurotics," that this sameness is an illusion based on poor discrimination of the actual circumstances. Therefore it may actually be that some individuals have much stronger conflicts than others. It may be that some are less well able to use higher mental processes than others and are therefore less well able to resolve traumatic tension. It may be that some are more "predisposed" than others in that they have stronger primary drives, or stronger tendencies to inhibition, or in other unknown respects. It is quite likely that the provocative circumstances of later life which precipitate neuroses are more severe in some cases than others; or that some are exposed to just those circumstances which for them excite neurotic behavior but that others are luckier and do not come into contact with just those adverse conditions which would set them off. . . .

Symptoms as Learned

Phobias

In a phobia acquired under traumatic conditions of combat the relevant events are recent and well known. Such cases provide one of the simplest and most convincing illustrations of the learning of a symptom.

The essential points are illustrated by the case of a pilot who was interviewed by one of the authors. This officer had not shown any abnormal fear of airplanes before being sent on a particularly difficult mission to bomb distant and well-defended oil refineries. His squadron was under heavy attack on the way to the target. In the confusion of flying exceedingly low over the target against strong defensive fire, a few of the preceding planes made a wrong turn and dropped their bombs on the section that had been assigned to the pilot's

---

Symptoms as Learned, from Dollard and Miller, *Personality and Psychotherapy,* pp. 157–81.

formation. Since not enough bombs were dropped to destroy the installations, the pilot's formation had to follow them to complete the job. As they came in above the rooftops, bombs and oil tanks were exploding. The pilot's plane was tossed violently about and damaged while nearby planes disappeared in a wall of fire. Since this pilot's damaged plane could not regain altitude, he had to fly back alone at reduced speed and was subject to repeated violent fighter attack which killed several crew members and repeatedly threatened to destroy them all. When they finally reached the Mediterranean, they were low on gas and had to ditch the airplane in the open sea. The survivors drifted on a life raft and eventually were rescued.

Many times during this mission the pilot was exposed to intensely fear-provoking stimuli such as violent explosions and the sight of other planes going down and comrades being killed. It is known that intense fear-provoking stimuli of this kind act to reinforce fear as a response to other cues present at the same time. In this case the other cues were those from the airplane, its sight and sound, and thoughts about flying. We would therefore expect the strong drive of intense fear to be learned as a response to all of these cues.

When a strong fear has been learned as a response to a given set of cues, it tends to generalize to other similar ones. . . . Thus one would expect the fear of this airplane and of thoughts about flying it to generalize to the similar sight and sound of other airplanes and thoughts about flying in them. This is exactly what happened; the pilot felt strongly frightened whenever he approached, looked at, or even thought about flying in any airplane.

Because he had already learned to avoid objects that he feared, he had a strong tendency to look away and walk away from all airplanes. Whenever he did this, he removed the cues eliciting the fear and hence felt much less frightened. But, as we have already said . . . a reduction in any strong drive such as fear serves to reinforce the immediately preceding responses. Therefore we would expect any response that produced successful avoidance to be learned as a strong habit. This is what occurred; the pilot developed a strong phobia of airplanes and everything connected with them.

Similarly, he felt anxious when thinking or talking about airplanes and less anxious when he stopped thinking or talking about them. The reduction in anxiety reinforced the stopping of thinking or of talking about airplanes; he became reluctant to think about or discuss his experience.

To summarize, under traumatic conditions of combat the intense drive of fear was learned as a response to the airplane and everything connected with it. The fear generalized from the cues of this airplane to the similar ones of other airplanes. This intense fear motivated responses of avoiding airplanes, and whenever any one of these responses was successful, it was reinforced by a reduction in the strength of the fear.

When all of the circumstances are understood, as in this case, there is no mystery about the phobia. In fact, such things as the avoidance of touching hot stoves or stepping in front of speeding cars usually are not called *phobias* because the conditions reinforcing the avoidance are understood. Our contention is that the laws of learning are exactly the same, although the conditions are often different and much more obscure, especially when the fear is elicited by the internal cues of thoughts or drives. . . .

Hysterical Symptoms

Our analysis of how hysterical symptoms are learned will start with a case of war neurosis when the causation is relatively recent and clear. This is case 12 reported by Grinker and Spiegel. . . . The patient had been directing the firing of an artillery platoon under great danger and with heavy responsibilities. After the acute phase of battle, he was lying on the ground exhausted when three shells landed nearby and exploded, blowing him off the ground each time. He was somewhat shaken up but otherwise fit. Half an hour later he found that he could not remove his right hand from his trouser pocket, having almost complete paralysis. He did not report sick and stayed with his company, regaining some strength in his arm but still suffering partial paralysis. Then he was sent to the hospital, where he was calm and cooperative and had no anxiety, tremor, or terror dreams.

His condition was not organic (i.e., it must have been learned) because under pentothal narcosis he was able to move his arm in all directions with ease. With reeducation and a short series of therapeutic interviews the condition cleared up. When it became obvious, however, that he was fit to return to his unit, he developed frank anxiety and tremor in both arms. The anxiety now appeared directly in relation to his battle experience and had to be dealt with as a separate problem. . . .

Regression

When the dominant habit is blocked by conflict or extinguished through nonreward, the next strongest response will be expected to occur. In an adult this often is a response that was reinforced and learned as a strong habit during childhood. When this happens, it is called regression. The more strongly the earlier habit was reinforced in the past (fixation), the more likely it is to be the next strongest one and hence to recur. Similarly, the more weakly the adult habit is established, the less interferences will be required to reduce its strength below that of the childhood one. . . .

Displacement

When the dominant response is prevented from occurring, the next strongest one will occur. As we have seen, when this other response owes its strength to the fact that it was reinforced during an earlier stage of the person's development, the process is called regression. But it is also possible for a response to be strong because of generalization. In this case the process is called displacement. . . .

Rationalization

. . . According to our analysis a rationalization involves the following steps: Social training of the type described . . . produces a need to have a logical explanation for obvious features of one's behavior and plans; the person tends to feel uneasy in the presence of any behavior that is illogical or unexplained. In some instances, however, the true explanation would provoke anxiety, guilt, or some other drive. Thus the person is motivated to find *some* explanation but to avoid the true one. When he happens to hit upon a rationalization that meets cultural standards of sensibleness, it is reinforced by a reduction in anxiety about unexplained behavior. Furthermore, if some of the sentences that would constitute a true explanation have been tending to come into the subject's mind and elicit anxiety or guilt, the alternative sentences in the rationalization tend to block them out and hence remove the anxiety or guilt that they felt. When this occurs, it serves as an additional reinforcement. . . .

Hallucinations

In connection with phobias and displacements we have already made use of the principle that increasing the strength of the drive raises the entire gradient of generalization, increasing the strength of all generalized responses and the range of stimuli that will elicit them. We have also found it useful to advance the hypothesis that internal cue-producing "responses," including images and perceptions, follow the same laws, including the principle of generalization, as do external responses. By putting these two together, we find that we have the nucleus of a theory for the influence of drive on perception. In extreme cases this might produce hallucinations. . . .

Projection

According to our analysis, the fact that members of our society tend to react in the same way to similar situations is one of the origins of projection. People tend to react in the same way because they are highly similar as biological organisms. Furthermore those people who frequently associate with each other usually come from similar social backgrounds and thus have been subjected to similar conditions of learning. Therefore each individual learns to expect his associates to react in the same way that he does; he learns that it is useful to judge others by himself. For example, the host who is cold may think that his guests are probably cold, verify this, and then build a fire in the fireplace.

Social interaction provides another origin of projection. When one is friendly, he is likely to behave in a way that elicits friendly behavior and feelings in others. When others are friendly, they are likely to elicit friendly behavior and feelings in you. Conversely, anger and aggressive behavior are likely to arouse anger in the other person and motivate "tit-for-tat" counteraggression. People thus learn to be on guard against others toward whom they are hostile. Furthermore, if someone hates you, he is likely to make you miserable so that you hate him. . . .

Repression as Learned

Repression is similar to suppression except it is much more strongly motivated and is automatic; that is, the patient does not say "I want to repress this." Because it is not under the control of verbal cues and is so strongly motivated, it is not within the patient's power to revoke. The patient may try to remember but be unable to, just as someone who is afraid of high places may try to jump across a narrow gap at a great height but may involuntarily come to a halt at the brink. According to our analysis, repression is the symptom of avoiding certain thoughts; it is reinforced by drive reduction in exactly the same way as the symptoms that have already been discussed. . . .

A serious misunderstanding of the goal of therapy often arises from the tendency of the general public to identify repression with all forms of restraint. Thus freedom from repression is confused with complete license. We are now in a position to clear up this misunderstanding and lay the basis for a rational policy by pointing out the proper distinctions.

Repression refers to the automatic tendency to stop thinking and avoid remembering. It is not under verbal control; the patient is not helped by being told or by telling himself to think. Its chief consequences have just been described. It eliminates the possibility of planned action but not the direct, unreasoned responses to drives and cues. Sometimes it may help to eliminate certain learned drives, but the primary, unlearned ones are unaffected.

Suppression also refers to stopping thinking and avoiding remembering. As long as it is operating its consequences are similar to those of repression, but since it is elicited by verbal cues, it can be highly selective and easily reversible and can show all the adaptive subtleties of the higher mental processes.

Repression as Learned, from Dollard and Miller, *Personality and Psychotherapy,* pp. 201–2, 220–21.

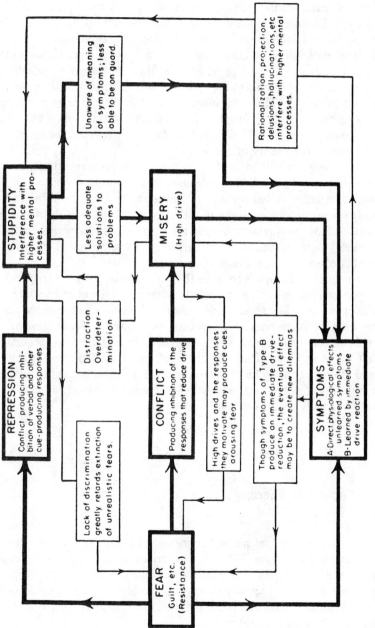

FIGURE 7.1 Interactions among factors in neurosis. Schematic diagram of some basic factors involved in neuroses. Arrows indicate "produces" or "tend to contribute to." Heavy arrows indicate major causal sequences; lighter arrows, subsidiary ones.

SOURCE: Dollard and Miller, *Personality and Psychotherapy* (New York: McGraw-Hill, 1950), p. 223.

Overt inhibition will be used by us to refer to the prevention of instrumental responses by strong conflicting responses that are not under verbal control. Thus a patient is sexually inhibited when he is unable to perform normal sexual responses. Because the same social conditions are likely to produce both repressions and inhibitions, repressions that stop thinking are likely to be correlated with inhibitions that stop action. Similarly the reduction in the fear that motivates one is likely to relieve the other. Whenever the conditions for learning or unlearning them are different, however, they will be expected to vary independently. Thus, it is often observed in the course of psychotherapy that a person may have "insight," i.e., have the correct sentences to describe his behavior, but may still be "sick," i.e., be unable to make the responses that would relieve the misery of conflict.

Over restraint will be used by us to refer to the prevention of an instrumental response by conflicting responses that are under verbal control. Since restraint is under verbal control, it can be much more highly selective and readily reversible and can show all the adaptive subtleties of the higher mental processes. Since suppression and restraint are both under verbal control, they are likely to be correlated. Furthermore, the suppression of provocative thoughts often aids in restraining undesirable acts.

The goal of therapy is to cause the patient to unlearn the crude responses of repression and inhibition, especially when they are out of line with current social conditions. For these crude responses he learns to substitute the much more discriminative ones of suppression and restraint. Since these are under verbal control, they have all the advantages of the higher mental processes. The result is not an escape from the mores of his group. To attempt this escape would almost certainly be maladaptive. In fact the foresight that comes with the removal of repression may help the patient to be on his guard and to exercise socially useful restraint. . . .

Main Factors in Therapy

The normal person uses his higher mental processes to solve emotional and environmental problems. When strong drives arise, he learns the responses that reduce these drives. The neurotic has failed to solve his problems in this way. Since he has not learned to solve his problems under the old conditions of his life, he must have new conditions before he can learn a better adjustment. What are these new conditions? . . .

Main Factors in Therapy, from Dollard and Miller, *Personality and Psychotherapy*, pp. 230–32.

In the therapist the patient finds someone with prestige who pays favorable attention, listens sympathetically, and holds out hope by having enough faith in an eventual cure to attempt treatment. The therapist shows exceptional permissiveness; he encourages the patient to express feelings in speech (but not in direct action) in the therapeutic situation. He does not condemn and is exceptionally able to tolerate the discussion of matters that have caused the patient's friends to show anxiety or disgust. The therapist's composure tends to be imitated by the anxious patient and thus has a reassuring effect. When the patient has always received severe disapproval, the therapist's calm accepting silence is experienced as a great relief and a striking intervention.

In addition to permitting free speech, the therapist commands the patient to say everything that comes to mind. By the free-association technique the therapist sets the patient free from the restraint of logic. The therapist avoids arousing additional anxiety by not cross-questioning. By encouraging the patient to talk and consistently failing to punish him, the therapist creates a social situation that is the exact opposite of the one originally responsible for attaching strong fears to talking and thinking. The patient talks about frightening topics. Since he is not punished, his fears are extinguished. This extinction generalizes and weakens the motivation to repress other related topics that were originally too frightening for the patient to discuss or even to contemplate. Where the patient cannot say things for himself, the therapist helps by attaching a verbal label to the emotions that are being felt and expressed mutely in the transference situation.

The therapist helps the patient to discriminate. First he helps to locate the problem by ruling out false hopes of miracle cures and by subtle means of emphasis. He points out the important difference between thoughts and actions. He contrasts disproportionate fears and actions with the realities of the situation. He brings out the contrast between the helpless past conditions of childhood, in which the fears were learned, and the present social conditions of the adult.

As the fears motivating repression are reduced by reassurance, extinction, and discrimination, and the patient is urged to think about his problems, mental life is greatly intensified. The removal of repressions restores the higher mental processes, which in turn help with further fear-reducing discriminations, reasoning, foresight, hope, and adaptive planning.

The patient begins to try better solutions in real life as fears are reduced and planning is restored. Some of the fear reduction generalizes from thinking and talking to acting. Becoming clearly aware of the problem and of the unrealistic basis of the fear serves as a challenge to try new modes of adjustment. As these new modes of adjustment are tried, the fears responsible for inhibitions are extinguished. When the new responses produce more satisfactory drive reduction, they are strongly reinforced. The reduction in drive and the extinction of fear reduce the conflict and misery. As the motivation behind the symptoms is reduced, they disappear.

In addition to permissiveness, to skill in decoding conflict, and to the ability to aid the patient to label and discriminate, the therapist has skill in "dosing" anxiety. Others have tried to punish the symptoms or force the patient to perform the inhibited act. Both of these methods tend to increase the fear and the conflict. The therapist concentrates on reducing the fears and other drives motivating repression and inhibition, or in other words, on analyzing "resistance." He tries to present the patient with a graded series of learning situations. He realizes that the patient must set his own pace and learn for himself; that it is the patient, not the therapist, who must achieve insight. He does not try to force the patient into any preconceived mold but helps him to develop his own potentialities in his own way within the limits imposed by our culture.

Each of the processes that we have just described goes on bit by bit with the others, and all interact. As fears are reduced by reassurance and extinction, the most lightly repressed thoughts begin to occur and may help the patient in some discriminations and problem solutions. As more strongly repressed and inhibitied responses appear, the cues that they produce elicit new and intense fears which must be eliminated by further extinction and discrimination. . . .

Selecting Patients Who Can Learn

A Learned, Not Organic, Disorder.   Sometimes it is possible for learning to compensate for a deficit produced by organic factors, but in order for the disorder itself to be unlearned it must obviously be one that is the product of learning. Thus learned (i.e., functional) disorders will be candidates for psychotherapy while organic ones will not. Sometimes the symptoms will be of mixed origin so that it will be difficult to decide whether psychotherapy will be effective. In case of doubt, organic factors must be ruled out by a thorough medical examination before psychotherapy is attempted. . . .

Reinforcement of Symptoms.   The more strongly the symptoms are reinforced the harder it will be to get rid of them, and hence the poorer the prognosis. Symptoms that produce an immediate great reduction in the drives involved in the neurotic conflict will be strongly reinforced even though their delayed effect may be an eventual increase in misery. The strong immediate reinforcement from relatively rapid drive reduction is another reason why drug addictions and perversions are difficult to treat. Secondary gains, such as financially important pensions or compensations in the case of an hysterical

---

Selecting Patients Who Can Learn, from Dollard and Miller, *Personality and Psychotherapy,* pp. 223–35.

paralysis, may also help to reinforce the symptoms and reduce the motivation for therapy. In this case the reinforcement is mediated by thoughts about the pension, but the causal relationship between these thoughts and reinforcement of the symptoms is not labeled by the patient.

Potential Rewards for Improvement.   The prognosis for therapy should be more favorable "the more the patient has to live for," or, in other words, the more rewards he will receive for improvement. . . .

Prerequisite Types of Social Learning.   The type of psychotherapy that we are describing (essentially the psychoanalytic technique for adult neurotic patients) was devised to remove repression and thus restore the higher mental processes. Certain minimum units of social learning are required before it can be used; it does not provide the conditions for giving the fundamental types of training that the small child receives in the family. Patients with basic deficits in this training will therefore be poor prospects. . . .

Free Association

Repression interferes with the neurotic's higher mental processes and prevents him from using these effectively in solving his emotional problems. This repression was learned in a social situation in which fear, shame, or guilt was attached to certain spoken words and generalized from them to thoughts. In therapy a new type of social situation is created, the opposite of that responsible for the learning of repression. In this new type of social situation the patient is urged to say whatever comes into his mind and to be especially sure to resist suppressing those words that he finds himself afraid, ashamed, or reluctant to say. As the patient says words that provoke fear or shame, the therapist does not punish him or show any signs of disapproval; he remains warm and accepting. In this way, the fear, shame, and guilt attached to talking about tabooed topics are extinguished. This extinction generalizes from speaking to thinking. It also generalizes from the painful but not completely repressed topics that are disucssed to similar topics that could not be discussed because they were repressed. As the drives motivating repression are weakened by such generalization, it becomes possible to talk about those additional topics that had been weakly repressed, and another cycle of extinction and generalization is initiated. Thus repression is gradually unlearned under permissive social conditions that are the opposite to the punitive ones under which it was learned. . . .

Free Association, from Dollard and Miller, *Personality and Psychotherapy,* p. 240.

Transference as a Generalized Response

The therapist is seeking data to make a construction about the patient's life. The patient gives some of these data directly in verbal form. The phenomenon of the transference gives other and new information which the patient cannot give directly. During the course of therapeutic work the patient transfers, or generalizes, to the therapist many strong emotional responses. A large part of these responses have never been labeled, so the patient cannot speak about what he is feeling. The patient fears, hates, pleads, but is not aware that he is doing so. These unwitting reactions are called *transference*. They provide important data because the therapist can label the reactions correctly though the patient cannot. . . .

Transferred Behavior in Everyday Life. The ordinary social presumption is that the responses of an individual are appropriate to the cues which excite them; that is, if a man is angry, he has been provoked; if a girl is in love, someone has been making love to her; if a person is frightened, he has reason to believe that danger threatens. In developing his technique of psychotherapy, Freud introduced a presumption of an opposite kind, i.e., that many responses of the patient are transferred to the therapist and not, in the ordinary sense of the word, learned. In the situation of free communication which Freud set up, he had excellent opportunity to observe that anger, love, or fear may appear in the absence of what, in ordinary life, would be considered adequate stimuli for them. These responses he viewed as transferred and called *transference.*

Transferred responses are not in any way unusual. They are everyday phenomena. A tennis player, meeting a new opponent, transfers his habits—good and bad—to this opponent. These responses will include more than his repertory of strokes. He may show his characteristic anger at losing, his intense competitiveness by playing better when he is at a disadvantage, or his "fear of success" by losing inexplicably just when the match is in his grasp. Such idiosyncrasies of top-flight players are well known to close followers of the sport.

Similarly, our immediate likes and dislikes of other persons in the ordinary course of life are transferred responses. Without knowing it themselves, strangers may present us with cues to which we immediately generalize love or hate. Sometimes these reactions persist, but often they are changed and we fail to understand how we could at first sight have "fallen so hard" for Jones or how we could have disliked so fine a person as Smith. Ordinarily, we pay little attention to these reactions, counting ourselves lucky when they win us

Transference as a Generalized Response, from Dollard and Miller, *Personality and Psychotherapy,* pp. 260-62, 280.

a strong friend and charging it off to "life" when someone appears instinctively prejudiced against us.

In psychotherapy, the case is different. Therapists notice these transferred reactions because they are part of the essential information which is needed to aid the patient. However earnestly he may try, if the patient does not know that he is capable of a certain kind of emotional reaction he may never be able to tell the therapist about it. He may be able to "reveal" himself only by having the reaction and directing it toward the therapist. The mildest patient will, for this reason, frequently surprise himself at the responses and emotions of which he is proved to be capable. . . .

Strong emotions occur during the course of therapeutic work. They are directed at the therapist and are felt by the patient to be real. They occur because the permissive conditions of therapy weaken repression and inhibition and thus increase the net strength of inhibited tendencies. These tendencies generalize more strongly to the therapist than to others just because the avoidance responses to him are less strong. These responses are ones which, having been long inhibited, have frequently never been labeled. By labeling these emotions while they are occurring, the therapist makes it possible for them to be represented in the patient's reasoning and planning activity. Frequently these responses block therapeutic progress. By identifying them and showing that they are generalized, the therapist mobilizes the learned drives to be reasonable and healthy, thus helping the patient to return to his project of self-understanding. Generalization of emotional response is not only useful but inevitable; it is not purposive and should not be thought of as a duel. . . .

Labeling

The neurotic is a person who is in need of a stock of sentences that will match the events going on within and without him. The new sentences make possible an immense facilitation of higher mental processes. With their aid he can discriminate and generalize more accurately; he can motivate himself for remote tasks; he can produce hope and caution within himself and aid himself in being logical, reasonable, and planful. By labeling a formerly unlabeled response he can represent this response in reasoning. . . .

If the patient is acting under strong emotional stimulation but has no label, the therapist will tentatively label the emotion within his own mind. If the patient has sentences without having the appropriate emotions attached, the therapist notes this (often dangerous) sign. If the patient fears without

---

Labeling, from Dollard and Miller, *Personality and Psychotherapy,* pp. 281–93.

reason, the therapist rehearses the fears and supplies the consolation to himself. Depending on his strategy, he may give such consolation then or withhold it.

If the patient lags, the therapist thinks the sentence which arouses learned drive within himself and communicates it to the patient—and so on throughout the range of behavior possibilities. The therapist sees the missing connections, makes the discriminations and generalizations, sees the hidden forces of the dream. The whole transaction must go on in his mind. He may use the construction gained in several different ways, i.e., to verify an innovation of the patient's, to select and repeat a chosen part of the patient's statement, or to announce a novel verbal unit which the patient cannot hit upon—but the therapist must have a correct construction or he cannot perform his function. . . .

Three Methods by Which Patients Learn New Verbal Responses

Apparently there are at least three ways in which the patient can acquire new verbal units. First, he can hit upon them by himself in the course of thinking out loud, with silent verification by the therapist. Second, certain of his responses can be strengthened by selective repetition on the part of the therapist. The therapist notes and repeats some things the patient says but neglects others. Third, the patient can acquire new responses by rehearsal from the therapist. The therapist can provide labeling when it is missing in the account that the patient gives. Only the last has traditionally been called "an interpretation." . . .

Method I: The Patient Himself Hits on Verbal Novelties.   The situation of free association helps the patient himself to create verbal novelties in a number of different ways. In the first place it puts upon him the compulsion to verbal experimentation and holds him to considerable periods of practice at the new skill. This experience is likely to be the first of the kind he has had. The therapist selectively encourages this freedom and fails to reward falling silent or thinking in routine ways. Further, as the patient hits on new lines of thought, the new verbal cues evoke anxiety responses. Such fearful reactions are gradually extinguished in the permissive situation of therapy. The patient speaks with reluctance or fright and finds that no punishment follows. Thereupon the patient "gains confidence"; that is, extinction effects generalize from the cues of sentences which have not been punished to other incipient sentences to which fear is attached. Both enforced experimentation and extinction of fear tend to create a new habit of "freedom of thought" which helps the patient to hit on verbal novelties. Some of these novelties constitute solutions to his problem at the mental level. It could be said of psychotherapy, therefore, that it tends automatically to make the patient more intelligent. . . .

Method II: Patient's Responses Strengthened by Selective Repetitions.
It is possible to have a marked effect on the patient's thinking even though the
therapist never "tells him anything new." The patient will be saying a great
many things. Some of these will seem more important to the therapist than
others. If the therapist will merely notice those that he thinks important and
neglect those he thinks not important, he can materially affect the patient's
thinking. Method II is appropriate when the patient presents a number of
different, confused, and jumbled facts and hypotheses. Since the therapist's
attention is a strong reward, any one of the patient's thoughts that he chooses
to notice is likely to be strengthened to its attendant cues. Such thoughts are
more likely to recur than those which are neglected. ...

Method III: Rehearsal: Teaching New Verbal Units. ... Rehearsal is
matched-dependent imitative behavior in the verbal sphere. It is learned with
considerable difficulty and over long periods of time in early life. In ordinary
terms, it constitutes listening.

If a verbal response is strongly opposed by anxiety, acquiring it by rehearsal has great advantages over waiting to hit upon the same response
oneself. Rehearsal causes the needed verbal response to occur in the patient
while the relevant cues are present. The patient may never learn to label an
emotion by himself because the label and the cues produced by the emotion
never occur at the same time. By his comment and the patient's rehearsal of
it, the therapist can make sure that the verbal response and cue and the
emotional response and cue are occurring at approximately the same time. ...

Reward for Rehearsal. Rehearsal, like any other habitual response,
must be rewarded, and it is. Many statements of the therapist which are
rehearsed provide secondary rewards, i.e., inhibit anxiety and offer hope.
Rehearsed responses frequently enable the patient to make discriminations
which reduce fear and thus reward rehearsal. ...

By teaching new verbal units we mean that the patient acquires such
responses and that they are attached to the correct cues—emotional, environmental, verbal, and instrumental. If the patient can hit upon these new units
himself or if cautious repetition will serve to teach him, there is no need for
the therapist to intervene further. However, the learning required is difficult.
The patient may not spontaneously produce the desired sentences when emotional stimuli are active; or he may fail correctly to pair the verbal with the
environmental event. Selective repetition may not have the opportunity to
strengthen responses which the patient makes because the needed responses do
not occur. In such a case, the therapist who does not actively teach new verbal
units must content himself with inferior results. If the patient cannot make the
required innovation in some manner, the therapist cannot help him by repetition or clarification. If the therapist is prevented by his theory from originating

and offering verbal units at the appropriate time and place, he may have to be satisfied at the end of therapy with a patient who is still befuddled on important issues. . . .

Teaching the Patient New Discriminations

Much of therapy consists of teaching the patient new discriminations. Some of these are achieved by directing the patient's attention toward relevant aspects of his environment or behavior. Some are achieved by contrasting the patient's present inhibitions with the lack of punishment in his present environment. Others are achieved by reviving memories of traumatic conditions of childhood, so that they can be contrasted with the different conditions of adult status. When the contrast is clear and immediate, the effect can be direct and automatic. Verbal responses play an important role in discriminations. They can help to revive memories of the past and to direct attention toward relevant details. They can function to make past neurotic habits seem similar to present ones but to make past conditions of reinforcement seem highly different from those of the present. They can also be the means of contrasting neurotic inhibitions of the present with real-life possibilities of gratification. Verbal cues can prevent generalization of anxiety from past to present. They can mediate responses inhibitory of anxiety. They can excite acquired drives which impel the patient to view the world realistically and to act intelligently. As anxiety is reduced by discrimination, reassurance, and extinction, new responses occur. When they reduce neurotic drives, these responses can be the basis of new habits which will permanently resolve the neurotic conflict. . . .

Gains from Restoring the Higher Mental Processes

This chapter will summarize and illustrate the therapeutic effects produced by removing repression, improving labeling, and thus restoring the higher mental processes. Before emphasizing the importance of these factors, however, it should be made perfectly clear that *significant therapeutic effects can also be produced in other ways without any improved labeling or "insight"* on the part

---

Teaching the Patient New Discriminations, from Dollard and Miller, *Personality and Psychotherapy,* p. 320.

Gains from Restoring the Higher Mental Processes, from Dollard and Miller, *Personality and Psychotherapy,* pp. 321–22.

of the patient. As has already been pointed out, we would expect the general reassuring and permissive attitude of the therapist to be able to produce a considerable reduction in fear. This reduction in fear should generalize from the therapeutic situation to the rest of the patient's life and thus reduce somewhat his conflict, misery, and motivation for symptoms. . . .

As has been pointed out, repression is not an all-or-none matter; the patient may be able to remember or think about certain things but have a strong disinclination to do so. Reducing the fear-motivating avoidance will not uncover any additional thoughts but will enable the patient to use the thoughts he has more freely and flexibly. Thus the patient's behavior will become more intelligent and adaptive.

Why Improved Labeling is Important.   The gains that have just been described usually are not enough to produce a complete cure in a severe neurosis. They must be supplemented by the removal of repression, by new labeling, and by the consequent improvement in discrimination and the higher mental processes. There are two reasons why the recovery of a repressed memory is likely to be especially significant in therapy: (1) the fact that the patient is able to overcome the repression means that the fear motivating it has *already* been considerably reduced, and (2) the restoration of the ability to think about the events and impulses involved is a useful addition to the higher mental processes. The removal of a repression is thus both a sign that therapy has occurred and the cause for additional therapeutic effects.

According to our hypothesis, the higher mental processes are carried on by means of verbal and other cue-producing responses. Therefore the failure to learn the proper verbal responses, or their removal by repression, eliminates the possibility of the specific higher functions that the missing responses would have performed. Conversely, when the repression is removed or the missing labels are learned, the patient begins to get the advantages of using these responses in the superior types of adaptive behavior that the higher mental processes allow. . . .

Eradicating Symptoms

Eliminating Symptoms by Eliciting Strong Incompatible Responses

A learned symptom, like any other response, can be eliminated by a stronger response that is incompatible with it. A therapist with sufficient authority can sometimes elicit a response strong enough to do this by issuing a command or

---

Eradicating Symptoms, from Dollard and Miller, *Personality and Psychotherapy,* pp. 383–91.

prohibition. The effect of such a command or prohibition can be strengthened greatly by hypnotism.

Another way of eliciting a strong response incompatible with the symptom is by severe physical punishment. Similarly, as has been pointed out, interpreting the function of a symptom or demonstrating its lack of organic basis elicits strong guilt that tends to cancel out the drive reduction and motivate the stopping of the symptom.

Finally the patient may find the therapeutic situation so anxiety-provoking that he is motivated to stop his symptoms so that he can leave therapy with a clear conscience. This process can occur unconsciously. . . .

Increased Drive from Interfering with Symptom.   According to our hypothesis, a learned symptom must produce a certain amount of reduction in the state of high drive motivating it. Therefore interfering with the symptom by any of the foregoing methods will be expected to throw the patient back into a state of high drive and conflict. This will tend to motivate the learning of new responses. These new responses may be either more adaptive ones or new, and possibly worse, symptoms. . . .

Increased Repression and Inhibition

Our analysis of the approach-avoidance conflict showed that making the feared goal seem less dangerous will cause the subject to come nearer, and that when he comes nearer, both the tendencies to approach and to avoid will be stronger. Thus, paradoxically, it will increase the amount of fear and conflict elicited and produce a negative therapeutic effect.

Conversely, an increase in the motivation to avoid can cause the subject to remain so far away from the feared goal that he is much less tempted and frightened. Although the example is clearest in a simple spatial situation, the same phenomenon will be expected in nonspatial situations. The first incipient responses will produce additional cues with learned connections for further responses in the sequence; and the cues produced by responses nearer the time of reinforcement elicit a still stronger tendency to continue. Similarly drive-producing responses seem to become stronger nearer the point of reinforcement. In this way a sequence of responses seems to pick up something analogous to momentum; it is much easier to stop the sequence before it gets started than after it is well under way. Therefore there is less conflict if the fear is strong enough to prevent any responses from getting started, or, in other words, if the patient gives up completely. This reduction in temptation, fear, and conflict will be expected to reduce somewhat the misery and motivation for symptoms. Therefore, increasing the strength of inhibition and repression by making the feared goal response seem much more dangerous can reduce some of the motivation for symptoms. This will be especially true if a large part of the drive is learned so that it can be prevented by inhibiting the responses producing it.

On the other hand, if a strong primary drive is involved, it will persist and be a chronic source of misery and motivation for symptoms. Therefore, whenever a socially acceptable goal response is available, the technique of reducing the conflict by increasing the inhibition would not be expected to be as effective as that of getting rid of the inhibition that is preventing the goal response from reducing the drive. . . .

Effects of Supportive Therapy

A child usually feels braver when one of its parents is present to defend it or rescue it from any danger. Similarly the moral support of the therapist as a prestigeful person may produce a considerable reduction in the strength of the patient's fear. Where the symptoms are the direct product of the fear, this will tend to weaken them. Furthermore, if the patient has strong needs for companionship, sympathetic attention, and encouragement, these can be gratified by the therapist. The net effect of this kind of a therapeutic relationship can be to reduce a considerable number of the learned drives motivating the symptoms and thus produce a remission in them. This is another mechanism that may be involved in the "transference cure." . . .

Removal of Inhibition and Repression

When the fear motivating repression is reduced, the patient is able to think of more adaptive ways to achieve his goals. When the fear motivating the inhibition of the goal responses is reduced, he is able to perform them and reduce his strong drives. Both the reduction in fear and the reduction in drive alleviate conflict and misery. Therefore, the subject is much less motivated to perform symptoms and is less reinforced for performing them. When this happens, the symptoms tend to drop out as the response of drinking water does when a person is no longer thirsty. . . .

Techniques of Therapeutic Intervention

Reward and Punishment: Approval and Disapproval

Approval and disapproval have strong learned reward and punishment value. They may be expressed either direcly and openly, or indirectly and subtly. In

Techniques of Therapeutic Intervention, from Dollard and Miller, *Personality and Psychotherapy,* pp. 394 –96.

ordinary social life they are commonly used methods of influencing another person's behavior. . . .

Permissiveness: Failing to Criticize or Show Alarm as a Powerful Intervention

When the patient has said something that frightens him, the therapist's calm, accepting manner can be a striking contrast to the type of social response that has reinforced the patient's fears. Under the right circumstances, merely saying nothing can therefore be a powerful intervention that reduces fear and is a condition for its extinction. We believe that this is a necessary condition for "catharsis," and that, by contrast, no relief is secured by expressing a suppressed feeling of emotion if the other person shows signs of strong disapproval. It is permissive also, when the patient asks about topics that are usually shied away from or discussed with embarrassment, for a therapist to give him calmly and objectively the information he wants. It is important for the therapist to be a good model. Since he has a great deal of prestige, his calmness, courage, and reasonableness are imitated by the patient, who thus tends to become somewhat calmer, more courageous, and more reasonable. Because it reduces the fear motivating repression and inhibition, the therapist's permissiveness is an effective form of intervention. . . .

Sympathetic Interest and Understanding

Warm, sympathetic interest and understanding are powerful rewards, particularly for those who are usually misunderstood and who have worn out the sympathy and interest of their friends. This is further heightened by the social prestige of the therapist. It rewards the patient for coming to therapy and continuing to try. Specific signs of interest may also reinforce specific types of behavior. . . .

Reassurance

Reassurance is a common way of reducing fear. By reducing fear, it can serve as a strong reward. The patient's friends usually have tried to reassure him, but this has not been entirely effective or else he would not have been forced to come to the therapist. The therapist is able to use this technique somewhat better than the friends because he is freer from anxiety himself and has more prestige. He will not have much better luck than the friends, however, with blanket reassurance. In order to succeed when they have failed, he must be better able to locate the important sources of fear and thus to give the right kind of reassurance exactly when and where it is most needed. Reassurance must be used to reduce fear so that new thoughts and acts can occur, and then to reward those new thoughts and actions. If it is used merely to make the patient feel better, it will only teach the patient to come for more reassurance. . . .

Motivating the Patient to Continue Therapy

The neurotic patient's basic conflicts are between thinking and repression and between goal responses and inhibitions. In addition to these, he also is in a conflict between seeking and avoiding therapy. This conflict is of special interest to the therapist. He must see that the balance is kept in favor of seeking therapy until the patient has completed his new learning. . . .

Since the outcome of a conflict is determined by the relative strength of the opposing tendencies, the stronger the patient's motivation is to continue, the more he will be able to bear fear, guilt, shame, and other drives motivating him to quit. It is therefore the therapist's task to maintain the patient's motivation for therapy at a reasonably high level.

The patient's motivation for therapy comes from his misery, the inconvenience of his symptoms, his desire to achieve better goals in life, his fears that he may be going crazy or will "do something awful," and pressure from his friends and relatives. Different ones of these motives may be in the foreground with different patients. If the patient thinks that the therapist will cure him, these motivations elicit the response of seeking therapy. . . .

Prerequisites of a Psychotherapist

It may be worthwhile to name four attributes of the therapist as a teacher in the situation of psychotherapy. We suggest that he should be *mentally free, empathic, restrained,* and *positive.* These words refer only roughly to what we mean so we shall enlarge upon each.

Mental Freedom

The therapist must have much less anxiety than the patient or the general public about the "worst" things that bother patients. He must be able to

---

Motivating the Patient to Continue Therapy, from Dollard and Miller, *Personality and Psychotherapy,* pp. 399, 403.

Prerequisites of a Psychotherapist, from Dollard and Miller, *Personality and Psychotherapy,* pp. 409–13.

rehearse what the patient says without anxiety. No degree of fear should compete with his tendencies to "complete the account." When the patient stops, the therapist should be able to carry on where the patient and others would be afraid. This lack of fear on his own part enables him to be permissive and therefore to set up one of the fundamental conditions which aid the patient. . . .

Empathy

Except in the case of excessive fear, the therapist should have the conventional emotional responses attached to the sentences that he rehearses. If the patient refers to a pitiable situation, the therapist should, as he silently repeats the patient's words, feel a twinge of pity. When the patient reports a situation where rage is appropriate, the therapist should feel the stirring of those rage responses. The account of a fearful situation should have its appropriate effect on the therapist.

When the therapist feels an emotional response along with the common humankind but the patient apparently does not, the therapist is in possession of some important information, i.e., that the patient does not have appropriate emotions attached to his sentences. The therapist should likewise feel in miniature the relaxation and relief which the patient feels when a correct verbal solution has been hit on. It may also be that various other kinds of empathy are important, such as a "sense of humor." . . .

Restraint

The therapist must resist the strong tendency to conduct the therapeutic interview as a conversation. He must subordinate himself to his strategy of cure and say nothing that does not further this strategy. Whereas the patient vows "utterance," the therapist vows relative silence. It is our belief, incidentally, that almost all therapists talk too much or, rather, too loosely. They find it hard to subordinate themselves to the listening role. They interrupt the patient, prompt the patient, give him unnecessary reassurance, paraphrase his statements without essential clarification, and otherwise vocalize in a useless manner. . . .

Positive Outlook

The therapist must believe—and, better, believe on the basis of his own experience—that repression can be revoked and that neurotic conflicts can be eliminated. How else can he have the courage to drive and to help the patient along the blind way he must go? He must believe in the patient's capacity to learn. . . .

Confronting Failure in Psychotherapy

Assuming, however, that we have in hand a patient with strong repressions and severe conflict, we will indicate some of the circumstances under which therapy may fail.

1. If the Patient Is Too Proud to Come to the Therapist.   Mention of this may seem naïve, but many who do need help do not try therapy for this reason. If they do not try they cannot change. Such persons may feel that it is a humiliation to admit being in need of help, and their resentment of the therapist is immediately raised by this circumstance. Friends and family may stand helplessly by while such a proud person destroys himself.

2. If the Patient Cannot Meet the Therapist's Conditions of Treatment.   Obviously, in this case again, the therapeutic relationship never occurs. We mention this case because, though the individual therapist does not fail, the craft or institution of psychotherapy does. Psychotherapy fails in its full social effect if all who need it cannot avail themselves of it. The patient may not be able to pay the therapist's fees—as is true of many lower-class and middle-class patients. They may not be able to come at the hours when the therapist can see them. Or they may not be able to pay long enough and stay long enough to the necessary therapeutic work. . . .

3. If the Patient Is Unable to Learn.   Since psychotherapy is by its nature a learning situation, the patient who is for any reason unable to learn cannot profit by it. The stupid, defective, or brain-injured are thus at a disadvantage. The therapist cannot restore higher mental processes if the necessary brain mechanisms do not exist. . . .

4. If the Patient Is Not Strongly Motivated to "Bear Therapy."   Many patients who urgently need psychotherapy attempt the relationship but then stop. They find the work required of them too painful and their own motivation to continue is too weak to overcome this avoidance. It is important for the therapist at the earliest possible moment to show the patient that psychotherapy is the *only* way out of his neurotic conflict and thus get the full benefit of neurotic pain as a motive for the work. Persons without intense conflict are little likely to continue when the attempt at free association produces much pain.

5. If Conditions of Therapy Are Not Arranged in a Proper, Benign Way.   The therapist may not know how to set up a permissive atmosphere.

Confronting Failure in Psychotherapy, from Dollard and Miller, *Personality and Psychotherapy,* pp. 424–27.

He may cross-question his patient and thus raise unbearable anxiety. He may fail to compel the patient to utterance and so never get him started on his proper work. Under such circumstances, naturally, the anxiety attached to verbal cues cannot be extinguished and the patient will remain without the benefit of improved higher mental life.

6. If the Therapist Cannot Spot Repression Areas.   The therapist cannot repair what he cannot locate. His failure may be due to lack of correct theory, lack of specific, controlled practice, or presence of some repression in the therapist. Psychotherapy is a special skill which requires special training. It must be actually practiced under supervision. It is hard to learn from books. Psychotherapeutic skill does not come as a by-product of any academic degree whatsoever. It is an applied science based on a fundamental science whose nature is not yet entirely understood. We believe, however, that the laws of learning must be fundamentally involved.

7. If the Therapist Does Not Understand Transferred Behavior.   In this case, the therapist cannot keep the patient "on the rails" and at his proper work. He loses essential knowledge as to the nature of inhibited drives. The therapist will find his patient motionless and the work blocked. He must be able to identify the transferred emotional response, convince the patient that it has not been "earned" in the course of therapy, and demonstrate that it does obstruct therapeutic advance. Motives to be reasonable and to be well are thus called out to compete with the tendency to luxuriate in obstructive behavior. Skill in identifying and exposing the negative transference is thus essential to getting the patient back at his work.

8. If the Patient Does Not Try New Responses Outside the Therapeutic Situation.   The patient must generalize the new verbal units learned in the therapeutic situation. He must likewise generalize emotional responses, first practiced toward the therapist, to persons in his actual life. If the patient cannot thus generalize, he remains fixed in the impermanent and unreal therapeutic situation. . . .

9. If Real Life Does Not Reward New Responses of Patient.   The goal of the whole therapeutic situation is to resolve the neurotic conflict and to set in place of it a positive, drive-reducing habit. The conditions of real life must be favorable if new responses are to become strong habits. On the one hand, the real-life conditions must fail to reinforce the inhibitory arm of the conflict, i.e., the patient must find in fact that self-expression is not dangerous. On the other hand, the responses produced by the inhibited drive of the conflict must be strongly rewarded. . . .

10. If Reality Circumstances Do Not Remain Favorable.   After therapy, habits retain the same changeability that they had before. Favorable circumstances must not only prevail at the time of the therapeutic sessions, but must be maintained; otherwise the misery of an unsatisfied drive, if not the conflict, will return. Such real-life conditions may improve or deteriorate after therapy. If the latter, therapeutic results may be lost. When this is the case, the therapist is powerless. There is no way of guaranteeing a permanent therapeutic result when the therapist cannot control the conditions which permit the reduction of strong drives.

8

PSYCHOTHERAPY AS MODELING AND VICARIOUS PROCESSES

Albert Bandura

Albert Bandura was born in Canada in 1925 and studied at the University of British Columbia and then at the University of Iowa, where he earned a Ph.D. in 1952. He has spent virtually his entire career at Stanford University, an affiliation he has held since 1953. Bandura was a fellow of the Center for Advanced Study in the Behavioral Sciences during the 1969–70 season. In 1969 he issued his *magnum opus* in which he articulated his comprehensive system of *humanistic behaviorism* under the title of *Principles of Behavior Modification.* In 1974 Bandura was elected president of the American Psychological Association.

Unlike B. F. Skinner, who saw the environment as extraneously controlling the individual, Bandura views individuals as capable of autonomously structuring the contingencies of the environment to their own good or ill. His system is further differentiated from Skinner's operant behaviorism due to his emphasis on social-learning theory: that is, the role played by vicarious reinforcement and modeling or the observation of consequences accruing to others because of their behavior. Individuals can even regulate their own behavior by virtue of self-administered consequences.

Bandura has been remarkably successful in modifying phobic disorders through modeling techniques, i.e., by (1) structuring conditions so that the client can perform the desired behavior to a point of being fearless and skillful; (2) seeing that the experiences issue in success; and (3) having the client perform acts progressively from the simple or easy to the more difficult, resulting not only in enduring behavioral change but in a sense of personal efficacy. By refining modeling procedures, Bandura produced a potent therapeutic technique for coping with phobic behavior. For example, to enable a phobic to cope with an aversion to snakes, the phobic is induced to be present in a room with a person unafraid of snakes. Gradually approaching more closely to the snake, the phobic then touches the snake with a heavy gloved covering extending almost to the shoulders. Successive stages follow: one of a lighter glove, then barehanded, and finally actually holding the snake during increasingly longer periods. By this technique the phobic conquers fear within a matter of a few hours. Bandura also maintains that learning is peculiarly social, occurring by observation, by example, and even vicariously.

Behavior Modification Through Modeling And Vicarious Processes

One of the fundamental means by which new modes of behavior are acquired and existing patterns are modified entails modeling and vicarious processes. Indeed, research conducted within the framework of social-learning theory . . . demonstrates that virtually all learning phenomena resulting from direct experiences can occur on a vicarious basis through observation of other persons' behavior and its consequences for them. Thus, for example, one can acquire intricate response patterns merely by observing the performances of appropriate models; emotional responses can be conditioned observationally by witnessing the affective reactions of others undergoing painful or pleasurable experiences; fearful and avoidant behavior can be extinguished vicariously through observation of modeled approach behavior toward feared objects without any adverse consequences accruing to the performer; inhibitions can be induced by witnessing the behavior of others punished; and, finally, the expression of well-learned responses can be enhanced and socially regulated through the actions of influential models. Modeling procedures are, therefore, ideally suited for effecting diverse outcomes including elimination of behavioral deficits, reduction of excessive fears and inhibitions, transmission of self-regulating systems, and social facilitation of behavioral patterns on a group-wide scale.

Vicarious phenomena are generally subsumed under a variety of terms. Among those in common usage are *modeling, imitation, observational learning, identification, copying, vicarious learning, social facilitation, contagion,* and *role-playing.* . . .

Three Effects of Modeling Influences

To elucidate vicarious influences it is essential to distinguish among different types of behavioral modifications resulting from exposure to modeling stimuli, but the differentiation must be made in terms of more fundamental criteria than those discussed above. There is abundant evidence . . . that exposure to

---

Albert Bandura, *Principles of Behavior Modification* (New York: Holt, Rinehart and Winston, 1969), pp. 118, 120, 133, 136, 138, 139, 141, 142, 143, 151, 152, 175, 192.

modeling influences has three clearly different effects, each of which is determined by a separate set of variables. First, an observer may acquire new response patterns that did not previously exist in his behavioral repertoire. In demonstrating this *observational learning* or *modeling effect* experimentally, it is necessary for a model to exhibit novel responses which the observer has not yet learned to make and which he must later reproduce in a substantially identical form. Any behavior that has a very low or zero probability of occurrence in the presence of appropriate stimuli qualifies as a novel response.

Second, observation of modeled actions and their consequences to the performer may strengthen or weaken inhibitory responses in observers. These *inhibitory* and *disinhibitory effects* are evident when the incidence of imitative and nonmatching behavior is increased, generally as a function of having witnessed a model experience positive outcomes, and decreased by having observed a model undergo punishing consequences.

Third, the behavior of others often serves merely as discriminative stimuli for the observer in facilitating the occurrence of previously learned responses in the same general class. This *response facilitation effect* can be distinguished from disinhibition and modeling by the fact that no new responses are acquired; disinhibitory processes are not involved because the behavior in question is socially sanctioned and, therefore, has rarely, if ever, incurred punishment. A simple example of social facilitation is provided in situations where a person gazes intently into a display window and passersby respond in a similar manner. . . .

No Trial Learning Therapy

When a person observes a model's behavior, but otherwise performs no overt responses, he can acquire the modeled responses while they are occurring only in cognitive, representational forms. Any learning under these conditions occurs purely on an observational or covert basis. This mode of response acquisition has accordingly been designated as no-trial learning, . . . because the observer does not engage in any *overt responding trials,* although he may require multiple *observational trials* in order to reproduce modeled stimuli accurately. Several theoretical analyses of observational learning . . . assign a prominent role to representational mediators that are assumed to be acquired on the basis of a contiguity learning process. According to the author's formulation, observational learning involves two representational systems—an *imaginal* and a *verbal* one. After modeling stimuli have been coded into images or words for memory representation they function as mediators for subsequent response retrieval and reproduction. . . .

Attentional Processes

Since repeated contiguous stimulation alone does not always result in response acquisition, it is evident that additional conditions are required for the occurrence of observational learning. Simply exposing persons to distinctive sequences of modeled stimuli does not in itself guarantee that they will attend closely to the cues, that they will necessarily select from the total stimulus complex the most relevant events, or that they will even perceive accurately the cues to which their attention has been directed. An observer will fail to acquire matching behavior, at the sensory registration level, if he does not attend to, recognize, or differentiate the distinctive features of the model's responses. To produce learning, therefore, stimulus contiguity must be accompanied by discriminative observation. . . .

Retention Processes and Rehearsal Operations

The discussion thus far has been concerned with sensory registration and symbolic coding of modeling stimuli. Another basic component function involved in observational learning, but one that has been virtually ignored in theories of imitation, concerns the retention of modeled events. In order to reproduce social behavior without the continued presence of external modeling cues a person must retain the original observational inputs in some symbolic form. This is a particularly interesting problem in instances where persons acquire social patterns of behavior observationally and retain them over extended periods of time, even though the response tendencies are rarely, if ever, activated into overt performance until attainment of the age or social status at which the activity is appropriate and permissible. . . .

Among the many variables governing retention processes, *rehearsal operations* effectively stabilize and strengthen acquired responses. The level of observational learning can, therefore, be considerably enhanced through practice or overt rehearsal of modeled response sequences, particularly if the rehearsal is interposed after natural segments of a larger modeled pattern. . . .

Symbolic Representations of Modeled Patterns

The third major component of modeling phenomena involves the utilization of symbolic representations of modeled patterns in the form of imaginal and verbal contents to guide overt performances. It is assumed that reinstatement of representational schemes provides a basis for self-instruction regarding the manner in which component responses must be combined and sequenced to produce new patterns of behavior. The process of representational guidance is essentially the same as response learning under conditions where a person behaviorally follows an externally depicted pattern, or is directed through a series of instructions to enact novel response sequences. The only difference is that, in the latter cases, performance is directed by external cues, whereas, in delayed modeling, behavioral reproduction is monitored by symbolic counterparts of absent stimuli. . . .

Incentive and Motivational Processes

A person may acquire and retain modeled events and possess the capabilities for skillful execution of modeled behavior, but the learning may rarely be activated into overt performance if negative sanctions or unfavorable incentive conditions obtain. Under such circumstances, when positive incentives are introduced observational learning is promptly translated into action. . . . Incentive variables not only regulate the overt expression of matching behavior, but they also affect observational learning by exerting selective control over the modeling cues to which a person is most likely to be attentive. Further, they facilitate selective retention by activating deliberate coding and rehearsal of modeled responses that have high utilitarian value. . . .

Establishment of New Response Patterns through Modeling

Research and theoretical interpretations of learning processes have focused almost exclusively on a single mode of response acquisition which is exemplified by the operant or instrumental conditioning paradigm. In this procedure an organism is instigated, in one way or another, to perform responses, and approximations progressively closer to the desired final behavior are selectively reinforced. It is generally assumed that complex human behavior is likewise developed under naturalistic conditions through this type of gradual shaping process. . . .

Treatment of Autism through Modeling

Many of the generalized behavior disorders that are most intractable are characterized by gross deficits not only in behavior but also in the basic psychological functions essential for learning. The more severe cases, such as autistic children and adult schizophrenics, generally manifest little or no functional speech; they lack social skills that are conducive to reciprocally rewarding relationships; and interpersonal stimuli, which ordinarily serve as the principle medium of social influence, often have relatively little impact on them. Since human behavior is largely acquired through modeling and regulated by verbal cues and symbolic reinforcers, profound deficiencies in functions of this nature create major obstacles to treatment. These issues are best exemplified by the treatment of autism. . . .

One of the most provocative behavioral approaches to the treatment of autism, in which modeling procedures figure prominently, has been developed by Lovaas and his colleagues. . . . The therapeutic program is based on the view that the total rehabilitation of autistic and schizophrenic children can be best achieved through the establishment of stimulus functions which make one amenable to social influence. This process primarily involves developing children's responsiveness to modeling cues, increasing the discriminative value of stimulus events so that children attend and respond appropriately to aspects of their environment that they have previously ignored, and endowing social approval and other symbolic stimuli with reinforcing properties. After a strong modeling set has been created, and children have become adequately responsive to environmental influences, the major task of broadening children's social and intellectual competencies can be effectively carried out by parents, teachers, and other agents. Since interpersonal communication and social learning are extensively mediated through language, the development of linguistic skills is also selected as a central objective of treatment. . . .

Vicarious Extinction

Emotional response patterns can be extinguished as well as acquired on a vicarious basis. Vicarious extinction of fears and behavioral inhibitions is achieved by having persons observe models performing fear-provoking behavior without experiencing adverse consequences. How avoidance response can be extinguished without having been elicited can be best explained in terms of a dual-process theory of avoidance behavior. As noted in the previous discussion of causal processes, conditioned aversive stimuli evoke emotional arousal that exerts some degree of control over instrumental responding. It would follow from this theory that if the arousal capacity of a threatening stimulus is extinguished, then both the motivation and one set of controlling stimuli for avoidance behavior are removed. Black has shown that neutralization of an aversive stimulus through classical extinction procedures alone markedly facilitates subsequent elimination of avoidance behavior. . . .

Vicarious Learning

In addition to the acquisition of instrumental and emotional behaviors through observational experiences, exposure to modeled events may strengthen or weaken observers' inhibitions of well-learned response patterns. The occurrence of *inhibitory effects* is indicated when, as a function of observing negative response consequences to a model, observers show either decrements in the same class of behavior, or a general reduction of responsiveness. It should be noted that when the subject witnesses behavior that is subsequently punished, the response-facilitative effects of modeling cues are counteracted by the suppressive effects of adverse outcomes. When these opposing influences are of comparable strength, persons who have observed modeled behavior punished and those who have had no exposure to the model may display an equally low incidence of response.

9

PSYCHOTHERAPY BY RECIPROCAL INHIBITION

Joseph Wolpe

The following is a brief autobiography by Joseph Wolpe.

I was born on April 20, 1915. I spent my entire childhood in the Union of South Africa where my parents had immigrated as children at the very beginning of the twentieth century. They followed Jewish religious custom but not very strictly. My maternal grandmother, a very religious woman, lived either with us or near us at all times until she died when I was about sixteen. Though she failed to imbue me with her own piety, her influence was considerable and led to a strongly theistic orientation that made me feel very much at one with the writings of Maimonides.

During my later years at high school and at the beginning of my university career I inevitably came into contact with people who held materialist beliefs. The strongest attacks upon my theism came from a cousin three years older, Maurice A. Millner, now a scintillating member of the Law Faculty at University College, London. We had many long arguments, but though I fought valiantly and stuck to my beliefs, I always felt uncomfortably at a disadvantage because the concrete facts were always on his side. At the age of twenty I immersed myself in all the Kantian critiques, especially the *Critique of Pure Reason,* and subsequently went on to Hume and a chain of later philosophers, of whom the most impressive were Bergson, Whitehead, G. E. Moore, and Bertrand Russell. The last two were particularly influential, Russell most of all in his *Inquiry into Meaning and Truth.* Through the additive influence of these philosophers my theoretical dualism was replaced by a physical monism. In the meantime, the medical curriculum had been supplying many kinds of information which really did seem to favor a materialist conception of the universe. From that time onward I became more and more firmly convinced that the only reality is material reality—of different forms and different degrees of complexity.

As far as psychology is concerned, after an initial skepticism about psychoanalytic theories, I came during my early university years to accept Freud's ideas about human behavior. To begin with, Freud seemed to share my materialist orientation. My first doubt arose when in 1944 I read a book called *Sigmund Freud* by Bartlett, who claimed that Malinowski had shown the inapplicability of Freud's theory of oedipal development, and that failed to support that theory. Finally I gathered from various sources that psychoanalytic theory was not accepted by the Russians. Puzzled by this, I turned to Pavlov towards whose works I had already cast a lingering eye toward the end of my medical student days. For several months in 1945–46 I spent many of the vacant hours of a declining military establishment with *Conditioned Reflexes,* summarizing every experiment and writing comments. I was greatly impressed by the experiments but quite unhappy about Pavlov's theoretical formulations.

At the end of 1945 I went on holiday to Capetown where a friend of mine was doing postgraduate studies in psychology under James G. Taylor. The latter had become an enthusiastic follower of Hull and incited me to read *Principles of Behavior.* I found this much more satisfactory as a framework for Pavlovian experiments, and readily translatable into neurophysiological terms.

Early in 1946 I came across Masserman's *Behavior and Neurosis* and was entranced by his experiments but repelled by the contortions by which he consistently tried to squeeze his findings into psychoanalytic theory. I decided to do experiments along the lines of his in order to clarify some points that his work left obscure. These experiments revealed principles of learning that applied to both animal neuroses and those of human beings.[1] . . .

Wolpe was born in Johannesburg, South Africa. He was educated at the University of Witwatersrand in Johannesburg, where in 1939 he received the M.B. and B.Ch. (medical qualifying degree), and the M.D. in 1948. He began his professional career in 1939 with a medical and surgical internship at Johannesburg General Hospital, and engaged in general practice in 1940. During the war years he served as captain in the South African Medical Corps. With the termination of this post in 1946, he undertook postgraduate studies in psychiatry for two years, which included investigations on experimental neuroses. While conducting private psychiatric practice, he inaugurated his academic career in 1948 as a lecturer in psychiatry at the University of Witwatersrand. During the 1956–57 school year, he was a fellow at the Center for Advanced Study in the Behavioral Sciences at Stanford University; then he returned to his former position at the University of Witwatersrand, but confined himself to the treatment of neuroses. From 1960–65 he was professor of psychiatry at the University of Virginia, except for a leave of absence to the University of London during the 1962–63 school year. In 1965 he became professor of psychiatry at Temple University Medical School.

Wolpe's psychotherapy by reciprocal inhibition restricts itself to the treatment of neurotics. Psychotics, such as schizophrenics, are organically disordered, whereas neurotic disturbance is grounded in anxiety. Reciprocal inhibition calls for the association of a response that is antagonistic to the one selected for extinction. This technique, which he discovered in his research with cats, calls for a systematic desensitization of anxiety by training the patient in progressive relaxation.

---

[1]Correspondence from Joseph Wolpe to the editor.

Then (after constructing a list of hierarchically ordered anxieties) he begins by stimulating the patient with desirable responses antagonistic to the anxiety-provoking ones and works from the weakest anxiety upward until all anxiety is displaced by inhibition. Neurotic cures may occasionally take place spontaneously as the consequence of fortuitous reciprocal inhibition.

Wolpe is best known for his *Psychotherapy by Reciprocal Inhibition* (1958), an expanded version of his paper "Reciprocal Inhibition as the Main Basis of Psychotherapeutic Effects" (1954). He also has to his credit approximately fifty papers, most of them treating some phase of his theory of psychotherapy. He is one of the editors (with Andrew Salter and L. J. Reyna) of *The Conditioning Therapies* (1964) and (with A. A. Lazarus) of *Behavior Therapy Techniques* (1966). His more recent publication, *The Practice of Behavior Therapy* (1969, 1974), is the most definitive statement of his system of psychotherapy.

Learning Theory as the Basis of Behavior Therapy

Counterconditioning: Reciprocal Inhibition Principle

We may note, in passing, some resemblances between the experimental and human neuroses. The latter, too, are persistent, and exhibit generalization; and while severe inhibition of eating is only occasionally seen, interferences with other adaptive functions are extremely common. A person will be unable to work if agoraphobia keeps him at home, of if claustrophobia makes his office unbearable. Fears of people may impair his social life; and anxieties related to sexual stimuli may cause sexual inadequacies—impotence or frigidity.

Because anxiety so decisively inhibited feeding in the neurotic cats, it seemed reasonable to think that if food were made available in circumstances in which anxiety was much weaker, feeding might occur and the anxiety be inhibited. It was possible to experiment with this idea in the various rooms mentioned above to which anxiety had generalized. The animal was offered food in them in descending order of similarity to the experimental laboratory. A room could always be found where the animal would eat despite showing some anxiety. In the course of eating a number of pellets of meat there, its anxiety in that room would subside entirely, and it would then accept food in a room more like the experimental laboratory. Proceeding systematically from room to room, it became possible to get the animal to eat in the experimental cage, and eventually entirely to overcome the anxiety responses that previously had been so powerfully aroused there.

Learning Theory as the Basis of Behavior Therapy, from Joseph Wolpe, *The Practice of Behavior Therapy,* 2nd ed. (New York: Pergamon, 1974), pp. 17–19.

These experiments led to the formulation of the reciprocal inhibition principle: *If a response inhibiting anxiety can be made to occur in the presence of anxiety-evoking stimuli, it will weaken the bond between these stimuli and the anxiety.*

In human neuroses, a considerable number of anxiety-inhibiting responses have been successfully used to overcome neurotic anxiety-response habits as well as other neurotic habits. For example, assertive responses are used to overcome neurotic anxieties that inhibit effective action towards those persons with whom the patient has to interact. The essence of the therapist's role is to encourage the outward expression, under all reasonable circumstances, of the feelings and action tendencies previously inhibited by anxiety. Each act of assertion to some extent reciprocally inhibits the concurrent anxiety and slightly weakens the anxiety-response habit. Similarly, relaxation responses can be employed to bring about systematic decrements of anxiety-response patterns to many classes of stimuli.

There are a number of ways of bringing about inhibition of anxiety in which it is not obvious that the activity concerned is reciprocally inhibitory of anxiety. In one such process, one makes use of the consistent reinforcement of the motor responses to inhibit an accompanying anxiety—intra-response reciprocal inhibition. Another possibility is to employ a mild electrical stimulus as an anxiety inhibitor—apparently as a function of external inhibition.[2] Then, it is possible to condition a neutral stimulus to counter-anxiety activity by repeatedly presenting that stimulus at the moment of cessation of a strong electrical stimulus; and subsequently, the counter-anxiety effect of that stimulus can be used to inhibit anxiety from various sources.

Finally, it seems likely that anxiety can sometimes be inhibited as a kind of "protective" reaction to its own strong and sustained evocation—transmarginal inhibition.[3] This process may well be the basis of the effects of "flooding."

The reciprocal inhibition principle also comes into play in overcoming responses other than anxiety. It has a vital role in verbal and conceptual (cognitive) relearning. The reciprocal inhibition of a previously learned verbal response by a newly evoked one is the basis of "retroactive" inhibition—the weakening of the original response.[4] Reciprocal inhibition is also the basis of the conditioned inhibition of obsessional and compulsive habits by aversive therapy. A painful faradic shock, or other strong stimulus, inhibits the undesirable behavior, with the result that a measure of conditioned inhibition of the latter is established. Again, in the process of replacing an established motor habit by a new one, the evocation of the new motor response involves an

---

[2]I. P. Pavlov, *Conditioned Reflexes*, trans. G. V. Anrep (New York: Dover, 1927).

[3]Pavlov, *Conditioned Reflexes;* B. M. Teplov, "Some Results of the Study of Strength of the Nervous System in Man," in *Typological Features of Higher Nervous Activity in Man,* vol. 2, ed. B. M. Teplov (Moscow: Akademiia Pedagogicheskikh, RSFSR).

[4]C. E. Osgood, "Meaningful Similarity and Interference in Learning," *Journal of Experimental Psychology* 38 (1946):132.

inhibition of the old. For example, when assertive behavior is being instigated, at the same time that the expression of "positive" feelings reciprocally inhibits anxiety, the new motor action inhibits the preexisting motor response tendency. To take a simpler example, if one is being taught to play a backhand tennis stroke by rotating on the right foot, one inevitably inhibits one's tendency to play off the left foot.

Positive Reconditioning

The conditioning of new motor habits or ways of thinking may accompany elimination of unadaptive autonomic responses, as in the example of assertive training just given. But frequently new habits of action or of thought are induced in contexts that do not involve anxiety. An instance of this is the conditioning treatment of enuresis nocturna. By arranging for the patient to be awakened by an alarm as soon as the first drop of urine is excreted during sleep, the waking reaction is conditioned to the imminence of urination, and this subsequently leads to the development of an inhibition of the tendency to urinate in response to bladder stimulation during sleep.[5] Another example is the conditioning of effective study behavior in individuals who have unproductive habits or fritter away their time when they should be working.

Successful conditioning of new habits always involves the use of "reward" of one kind or another. It sometimes suffices to supply these on an *ad hoc* basis, but in recent years there has been increasing formal use of Skinner's operant conditioning principles to remove and replace undesirable habits.[6] In order to establish a new behavior pattern in a particular situation, the desired response has to be elicited and frequently rewarded, while the undesired behavior is consistently not rewarded and even punished. For example, anorexia nervosa has been successfully treated by making social rewards such as the use of a radio or the granting of companionship contingent on eating, withdrawing these rewards when the patient fails to eat.[7] Various types of behavior in schizophrenics have been treated on the same principle and major and lasting changes of behavior have been procured, even in patients who had been hospitalized for years.[8]

---

[5]H. G. Jones, "The Behavioral Treatment of Enuresis Nocturna," in *Behavior Therapy and the Neuroses*, ed. H. J. Eysenck (Oxford: Pergamon Press, 1960); S. H. Lovibond, "The Mechanism of Conditioning Treatment of Enuresis," *Behavior Research and Therapy* 1 (1963):17.

[6]B. F. Skinner, *Science and Human Behavior* (New York: Macmillan, 1953).

[7]A. J. Bachrach, W. J. Erwin, and J. P. Mohr, "The Control of Eating Behavior in an Anorexic by Operant Conditioning Techniques," in *Case Studies in Behavior Modification*, ed. L. Ullmann and L. Krasner (New York: Holt, Rinehart & Winston, 1965).

[8]O. R. Lindsley, "Operant Conditioning Methods Applied to Research in Chronic Schizophrenia," *Psychiat. Res. Rep.* 5 (1956):118; C. D. Williams, "The Elimination of Tantrum Behavior by Extinction Procedures: Case Report," *Journal of Abnormal Social Psychology* 59 (1959):269; T. Ayllon, "Intensive Treatment of Psychotic Behavior by Stimulus Satiation and Food Reinforcement," *Behavior Research and Therapy* 1 (1963):53;G. C. Davison, "A Social Learning Therapy Programme with an Autistic Child," *Behavior Research and Therapy* 2 (1964): 149.

Experimental Extinction

This is the progressive weakening of a habit through the repeated evocation without reinforcement of the responses that manifest it. Thus, behavior that has usually been followed by food reinforcement becomes progressively weaker if its elicitations cease to be followed by food. Similarly, avoidance behavior usually diminishes if it is not at least sometimes reinforced by a noxious event such as shock. The performance of a motor response has consequences that weaken its habit unless their effects are counteracted by the effects of reinforcement. The exact mechanism of experimental extinction has not been unequivocally established, but it is likely that it depends at least partly on the fatigue-associated reactive inhibition mechanism proposed by Hull.[9] I have elsewhere proposed a possible neurophysiological mechanism for the extinction process thus conceived.[10]

Assertive Training

Assertive training is preeminently applicable to the deconditioning of unadaptive anxiety habits of response to people with whom the patient interacts. It makes use of the anxiety-inhibiting emotions that life situations evoke in him. A great many emotions, mostly "pleasant" in character, seem to involve bodily events competitive with anxiety.[11] All categories of stimuli—sights, smells, sounds, words—may be sources of such emotions because of their immediate perceptual harmoniousness (esthetic effect) or because of previous conditioning. A perfume, for example, may be conditioned to strong romantic feelings. In like fashion, another person may arouse approval, affection, admiration, annoyance, or anger or other feelings, each of which produce bodily responses different from anxiety and possibly competitive with it. It seems that when such emotions are exteriorized in motor behavior their intensity is enhanced; and any anxiety that is evoked by the situation is more likely to be inhibited. *Assertive behavior is defined as the proper expression of any emotion other than anxiety towards another person. . . .*

Preliminary Measures

A suitable context for starting assertive training often emerges in a very natural way from the patient's narration of some recent incident. An alternative start-

---

[9]C. L. Hull, *Principles of Behavior* (New York: Appleton-Century-Crofts, 1966).
[10]J. Wolpe, *Psychotherapy by Reciprocal Inhibition* (Stanford: Stanford University Press, 1958), p. 27.
[11]Wolpe, *Psychotherapy by Reciprocal Inhibition,* p. 99.

ing point may be found in the patient's responses to the Willoughby Personality Schedule (Appendix 1)—particularly if there are high numerical responses to the following questions: Are your feelings easily hurt? Are you shy? Does criticism hurt you badly? Are you self-conscious before superiors?

To take the first of these as an example, the therapist would ask for an example of a situation that hurts the patient's feelings, and follow this up by inquiring how he would handle the situation. If the handling was unassertive, he would propose an assertive substitute.

A useful route to the initiation of assertion in "outgroup" contexts takes off from asking the patient how he behaves in a number of set situations. For some years I have been presenting these five questions:

1. What do you do if after having bought an article in a shop you walk out and find that your change is a dollar short?

2. Suppose that, arriving home after buying an article on the way, you find it slightly damaged. What will you do?

3. What do you do if somebody pushes in front of you in line (e.g., at the theater)?

4. At a shop, while you wait for the clerk to finish with the customer ahead of you, another customer arrives and also waits. What do you do if the clerk subsequently directs his attention to that customer ahead of you?

5. You order a steak rare and it arrives well done. How do you handle the situation?

In all these situations, a person ought to be able to stand up for himself. Insofar as he does not, assertive training is indicated.

Instigating Assertive Behavior

Let us trace how assertive instigation may develop out of the third of the above questions:

THERAPIST: What do you do if you are standing in line for theater tickets and somebody gets in front of you?

PATIENT: I don't do anything.

THERAPIST: Well, how do you feel?

PATIENT: I feel mad. I boil up inside.

THERAPIST: So, why don't you do anything?

PATIENT: I'm afraid of making a scene.

Thus, it is the fear of making a scene which prevents him from taking action. But at the same time he is angry. The therapist must try to get him to inflate this anger by giving vent to it. Then the anger may be great enough to inhibit the anxiety.

THERAPIST: People are taking advantage of you. Here, this person is taking advantage of you. You cannot allow it. You must say to him, "Will you kindly go to the back of the line?" In doing this, you will be expressing your anger in a way that is appropriate to the situation and socially acceptable. . . .

Behavior Rehearsal

This techinque was originally called *behavioristic psychodrama.* [12] It consists of the acting out of short exchanges between the therapist and the patient in settings from the patient's life. The patient represents himself, and the therapist someone towards whom the patient is unadaptively anxious and inhibited. The therapist starts with a remark, usually oppositional, that the other person might make, and the patient responds as if the situation were "real." His initial response will usually be variously hesitant, defensive, and timid. The therapist then suggests a more appropriate response; and the exchange is run again, revised. The sequence may be repeated again and again until the therapist is satisfied that the patient's utterances have been suitably reshaped. It is necessary to take into account not only the words the patient uses, but also the loudness, firmness, and emotional expressiveness of his voice, and the appropriateness of accompanying bodily movements. (For the last-mentioned purpose, the Behavior Therapy Unit has recently made good use of the modeling of behavior by a well-trained actress.) The aim of such modelling, shaping, and rehearsing is frequently an effective preparation for the patient to deal with his real "adversary" so that the anxiety the latter evokes may be reciprocally inhibited, and the motor assertive habit established.

Case 4 is a typical example of the shaping that is done during behavior rehearsal, excerpted from a case study. [13] The patient had been brooding over having been unfairly criticized by her father and wanted to rectify the matter.

THERAPIST: Well, let's do an experiment. Let's sort of act it out. Suppose you just go ahead and pretend I am your father and say to me what you think you would like to say to him.

PATIENT: About the other night, I would like to say that I think you were exceptionally unfair in assuming that I did not want to come up and that I was the one who was being unjust or the villain because I wasn't coming up to make the family happy. The family hasn't been much of a family actually for a number of years and that when it comes down to it, the family doesn't mean that much to me. I would be much happier spending Christmas by myself. And then he would probably say, "Well, you just go ahead and do that."

THERAPIST: Wait a minute. Never mind. Don't you worry about him. I am he, so don't put words in my mouth. Besides this, in general I would like to correct your approach. You are doing it in a way that leaves you too

---

[12]Wolpe, *Psychotherapy by Reciprocal Inhibition.*
[13]J. Wolpe, "The Instigation of Assertive Behavior: Transcripts from two Cases," *Journal of Behavior Therapy and Experimental Psychiatry* 1 (1970):145.

vulnerable. First of all, it is very unsatisfactory for you to complain to some-body that he is *unfair,* because if you do that you are really in some sense putting yourself at his mercy. A better line of approach would be: "I want to tell you that you had no right to assume the other night that I had no intention of coming for Christmas. You know very well that I have always come. You accused me of lacking feeling. I have a great deal of feeling, and perhaps too much. Your attack was absolutely unwarranted." In saying this, you are not asking for justice or fairness, you are simply stating what you feel was wrong in his behavior. Now, do you think you could redo it in some fashion?

PATIENT: Okay. I would like to set some matters straight—about your call the other night. When you called me I just couldn't think of this right away. I was so taken by surprise, but I have been thinking about it and I would just like to say a couple of things.

THERAPIST: I must interrupt you again. You started fine—the first sentence was fine, but when you begin to explain why you didn't say it the other night, that weakens your position. For example, it might invite him to say, "Yes, that is like you, isn't it? You never answer at the right time. You always have to brood for three days before you can say anything." He *could* say something of that sort. But in any case, it is a kind of underdog statement, and we don't want that.

PATIENT: All right. About the call the other night, I had not entirely given up on the idea of coming up to have Christmas with you and Mom. I was doing what I thought was best according to what I gathered from the conversation I had with Mom. I felt that Mom wanted me to have Christmas with grandma and grandpop—have Christmas dinner, and I wanted to be both places, but I just felt that the drive might be too much.

THERAPIST: I am sorry, but I must interrupt you again. You see, you are explaining yourself. You are giving a kind of excuse. Actually, the impor-tant part of this conversation is to bring out the point that it was not right for him to plunge into a criticism that assumed that you had made up your mind not to come.

PATIENT: How about—I don't think it was right for you to call me last night and say what you did, because I don't think you had the facts straight from Mom. I think you should have checked with her first and be sure you understood the situation. I had talked with Mom earlier and felt that this was what we had worked out and I think you should have checked with her and made sure that—

THERAPIST: That's enough. The fact that you keep on suggests that you are not very confident; so stop. Now, let him say something.

Actually, a *good deal of deconditioning of anxiety frequently takes place during the behavior rehearsal itself.*

Systematic Desensitization

The Formal Basis of Systematic Desensitization

Conditioning theory requires that to eliminate or change a habit of reaction to a stimulus, that stimulus must be present in the deconditioning situation. Such deconditioning as occurs through acts of assertion can affect only the anxiety-response habits to stimuli that are present. If a patient has a fear of being alone, this will not be diminished by assertive behavior (if only because assertion implies the presence of another person). Certainly, now and then, benefit is noted in special cases in which a chain of other habits may be secondarily altered when interpersonal fear has been diminished (for example, in certain cases of agoraphobia; *see below.*) In general, however, assertion towards persons is irrelevant where anxiety responses are to such nonpersonal stimulus constellations as enclosed spaces, animals, heights, the sight of blood —in short, in most classical phobic reactions. It is also irrelevant in the case of anxiety responses that other people elicit in contexts where action on the part of the patient would be inappropriate—for example, where the fear is evoked by the mere presence of particular persons, by being the center of attention, or by a feeling of "rejection," such as in a social situation where it seems to the patient that too little attention is being directed to him.

A case which at that time starkly displayed the irrelevancy of interpersonal expressiveness was that of a woman who was severely anxious at manifestations of illness in other people. Successful schooling in expressive behavior failed to diminish her anxiety and the case was sorrowfully abandoned as a failure. At that time I knew no way to inhibit anxieties aroused by stimuli to which no relevant *action response* could be proposed for the patient—stimuli that oppress the patient "without *animus.*"

Soon afterwards, I had the good luck to come across Edmund Jacobson's *Progressive Relaxation* (1938). Here was described an anxiety-inhibiting response that did not call from the patient *any kind of motor activity towards the source of his anxiety.* I began to give relaxation training to patients for whose neuroses assertion was not applicable. However, an enormous relaxation potential was necessary to inhibit the anxiety evoked by a major real-life phobic stimulus. I conjectured that Jacobson's patients were enabled to inhibit *high* levels of anxiety because of their assiduous training and long and diligent practice.

I began to organize programs of exposure to graduated phobic stimuli *in vivo* for patients who had acquired some facility in relaxing, usually after six to ten sessions. But since it is often very awkward to arrange for graded real-life situations, I began to explore the possibility of making use of imagi-

---

Systematic Desensitization, from Wolpe, *The Practice of Behavior Therapy,* pp. 97–123.

nary situations in the place of real ones—being encouraged in this by the writings of practitioners of hypnosis. I was gratified to find that magnitudes of experienced anxiety diminished progressively at repeated presentations of imaginary situations that were weakly anxiety-arousing. Increasingly strong imaginary stimuli could one by one be divested of their anxiety-evoking potential. Furthermore, there was transfer of the deconditioning of anxiety to the corresponding real situations. At first, influenced by certain of Pavlov's experiments, I presented only one stimulus of any class at a session, but cautious trials of multiple presentations revealed no adverse effects. This opened up the prospect of greatly accelerating therapy.

General Statement of Desensitization Paradigm

The autonomic effects that accompany deep relaxation are diametrically opposed to those characteristic of anxiety. Jacobson long ago showed that pulse rate and blood pressure were diminished by deep muscle relaxation.[14] It was subsequently demonstrated that skin resistance increases and respiration becomes slower and more regular during relaxation.[15] More thoroughgoing studies have recently appeared. Paul has shown that muscle relaxation produces effects opposite to those of anxiety on heart rate, respiratory rate, and skin conductance.[16] Obvious effects can be obtained even by simple instructions to relax; but they are significantly enhanced if the instructions are given in an hypnotic setting and even more significantly if they follow relaxation training. Van Egeren, Feather, and Hein, in an elaborate psychophysiological study involving skin conductance, heart rate, digital pulse amplitude, and rate of respiration, found that relaxed subjects showed less decrease in skin resistance to phobic stimuli than those who were not relaxed.[17] These autonomic effects of relaxation (and the related subjective calmness) cannot be secondary to the relaxed state of the muscles. The complete or almost complete relaxation induced by curare-like drugs may be accompanied by very severe anxiety. The

---

[14]E. Jacobson, "Variation of Blood Pressure with Skeletal Muscle Tension and Relaxation," *Annals of Internal Medicine* 12 (1939): 1194; idem, "Variation of Pulse Rate with Skeletal Muscle Tension and Relaxation," *Annals of Internal Medicine* 13 (1940): 1619.

[15]S. Drvota, "Personal Communication," 1962; D. E. Clark, "The Treatment of Monosymptomatic Phobia by Systematic Desensitization," *Behaviour Research and Therapy* 1 (1963): 63; J. Wolpe, "Behavior Therapy in Complex Neurotic States," *British Journal of Psychiatry.* 110(1964):28.

[16]G. L. Paul, "Physiological Effects of Relaxation Training and Hypnotic Suggestion," *Journal of Abnormal Psychology* 74(1969):425.

[17]L. F. Van Egeren, B. W. Feather, and P. L. Hein, "Desensitization of Phobias: Some Psychophysiological Propositions," *Psychophysiology* 8 (1971):213.

calming effects of Jacobsonian relaxation appear to be concomitants or consequences of the voluntary efforts the subject makes to diminish the tonus of his
muscles.

A pilot psychophysiological study by Wolpe and Fried provided evidence
that the galvanic skin response (on Lathrop's variability measure) shows decrements during desensitization that are parallel to the decrements of anxiety that
patients report. ....[18]

Thus, not only are the effects of relaxation opposite in kind to those of
anxiety, but, if counterposed to anxiety-evoking stimuli, they diminish the
anxiety responses that these stimuli are able to evoke. Van Egeren reported
that with repetitions of the phobic stimuli, the magnitude of their effects
decreased progressively in relaxed subjects, but remained much the same in the
unrelaxed.[19]

The Technique of Systematic Desensitization

If systematic desensitization is indicated, it is started as soon as possible and
may be conducted in parallel with any measures that may have been prescribed
for the life situation. The technique involves four separate sets of operations:

1. Training in deep muscle relaxation.
2. The establishment of the use of a scale of subjective anxiety.
3. The construction of anxiety hierarchies.
4. Counterposing relaxation and anxiety-evoking stimuli from the hierarchies.

Training in Relaxation.   The method of relaxation taught is essentially
that of Jacobson, but instruction is completed in the course of about six
interviews, in marked contrast to Jacobson's very prolonged training schedule.
The patient is asked to practice at home for two fifteen-minute periods a day.

In introducing the subject of relaxation, I tell the patient (who has by now
usually gained a general idea of the nature of conditioning therapy) that
relaxation is just one of the methods in our armamentarium for combating
anxiety. I continue as follows:

> Even the ordinary relaxing that takes place when one lies down often
> produces quite a noticeable calming effect. It has been found that there is
> a definite relationship between the extent of muscle relaxation and the
> production of emotional changes opposite to anxiety. I am going to teach
> you how to relax far beyond the usual point, and with practice you will
> be able to "switch on" at will very considerable emotional effects of an
> "anti-anxiety" kind.

---

[18]J. Wolpe and R. Fried, "Psychophysiological Correlates of Imaginal Presentations of
Hierarchical Stimuli. I, The Effect of Relaxation," 1968.

[19]L. F. Van Egeren, "Psychophysiology of Systematic Desensitization: The Habituation
Model," *Journal of Behavior Therapy and Experimental Psychiatry* 1 (1970):249.

There is no necessary sequence for training the various muscle groups in relaxation, but the sequence adopted should be orderly. My own practice is to start with the arms because they are convenient for purposes of demonstration and their relaxation is easy to check. The head region is done next because the most marked anxiety-inhibiting effects are usually obtained by relaxations there.

The patient is asked to grip the arm of his chair with one hand to see whether he can distinguish any qualitative difference between the sensations produced in his forearm and those in his hand. He is told to take special note of the quality of the forearm sensation because it is caused by muscle tension in contrast to the touch and pressure sensations in the hand. He is also enjoined to note the exact location of the forearm tensions in the flexor and extensor areas. Next, the therapist grips the patient's wrist and asks him to bend his arm against this resistance, thus making him aware of the tension in his biceps. Then, by instructing him to straighten his bent elbow against resistance, he calls his attention to the extensor muscles of the arm. The therapist goes on to say:

> I am now going to show you the essential activity that is involved in obtaining deep relaxation. I shall again ask you to resist my pull at your wrist so as to tighten your biceps. I want you to notice very carefully the sensations in that muscle. Then I shall ask you to let go gradually as I diminish the amount of force exerted against you. Notice, as your forearm descends, that there is decreasing sensation in the biceps muscle. Notice also that the letting go is an activity, but of a negative kind—it is an "uncontracting" of the muscle. In due course, your forearm will come to rest on the arm of the chair, and you may then think that you have gone as far as possible—that relaxation is complete. But although the biceps will indeed be partly and perhaps largely relaxed, a certain number of its fibers will still, in fact, be contracted. I shall, therefore, say to you, "Go on letting go. Try to extend the activity that went on in the biceps while your forearm was coming down." It is the act of relaxing these additional fibers that will bring about the emotional effects we want. Let's try it and see what happens.

The therapist then grips the patient's wrist a second time, and asks him to tense and then gradually to relax the biceps. When the forearm is close to the arm of the chair, the therapist releases the wrist, allowing the patient to complete the movement on his own. He then exhorts him to "go on letting go," to "keep trying to go further and further in the negative direction," to "try to go beyond what seems to you to be the furthest point."

When the patient has shown by relaxing his biceps that he fully understands what is required, he is asked to put both hands comfortably on his lap and try to relax all the muscles of both arms for a few minutes. He is to report any new sensations that he may feel. The usual ones are tingling, numbness, or warmth, mainly in the hands. After a few minutes the therapist palpates the relaxing muscles. With practice he learns to judge between various grosser degrees of muscle tension.

Most patients have rather limited success when they first attempt to relax, but they are assured that good relaxation is a matter of practice, and whereas initially twenty minutes of relaxation may achieve no more than partial relaxation of an arm, it will eventually be possible to relax the whole body in a matter of a minute or two. However, there are some fortunate individuals who from the first attempt experience a deepening and extending relaxation, radiating, as it were, from the arms, and accompanied by general effects, like calmness, sleepiness, or warmth.

I customarily begin the *second lesson* in relaxation by telling the patient that, from the emotional point of view, the most important muscles in the body are situated in and around the head, and that we shall, therefore, deal with this area next. We begin with the muscles of the face, demonstrating the tensions produced by contracting the muscles of the forehead. These muscles lend themselves to a demonstration by the therapist of the "steplike" character of deepening relaxation. The therapist simultaneously contracts the eyebrow raising and frowning muscles in his own forehead very intensely, pointing out that an anxious expression has thus been produced. He then says: "I am going to relax these muscles in a controlled way to give you an impression of the steplike way in which decrements of tension occur during attempts at deep relaxation, although, when you are learning to relax, the steps take much longer than in my demonstration." The muscles are then relaxed, making an obvious step-down about every five seconds until, after about half-a-dozen steps, no further change is evident. At this point, it is clearly stated that relaxation is continuing and that this relaxation "beneath the surface" is the part that matters for producing the desired emotional effects. The patient is then told to contract his own forehead muscles, and given about ten minutes to relax them as far as possible. Many report spontaneously the occurrence of "relaxation feedback" in their foreheads, which they may feel as tingling, warmth, or "a feeling of thickness, as though my skin were made of leather." These sensations are, as a rule, indicative of a degree of relaxation beyond the normal level of muscle tone.

This lesson usually concludes by drawing attention to the muscles in the region of the nose by getting the patient to wrinkle his nose, and to the muscles around the mouth by making him purse his lips and then smile. All these muscles are now relaxed.

At the *third lesson* the patient is asked to bite on his teeth, thus tensing his masseters and temporales. The position of the lips is an important indicator of relaxation of the muscles of mastication. When these are relaxed, the lips are parted by a few millimeters. The masseters cannot be relaxed if the mouth is resolutely closed. On the other hand, an open mouth is no proof of their relaxation.

At the same lesson, I usually also introduce the muscles of the tongue. These may be felt contracting in the floor of the mouth when the patient presses the tip of his tongue firmly against the back of his lower incisor teeth. Relaxing the tongue muscles may produce such local sensations as tingling or a feeling of enlargement of that organ.

Patients who have special tensions in the neck region are now shown how to relax the pharyngeal muscles—which can be located by preparing to clear the throat. Other muscle groups that receive attention only for special purposes are those of the eyeball (which are first identified by having the eyes turned in succession left, right, up, and down), and the infrahyoid group (which the patient can be made to feel by trying to open his jaws against resistance).

The *fourth lesson* deals with the neck and shoulders. The main target in the neck is the posterior muscles that normally maintain the head's erect posture. Most people become aware of them merely by concentraing on sensations at the back of the neck. Relaxing these muscles makes the head fall forward, but because in the unpracticed individual the relaxation is incomplete, the head's whole weight is imposed on the few muscle fibers that are still contracted, producing discomfort and even pain in the neck. As Jacobson pointed out, persistent practice, in spite of the discomfort, leads to a progressive yielding of these muscles; and usually in a week or so the patient finds his neck comfortable with his chin pressing against his sternum. Those who find the discomfort of the forward leaning head too great are instructed to practice relaxing the neck muscles with the back of the head resting against a high-backed chair.

Shoulder muscle tensions are demonstrated by the following routine. The deltoid is contracted by abducting the arm to the horizontal, the lateral neck muscles by continuing this movement up to the ear, the post-humeral and scapulo-spinal groups by moving the horizontal arm backward, and the pectorals by swinging it forward across the chest. In relaxing these muscles the patient is directed to observe their functional unity with those of the arm.

The *fifth lesson* deals with the muscles of the back, abdomen, and thorax. The procedure with respect to the first two areas follows the usual pattern. The back muscles are contracted by backward arching of the spine. The abdominal muscles are tensed as if in anticipation of a punch in the belly. After contracting these muscles, the patient lets them go as far as he can. The thoracic muscles, or, more accurately, the muscles of respiration, are necessarily in a different category—for total inhibition of breathing is not an achievement to try to promote! But the respiratory rhythm can often be used to augment relaxation. Attention to the musculature during a few fairly deep breaths soon reveals that while some effort is involved during inhalation, expiration is essentially a "letting-go." Some patients find it very helpful to coordinate relaxation of various other muscles with the automatic relaxation of the respiratory muscles that takes place with the exhalation during *normal* breathing.

In making patients aware of the muscles to be relaxed in the lower limbs, during the *sixth lesson,* it has been my custom to start with the feet, and work upwards. The flexor digitorium brevis is felt in the sole by bending the toes within the shoe, the calf muscles by placing some weight on the toe, the peroneal and anterior tibial muscles by dorsiflexing the foot, the quadriceps femoris by straightening the knee, the hamstrings by trying to bend the knee against resistance, the adductors of the thigh by adduction against hand pressure on the inner aspect of the knee, and the abductors (which include some of the gluteal muscles) by abduction against pressure. All these muscles are the subject of the sixth lesson, and the patient should be allowed enough time for relaxing them.

The assessment of a patient's ability to relax depends partly upon his reports of the degree of calmness that relaxing brings about in him, and partly upon impressions gained from observing him. By the second or third lesson, most patients report ease, tranquility, or sleepiness. A few experience little or no change of feeling. It is an advantage to have objective indicators of relaxation. Jacobson has used the electromyogram, but mainly as a corroborative measure.[20] Recently, more convenient equipment has become available that translates muscle potentials into auditory signals whose pitch drops as tension decreases.[21] This also facilitates relaxation by providing feedback to the patient. Fortunately, the reports of patients usually serve as a sufficiently reliable guide to their emotional state, especially with the help of the subjective anxiety scale. Quite a number of them, especially those who start with little or no ongoing anxiety, report a positive feeling of calm after only one or two sessions of relaxation training. Some fortunate individuals appear to possess a kind of relaxation-radiation zone (usually in the arms or face), from which relaxation spreads to other regions when the radiation zone is relaxed.

The Construction of Hierarchies.   An anxiety hierarchy is a list of stimuli on a theme, ranked according to the amount of anxiety they evoke. My own practice has always been to place the stimulus evoking greatest anxiety at the top of the list. Sometimes hierarchy construction is an easy matter: the themes are clear and the rank order of the stimuli obvious. . . .

It is not necessary for the patient actually to have experienced each situation that is included in a hierarchy. The question posed is, "If you were today confronted by such and such a situation, *would you expect* to be anxious?" To answer this question he has to *imagine* the situation concerned, and it is generally almost as easy to imagine a supposed event as one that has at some time occurred. The temporal setting of an imagined stimulus configura-

---

[20]Jacobson, "Variation of Blood Pressure"; idem, *Anxiety and Tension Control* (Philadelphia: Lippincott, 1964).

[21]T. Budzinski, J. Stoyva, and C. Adler, "Feedback-Induced Muscle Relaxation: Application to Tension Headache," *Journal of Behavior Therapy and Experimental Psychiatry* 1 (1970): 205.

tion scarcely affects the responses to it. A man with a phobia for dogs will usually have about as much anxiety at the idea of meeting a bulldog on the way home tomorrow as at recalling an actual encounter with this breed of dog.

The following list of fears supplied by a patient will be used to illustrate some of the intricacies of hierarchy construction. This list is reproduced exactly as the patient presented it.

Raw List of Fears

1. High Altitudes
2. Elevators
3. Crowded Places
4. Church
5. Darkness—Movies, etc.
6. Being Alone
7. Marital Relations (pregnancy)
8. Walking any Distance
9. Death
10. Accidents
11. Fire
12. Fainting
13. Falling Back
14. Injections
15. Medications
16. Fear of the Unknown
17. Losing My Mind
18. Locked Doors
19. Amusement Park Rides
20. Steep Stairways

With the help of a little clarification from the patient the items were sorted into categories, thus:

A. ACROPHOBIA
1. High Altitudes
19. Amusement Park Rides
20. Steep Stairways

B. CLAUSTROPHOBIA
2. Elevators
3. Crowded Places
4. Church
5. Movies (darkness factor)
18. Locked Doors

C. AGORAPHOBIA
6. Being Alone
8. Walking any Distance (alone)

D. ILLNESS AND ITS ASSOCIATIONS
12. Fainting
13. Falling Back
14. Injections
15. Medication

E. BASICALLY OBJECTIVE FEARS
7. Marital Relations (pregnancy)
9. Death
10. Accidents
11. Fire
16. Fear of the Unknown
17. Losing My Mind. . . .

The Subjective Anxiety Scale. Knowledge of the magnitude of the patient's anxiety responses to specific stimuli being indispensable to desensitization, it is desirable to have reliable ways of gauging it.

The scale is introduced to the patient by addressing him as follows: "Think of the worst anxiety you have ever experienced, or can imagine experiencing, and assign to this the number 100. Now think of the state of being absolutely calm and call this zero. Now you have a scale of anxiety. On this scale how do you rate yourself at this moment?" Most subjects give a figure without much hesitation, and with practice come to be able to indicate their feelings with increasing confidence in a way that is much more informative than the usual adjectival statements. The unit is the *sud* (subjective unit of disturbance). It is possible to use the scale to ask the patient to rate the items of the hierarchy according to the amount of anxiety he would have upon exposure to them. If the differences between items are similar, and, generally speaking, not more than five to ten *suds,* the spacing can be regarded as satisfactory. On the other hand, if there were, for example, forty *suds* for item number 8, and ten *suds* for item number 9, there would be an obvious need for intervening items.

Desensitization Procedure: Counteracting Anxiety by Relaxation. The stage is set for the desensitization procedure when the patient has attained a capacity to calm himself by relaxation, and the therapist has established appropriate hierarchies. Many of them are adequately calm when relaxation training has gone halfway or less. While a desensitization program makes it highly desirable for the patient to achieve a positive feeling of calm, i.e., a negative of anxiety, it is not mandatory, and one can be well satisfied with zero subjective units of disturbance. In a fair number who have considerable levels of current anxiety (whether or not this is pervasive—"free-floating"—anxiety), it has been found that a substantial lowering of the level—say, from fifty to fifteen *suds*—may afford a sufficiently low anxiety baseline for successful desensitization. Apparently, an anxiety-inhibiting "dynamism" can inhibit small quanta of intercurrent anxiety even when it does not fully overcome current anxiety. Desensitizing effects are only rarely obtainable with levels in excess of twenty-five *suds;* and in some individuals a zero level is indispensable.

It is natural to hope for a smooth therapeutic passage, and such is often the case, but there are many difficulties that may encumber the path. I shall first describe the technique and the characteristic course of uncomplicated desensitization.

The first desensitization session is introduced by saying, "I am now going to get you to relax; and when you are relaxed I will ask you to imagine certain scenes. Each time a scene is clear in your mind indicate this by raising your index finger about one inch."

While the patient sits or lies comfortably with his eyes closed, the therapist proceeds to bring about as deep as possible a state of relaxation by the use of such words as the following: "Now, your whole body becomes progressively heavier, and all your muscles relax. Let go more and more completely. We shall give your muscles individual attention. Relax the muscles of your forehead. (Pause five to ten seconds.) Relax the muscles of your jaws and those of your tongue. (Pause) Relax the muscles of your eyeballs. The more you relax, the calmer you become. (Pause) Relax the muscles of your neck. (Pause) Let all the muscles of your shoulders relax. Just let yourself go. (Pause) Now relax your arms. (Pause) Relax all the muscles of your trunk. (Pause) Relax the muscles of your lower limbs. Let your muscles go more and more. You feel so much at ease and so very comfortable."

At the first desensitization session, which is always partly exploratory, the therapist seeks some feedback about the state of the patient, asking him to state on the subjective scale how much anxiety he feels. If it is zero or close thereto, scene presentations can begin. If the patient continues to have some anxiety despite his best efforts at direct relaxation, various imaginal devices may be invoked. Those most commonly used are:

1. "Imagine that on a calm summer's day you lie back on a soft lawn and watch the clouds move slowly overhead. Notice especially the brilliant edges of the clouds."

2. "Imagine an intense, bright spot of light about eighteen inches in front of you." (This image is due to Milton Erickson.)

3. "Imagine that near a river's bank you see a leaf moving erratically on little waves."

There is a routine manner of proceeding with the introduction of the scenes at the first desensitization session. The observations that the therapist makes at this session frequently lead to modifications of technique to fit in with particular requirements of the patient.

The first scene presented is a "control." It is neutral in the sense that the patient is not expected to have any anxious reaction to it. I most commonly use a street scene. Sometimes it is "safer" to have the patient imagine himself sitting in his living room, or reading a newspaper; but there is no guarantee of safety unless the subject matter has actually been explored beforehand. At one time I used to employ a white flower against a black background as a standard control scene. One day, a patient evinced considerable anxiety to it, because he associated it with funerals, and, as it subsequently turned out, he had a neurosis about death.

There are two reasons for using a control scene. First, it provides information about the patient's general ability to visualize anxiety-free material. Second, it provides indications of certain contaminating factors: the patient may have anxiety about relinquishing control of himself, or about "the unknown." In either case, anxiety is present that has nothing to do with the target of desensitization, and that must be dealt with if therapy is to succeed. . . .

The patient is asked to imagine a number of scenes that will be described to him. He is to raise his left index finger about one inch the moment the image is clearly formed. The therapist then presents a scene and lets it remain for exactly as long as he wants to—usually five to seven seconds. He terminates it by saying, "Stop the scene"; and then asks the patient to state how much it disturbed him in terms of *suds*. After a few sessions, the patient gets into the habit of stating the number of *suds* automatically upon the termination of the scene. While the use of a verbal report possibly disrupts relaxation more than the raising of a finger, the adverse effects have to date in no case seemed to be important. Any disadvantages are certainly outweighed by dispensing with the need to allow "long enough time" to be sure that the patient has visualized the scene, and by the immediate and precise feedback of amount of disturbance.

Aversion Therapy

Aversion therapy consists, operationally, of administering an aversive stimulus to inhibit an unwanted emotional response, thereby diminishing its habit strength. For example, a painful stimulus may be employed to inhibit sexual arousal by a fetishistic object. It is thus a special application of the reciprocal inhibition principle. Aversion must be clearly distinguished from punishment, in which the aversive stimulus follows the response of concern instead of coinciding with it. . . .

Description of Techniques

Electrical Stimulation. An important advantage of electrical stimulation is that it can be precisely timed in relation to the behavior to be modified. Depending upon the circumstances of the case, one may administer the shock either in the presence of the actual objects or situations that form the basis of the obsessional or other undesirable behavior, or in relation to imaginary or pictorial representations of them. The preferred source of aversive stimulation is either faradic current or alternating current because these can, if necessary, be kept at steady levels for prolonged periods. The electrodes are usually attached to the patient's forearm. The baseline shock setting is determined by gradually increasing the current to a point where the patient reports it to be distinctly unpleasant. The starting point for aversive trials is then usually a current 25–50 percent stronger. The most satisfactory electrode is the concentric electrode, which greatly minimizes the risk of burning the skin.[22] Wet

---

[22]B. Tursky, P. D. Watson, and D. N. O'Connell, "A Concentric Shock Electrode for Pain Stimulation," *Psychophysiology* 1 (1965):296.

electrodes of saline-soaked gauze are also quite satisfactory. Ordinary electrocardiographic silver electrodes may be used if necessary. . . .

Aversion Therapy by Drugs.   The treatment of alcoholism by an aversion method based on the nauseating effects of drugs was introduced many years ago by Voegtlin and Lemere (1942), and has been the subject of many subsequent reports.[23] It consists of giving the patient a nausea-producing drug, such as tartar emetic, emetine, apomorphine, or gold chloride, and then having him drink a favored alcoholic beverage. The combination of alcohol and emetic is given daily for a week to ten days, after which the effectiveness of the procedure is tested by giving the patient alcohol alone. If there is sufficient conditioning, the very sight of alcohol will produce nausea. Booster treatments are given two or three times during the following year.

Typically, the patient is given two ten-ounce glasses of warm saline solution containing 0.1 gram of emetine and 1 gram of sodium chloride to 20 ounces of water. This is just sufficient salt to mask the bitter taste of emetine. Immediately after this, he is given a hypodermic injection of 30 milligrams of emetine hydrochloride to produce emesis, 15 milligrams of pilocarpine hydrochloride for diaphoresis, and 15 milligrams of ephedrine sulphate for "support." The alcoholic beverage, e.g., whiskey, is held in front of the patient's nose and he is asked to smell deeply. He is then requested to sip the beverage and taste it thoroughly, swishing it around in his mouth and then swallowing it so that the sensory impact is at a maximum. Another drink is poured and the same procedure repeated. Nausea should begin immediately after this second drink if the timing has been right—as it must be if the treatment is to have its maximum effect.

---

[23]F. Lemere and W. L. Voegtlin, "An Evaluation of the Aversion Treatment of Alcoholism," *Quarterly Journal of Studies on Alcohol* 11 (1950):199.

10

INTERFERENCE THEORY:
ASSERTION-STRUCTURED THERAPY

E. Lakin Phillips

Ewing Lakin Phillips was born on April 29, 1915, in Higginsville, Missouri. He earned degrees at Missouri State College (B.S., 1937), the University of Missouri (M.A., 1940), and the University of Minnesota (Ph.D., 1949). Child psychology was his field of specialization. From 1939–40 he was with the LaGrange Public School system in Missouri and at the same time he was an assistant at the University of Missouri. He spent one year with the U.S. Army Air Force (1942 – 43) and two years as a clinical psychologist with the U.S. Army. After the war, he worked for the St. Paul Department of Education for a year. During 1947 – 48 he was with the Minneapolis Board of Education, while at the same time working as a teaching assistant at the University of Minnesota and as an instructor at Macalester College. From 1948–52, he was associated with George Washington University as assistant professor of psychology. He served as a clinical psychologist for the Arlington County Guidance Center in Virginia from 1949–56. During 1952–55 he was associated with the Anderson Orthopedic Hospital in Arlington and with the Arlington County Juvenile Court. He accepted an appointment as chief psychologist with the National Orthopedic and Rehabilitation Hospital in 1956 and in 1958 became codirector of the Psychological Testing Center. He gave up both posts in 1962 when he was appointed professor and director of the Testing and Counseling Center at George Washington University. In 1967 he added to his duties that of executive director of the School for Contemporary Education. Since 1952 he also has conducted his own private practice.

The interference theory of psychotherapy, nondepth therapy grounded on the findings of learning theory or experimental psychology, is an assertion-structured therapy. In order to alter individuals' behavior, it is necessary to interfere with their activities, their assertions, and the entire bases of their assumptions. Patients should be committed to another set of probabilities upon which to structure their life or behavior. The psychodynamics involved are not defense mechanisms or the unconscious, but intelligence and choice, utilized for constructive living. An ill organism is restored to health by abandoning old assumptions that lead to circularity and redundancy (neurotic behavior), and by acquiring a new set of assumptions or assertions, a set which is constructive, free from redundancy, and strong. While redundant behavior lacks confirmation, wholesome behavior developed through the therapeutic process of interference is environmentally confirmed.

Phillips has published a number of papers, but his system of psychotherapy is found principally in his two books *Psychotherapy: A Modern Theory and Practice* (1956) and *Short-term Psychotherapy and Structured Behavior Change* (with D. W. Weiner, 1966).

The Nature of Assertion-Structured Psychotherapy

What of the present position? Wherein does it differ from the main characteristics of depth psychology and clinical theory?

In essence, there are three major differences: (1) A difference in methodological emphasis; (2) a difference in the theory of the mind (or of personality or of behavior) used; and (3) a difference in the *practical implications* of the first two, especially as these implications involve psychotherapy and the general problems of diagnosis of personality ills.

The difference in methodology is pivoted around the idiographic-nomothetic controversy. The position taken here is that there is no difference between the method of the clinician and that of the experimental or research psychologist. There is no *individual* lawfulness in the sense of opposition to or difference from actuarial lawfulness; that is, the laws that apply to one person are those that apply to all persons. The emphasis in the former, however, has to do with a given person at a given time or in relation to a given set of conditions. The misapprehension of this problem has allowed the clinician to grow careless about his assertions, his theory, his research (except where he researches in a nomothetic framework), and his practice. The position taken classically by the clinician allows him to get mired down in his own image of himself and his function; it does not make for scientific communication and testability and the formulation of useful theories. . . .

The present view of mind is much more like that of the learning theorist, whose ideas are well enough known and often invoked in limited ways in clinical-personality theory making. But there has not been a systematic reapplication of the learning position to clinical phenomena. If there should be—and this is where much of the purpose of the present work is illustrated—it

---

The Nature of Assertion-Structured Psychotherapy, from E. Lakin Phillips, *Psychotherapy: A Modern Theory and Practice* (Englewood Cliffs, N.J.: Prentice-Hall, 1956), pp. xiv–xvii.

would change the clinician's thinking and his practice. We begin to see behavioral possibilities in terms of varying probabilities; we begin to see that what the person does is a function of how he estimates these probabilities, how he makes choices. He puts forward notions or works on the basis of assumptions or lives by hypotheses—these are subsumed under the general, non-value-laden rubric of *assertions.* These assertions have varying probabilities of confirmation—depending on the environmental possibilities—or other assertions have varying degrees of application in a given situation. The organism selects, as it were, in the way that the gambler selects a number to bet on. We are all betting on life's contingencies all the time, although we do not stop to think about it nor do we conceptualize the odds at every turn.

If one is going to change a person's behavior, he has to interfere with what the person is doing, with his assumption-system, with his assertions, or with their degree. The clinician teaches the patient to bet less, or to bet on different probabilities.

This position, then, allows us to do away with all the notions of defense, with the unconscious, with the view that organisms are always pushed from behind in some blind fashion. It puts more choice, more control, more intelligence into the organism and utilizes these for constructive purposes. This is where psychotherapy and diagnostic work come in.

The third difference, that of the implication of the theory for practical situations such as diagnostic and therapeutic work, is extremely important. In the interference theory, we can see our way to conducting psychotherapy on a more practical basis; we do not set up a mind-structure so formidable that it has to be beaten down or broken into a defenseless position, or plumbed to its depth. We can change probabilities of behaving by rather modest, practical, and surprisingly economical and efficient means. We can apply psychotherapy to far more people, under less austere and expensive conditions, and we can relate psychotherapy to the host of knowledge we have from other areas of science.

If we can do these things well in psychotherapy, our circle has been completed, as it were. We started off with different assumptions about mind and about psychopathology, and we can bring these different assumptions to fruition; this, of course, increases the confidence we place in the assumptions. This is all to the good; and it raises another important theoretical problem.

Something has been said about coming out where we started; about returning to the beginning. Is this process circular? Yes! But not *circular* in the sense in which the term applies to methodology that has no independent, testable conditions.

The idea of circularity brings to mind recent advances in information-communication theory. The view advanced by this book is that these new ideas can be joined to a learning-theory, conflict-theory formulation of psychopathology and used to broaden our concepts of the problems we are dealing with and net new practical results at the same time.

The circularity—*redundancy*—of neuroses (and of other psychopathological conditions, too) has not been adequately explained to date. It is one
purpose of the present volume to indicate an explanation. It considers the
strength of the assertion, its probability of confirmation, and the probability
of building into the organism new assumptions that will free it from the
redundancy aspect. The stronger the assertiveness, though, the greater the
probability of the redundancy. This kind of thinking most likely would not
evolve from a "depth" theory of mind. . . .

Interference Theory of Psychotherapy

Very briefly considered, interference theory constitutes the viewpoint that
behavior—pathological or otherwise—is a result of various *assertions* made by
the individual about himself or about his relationship with others. The person
chooses now one kind of behavior, now another, depending on what kind of
behavior seems likely to bring (from the environment) confirmation of his
assertions. Certain behavior possibilities "interfere" with each other; that is,
the person cannot do both at the same time. However, since possible behavior
is always selected by a person on the basis of its appropriateness to the
environment, the whole process with which we are concerned goes on "in the
open." Depth views, which regard the mental life of people as having a kind
of deep-going reservoir from which diabolical forces spring, are entirely anathema to the present viewpoint. The depth view is essentially untestable—an
elementary, too elementaristic view, one that cannot meet the complexity of
problems that we contrive in the laboratory, see in the nursery school, or meet
daily in a myriad of practical situations.. . .

A Case Study

After having been seen in therapy ten times, the subject of this case, a young
woman of twenty-two years, was forced to discontinue treatment owing to the
necessity of her moving some distance away. She had previously had between
90 and 100 hours of psychoanalytically oriented therapy on an out-patient,
once-a-week basis. Current treatment had also been once a week. She was quite
ill-at-ease, hyperactive, and self-stimulating (face, arms, legs were rubbed all
the time) but was sincerely interested in doing something to overcome her
misery. Some of the presenting problems were: inability to fall asleep at night;
awakening for long periods if she'd been asleep; a tense, isolated feeling on the
job (clerical work); frequent and violent fights with her husband; several

Interference Theory of Psychotherapy, from Phillips, *Psychotherapy: A Modern Theory and
Practice,* pp. 2–6, 42–43, 45–46.

hour-long crying spells each week, usually in connection with discord with her husband; constant talking to herself about her present or future activities ("Now I'm riding the bus to work," "Now I'm cooking dinner and next I'll eat and then go meet my husband," "Now I'm getting ready to go down town where I'll buy something I like," and so on); great strain and discomfort in social situations and considerable envy of her husband's more relaxed attitude; and a tendency to provoke conflict with her husband in social situations in order to get him to do her bidding ("Are you going to stay here and leave me helpless and ill like this?"). Many other overt (as well as covert) symptoms added up to a miserable day each day. The violent storms were patched up between her and her husband mainly on the strength of her instigation, her profuse apologies (and sometimes his in those instances when he had lost perspective in the heat of controversy), and fairyland types of promises and statements of affection. She required frequent reassurances that he loved her, and that things were as they used to be before a recent fight. To spend an evening in quiet reading or the like was anathema to her, because her husband would thus be "paying attention to the book and not to me." This attitude became embellished in a variety of ways and in many situations.

In the therapy, effort was made immediately to bring her to terms with her assertions, her expectations, and her assumptions about herself. (Later development of the viewpoint will illustrate that people live by *assertions,* not by denials.) She was trying to have notions concerning herself and others (in relation to herself) confirmed at any or all costs. She had to be attended to, to be noticed, to be taken into consideration—first, last, and always. She wanted what she wanted, as she wanted it, when she wanted it! If she awakened at night and could not fall asleep again, she would also awaken her husband, as if he could do something about it. His attempts to do something sympathetic would naturally fail to meet her requirements (either on a subjective basis or on a "reality" basis) and so would worsen the situation. When he acted as if he *could* do something to permanently relieve his wife's tension, thereby increasing her expectations of relief it was all the more disappointing to her when relief was not forthcoming. This left her more helpless. If, on the other hand, the husband fought back, as he might well do, this enraged the patient, since this act constituted not only a failure to "help her" but also a critical attitude toward her. Usually such an episode ended in the patient's exhaustion, or in her leaving the house for a long walk in the middle of the night.

So much for symptoms; the conceptualization is the thing. What did these symptoms mean? All of these difficulties were grouped, through discussion with the patient, under four rubrics:

1. Assertion.   She wanted constant attention, accord, recognition, approval. This constituted her assertions, her assumptions, her movement toward others, her essential views of herself.

2. Disconfirmation.   But these demands were too stringent for anyone to consistently accept; they were too recurrent, too persistent for others to meet. They were therefore disconfirmed in personal ways (as by the husband) or in impersonal ways (through social isolation, through strains on the job), and this disconfirmation, together with the requirement itself, constituted the conflict situation. On the one hand, she asserted, expected, required; on the other hand, she could not have her demands fulfilled.

3. Tension resulted.   As always, it was shown in a variety of ways, both overtly and covertly. This discomfort was unbearable, being directly related (it is hypothesized) to the strength of her assertion and/or to the finality of the disconfirming experiences.

4. Redundancy.   This led to the redoubling of her assertive efforts and to side tactics, as it were, to throwing tantrums—all of which illustrated the tension-reducing objectives she had as well as the reassertive intentions; after the heat of the matter had passed, it would eventually lead to guilt over the way she had acted.

Explanations following this four-point model—but in nontechnical language—were given her with respect to concrete experiences she had reported during the therapy hours. The paradigm or model was made clearer and clearer each week with respect to new data or with regard to old concerns. Each time she reported difficulty—which was often—the effort was extended in the therapy to learn what she was putting into the situation, what she was expecting, and what her self-others hypotheses were at the moment; and to discover how these expectations and hypotheses were disconfirmed in the reality of the exchange with others. What was actually happening in the give-and-take with others, in the bobbing up and down of her symptoms, was seen to be the confirmation or disconfirmation of the assertion and reassertion of a given notion.

This explanation gave her a tool to work with—a means of analyzing her own reactions, a means of extending self-knowledge from one situation to another. Each success in these undertakings brought about an increased confidence that she could cope better and better with her life. By the same token, this tended to reduce the potency of the "vicious circle" in which she was caught and to replace it with constructive exchanges with others (a positive circle, as it were, based on positive feedback from others).. . .

A brief digression into the mechanics (dynamics) of the *assertion-disconfirmation-tension-redundancy* paradigm is indicated at this point. . . .

Is this *assertion* paradigm really different from the *motivation-blocking-tension reduction* formula that learning theorists have used for some time? Yes —there are important differences between the older formulation and the one proffered here.

First. In the older formulation, no effort has been expended to relate motivation and blocking to various symptom complexes as a function of what was motivated and of how the motivation was blocked. The motivation-blocking formula was and remains very abstract; and it is not rigorous enough to allow any specific deductions to be derived that would have direct or incisive application to particular symptom complexes (diagnostic categories).

Second. Blocking or frustration is subsumed here under approach-avoidance conflict and the old emphasis on blocking per se, is largely superseded by emphasis on the environment's indirect effect on the person who over-asserts (or too narrowly asserts). It is not so much a question of blocking or frustration as it is of betting on too great odds, of asserting expectations that cannot be fulfilled. Hence the conflict between assertion and disconfirmation.

Third. The *assertion* in the present viewpoint is seen to come from honest organismic efforts to cope with the environment, not from the pressure of childhood frustrations and deprivations (such, for example, as one finds emphasized in the explanation that present pleasures are derived from previous deprivations).

Fourth. The playing down of symptoms in therapy is not allowed by the old formulations. The older versions are ostensibly compatible with depth theory, as exemplified in the work of the various Yale theorists-experimentalists. In the present version, symptoms are tension-derived; one might speak here of a "tension theory" of symptoms in contrast to the "specificity theory" that asserts for the important symptoms a separate history of their own. In the latter view, the contemporary value of symptoms is to point, as it were, back to the relevant developmental epoch when the dirty work took place. This implies, in therapy, the necessity of going-back-to-the-origin and the consequent digging out, restructuring, reliving, and relieving activities necessary for recovery.

Fifth. Perhaps most important for theoretical considerations is the observation that the old *motivation-blocking-tension reduction* formulation has no built-in readiness to handle the circularity of behavior, the vicious-circle phenomena, or the *redundancy* aspect of psychopathology as it is herein referred to. Without this capacity, the motivation-blocking formulation can handle only a small aspect of psychopathology. If this and tension reduction were the whole matter, how does it happen that the tension reduction does not allow the pathological behavior to desist? However, in the present, formulation on the tension reduction value of symptoms is largely nil, and the persistence of the pathological behavior is explained on the basis of the strength of the assertion. ... We would expect the conflict to persist if information suitable to the reduction of the original assertion were not forthcoming, no matter how much tension-reducing symptom activation took place. ...

Characteristics of Assertion-Structured Therapy

1. Anxiety is treated as a result of conflict, not as a "separate" to be pursued for its own sake. This allows us to deal with more symptoms and with more "severe" symptoms in a more functional manner.

2. The healthy part of the person is stressed more.

3. Psychopathology is treated from a problem-solving vantage point and this helps the patient to fear his problems less, to view them with more patience and with more positive and workable hope for improvement.

4. Over-all features of the patient's problem behavior are discussed—frequency in general population, relation of problem to developmental status, the methods that generally work and those that do not and reasons for same (applies most directly to parent-child cases).

5. The individual's problems are named and conceptualized as early as possible in therapy. This allows for progressive clarification of the problem and for testing out the presumptive solutions to it.

6. Most instances of "anxiety" are regarded as anger, resentment, disappointment, stemming from the disconfirmation of expectations. This affords a more specific and a more germane treatment of symptoms and an earlier testing out of proposed solutions.

Precepts of Assertion-Structured Therapy

Our precepts are (1) develop structure, (2) change behavior as directly and efficiently as possible, and (3) realign variables. Set tasks and do follow-up. Use any reasonable and ethical means effectively to change behavior. Try many devices, recognizing that changing behavior can take many directions. Above all, judge results critically, and change accordingly.

Time was our first consideration; then the notion of structure followed quickly. Structure is important because it subsumes time and measures many other variables as well. Structure is an abstraction; time is concrete, easily identified, and readily measured. Action and responsibility are more vague, although they can be related to specific acts, instruments, and conditions.

Precepts of Assertion-Structured Therapy, from E. Lakin Phillips and Daniel W. Wiener, *Short-Term Psychotherapy and Structured Behavior Change* (New York: McGraw-Hill, 1966), pp. 9–10, 25–26.

To sum up, the psychotherapist is only one of many behavior changers, and psychotherapy is only one of many methods for behavior change. Hopefully, since he is especially trained and skilled, the psychotherapist is capable of directing the work of others who will help in accomplishing change and is not limited to the practice of psychotherapy in the consulting room. Krasner . . . writes of the psychotherapist as a "reinforcement machine." Granted, this is one role, but priority should be given to the choice and control of change media and goals. Otherwise, what is reinforced may be a matter of chance or drift. The highest priority should be given to what is chosen to be regulated, controlled, directed, and shaped. The reinforcement should come naturally from the (new) behavior outside therapy, after it has been generated in some behavior-change situation. This natural reinforcement is vital in our concept of behavior change.

The therapist is to be an "architect of change." He may act as a reinforcer himself; he may teach others, such as parents and teachers, to take this role; he may act to manipulate variables as well as people (who may be considered "variables") in order to bring structure to a given person or situation; and he may work in the consulting room with a single human being. But, as an architect of change, he should be able to work in a school, in a clinic, in the laboratory, or in large units of society. He should be able to work on emotional problems in individual behavior or on the social problems of individuals or groups. . . .

This approach is derived from, and supported by, research (including original research), learning theory, and cybernetics. It is intended to contribute a useful set of principles about behavior change for use by the tyro therapist, the laboratory-minded experimental clinician, the classroom teacher of psychotherapy, those responsible for the direction of others (such as parents and teachers), and all others who attempt, systematically and professionally, to change behavior to benefit the developing or troubled human being. . . .

Our conclusion is that structure is what makes human relations satisfying and provides the basis for problem solving. This is particularly evident when the person is suffering from relatively serious emotional disturbance. The example of the Hutterite society is not offered in support of any type of therapy, but as evidence that a highly structured set of living conditions need not injure mental health and that such structuring can be of substantial benefit. . . .

There are many interpretations of "structure." Here the emphasis is on the therapist's use of external controls and manipulations that will lead to self-control and direction where needed. More specifically, structure in therapy means observing the relationship between given antecedent and resultant elements; interfering in pathology to realign variables so as to produce a different outcome or effect; using environmental manipulations (encompassing persons outside of therapy) to bring about desired effects; introducing and assuring as much certainty and dependability and control in heretofore uncontrolled and uncertain situations as possible; and, above all, making these changes in ways consonant with the integrity and values of the individual (or social unit). . . .

To sum up, this view of structure subsumes verbal therapy measures that are engineered to change behavior, as well as many types of laboratory methods (related chiefly to conditioning, either of a classical or operant variety). And, finally, it embraces a wide range of social measures that seek to control variables entirely outside the classroom, laboratory, or consulting room.

Learning Theory in Assertion-Structured Therapy

Such older learning-theory-psychotherapy formulations can be put in terms of Woodworth's *S-O-R* formula, where *S* refers to the stimulus; *O* refers to the organism (cognitive states, central processes, feeling states, or phenomenological events); and *R* refers to the response. If the Woodworth statement were rewritten to fit the learning-theory position just cited, it would include a large *S*:

$$S\text{-}O\text{-}R$$

If Rogerian therapy were translated into the same statement, it would emphasize the *O*:

$$S\text{-}O\text{-}R. . . .$$

But what difference does it make to the choice of working variables and to the therapeutic process if *S*-centered and *O*-centered variables are replaced with *R*-centered ones? Although there are no good proofs yet, some tentative answers are possible:

1. There would be less interest in the presumptive origins of a patient's difficulties, that is, little effort to find the original stimuli for the problem.

2. The client would be taught to develop new responses to troublesome situations by manipulating his behavior, his environment, or both. He often states his objectives in simple terms, such as "to control my temper," "to overcome sexual impotence," "to feel happier," or "to stop changing jobs so often." Since the therapist may not agree with the objective as stated, in response-centered therapy the therapist and the patient would then seek agreement upon an objective and upon steps to attain it.

Learning Theory in Assertion-Structured Therapy, from Phillips and Wiener, *Short-Term Psychotherapy*, pp. 61, 66–68.

3. Other people would be involved where needed to aid the patient—wherever they were able to act as change agents—in addition to, or even in lieu of, the patient where he was too young, handicapped, or otherwise ineffectual or uninterested.

4. There would be less need to depend on verbal-talking-insight therapy, either partially or totally, if more effective means were available. Many other techniques exist—including reconditioning and restructuring the environment.

5. Any problem-solving responses would be identified and encouraged. The means to this encouragement could be as pervasive and inventive as the client and therapist could contrive.

6. Undesired behavior would be prevented from occurring whenever possible, rather than being allowed to occur or studied in the hope that the analysis of it would "cure" or automatically produce behavior change. The extinction process through analysis appears, at best, to be a weak method of changing behavior.

7. The general task becomes that of finding and instituting new, desired behavior in place of the problem behavior. Since the new behavior is to be set up for reinforcement, the situation must be structured accordingly. In restructuring a situation for reinforcement purposes, the therapist has many procedures available, including simplifying the choices available, reducing external stimuli, and putting the individual on various schedules to ward off undesired behavior. Restructuring is essentially an experiment; as in experimental control, it must hold unwanted variables in check and allow other variables to operate to reinforce the desired behavior.

8. The solution to most problems would be approached step by step, and not by depending upon "insightful" bursts. These gradual steps would be scheduled, with more specific ordering of behavior, setting of limits, blocking of self-defeating behavior, and similar structuring. At times the solution will appear hesitant or tentative, in the way that most habits develop.

9. Corrective behavior, whether it is only a simple act or a large response system, would be considered to occur only on a very specific basis. The behavior that directly opposes the problem-bearing tendency would be identified and promoted through such methods as desensitization, operant conditioning and reconditioning, and aversive stimulation. Specific corrective measures could be forward-looking; they would deal with what is needed to solve the problems *now*, not with what may have caused them originally (although the original causes are probably similar to the causes of the present problems).

10. Clinical terms and descriptions, such as anxiety in most of its uses, complexes, unconscious motivational states, and most diagnostic classifications, if they are used at all, would be reduced to behavioral descriptions and discriminable responses. There would be no need for a separate, esoteric clinical language or explanation.

Writing Therapy

If the patient is reasonably articulate and can write with a degree of clarity, and if he is willing to accept writing as a therapeutic tool, it is relatively easy to find out what his problems are. Many patients prefer this to a face-to-face interview and can write more directly and openly about themselves than they can talk. In general, however, the comparative advantages and disadvantages of writing and of direct oral communication are not the focus here; this chapter is intended only to point out the efficiency and effectiveness of this relatively new approach as another way of helping to solve some of the client's specific problems.

Patients often report that setting down their problems in writing enables them to communicate more effectively with others outside the therapy hour. Whether this is true and, if so, whether it occurs in other modalities equally is of course an open question.

In this procedure, the patient is not simply given a notebook and told to write about himself, but is given guiding instructions. He has a regular weekly appointment which is scheduled at a given hour, just as if he were appearing for a personal interview. Inside the cover of the notebook assigned to him is a one-page description of what is expected of each patient. These instructions are as follows:

1. This procedure—called *writing therapy*—is intended to help you in regard to personal, social, and academic problems.
2. You are to keep your appointments as precisely and conscientiously as if you were appearing for an interview with a staff member.
3. Your writing is kept confidential; your notebook is kept under lock and key.
4. Please be frank, complete, and cooperative with us, and we shall be the same toward you.
5. Some specific suggestions regarding the procedure, intended to help you get along, are the following:
   a. Write out as completely as you desire your ideas about yourself, your observations, etc., spelling out your problems or concerns as clearly as you can.
   b. These problems or concerns may include study habits, concentration, worrry about exams; they may include difficulties with other students, with instructors; they may include difficulties with yourself, or with family members.
   c. Think of ways in which you have tried to cope with these problems, either with or without success.

Writing Therapy, from Phillips and Wiener, *Short-Term Psychotherapy.* pp. 162–63, 183, 185.

d. No problem is either too minor or too gross to report. Only with your candid cooperation can we be of the greatest help to you.

6. At the close of this series of writing therapy sessions, you will be asked to retake some of the initial assessment procedures, in order for us to help evaluate, along with you, the value of these sessions. . . .

Several guidelines can be suggested for the therapist who is interested in trying out writing therapy:

1. Establish a set time for the writing session, just as for an oral therapy session.

2. Allow the patient to write as he wishes, but suggest topics that might get him started if he is blocked.

3. Have the writings go on for about one hour or for some other regular period of time practical for the patient and the therapist. Such structuring of procedural details is just as important here as it is for personal interviews.

4. Ask the patient to write down as specific a description of his problems as possible. If these are not described adequately in the first writing session, ask him to describe them again and give an illustration or two to guide him.

5. Underline the words or phrases that seem to represent the essence of the patient's problems (or write in the margin) and use these as the basis for your reply. Accept the patient's statement of the problem and proceed from there toward solutions, additions, and revisions.

6. Stress the importance of action at all times. Emotional problems are conceived of as reflecting the fact that appropriate behavior has not occurred at the right time or to the right extent. The emphasis on behavior is uppermost.

7. Clarify rewards if there is any evidence that the patient is moving toward solving his problems. The patient's hesitant and perplexed state of mind in meeting the requirements of daily living makes it imperative that any small amount of progress be clearly registered and reinforced. (Generally, the environment will, if properly perceived, provide inherent rewards. The therapist's reinforcement comes primarily from his labeling progress and his tying together of bits of new behavior with desired goals.)

8. Encourage the patient to set even more specific goals. This in turn helps to refine his present goals and to move the therapy along, with the patient and therapist working together.

9. If the patient's reports seem inaccurate, ask him to cite the evidence for his statements. People who are disturbed frequently misperceive and misinterpret events; situations must be described as specifically as possible.

10. Feel free to differ with the patient, but state your reasons, cite evidence to support your position, and be prepared to admit and learn from errors. Differences will inevitably exist, almost to the extent that the therapist and patient adopt the experimental behavior modification view and are active.

11. While writing therapy by itself can succeed as a therapeutic technique, the door should always be left open for the patient to request a personal interview or to switch to oral interviews. More research is needed on writing therapy with other populations. For purposes of research, however, writing therapy can apparently be used effectively without introducing any additional modes of therapy.

PART THREE

Cognitive Approaches to Psychotherapy

11

LOGOTHERAPY

Viktor E. Frankl

Viktor E. Frankl, born on March 26, 1905, was educated at the University of Vienna, where he received his M.D. in 1930 and his Ph.D. in 1949. From 1930 to 1938, he served at the Neuropsychiatric University Clinic. Since 1936 he has been a specialist in neurology and psychiatry. He headed the Department of Neurology at the Poliklinik Hospital in Vienna from 1946 until his retirement. In 1947 he also was appointed assistant professor of psychiatry and neurology at the University of Vienna, and he became a full professor there in 1955.

A frequent lecturer in the United States, Frankl has been visiting professor at Harvard and Southern Methodist University. Recently he began lecturing at the Institute of Logotherapy at the United States International University. Elsewhere he has been a guest lecturer in England, Argentina, Australia, Sri Lanka, India, Israel, Japan, Hawaii, Mexico, and South Africa. He has made twenty-two lecture tours around the world.

Logotherapy is based on the principle of one's "will-to-meaning," one's deep-seated striving for a higher and ultimate meaning to existence. Logotherapy offers a positive approach to the mentally and spiritually disturbed personality.

Regarded as the third Viennese school of psychotherapy (the first being the psychoanalysis of Freud, the second the individual psychology of Adler), logotherapy extends the frontiers of psychiatric knowledge and insight by introducing a new concept of the "will to meaning" in life. (Freudianism is based on the "will to pleasure" and Adlerianism is founded on the "will to power.") In logotherapy, the emphasis is on a psychiatric approach that ministers to the frustration of boredom, automation, and lack of an aim in life.

Frankl's school of psychotherapy aims to give patients the feeling that they are responsible to life for something. Having a goal and responsibility not only give life meaning but can even save life, evidenced by Frankl's experience in concentration camps. Frankl employs the dialectical method in a number of his psychotherapeutic techniques: paradoxical intention; dereflection; the search for meaning, or deriving a meaning in irremedial suffering; self-detachment; logo-drama; medical ministry; technique of the common denominator; humor; and attitudinal stances toward life's irresolute problems. In logotherapy, meaning and value are found in all levels of life's experiences, notwithstanding pain and suffering. Provide individuals with sufficient meaning in life and they can withstand any obstacle.

Frankl's first article, published in 1924 in the *International Journal of Psychoanalysis,* was followed by a number of books, ten of which have been translated into Spanish, Italian, Japanese, Dutch, Swedish, Polish, Norwegian, Portuguese, Danish, French, Chinese, and English. Frankl's best-known book, *Man's Search for Meaning: An Introduction to Logotherapy* (1962), is a revised and enlarged edition of his *From Death-Camp to Existentialism* (1959), which speaks of the survival of human values under conditions of utmost horror and stress. Frankl spent three years as a prisoner in four different Nazi concentration camps, including the notorious Auschwitz. The book depicts his experiences and his search for the meaning of life, leading to the discovery of logotherapy. Among his other important works are *The Doctor and the Soul* (rev. ed., 1966); *Psychotherapy and Existentialism* (1967), a collection of his papers; *The Will to Meaning* (1969), containing his more recent thoughts along with his philosophy; *The Unconscious God* (1975); and *Encyclopedia of Psychotherapeutics,* a five-volume work that he edited with V. E. von Gebsattel and J. H. Schultz.

His more important papers include:

"Paradoxical Intention: A Logotherapeutic Technique," *American Journal of Psychotherapy* 14(1960):520–35.

"Logotherapy and Existential Analysis—A Review," *American Journal of Psychotherapy* 20 (1966):252–60.

"Psychiatry and Man's Quest for Meaning," *Journal of Religion and Health* 1(1962):93–103.

"The Spiritual Dimension in Existential Analysis and Logotherapy," *Journal of Individual Psychology* 15 (1959):157–65.

"Logotherapy and Existentialism," *Psychotherapy: Theory, Research and Practice* 4(1967):138–43.

"Self-Transcendence as a Human Phenomenon," *Journal of Humanistic Psychology* 6(1966):97–106.

"Basic Concepts of Logotherapy," *Journal of Existential Psychiatry* 3(1962):111–18.

"Logotherapy and the Challenge of Suffering," *Review of Existential Psychology and Psychiatry* 1(1961):3–7.

"On Logotherapy and Existential Analysis," *American Journal of Psychoanalysis* 18:(1958):28–37.

"Logos and Existence in Psychotherapy," *American Journal of Psychotherapy* 7(1953):8–15.

"Group Psychotherapeutic Experiences in a Concentration Camp," *Group Psychotherapy* 7(1954):81–90.
"The Concept of Man in Psychotherapy," *Pastoral Psychology* 6(1955):16–26.

Chapters in books include:

"Logotherapy and the Collective Neuroses," in *Progress in Psychotherapy*, ed. J. H. Masserman and J. L. Moreno (1959).
"From Psychotherapy to Logotherapy," in *Psychology*, ed. Annette Walters (1963).
"The Philosophical Foundations of Logotherapy," in *Phenomenology: Pure and Applied*, ed. E. W. Straus (1964).

The Meaning of Logotherapy

The Existential Vacuum

More and more a psychiatrist today is confronted with a new type of patient, a new class of neurosis, a new sort of suffering the most remarkable characteristic of which is the fact that it does not represent a disease in the proper sense of the term. This phenomenon has brought about a change in the function—or should I say mission?—of present-day psychiatry. In such cases, the traditional techniques of treatment available to the psychiatrist prove themselves to be less and less applicable.

More specifically, I have called this phenomenon, which the psychiatrist now has to deal with so frequently, *the existential vacuum.* What I mean thereby is the experience of a total lack, or loss, of an ultimate meaning to one's existence that would make life worthwhile. The consequent void, the state of inner emptiness, is at present one of the major challenges to psychiatry. In the conceptual framework of logotherapeutic teaching, that phenomenon is also referred to as *existential frustration,* or the frustration of *the will to meaning.*

By the latter concept, logotherapy denotes what it regards as the most fundamental motivational force in man. Freudian psychoanalysis centers its motivational theory on the pleasure principle or, as one might call it, the *will to pleasure,* whereas Adlerian individual psychology focuses on what is generally called the *will to power.* [1] In contrast to both theories, logotherapy consid-

The Meaning of Logotherapy, from Viktor E. Frankl, "Psychiatry and Man's Quest for Meaning," *Journal of Religion and Health* 1(1962): 93–103. Some internal references have been deleted.

[1]According to Freud's own statement, the reality principle is nothing but an extension of, and ultimately operates in the service of, the pleasure principle.

ers man to be primarily motivated by a groping for a meaning to his existence, by the striving to fulfill this meaning and thereby to actualize as many value potentialities as possible. In short, man is motivated by the will to meaning.

In former days, people frustrated in their will to meaning would probably have turned to a pastor, priest, or rabbi. Today, they crowd clinics and offices. The psychiatrist, then, frequently finds himself in an embarrassing situation, for he now is confronted with human problems rather than with specific clinical symptoms. Man's search for a meaning is not pathological, but rather the surest sign of being truly human. Even if this search is frustrated, it cannot be considered a sign of disease. It is spiritual distress, not mental disease.

How should the clinician respond to this challenge? Traditionally, he is not prepared to cope with this situation in any but medical terms. Thus he is forced to conceive of the problem as something pathological. Furthermore, he induces his patient to interpret his plight as a sickness to be cured rather than as a challenge to be met. By so doing, the doctor robs the patient of the potential fruits of his spiritual struggle.

The doctor should not let himself be seduced by the still prevalent reductionism into devaluating man's concern for meaning and values to "nothing but" a defense mechanism, a reaction formation, or a rationalization. The "nothing-but-ness" of human phenomena is indeed one of the foremost features in the reductionist image of man. But would it be wise to base therapy on, or even to start therapy with, Freud's assumption, for example, that philosophy is "nothing more" than a form of sublimation of repressed sexuality? A sound philosophy of life, I think, may be the most valuable asset for a psychiatrist to have when he is treating a patient in ultimate despair. Instead of stubbornly trying to reduce meaning and values to their alleged psychodynamic roots, or to deduce them from psychogenetic sources, the psychiatrist should take these phenomena at face value rather than press them into the Procrustean bed of preconceived ideas regarding their function and origin. Preserving the humanness of human phenomena is precisely what the phenomenological approach, as propounded by Husserl and Scheler, has attempted to do.

Certainly both the meaning of human existence and man's will to meaning are accessible only through an approach that goes beyond the plane of merely psychodynamic and psychogenetic data. We must enter, or better, we must follow man into the dimension of the specifically human phenomena that is the spiritual dimension of being. To avoid a confusion arising from the fact that the term *spiritual* usually has a religious connotation in English, I prefer to speak of noetic in contrast to psychic phenomena and the noological in contrast to the psychological dimension. The noological dimension is to be defined as that dimension in which the specifically human phenomena are located.

Through a merely psychological analysis, the human phenomena are, as it were, taken out of the noological space and leveled down into the psychological plane. Such a procedure is called psychologism.[2] It entails no less than the loss of a whole dimension. Moreover, what is lost is the dimension that allows man to emerge and rise above the level of the biological and psychological foundations of his existence. This is an important issue, for transcending these foundations and thereby transcending oneself signifies the very act of existing. Self-transcendence, I would say, is the essence of existence, which in turn means the specifically human mode of being. To the extent to which this mode of being exceeds the psychological frame of reference, the appropriate and adequate approach to existence is not psychological, but existential.

Logotherapy and Noology

This holds true even for therapy. Logotherapy is that psychotherapy centering on life's meaning as well as man's search for this meaning. In fact, *logos* means "meaning." However, it also means "spirit." And logotherapy takes the spiritual or noological dimension fully into account. In this way, logotherapy is also enabled to realize—and to utilize—the intrinsic difference between the noetic and psychic aspects of man. Despite this ontological difference between the noetic and psychic, between spirit and mind, the anthropological wholeness and unity is not only maintained by our multidimensional concept of man, but even supported. Speaking of man in terms of his spiritual, mental, and bodily levels, or layers, may well prompt one to assume that each of these aspects can be separated from the others. Nobody, however, can claim that viewing a human being in his manifold dimensions would destroy the wholeness and unity inherent in man.

There is a practical implication involved in our "dimensional ontology." I refer to the specific capacity of man to detach himself from himself. Through the emergence into noological dimension, man becomes able to detach himself from his psychological condition. This specifically human capacity for self-detachment is mobilized by logotherapy particularly against pathological events within the psychological dimension, such as neurotic and psychotic symptoms. In spite of the emphasis that it places upon responsibleness as an essential quality of being human, logotherapy is far from holding man responsible for psychotic, or even neurotic, symptoms. However, it does hold him accountable for his *attitude* toward these symptoms. For it regards man as *free* and responsible and considers this freedom not to be freedom from conditions, but rather freedom to take a stand, to choose a stand toward conditions. What is called paradoxical intention is a logotherapeutic technique designed to make use of the human capacity for noopsychic detachment.

---

[2]Insofar as psychoanalysis is more or less linked to abnormal phenomena such as neuroses and psychoses, the spiritual aspirations of man are likely to be dealt with not only in psychological but also in pathological terms. Thus the pitfall of psychologism is increased by the fallacy that I have termed *pathologism*.

A multidimensional view enables us to avoid not only psychologism, but also noologism. . . .

An example of flagrant noologism would be the contention by some psychiatrists that a patient suffering from endogenous depression not only feels guilty, but really is guilty, "existentially guilty," and hence depressed. I regard endogenous depression as somatogenic rather than noogenic—not even psychogenic—in origin. This somatogenic psychosis in turn engenders an abnormal awareness of the guilt that is normally linked to the "human condition." One could compare this to a reef that emerges during low tide. Yet no one could claim that the reef causes the low tide. Likewise, the guilt has not caused the psychotic depression but, on the contrary, the depression—an emotional low tide, as it were—has caused the guilt to be felt so acutely. But imagine the potential effect of confronting the psychotic patient with such a spiritualistic, even moralistic, interpretation of his illness in terms of "existential guilt." It just would offer additional content to the patient's pathological tendency toward self-accusations, and suicide might well be his response.

In itself, the existential vacuum is not anything pathological. Nonetheless, it may eventuate in a neurotic illness for which logotherapy has coined the term *noogenic neurosis*. This neurosis is not the result of instinctual conflicts or clashes between the claims of ego, id, and superego, but rather the effect of spiritual problems and existential frustration. What is required in such cases is a psychotherapy that focuses on both spirit and meaning—i.e., logotherapy. However, logotherapy, as a psychotherapeutic approach and procedure, is also applicable in psychogenic, and even somatogenic, neuroses. As an example of the latter, hyperthyroidism brings about an inclination to anxiety states to which the patient often responds in terms of what is called *anticipatory anxiety*. That is to say, he is afraid of the recurrence of anxiety, and the very expectation of such an attack precipitates it again and again. Increasingly, the patient is thus caught in a feedback mechanism that becomes established between the primary somatic condition and the secondary psychic reaction. This vicious circle must be attacked on its somatic as well as its psychic side. In order to achieve the latter, one must use logotherapy, more specifically paradoxical intention, which "takes the wind out of the sails" of anticipatory anxiety, while tranquilizing drugs accomplish the other requirement: namely, to remove the somatic foundation and basis of the whole disorder. According to the observation of the author, mild hyperthyroidism frequently results in agoraphobias just as masked tetany does in claustrophobias. And it happens that the first tranquilizer ever brought out on the European continent (it was developed by the author as early as 1952, even before the "march to Miltown" had begun) has proved itself to be the most effective drug treatment of choice in cases of somatogenic phobias.

Again and again, however, it turns out that the feedback mechanism called anticipatory anxiety thrives in the existential vacuum. Filling this vacuum prevents the patient from having a relapse. Refocusing him on meaning and purpose and decentering him away from obsession and compulsion cause these symptoms to atrophy. In such cases, the source of pathology is psychological or even biological; but the resource of therapy, the therapeutic agent, is noological. . . .

Self-Transcendence and Noodynamics

It is a tenet of logotherapy that transcendence is the essence of existence. What is meant by this tenet is that existence is authentic only to the extent to which it points to something that is *not* itself. Being human cannot be its own meaning. It has been said that man must never be taken as a means to an end. Is this to imply that he is an end in itself, that he is intended and destined to realize and actualize himself? Man, I should say, realizes and actualizes values. He finds himself only to the extent to which he loses himself in the first place, be it for the sake of something or somebody, for the sake of a cause of a fellowman, or "for God's sake." Man's struggle for his self and identity is doomed to failure unless it is enacted as dedication and devotion to something beyond his self, to something above his self. As Jaspers puts it, "What man is, he becomes through that cause which he has made his own."

Being human fades away unless it commits itself to some freely chosen meaning. The emphasis lies on free choice. An outstanding American psychoanalyst reported after his trip to Moscow that behind the Iron Curtain people were less neurotic because they had more tasks to fulfill. When I was invited to read a paper before the psychiatrists of Krakow, I referred to this report, but remarked that even though the West might well confront man with fewer tasks than does the East, it leaves to him the freedom to choose among the tasks. If this freedom is denied to him, he becomes a cogwheel that has a function to carry out, but no opportunity to choose it.

A psychotherapy that confronts man with meaning and purpose is likely to be criticized as demanding too much of the patient. Actually, however, man of today is less endangered and threatened by being overdemanded than by being underdemanded. There is not only a pathology of stress, but also a pathology of the *absence* of tension. And what we have to fear in an age of existential frustration is not so much tension per se as it is the *lack* of tension that is created by the loss of meaning. I deem it a dangerous misconception of mental health that what man needs in the first place is homeostasis *à tout prix*. What man really needs is a sound amount of tension aroused by the challenge of a meaning he has to fulfill. This tension is inherent in being human and hence indispensable for mental well-being. What I call noodynamics is the dynamics in a field of tension whose poles are represented by man and the meaning that beckons him. By noodynamics man's life is put in order and structure like iron filings in a magnetic field of force. In contrast to psychodynamics, noodynamics leaves to man the freedom to choose between fulfilling or declining the meaning that awaits him.

Theodore A. Kotchen explored the relation of the concept of meaning to mental health by constructing a questionnaire and administering it to mental patients and to nonpsychiatric control groups. The results gave empirical validity to a conception of mental health as offered by "logotherapy, or any other variety" of existential analysis: a mind is healthy when it has achieved a sufficient store of "meaning."

Will to Meaning

We maintain: only when the primary, objective orientation is lacking and has run aground does that interest in one's condition arise which is so strikingly manifest in neurotic existence. Therefore the striving for self-actualization is in no way something primary; rather we see in it a deficient mode and a reduced level of human existence. Man's primary concern is not self-actualization, but fulfillment of meaning. In logotherapy we speak of a will-to-meaning; with this we designate man's striving to fulfill as much meaning in his existence as possible, and to realize as much value in his life as possible.

The will to meaning is something elementary, something genuine and authentic, and as such ought to be taken seriously by psychotherapy. But a psychology that designates itself as an unmasking one is out to unmask this too; it presents man's claim to a maximally meaningful existence as a camouflage of unconscious instincts, and disposes of it as a mere rationalization. What is needed, I would say, is an unmasking of the unmasker! Although in some cases unmasking may be right, the tendency to unmask must be able to stop in front of that which is genuine in man; else, it reveals the unmasking psychologist's own tendency to devaluate.

Least of all can psychotherapy afford to ignore the will to meaning; instead, calling upon it involves a psychotherapeutic principle of the first rank. This can, under some circumstances, not only effect the preservation of psychic or somatic health but may be outright life-saving. Here not only clinical but other types of experiences, though no less empirical and practical, present themselves. In the tormenting "experiment" *(experimentum crucis)* of war prisons and concentration camps scarcely anything enabled one more to sur-

Will to Meaning, from Viktor E. Frankl, "The Spiritual Dimension in Existential Analysis and Logotherapy," *Journal of Individual Psychology* 15(1959):157–65. Also published as "Existential Analysis and Dimensional Ontology" in Viktor E. Frankl, *Psychotherapy and Existentialism: Selected Papers on Logotherapy* (New York: Simon & Schuster, 1968). Internal references have been deleted.

vive all these "extreme situations" (*Grenzsituationen,* in the sense of Karl Jaspers) than the knowledge of a life task. This "experiment" has confirmed Nietzsche's words: "He who has a *why* to live for, can bear almost any *how*." The validity of these words depends, however, upon the fact that such a "why" pertains not just to any situation: it *must* pertain to the unique life task, the singularity of which corresponds to the fact that each man's life is singular in its existence and unique in its essence.

Existential Frustration

The will to meaning can become frustrated. In logotherapy we speak of an *existential frustration* since it appears justified to designate as existential that which applies to the meaning of existence, including the will to meaning. The feeling of meaninglessness is not pathological; it is something generally human, even the most human of all that there may be in man; it is not something all-too-human, something morbid. We must learn to distinguish between the human and the morbid, lest we confuse two essentially different things, viz., spiritual distress and psychic illness. In itself existential frustration is far from being morbid.

> A patient of our acquaintance, a university professor of Vienna, had been assigned to us because he had tormented himself with the question of the meaning of his life. It turned out that he suffered from a recurrent endogenous depression; however, he brooded over and doubted the meaning of his life not during the phases of his psychic illness, but rather in the intervals, that is, during the time of healthiness.

Today existential frustration plays a more important role than ever. Man today suffers not only an increasing loss of instinct but also a loss of tradition, and herein may well be one of the causes of existential frustration. We see its effect in a phenomenon which we in logotherapy call *existential vacuum,* that is, inner emptiness, the feeling of having lost the meaning of existence and the content of life. This feeling then spreads and permeates the whole of life.

> The existential vacuum may become manifest or remain concealed. It becomes manifest in the condition of boredom. The phenomenon of boredom, incidentally, invalidates the principle of homeostasis as applied to man's psychic life. If complete satisfaction of our needs were our primary aim, then such satisfaction would not result in existential fulfillment but rather in emptiness in the deepest sense of existential vacuum.
>
> When Schopenhauer once said that humanity apparently is doomed to swing back and forth between the two extremes of need and boredom,

---

Existential Frustration, from Frankl, "The Spiritual Dimension," pp. 157–66.

he was not only quite correct; he seems to have foreseen that in our generation boredom gives us psychiatrists more work than does need, including the sexual need. Increasing automation gives man a greater amount of leisure time than he has previously had and than he knows how to use. Also the aging population is faced with the problem of how to fill its time and its own existential vacuum. Finally, we can also see many ways in which the will-to-meaning is frustrated in youth and adolescence. Delinquency can only in part be traced to the acceleration of physical development; spiritual frustration, as is more and more being recognized, is also decisive.

Existential frustration can certainly also lead to neurosis. And so we speak in logotherapy of a *noogenic neurosis,* by which we understand a neurosis which has originally and genuinely been caused by a spiritual problem, a moral conflict, or an existential crisis; and we place the noogenic neurosis heuristically over against neurosis in the strict sense of the word, which is by definition a psychogenic illness.

Noetic Therapy

The specific therapy of noogenic neurosis can only be a psychotherapy which dares to follow man, his sickness and its etiology into the noetic, spiritual dimension. Such a therapy is logotherapy. When we distinguish between logotherapy and psychotherapy, we use the latter term in the narrow sense, and, at that, intend the distinction only in a heuristic way. *Logos* now means not only "meaning," but also the "spiritual." The will-to-meaning is the subjective side of a spiritual reality in which the meaning is the objective side; at least it is objective insofar as the will is concerned with "finding" meaning and not at all with "giving" it.

Noetic therapy is, however, not only applicable in cases of noogenic neuroses; rather, a psychogenic neurosis often represents a psychic development that has become rampant because of a spiritual vacuum, so that the psychotherapy will not be complete unless the existential vacuum is filled and the existential frustration is removed.

Logotherapy is more concerned with the attitude of the patient toward the symptom than with the symptom itself; for all too often it is the wrong attitude that is really pathogenic. Logotherapy, therefore, distinguishes different attitude formations, and attempts to bring about within the patient a transformation of attitude; in other words, it is really a conversion therapy (not implying the religious connotation). To this end it provides specific methods

---

Noetic Therapy, from Frankl, "The Spiritual Dimension," pp. 157–66.

and techniques such as *dereflection* and *paradoxical intention* which have been described elsewhere.

Logotherapy attempts to orient and direct the patient toward a concrete, personal meaning. But it is not its purpose to *give* a meaning to the patient's existence; its concern is only to enable the patient to *find* such a meaning, to broaden, so to speak, his field of vision, so that he will become aware of the full spectrum of possibilities for personal and concrete meanings and values.

If the patient is to become conscious of a possible meaning, then the doctor must know and remain conscious of all the possibilities for meaning, above all the meaning of suffering. Suffering from an incurable disease, for example, conceals in itself not only the last possibility for the fulfillment of meaning and the realization of value, but the possibility for deepest meaning and highest value. In this view, life up to the last moment never ceases to have a meaning. Logotherapy, then, will not only aim toward the recovery of the patient's capacity for work, enjoyment, and experience, but also toward the development of his capacity to suffer, viz., his capacity to fulfill the possible meaning of suffering.

Logotherapy

Today, the will to meaning is often frustrated. In logotherapy, one speaks of existential frustration. Patients who fall into this diagnostic category usually complain of a sense of futility and meaninglessness or emptiness and void. In logotherapy, this condition is termed *existential vacuum*. It constitutes the mass neurosis of our age. In a recent publication, a Czechoslovakian psychiatrist, Stanislav Kratochvil, has pointed out that existential frustration makes itself felt even in Communist countries.

In cases in which existential frustration produces neurotic symptoms, one is dealing with a new type of neurosis which I call *noogenic neurosis*. In order to substantiate this concept, Crumbaugh and Maholick, the directors of a research center in the United States, devised their Purpose in Life (PIL) test and administered it to 225 subjects. "The results," they write, "consistently support Frankl's hypothesis that a new type of neurosis—which he terms *noogenic neurosis*—is present in the clinics alongside the conventional forms. There is evidence," the authors conclude, "that we are in truth dealing with a new syndrome." As to the frequency of its occurrence, let me refer to the statistical research conducted by Werner in London, Langen and Volhard in Tübingen, Prill in Würzburg, and Niebauer in Vienna. They estimate that about 20 percent of the neuroses one encounters are noogenic in nature and origin.

Logotherapy, from Viktor E. Frankl, "Logotherapy and Existential Analysis—A Review," *American Journal of Psychotherapy* 20(1966):252–60. Some internal references have been deleted.

It goes without saying that meaning and purpose in life cannot be prescribed like a drug. It is not the job of a doctor to *give* meaning to the patient's life. But it may well be his task, through an existential analysis, to enable the patient to *find* meaning in life. And in my opinion, meaning is something to be found rather than to be given. At least, meaning cannot be given in an arbitrary way. Again it was Crumbaugh and Maholick who, to my knowledge for the first time, have pointed to the fact that finding meaning in a situation has something to do with a Gestalt perception. This assumption is confirmed by a Gestaltist, Wertheimer, who explicitly states that a quality of "requiredness" is inherent in the situation and, what is even more, "the demands and 'requirements' " of the situation "are objective qualities."

Dereflection, Hyperintention, and Hyperreflection

According to logotherapeutic teachings, meaning is not really lacking in any life situation. This is due to the fact that even the negative aspects of human existence such as suffering, guilt, and death can still be turned into something positive, provided that they are faced with the right attitude. Needless to say, meaning can be found only in unavoidable suffering whereas accepting avoidable pain would form some sort of masochism rather than heroism. As a matter of fact, unavoidable suffering is inherent in the human condition and the therapist should take heed not to reinforce the patient's evasive denial of this existential fact.

Alongside the will to meaning stands the will to power and what one could call the will to pleasure. In the final analysis, however, the will to pleasure proves to be self-defeating. The more one tries to gain pleasure, the less one is able to obtain it. Therein lies one of the major factors underlying sexual neuroses, be it impotence or frigidity. Sexual performance or experience are strangled to the same extent to which they are made either an objective of intention or an object of attention. In logotherapy, one speaks of hyperintention or hyperreflection, respectively. In cases of impotence, hyperintention is frequently due to the fact that the patient approaches sexual intercourse as something which is demanded of him. Correspondingly, a logotherapeutic technique has been developed in order to remove this demand quality.[3] This technique is termed *dereflection*. Yet the logotherapeutic treatment of sexual

---

[3]It is often possible to overcome the "demands of the partner" through a trick: We advise the patient to inform the partner that he consulted a doctor who considered the patient's case as not serious and the prognosis favorable. It is most important for him, however, to tell his partner that the doctor also has absolutely forbidden coitus. His partner now expects no sexual activity and the patient is "released." This release from the demands of the partner enables the patient to express his sexuality again, undisturbed and unblocked by the feeling that something is demanded or expected from him. Often, in fact, the partner is not only surprised when the potency of the patient becomes apparent, but she goes so far as to reject him because of the doctor's orders. It is then, usually, with the *fait accompli,* that the vicious circle of apprehension and compulsion to self-observation is completely broken.

neurosis is applicable regardless of whether or not one adopts the logotherapeutic theory. In the neurological department of the Poliklinik Hospital in Vienna, I have entrusted an outpatient ward for patients with sexual neuroses to a doctor who is a strict Freudian, but in the given setting, where only short-term procedures are indicated, he uses the logotherapeutic rather than the psychoanalytic technique.

Paradoxical Intention and Anticipatory Anxiety

Along with deflection, there is another logotherapeutic technique which lends itself to the short-term treatment of obsessive-compulsive and phobic patients rather than those with sexual neuroses. This technique is called *paradoxical intention.* I have described it as early as 1946 in the original German version of one of my English books, *The Doctor and the Soul,* and in other papers. Again, it should be noted that even doctors who adhere to theories different from the one which underlies logotherapy include paradoxical intention in their armamentarium. For example, many psychoanalysts have been using the paradoxical intention technique successfully. Now they try to explain this success and specifically to explain it in psychodynamic terms. To cite another instance, Müller-Hegemann interprets paradoxical intention in terms of a "neurophysiologically oriented approach." He "has observed favorable results in the last years in patients suffering from phobias" and therefore considers paradoxical intention "to have much merit."

What is going on when paradoxical intention is applied? In order to understand it one must consider the phenomenon called *anticipatory anxiety.* By this I mean the response and reaction to an event in terms of the fearful expectation of the recurrence of the event. However, fear tends to make come true precisely that which one is afraid of and in the same vein anticipatory anxiety triggers off what the patient so fearfully expects to happen. Thus a vicious circle is established. A symptom evokes a phobia and the phobia provokes the symptom. The recurrence of the symptom then reinforces the phobia.

How can one break up this vicious circle? It can be managed in two ways, first by psychotherapy and second by pharmacotherapy. With regard to pharmacotherapy, let me refer to those cases with agoraphobic symptoms in which I could show that hyperthyroidism is an underlying factor. Or cases of claustrophobia which I could trace to latent tetany. Incidentally, the first tranquilizer ever developed on the Continent—it was developed by me as early as 1952 —even lends itself to the drug treatment of these claustrophobias in a specific way. One should bear in mind, however, that the organic factor involved in such cases provides no more than a mere inclination to anxiety while the full-fledged anxiety neurosis does not develop unless the anticipatory anxiety mechanism comes into play. Therefore, to unhinge the circle one must attack it both psychically and organically. And taking the wind out of the sails of anticipatory anxiety is precisely the job done by paradoxical intention. To put it in a nutshell, the patient is thereby encouraged to do, or wish to happen, the very things he fears. In other words, the pathogenic fear is replaced by a paradoxical wish.

Alongside the circle formation built up by anticipatory anxiety in phobic cases, there is another feedback mechanism which one may encounter in obsessive-compulsive neurotics. They are plagued by the idea that they might commit suicide or even homicide or that the strange thoughts which haunt them might be signs of imminent, if not present, psychosis. For these reasons the patients fight their obsessions and compulsions. But pressure induces counterpressure, and counterpressure, in turn, increases pressure. Conversely, if one succeeds in making the patient stop fighting his symptoms—and this may well be accomplished by paradoxical intention—the symptoms soon diminish and finally atrophy.

Most of the authors who have practiced paradoxical intention and published their work agree that it is a short-term procedure. The assumption, however, "that the durability of results corresponds to the length of therapy" is one of "the illusions of Freudian orthodoxy," to quote Emil A. Gutheil, the late editor of the *American Journal of Psychotherapy.* It is also "a completely baseless assertion," to cite the grand old man of German psychotherapy, J. H. Schultz, "that symptom removal must be followed by substitute symptoms."

Self-Detachment

There is evidence that paradoxical intention even works in chronic cases. For example, in the German *Encyclopaedia of Psychotherapy* the case of a sixty-five-year-old woman is described who for sixty years had suffered from a hand-washing compulsion. A member of my staff successfully applied the paradoxical intention technique in this case. The patient was finally able to joke about her compulsion, to develop a sense of humor. In fact, paradoxical intention should always be formulated in as humorous a manner as possible. Humor is indeed a definitely human phenomenon. After all, no beast is capable of laughing. What is even more important, humor allows man to create a perspective, to put a distance between himself and whatever may confront him. By the same token, humor allows man to become detached and thereby to attain the fullest possible control over himself. To make use of the human capacity for self-detachment is what paradoxical intention basically achieves. . . .

Man's primary concern is to find and fulfill meaning and purpose in life. Today, however, ever more patients relate the feeling of a profound meaninglessness or, as one could call it—in contradistinction to Maslow's peak-experience—an *abyss-experience.* In logotherapy, this inner void is referred to as the *existential vacuum.* In cases in which it results in a neurosis, this is termed in logotherapy a *noogenic neurosis*—in contradistinction to the psychogenic neurosis which is the neurosis in the conventional sense of the word.

According to existential analysis [*Existenzanalyse*] which underlies logotherapy, there are two specifically human phenomena, the "capacity of self-transcendence" and the "capacity of self-detachment." They are mobilized by two logotherapeutic techniques, "dereflection" and "paradoxical intention," respectively. Both lend themselves particularly to the short-term treatment of sexual as well as obsessive-compulsive and phobic neuroses, especially in cases in which the anticipatory anxiety mechanism is involved. It is the contention of some authors that in existential psychiatry, logotherapy is the only school which has evolved psychotherapeutic techniques.

Paradoxical Intention as a Principal Logotherapeutic Technique

In order to understand fully what takes place when this technique is utilized, we shall use as a starting point a phenomenon which is known to every clinically trained psychiatrist, namely anticipatory anxiety. It is commonly observed that such anxiety often produces precisely that situation of which the patient is afraid. The erythrophobic individual, for example, who is afraid of blushing when he enters a room and faces a group of people, will actually blush at precisely that moment.

In case histories which display anticipatory anxiety, the fear of some pathogenic event (thus, ironically, precipitating it), one may frequently observe an analogous phenomenon. This is the compulsion to self-observation. For instance, in cases of insomnia, the patients often report in the anamnesis that they become especially aware of the problem of falling asleep when they go to bed. Of course this very attention inhibits the sleeping process.

In addition to the fact that excessive *attention* proves to be an intrinsically pathogenic factor with regard to the etiology of neuroses, we also observe in many neurotic patients that excessive *intention* may also be pathogenic. Many sexual neuroses, at least according to the findings and teachings of logotherapy, may be traced back to the forced intention of attaining the goal of sexual intercourse—be it the male seeking to demonstrate his potency, or the female her ability to experience orgasm. The author has discussed this subject at

Paradoxical Intention as a Principal Logotherapeutic Technique, from Viktor E. Frankl, "Paradoxical Intention: A Logotherapeutic Technique," *American Journal of Psychotherapy* 14(1960):520–35. Also found in Viktor E. Frankl, *Psychotherapy and Existentialism: Selected Papers on Logotherapy* (New York: Simon & Schuster, 1968). Internal references have been deleted.

length in various papers, pointing out that as a rule the patient seeks pleasure intentionally (one might say that he takes the "pleasure principle" literally). However, pleasure belongs to that category of events which cannot be brought about by direct intention, but, on the contrary, is a mere side-effect or by-product. Therefore, the more one strives for pleasure, the less one is able to attain it. Thus we see an interesting parallel in which anticipatory anxiety brings about precisely what the patient had feared, while excessive intention, as well as excessive self-observation with regard to one's own functioning, makes this functioning impossible.

It is this twofold fact upon which logotherapy bases the technique known as *paradoxical intention.* For instance, when a phobic patient is afraid that something will happen to him, the logotherapist encourages him to intend or wish, even if only for a second, precisely what he fears.

The following clinical reports will indicate what I mean:

> A young physician came to our clinic because of a severe hidrophobia. He had for a long time been troubled by disturbances of the autonomic nervous system. One day he happened to meet his chief on the street and, as the young man extended his hand in greeting, he noticed that he was perspiring more than usually. The next time he was in a similar situation he expected to perspire again and this anticipatory anxiety precipitated excessive sweating. It was a vicious circle; hyperhidrosis provoked hidrophobia and hidrophobia, in turn, produced hyperhidrosis. We advised our patient, in the event that his anticipatory anxiety should recur, to resolve deliberately to show the people whom he confronted at the time how much he could really sweat. A week later he returned to report that whenever he met anyone who triggered his anticipatory anxiety, he said to himself, "I only sweated out a liter before, but now I'm going to pour out at least ten liters!" What was the result of this paradoxical resolution? After suffering from his phobia for four years, he was quickly able, after only one session, to free himself of it for good by this new procedure.

The reader will note that this treatment consists not only in a reversal of the patient's attitude toward his phobia—inasmuch as the usual "avoidance" response is replaced by an intentional effort—but also, that it is carried out in as humorous a setting as possible. This brings about a change of attitude toward the symptom which enables the patient to place himself at a distance from the symptom, to detach himself from his neurosis. This procedure is based on the fact that, according to logotherapeutic teaching, the pathogenesis in phobias and obsessive-compulsive neuroses is partially due to the increase of anxieties and compulsions that is caused by the endeavor to avoid or fight them. A phobic person usually tries to avoid the situation in which his anxiety arises, while the obsessive-compulsive tries to suppress, and thus to fight, his threatening ideas. In either case the result is a strengthening of the symptom. Conversely, if we succeed in bringing the patient to the point where he ceases to flee from or to fight his symptoms, but, on the contrary, even exaggerates them, then we may observe that the symptom diminishes and that the patient is no longer haunted by it.

Such a procedure must make use of the unique potentiality for self-detachment inherent in a sense of humor. Along with Heidegger's assertion that "sorrowful concern" [*Sorge*] is the essential feature permeating human existence, and Binswanger's subsequent substitution of "loving togetherness" [*liebendes Miteinandersein*] as the chief human characteristic, I would venture to say that humor also deserves to be mentioned among the basic human capacities. No animal is able to laugh.

As a matter of fact, when paradoxical intention is used, the purpose is to enable the patient to develop a sense of detachment toward his neurosis by laughing at it, to put it simply. . . .

A few more case reports may serve to develop and clarify this method further:

I once received a letter from a young medical student who had in the past listened to my clinical lectures on logotherapy. She reminded me of a demonstration of paradoxical intention that she had attended, and continued: "I tried to apply the method which you had used in the classroom demonstration to myself. I, too, suffered continually from the fear that, while dissecting at the Institute of Anatomy, I would begin to tremble when the anatomy instructor entered the room. Soon this fear actually did cause a tremor. Then, remembering what you had told us in the lecture that dealt with this very situation, I said to myself whenever the instructor entered the dissecting room "Oh, here is the instructor! Now I'll show him what a good trembler I am—I'll really show him how to tremble!" But whenever I deliberately tried to tremble, I was unable to do so!" . . .

Once I encountered the most severe case of stuttering that I have seen in my many years of practice: I met a man who had stuttered severely all his life—except once. This happened when he was twelve years old, and had hooked a ride on a street car. When he was caught by the conductor, he thought that the only way of escape would be to evoke his sympathy, and so he tried to demonstrate that he was just a "poor, stuttering boy." But when he tried to stutter, he was utterly unable to do it! . . .

Another case, which was treated by one of my assistants, Dr. Kurt Kocourek, concerned a woman, Mary B., who had been undergoing various treatment methods for eleven years, yet her complaints, rather than being alleviated, had increased. She suffered from attacks of palpitation accompanied by marked anxiety and anticipatory fears of a sudden collapse. After the first attack she began to fear that it would recur and, consequently, it did. The patient reported that whenever she had this fear, it was followed by palpitations. Her chief concern was, however, that she might collapse in the street. Dr. Kocourek advised her to tell herself at such a moment: "My heart shall beat still faster! I will collapse right here on the sidewalk!" Furthermore, the patient was advised to seek out deliberately places which she had experienced as disagreeable, or even dangerous, instead of avoiding them. Two weeks later, the patient reported: "I am quite well now and feel scarcely any palpitations. The fear has completely disappeared." Some weeks after her discharge, she reported: "Occasionally mild palpitations occur, but when they do, I say to myself, 'My heart should beat even faster,' and at that moment the palpitations cease."

Paradoxical intention may even be used therapeutically in cases which have an underlying somatic basis:

The patient was suffering from a coronary infarct. Subsequently he developed anxiety as a psychic response to his somatic illness, and this anxiety became so intense that it became his main complaint. He began to withdraw from his professional and social contacts and finally could not bear to leave the hospital where he had been a patient for six months and where a heart specialist was at hand. Finally the patient was transferred to our clinic and logotherapeutic treatment was begun by Dr. Gerda Becker. The following is a brief summary of tape-recorded comments of the patient:

"I felt very anxious and the pain in my heart region began to trouble me again. Then I asked the nurse to call the doctor. She stopped in for a moment and told me to try to make my heart beat faster and to *increase* the pain and fear until she could return a little later. I tried this and when she came back after about a quarter of an hour, I had to confess to her that, to my great surprise, my endeavors had been in vain—I could increase neither the pain nor the palpitations but, as a matter of fact, both had disappeared! . . . Encouraged by this turn of events, I left the clinic for an hour or so and went for a walk through the streets—something that I had not attempted for more than six months. Upon entering a store I felt a slight palpitation but, as the doctor had suggested, I immediately started saying to myself, 'Try to feel even more anxiety!' Again it was in vain, I simply could not do it! I returned to the clinic happy over my achievement of leaving the hospital and strolling around alone." We invited the patient to visit us six months later and he reported that he was free of any complaints and had, meanwhile, resumed his professional work.

Now let us turn to the following case:

Mrs. H. R. had been suffering for fourteen years when she came to the clinic. She was severely handicapped by a counting compulsion as well as the compulsion to check whether her dresser drawers were in order and securely locked. She did this by continually checking the contents of the drawers, closing them by a sharp rapping of her knuckles, and finally by attempting to turn the key in the lock several times. Eventually this condition became so chronic that her knuckles were often bruised and bleeding and the keys and locks on the bureau were ruined.

On the day of her admission, Dr. Eva Niebauer demonstrated to the patient how to practice paradoxical intention. She was shown how to throw things carelessly into her dresser and closet, to try to create as much disorder as possible. She was to say to herself, "These drawers should be as messy as possible!" The result was that two days after admission her counting compulsion disappeared and, after the fourth day, she felt no need to recheck her dresser. She even forgot to lock it—something that she had not failed to do for decades! Sixteen days after hospitalization she felt free of any complaints or symptoms, was very proud of her achievement, and was able to do her daily chores without compulsive repetition. She admitted that obsessive-compulsive ideas occasionally recurred but reported that she was able to ignore them, or, to make light of them. Thus she overcame her compulsion not by frantically fighting it (which only strengthens it) but, on the contrary, by "making a joke of it"; in other words, by applying paradoxical intention.

A remarkable fact about this case is that after her symptoms had cleared up, the patient spontaneously, during a psychotherapeutic interview, revived some significant memories. She remembered that when she was five years old, her brother had destroyed a favorite doll and thereafter she began locking her toys in her dresser drawer. When she was sixteen, she caught her sister in the act of putting on some of the patient's best party clothes without her permission. From that time on she always carefully locked up her clothes. Thus, even if we take it for granted that her compulsions were rooted in these traumatic experiences, it is, nevertheless, the radical *change of attitude* toward her symptoms which was therapeutically effective. The bringing to consciousness of such psychic traumata cannot, at any rate, *in itself* be the appropriate treatment, inasmuch as a method which does not include such a procedure proved to be so effecient. This brings to mind a statement made by Edith Weisskopf-Joelson in her article "Some Comments in a Viennese School of Psychiatry," which seems to me to be noteworthy: "Although traditional psychotherapy has insisted that therapeutic practices have to be based on findings on etiology, it is possible that certain factors might cause neuroses during early childhood and that entirely different factors might relieve neuroses during adulthood." Even psychoanalysts are more and more inclined to assume that traumata in themselves do not directly cause neuroses. The traumata merely provide the contents of the respective obsessions, compulsions, and phobias. In some cases, I would dare to say that even the opposite is true: The trauma does not cause the neurosis, but rather, the neurosis makes the trauma reappear. One illustration may serve to clarify this point. A reef which appears at low tide is not the cause of the low tide; rather, it is the low tide which causes the reef to appear. Be that as it may, the therapy that we use must be independent of the validity of the etiologic assumptions of any particular neurotic symptoms. Thus Weisskopf-Joelson's comment is pertinent. At any rate, it is interesting to note that more or less "free associations" leading back to the traumatic experiences which produced certain habits and symptoms may occur *after* therapy has brought relief.

Thus we see that paradoxical intention works even in cases in which either the actual *somatic* basis (the patient with the coronary infarct) or the presumed *psychic* cause (the case of H. R.) were not touched upon. Paradoxical intention is effective irrespective of the underlying etiologic basis; in other words, it is an intrinsically nonspecific method. According to the author's opinion, based upon clinical experience, in every severe case involving phobic symptoms, one has to reckon with an autonomic-endocrine or an anankastic substructure. This does not entail a fatalistic viewpoint, however, for a full-fledged neurosis is nothing but a superstructure built upon these constitutional elements; it may well be that it can be psychotherapeutically alleviated without necessarily removing, or even taking into account, the underlying basis. Such a therapy is palliative rather than causal. This is not to say that it is a symptomatic therapy, however, for the logotherapist, when applying paradoxical intention, is concerned not so much with the symptom in itself but, rather, the patient's *attitude* toward his neurosis and its symptomatic manifestations. It is the very act of changing this attitude that is involved whenever an improvement is obtained. . . .

Paradoxical intention can also be applied to cases of sleep disturbance, as mentioned before. The fear of sleeplessness increases sleep disturbance because anticipatory anxiety completes and perpetuates the vicious circle. In addition, it results in a forced intention to sleep which incapacitates the patient to do so. Dubois, the famous French psychiatrist, once compared sleep with a dove which has landed near one's hand and stays there as long as one does not pay any attention to it; if one attempts to grab it, it quickly flies away. But how can one remove the anticipatory anxiety which is the pathologic basis of forced intention? In order to take the wind out of the sails of this specific fearful expectation, we advise the patient not to try to force sleep, since the necessary amount of sleep will be automatically secured by the organism. Therefore, he can safely try to do just the opposite, to stay awake as long as possible. In other words, the forced intention to fall asleep, arising from the anticipatory anxiety of not being able to fall asleep, should be replaced by the paradoxical intention of not falling asleep at all! (Which in turn will be followed very rapidly by sleep.) . . .

We have previously stated that a compulsion to self-observation accompanies anticipatory anxiety, and in the etiology of a neurosis one often finds an excess of attention as well as intention. This is especially true in insomnia in which the forced intention to sleep is accompanied by the forced attention to observe whether the intention is becoming effective or not. This attention thus joins in perpetuating the waking state.

In reference to this phenomenon, logotherapy includes a therapeutic device known as *dereflection*. Just as paradoxical intention is designed to counteract anticipatory anxiety, dereflection is intended to counteract the compulsive inclination to self-observation. In other words, what has to be achieved in such cases is more than trying to ridicule the trouble by using paradoxical intention and its humorous formulation; one should also be able to *ignore* the trouble to some degree. Such ignoring, or dereflection, however, can only be attained to the degree in which the patient's awareness is directed toward positive aspects. Dereflection, in itself, contains both a negative and a positive aspect. The patient must be dereflected *from* his anticipatory anxiety *to* something else. . . .

Let us, in conclusion, review the indications of paradoxical intention from the perspective of what logotherapy presents as the four characteristic patterns of response toward neurotic problems:

A. Wrong Passivity: By this is meant the behavioral pattern which may be observed in cases of anxiety neurosis or phobic conditions, or both. It is the withdrawal from those situations in which the patient, because of his anticipatory anxiety, expects his fears to recur. What we have to deal with in this case is the "*flight* from fear"—most commonly fear of collapsing on the street or having a heart attack.

B. Wrong Activity: This behavioral pattern is characteristic, in the first place, of obsessive-compulsive neurosis. 1. The individual, rather than trying to avoid conflict situations, *fights* against his obsessive ideas and neurotic compulsions and thus reinforces them. This struggle is motivated by two basic fears: (a) that the obsessive ideas indicate an imminent, or actual, psychotic condition, and (b) that the compulsions will someday result in a homicidal or suicidal attempt. 2. Another aspect of "wrong activity" may be observed in sexual neurosis, namely, a struggle *for* something, rather than *against* something: a striving for orgasm and potency. The underlying motivation is usually as follows: the patient feels that competent sexual performance is "demanded" of him either by the partner, by the situation, or by himself, in the event that he may have, so to speak, "scheduled" it for that moment. Due to this very "pursuit of happiness" the sexually neurotic individual founders just as the obsessive-compulsive neurotic does due to responses that are inappropriate to the situation; pressure precipitates counterpressure.

In contrast to these negative, "wrong" behavioral patterns, there are two positive, normal ones:

C. Right Passivity: This is the case when the patient, by means of paradoxical intention, ridicules his symptoms rather than trying to either run away from them (phobias) or to fight them (obsessive compulsions).

D. Right Activity: Through dereflection, the patient is enabled to ignore his neurosis by focusing his attention away from himself. He will be directed to a *life full of potential meanings and values with a specific appeal to his personal potentialities.*

In addition to this personal aspect, a social factor is involved as well. More and more we meet individuals who are suffering from what logotherapy calls man's *existential vacuum.* Such patients complain of a feeling of a *total and ultimate meaninglessness* in their lives. They display an inner void or emptiness in which neurotic symptoms may abound. Filling this vacuum may thus assist the patient in overcoming his neurosis by helping him become aware of the full spectrum of his concrete and personal meaning and value possibilities, or, in other words, by confronting him with *the "logos" of his existence*. . . .

Paradoxical intention consists in a reversal of the patient's attitude toward his symptom, and enables him to detach himself from his neurosis. This technique mobilizes what is called in logotherapeutic terms the *psychonoetic antagonism,* i.e., the specifically human capacity for self-detachment. Paradoxical intention lends itself particularly as a useful tool in short-term therapy, especially in cases with an underlying anticipatory anxiety mechanism.

Counterindications

Attempts have been made to clarify the indications for logotherapy. In my opinion, however, it is even more important to delineate where paradoxical intention is counterindicated. It is strictly counterindicated in psychotic depressions. For such patients a special logotherapeutic technique is reserved whose guiding principle is the decrease of that burden of guilt feelings on the part of the patient which is due to his tendency to self-accusations. It would be a misconception of existential psychiatry to interpret these self-accusations as indicating that a patient suffering from endogenous depression not only feels guilty, but really is guilty, "existentially guilty," and hence depressed. This would amount to mistaking an effect for the cause. Even more, such an interpretation would reinforce the patient's guilt feelings to the extent that his suicide might well be the result. Incidentally, logotherapy offers a special test to evaluate the suicide risk in a given case, as was pointed out by Kaczanowski and Wallace.

As far as schizophrenic patients are concerned, logotherapy is far from providing a causal treatment. As a psychotherapeutic adjunct, however, the aforementioned logotherapeutic technique called dereflection is also recommended for such patients.

Counterindications, from Frankl, "Paradoxical Intention," p. 527.

12

RATIONAL-EMOTIVE PSYCHOTHERAPY

Albert Ellis

Albert Ellis, born in Pittsburgh on September 27, 1913, was educated at the College of the City of New York and Columbia University. From the former institution he received his B.B.A. in 1934, and from the latter his M.A. in 1943 and his Ph.D. in 1947. After careers of free-lance writer (from 1934 and 1938) and personnel manager (for the next ten years), Ellis became senior clinical psychologist at the New Jersey State Hospital at Greystone Park. At the same time he was an instructor in psychology at Rutgers University. In 1949 he took the post of chief psychologist with the New Jersey State Diagnostic Center in Menlo Park. After a year he joined the New Jersey Department of Institutions and Agencies at Trenton. Concurrently with these appointments, Ellis was engaged in private practice from 1943, specializing in psychotherapy and marriage counseling. Since 1959 he has been executive director at the Institute for Rational Living. He is also executive director of the Institute for Advanced Study in Rational Psychotherapy in New York City. A fellow of the American Psychological Association, Ellis has been president of its Division of Consulting Psychology (1961–62).

Ellis's rational-emotive psychotherapy theorizes that irrational philosophies that are expressed in overt action in the form of emotion underlie neurotic behavior. One can structure one's thinking rationally, and rational behavior patterns follow. At the base of irrational behavior are emotive, groundless suppositions. A person is rationally organized in such a way that self-interest harmonizes with social interest; by nature one seeks to love, to be interested in, and to help others. Irrational thinking is responsible for self-destruction or a hatred of self. Those persons who are relatively free from psychosis, moderately intelligent, and free from the dogmas of other psychotherapies (e.g., Freudianism) respond best to rational-emotive psychotherapy.

He has authored a number of psychological works, including: *An Introduction to the Principles of Scientific Psychoanalysis* (1950); *The Folklore of Sex* (1951); *Sex, Society and the Individual* (1953); *The American Sexual Tragedy* (1954); *New Approaches to Psychotherapy Techniques* (with Ralph Brancale, 1955); *The Psychology of Sex Offenders* (1956); *How to Live with a "Neurotic"* (1957); *Sex without Guilt* (1958); *Art and Science of Love* (1960); *Creative Marriage* and *Guide to Rational Living* (both with R. A. Harper, 1961); *Encyclopedia of Sexual Behavior* (coeditor with A. Abarbanel, 1961); *Reason and Emotion in Psychotherapy* (1962); *The Intelligent Woman's Guide to Manhunting* (1963); *If This Be Sexual Heresy* (1963); *Sex and the Single Man* (1963); *The Origins and Development of Incest Taboo* (1963); *Homosexuality* (1965); *Nymphomania: A Study of the Oversexed Woman* (with E. Sagarin, 1965); *Growth through Reason* (1971); *Executive Leadership* (1972); and *Humanistic Psychotherapy: The Rational-Emotive Approach* (1973).

Rational-Emotive Psychotherapy Defined

Rational-emotive psychotherapy is a comprehensive approach to psychological treatment and to education that not only employs emotive and behavioristic methods but also significantly stresses and undermines the cognitive element in self-defeating behavior. Humans are exceptionally complex, so that there is no simple way in which they become "emotionally disturbed," nor no single manner in which they can be helped to overcome their disturbances. Their psychological problems arise from their misperceptions and mistaken cognitions about what they perceive; from their emotional underreactions or overreactions to normal and to unusual stimuli; and from their habitually dysfunctional behavior patterns, which encourage them to keep repeating nonadjustive responses even when they know they are behaving poorly. Consequently, a three-way, rational-emotive-behavioristic approach to their problems is desirable; and rational-emotive therapy (RET, for short) provides this multifaceted attack.[1]

Primarily, RET employs a highly active, cognitive approach. It is based on the assumption that what we label our "emotional" reactions are mainly caused by our conscious and unconscious evaluations, interpretations, and philosophies. Thus, we feel anxious or depressed because we strongly convince ourselves that it is not only unfortunate and inconvenient but that *it is terrible and catastrophic* when we fail at a major task or are rejected by a significant person. And we feel hostile because we vigorously believe that people who behave unfairly not only *had better not* but *absolutely should not* act the way they indubitably do and that it is *utterly insufferable* when they frustrate us.

This chapter was written by Albert Ellis specifically for this volume with heads and subheads supplied by the editor. The author's original title was "The ABC's of Rational-Emotive Psychotherapy." Footnotes appear at the end of the chapter.

The Rational-Emotive Orientation

Like stoicism, a school of philosophy that originated some twenty-five hundred years ago, RET holds that there are virtually no legitimate reasons for people to make themselves terribly upset, hysterical, or emotionally disturbed, no matter what kind of psychological or verbal stimuli are impinging on them. It encourages them to feel strong *appropriate* emotions—such as sorrow, regret, displeasure, annoyance, rebellion, and determination to change unpleasant social conditions. But it holds that when they experience certain self-defeating and *inappropriate* emotions—such as guilt, depression, rage, or feelings of worthlessness—they are adding an unverifiable, magical hypothesis (that things *ought* or *must* be different) to their empirically based view (that certain things and acts are reprehensible or inefficient and that something *had better* be done about changing them).

Because rational-emotive therapy is a highly structured and workable theory, the therapist can almost always see the few central irrational philosophies that clients are vehemently propounding to themselves and through which they are foolishly upsetting themselves. The therapist can show clients how these ideas cause their problems and their symptoms; can demonstrate exactly how clients may forthrightly question and challenge these ideas; and can often induce them to work to uproot these ideas and to replace them with scientifically testable hypotheses about themselves and the world that are not likely to get them into future emotional difficulties.

The Cognitive Aspect of the Theory

The cognitive part of the theory and practice of RET may be briefly stated in ABC form as follows:

At Point A there is an **activity, action,** or **agent** that you become disturbed about. Example: You go for an important job interview; or have a fight with your mate, who unfairly screams at you.

At point (R)B, you have a **rational belief** (or a **reasonable belief** or a **realistic belief**) about the **activity, action** or **agent** that occurs at point A. Example: "It would be unfortunate if I were rejected at the job interview." Or: "How annoying it is to have my mate unfairly scream at me!"

At point (I)B, you have an **irrational belief** (or an **inappropriate belief**) about the **activity, action,** or **agent** that occurs at point A. Example: "It would be catastrophic if I were rejected at the job interview." Or: "My mate is a horrible person for screaming at me!"

Point (R)B, the **rational belief,** can be supported by empirical data and is appropriate to the reality that is occurring, or that may occur, at point A. For it normally *is* unfortunate if you are rejected at an interview for an important job; and it *is* annoying to be unfairly screamed at by your mate. It would hardly be rational or realistic to think: "How great if I am rejected at the job interview!" Or: "It is wonderful to have my mate scream at me!"

Point (I)B, the **irrational belief,** cannot be supported by any empirical evidence and is inappropriate to the reality that is occurring, or that may occur, at point A. For it hardly would be truly catastrophic, but only (at worst) highly inconvenient, if you were rejected for an important job interview. It is unlikely that you would never get another job; that you would literally starve to death; or that you would have to be utterly miserable at any other job you could get. And your mate is not a horrible person for screaming at you, but merely a person who behaves (at some times) horribly and who (at other times) has various lovable traits.

(I)B's or **irrational beliefs,** moreover, state or imply a *should, ought,* or *must*—an absolutistic *demand* or *dictate* that you obtain what you want. For, by believing it *catastrophic* or *awful* to be rejected for an important job interview, you explicitly or implicitly believe that you *should* or *must* be accepted at that interview. And by believing that your mate is a horrible person for screaming at you, you overtly or tacitly believe that he or she *ought* or *must* be nonscreaming. There is, of course, no law of the universe (except in his or her muddled head!) that says that you *should* do well at an important job interview, nor that your mate *must* not scream at you.

At point (R)C, you feel **rational consequences** or **reasonable consequences** of (R)B's **(rational beliefs).** Thus, if you rigorously and discriminately believe, "It would be unfortunate if I were rejected at the job interview," you feel concerned and thoughtful about the interview; you plan in a determined manner how to succeed at it; and if by chance you fail to get the job you want, you feel disappointed, displeased, sorrowful, and frustrated. Your actions and feelings are *appropriate* to the situation that is occurring or may occur at point A; and they tend to help you succeed at your goals or feel suitably regretful if you do not achieve these goals.

At point (I)C, you experience **irrational consequences** or **inappropriate consequences** of your (I)B's **(irrational beliefs.)** Thus, if you childishly and dictatorially believe "It would be catastrophic if I were rejected at the job interview. I couldn't stand it! What a worm I would then prove to be! I *should* do well at this important interview!" you tend to feel anxious, self-hating, self-pitying, depressed, and enraged. You get dysfunctional, psychosomatic reactions, such as high blood pressure and ulcers. You become defensive, fail to see your own mistakes in this interview, and rationalizingly blame your failure on external factors. You become preoccupied with how hopeless your situation is, and refuse to do much about changing it by going for other interviews. You generally experience what we call *disturbed, neurotic,* or *overreactive* symptoms. Your actions and feelings at point (I)C are *inappropriate* to the situation that is occurring or may occur at point B, because they are based on magical demands regarding the way you and the universe presumably *ought to* be. And they tend to help you fail at your goals or feel horribly upset if you do not achieve them.

These are the ABC's of emotional disturbance or self-defeating attitudes and behavior, according to the RET theory. Therapeutically, these ABC's can be extended to (D)E's, which constitute the cognitive core of the RET methodology.

At point D, you can be taught (or can teach yourself) to **dispute** your (I)B's **(irrational beliefs).** Thus, you can ask yourself, "*Why* is it catastrophic if I am rejected in this forthcoming job interview? How would such a rejection *destroy* me? Why couldn't I *stand* losing this particular job? Where is the evidence that I would be a *worm* if I were rejected? Why *should* I have to do well at this important interview?" If you persistently, vigorously **dispute** (or *question* and *challenge*) your own (I)B's **(irrational beliefs)** which are creating your (I)C's **(inappropriate consequences),** you will sooner or later come to see, in most instances, that they are unverifiable, unempirically based, and superstitious; and you will be able to change and reject them.

At point (C)E, you are likely to obtain the **cognitive effect** of **disputing** your (I)B's **(irrational beliefs).** Thus, if you ask yourself, "Why is it catastrophic if I am rejected in this forthcoming job interview?" you will tend to answer: "It is not; it will merely be inconvenient." If you ask, "How would such a rejection destroy me?" you will reply: "It won't; it will only frustrate me." If you ask, "Why couldn't I stand losing this particular job?" you can tell yourself: "I can! I won't like it; but I can gracefully lump it!" If you ask, "Where is the evidence that I would be a worm if I were rejected?" you can respond: "There isn't any! I will only feel like a worm if I *define myself as, think of myself as* a worm!" If you ask, "Why *should* I *have* to do well at this important interview?" you will tell yourself: "There's no reason why I should *have* to do well. There are several reasons why *it would be nice; it would be very fortunate* if I succeeded at this job interview. But they never add up to: "Therefore I *must!*"

At point (B)E, you will most likely obtain the **behavioral effect** of **disputing** your (I)B's **(irrational beliefs).** Thus, you will tend to be much less anxious about your forthcoming job interview. You will become less self-hating, self-pitying, and enraged. You will reduce your psychosomatic reactions. You will be able to act less defensively. You will become less unconstructively preoccupied with the possibility or the actuality of failing at the job interview and will more constructively devote yourself to succeeding at it or taking other measures to improve your vocational condition if you fail at it. You will become significantly less "upset," "disturbed," "overreactive," or "neurotic."

On the cognitive level, then, rational-emotive therapy largely employs direct philosophic confrontation. The therapist actively demonstrates to clients how, every time they experience a dysfunctional emotion or behavior or **consequence,** at point C, it only indirectly stems from some **activity** or **agent** that may be occurring (or about to occur) in their life at point A, and it much more directly results from their interpretations, philosophies, attitudes, or **beliefs,** at point B. The therapist then teaches the clients how to scientifically (empirically and logically) **dispute** these beliefs, at point D, and to persist at this **disputing** until they consistently come up, at point E, with a set of sensible **cognitive effects,** (C)E's, and appropriate **behavioral effects,** (B)E's. When they have remained, for some period of time, at point E, the clients have a radically changed philosophic attitude toward themselves, toward others, and toward the world. They are thereafter much less likely to keep convincing themselves of (I)B's **(irrational beliefs)** and thereby creating (I)C's **(inappropriate consequences)** or emotional disturbances.

Behavioristic Techniques of Rational-Emotive Therapy

In addition to its cognitive methods, RET has exceptionally important behavioristic techniques that it consistently uses. It especially uses activity homework assignments, which the therapist or the client's therapy group assign to the client during various sessions, and later check up to see whether they are completed. Such assignments may consist of the client's being asked to initiate contacts with three new people during a week's period; to visit her nagging father-in-law instead of trying to avoid him; or to make a list of her job-hunting assets and of several means of looking for a better job. These assignments are given in order to help the clients take risks, gain new experiences, interrupt their dysfunctional habituations, and change their philosophies regarding certain activities. Eysenck, Pottash and Taylor, and A. Lazarus have indicated that the RET homework assignments overlap significantly with some of the methods of behavior therapy.[2] In any event, they are an integral and important part of RET.[3]

Emotive Release

A third major emphasis in RET is on emotive release. Thus, the rational-emotive therapist usually takes a no-nonsense-about-it, direct-confrontation approach to clients and their problems. She forces or persuades the clients to express themselves openly and to bring out their real feelings, no matter how painful it may first be for them to do so. Frequently, the therapist ruthlessly reveals and attacks the clients' defenses—while simultaneously showing them how they can live without these defenses and how they can unconditionally accept themselves whether or not others highly approve of them. The therapist does not hesitate to reveal his or her own feelings, to answer personal questions, and to participate as an individual in rational marathon encounters. She gives the clients unconditional rather than conditional positive regard and teaches them the essence of rational-emotive philosophy: namely, that no humans are to be condemned for anything, no matter how execrable their acts may be. Their *deeds* may be measurable and heinous, but they are never to be rated or given report cards *as people*. Because of the therapist's full acceptance of them as human beings, the clients are able to express their feelings much more openly than in their everyday life and to accept *themselves* even when they are acknowledging the inefficiency or immorality of some of their *acts*.

In many important ways, then, RET uses expressive-experiential methods and behavioral techniques. It is not, however, primarily interested in helping clients *feel* better but in showing them how they can *get* better. In its approach to marathon group therapy, for example, RET allows the participants plenty of opportunity to encounter each other on a gut level, to force themselves to stay in the here and now, to face their own emotional and sensory reactions to themselves and to other members of the group, and to be ruthlessly honest with themselves and others. RET, however, does not merely begin and end on a purely basic encounter or sensitivity training level—and thereby risk opening up many people without showing them how to put themselves together again. Instead, the rational-oriented marathon also shows the participants exactly what they are telling themselves to create their negative feelings toward themselves and others, and how they can change their internalized and uncritically accepted (I)B's **(irrational beliefs)**. Ultimately they can spontaneously feel and behave in a less self-defeating manner and actualize their potential for happy, nondefeating lives.

RET as the Application of Logic and Scientific Method

Basically, RET is an extension of the scientific method to human affairs. People, for biological as well as environmental reasons, tend to think magically, superstitiously, unrealistically, and unscientifically about themselves and the world around them. In science, we teach people to set up hypotheses about external reality and then to vigorously question and challenge these hypotheses —to look for empirical evidence for and against them, before they are cavalierly accepted as truths. In rational-emotive therapy, the therapist teaches his clients to scientifically question (to dispute) their self-defeating hypotheses about themselves and others. Thus, if you believe—as, alas, millions of people tend to believe—that you are a worthless person because you perform certain acts badly, you are not merely taught to ask, "What is truly bad about my acts? Where is the evidence that they are wrong or unethical?" More importantly, you are shown how to ask yourself, "Granted that some of my acts may be mistaken, why am *I* a totally bad *person* for performing them? Where is the evidence that I must always (or mainly) be right in order to consider myself worthy? Assuming that it is *preferable* for me to act well or efficiently rather than badly or inefficiently, why do I *have* to do what is preferable?"

Similarly, when you perceive—and let us suppose that you correctly perceive—the erroneous and unjust acts of others, and when you make yourself (as you may all too frequently make yourself!) enraged at these others and try to hurt or annihilate them, you are taught by the rational-emotive therapist to stop and ask yourself: "Why is my hypothesis that these error-prone people are no damned good a true hypothesis? Granted that *it would be better* if they acted more competently or fairly, why *should* they have to do what would be better? Where is the evidence that people who commit a number of mistaken or unethical acts are doomed to be forever wrong? Why, even if they persistently behave poorly, should they be totally damned, excommunicated, and consigned to some kind of hell?"

Rational-emotive therapy teaches the individual to generalize adequately but to watch his *over*generalizing; to discriminate his desires, wants, and preferences from his assumed needs, necessities, or dictates; to be less suggestible and more thinking; to be a long-range hedonist, who enjoys himself in the here and now and the future, rather than merely a short-range hedonist, who thinks mainly of immediate gratification; to feel the appropriate emotions of sorrow, regret, annoyance, and determination to change unpleasant aspects of his life while minimizing the inappropriate emotions of worthlessness, self-pity, severe anxiety, and rage. RET, like the science of psychology itself and like the discipline of general semantics, particularly teaches the client how to *discriminate* more clearly between sense and nonsense, fiction and reality, superstition and science.[4] While using many behavioristic and teaching methods, it is far from being dogmatic and authoritarian. Rather, it is one of the most humanistically oriented kinds of therapy in that it emphasizes that humans can fully accept themselves just because they are alive, just because they exist; that they do not have to prove their worth in any way; that they can have real happiness whether or not they perform well and whether or not

they impress others; that they are able to create their own meaningful purposes; and that they need no magic nor gods on whom to rely. The humanistic-
existentialist approach to life is therefore as much a part of rational-emotive
psychotherapy as is its rational, logical, and scientific methodology.[5]

Validation of Rational-Emotive Psychotherapy

RET, like many other modern forms of psychotherapy, is backed by a good
many years of clinical experience by the author and various other rational-
emotive therapists.[6] RET is also supported by several studies demonstrating
its clinical effectiveness under controlled experimental conditions.[7] Finally,
RET has been empirically confirmed, in terms of some of its major theoretical
hypotheses, by a great many experimental studies.[8]

A concrete example of the rational-emotive approach to psychotherapy
is given in a paper entitled "Rational-Emotive Therapy."[9]

Let me quote from this paper:

> One of my recent clients, a young male, came to therapy because he was
> becoming increasingly impotent with his bride of four months, and he was
> also losing confidence in his work as a dentist. He had the usual kind of
> family history, with an overly protective mother, a highly critical father,
> and a competitive younger brother; but we hardly mentioned this in the
> course of our sessions, except for a ten-minute exposition during the first
> session. Most of our time together, at the beginning, was spent in directly
> showing him that he believed very strongly that he had to succeed in life
> in order to be a worthwhile human being, and that he especially had to
> succeed in penile-vaginal intercourse in order to prove himself as a man.
> When I demonstrated to him that with this kind of demanding, self-
> denigrating view of himself he couldn't help being terribly anxious sexu-
> ally, and when he vigorously began to ask himself, "Why *must* I be great
> in bed in order to accept myself as a person?" he immediately began to
> function better sexually. Then, when I gave him the homework assignment
> of letting himself come to full orgasm through oral-genital relations—
> which he had previously never even considered doing, because he thought
> it unmanly to use this method for anything but love play preceding inter-
> course—he radically changed his sexual philosophy, began to have sex
> with his wife for enjoyment rather than for the purpose of proving himself,
> and became more potent than he had ever previously been in his life. Also,
> although we had rarely talked about his work, he clearly saw that he was
> demanding perfection of himself as a dentist, just as he was insisting that
> he be a perfect lover. He took a much more enjoying and less obligatory
> attitude toward his profession; and he gained considerably more confi-

dence and skill in this activity. Although I saw this client for a total of only ten sessions, his symptomatic improvement as well as his basic personality structure were helped more than those of many other clients I have seen for scores of sessions when I employed psychoanalytic or other more passive therapeutic methods.

Applications of Rational-Emotive Psychotherapy

Rational-emotive psychotherapy has a great many therapeutic applications, some of which are unavailable to various other modes of psychotherapy. For one thing, it is relevant and useful to a far wider range of client disabilities than are many other therapies. Harper, Patterson, and others have shown that many techniques, such as classical psychoanalysis, can only be effectively employed with a relatively small number of clients and are actually contraindicated with other individuals (such as schizophrenics).[10] Rational-emotive therapy, however, can be employed with almost any kind of person the therapist is likely to see, including those who are conventionally labeled as psychotic, borderline psychotic, psychopathic, and mentally retarded. This is not to say that equally good results are obtained when it is employed with these most difficult individuals as are obtained with run-of-the-mill neurotics. But the main principles of RET can be so simply and efficiently stated that even individuals with very serious problems, some of whom have not been reached by years of previous intensive therapy, can often find significant improvement through RET.

Rational-emotive principles can be used with many kinds of individuals to help prevent them from eventually becoming emotionally disturbed. Outstanding in this respect is RET's application to education. The Institute for Advanced Study in Rational Psychotherapy in New York City not only operates a postdoctoral training institute and a moderate-cost clinic but also runs a private school for normal children. At this school, the pupils are taught a rational-emotive philosophy by their regular teachers, in the course of classroom activities, recreational affairs, therapy groups, and other games and exercises. They are taught, for example, not to catastrophize when they do not achieve perfectly, not to enrage themselves against others when these others act badly, and not to demand that the world be nicer and easier than it usually is. As a result of this teaching, these pupils seem to be becoming remarkably less anxious, depressed, self-hating, and hostile than other children of equivalent age."[11]

Rational-emotive ideas also have application to politics, to problems of the generation gap, to the treatment and prevention of violence and murder, and to various other areas of life.[12] Because it is deeply philosophic, because it realistically accepts individuals where they are and shows them how they can obtain their fuller potentials, and because it is not only oriented toward individuals with emotional disturbances but toward all types of people everywhere, RET is likely to be increasingly applied to the solution of many kinds of human problems.

Is RET really more effective than other forms of psychotherapy? The evidence is not in that will answer this question. Clinical findings would seem to indicate that it benefits more people than do most other methods; that it can obtain beneficial results in surprisingly short order in many instances; and that the level of improvement or cure that is effected through its use is more elegant and deep-seated than that obtained through other methods. This clinical evidence is partly substantiated through controlled studies of therapeutic outcome. My hypothesis, backed by almost a hundred such studies, is that RET is a more effective procedure than methods that emphasize purely cognitive or emotive or behavioral approaches because it is active-directive, comprehensive, unusually clear and precise, and hard-headed and down-to-earth.

Characteristics of RET

Rational-emotive therapy is also philosophically unambiguous, logical, and empirically oriented. This can be especially seen in its viewpoint on the most important of therapeutic problems: that of human worth. Nearly all systems of psychotherapy hold that people are worthwhile and can esteem themselves when they discover how to relate well to others and win the love they need or when they perform adequately and fully actualize themselves. Freud held that people solve their basic problems through work and love.[13] Adler emphasized the necessity of their finding social interest.[14] Sullivan stressed achieving adequate interpersonal relations.[15] Glasser insists that they need both love and achievement.[16] Branden demands competence and extreme rationality.[17] Even Rogers, who presumably emphasizes unconditional positive regard, actually holds that the individual can truly accept himself only when someone else, such as a therapist, accepts him or loves him unconditionally; so that this self-concept is still dependent on some important element outside himself.[18]

RET, on the contrary, seems to be almost the only major kind of psychotherapy that holds that humans do not need *any* trait, characteristic, achievement, purpose, or social approval in order to accept themselves. In fact, I contend, they do not have to rate themselves, esteem themselves, or have any self-measurement or self-concept whatever.

I have elsewhere shown in detail how it is really impossible for people to have valid self-images and why it is enormously harmful if they attempt to construct one.[19] Suffice it to say here, in brief summation, that ego ratings depend on the summation of the ratings of the individual's separate traits (such as competence, honesty, talents, etc.). It is not legitimate to add and average these traits any more than it is legitimate to add apples and pairs. Moreover, if you finally arrive, by some devious means, at a global rating of your being (or of your "self"), you thereby invent a magical heaven (your "worth," your "value," your "goodness") and a mystical hell (your "worthlessness," your "valuelessness," your "badness"). This deification or devilification of the individual is arrived at tautologically, by definition. It has no real relation to objective reality. It is based on the false assumption that you *should* or *must* be a certain way and that the universe truly *cares* if you are not what you *ought to* be. It refuses to acknowledge the fact that all humans are, and probably always will be, incredibly *fallible.* And it almost always results in your harshly condemning and punishing yourself or defensively pretending that you are "worthy" and "good" in order to minimize your anxiety and self-deprecation. Finally, since self-ratings invariably involve ego-games wherein you compare your self-esteem to that of others, they inevitably result in your deifying and damming other humans in addition to yourself; and the feelings of intense anxiety and hostility that thereby occur constitute the very core of what we usually call *emotional disturbance.*

Rational-emotive therapy, by solidly teaching people to avoid *any* kind of self-rating (and only, instead, to measure their characteristics and performances, so that they may help correct them and increase their enjoyment), gets to the most elegant and deepest levels of personality change. It offers no panacea to human unhappiness, sorrow, frustration, and annoyance. But it importantly reveals, attacks, and radically uproots the major sources of needless self-defeating and socially destructive behavior.

Footnotes

[1]A. Ellis, "What *Really* Causes Therapeutic Change," *Voices* 4, no. 2 (1968):90–97.

[2]H. J. Eysenck, ed., *Experiments in Behaviour Therapy* (New York: Macmillan, 1964); A. Lazarus, *Beyond Behavior Therapy* (New York: McGraw-Hill, 1971); R. R. Pottash and J. E. Taylor, "Discussion of Albert Ellis: Phobia Treated with Rational-Emotive Psychotherapy," *Voices* 3, no. 3 (1967):38–41.

[3]A. Ellis, *How to Live with a "Neurotic,"* rev. ed. (New York: Crown, 1975); A. Ellis, *Reason and Emotion in Psychotherapy* (New York: Lyle Stuart, 1962); A. Ellis, *Homosexuality* (New York: Lyle Stuart, 1965); A. Ellis, *Sex and the Single Man,* rev. ed. (New York: Lyle Stuart, 1976); A. Ellis, J. L. Wolfe, and S. Moseley, *How to Prevent Your Child from Becoming a Neurotic Adult* (New York: Crown, 1966); A. Ellis and R. A. Harper, *A New Guide to Rational Living* (Englewood Cliffs, N.J.: Prentice-Hall, and Hollywood, Calif.: Wilshire, 1975); A. Ellis and R. A. Harper, *A Guide to Successful Marriage* (New York: Lyle Stuart, and Hollywood, Calif.: Wilshire, 1968); M. Maultsby, Jr., *Help Yourself to Happiness* (New York: Institute for Rational Living,

1975); K. T. Morns and H. M. Konitz, *Rational-Emotive Therapy* (Boston: Houghton Mifflin, 1975).

[4]A. Korzbyski, *Science and Sanity* (Lancaster, Pa.: Lancaster Press, 1933); Ellis, *How to Live with a "Neurotic."*

[5]A. Ellis, "A Weekend of Rational Encounter," in *Encounter;* ed. A. Burton (San Francisco: Jossey-Bass, 1969), pp. 112–27; idem, *Humanistic Psychotherapy* (New York: Julian Press/ McGraw-Hill Paperbacks, 1974).

[6]B. Ard, "Bruising the Libido," *Rational Living* 1, no. 2 (1966):19–25; B. Ard, "The A-B-C of Marriage Counseling," *Rational Living* 2, no. 2 (1967):10–12; B. Ard, "Rational Therapy in Rehabilitation Counseling," *Rehabilitation Counseling Bulletin* 12 (1968):84–88; R. Callahan, "Overcoming Religious Faith," *Rational Living* 2, no. 1 (1967):16, 21; L. Diamond, "Defeating Self-Defeat; Two Case Histories," *Rational Living* 2, no. 1 (1967): 13–14; L. Diamond, "Restoring Amputated Ego," *Rational Living* 2, no. 2 (1967):15; Ellis, *Reason and Emotion in Psychotherapy;* Ellis, *Homosexuality;* A. Ellis, *The Art and Science of Love* (New York: Lyle Stuart and Bantam, 1965); A. Ellis, Wolfe, and S. Moseley, *How to Prevent Your Child from Becoming a Neurotic Adult;* A. Ellis and J. M. Gullo, *Murder and Assassination* (New York: Lyle Stuart, 1971); A. Ellis and R. A. Harper, *A New Guide to Rational Living;* A. Ellis and R. A. Harper, *A Guide to Successful Marriage;* M. D. Glicken, "Counseling Children," *Rational Living* 1, no. 2 (1966):27, 30; M. D. Glicken, "Rational Counseling: A New Approach to Children," *Journal of Elementary Guidance and Counseling* 2, no.4 (1968):261–67; I. Greenberg, "Psychotherapy: Learning and Relearning," *Canada's Mental Health,* supplement no.53 (1966); M. Grossack, "Why Rational-Emotive Therapy Works," *Psychological Reports* 16 (1965):464; M. Grossack, *You Are Not Alone* (Boston: Marlborough Books, 1975); J. M. Gullo, "Useful Variations on Rational-Emotive Therapy," *Rational Living* 1, no. 1 (1966):44–45; J. M. Gullo, "Counseling Hospital Patients," *Rational Living* 1, no.2 (1966):11–15; P. A. Hauck, *The Rational Management of Children* (New York: Libra, 1967); Lazarus, *Behavior Therapy and Beyond* (New York: McGraw-Hill, 1971); W. Knaus, *Rational-Emotive Education* (New York: Institute for Rational Living, 1974); E. E. Wagner, "Techniques of Rational Counseling," *High Spots* 3, no. 6 (1963):2; E. E. Wagner, "Counseling Children," *Rational Living* 1, no. 2 (1966):26, 28–30; M. C. Maultsby, Jr., *Help Yourself to Happiness* (New York: Institute for Rational Living, 1975); P. Hauckel, *Overcoming Depression* (Philadelphia: Westminster Press, 1973; P. Hauck, *Overcoming Frustration and Anger* (Philadelphia: Westminster Press, 1974).

[7]A. Deloreto, "A Comparison of the Relative Effectiveness of Systematic Desensitization, Rational-Emotive and Client-Centered Group Psychotherapy in the Reduction of Interpersonal Anxiety in Introverts and Extroverts," Ph.D. thesis, Michigan State University, 1969; P. L. Russell and J. M. Brandsma, "A Theoretical and Empirical Integration of the Rational-Emotive and Classical Conditioning Theories," *Journal of Consulting and Clinical Psychology* 42(1974): 389–397; D. E. Burnhead, "The Reduction of Negative Affect in Human Subjects," Ph.D. thesis, Western Michigan University, 1970; A. P. MacDonald and R. G. Ganes, "Ellis' Irrational Values," *Rational Living* 7(2) (1972):25–28; D. H. Michenbaum, *Cognitive Behavior Modification* (Morristown, N.J.: General Learning Press, 1974); L. D. Trexler, "Rational-Emotive Therapy, Placebo, and No-Treatment Effects on Public-Speaking Anxiety," Ph.D. thesis, Temple University, 1971; M. Grossack, T. Armstrong, and G. Lussiev, "Correlates of Self-Actualization," *Journal of Humanistic Psychology* 6 (1966):87; T. O. Karst and L. D. Trexler, "Initial Study Using Fixed-Role and Rational-Emotive Therapy in Treating Public-Speaking Anxiety," *Journal of Consulting and Clinical Psychology* 34(1970):360–66; S. Krippner, "Relationship Between Reading Improvement and Ten Selected Variables," *Perceptual and Motor Skills* 19(1964):15–20; J. C. Lafferty, D. Dennerll, and P. Rettich, "A Creative School Mental Health Program," *National Elementary Principal* 43, no.5 (1964):28–35; M. Maultsby, "Psychological and Biochemical Test Change in Patients Who Were Paid to Engage in Psychotherapy," mimeographed (Department of Medicine, University of Wisconsin, 1970); M. Maultsby, "Systematic, Written Homework in Psychotherapy," *Rational Living* 5, no.1 (1970) (A clinical study of 87 unselected OPD patients); K. L. Sharma, "A Rational Group Therapy Approach to Counseling Anxious Underachievers," Ph.D thesis, University of Alberta, 1970; H. W. Zingle, "A Rational Therapy Approach to Counseling Underachievers," Ph.D. thesis, University of Alberta, 1965; W. R. Maes and R. A. Heimann, "The Comparison of Three Approaches to the Reduction of Test Anxiety in High School Students," (Washington, D.C.: U.S. Office of Education, 1970).

[8]A. H. Argabrite and L. J. Nidorf, "Fifteen Questions for Rating Reason," *Rational Living* 3, no.1 (1968):9–11; T. X. Barber, *Hypnosis: A Scientific Approach* (Cincinnati: Van Nostrand Reinhold, 1969); L. Berkowitz, J. P. Lepinsky, and E. J. Angulo, "Awareness of own Anger Level and Subsequent Aggression," *Journal of Personality and Social Psychology* 11 (1969):293–300; W. A. Carlson, R. M. W. Travers, and E. A. Schwab, "A Laboratory Approach to the Cognitive Control of Anxiety" (Paper presented at the American Personnel and Guidance Association Meeting, Las Vegas, March 31, 1969); R. C. Conklin, "A Psychometric Instrument for the Early Identification of the Underachievers," Master's thesis, University of Alberta, 1965; S. W. Cook and R. E. Harris, "The Verbal Conditioning of the Galvanic Skin Reflex," *Journal of Experimental Psychology* 21(1937):201–10; R. L. Davies, "Relationship of Irrational Ideas to Emotional Disturbance," M.Ed. thesis, University of Alberta, 1970; A. Ellis, "Outcome of Employing Three Techniques of Psychotherapy," *Journal of Clinical Psychology* 13(1957):344–50; H. J. Geis, "A Study of Shame and Guilt," Ph.D. thesis, New York University, 1968; B. J. Hartman, "Sixty Revealing Questions for Twenty Minutes," *Rational Living* 3, no.1 (1968):7–8; R. G. Jones, "A Factored Measure of Ellis's Irrational Belief System, with Personality and Maladjustment Correlates," Ph.D. thesis, Texas Technological College, 1968; R. Lazarus, *Psychological Stress and the Coping Process* (New York: McGraw-Hill, 1966); Maultsby, "Systematic, Written Homework in Psychotherapy"; N. Miller, "Learning of Visceral and Glandular Responses," *Science* 163 (January 31, 1969):34–45; O. H. Mowrer, "Preparatory Set (Expectancy)—A Determinant in Motivation and Learning," *Psychological Review* 45 (1938):62–91; S. Schacter, "The Interaction of Cognitive and Physiological Determinants of Emotional States," *Advances in Experimental Social Psychology*, vol. 1, ed. L. Berkowitz (New York: Academic Press, 1964); S. Schacter and J. E. Singer, "Cognitive, Social and Physiological Determinants of Emotional State," *Psychological Review* 69 (1962):379–99; G. L. Taft, "A Study of the Relationship of Anxiety and Irrational Beliefs," Ph.D. thesis, University of Alberta, 1965; S. Valins, "Cognitive Effects of False Heart-Rate Feedback," *Journal of Personality and Social Psychology* 4 (1966):400–408; E. Velten, "A Laboratory Task for Induction of Mood States," *Behavior Research and Therapy* 6 (1968):473–82.

[9]A. Ellis, "Rational-Emotive Therapy," *Journal of Contemporary Psychotherapy* 1 (1969): 82–90.

[10]R. A. Harper, *Psychoanalysis and Psychotherapy: Thirty-Six Systems* (Englewood Cliffs, N.J.: Prentice-Hall, 1959); R. A. Harper, *The New Psychotherapies* (Englewood Cliffs, N.J.: Prentice-Hall, 1975); C. H. Patterson, *Theories of Counseling and Psychotherapy* (New York: Harper & Row, 1966).

[11]A. Ellis, "Teaching Emotional Education in the Classroom," *School Health Review* (November 1969): 10–14; W. Kraus, Rational-Emotive Education (New York: Institute for Rational Living, 1974).

[12]A. Ellis, "Toward the Understanding of Youthful Rebellion," in *A Search for the Meaning of the Generation Gap,* ed. P. R. Frank (San Diego: San Diego County Department of Education, 1969):85–105; Ellis and Gullo, *Murder and Assassination* (New York: Lyle Stuart, 1972).

[13]S. Freud, *Collected Papers* (New York: Collier, Macmillan, 1963).

[14]A. Adler, *What Life Should Mean to You* (New York: Capricorn Books, 1958); idem, *Social Interest* (New York: Capricorn Books, 1964).

[15]H. S. Sullivan, *The Interpersonal Theory of Psychiatry* (New York: Norton, 1968).

[16]W. Glasser, *Reality Therapy* (New York: Harper & Row, 1964); idem, *Schools without Failure* (New York: Harper & Row, 1969).

[17]N. Branden, *The Psychology of Self-Esteem* (Los Angeles: Nash, 1970).

[18]C. R. Rogers, *On Becoming a Person* (Boston: Houghton Mifflin, 1961).

[19]A. Ellis, "Psychotherapy and the Value of a Human Being," in *Value and Evaluation: Essays in Honor of Robert S. Hartman,* ed. J. W. Davis (Knoxville: University of Tennessee Press, 1972).

13

PHILOSOPHICAL PSYCHOTHERAPY

William S. Sahakian

William S. Sahakian completed his graduate studies at Harvard University and Boston University, receiving his Ph.D. from the latter institution in 1951. The bulk of his career has been as professor of psychology and philosophy at Suffolk University in Boston. In the 1960s he was professorial lecturer in psychology at the Massachusetts College of Pharmacy and taught Massachusetts Department of Education courses at Harvard University. More recently, he lectured in psychology for the Graduate School of Education at Northeastern University. A fellow of the American Psychological Association, he has been a consultant in psychology and has practiced psychotherapy for a number of years.

Philosophical psychotherapy, as Sahakian calls his system, is a cognitive approach to therapy, whereby it is held that thoughts and attitudes profoundly influence behavior and well-being. Philosophical attitudes can produce and eliminate symptoms; especially do they affect the misery and discomfort attending neurotic symptoms. The most distressing element in neurosis, the anxious, emotional stress exerted in order to combat neurotic symptoms and their accompanying emotional draining, self-doubt, and insecurity, is removed through philosophical psychotherapy.

Sahakian's more than forty publications include *Psychopathology Today* (1970), *Psychology of Personality* (rev. ed., 1974), *Systematic Social Psychology* (1974), and *History and Systems of Psychology* (1975). The last mentioned book contains a historical analysis of psychotherapy. Three of his more important papers on philosophical psychotherapy are: "Stoic Philosophical Psychotherapy" (1969), "Philosophical Psychotherapy" (1974), and "Philosophical Psychotherapy: An Existential Approach" (1976). He was also a contributor to the *International Encyclopedia of Neurology, Psychiatry, Psychoanalysis, and Psychology* and the *Encyclopaedia Britannica.*

Philosophical Background of the Theory

Philosophical psychotherapy is not an innovation that has emerged as a gimmick, but has had years of testing in classroom and clinical settings. With the author, it first appeared in classroom lectures and discussions when students reported with amazing regularity that his lectures were more than the usual informative talks; they were psychologically therapeutic experiences. Since the lectures were not planned to possess therapeutic value, it seemed worthwhile to analyze, review, and research the entire lecture series for an explanation as to why certain lectures and classroom discussions should affect students therapeutically. It was during this study that philosophy as a psychotherapeutic instrument was discovered and transferred to client-oriented situations.

It is not new that a person's psychological stance is often and to a considerable extent predicated on his philosophical convictions. But William James (1907) believed the opposite, namely, that a person's psychological constitution determined his philosophy so that the tough-minded personality was empiricistic, materialistic, pessimistic, fatalistic, and sceptical; whereas the tender-minded person was rationalistic, idealistic, optimistic, "free-willist," and dogmatic. Perhaps it was the enormous influence engendered by James that had scholars thinking in terms of the psychological affecting the theoretical beliefs of an individual that detoured us from the possibility that the reverse could be equally effective, if not entirely true. That is, it may be the case that the philosophical convictions of a person determine his psychological attitude, and it was mistakenly taken to be the opposite. The author's current position is that both are active, with one's philosophical *Weltanschauung* being in the ascendency.

The conception of one's philosophical beliefs affecting his psychological outlook and behavior is far from new, for it dates as far back as Epicurus and Epictetus. Epicurus, dealing with the anxieties of a youth, admonished him [the youth, Menoeceus] to have a salutary philosophy, for anxieties are couched in jaundiced philosophies.[1] The Stoics also dealt with psychological tensions from a philosophical orientation. Epictetus counselled that when life's vicissitudes that cannot be changed become an inscrutable problem, then a shift in attitude from one of anxious concern to one of stoical indifference will transform the situation into a reasonably tolerable one.[2] Moving from these ancient philosophers to the modern period, at least two notable philosophers can be found who have espoused a philosophical base for psychotherapy. The

---

Philosophical Background of the Theory, from William S. Sahakian, "Philosophical Psychotherapy," *Psychologia* 17, no. 4 (1974): 12–18.

[1] Epicurus, "The Extant Writings of Epicurus," in *The Stoic and Epicurean Philosophers,* ed. W. J. Oates (New York: Random, 1940).

[2] Epictetus, *The Works of Epictetus* (Boston: Little, 1865).

first of these, Schopenhauer, offered two recommendations: (1) the mental immersion into the depths of profound philosophy results in an alleviation of one's mental anguish, and (2) the psychological embracement of one's miseries, as it were, has the effect of attenuating their painful affects.[3] The first is effected by psychologically soaring to a realm above one's passions, anxieties, and driving forces to an elevated state of relative tranquility or escape from them, while the latter eliminates the intensity of *pressure* of painful experiences such as fears, crises, impending calamities, and the like. The second of these modern philosophical psychologists, Nietzsche, propounded the hypothesis that if a person has a "why" of living, he can overcome any "how."[4] That is, if a person has a reason for living, then he can endure any obstacle that he may confront in life.[5] Alfred Adler's theory of fictional finals,[6] a view that he derived from the philosopher Hans Vaihinger's *Philosophy of "as if,"*[7] possesses a comparable effect to Nietzsche's dictum.

Philosophical Psychotherapy Defined

From what has been said it can be surmised that philosophical psychotherapy may be defined as any system that utilizes beliefs, attitudes, convictions, a person's *Weltanschauung* or philosophy of life, as a vehicle to alter, control or cope with his psychological or emotional problems, thereby changing his behavior pattern, psychological or emotional state, hence rectifying a maladjusted condition.

That beliefs affect our psychological state and behavior is an experience common to everyone. Evidence of this fact is so abounding that a simple instance or example attesting to it should suffice. If, while flying aboard a passenger airplane, the captain should announce that the landing gear is jammed and that the plane may have to crash-land, the passengers would be anxiously apprehensive even though the captain for some ulterior motive may have fabricated this deceit (or even if the landing gear is operative, but the captain's signaling device is in error). Note that a belief, notwithstanding its being an erroneous one, has potent psychological effects upon us and our behavior. Another example is that of a representative of the police or army

---

[3]A. Schopenhauer, *The World as Will and Idea* (London: Trubner, 1883).

[4]F. Nietzsche, "The Twilight of the Idols," in *The Complete Works of Friedrich Nietzsche,* ed. O. Levy (New York: Macmillan, 1909–11).

[5]Maxim 12 of "The Twilight of the Idols."

[6]A. Adler, *The Practice and Theory of Individual Psychology* (New York: Littlefield, 1929; reprint by Humanities, 1971).

[7]H. Vaihinger, *The Philosophy of "as if "* (New York: Barnes & Noble, 1935).

delivering an erroneous message to a person informing him that his son has been killed. The news, despite its being false, can have severe psychological effects upon one as long as it is believed. It is said that Abraham Lincoln suffered more from worries about things that never occurred than from those that materialized.

Although many neurotics and others suffer in the same manner as do those victimized by false calamitous beliefs, the point is not whether beliefs are false (these illustrations were merely supplied to demonstrate the potency of even false notions), but that beliefs per se, whether true or false, motivate the individual. But philosophical psychotherapy is not simply a question of beliefs, it is a question of conviction, attitude, response, and choice. It is a question of undermining unsavory beliefs, disarming their power, establishing a posture toward them.

The author has had a number of individuals who, after having undergone Freudian psychotherapy, despairingly report that their maladjusted behavior (neurosis) is an indelible product of their childhood years and consequently is unavoidable. Their fatalistic beliefs derived from psychoanalysis rendered the wills of these individuals paralyzed with the resultant belief that they could not by choice extricate themselves from their predicament by a deliberate change of their behavior. These are cases where a belief in one's inability to choose to change left his autonomous will in a prostrate condition.

The reason why a person is the victim of his past experiences and of his complexes is that he *believes* that he has been duped, "brain-washed," or psychologized by his own tragic misinformation or an imprudent psychotherapist's unsalutary philosophy. As soon as a person *ceases* to believe that he can do no other but what his past experiences dictate that he must do, then he will experience a liberation that allows him the free choices that are truly within his possession and power of exercise. Beliefs possess the power to condition a person, and beliefs gained in therapy are a form of the conditioning process. The author has known individuals in therapy who (on advice to exercise their choices) do so with laborious effort because they have been in a sense hypnotically conditioned to believe in the paralysis of their genuinely autonomous state.[8] As the perceptive mind of Peirce observed, a belief is "that upon which a man is prepared to act"; and "beliefs are really rules for action, and the whole function of thinking is but one step in the production of habits of action."[9] Adler was convinced of the effect philosophy exerts on man. He saw "no reason to be afraid of metaphysics; it has had a great influence on human life and development."[10]

---

[8]W. S. Sahakian, "A Social Learning Theory of Obsessional Neurosis," *Israel Annals of Psychiatry and Related Disciplines* 7(1969):70–75.

[9]C. S. Peirce, *Collected Papers* (Cambridge, Mass.: Harvard University Press, 1931–36). 8 vols.

[10]A. Adler, *Social Interest: A Challenge to Mankind* (New York: Capricorn Books, 1964): 275.

The Character of Philosophical Psychotherapy

In philosophical psychotherapy, a person's attitude, which is inextricably interwoven with his beliefs, is of paramount importance. The Stoics believed that if a condition was unalterable, then it was imperative to change one's attitude in order to cope with the confronting situation. If concern for one's predicament is incapable of bringing about a suitable alteration of conditions, then alter your attitude. External conditions and internal attitudes play such a reciprocal role that a restructuring of one causes a concomitant reorganization of the other. The Stoic, Epictetus, advises that if you cannot change your situation, then assume an attitude of indifference toward it. The failure to be concerned about a situation causes a discharge in the forces that the distasteful condition may have exerted upon you. A young college student who was once faced with close prospects of death and its attending anxiety came abruptly to the rude realization that death is much too imminently near even for a young man. Subsequent to this experience his attitude was of extreme indifference to the values ordinarily countenanced by the general public, and he with an air of indifference was free from most of the petty anxieties that disturb the tranquility of the average person. One technique the author has advised in dealing with daily anxieties is to assume the mental stance that life is too brief to be concerned with them and a carefree attitude (of "Who cares," "I can't be bothered, life is too short," or "Who gives a damn,") will often aid in alleviating tension.

Another stoically philosophical stance is a device used to remain emotionally unperturbed, or to set oneself emotionally beyond the distance of persons who normally would prove distressing. The Stoics believed that you cannot be emotionally disturbed unless you will to become so, that is, unless you allow your will to be broken. For example, if you are emotionally upset by an insulting word or action of a person, it is not he that is distressing but the fact that you permitted him control over yourself. You granted him the emotional powers by allowing him to break your will. Had you retained your will in your own discrete possession, then no person could inflict emotional disturbances upon you. The author recommends that in cases where many persons or situations are emotionally distressing, one can often maintain a composure free from repression by understanding the matter and readjusting his attitude. To illustrate, there was a man who asserted that he was fast reaching the point where he was no longer going to drive his car because the reckless and discourteous drivers on the road were more than he could cope with emotionally. It was recommended to this man that he readjust his attitude toward driving by making up his mind that in venturing upon the road one must expect a certain percentage of discourteous drivers out of the enormous numbers of cars on the congested city roads. He found that with the necessary change of attitude, not only was he able to cope with those drivers causing him perturbation but that it seemed as if there were fewer of this type of driver on the road than he realized.

Another individual who was easily provoked by others found that attitudinal changes provided a decided control over the matter. Instead of becoming disturbed when insulted, he assumed a philosophical attitude of indifference by thinking to himself that the would-be insulter was simply ignorant of the facts or that he was simply a stupid person who knew no better. Thoughts such as these do more than acquiesce the emotions; they remove the tension required for emotions to generate. Accordingly, it is not a question of repressing the emotions, since emotional pressure is not present to repress. This method is far superior to the Freudian technique of giving vent to one's emotions, for Freud's recommendation often proves detrimental to self and others, to others because they become the object of one's emotional venom and its destructive effects, to oneself because the regular unbridled expression of one's feelings develops into a trait, a personality characteristic dominating the individual and potent enough to motivate the personality by its own functional autonomy as Allport has argued.[11]

The Effectiveness of Philosophical Psychotherapy

Philosophical psychotherapy may require other therapeutic techniques to supplement it, but it is an unusually effective complement to nearly all systems. The value of philosophical psychotherapy can be readily seen and appreciated by those who are aware of the importance of changing a patient's attitude under the assumption that "the conscious as well as the unconscious is determined by subjective values and interests."[12] One of the most efficient methods of altering a person's psychological posture is by changing his philosophical outlook. One may even go so far as to assert that in certain instances a symptom is produced or controlled or eliminated by a change in a patient's philosophical attitude. One's beliefs play an important role in reinforcing or eliminating symptoms.

The present section deals with the application of Stoic philosophy to psychotherapy. According to the psychology of the Stoics, what cannot be changed should be accepted or else treated with philosophical indifference.[13] A fact which is not accepted by a person may cause him great distress; that

---

[11]G. W. Allport, *Personality: A Psychological Interpretation* (New York: Henry Holt, 1937); idem, *Pattern and Growth in Personality* (New York: Holt, Rinehart and Winston, 1961).

The Effectiveness of Philosophical Psychotherapy, from William S. Sahakian, "Stoic Philosophical Psychotherapy," *Journal of Individual Psychology,* 25 (1969): 32.

[12]H. L. Ansbacher and R. R. Ansbacher, eds., *The Individual Psychology of Alfred Adler* (New York: Basic, 1956), p. 9.

[13]Epictetus, *Discourses* (Oxford: Clarendon, 1916).

is, if he is confronted with a problem or situation that he cannot change but nevertheless strives doggedly to dispel, he will merely succeed in intensifying the emotional tension and stress, causing him more misery than the problem that he is seeking to resolve. Emotional exhaustion compounded by a sense of defeat or despair in combatting one's psychological disturbances is often more distressing than the original ailment. It is in these cases that philosophical psychotherapy is definitely indicated: Instead of removing the object of complaint of a person, you alter his philosophical attitude or posture.

Technique of Philosophical Psychotherapy

Philosophical psychotherapy lends itself to phenomenological theories of personality such as those of Rogers and Frankl.[14] For Rogers, the important consideration is that which the individual experiences as reality, his phenomenological field of experience and not reality per se. For example, a thirsty person races anxiously to a pool of water whether it is actually a mirage or genuine reality. For Rogers, anxiety is an alarm, but in philosophical therapy (after an attempt via the usual modes of therapy have failed to eliminate the cause or source of anxiety), one seeks to shut off the alarm, because it is then regarded as a false alarm. Anxiety is triggered off unnecessarily. In this situation and at this point, it is no longer advisable to continue to remove the threat, since continued failure often proves demoralizing. At this point, philosophical therapy is indicated, that is, ignore the threatening object, and attenuate the pressure. Ordinarily, in such cases, the object of threat is not the primary or direct source of discomfort, for the primary source is the attempt to combat or cope with the object of tension. Not only is this a common experience in the life of a neurotic, but it is found in everyday experiences of reasonably well-adjusted persons. There was the predicament of a clergyman who was about to perform religious services and reported that the prospects of performing such services were overwhelmingly terrifying, because the clergyman felt that it was impossible to measure up to the expectations of the congregation either morally or academically. The clergyman sought to remove the source of tension (performing services) by providing a socially acceptable excuse, such as obtaining a substitute cleric to conduct the services. The author's counsel in this matter, proceeding along the lines of philosophical psychotherapy, was

---

[14]V. E. Frankl, *The Will to Meaning: Foundations and Applications of Logotherapy* (New York: World Publishing, 1969); C. R. Rogers, "A Theory of Therapy, Personality, and Interpersonal Relationships, as Developed in the Client-Centered Framework," in *Psychology: A Study of a Science,* ed. S. Koch (New York: McGraw-Hill, 1959), vol. 3; C. R. Rogers, "The Phenomenological Theory of Personality," in *Psychology of Personality,* ed. W. S. Sahakian (Chicago: Rand McNally, 1965).

to allow the assumed source of tension (conducting services) remain as it was but to remove the actual source of tension, namely, the beliefs and attitudes displayed. Our dialogue proceeded in the following manner (after the expression of the clergyman's feeling of tension owing to a sense of moral and intellectual incompetence):

> "In a religious service does the clergyman perform for the congregation? Is the congregation gathered together to observe how marvelous the clergyman is?"
>
> "No, he performs for no one."
>
> "Is he there to display his intellectual talents in order to win the praise and admiration of his congregation?"
>
> "No, the purpose of a religious service is to praise God, the clergy being merely the instrument toward this end. The people are in church for the sole purpose of worshipping God, and it would be improper for the clergyman to display ostentatiously his charming personality or anything else to distract the people from the principal purpose of the church service."
>
> "Then, you are not on exhibition?"
>
> "You are right! I feel a great deal better."

Frankl often uses a form of philosophical psychotherapy in his logotherapy, especially in relation to what he terms the *tragic triad* (pain, death, and guilt).[15] In cases where a person cannot remove suffering, he can alter his attitude toward it. The author was confronted with a case in which the individual concerned suffered a calamitous experience, his best friend being killed tragically by a tractor overturning upon him. Our conference proceeded somewhat as follows:

> "I'm distraught, angry, and want to curse someone for what happened. If there is a God, why did he allow it to occur?"

Ironically, this man said that he did not believe in God; then he proceeded to curse God—his emotional upheaval causing his irrational outburst and contradiction. He went on to say:

> "I can't understand it. Here is a fine young man, a good person with a good family that needed him. Now what are they supposed to do? I hate the world; there is no justice in it. Why is there evil? Why do good people have to suffer? What is the meaning of it all?"

Ordinarily, in such a case the psychotherapist would permit the emotionally troubled man to continue to expel all of his emotional ejaculations to the point of emotional depletion as a cathartic experience. Allport would argue that this man may continue to express his emotional evincings to a point where it becomes not only a personality trait but one that is cardinal and functioning

---

[15]V. E. Frankl, *Psychotherapy and Existentialism* (New York: Washington Square Press, 1967).

autonomously, and that would be disastrous. In this instance, the man was allowed to vent his feelings until he reached a point where he sought a respite from emoting and awaited a response from the psychotherapist. At this juncture he was sympathetically told:

> "Suffering has a peculiar effect on persons, usually developing in them one of two types of characteristics: The first is a vengeful personality, with a profound hatred of everything and everyone because of the injustice sensed in his experience of suffering. His embittered attitude permeates his world as a style of life. The second, however, is a mellowed personality who has emerged with insight and maturity, and exhibits a profound compassion and understanding for the suffering of others as a fellow-sufferer, as a comrade in misery. Misery often units people together as Albert Schweitzer noted in his experiences in darkest Africa and as members of Alcoholics Anonymous are keenly aware. Which type will you choose to be, or which type will you allow yourself to fall prey to becoming?"

To my amazement, he retorted:

> "You are absolutely right, the experience of suffering does place a person in an advantageous position to appreciate the suffering of others, and he can become mellowed and matured in a manner that no one else can. In a sense, one is privileged to suffer, for it can make him superior to others, sharing experiences and a level of living unknown to others."

Note the philosophical and not the psychological approach employed. It was not necessary to see this man for a number of times and permit him to expel his emotions, excusing it as catharsis. His emotions were self-contained once his philosophical attitude was altered and he accepted his circumstances. His emotional tensions were not principally aroused from the tragedy but from his attitude toward, and philosophical interpretation or beliefs concerning, the tragedy.

Case Studies

Case One

A woman in her fifties, after having undergone brain surgery, complained of headaches localized behind the left ear. After careful examination, her physicians concluded that the operation was quite successful and that they could find nothing physically wrong with her, and recommended that she see the clinic's psychiatrist. Some months later, when she came to my attention, she had had no less than a dozen visits with the clinic's psychiatrist but to no avail.

Sahakian, "Stoic Philosophical Psychotherapy," pp. 33–35.

Knowing that she had competent psychiatric care, I decided to proceed along another approach, namely philosophical psychotherapy. On the conclusion of a brief introductory chat, enabling us to become better acquainted with each other, I explored her attitude regarding her ailment by engaging in the following dialogue with her:

"Is the pain severe?"

"Yes, at times."

"Is it endurable?"

"Not at times, and I think that it is getting worse."

"Is it very painful at this moment?"

"Excruciating!"

"Do you feel that the pain will become so intense that it will drive you out of your mind?"

"How did you know that? That is precisely what terrifies me; I am afraid that I am going insane, that is, the pain will get worse until I lose my mind."

At this point it was decided to employ Stoic psychotherapy. The patient would be offered the choice of accepting her condition laden with pain instead of fighting it, which she had been doing up to now. What she did not realize was that she was suffering from a dual pain, one which she had localized in the brain, and the other, the strain of emotional tension. Apparently, the latter was the less endurable of the two and had a concomitant aggravating effect upon the former.

The dialogue with the patient continued:

"Why do you want to get rid of the pain?"

"Nobody wants pain," she said looking at me as if I were rather peculiar for asking such an asinine question.

"If you could feel confident that no matter how severe the pain in your head becomes it will, nevertheless, not drive you to 'insanity' as you put it, do you think it would then be possible for you to endure the headache?"

"Why? Won't it?"

"But do you think that you could endure it?"

"Yes, I'm sure that I can."

"What if I were to tell you that your headache will never cause 'insanity'; and if you were ever to become 'insane,' it would not be from your head pain?"

"Is that true?"

"Actually, a person becomes adapted to pain."

"Truly?"

"It is true."

Then smilingly she said: "I don't think that you will believe it but the pain in my head has subsided considerably, and I know that I can endure it."

When the tension that she had suffered was alleviated, she accepted her condition and was reasonably content, which indicates that it was not the head pain (regardless of whether it was psychological, psychosomatic, or otherwise) that distressed her, but the strenuous emotional confrontation with what she thought was a grave problem. Note that the symptom had "subsided considerably" through this dialectical method.

Case Two

This second case is that of a man in his late thirties complaining of neurotic symptoms though he had been to a number of psychiatrists. When he came to me it was uncertain whether he expected a miracle or was just shopping for another psychotherapist. It was quite obvious in this case that, owing to the failure of a number of psychiatrists, Stoic philosophical psychotherapy might possibly succeed where the other methods had failed. At least it was worth the attempt. He had a number of persistent neurotic symptoms with which he was wrestling, with the hope of conquering them. Instead of gaining any control over them, he had become worse by succumbing to despair and by depleting himself emotionally. It became quite clear that the tense, emotional strain exerted in combatting his neurosis was more painfully distressing than the neurosis itself. After some time, our session took the following dialectical course:

> "You have told me of some of your neurotic symptoms and you say that you want me to help you to eradicate them. Why?"
>
> "What do you mean, 'Why?' Any normal person would want to get rid of them. They are tormenting problems and disturb me terribly. They have made me miserable for a long time."
>
> "Have you ever tried to live with them; accept them? Some crippled people have learned to live with their ailment. They do not spend every hour of their waking day or an entire lifetime striving to gain mastery over their problem. They accept their plight and learn to live with it, as do many other people who are handicapped victims. Some persons with the loss of an arm or with a heart condition learn to live within the limitations of their handicap; they do not waste their time and exhaust themselves vainly combatting their problem. Is it not possible for you also to do something comparable?"
>
> After staring at me with a meaningless look for almost a minute, the patient's eyes and face lit up, and he smiled broadly (a smile that never left his face for the remainder of the session) and said: "Why didn't the other psychotherapists tell me this long ago? Of course I can accept it and live with it. In fact, I feel better already. It is most ironic that I should come to a therapist, requesting that he cure me, and then have him tell me to keep my problem."

Two weeks later I saw this man, and with a similar smile and sense of relief he reported that he was "all better." Six months later, he was still content. The goal of Stoic psychotherapy is not happiness, but tranquility. In Stoic tranquility, there is neither anguish nor joy.[16]

Conclusion

Actually, what is most distressing to many neurotics and others is the emotional stress exerted to combat their problem, creating an emotional exhaustion, a state of doubt and insecurity, that readily stimulates or triggers anxiety at the slightest provocation. What needs to be accomplished in these cases is the removal of the superimposed emotional stress that comes with the fighting of the symptoms and not the symptoms per se.

Stoic psychotherapy may work here. The emotional block is removed by eliminating the driving force, namely, the unrelenting determination to control neurotic symptoms. Eliminate the tension created by the determination to gain mastery over the symptoms and the symptoms themselves may dissipate. If you cannot remove the problem, then change the attitude that is assumed toward it, and you will discover that you may have effectively dealt with two problems: the original neurosis and the distressing emotional tension expended in wresting it.

In closing we should like to point out that the motto of the "Introduction" of Adler's *The Neurotic Constitution* is a quotation from a leading Stoic, Seneca: "Everything depends on one's opinion. . . . We suffer according to our opinion. One is as miserable as one believes oneself to be.—*Epist.* 78, 13."[17]

Philosophical Psychotherapy: An Existential Approach

The Nature of Existential Psychotherapy

In this section, attention is centered on existential philosophy as a psychotherapeutic vehicle. Philosophical psychology in the nonscholastic and nonrational-

---

[16]H. N. Simpson, *Stoic Apologetics* (440 Linden Ave., Oak Park, Ill. 60302: Author, 1966).
[17]A. Adler, *The Neurotic Constitution* (New York: Dodd, 1926; reprint by Books for Libraries, 1972).
This section has also been published as a separate article in *Journal of Individual Psychology* (spring 1976).

istic sense is not new to empirical or clinical psychology, as is evidenced by the writings of Kierkegaard.[18]

Adherents of contemporary existential psychology and psychotherapy have learned of Kierkegaard's existential psychology through Heidegger,[19] but the philosopher who applied it directly to psychotherapy, terming it *existential psychoanalysis*, was Sartre.[20] Sartre also developed a phenomenological or existential theory of consciousness. Psychologists such as May[21] and psychiatrists such as Binswanger,[22] Condrau and Boss[23] look to Heidegger for their lead, while the psychiatrist Frankl[24] takes his lead from the phenomenological philosopher Scheler.[25] Rogers also identifies himself as a phenomenologist.[26] Recently, Maddi has joined the ranks of existentialist psychologists,[27] as has Thorne.[28] Adler is seen as related to the existentialist stream of development.[29] "The ceaseless task of unfolding issues of freedom, choice, and meaning is essential to the notion of humanism. This has been a cornerstone of Adlerian psychology."[30] Stern asserts that Sartre's position is decidedly nearer to Adler's than to Freud's. "There is no doubt that Sartre's 'original choice' is the counterpart of Adler's goal, and Sartre's 'fundamental project' is the replica of Adler's life plan."[31]

Objective of Existential Psychotherapy

The goal of existential therapy is *authenticity*, not tranquility as is the aim in Stoic therapy, nor happiness as is the goal in some other forms of therapy. For

---

[18]S. Kierkegaard, *Fear and Trembling*, 2d ed. (Princeton: Princeton University Press, 1954); idem, *The Concept of Dread*, 2d ed. (Princeton: Princeton University Press, 1957).

[19]M. Heidegger, *Being and Time* (New York: Harper & Row, 1962).

[20]J.-P. Sartre, *Being and Nothingness* (New York: Philosophical Library, 1956), pp. 557–75; idem, *The Transcendence of the Ego: An Existentialist Theory of Consciousness* (New York: Noonday, 1957).

[21]R. May, ed., *Existential Psychology*, 2d ed. (New York: Random, 1969).

[22]L. Binswanger, *Being-in-the World* (New York: Basic, 1963).

[23]G. Condrau and M. Boss, "Existential Analysis," in *Modern Perspectives in World Psychiatry*, ed. J. G. Howells (Edinburgh and London: Oliver & Boyd, 1968), pp. 488–518; M. Boss, *Psychoanalysis and Daseinsanalysis* (New York: Basic, 1953).

[24]V. E. Frankl, *The Will to Meaning: Foundations and Applications of Logotherapy* (New York: World Publishing, 1969).

[25]M. Scheler, *Formalism in Ethics and Non-Formal Ethics of Values* (Evanston, Ill.: Northwestern University Press, 1973).

[26]C. R. Rogers, *Client-Centered Therapy: Its Current Practice, Implications, and Theory* (Boston: Houghton Mifflin, 1951); p. 532.

[27]S. R. Maddi, "The Existential Neurosis," *Journal of Abnormal Psychology* 72 (1967): 311–25.

[28]F. C. Thorne, "An Existential Theory of Anxiety," *Journal of Clinical Psychology* 19 (1963): 35–43.

[29]A. Adler, *The Science of Living* (Garden City, N.Y.: Doubleday, 1969); p. vii.

[30]R. D. Waldman, "A Theory and Practice of Humanistic Psychotherapy," *Journal of Individual Psychology* 25 (1969): 19–31.

[31]A. Stern, "Existential Psychoanalysis and Individual Psychology," *Journal of Individual Psychology* 14 (1958): 40.

Kierkegaard, authenticity is the willingness to be oneself, standing "transparently" before God;[32] for Heidegger, it is to be genuine, to make one's own (autonomous) choices, to avoid losing one's identity by blending in with the crowd.

Pleasure or happiness is not desired, because the pursuit of pleasure inevitably terminates in despair.[33] The person who constantly seeks pleasure is fundamentally a desperate individual, as exemplifid by the so-called jet set whose members are driven to such lengths for a taste of pleasure: by breakfasting in New York, lunching in Los Angeles, and supping in Acapulco to extract a "kick" out of life. Such behavior is an act of desperation, as is the "doing-the-town" itinerary of those who go from nightclub to nightclub to escape ennui.

A philosophy of pleasure is a philosophy of despair. It is an indication of extreme boredom from which one is prepared to do virtually anything to extricate oneself. A Freudian system of psychological hedonism tends toward despair, hence to "existential frustration" or "existential neurosis." Frankl, repudiating pleasure as the goal of human existence, cited the case of a woman in a concentration camp who sought to take her own life because the future offered no promise of pleasure. Frankl, challenging this hedonistic philosophy, countered that the woman was posing the wrong question. Her query should have been: "What can life expect from me?"[34]

In existential philosophy and psychotherapy, *choice, freedom,* and *responsibility* are the aims, not pleasure. Pleasure will not see a person through life, but a *raison d'être* will, and this will carry a person through life's severest vicissitudes. As Nietzsche said: "If we have our own reason for living, we shall endure almost any mode of life."[35] By freely choosing our mode of existence, we develop our personality according to our individual preference.

Characteristics of Existential Psychotherapy

The existential psychotherapist is convinced that his client can freely choose his personality at any stage of life, and in any condition of human existence. "Empirical psychoanalysis tries to determine the complex," asserted Sartre, "while existential analysis tries to determine the original choice."[36] A patient's past does not have the control over him that psychoanalysts fancy; an individual's future rests in his own hands. A person is a *being-for-the-future,* not the victim of the past. The reason a person is victimized by his past experiences

---

[32]S. Kierkegaard, *Either/Or,* 2 vols. (Princeton: Princeton University Press, 1944).

[33]S. Kierkegaard, *Concluding Unscientific Postscript* (Princeton: Princeton University Press, 1941); idem, *Either/Or.*

[34]V. E. Frankl, *The Doctor and the Soul: From Psychotherapy to Logotherapy,* rev. ed. (New York: Knopf, 1965).

[35]F. Nietzsche, *Twilight of the Idols: Or, How to Philosophize with a Hammer,* in COMPLETE WORKS OF FRIEDRICH NIETZSCHE, 17 vols., ed. O. Levy (New York: Macmillan, 1901-11), vol. 16, maxim 12.

[36]Sartre, *Being and Nothingness,* p. 657.

is that he *believes* he is, and so is committed in practice to that belief. Actually, he has been "brainwashed" by a fatalistic philosophy as found in psychoanalysis. As soon as a person ceases to believe that he can do no other but what his past dictates, then he will experience the freedom that he genuinely possesses and can now exercise it. Belief directs a person. Many people have become so committed to the deterministic views of psychoanalysis that when they think and act independently, they do so only with enormous effort and difficulty.[37] As Peirce observed, a belief is "that upon which a man is prepared to act. Beliefs are really rules for action, and the whole function of thinking is but one step in the production of habits of action."[38] Adler, too, was convinced of the effect philosophy exerts on an individual. He saw "no reason to be afraid of metaphysics; it has had a great influence on human life and development."[39]

Existentialists hold that the essential nature of a person is freedom. It is necessary for this freedom to be expressed for one to find one's wholesome self. According to Sartre, we are our choices, and psychoanalysis results in "a lie without a liar; it allows me to understand how it is possible for me to be lied to without lying to myself . . . ; it replaces the duality of the deceiver and the deceived, the essential condition of the lie, by that of the 'id' and the 'ego.' "[40] Stern and Sartre emphasize the unity of the individual, his relative indeterminism, and his responsibility for his choices.[41]

Prior to Sartre, both Kierkegaard and Heidegger asserted that we are our choices, but with a different inflection. Kierkegaard modified Socrates's dictum from "know thyself" to "choose thyself." An authentic self (Heidegger) or a transparent self (Kierkegaard) is not alienated from the past, or even from the present, but integrates past and present with the *future*. A person's future is as much a part of him as is the past and present, directing him to his authentic self. An individual is more than a being-in-the-world (a phenomenological existence incorporating surrounding reality), he is a being-for-the-future. His futural existence has a bearing on his present existence—his motivation and behavior. Adlerian therapy aims at a durable adjustment by integrating the future with the present. "When I speak of active adaptation," remarked Adler, "it is a question rather of adaptation *sub specie aeternitatis* [under the aspect of the eternal], for only that physical and psychical development is 'right' which can be reckoned as right for the uttermost future."[42]

[37]W. S. Sahakian, "A Social Learning Theory of Obsessional Neurosis," *Israel Annals of Psychiatry and Related Disciplines* 7 (1969): 70–75.

[38]C. S. Peirce, *Collected Papers,* 8 vols. (Cambridge, Mass.: Harvard University Press, 1931–66).

[39]A. Adler, *Social Interest: A Challenge to Mankind* (New York: Capricorn Books, 1964), p. 275.

[40]Sartre, *Being and Nothingness,* p. 51.

[41]P. Rom and H. L. Ansbacher, "An Adlerian Case of a Character by Sartre?" *Journal of Individual Psychology* 21 (1965): 37.

[42]Adler, *Social Interest,* p. 271.

To appreciate existential psychotherapy, two case studies will serve to elucidate its tenets in practice.

Case Studies

Case One (Illustrating Being-of-the-Future)

A male in his thirties, despondent over an affair of unrequited love, sought to do away with himself. Insisting on immediate psychotherapy, he came to the therapist's office without an appointment and there played his small portable tape recorder, containing his final statement to those he loved. He announced that although he had wanted to take his life in the past, this was the first time that he knew for certain he would follow through with his suicidal plan.

In this session he spent a considerable period of time dwelling on his bleak past, and he talked incessantly of episodes in his life which terminated in failure, discouragement, and misfortune. After summarizing his life as one of disvalue, he pointed out that the pattern of his existence was miserable and fixed by previous experiences. To validate what the future held in store for him, he used the past as his monitor, as if it held the reins of the future.

The client, who was a person of high potential, had moderate ambitions well within his grasp. During this and subsequent sessions, it was pointed out that he was much more than a being-of-the-past, that he was also a being-for-the-future and must allow that future to assist him. The therapist said he believed his patient had great potential that made for a promising future, and that he could "cash in" and live on the promise of that future.

The client constantly harped on past episodes of unhappiness, using them as a forecast of the future. Eventually, he learned to see past experiences as unreliable predictors and to draw on the future for direction in decision-making.

Once he became identified with the future instead of the past, his attitude changed to his benefit. With this philosophical conversion, there was a concomitant transformation in emotions, attitude, behavior, and other personality factors. Subsequent to the first session, this man required only reinforcement of the philosophical attitude acquired during the initial meeting. A year later, he was still doing well, free from suicidal inclinations.

Case Two (Illustrating Choice, Decision, and Authenticity)

A married woman of thirty, who had previously undergone psychoanalysis, said she hated herself and had wanted to take her life on several occasions. She suffered from what one might identify as an existential neurosis, since she had lost her purpose in life, was floundering mentally, and was confused as to her identity. Fearing that life was "passing her by" before she had an opportunity to live, she wanted to know before it was too late precisely what truth or meaning life had for her, and if indeed it had any meaning at all.

Behind her search for answers was a desire to be told exactly what to think and do. She revealed that since childhood she never was allowed to make a decision. Her mother invariably made them for her, even to this day, and now the situation was compounded by three in-laws joining mother in making choices for her. After six months of therapy, she (for the first time in her life that she could remember) made two decisions that she felt were autonomous. Having made them, she experienced a feeling of exhilaration because she sensed that she was now a person in her own right, free and independent.

Her new-found autonomy was complicated owing to an emergence of a sense of responsibility, a concomitant of her new autonomy. Now able to make choices, she realized she was responsible for her decisions and her behavior, whereas previously she could lean on others.

She now yearned to find her authentic self, hoping that her inner integrity would accord her the values that she prized in human existence. She wanted to make responsible choices. She sought to divorce her husband but did not want this action to be detrimental to her two young sons. She had a lover, but she did not want this to affect her children or herself adversely. In her search for authenticity, she realized that she would have to reexamine her scale of values and decide responsibly, whereas previously she allowed her mind to entertain only those desires to which her personality was predisposed, without engaging in any critical evaluation. That is to say, she would permit herself to drift toward amorous pursuits without questioning their consequences. In consequence of her existential analysis an entirely different perspective and value orientation on her life and behavior resulted.

Summary

Unlike other systems of psychotherapy whose objectives are happiness or tranquility, existential analysis seeks to bring about an authentic person through the exercise of choices. One must bring his true self to realization through commitment, decisions, and choices. Inasmuch as personality change is effected through choice, an individual chooses himself: that is, his personality is the product of his choices. While the therapist does not make choices for his client, he facilitates his client's endeavors toward this end.

14

MORITA THERAPY: ZEN BUDDHISM APPLIED TO PSYCHOTHERAPY

Shoma Morita

Shoma Morita (1874–1938) was professor of neuropsychiatry at Tokyo Jikeikai School of Medicine. A neurotic himself, Morita directed his therapy toward neurosis. As early as 1919 and especially during the 1920s, he developed his psychotherapy to treat *shinkeishitsu* (*Nervosität* in German, *nervosity* in English). The term, which shows the influence of German psychiatry, is not the only influence on Morita therapy. Morita researched Kraepelin's biological psychiatry and, influenced by it, arrived at the theory of a *hypochondriacal constitution*. He meant by this term a predisposition toward anxiety neurosis, obsessive neurosis, and neurasthenia, phenomena characteristic of *Nervosität*. The hypochondriacal constitution, one marked by excessive instinctive fear, is not in itself sufficient to produce symptom formation of neurosis. Certain stimuli form reactions due to this hypochondriacal mood; these reactions, which ordinarily would have merely short-term consequences, grow in intensity because of hypochondriacal fear. The result is a vicious circle of ever-increasing reaction and fear.

This vicious circle is a process he termed *toraware,* meaning "to be caught," that is, preoccupied with excessive concern or "to be bound over with self-consciousness." In order to cope with *toraware, arugamama* is invoked. Arugamama, identical with the *satori* of Zen Buddhism, means "taking things as they are," or "the acquisition of insight." Arugamama calls for resigning oneself to one's fate in the sense of accepting one's condition. For example, by arugamama (letting nature take its course), neurotics can effectively deal with insomnia because it is not insomnia that keeps them awake but "fear" of insomnia. Permitting nature to takes its course will produce sleep instinctively when it is required. Accordingly, arugamama implies living with symptoms, accepting things as they are, facing agony, etc. The four states of Morita therapy include: (1) bed rest in isolation, (2) manual tasks, (3) increased or heavier tasks, and (4) a preparatory period designed for a return to everyday living in the world at large.

The books published on psychotherapy by Morita include the following (their titles have been translated into English): *Theory of Nervosity and Neurasthenia* (1921); *Lectures on Psychotherapy* (1921); *Nature and Therapy of Nervosity* (1928, with a new edition in 1956); and *Ways to the Therapy of Nervosity* (1935).

The Origin and Development of Morita Therapy

The Morita therapy is a unique psychotherapy which was originated and developed in Japan. Dr. Shoma Morita (1874–1938), professor of neuropsychiatry at Tokyo Jikeikai School of Medicine, as a result of his twenty years of effort towards effective medical treatment of neurasthenia, arrived at this form of therapy. Around 1919 he founded this theory on his experience of a successful "Conducting therapy in home setting," which was tried at his home on a few neurotic people.[1] Among references which, employed critically, became part of the background of this therapy, are the work therapy applied to psychotic patients, the fattening therapy of W. Mitchel of Philadelphia, the regulated living method of L. Binswanger, and the persuasive therapy of P. Dubois. During ten years preceding his therapy, Morita had made experiments with interest on hypnosis. In the end he had become doubtful about this hypnotic method and, discarding it, began his new therapy. It must be emphasized here that the psychoanalytical therapy was well criticized in its early stage of development and incorporated into his novel therapy.

Shuzo Kure, a teacher of S. Morita's and pioneer of Japanese psychiatry, introduced and popularized the scholastic system of Kraepelin in Japan. He also recognized the therapeutic value of the scientific psychotherapy which was prevailing in Europe at that time. He presented the theme of psychotherapy to Morita, who was motivated to study this field. (Since his sixteenth year of age Morita had suffered from neurasthenia, with palpitation, heavy feeling in his head and the like, but he was not cured by any kind of internal treatment.

Memoshige Miura and Shin-ichi Usa, "A Psychotherapy of Neurosis," *Psychologia* 3 (1970): 18–34. Originally reprinted from *Yonago Acta Medica* 14 (1970): 1–17, organ of the School of Medicine, Tottori University, Yonago City, Tottori Prefecture.

[1] "Among some patients whom Dr. Morita was taking care of at his home there was a certain female, Miss Yatabe. She suffered from obsessive neurosis of mysophobia. She had been treated at the Sugamo Psychiatric Hospital for a long time, and had left the hospital without being cured. At his home Dr. Morita tried hypnosis, other usual methods of treatment, and his own method of persuasion, but had no success. He told me that sometimes he had lost his temper and struck her. To his surprise, however, the patient had been cured suddenly by herself when she abandoned herself in agony and despair. Dr. Morita studied this accidental case, and found the necessary conditions for this wonderful cure, which became the basis of his unique therapeutic method.

This may be also one reason why he took an interest in psychotherapy.) Morita had studied the German orthodox biological methods founded by Kraepelin, so it was natural that he should have opposed Freud's theory. But the so-called neurasthenia was classified, at that time, in the field of somatology which is concerned with etiology as well as treatment, so that not only the psychoanalysis introduced by Freud but also the psychogenic theory on nervous disease introduced by Morita, on which the psychotherapy was based, were out of the main current of psychiatry for a long time. Mitsuzo Shimoda, former professor of psychiatry at Kyushu University, however, was one of the few who supported this therapy.

The therapy was successfully applied and further developed by Morita's disciples, Gen-yu Usa, Takehisa Kora, Yoshiyuki Koga, and Akichika Nomura, disciples of Shimoda and Koji Sato, a psychologist who was professor at the Third National College at that time (now Kyoto University). As G. Usa originally was a Zen monk, he naturally inevitably developed the Morita therapy along the line of Zen. So this therapy in the end also included the Zen mode of thought, though Morita did not receive it directly from Zen. Kora developed it with the background of European characterology and Koga studied it in his field of psychosomatic medicine. Sato employed this method for student counseling and developed it in connection with Lewin's theory of causality. The actual value of the Morita therapy was gradually recognized by Japanese psychiatrists and psychologists, and after the Second World War it was introduced into the United States by the psychiatrists or clinical psychologists who had stayed in Japan as medical officers of the American army.

Karen Horney, who came to Japan in the summer of 1952, receiving a suggestion by Daisetz T. Suzuki, Zen philosopher, studied the Morita therapy and Zen. She discussed the Morita therapy with Kora in Tokyo, and G. Usa and Sato in Kyoto. But she could not utilize what she had found because of her sudden death at the end of the year. Akihisa Kondo, who was a disciple of Kora, and Horney wrote a treatise on the Morita therapy in Horney's journal in 1953. Sato read a paper on a case of treatment of stammering by the Morita therapy in the Inter-American Congress of Psychology in December 1955 and delivered lectures in the U.S. and Europe to make it known worldwide. About this time Erich Fromm showed interest in the Morita therapy and sought much explanation from D. T. Suzuki and Sato. In the same year Kora contributed an article to L'Hygiène mentale, and since 1957, Ingeborg Y. Wendt, a German psychologist, had shown her interest in the Morita therapy and Zen. She visited Japan twice and then wrote articles with a view in mind that the therapy should be adopted also in Europe. In the summer of 1958, Harold Kelman, successor of K. Horney in the American Institute for Psychoanalysis, visited Japan and emphasized the points of similarity between the Morita therapy and Zen. In the same year Kora and Sato introduced the therapy abroad from the point of view of "Zenish" psychotherapy. In 1962 Takeo Doi reported on "Morita therapy and psychoanalysis" and argued on psychopathology of *toraware* (to be caught) at the conference of the National Institute of Mental Health. In 1963 Nomura explained the genealogy of the Morita therapy and discussed it in comparison with American and European psychotherapy at the Joint Psychiatric Meeting of Japan and U.S.A. held in Tokyo. In the *International Journal of Psychiatry* of October 1965, "Morita Therapy" written in 1964 by Kora was reported in full, and a psychiatrist and two psychologists presented their opinions about it, to which Kora gave his answers.

Morita's Theory of "Nervosity"

The so-called neurasthenia or neurosis has been classified under many headings and there have been many opinions about its true form of cause. Morita summarized such diseases under the name of *shinkeishitsu* (nervosity), because neurasthenia, hypochondriasis, and obsession are based on the same predispositons. This denies the theory that they are caused by nervous exhaustion, and it is at the same time in opposition to the psychoanalysis and the psychogenic theories. His explanation is based on his view that a hypochondriac temperament is the generation of nervosity and that the mechanism of psychic interaction is the condition inducing development of the disease.

Hypochondriac temperament is a kind of introvert inclination or predisposition, an extreme self-communion; that is, hypersensitivity to one's own physical and mental indisposition or any unusual, morbid sensation which threatens one's own existence. But it is the manifestation of the desire for existence which is inherent in human nature, a characteristic of every human. In cases of an extreme inclination, there develop a nervous tendency and then complicated symptoms of nervosity. This means that a man of nervous temperament has a sensitive, delicate feeling and also an extreme desire for completeness, an idealistic intellectual attitude, and will to live. Kora gave it the name *inadaptability,* which means the anxiety of a man who under his present conditions cannot adapt himself to the given circumstances. This idea of his gives a broader meaning to the notion of hypochondriac temperament. He recognized its similarity with the basic anxiety alleged by Horney, but he thought the anxiety called "basic" was unnatural because the fear of death derives from the desire for existence.

Both hereditary and environmental elements influence the creation of hypochondria. Shimoda emphasized the element of environment and considered that one factor for its creation is overdiscipline or overprotection in infancy. The intelligence of people of nervous temperament is on a level with that of normal men. Their extreme intellectual attitude is in striking contrast to the emotional inclination in cases of hysteria.

The second element of Morita's theory is the mechanism of psychic interaction. The mental process that Morita paid attention to in respect to nervosity is explained as follows: If attention is paid to some sensation, the sensation becomes very sharp; and by mutual interaction of sensation and attention the sensation will become more and more excessive. This process is named the mechanism of psychic interaction.

This is a kind of vicious circle which grows out of hypochondriac temperament, out of being prepossessed with one's own oversensitiveness, for example, headache, giddiness, absence of mind, heart acceleration, distraction, insomnia, inflating sensation of stomach, fear of epidemics, bashfulness when made an object of attention, sudden association of sexual excitation at the sight of the opposite sex, accidental fit of fear, fit of pain, and so on. But if these symptoms are retraced back to their beginning, it will be made clear that these are normal sensations experienced by any normal man. The nervosity patient, however, out of his hypochondriac feeling, regards such reactions as unsound and unusual, is struck with fear of them, and at the same time anticipates them, so that by such mechanism of psychic interaction, these symptoms become worse and worse, he is captured therein, and the symptoms will be fixed for a long time in life.

Once having these symptoms, the patients believe in their reality and will continuously feel the distress of being confined in the subjectivity, as is shown in the dream. (G. Usa showed a case of mechanism of interaction in the afterimage of sensation of nervosity under the guidance of one of us [M. M.].) Autosuggestion is also one cause for the acceleration of adherence to those symptoms.

The patients cannot compare themselves with others correctly because they are captives to their subjectivity; they cannot feel sympathy for others and are not apt to take care of others in view of their own fear and distress. Therefore, the patients become egocentric and pity themselves and envy others; in their longing for sympathy they are always irritable and impatient. Such sadness and irritability are secondary emotions based on pessimistic thoughts caused by the misunderstanding of self-criticisms.

Classification and Statistics of Nervosity

Dr. Morita specified *nervosity* as the condition of mind in which, because of being self-introspective (introverted), one tends to become intellectual in the end. Therefore, he drew a clear line between nervosity and hysteria, because the former shows quite a different tendency from the latter in that hysteria means highly sensitive feeling in conjunction with extrovert mentality.

In classifying nervosity according to its elemental characteristics and not according to its external appearances, Morita regarded neurasthenia, anxiety neurosis, and obsession as diseases of the same type in their basic nature. The results of the therapy, and the fact that medical cures of these diseases require the same psychotherapy and almost the same period of treatment, demonstrate the sameness of the nature of these diseases.

Morita classified nervosity under the following three headings according to simplicity and complexity and general appearance. Of course, these three types of diseases may grade into or combine with one another.

Ordinary Nervosity (So-Called Neurasthenia)

This means a peculiar nervosity in a narrow sense, including: heavy feeling in the head, headache, insomnia, stunned feeling, abnormality in senses, gastroenteric neurosis, increase of fatigue, reduced productivity, reduced strength, bad memory, distraction of mind, vertigo (giddiness), ringing in the ears, tremor, writer's cramp, inferiority complex, shyness and worry for the future, sexual trouble, etc.

Paroxysmal Neurosis (Anxiety Neurosis)

This is a kind of fit which a patient has subjectively: the excitement of fear accompanied by the fear evoked in expectation of fit. The following come under this category: palpitation-fit, debility of arms and legs, vertigo, fainting-fit, nympholepsy, anxiety-fit, cold-fit, shivering-fit, pain-fit, dyspnea-fit, etc.

Obsession (Phobia)

This is a kind of mental complication caused by an antagonism in which a patient tries, by some means, neither to feel nor to think about certain unpleasant feelings or thoughts, regarding them with a hypochondriac feeling as morbid abnormality. The following come under this classification: homophobia (erythrophobia, look-in-the-face phobia, self-expression phobia, etc.), mysophobia, nosophobia, imperfection phobia, reading phobia, fainting phobia, agoraphobia, stammering phobia, crime phobia, aichmophobia, earthly thought phobia, acrophobia, inquiry phobia, etc.

As to the frequency of evocation of these diseases, the data issued by the Kora Kosei-in Hospital (1950–52) show that homophobia ranks first (38 percent), followed by heavy feeling in the head (11 percent), unstable nervous disease (8 percent), insomnia (5 percent) and nosophobia (4 percent).[2] However, a study of the materials of nervous diseases published by the Neuro-Psychiatry Department of Tokyo Jikeikai School of Medicine (1953–62) reveals that as the prime subject of complaint the physical condition comes first, showing almost the same percentage (34– 40 percent) for every age.[3] In regard to age and sex, the patients in their twenties lead the list, and of all patients examined, 47 percent males and 41 percent females belong to this age. According to the statistics showing diagnostic distinction, of all the victims of nervous diseases, 55 percent are patients of nervosity (ordinary nervosity 35 percent, obsession 19 percent, anxiety neurosis 11 percent). As to the ratio of distribution by age of the three types of nervosity, ordinary nervosity is distributed almost equally (approximately 35 percent), while fear complex reaches a percentage of 36 at an age between 15 and and 19 and shows a gradual decrease in percentage with increasing age. Anxiety neurosis occupies a little over 20 percent between the thirties and fifties. No children under fourteen years old are diagnosed as having nervosity. When classified according to sex it is found that more persons of ordinary nervosity or obsession are found among the males, whereas more patients of anxiety neurosis (hysteria and psychogenic reaction, too) are among the females. In 1961, as against 1953, the victims of ordinary nervosity showed some decrease in number, while an increase in number was seen with the patients of obsession. Investigation with regard to the chief causes of the diseases reveals that in most cases domestic trouble and physical disorder result in sudden ailments. These are some of the causes of mental ailments: school problems of patients under the age of nineteen; domestic problems of people in their thirties or after; and various kinds of problems ranging from character disposition to love affairs of those who are between twenty to twenty-nine years of age. The individual causes, however, do not greatly differ in percentage. Males are more troubled with problems concerning character, job, and school affairs, while more domestic or housing problems worry females. More sexual problems are revealed by people below twenty. Insomnia gradually takes a more important position among the chief complaints with increase in age. The factors of heredity were found to be around 15 percent with all the patients of nervous disease examined. Among the factors, neurotic factors are the largest in number. The statistics published in 1960 by T. Suzuki reveal that among 1330 cases of nervosity, 31.1 percent

[2]T. Kora, "Morita Therapy," *International Journal of Psychiatry* 1 (1965):611–40.
[3]T. Takeyama et al., "Materials on Neurosis," *Shinkeishitsu* 6 (1966):18–29. (Written in Japanese)

of patients had close relatives who were suffering from nervosity or had strong disposition to nervosity. He also reported that there is a high percentage of firstborn children among nervosity patients, at a 1 percent level of reliability.

Principles of Morita Therapy

Since those who have a special psychical inclination towards nervous disease are apt to have an attack of nervosity due to some psychological mechanism, the method of treatment of this disease ought to be psychotherapy. The point aimed at by Morita's method is a training or drilling treatment of hypochondriac temperament underlying the disease, as well as the destruction of the psychic interaction in which the patient is caught. Some psychological bases in this therapy are as follows:

Contradiction of Thought

Our thinking of what we wish to be or what we should be often brings about a contradictory result or a "fact," which was referred to as contradiction of thought by Morita. An idea or a thought is not always the same as the substance or the fact itself. Being unaware of this difference between idea and fact, not only the patients of nervosity but also sane people think of things that are not real just as if they were actually real. They do their best trying to change what is imagined into real facts by intellectual means, which results in contradiction of thought. The victims of nervosity may easily fall into contradiction of thought all the more because they so strongly long for perfection and they are such idealists. Generally speaking, our subjectivity and objectivity, our sentiment and intelligence, our understanding and realization —these things are frequently and very much contradictory, and hence do not accord with each other. The indistinctness in discrimination gives rise to the contradiction of thought. If a doctor tries to objectively persuade and control a patient of nervosity by telling him, "Try not to think of such a thing" or "Don't worry about that," he will not be able to succeed in attaining his object of curing this illness which is, after all, subjective. The unpleasant feeling we may have when we see cockroaches, for example, is feeling made into fact. In such a case, the patient of nervosity, if occasion demands, does not try to destroy the cockroaches, but by preserving this unpleasant feeling first suppresses his aversion against the insects, then becomes cool, and tries to do his best to approach them. This is also a feeling made into a fact by objective criticism, the fruit of intelligence, just like an attempt at the exclusion of fear of subjective death by saying, "Death is nothing to fear," which is nothing but a contradiction of thought. This attitude becomes one of the most important prerequisites in establishing an obsession.

Realization and Understanding

Realization is self-consciousness obtained through the actual performance and experiences of our own, while understanding is abstract intelligence which fosters our judgment provoking us to say, "This ought to be so," or "That must be so," etc. by using our reasoning power. And, the deepest understanding is acquired through concrete experiences we actually go through, just as we can appreciate the taste of food only after we have actually eaten it. Our interests or hobbies, also, come to have meaning only after we have had actual experience. A patient of nervosity puts too much weight on his understanding by neglecting his own practical experience, so that he hastily concludes that the condition of his body and mind is so and so. Or if he thinks that interest is needed in the work he is to do, he does not try to set to work until his interest has been aroused. In such a situation, infused knowledge or thoughts prove to have little power of persuasion, unless the patient actually works and consequently creates a real situation. If the underlying tone of feeling of the patient is ignored, intellectual persuasion will bring him even further away from the realization.

Obedience to Nature

It is a fact that the activity of our body and mind is a natural phenomenon. We cannot control it by artificial means. However, our rational thinking suggests that we can control it as desired. The same is the case with mental phenomena. We have made the mistake of thinking that "only we know our own mind," or that "we can feel things just as we think we should," or that "we are free in thinking." To fear death, to hate discomfort, to grieve over a sad event, to complain about things that do not conform to our wishes—each of these is a natural manifestation of human sentiment. Even if we try to control ourselves as we want by such artificial means to our own advantage, after all matters will not go on as we wish. This frustration will begin to weigh heavy on our mind to no good and we will become incapable. Finally we will not be able to stand the pain. Then what we should do for our sake is to definitely abandon such artificial, poor behavior and to obey nature. Thereby, we will be able to attain the object of breaking down such contradiction of thought by feeling cold as cold, by accepting pain or fear as it is, or by going through the agony itself. But we will never be able to succeed if we devise an artificial intellectual counterplan. As the result of submitting to nature we will lack a clear attitude of mind, and both physical and mental uncertainty will arise. Consequently the mind is always in a strain. But if the patient will adapt himself to the changes occurring in his environments, his attention will come into free play. As the symptoms of nervosity are caused by concentrated attention upon a point, the doctor should start by increasing the natural mental activity of the patient, enlarge the sphere of this activity, and guide him to a free mental attitude.

Practice of Morita Therapy

Because nervosity is not directly related to nervous fatigue, rest and tranquilizers are not effective. Therefore, the Morita therapy treats hypochondriac dispositions by training the patients' characters and treats psychic interaction, which is the mechanism that aggravates the symptoms, by breaking the contradiction of thought, thereby breaking down the vicious circle of attention and sensation. We always endeavor to make patients grasp an attitude of life natural and obedient to their environment by their personal experiences and feelings.

Morita therapy is a fundamental and natural method of treatment. It teaches the patients to obey their own nature and to have an attitude towards life appropriate to things as they are. Therefore, we do not stress suggestion or persuasion; nor is it necessary to pursue psychic conflicts to their sources. Instead, we direct the patients' lives, actions, and mental attitudes by the following method: We only criticize them through diaries and lectures. These directions and criticisms for their mental attitude are unique to the Morita therapy. The therapist does not direct the patients' attitude of mind to their symptoms but has them renounce all their intellectualized attitudes of mind, allow their symptoms to change as they will, and avoid being consciously concerned with their attitude of mind. As a general rule we have them enter the hospital but also treat out-patients as an expedient means.

Four Stages of Treatment in the Hospital

First stage: Period of absolute bed rest (four to seven days). In this period we isolate patients. Meeting with others, talking, reading and writing, smoking, eating between meals, and singing are forbidden. We have them be in bed except when they take meals, bathe, and excrete. We make them endure worldly thoughts and all of the pain which accompanies them, advising them not to avoid facing the agony. At the beginning patients are in great distress, but after about four days they are bored and tired of lying in bed. They want to get up and do something. And then, we direct them to get up. We give them printed instructions so that they will know and observe the rules. If they do not follow our directions, we sometimes tell them to leave the hospital. We interview patients every day for several minutes to see whether they are observing the instructions honestly or not. But the interview may be omitted, if during the period the patient complains of his symptoms.

Second stage: Period of light work after getting out of bed (three to seven days).   This period is for an insulation method of treatment, too. Talking, associating with others, playing, and reading are forbidden. Sleeping is limited to seven or eight hours. They must be out-of-doors in the daytime. To take a rest in the room is not allowed. On the first and the second day, we prohibit all actions requiring the use of muscles, such as looking at the sky, climbing an elevation, or using a bamboo broom, and also prohibit purposeless use of time in taking a walk without necessity, doing physical exercises, or playing with children or dogs, etc. We let the symptoms change as they occur, at the same time arousing a spontaneous desire to work, promote exact observation of animals or plants, and allow hand work like weeding or gathering dead leaves. Every day after supper they make entries in a diary, so that both their physical and mental conditions will become clear and the doctor will be able to criticize the contents of the diary and to make hints with regard to the mental attitude of the patients. For all the patients who are at the second stage or higher, lectures are held three times a week explaining the process of recovery in reference to the diary and leading the patients to be able to discern between desires and facts. After having washed themselves in the morning and before going to bed at night, that is twice a day, they are required to read a convenient portion (or for five minutes) of a difficult classic book like the *Kojiki,* always from the beginning. But we induce them to read accurately only in pronunciation regardless of the meaning of the contents.

At this stage we let them perform necessary work at hand, not for fun or interest, but for them to be always in action, leave them in doubt about whether they will recover or not, keep them from devising treatment by themselves, and make them rely on the leadership of the doctor without reserve. We lead them not to tell the therapist about their symptoms in order to prevent them from observing their own progress and leave them to themselves according to the so-called ignoring therapy to ignore their complaints of pains. We lead them to stop taking an attitude of being ill, but rather to pretend that they are healthy, and to dissolve their fascination with contrasting phenomena of pleasure and displeasure by stopping any discussion of a discriminating nature. There is no clear boundary in advancing to the next stage.

Third stage: Period of choices (seven to twenty days).   In this period we have the patients work according to their state of health. They will become patient in working before they know it and happy in the discovery of their own courage and capacity for satisfaction in work. But we have to take care in this period not to let the patients be concerned with how they appear to others or with the dignity of their task. It is best for them not to have a choice as to what work to do; we have them do whatever they can. Their work extends to washing, cleaning the lavatory, kitchen work, and so on. As they are working they come to realize that happiness lies, not far away, but in the immediate experience of daily life. Therefore, it is necessary for the therapist to devise directions so that they will gradually develop the ability to act voluntarily in any work. When the patients are so fully occupied with their work that they are unconscious of the passage of time, they are ready for the next stage.

Fourth stage: Period of complicated practical life (ten days).   They learn patience through steady application of effort in work. While at the third stage their work depends on their interest, in this period they must work whether they are interested or not. Then they will come to adjust themselves to their varied situation. At the beginning of this period, patients are trained to lead a practical, ordinary life. They are permitted to read books and to go shopping. However, their reading is restricted to simple practical, descriptive, and scientific works; amusing, philosophical, and literary ones are to be avoided. We do not permit patients to sit and read in their rooms; they read at scattered odd moments during the day when they are free from work. We have them read any part of books and repeat several lines time and again without endeavoring to understand or memorize, whether they are difficult or not. During this period they are sometimes given permission to go to work or school outside the hospital. In this way, by continuing to have a realistic attitude towards life and work, the patients will be able, we hope, to fully experience their own lives and gradually realize what Morita called *pure mind.* The Morita therapy achieves its aim when patients spontaneously concentrate on daily real life.

Kazuyoshi Ikeda, professor at the Kyushu University Psychiatric Institute, explained very well the meaning of these four stages in his paper.[4] Let me quote some of his passages:

> The first stage: The principle is to minimize the working span of "contradiction of thought" or "bad intellect," and to reduce the conflict to a simpler form of psychic interaction. The subsidiary meaning of taking rest is to recover from exhaustion and to induce spontaneous activities of the patient.

---

[4]K. Ikeda, "Nervosity (Morita) and Morita Therapy," *Clinical Psychiatry* 1 (1959):461–73. (Written in Japanese)

The second stage: A period of transition from rest to spontaneous activity. Here comes out the positive aspect of the Morita therapy, that is, to break the contradiction of thought by making the patient concentrate on unrelated activities, and help him get insight into the dynamics of the paradox. At this stage the amount of work must be reserved so as to stimulate further spontaneous activity.

The third stage: An extension of the second stage. Varieties and heaviness of work increase, and they help the patient acquire self-confidence in his capacity. Individual differences come to appear at this stage in the type and the progress of cure.

The fourth stage: The preparation period for returning to actual life. Almost all the restrictions of life, including interpersonal relationships, are taken away. The responses of the patients show much more variety and complexity than in the previous stages. The theory of neurosis in the Morita school has not taken up the problem of character structure which underlies the symptom and has no hypothesis concerning it. The goal of treatment here is rather to bring about conditions under which the patient can develop his capacities to the utmost, keeping his native character as it has been.

Though the period of treatment is not fixed owing to the individual differences of the patients, an early recovery takes two weeks, and a slow recovery ten weeks, forty days being the average. What makes it possible to build up such ability to adapt oneself to normal life in such a comparatively short period of time is the excellent originality of the Morita therapy. The problem of returning to their places in society after having left the hospital is not so difficult, because the patients, while in the hospital, have already been able to go to school or practice a profession at the fourth stage. Since the egocentric aspect of life has been broken down and a living attitude in which the patients are not too particular about the choice of the conditions of life has been cultivated, they are not forced to suddenly adapt themselves to changed conditions.

Though Morita therapy originally was directed at a homelike therapy, there was also a kind of group therapy which only aimed at persons of nervosity, Morita himself living together with them. In the orthodox Morita therapy, it is obligatory that the therapist lives not too far from the patients and passes much of his time with them; the doctor and his family, the nurses, and the cooks take a consistent attitude towards the people of nervosity, and they treat them rather as lodgers than as patients, sometimes even as members of the family. Morita maintains that, "A man of nervosity cannot get well if treated as sick, but will soon get healthy when treated as if he were healthy." Therefore, the specific atmosphere in the therapeutic community is considered by William Caudill to be of great importance.[5]

[5] W. Caudill, *The Psychiatric Hospital as a Small Society* (Cambridge, Mass.: Harvard University Press, 1958).

Thus the therapeutic community is beyond the mere relationship between a doctor and a patient. This is one of the important characteristics of this therapy, since the lack of the usual one-to-one, doctor-patient relationship is useful to raise the independence of the patients and eliminate their dependence upon others.

Also the Sansei Hospital (Kyoto), which at present has fifty to sixty patients of nervosity, has adopted this therapy and gradually perfected group psychotherapy. In this hospital, since 1956, leaders have been elected from among the patients of the third stage or higher. A group of fifteen leaders takes charge of several tasks like cooking, gardening, postal service, and fire warden, and instructs the juniors, which system produces satisfactory results. The main points to be observed in guiding the patients by having them write a diary and hear lectures are as follows:

1. Lead them not to write about the symptoms of their disease and about their own character in the diary and not to speak with others about such things.

2. Lead them to stop self-observing feelings and mental conditions and urge them to draw their attention to the things happening around them.

3. As to the symptoms, advise them to leave them as they are, i.e., to let them change as they do without any treatment.

4. The doctor does not attach importance to the symptoms, nor does he put any evaluating criticism on them, but tells the patients to bear distress even if it is painful.

5. Let them do necessary work without delay. In case the patients do not take pleasure in it, lead them to begin the work without noticing their aversion.

6. Let them know through experience that a change in the kind of work means relaxation, and that it is possible to carry out two kinds of tasks or more at the same time (including mental work).

7. Emphasize that the purpose of the work is not to expedite the recovery of the patient but to complete the work itself.

8. Lead them not to accumulate self-confidence from various experiences; aiming at attaining a specific mental state like the feeling of relief gives rise to an illusion of the reality of one's feeling and results in establishing an imaginary self gain.

9. Let them assume full responsibility for their work, make them always bear the strains of life, and above all, meet the requirements of the public. And it is important that, when they are with other people, they always should try to be tactful.

10. It is not absolutely necessary that an explanation of the psychological mechanism of nervosity be given. On the contrary, intellectual interpretations and rationalistic comments may be a cause of strengthening the captivity in nervous temperament. C. Suzuki and A. Kumano pointed out that in the case

of three physicians who tried to cure their own nervosity, their medical knowledge was absolutely of no value in the dissolution of this disease.[6]

11. Always give the patients a chance to behave like healthy members of society. Whether their feeling of being ill or imperfect still remains or not, they may even obtain an attitude aiming at lending their assistance to others.

Recovery by Morita Therapy

Patients who have been cured by this therapy have confessed to being in a mental state as if "having just awakened from a dream," or "the day has broken," or "the world has changed." But this does not mean that the anxiety and the feeling of discontentment have suddenly been taken away. As human life is a flexible thing, feeling is fixed in a stream of ups and downs and follows it obediently, but if once feeling has come in accord with nature, this means a first arrival at the absolute calmness of mind. The patients who have been cured by breaking down their hypochondriac temperament that had veiled their basic will to live gain a more constitutive behavior and even a more active attitude towards society than they had in the days before they fell ill. When they do no longer need an intellectual support, intellect does not hamper their mind any more and can freely fulfill its original role of functioning as an outwardly directed structure. Also from this point of view, the self-insight, as devised in the Morita therapy, is not limited, in its deepest meaning, to an intellectual understanding, but is that very condition which is brought to reality in the practice of daily life that may conveniently be called *intuitive vision.*

For measuring the results of the Morita therapy by means of psychological tests, Kataguchi used the Rorschach test and showed on the basis of the Basic Rorschach Score (BRS) that Morita therapy, as compared with nondirective therapy, does not so easily bring about a change in human character.[7] But Nakae, also by using the BRS, found that in other clinics, after the therapy had been finished, a remarkable change was observed,[8] and he concluded that dissolution of the inclination to repressions, mental stability, feeling of sympathy, self-acceptance, and a nature-obeying attitude had been more improved than before. Using the RPRS (Rorschach Prognostic Rating Scale) according

---

[6]T. Suzuki, *One Way of Life* (Tokyo: Hokuyosha, 1960).

[7]Y. Kataguchi, "The Application of Rorschach Test to Psychotherapy," *Shinrigaku-Hyoron* 2 (1958):216 –32. (Written in Japanese)

[8]S. Nakae, "A Study on the Therapeutic Effects Reflected upon the Personality Changes of 'Nervosität' by the Morita Therapy. By Means of the Rorschach Test," *Rorschachiana Japonica* 2 (1959):86 –101. (Written in Japanese with English summary)

to Klopfer, one of us (S.U.) obtained the following results on personality changes in 114 patients who had been cured by the Morita therapy.[9]

1. Between the prognostic rating score and the evaluation of results of treatment there exists a significant connection, and among the RPRS-factors, M [the human movement response in Rorschach scoring], Sh [any delay or failure in responding to the ink blot in Rorschach testing], as well as FL indicate the efficiency in the healing prognosis.

2. Concerning the personality changes before and after the treatment, a significant increase is obvious in the RPRS-factors, Sh and Col [re: Rorschach tests; color response type. The two response personality types are M, or human movement, and C, or color response.], of the treated group in comparison with the other groups, and also an improvement towards emotional integration.

3. Among those who left the hospital after three to thirty-five years of treatment, the group that possessed a specific adaptability showed significant increase in M and Sh of RPRS as compared with the other groups, and for a long time they lived a community life tiding over difficulties they had never been faced with while they were in the hospital. H. Kawai and S. Yamamoto found the score of the RPRS to be high on nervosity and pointed out that the "unused ego-strength" of nervosity is strong.[10]

There are further studies on the relationship between the afterimage time and the treatment process conducted by G. Usa,[11] on character tests by T. Abe,[12] on the P-F study by K. Takano,[13] on the urine test by Y. Takahashi,[14] and on the mecholyl test by B. Fujita and Okuda,[15] and these researchers have obtained quantitative figures of the therapeutic effects of the Morita therapy.

The favorable results of the treatment are as indicated. About 60 percent of the patients were completely cured on an average after they had been in the hospital for about forty days. But even those who only improved in health will

[9]S. Usa, "A Study of the Effects of the Morita Therapy on Neurosis as Evaluated by Rorschach Test," *Psychiatria et Neurologia Japonica* 63(1961):575–91. (Written in Japanese with English summary)

[10]H. Kawai, S. Yamamoto, and S. Usa, "A Study on the Validity of the Rorschach Prognostic Rating Scale—Applied to Morita-Therapy," *Rorschachiana Japonica* 1 (1958):95–106. (Written in Japanese with English summary)

[11]G. Usa, "Relations between After-Image and Mental Set," Psychiatric Department contribution in memory of the late Dr. Morita, ed. Tokyo Jikeikai School of Medicine, 1938, pp. 83–108. (Written in Japanese)

[12]T. Abe, "Supplementary Study on Nervosity, with Special Reference to Personality Tests," *Shinkeishitsu* 1 (1960):137–56. (Written in Japanese)

[13]K. Takano, "Results of Pictures Frustration Test with Nervosity," *Shinkeishitsu* 2 (1961): 101–16. (Written in Japanese)

[14]Y . Takahashi, "Psychophysiological Study on Neurotic Patients Treated with Morita Therapy," *Shinkeishitsu* 1 (1960):21–42. (Written in Japanese)

[15]B. Fujita, "Psychophysiological Significance of the Mecholyl Test as Applied in Mental Disorders, Especially with Reference to Morita's Psychotherapy," *Psychiatria et Neurologia Japonica.* 62 (1960):831–53. (Written in Japanese with English summary); Y. Okuda, "Reaction on Autonomic Nervous System in Mental Illness," *Shinkeishitsu* 1 (1960):43–64.

lead everyday life even if a few symptoms of the disease remain, and there are many who have completely regained their health after several months or years. There are also some who are suffering a renewed attack of disease and must once more enter a hospital, but according to Kobayashi's catamnestic observations over a long period of time, a comparatively great number of those who had to resort to the hospital for a second time were hereditarily afflicted.[16]

Criticism of Morita Therapy

Even in Japan the Morita therapy was not taken seriously at the beginning, since at the time the influence of the German psychiatric line of thought was considerable and no great importance was attached to psychotherapy in general. Today the actual value of the Morita therapy has been widely acknowledged, but nevertheless there is some criticism. From its early period this therapy has been in contradiction to the Freudian psychoanalysis, as seen in the dispute between Morita, Sato, and S. Marui who had introduced psychoanalysis into Japan,[17] and has encountered much criticism from this side. But properly speaking, there are only a few in Japan who have completed an exact training in the psychoanalytic way of thinking. Takamizu criticizes the Morita therapy from the psychoanalytic viewpoint, pointing out that it is not built up on a foundation of scientific theory, and that there is insufficient analysis of the complications occurring in the unconscious which may be the true cause for a neurosis.[18] A. Jacobson and A. R. Berenberg, two American psychiatrists, stayed in Japan from 1950 through 1951 to participate in clinical practice and seminars at the Medical Department of Kyushu University. Their criticism of the Morita therapy was as follows: "They don't investigate the foundations and origins of neurotic behavior." "Techniques aimed at derepression are looked upon as wasteful of time and antithetical to the goals they have set themselves." "Sources of conflict material are not sought after." "Dreams are given but scant attention." "Transference phenomena are not referred to." But their final conviction was that "Suppression is the dominant theme in therapy; conformity the goal!"[19] From their point of view, the cure seemed to be chiefly "conforming behavior" rather than for the patient himself to have

---

[16] J. Kobayashi, "Catamnestic Study on Neurosis," *Psychiatria et Neurologia Japonica* 62 (1960):40–59. (Written in Japanese with English summary)

[17] S. Marui, "On Neurosis," *Psychiatria et Neurologia Japonica* 42 (1938):741–54, 797. (Written in Japanese); K. Sato, "A Criticism of the Psychoanalytic Studies of Prof. Marui and Others," *Psychiatria et Neurologia Japonica* 31 (1930):687.

[18] R. Takamizu, "A Medical View on Insomnia," *Psychoanalysis* 10, no. 3 (1952):12–15. (Written in Japanese)

[19] A. Jacobson and A. N. Berenberg, "Japanese Psychiatry and Psychotherapy," *American Journal of Psychiatry* 109 (1952):321–29.

the feeling of being well without any conflicts. But with the above views in mind it was only natural that they were skeptical about the correctness of the very high recovery rate (cured, 76.2 percent; favorable progress, 7.6 percent) set forth by the Department of Psychiatry at Kyushu University. If emphasis is put on the cultivation of "personality," the lack of analytical research may be a weak point of the Morita therapy. But such arguments of these two American psychiatrists show the difficulty in understanding the intrinsic value of the Morita therapy.

A. Kondo, a disciple of Kora and Horney, argues on the future development of the Morita therapy as follows: In the first place, "It must utilize the rich achievements gained by the recent development of analysis in the Western world, especially of the neurotic structure. Also the study of the patient's relationship with the doctor in the analysis surely will contribute a great deal to it." In the second place: "Reexamination of the whole system in the light of a reappreciation of Zen Buddhism can help this therapy develop more effectively and profoundly."[20]

In a discussion about oriental psychology and psychotherapy held on the occasion of the Fourth International Psychotherapeutic Association Meeting in 1958, according to M. Kato's report, Kelman declared that in recent times in Japan there is an endeavor to unite the Morita therapy and psychoanalysis. It is true that in the previous two articles Kondo endeavored to make clear the fact that although there are strong differences between the Freudian orthodox school, Horney's school, and the Morita Therapy concerning the theoretical structure, they have many factors in common with regard to the therapeutic mechanism. He demands the "acceptance" of those,[21] and states: "There is some possibility of finding a method to adopt intellectual insight and emotional insight of psychoanalysis also into the Morita therapy."[22] According to T. Doi's opinion, when explaining nervosity with the aid of the psychoanalytical method, it is found that the substantial common feature is "to be caught," which means something like "one cannot depend and presume upon another's benevolence even if one wants to."[23] And again, by elucidating the basic psychological structure of nervosity, he thinks that there exists no substantial difference between Japan and the Western countries, the

---

[20]A. Kondo, "Morita Therapy: A Japanese Therapy for Neurosis," *American Journal of Psychoanalysis* 13 (1953):31–37.
[21]A. Kondo, "Acceptance: Its Meaning in Psychotherapy," *Shinkeishitsu* 3 (1962):13–18. (Written in Japanese)
[22]A. Kondo, "Intellectual Insight, Emotional Insight and Intuitive Insight in Existential Situation," *Shinkeishitsu* 3 (1962):37–43. (Written in Japanese)
[23]L. T. Doi, "Psychopathology of 'Shinkeishitsu,' Espeically Regarding the Psychodynamics of its 'Toraware,' " *Psychiatria et Neurologia Japonica* 60 (1958):734–44. (Written in Japanese with English summary); idem, "Amae: A Key Concept for Understanding Japanese Personality Structure," *Psychologia* 5 (1962):1–7.

difference between Morita's concept and Freud's concept being rather due to sociocultural variations.[24]

According to K. Kakeda, in the Joint Japanese-American Conference of Psychiatry held in 1963 in Tokyo, the American participants critically commented on the report on the Morita therapy by A. Nomura, stating that in a strict sense, it cannot be classified under the notion of psychotherapy but under psychophysiological therapy.[25] With regard to this, Nomura pointed out that the difference is mainly due to the different viewpoints on the part of the therapists, and that the Morita therapy takes as a starting point the biological, psychological, and mental state, including the physical, and aims at normalizing the adaptability and leading the patients back to humanity in a wide sense. At this conference Z. Lebensohn said that the Sullivan school of psychotherapy, which puts emphasis on the peculiar human relations, has a deeper connection with the Morita therapy than the Horney school, and that the method of leading even the out-patients to write a diary on events really occurring in everyday life will possibly also be adopted in America.[26]

As Nomura also mentioned, many points of similarity between the Morita Therapy and V. Frankl's *Logotherapie* are recognized by many Japanese psychotherapists.[27] The practical techniques like the "paradox intention" or the "dereflexion" are identical with Morita's nature-obedience and the conquest of the contradiction of thought, respectively.[28] As devised by Morita, to give oneself completely up to the stream of natural feeling without putting any kind of significance on the things occurring is one special feature of oriental mentality.

As soon as Kora made public a detailed introduction to the Morita therapy in 1965, three American psychiatrists and psychologists responded with discussions on it.[29] It seems that these criticisms have a better grasp of the Morita therapy than former ones. Though the expressions of their opinions do not agree with eath other, they have a common doubt about this therapy. The doubt raised is whether the Morita therapy can be applied not only in Japan but also in America and Europe. Y. Kumasaka, while appreciating the Morita therapy, maintains that thing-as-it-is-ness cannot be accepted in America and Europe in the same way as in the East, for the American and European attitude towards nature consists not so much in merging into it as in challenging and conquering it. He adds that work therapy cannot be adopted, because

---

[24]L. T. Doi, "Morita Therapy and Psychoanalysis," *Psychologia* 5 (1962):117–23.

[25]A. Nomura, "Morita Therapy Found in Japan," *Folia Psychiatrica et Neurologica Japonica* 17, Supplement (1964):133–38.

[26]J. R. Ewalt, "East and West Look at Psychiatry," *MD. Medical Newsmagazine* 7 (1963): 77–81.

[27]A. Nomura, *Therapy of Neurosis and the Present-Day Life* (Tokyo: Nihonkyobun-sha, 1958). (Written in Japanese)

[28]V. E. Frankl, *Theorie und Therapie der Neurosen* (Wien: Urban Schwarzenburg, 1956).

[29]T. Kora, "Morita Therapy," 611–40.

work is not much valued for its own sake in America and Europe as it is in Morita therapy, in which work constitutes an important process in order to adapt to nature. Norman J. Levy considers that highly democratic countries would not adopt the Morita therapy because of its authoritative nature, even if it is applicable to the Japanese whose feelings easily submit to the will of authority. It is said that Kelman is of the same opinion. George A. Devos affirms by the results of a test on Japanese, which he did with Caudill, that Japanese tend to lose their confidence when they fail to fulfill the expectations of authorities and families, but that Americans do not admit readily their lack of ability, and that they unconsciously think that they should serve others. He cites diligence as a fundamental character of the Japanese. He seems to consider that diligence not only takes part in nervosity but forms a ground for adopting Morita therapy.

Kora answers to all these doubts: "It is often said that the Japanese easily accept nature, but actually it is not so. If the Japanese had been able to accept nature as easily as the Americans and Europeans think that they do, many cases of nervosity might have been avoided. If one could accept mental facts as they are, as we recognize sensual facts as they are, as 'Flower is red, willow is green,' it would not be difficult to understand the standpoint of Morita therapy irrespective of the East and West." He thus explains the possibilities of adopting the Morita therapy in America and Europe and refers to the fact that the Japanese do not behave so obediently as Americans suppose. He says that Americans and Europeans also, if they really want to cure their nervous diseases, have to follow doctors' directions. This probably isn't a question of being democratic or undemocratic. His proposal in his final passage corresponds to our own hope. "We hope that the Morita therapy should be applied to many European and American patients so that Europeans and Americans may concretely examine where it is unacceptable and what its merits are." I. Y. Wendt has often expressed the same hope and proposes, "Japanese and Western doctors have to cooperate for purposes of research. In the beginning, therapy with Western patients should be done by Japanese doctors (with Japanese nurses) since the character of the method is nearer to their natural disposition."

Finally, it is a well-known fact that Morita owed very much to oriental philosophy when he founded this treatment. Above all, so much importance to the influence of Zen is attached that Zen has sometimes been discussed in relation to "thing-as-it-is-ness" which forms the central tasks of this treatment. But, in fact, the Morita therapy was never constructed on the ideas of Zen, nor was it explained in accordance with Zen. On the contrary, Morita absorbed knowledge about Zen from his patients, and his disciples praised his treatment as being one with Zen. In 1952, G. Usa answered to Horney that the founding of the Morita therapy had nothing to do with Zen. Nevertheless the Zen monk G. Usa had believed that the Morita therapy had the same logic as Zen. He applied Zazen (Zen sitting) to his actual treatment. This was because he had known the ultimate result of Zen and the Morita therapy from the viewpoint of "life without theory." It may be on the same background that K. Yokoyama uses for the Morita therapy the Seiza (sitting still) which was founded in Japan apart from Zazen.

15

REALITY THERAPY

William Glasser

William Glasser, born in 1925, is an American psychiatrist who earned his M.D. from Western Reserve University in 1953 and served his internship and residency in Los Angeles at the Veterans Administration Center and the University of California Medical Center. A psychiatrist in private practice during the 1950s, during that decade Glasser also served as consultant to the Ventura School for Girls in California as well as at the Los Angeles Orthopaedic Hospital. During the 1960s, he taught his reality therapy to school teachers at the University of California (Los Angeles). He developed his theory in collaboration with G. L. Harrington. By 1967 he had founded the Reality Therapy Institute.

Glasser's system of psychotherapy, which he called *reality therapy,* found written expression in his *Mental Health or Mental Illness,* published in 1961. In this work he denied the concept of mental illness, thereby making individuals responsible for their behavior. In *Reality Therapy: A New Approach to Psychiatry* (1965), Glasser offered his developed system, calling for people to face reality. Reality is achieved by fulfilling two essential needs: (1) that of loving and being loved, and (2) that of feeling worthwhile to oneself and to others. Irresponsible people are inadequate in fulfilling these needs. Morality, an important tenet in reality therapy, encumbers the individual with a sense of responsibility. A person's basic need for identity finds its two fundamental pathways in love and self-worth. A sense of being a worthwhile human being arises from the feeling that one is loved by at least one person in the world. These two roads lead to success identity, while loneliness is a concomitant of failure identity.

The eight principles of reality therapy include: (1) a personal relationship, (2) behavior rather than emotions as the focal point, (3) the present as the focus of attention, (4) value judgments with respect to an individual's failure, (5) the development of a plan for the modification of behavior, (6) commitment to preferable choices, (7) rejection of excuses for not modifying behavior, and (8) the elimination of punishment and the stress on discipline.

Facing Reality

In their unsuccessful effort to fulfill their needs, no matter what behavior they choose, all patients have a common characteristic: *they all deny the reality of the world around them.* Some break the law, denying the rules of society; some claim their neighbors are plotting against them, denying the improbability of such behavior. Some are afraid of crowded places, close quarters, airplanes, or elevators, yet they freely admit the irrationality of their fears. Millions drink to blot out the inadequacy they feel, but that need not exist if they could learn to be different; and far too many people choose suicide rather than face the reality that they could solve their problems by more responsible behavior. Whether it is a partial denial or the total blotting out of all reality of the chronic backward patient in the state hospital, the denial of some or all of reality is common to all patients. Therapy will be successful when they are able to give up denying the world and recognize that reality not only exists but that they must fulfill their needs within its framework.

A therapy that leads all patients toward reality, toward grappling successfully with the tangible and intangible aspects of the real world, might accurately be called a therapy toward reality, or simply *reality therapy.*

As mentioned above, it is not enough to help a patient face reality; he must also learn to fulfill his needs. Previously when he attempted to fulfill his needs in the real world, he was unsuccessful. He began to deny the real world and to try to fulfill his needs as if some aspects of the world did not exist or in defiance of their existence.

The Need to Be Cared For

Before discussing the basic needs themselves, we must clarify the process through which they are fulfilled. Briefly, *we must be involved with other people,* one at the very minimum, but hopefully many more than one. At all times in our lives we must have at least one person who cares about us and whom we care for ourselves. If we do not have this essential person, we will not be able to fulfill our basic needs. Although the person usually is in some direct relationship with us as a mother is to a child or a teacher is to a pupil, he need not be that close as long as we have a strong feeling of his existence and he, no

William Glasser, *Reality Therapy: A New Approach to Psychiatry* (New York: Harper & Row, 1965), pp. 6 – 46.

matter how distant, has an equally strong feeling of our existence. One characteristic is essential in the other person: he must be in touch with reality himself and able to fulfill his own needs within the world. A man marooned on a desert isle or confined in a solitary cell may be able to fulfill his needs enough to survive if he knows that someone he cares for cares about him and his condition. If the prisoner or castaway loses the conviction that this essential human cares about what is happening to him, he will begin to lose touch with reality, his needs will be more and more unfulfilled, and he may die or become insane. . . .

Two Basic Needs: To Love and Be Loved

. . . Psychiatry must be concerned with two basic psychological needs: *the need to love and be loved and the need to feel that we are worthwhile to ourselves and to others.* Helping patients fulfill these two needs is the basis of reality therapy.

Although men of all societies, classes, colors, creeds, and intellectual capacity have the same needs, they vary remarkably in their ability to fulfill them. In every area of the world, including the most economically and culturally advanced, there are many people whose psychological needs are not satisfied, who are unable to give and receive love, and who have no feeling of worth either to themselves or to others. . . .

Responsibility

Responsibility, a concept basic to reality therapy, is here defined as the ability to fulfill one's needs and to do so *in a way that does not deprive others of the ability to fulfill their needs.* To illustrate, a responsible person can give and receive love. If a girl, for example, falls in love with a responsible man, we would expect him either to return her love or to let her know in a considerate way that he appreciates her affection but that he does not share her feelings. If he takes advantage of her love to gain some material or sexual end, we would not consider him responsible.

A responsible person also does that which gives him a feeling of self-worth and a feeling that he is worthwhile to others. . . .

Procedures of Reality Therapy

Easy or difficult as its application may be in any particular case, the specialized learning situation which we call reality therapy is made up of three separate but intimately interwoven procedures. First, there is the involvement; the therapist must become so involved with the patient that the patient can begin to face reality and see how his behavior is unrealistic. Second, the therapist must reject the behavior which is unrealistic but still accept the patient and maintain his involvement with him. Last, and necessary in varying degrees depending upon the patient, the therapist must teach the patient better ways to fulfill his needs within the confines of reality. . . .

In reality therapy we are much more concerned with behavior than with attitudes. Once we are involved with the patient, we begin to point out to him the unrealistic aspects of his irresponsible behavior. If the patient wishes to argue that his conception of reality is correct, we must be willing to discuss his opinions, but we must not fail to emphasize that our main interest is his behavior rather than his attitude. . . .

Characteristics of Reality Therapy

The way reality therapy differs from conventional therapy on each of the six points to be discussed contributes to the major difference in involvement. The six points may be considered briefly from the standpoint of involvement.

1. Because we do not accept the concept of mental illness, the patient cannot become involved with us as a mentally ill person who has no responsibility for his behavior.

2. Working in the present and toward the future, we do not get involved with the patient's history because we can neither change what happened to him nor accept the fact that he is limited by his past.

3. We relate to patients as ourselves, not as transference figures.

4. We do not look for unconscious conflicts or the reasons for them. A patient cannot become involved with us by excusing his behavior on the basis of unconscious motivations.

5. We emphasize the morality of behavior. We face the issue of right and wrong which we believe solidifies the involvement, in contrast to conventional psychiatrists who do not make the distinction between right and wrong, feeling it would be detrimental to attaining the transference relationship they seek.

6. We teach patients better ways to fulfill their needs. The proper involvement will not be maintained unless the patient is helped to find more satisfactory patterns of behavior. Conventional therapists do not feel that teaching better behavior is a part of therapy.

Synopsis of Reality Therapy

The first important step in correcting behavior is to find out what you are trying to correct. If we want to face reality we must admit that we cannot rewrite a person's history, no matter how much we understand the unfortunate circumstances which led to his behavior. There is nothing this information can do for us or for him except to reinforce the concept that, indeed, he has a reason to act the way he does and excuse this transgression on the ground that he is "sick." No matter what happened to him in the past, he still has the responsibility for what he does now.

Until an individual can accept the fact that he is responsible for what he does there can be no treatment in our field. It is not up to us to advance explanations for irresponsibility, but rather to recognize that individual responsibility must be the goal of treatment, and that unhappiness is the result and not the cause of irresponsibility.

The simple basic need that all people in all cultures possess from birth to death is the need for an identity; the belief that we are someone in distinction to others. The two basic need pathways are those of love and self-worth. In order to feel that one is a success in the world he must feel that at least one other person loves him and that he also loves another person. He must feel that at least one person "out there" feels that he is a worthwhile human being, and he, himself, must also feel it. If a person cannot develop an identity through these two pathways, he attempts to do so through two other identity pathways, delinquency and withdrawal, or "mental illness." These pathways do lead to an identity, but a failure identity. One outstanding feature of all individuals with a failure identity is that they are lonely.

In working with an individual we feel that unless he and the therapist are involved he is not motivated, that in therapy and counseling, motivation and involvement, in a general way, can be considered synonymous.

Following the concepts of reality therapy there are eight principles. (1) The relationship must be personal. (2) We must focus on behavior rather than

Synopsis of Reality Therapy, from William Glasser and Leonard M. Zunin, "Reality Therapy," in *Current Psychotherapies,* ed. Raymond Corsini (Itasca, Ill.: Peacock Publishers, 1973), pp. 314–15.

emotions, because only behavior can be changed. (3) We must focus on the present, on what the individual is doing now, and his present attempts to succeed. (4) We must have the individual make a value judgment about what he is now doing that is contributing to his failure. (5) The individual is assisted in developing a plan to alter his behavior and plan a better course. (6) He must choose a better way and commit himself to his choice. It is from commitment that individuals develop maturity. (7) When an individual has made a commitment to change his behavior, no excuse is accepted for not following through. The therapist, in a nonjudgmental manner, assists the individual in developing a new plan rather than focusing on the reasons the old ones failed. (8) The therapist eliminates punishment, which always reinforces failure identity, and instead invokes discipline.

Through accepting responsibility for their own behavior and acting maturely to constructively change their behavior, individuals find they are no longer lonely, symptoms begin to resolve and they are more likely to gain maturity, respect, love, and that most important success, identity.

16

GESTALT PSYCHOTHERAPY

Frederick S. Perls

Ralph F. Hefferline

Paul Goodman

Frederick (Fritz) S. Perls (1893–1970) was born in Berlin and educated at the University of Freiburg and the University of Berlin. He earned an M.D. degree from the University of Berlin. After serving as a medical officer in the German army during World War I, Perls began a career in psychotherapy. From 1927–28 he worked in Vienna as Paul Schilder's assistant, and the following year he accepted an appointment as assistant to Kurt Goldstein at the Frankfort Neurological Institute. Subsequently he was engaged in private psychotherapy practice in Berlin.

In the early 1930s Perls was at the Vienna Institute of Psychoanalysis and then attended the Berlin Institute of Psychoanalysis. In 1933 he stayed briefly in Holland before migrating to Johannesburg, South Africa, where in addition to establishing a private practice in psychotherapy, he founded an institute of psychoanalysis. It was in South Africa during 1941–42 that he wrote *Ego, Hunger and Aggression: A Revision of Freud's Theory and Method,* which is an introduction to a technique of psychotherapy known as Gestalt therapy. In 1946 Perls left for the United States, where he took up permanent residence and established a private practice in New York City. With his wife, Dr. Lore P. Perls (also a psychotherapist), and others he founded the New York Institute for Gestalt Therapy in the early 1950s. For a brief time he taught at the Cleveland Institute for Gestalt Therapy. In the 1960s he left for California (where he acquired a Ph.D. degree) and was associated with the Esalen Institute at Big Sur.

Perls initiated the writing of *Gestalt Therapy: Excitement and Growth in the Human Personality* (coauthored with Hefferline and Goodman, 1951). The year before he died, Perls published his autobiography, *In and Out of the Garbage Pail*

(1969), and transcripts of complete therapy sessions in *Gestalt Therapy Verbatim* (1969). In 1973 *The Gestalt Approach and Eye Witness to Therapy* was published posthumously. Perls's other contributions to the field of psychotherapy are in the form of papers, as follows: "Theory and Technique of Personality Integration" (*American Journal of Psychotherapy*, 1948); "The Anthropology of Neurosis" (*Complex*, 1950); "Morality, Ego-Boundary and Aggression" (*Complex*, 1955); "Gestalt Therapy and Human Potentialities" (in *Explorations in Human Potentialities,* ed. H. A. Otto, 1966); and "Workshop vs. Individual Therapy" (APA convention paper, 1966).

Ralph Franklin Hefferline, born in Muncie, Indiana, on February 15, 1919, was educated at Columbia University, where he received a B.S. degree in 1941, an M.A. in 1942, and a Ph.D. in 1947. He submitted as his dissertation "An Experimental Study of Avoidance." His career, devoted to Columbia University, consisted of an assistantship to H. E. Garrett from 1942 to 1946, followed by an instructorship until 1948, when he was promoted to assistant professor of psychology. In 1960 he was elevated to the rank of associate professor and from 1965 until his death in 1974 he was chairman of the Department of Psychology. Hefferline, a fellow of both the American Association for the Advancement of Science and the New York Academy of Sciences, was a review editor for *Science, Journal of Psychophysiology,* and *Journal of the Experimental Analysis of Behavior.* In addition to academic and administrative duties, he served as research consultant for the Menninger Foundation and was involved in psychological research. As well as coauthoring *Gestalt Therapy: Excitement and Growth in the Human Personality* Hefferline wrote approximately a dozen papers.

A native New Yorker, Paul Goodman was born on September 9, 1911. After receiving a B.A. from the College of the City of New York, he earned a Ph.D. in humanities at the University of Chicago. His academic career included teaching appointments at the University of Chicago, New York University, and Black Mountain College, plus holding faculty status at the Institute for Gestalt Therapy in both New York and Cleveland. In 1964, he became a professor at the University of Wisconsin and conducted a seminar on Problems of Interpretation at Columbia. He is a fellow of the Institute for Policy Studies in Washington, D.C.

Besides coauthoring *Gestalt Therapy,* he has written *The Facts of Life* (1946), *Growing Up Absurd: Kafka's Prayer* (1947), *People or Personnel* (1963), and *Compulsory Mis-Education* (1964).

Gestalt psychotherapy is interested in a here-and-now-and-around-us reality and the treatment of the organism-as-a-whole. One must not lose sight of the organism-environment unity, not only with respect to the patient's relationship with his surrounding physical world, but with his social world, including the therapist with whom the encounter must be that of one human being with another. Individual therapy must yield to social (group or workshop) therapy. The therapist's task is that of restoring a personality to his *gestalt,* his organized whole (for the whole determines the parts), entailing a structural and meaningful relationship with himself and the world, one in which unity, integration, and wholeness of being is achieved, and dualism of personality eliminated. That personality who has made a gestalt of himself through growth and maturation functions as a whole, thus attaining an elastic figure/ground relationship. The neurotic attains self-development through the aid of psychotherapy, a self with a toleration for frustration and anxiety, a self whose potential develops despite decreasing environmental support.

Gestalt Personality Development

Interaction of Organism and Environment

Now in any biological, psychological, or sociological investigation whatever, we must start from the interacting of the organism and its environment. It makes no sense to speak, for instance, of an animal that breathes without considering air and oxygen as part of its definition, or to speak of eating without mentioning food, or of seeing without light, or locomotion without gravity and supporting ground, or of speech without communicants. There is no single function of any animal that completes itself without objects and environment, whether one thinks of vegetative functions like nourishment and sexuality, or perceptual functions, or motor functions, or feeling, or reasoning. The meaning of anger involves a frustrating obstacle; the meaning of reasoning involves problems of practice. Let us call this interacting of organism and environment in any function the *organism/environment field;* and let us remember that no matter how we theorize about impulses, drives, etc., it is always to such an interacting field that we are referring, and not to an isolated animal. Where the organism is mobile in a great field and has a complicated internal structure, like an animal, it seems plausible to speak of it by itself— as, for instance, the skin and what is contained in it—but this is simply an illusion due to the fact that the motion through space and the internal detail call attention to themselves against the relative stability and simplicity of the background.

The human organism/environment is, of course, not only physical but social. So in any humane study, such as human physiology, psychology, or psychotherapy, we must speak of a field in which at least sociocultural, animal, and physical factors interact. Our approach in this book is "unitary" in the sense that we try in a detailed way to consider *every* problem as occurring in a social-animal-physical field. From this point of view, for in-

---

Gestalt Personality Development, from Frederick S. Perls, Ralph F. Hefferline, and Paul Goodman, *Gestalt Therapy* (New York: Dell Publishing, 1965 [Julian Press edition, 1951]), pp. 228–35.

stance, historical and cultural factors cannot be considered as complicating or modifying conditions of a simpler biophysical situation, but are intrinsic in the way any problem is presented to us.

The Subject Matter of Psychology

On reflection, the foregoing two sections must seem obvious and certainly not extraordinary. They assert (1) that experience is ultimately contact, the functioning of the boundary of the organism and its environment; and (2) that every human function is an interacting in an organism/environment field, sociocultural, animal, and physical. But now let us attend to these two propositions in combination.

Among the biological and social sciences, all of which deal with interacting in the organism/environment field, *psychology studies the operation of the contact-boundary in the organism/environment field. . . .*

Definition of Psychology and Abnormal Psychology

We must then conclude that all contact is creative and dynamic. It cannot be routine, stereotyped, or merely conservative because it must cope with the novel, for only the novel is nourishing. (But like the sense organs themselves, the internal noncontacting physiology of the organism is conservative.) On the other hand, contact cannot passively accept or *merely* adjust to the novelty, because the novelty must be assimilated. *All contact is creative adjustment of the organism and environment.* Aware response in the field (as both orientation and manipulation) is the agency of growth in the field. Growth is the function of the contact-boundary in the organism/environment field; it is by means of creative adjustment, change, and growth that the complicated organic unities live on in the larger unity of the field.

We may then define: *psychology is the study of creative adjustments.* Its theme is the ever renewed transition between novelty and routine, resulting in assimilation and growth.

Correspondingly, *abnormal psychology is the study of the interruption, inhibition, or other accidents in the course of creative adjustment.* We shall, for instance, consider anxiety, the pervasive factor in neurosis, as the result of the interruption of the excitement of creative growth (with accompanying breathlessness); and we shall analyze the various neurotic "characters" as stereotyped patterns limiting the flexible process of creatively addressing the novel. . . .

Creativity and adjustment are polar, they are mutually necessary. Spontaneity is the seizing on, and glowing and growing with, what is interesting and nourishing in the environment. (Unfortunately, the "adjustment" of much psychotherapy, the "conformity to the reality-principle," is the swallowing of a stereotype.)

The Figure of Contact Against the Ground of the Organism/Environment Field

Let us return to the idea we began with, that the wholes of experience are definite unified structures. *Contact, the work that results in assimilation and growth, is the forming of a figure of interest against a ground or context of the organism/environment field.* The figure (gestalt) in awareness is a clear, vivid perception, image, or insight; in motor behavior, it is the graceful energetic movement that has rhythm, follows through, etc. In either case, the need and energy of the organism and the likely possibilities of the environment are incorporated and unified in the figure.

The process of figure/background formation is a dynamic one in which the urgencies and resources of the field progressively lend their powers to the interest, brightness, and force of the dominant figure. It is pointless, therefore, to attempt to deal with any psychological behavior out of its sociocultural, biological, and physical context. At the same time, the figure is specifically psychological: it has specific observable properties of brightness, clarity, unity, fascination, grace, vigor, release, etc., depending on whether we are considering primarily a perceptual, feelingful, or motor context. The fact that the gestalt has specific observable psychological properties is of capital importance in psychotherapy, for it gives *an autonomous criterion of the depth and reality of the experience.* It is not necessary to have theories of "normal behavior" or "adjustment to reality" except in order to explore. When the figure is dull, confused, graceless, lacking in energy (a "weak gestalt"), we may be sure that there is a lack of contact, something in the environment is blocked out, some vital organic need is not being expressed; the person is not "all there," that is, his whole field cannot lend its urgency and resources to the completion of the figure.

Therapy as Gestalt Analysis

The therapy, then, consists in analyzing the internal structure of the actual experience with whatever degree of contact it has: not so much *what* is being experienced, remembered, done, said, etc., as *how* what is being remembered is remembered, or how what is said is said, with what facial expression, what tone of voice, what syntax, what posture, what affect, what omission, what regard or disregard of the other person, etc. By working on the unity and disunity of this structure of the experience here and now, it is possible to remake the dynamic relations of the figure and ground until the contact is heightened, the awareness brightened, and the behavior energized. Most important of all, *the achievement of a strong gestalt is itself the cure, for the figure of contact is not a sign of, but is itself the creative integration of experience.*

From the beginning of psychoanalysis, of course, a particular gestalt property, the "Aha!" of recognition, has held a sovereign place. But it has always seemed a mystery why "mere" awareness, for instance recollection, should cure the neurosis. Note, however, that the awareness is not a thought about the problem but is itself a creative integration of the problem. We can see, too, why usually "awareness" does not help, for usually it is not an aware gestalt at all, a *structured* content, but mere content, verbalizing or reminiscing, and as such it does not draw on the energy of present organic need and a present environmental help.

Destroying as Part of Figure/Background Formation

The process of creative adjustment to new material and circumstances always involves a phase of aggression and destruction, for it is by approaching, laying hold of, and altering old structures that the unlike is made like. When a new configuration comes into being, both the old achieved habit of the contacting organism and the previous state of what is approached and contacted are destroyed in the interest of the new contact. Such destruction of the status quo may arouse fear, interruption, and anxiety, the greater in proportion as one is neurotically inflexible; but the process is accompanied by the security of the new invention experimentally coming into being. Here as everywhere the only solution of a human problem is experimental invention. The anxiety is "tolerated" not by Spartan fortitude—though courage is a beautiful and indispensable virtue—but because the disturbing energy flows into the new figure.

Without renewed aggression and destruction every achieved satisfaction soon becomes a matter of the past and is unfelt. What is ordinarily called *security* is clinging to the unfelt, declining the risk of the unknown involved in any absorbing satisfaction, and with a corresponding desensitizing and motor inhibition. It is a dread of aggression, destroying, and loss that results, of course, in unaware aggression and destroying, turned both inward and outward. A better meaning of *security* would be the confidence of a firm support, which comes from previous experience having been assimilated and growth achieved, without unfinished situations; but in such a case, all attention tends to flow from the ground of what one is into the figure of what one is becoming. The secure state is without interest, it is unnoticed; and the secure person never knows it but always feels that he is risking it and will be adequate. . . .

Contact Is "Finding and Making" the Coming Solution

Concern is felt for a present problem, and the excitement mounts toward the coming, but as yet unknown, solution. The assimilating of novelty occurs in the present moment as it passes into the future. Its result is never merely a rearrangement of the unfinished situations of the organism but a configuration containing new material from the environment, and therefore different from what could be remembered (or guessed at), just as the work of an artist becomes unpredictably new to him as he handles the material medium.

So in psychotherapy we look for the urgency of unfinished situations in the present situation, and by present experimentation with new attitudes and new materials from the experience of the actual day to day, we aim at a better integration. The patient does not remember himself, merely reshuffling the cards, but "finds and makes" himself. (The importance of new conditions in the present was perfectly understood by Freud when he spoke of the inevitable transference of the childhood fixation to the person of the analyst; but the therapeutic meaning of it is not that it is the same old story, but precisely that it is now differently worked through as a present adventure: the analyst is not the same kind of parent. And nothing is more clear, unfortunately, than that certain tensions and blocks cannot be freed unless there is a real environmental change offering new possibilities. If the institutions and mores were altered, many a recalcitrant symptom would vanish very suddenly.)

Let us call the "self" the system of contacts at any moment. As such, the self is flexibly various, for it varies with the dominant organic needs and the pressing environmental stimuli; it is the system of responses; it diminishes in sleep when there is less need to respond. The self is the contact boundary at work; its activity is forming figures and grounds. . . .

But the self is precisely the integrator; it is the *synthetic* unity, as Kant said. It is the artist of life. It is only a small factor in the total organism/environment interaction, but it plays the crucial role of finding and making the meanings that we grow by.

The description of psychological health and disease is a simple one. It is a matter of the identifications and alienations of the self: If a man identifies with his forming self, he does not inhibit his own creative excitement in reaching toward the coming solution; and conversely, if he alienates what is not organically his own and therefore cannot be vitally interesting, but rather disrupts the figure/background, then he is psychologically healthy, for he is exercising his best power and will do the best he can in the difficult circumstances of the world. But on the contrary, if he alienates himself and because of false identifications tries to conquer his own spontaneity, then he creates his life dull, confused, and painful. The system of identifications and alienations we shall call the "ego."

From this point of view, our method of therapy is as follows: to train the ego, the various identifications and alienations, by experiments of deliberate awareness of one's various functions, until the sense is spontaneously revived that "it is I who am thinking, perceiving, feeling, and doing this." At this point the patient can take over on his own.

Fundamental Principles of Gestalt Therapy

Gestalt Therapy and Psychoanalysis

The psychotherapy proposed [earlier] ... emphasizes: concentrating on the structure of the actual situation; preserving the integrity of the actuality by finding the intrinsic relation of sociocultural, animal, and physical factors; experimenting; promoting the creative power of the patient to reintegrate the dissociated parts. ...

What we add is simply this: the insistence on the reintegration of normal and abnormal psychology, and with this the revaluation of what is taken for normal psychological functioning. To put it somewhat dramatically: from the beginning Freud pointed to the neurotic elements in everyday life, and he and others have increasingly uncovered the irrational bases of many institutions; now we come full circle and venture to assert that the experience of psychotherapy and the reintegration of neurotic structures often give better information of reality than the neurosis of normalcy.

Broadly speaking, we have said the trend of psychotherapy is toward concentration on the structure of the actual situation. On the other hand, psychotherapy (and the history of psychotherapy) makes a difference in our seeing the actual situation. And the closer the therapy concentrates on the actual here and now, the more unsatisfactory appear the usual scientific, political, and personal preconceptions of what "reality" is, whether perceptual, social, or moral. Consider simply how a physician, aiming at "adjusting the patient to reality" might find, as treatment proceeds (and as it has proceeded for half a century), that the "reality" begins to look very different from his own or the accepted preconceptions; and then he must revise his goals and methods.

In what direction must he revise them? Must he propose a new norm of human nature and attempt to adjust his patients to it? This is in fact what some therapists have done. In this book we attempt something more modest: to regard the development of the actual experience as giving autonomous criteria, that is, to take the dynamic structure of experience not as a clue to some "unconscious" unknown or a symptom, but as the important thing itself. This is to psychologize without prejudgment of normal or abnormal, and from this point of view, psychotherapy is a method not of correction but of growth.

Gestalt Therapy and Gestalt Psychology

On the other hand, let us consider our relation to the psychology of the normal. We work with the chief insights of Gestalt psychology: the relation of figure and background; the importance of interpreting the coherence or split of a

---

Fundamental Principles of Gestalt Therapy, from Perls, Hefferline, and Goodman, *Gestalt Therapy*, pp. 236–51.

figure in terms of the total context of the actual situation; the definite structured whole that is not too inclusive yet is not a mere atom; the active organizing force of meaningful wholes and the natural tendency toward simplicity of form; the tendency of unfinished situations to complete themselves. What do we add to this?

Consider, for instance, the unitary approach, to take seriously the irreducible unity of the sociocultural, animal, and physical field in every concrete experience. This is, of course, the main thesis of the Gestalt psychology: that phenomena which appear as unitary wholes must have their wholeness respected and can be analytically broken into bits only at the price of annihilating what one intended to study. Now applying this thesis mainly in laboratory situations of perception and learning, as the normal psychologists have done, one discovers many beautiful truths, can demonstrate the inadequacy of the associationist and reflex psychologies, and so forth. But one is protected from a too sweeping rejection of the usual scientific assumptions, because the laboratory situation itself sets up a limitation as to how far one will think and what one will discover. *This* situation is the total context that determines the meaning of what emerges, and what emerges from the limitation is the peculiarly formal and static quality of most gestalt theory. Little is said about the dynamic relation of the figure and ground, or about the urgent sequence in which a figure rapidly transforms itself into the ground for the next emerging figure, until there is a climax of contact and satisfaction and the vital situation is *really* finished.

Yet how *could* much be said about these things? For a controlled laboratory situation is not in fact a vitally urgent situation. The only one vitally concerned is the experimenter, and his behavior is not the subject of the study. Rather, with a laudable zeal for objectivity, the Gestaltists have shunned, sometimes with comical protestations of purity, all dealings with the passionate and interested; they have analyzed the solving of not exactly pressing human problems. They often seem to be saying, indeed, that everything is relevant in the field of the whole except the humanly interesting factors; these are "subjective" and irrelevant! Yet, on the other hand, only the interesting makes a strong structure. (With regard to animal experiments, however, such factors of urgency and interest are not irrelevant, especially since apes and chickens are not such docile laboratory subjects.)

Psychology of the "Conscious" and the "Unconscious"

Yet the bypassing of Gestalt psychology by the psychoanalysts has been most unfortunate, for Gestalt psychology provides an adequate theory of awareness, and from the beginning psychoanalysis has been hampered by inadequate theories of awareness, despite the fact that to heighten awareness has always been the chief aim of psychotherapy. . . .

As psychotherapists drawing on the Gestalt psychology, we investigate the theory and method of creative awareness, figure/background formation, as the coherent center of the powerful but scattered insights into the "unconscious" and the inadequate notion of the "conscious."

Reintegration of the Psychologies of the "Conscious" and the "Unconscious"

When, however, we insist on the unitary thesis, on the creativity of structured wholes, and so forth, not in the uninteresting situations of laboratories but in the urgent situations of psychotherapy, pedagogy, personal and social relations, then suddenly we find ourselves going very far—drawn very far and driven very far—in rejecting as fundamentally inadmissible, as "breaking into bits and annihilating the thing that it was intended to study," many commonly accepted assumptions and divisions and categories. Instead of truths stating the nature of the case, we find them to be precisely the expression of a neurotic splitting in the patient and in society. And to call attention to basic assumptions that are neurotic arouses anxiety (both in the authors and in the readers).

In a neurotic splitting, one part is kept in unawareness, or it is coldly recognized but alienated from concern, or both parts are carefully isolated from each other and made to seem irrelevant to each other, avoiding conflict and maintaining the status quo. But if in an urgent present situation, whether in the physician's office or in society, one concentrates awareness on the unaware part or on the "irrelevant" connections, then anxiety develops, the result of inhibiting the creative unification. The method of treatment is to come into closer and closer contact with the present crisis, until one identifies, risking the leap into the unknown, with the coming creative integration of the split. . . .

Fundamental Gestalt Concepts

"Body" and "Mind." This split is still popularly current, although among the best physicians the psychosomatic unity is taken for granted. We shall show that it is the exercise of a habitual and finally unaware deliberateness in the face of chronic emergency, especially the threat to organic functioning, that has made this crippling division inevitable and almost endemic, resulting in the joylessness and gracelessness of our culture.

"Self" and "External World." This division is an article of faith uniformly throughout modern Western science. It goes along with the previous split, but perhaps with more emphasis on threats of a political, and interpersonal nature. Unfortunately those who in the history of recent philosophy have shown the absurdity of this division have mostly themselves been infected with either a kind of mentalism or materialism.

"Emotional" (Subjective) and "Real" (Objective).   This split is again a general scientific article of faith, unitarily involved with the preceding. It is the result of the avoidance of contact and involvement and the deliberate isolation of the sensoric and motoric functions from each other. (The recent history of statistical sociology is a study in these avoidances raised to a fine art.) We shall try to show that the real is intrinsically an involvement or "engagement."

"Infantile" and "Mature."   This split is an occupational disease of psychotherapy itself, springing from the personalities of the therapists and from the social role of the "cure": on the one hand, a tantalizing preoccupation with the distant past, on the other, the attempt to adjust to a standard of adult reality that is not worth adjusting to. Traits of childhood are disesteemed the very lack of which devitalizes the adults; and other traits are called infantile that are the introjections of adult neuroses.

"Biological" and "Cultural."   This dichotomy, which is the essential subject matter of anthropology to eliminate, has in recent decades become entrenched precisely in anthropology, so that (not to mention the idiotic racialisms of one side) human nature becomes completely relative and nothing at all, as if it were indefinitely malleable. We shall try to show that this is the result of a neurotic fascination with artifacts and symbols, and the politics and culture of these, as if they moved themselves.

"Poetry" and "Prose."   This split, unitarily involved with all the preceding, is the result of neurotic verbalizing (and other vicarious experience) and the nausea of verbalizing as a reaction against it, and it leads some recent semanticists and inventors of languages of science and "basic" languages to disesteem human speech as though we had enough other media of communication. There are not, and there is a failure of communication. Universal terms, again, are taken as mechanical abstractions rather than expressions of insight. And correspondingly, poetry (and plastic art) becomes increasingly isolated and obscure.

"Spontaneous" and "Deliberate."   More generally, it is believed that the unsought and inspired belongs to special individuals in peculiar emotional states, or again to people at parties under the influence of alcohol or hashish, rather than being a quality of all experience. And correspondingly, calculated behavior aims at goods that are not uniquely appropriated according to one's fancy but are in turn only good for something else (so that pleasure itself is endured as a means to health and efficiency). "Being oneself" means acting imprudently, as if desire could not make sense; and "acting sensibly" means holding back and being bored.

"Personal" and "Social." This common separation continues to be the ruination of community life. It is both the effect and cause of the kind of technology and economy we have, with its division of "job" and "hobby," but no work or vocation; and of timid bureaucracies and vicarious "front" politics. It is to the credit of the therapists of interpersonal relations to try to heal this split, yet even this school, anxiously controlling the animal and sexual factors in the field, likewise usually comes to formal and symbolic rather than real communal satisfactions.

"Love" and "Aggression." This split has always been the result of instinctual frustration and self-conquest, turning the hostility against the self and esteeming a reactive passionless mildness, when only a release of aggression and willingness to destroy the old situations can restore erotic contact. But in recent decades this condition has been complicated by a new high esteem given to sexual love at the same time as the various aggressive drives are especially disesteemed as antisocial. The quality of the sexual satisfaction may perhaps be measured by the fact that the wars we acquiesce in are continually more destructive and less angry.

"Unconscious" and "Conscious." If taken absolutely, this remarkable division, perfected by psychoanalysis, would make all psychotherapy impossible in principle, for a patient cannot learn about himself what is unknowable to him. (He is aware, or can be made aware, of the distortions in the structure of his actual experience.) This theoretical split goes with an underestimation of the reality of dream, hallucination, play, and art, and an overestimation of the reality of deliberate speech, thought, and introspection; and in general, with the Freudian absolute division between "primary" (very early) thought processes and "secondary" processes. Correspondingly, the "id" and the "ego" are not seen as alternate structures of the self differing in degree—the one an extreme of relaxation and loose association, the other an extreme of deliberate organization for the purpose of identification—yet this picture is given at every moment of psychotherapy.

The Contextual Method of Argument

The foregoing are, in order, the chief neurotic dichotomies that we shall try to dissolve. With regard to these and other "false" distinctions, we employ a method of argument that at first sight may seem unfair, but that is unavoidable and is itself an exercise of the gestalt approach. Let us call it the *contextual method,* and call attention to it immediately so that the reader may recognize it as we use it.

Fundamental theoretical errors are invariably characterological, the result of a neurotic failure of perception, feeling, or action. (This is obvious, for in any basic issue the evidence is, so to speak, "everywhere" and will be noticed unless one will not or cannot notice it.) A fundamental theoretical error is in an important sense *given* in the experience of the observer; he must in good faith make the erroneous judgment; and a merely "scientific" refutation by adducing contrary evidence is pointless, for he does not *experience* that evidence with its proper weight—he does not see what you see, it slips his mind, it seems irrelevant, he explains it away, etc. Then the only useful method of argument is to bring into the picture the total context of the problem, including the conditions of experiencing it, the social milieu, and the personal "defenses" of the observer. That is, to subject the opinion and his holding of it to a gestalt analysis. . . .

The Contextual Method Applied to Theories of Psychotherapy

But if we say, and intend to show, that psychotherapy makes a difference to the usual preconceptions, we must also say what we ourselves take psychotherapy to be, for it is only in the process of becoming something. So in the following chapters, as we proceed with our critique of many general ideas, at the same time we must keep referring to many specialist details of therapeutic practice, for the attainment of every new stage of general outlook makes a difference in the goals and methods of practice. . . .

Creative Adjustment: The Structure of Art-Working and Children's Play

As examples of progressive integration, we shall frequently refer to creative artists and art-working and to children and child play.

Now the references to artists and children in psychoanalytical literature are amusingly inconsistent. On the one hand, these groups are invariably singled out as "spontaneous," and spontaneity is recognized as central in health; in a successful therapeutic session the curative insight is marked by its spontaneity. On the other hand, the artists are considered exceptionally neurotic and the children are—infantile. Also, the psychology of art has always had an uneasy connection with the rest of psychoanalytic theory, seeming to be strangely relevant and yet mysterious: for why is the artist's dream different from any other dream? And why is the artist's conscious calculation more valuable than any other conscious calculation?

The solution of the mystery is fairly simple. The important part of the psychology of art is not in the dream or in the critical consciousness; it is (where the psychoanalysts do not look for it) in the concentrated sensation and in the playful manipulation of the material medium. With bright sensation and play in the medium as his central acts, the artist then accepts his dream and uses his critical deliberateness: and he spontaneously realizes an objective form. The artist is quite *aware* of what he is doing—after it is done, he can show you the steps in detail; he is not unconscious in his working, but neither is he mainly deliberately calculating. His awareness is in a kind of middle mode, neither active nor passive, but accepting the conditions, attending to the job, and *growing* toward the solution. And just so with children: it is their bright sensation and free, apparently aimless, play that allows the energy to flow spontaneously and come to such charming inventions.

In both cases it is the sensory-motor integration, the acceptance of the impulse, and the attentive contact with new environmental material that result in valuable work. Yet after all, these are rather special cases. Both art works and children's play use up little social wealth and need have no damaging consequences. Can the same middle mode of acceptance and growth operate in adult life in more "serious" concerns? We believe so.

Creative Adjustment: In General

We believe that the free interplay of the faculties, concentrating on some present matter, comes not to chaos or mad fantasy but to a gestalt that solves a real problem. We think that this can be shown again and again with striking examples (and that, on careful analysis, nothing else can be shown). Yet it is this simple possibility that modern man and most modern psychotherapy refuse to entertain. Instead, there is a shaking of the head and a timid need to be deliberate and conform to the "principle of reality." The result of such habitual deliberateness is that we are more and more out of contact with our present situations, for the present is always novel; and timid deliberateness is not ready for novelty—it has counted on something else, something like the past. And then, if we are out of touch with reality, our abortive bursts of spontaneity are indeed likely to miss the mark (though not necessarily worse than our carefulness misses the mark); and this then becomes a disproof of the possibility of creative spontaneity, for it is "unrealistic."

But where one is in contact with the need and the circumstances, it is at once evident that the reality is not something inflexible and unchanging but is ready to be remade; and the more spontaneously one exercises every power of orientation and manipulation, without holding back, the more viable the remaking proves to be. Let anyone think of his own *best* strokes, in work or play, love or friendship, and see if this has not been the case.

Creative Adjustment: "Organismic Self-Regulation"

With regard to the working of the organic body, there has recently been a salutary change in theory in this respect. Many therapists now speak of "organism self-regulation," that is, that it is not necessary deliberately to schedule, to encourage or inhibit, the promptings of appetite, sexuality, and so forth, in the interests of health or morals. If these things are let be, they will spontaneously regulate themselves, and if they have been deranged, they will tend to right themselves. But the suggestion of the more total self-regulation of all the functions of the soul, including its culture and learning, its aggression and doing the work that is attractive, along with the free play of hallucination, is opposed. The possibility that if these things are let be, in contact with the actuality, even their current derangements will tend to right themselves and come to something valuable, is met with anxiety and rejected as a kind of nihilism. (But we reiterate that the suggestion is a spectacularly conservative one, for it is nothing but the old advice of the Tao, "stand out of the way.")

Instead, every therapist knows—how?—what the "reality" is to which the patient ought to conform or what the "health" or "human nature" is that the patient ought to realize. How does he know it? It is only too likely that by the *reality principle* is meant the existing social arrangements introjected and reappearing as immutable laws of man and society. We say the social arrangements, for note that with regard to physical phenomena no such need to conform is felt at all, but physical scientists generally freely hypothesize, experiment, and fail or succeed, quite without guiltiness or fear of "nature," and thereby they make ingenious machines that can "ride the whirlwind," or foolishly stir it up.

Creative Adjustment: The Function of the "Self"

We speak of creative adjustment as the essential function of the self (or better, the self *is* the system of creative adjustments). But if once the creative functions of self-regulating, welcoming novelty, destroying and reintegrating experience —if once this work has been nullified, there is not much left to constitute a theory of the self. And so it has proved. In the literature of psychoanalysis, notoriously the weakest chapter is the theory of the self or the ego. In this book, proceeding by not nullifying but by affirming the powerful work of creative adjustment, we essay a new theory of the self and the ego. The reader will come to this in its place. Here let us continue to point out what difference it makes in therapeutic practice whether the self is an otiose "consciousness" plus an unconscious ego, or whether it is a creative contacting.

Some Differences in General Therapeutic Attitude

1. The patient comes for help because he cannot help himself. Now if the self-awareness of the patient is otiose, a mere consciousness of what goes on that does not make any difference in his comfort—though to be sure it has already made the difference that *he* has come, moving his own feet—then the role of the patient is that something is done *to* him; he is asked only not to interfere. But on the contrary, if the self-awareness is an integrative force, then

from the beginning the patient is an active partner in the work, a trainee in psychotherapy. And the emphasis is shifted from the rather comfortable sentiment that he is sick to the sentiment that he is learning something, for obviously psychotherapy is a humane discipline, a development of Socratic dialectic. And the term of treatment is not to dissolve most of the complexes or free certain reflexes but to reach such a point in the technique of self-awareness that the patient can proceed without help—for here, as everywhere else in medicine, *natura sanat non medicus,* it is only oneself (in the environment) that can cure oneself.

2. The self only finds and makes itself in the environment. If the patient is an active experimental partner in the session, he will carry this attitude abroad and make more rapid progress, for the environmental material is much more interesting and urgent. Nor is this more dangerous, but indeed less dangerous, than his going abroad passively subject to the moods that come up from below.

3. If the self-awareness is powerless and only the reflex of the unconscious ego, then the very attempt of the patient to cooperate is obstructive; and so, in the usual character analysis, the resistances are "attacked," the "defenses" are dissolved, and so forth. But on the contrary, if the awareness is creative, then these very resistances and defenses—they are really counterattacks and aggressions against the self—are taken as active expressions of vitality, however neurotic they may be in the total picture.[1] Rather than being liquidated, they are accepted at face value and met accordingly man to man: the therapist, according to his own self-awareness, declines to be bored, intimidated, cajoled, etc.; he meets anger with explanation of the misunderstanding, or sometimes apology, or even with anger, according to the truth of the situation; he meets obstruction with impatience in the framework of a larger patience. In this way the unaware can become foreground, so that its structure can be experienced. This is different from "attacking" the aggression when the patient does not feel it, and then, when it has a modicum of felt reality, explaining it away as "negative transference." Is the patient never to have a chance to *exercise* his wrath and stubbornness in the open? But in the sequel, if he now dares to exercise his aggressions in real circumstances and meeting a normal response without the roof caving in, he will see what he is doing, remember who his real enemies are; and the integration proceeds. So again, we do not ask the patient not to censor, but to concentrate on *how* he censors, withdraws, falls silent, with what muscles, images, or blanks. Thus a bridge is made for him to begin to feel himself actively repressing, and then he can himself begin to relax the repression.

4. An enormous amount of energy and previous creative decision is invested in the resistances and modes of repression. Then to bypass the resistances, or "attack" them, means that the patient will end up by being less than

---

[1] Rank's *Gegenwille*—negative will.

he came, although freer in certain respects. But by realizing the resistances experimentally and letting them act and come to grips with what is being resisted in himself or in the therapy, there is a possibility for resolution rather than annihilation.

5. If the self-awareness is otiose, the suffering of the patient is meaningless and had as well be relieved by aspirin while the therapeutic surgeon continues to do something to his passivity. And indeed it is partly on this theory that the resistances are quickly dissolved, in order to avoid the anguish of real conflict, lest the patient tear himself to pieces. But suffering and conflict are not meaningless or unnecessary: they indicate the destruction that occurs in all figure/background formation, in order that the new figure may emerge. This is not in the absence of the old problem but *solving* the old problem, enriched by its very difficulties, and incorporating new material—just as a great researcher does not shun the painful contradictory evidence to his theory but seeks it out to enlarge and deepen the theory. The patient is protected not by easing the difficulty, but because the difficulty comes to be felt just in the areas where the ability and creative élan are also being felt. If instead one attempts to dissolve the resistance, the symptom, the conflict, the perversion, the regression, rather than to increase the areas of awareness and risk and let the self live out its own creative synthesis—this means, it must be said, that the therapist in his superiority judges such and such human material as not worthy of regaining a whole life.

6. Finally, no matter what the theory of the self, just as at the beginning the patient has come under his own steam, so at the end he must go under his own steam. This is true for any school. If in treatment the patient's past is recovered, he must finally take it as his own past. If he adjusts in his interpersonal behavior, he must himself be the actor in the social situation. If his body is brought to react in a lively way, the patient must feel that it is he and not his body that is doing it. But where does this new powerful self suddenly come from? Does it emerge waking as from a hypnotic trance? Or has it not been there all along, coming to the session, talking or falling silent, doing the exercise or lying rigid? Since *de facto* it exerts as much power as this in the proceedings, is it not plausible *de jure* to concentrate some attention on its proper actions of contact, awareness, manipulation, suffering, choice, etc., as well as on the body, the character, the history, the behavior? The latter are indispensable means for the therapist to find contexts of closer contact, but it is only the self that can concentrate on the structure of the contact.

We have tried to show what difference our approach makes in general outlook and in therapeutic attitude. [This approach] is a theory and practice of gestalt therapy, the science and technique of figure/background forming in the organism/environment field. . . .

For our present situation, in whatever sphere of life one looks, life must be regarded as a field of creative possibility, or it is frankly intolerable. By desensitizing themselves and inhibiting their beautiful human powers, most persons seem to persuade themselves, or allow themselves to be persuaded, that it is tolerable, or even well enough. They seem, to judge by the kind of their concern, to conceive of a "reality" that is tolerable, to which they can adjust with a measure of happiness. But that standard of happiness is too low, it is contemptibly too low; one is ashamed of our humanity. But fortunately, what they conceive to be the reality is not the reality at all, but a comfortless illusion (and what the devil is the use of an illusion that does not at least give consolation!).

The case is that, by and large, we exist in a chronic emergency and that most of our forces of love and wit, anger and indignation, are repressed or dulled. Those who see more sharply, feel more intensely, and act more courageously mainly waste themselves and are in pain, for it is impossible for anyone to be extremely happy until we are happy more generally. Yet if we get into contact with this terrible actuality, there exists in it also a creative possibility. . . .

The Self: Ego, Id, and Personality

. . . We explain the various neurotic configurations as various inhibitions of the process of contacting the present.

Self as the System of Present Contacts and the Agent of Growth

We have seen that in any biological or sociopsychological investigation, the concrete subject matter is always an organism/environment field. There is *no* function of any animal that is definable except as a function of such a field. Organic physiology, thoughts and emotions, objects and persons, are abstractions that are meaningful only when referred back to interactions of the field.

The field as a whole tends to complete itself, to reach the simplest equilibrium possible for that level of field. But since the conditions are always changing, the partial equilibrium achieved is always novel; it must be grown to. An organism preserves itself only by growing. Self-preserving and growing are polar, for it is only what preserves itself that can grow by assimilation, and it is only what continually assimilates novelty that can preserve itself and not degenerate. So the materials and energy of growth are: the conservative attempt of the organism to remain as it has been, the novel environment, the

---

The Self: Ego, Id, and Personality, from Perls, Hefferline, and Goodman, *Gestalt Therapy,* pp. 371–78.

destruction of previous partial equilibria, and the assimilation of something new.

Contacting is, in general, the growing of the organism. By contacting we mean food getting and eating, loving and making love, aggressing, conflicting, communicating, perceiving, learning, locomotion, technique, and in general every function that must be primarily considered as occurring at the boundary in an organism/environment field.

The complex system of contacts necessary for adjustment in the difficult field we call *self.* Self may be regarded as at the boundary of the organism, but the boundary is not itself isolated from the environment; it contacts the environment; it belongs to both, environment and organism. Contact is touch touching something. The self is not to be thought of as a fixed institution; it exists wherever and whenever there is in fact a boundary interaction. To paraphrase Aristotle, "When the thumb is pinched, the self exists in the painful thumb."

(Thus, supposing that, concentrating on one's face, one feels that the face is a mask and then wonders what one's "real" face is. But this question is absurd, for one's real face is a response to some present situation: if there is danger, one's real face is fright; if there is something interesting, it is an interested face, etc. The real face underlying a face felt as a mask would be the response to a situation kept in unawareness; and it is this actuality, of the keeping something in unawareness, that is expressed by the mask: for the mask is then the real face. So the advice, "Be yourself," that is often given by therapists, is somewhat absurd; what is meant is "contact the actuality," for the self is only that contact.)

Self, the system of contacts, always integrates perceptive-proprioceptive functions, motor-muscular functions, and organic needs. It is aware and orients, aggresses and manipulates, and feels emotionally the appropriateness of environment and organism. There is no good perception without involving muscularity and organic need; a perceived figure is not bright and sharp unless one is interested in it and focuses on it and scans it. Likewise there is no grace or skill of movement without interest and proprioception of the muscles and perception of the environment. And organic excitation expresses itself, becomes meaningful, precisely by imparting rhythm and motion to percepts, as is obvious in music. To put this another way: it is the sensory organ that perceives, it is the muscle that moves, it is the vegetative organ that suffers an excess or deficit; but it is the organism-as-a-whole in contact with the environment that is aware, manipulates, feels.

This integration is not otiose; it is creative adjustment. In contact situations the self is the power that forms the gestalt in the field; or better, the self *is* the figure/background process in contact-situations. The sense of this formative process, the dynamic relation of ground and figure, is excitement: excitement is the feeling of the forming of the figure/background in contact-situations, as the unfinished situation tends to its completion. Conversely, since self exists not as a fixed institution but especially as adjusting to more intense and difficult problems, when these situations are quiescent or approach equilibrium, the self is diminished. So it is in sleep or in any growth as it approaches assimilation. In food getting, the hunger, imagination, motion, selection, and eating are full of self; the swallowing, digestion, and assimilation occur with less or no self. Or so in the contact by proximity of charged surfaces, as in love: the desire, approach, touching, and total release of energies are full of self, the subsequent flowing occurs with diminished self. So again in conflicts: the destruction and annihilation are full of self, the identification and alienation occur with diminished self. In brief, where there is most conflict, contact, and figure/background, there is most self; where there is "confluence" (flowing together), isolation, or equilibrium, there is diminished self.

Self exists where there are the shifting boundaries of contact. The areas of contact may be restricted, as in the neuroses, but wherever there is a boundary and contact occurs, it is, in so far, creative self.

Self as Actualization of the Potential

The present is a passage out of the past toward the future, and these are the stages of an act of self as it contacts the actuality. (It is likely that the metaphysical experience of time is primarily a reading off of the functioning of self.) What is important to notice is that the actuality contacted is not an unchanging "objective" state of affairs that is appropriated, but a potentiality that in contact becomes actual. . . .

Neurosis as the Loss of Ego-Functions

The Figure/Background of Neurosis

Neurotic behavior is also a learned habit, the result of creative adjustment; and like other assimilated habits is no longer contacted, because it presents no novel problem. What differentiates this kind of habit from others, and what is the nature of neurotic unawareness (repression) as distinct from simple forgetting and available memory?

In the process of creative adjustment we have traced the following sequence of grounds and figures: (1) Fore-contact: in which the body is the ground and its urge or some environmental stimulus is the figure; this is the

---

Neurosis as the Loss of Ego-Functions, from Perls, Hefferline, and Goodman, *Gestalt Therapy*, pp. 429–33. Internal references have been deleted.

"given" or id of the experience. (2) Contacting: accepting the given and draw-ing on its powers, the self goes on to approach, estimate, manipulate, etc. a set of objective possibilities: it is active and deliberate with regard to both the body and the environment; these are the ego-functions. (3) Final contact: a sponta-neous, disinterested, middle mode of concern for the achieved figure. (4) Post-contact: diminishing self.

We saw also ... that at any stage the process could be interrupted, because of danger or inevitable frustration, and the excitement throttled, re-sulting in anxiety. The particular stage of interruption is important for the particular neurotic habit that is learned. ... But now let us consider how any interruption and anxiety leads also to an attempt to inhibit the original drive or response to the stimulus, for these are most available to control. There is thus set up a reverse sequence that we must explore.

1. The deliberate effort to control is the ground. The figure is the inhibited excitation or response to stimulus; this is a painful feeling of the body. It is painful because the excitation seeks discharge in out-going and the control is a contraction of the expansion (gritting the teeth, clenching the fists, etc.).

This figure-ground does not as such, of course, lead further. One relaxes the control and tries again. But supposing now the danger and frustration are chronic and one cannot relax the control; meantime there are other matters to attend to. Then,

2. A new situation arises and the old situation is still unfinished. The new situation may be either a new stimulus or a distraction sought to lessen the pain, disappointment, etc. In meeting the new situation, the old unfinished situation is necessarily suppressed: one swallows one's anger, hardens oneself, pushes the urge out of mind. Yet in the new situation, the painful suppressed excitation persists as part of the ground. The self turns to cope with the new figure, but it cannot draw on the powers engaged in keeping down the sup-pressed excitation. Thus the ground of contacting the new figure is disturbed by the existence of the painful suppression, which is immobilizing certain of the ego-functions.

Beyond this, the sequence cannot develop. This is because the body cannot be annihilated. The suppressed urge belongs to the physiological self-regula-tion and conservatively persists, recurs acutely whenever sufficient tension accumulates or there is a stimulus, and always remains as a coloration of whatever looms in the foreground of interest. The excitation cannot be re-pressed but only kept out of attention. All further developments are again in the other direction, of confronting the new problem, except that the process is now hampered by the disturbed ground of the unfinished situation. This persisting disturbance prevents final contact in the new adjustment, for all concern is not given to the figure. It prevents the new problem from being addressed on its merits, for every new solution must also "irrelevantly" solve the unfinished situation. And perceptual and muscular powers are bound in maintaining the deliberate suppression.

The excitation cannot be forgotten; but the deliberate control can be forgotten and remain unaware. This is simply because, being a motoric pattern, after a while the situation is learned; if the inhibition is chronic, the means of effecting it are no longer novel and contacted; they are a kind of useless knowledge that would occupy the attention apparently without function. So long as nothing is to be changed in the ground inhibition, the self forgets how it is being deliberate, as it turns to new problems. The motor and perceptual powers involved in the inhibition cease to be ego-functions and become simply strained bodily states. In this first step, thus, there is nothing remarkable about the transition from aware suppression to repression; it is ordinary learning and forgetting how one learned it; there is no need to postulate a "forgetting of the unpleasant."

(Further, in every important case of repression, one quickly attends to quite different matters and therefore quickly forgets.)

But let us follow the process further, for as yet the means of inhibiting is an available memory. We have seen that any uncontacted habit is "second nature"; it is part of the body, not of the self. So our posture, whether correct or incorrect, seems "natural," and the attempt to change it rouses discomfort; it is an attack on the body. But unaware inhibiting has this peculiar property, that if the attempt is made to relax it, there is immediate anxiety, for the situation of excitement is revived, and promptly must be throttled. Suppose, for instance, the inhibited excitation is surprised by an unusual stimulus, or vice versa that the control is temporarily loosed by a therapeutic exercise: then the sight habitually dulled is threatened, it seems, with blindness, the ears ring, the muscle is threatened with a fatal cramp, the heart pounds, etc. The self—unaware that these are the effects of a simple contraction and that all that is called for is to bear a slight discomfort, to locate the contraction, and loosen it deliberately—imagines that the body itself is in danger, and it responds with fright, throttling, and a secondary aware deliberateness to protect the body. It avoids the temptation, resists the therapy; being unaware close-mouthed against something savory but once dangerous, it reacts now with vomiting, as if the thing were poison. Further, since the nascent excitement is painful in any case, it easily lends itself to the extreme interpretation. The attitude and interpretation of defending the one-time ego-functions as if they were vital organs rather than learned habits are reaction-formations. (Throughout this process there is evident the aggressive attempt to annihilate the more basic physiology.)

We are thus elaborating the following theory of repression: Repression is the forgetting of deliberate inhibiting that has become habitual. The forgotten habit becomes unavailable because of further aggression reaction-formations turned against the self. What is not, and cannot be, forgotten is the urge or appetite itself; but this persists as a ground of pain because [it is] undischarged and obstructed. (This is the "reversal of affect.") To the extent that the drive maintains its original quality and can enliven objects in the foreground, there are "sublimations," direct but imperfect gratifications.

Analysis of Neurosis: Loss of Ego-Functions

Neurosis is the loss of ego-functions to the secondary physiology as unavailable habits. The therapy of neurosis, conversely, is the deliberate contacting of these habits through exercises graded so as to make anxiety tolerable. . . .

As a disturbance of the self-function, neurosis lies midway between the disturbance of the spontaneous self, which is misery, and the disturbance of the id-functions, which is psychosis. Let us contrast the three classes.

The one who gives himself spontaneously may not achieve final contact: the figure is disrupted in frustration, rage, exhaustion. In this case he is miserable rather than happy. The harm his body suffers is starvation. His disposition is soured and he turns against the world; but he does not as yet turn against himself, nor have much sense of himself except that he is suffering, until he becomes desperate. The therapy for him must be to learn more practical techniques, and there must also be a change in social relations so that his efforts can bear fruit, and biding that, a little philosophy. This is the culture of the Personality. (This is a description of many small children who, however, are hard to make philosophical.)

At the other extreme is psychosis, the annihilation of some of the given-ness of experience, e.g., the perceptive or proprioceptive excitations. To the extent that there is integration at all, the self fills the experience: it is utterly debased, or immeasurably grand, the object of a total conspiracy, etc. The primary physiology begins to be affected.

Midway, neurosis is the avoidance of spontaneous excitement and the limitation of the excitations. It is the persistence of sensory and motor attitudes when the situation does not warrant them or indeed when no contact-situation exists at all, as a bad posture is maintained in sleep. These habits intervene in the physiological self-regulation and cause pain, exhaustion, susceptibility, and disease. No total discharge, no final satisfaction; disturbed by unfulfilled needs and unaware maintaining an inflexible grip on himself, the neurotic cannot become absorbed in his outgoing concerns nor successfully carry them through, but his own personality looms in awareness: embarrassed, alternately resentful and guilty, vain and inferior, brazen and self-conscious, etc.

Through the assimilation of experience under conditions of chronic emergency, the neurotic self has lost part of its ego-functions; the process of therapy is to change the conditions and provide other grounds of experience, till the self discovers-and-invents the figure, "*I* am deliberately avoiding this excitement and wielding this aggression." It may then go on again to a spontaneous creative adjustment. (But, to repeat it again, to the extent that the conditions of life inevitably involve chronic emergency and frustration, the chronic control will prove to be functional after all; the release during the session of therapy will provide nothing but an abreaction of rage and grief, or worse, vomiting up of situations which one "can't stomach.") . . .

Gestalt Therapy of the Neurosis

Stratagem of Therapy of "Neurotic Characters"

In this final chapter, let us try to explain the most important neurotic mechanisms and "characters" as ways of contacting the actual on-going situation, whatever it happens to be during the therapy session. Neurotic behaviors are creative adjustments of a field in which there are repressions. This creativity will spontaneously operate in any on-going present; the therapist does not have to get under the "ordinary" behavior or trick it out of the way in order to reveal the mechanism. His task is simply to pose a problem which the patient is not adequately solving and where he is dissatisfied with his failure; then the need of the patient will, with help, destroy and assimilate the obstacles and create more viable habits, just as with any other learning.

We have located the neuroses as loss of ego-functions. In the ego-stage of creative adjustment, the self identifies parts of the field as its own and alienates other parts as not its own. It feels itself as an active process, a deliberateness, of certain wants, interests, and powers that have a definite but shifting boundary. Progressively engaged the self is as if asking: "What do I need? Shall I act it? How am I aroused? . . . What is my feeling toward that out there? . . . Shall I try for that? Where am I in relation to that? How far does my power extend? What means do I dispose of ? Shall I press on now or hold back? What technique have I learned that I can use?" Such deliberate functions are spontaneously exercised by the self and are carried on with all the strength of the self, awareness and excitement and the creation of new figures. And ultimately, during close and final contact, the deliberateness, the sense of "I," spontaneously vanishes into the concern, and then boundaries are unimportant, for one contacts not a boundary but the touched, the known, the enjoyed, the made.

Gestalt Therapy of the Neurosis, from Perls, Hefferline, and Goodman, *Gestalt Therapy,* pp. 447–51, 457–66.

But during this process the neurotic loses his boundaries, his sense of where he is and what and how he is doing, and he can no longer cope; or he feels his boundaries as inflexibly fixed, he does not get on, and he can no longer cope. Therapeutically, this problem of the self is the obstacle to solving other problems and is the object of deliberate attention. The questions now are: "At what point do *I* begin not to solve this simple problem? How do I go about preventing myself? What is the anxiety I am feeling?"

Mechanisms and "Characters" as Stages of Interruption of Creativity

The anxiety is the interruption of creative excitement. We now want to present the idea that the various mechanisms and "characters" of neurotic behavior may be observed as the stages of creative adjustment at which the excitement is interrupted. That is to say, we want to elaborate a typology from the experiencing of the actual situation. Let us discuss the advantages of such an approach and the properties of a typology that can be useful in therapy (for of course it is a unique person and not a type of disease that is being treated).

Every typology depends on a theory of human nature, a method of therapy, a criterion of health, a selected run of patients. ... The scheme we shall offer here is no exception. The therapist needs his conception in order to keep his bearings, to know in what direction to look. It is the acquired habit that is the background for this art as in any other art. But the problem is the same as in any art: how to use this abstraction (and therefore fixation) so as not to lose the present actuality and especially the on-goingness of the actuality? and how—a special problem that therapy shares with pedagogy and politics—not to impose a standard rather than help develop the potentialities of the other?

1. If it is possible to find our concepts in the process of contacting, then at least it will be the actual patient that is there, not the past history or the propositions of a biological or social theory. On the other hand, of course, in order to be the means by which the therapist can mobilize the learning and experience of his art, these concepts must recognizably belong to his knowledge of human upbringing and his somatic and social theory.

2. The actual situation is always, we must remember, an example of all the reality that there ever was or will be. It contains an organism and its environment and an on-going-need. Therefore, we can ask the usual questions concerning the structure of the behavior: how does it cope with the organism? How does it cope with the environment? How does it fulfill a need?

3. Again, if we draw our concepts from moments in a present process (namely its interruptions), we can expect that, with awareness, these interruptions will develop into other interruptions; the on-goingness of the process will not be lost. The patient will be found not to have a "type" of mechanism, but indeed a sequence of "types," and indeed all the "types" in explicable series.

Now the case is that in *applying* any typology, rather than finding it in the actuality, one experiences the absurdity that none of the types fits any particular person, or conversely that the person has incompatible traits or even all the traits. Yet what does one expect? It is the nature of the creative—and so far as the patient has any vitality he is creative—to make its own concrete uniqueness by reconciling apparent incompatibilities and altering their meaning. Then instead of attacking or reducing the contradictory traits in order to get at the "real" underlying character that the therapist guesses at (character analysis), or of trying to uncover the missing connections to what must be the "real" drive (anamnesis), we need only help the patient develop his creative identity by his ordered passage from "character" to "character." The diagnosis and the therapy are the same process.

4. For the ordered passage is nothing but the remobilizing of fixations into wholes of experience. The most important thing to remember is that every mechanism and characteristic is a valuable means to live if it can only go on and do its work. Now the patient's behavior, in therapy and elsewhere, is a creative adjusting that continues to solve a problem of chronic frustration and fear. The task is to provide him a problem in circumstances in which his customary (unfinished) solutions are no longer the most adequate possible solutions. If he needs to use his eyes, and does not because it is not interesting and safe to use them, now he will alienate his blindness and identify with his seeing; if he needs to reach out, he will now become aware of his muscular aggression against reaching out and relax it, etc.; but this is not because blindness and paralysis are "neurotic," but because they no longer achieve anything: their meaning has changed from technique to obstacle.

To sum up, we offer the following sketches of "character" as a kind of bridge between the therapy of the actual situation and the therapist's concepts. These characters and their mechanisms are not types of persons, but taken as a whole they are a description of the neurotic "ego" in process. So we try in each case to (1) start from a moment of actual interruption, (2) indicate the normal functioning of the interruption, (3) show how, against the background of repressions, it copes with the organism and the environment and gives a positive satisfaction, (4) relate it to the cultural and somatic history. Finally (5) we discuss the sequence of characters when mobilized.

The Moments of Interruption

The question in the loss of ego-functions is, we saw, "At what moment do *I* begin not to solve this simple problem? How do I prevent myself?"

Let us return again to our schematized sequence of grounds-and-figures in excitement and the reverse sequence in inhibition. In the neurotic inhibition the sequence was reversed and the body became a final object of aggression: the background is occupied by a repression, a chronic inhibiting that has been forgotten and is kept forgotten.[2] Against this ground, the present interruption (loss of ego-functions) occurs.

The difference in types consists in whether the interruption occurs
1. Before the new primary excitation. Confluence.
2. During the excitation. Introjection.
3. Confronting the environment. Projection.
4. During the conflict and destroying. Retroflection.
5. At final contact. Egotism. . . .

Schematic of Moments of Interruption

We may summarize these moments of interruption and their "characters" in the following scheme. (O is the aggression toward the organism, E toward the environment, and S the direct satisfaction possible in the fixation.)

Confluence: no contact with excitation or stimulus
    O: clinging, hanging-on bite
    E: paralysis and desensitized hostility
    S: hysteria, regression
Introjection: not accepting the excitation
    O: reversal of affect
    E: resignation (annihilation by identification)
    S: masochism
Projection: not confronting or approaching
    O: disowning the emotion
    E: passive provocation
    S: fantasy (chewing it over)
Retroflection: avoiding conflict and destroying
    O: obsessive undoing
    E: self-destructiveness, secondary gain of illness
    S: active sadism, busyness
Egotism: delaying spontaneity
    O: fixation (abstraction)
    E: exclusion, isolation of self
    S: compartmenting, self-conceit

---

[2]The *repression, sublimation,* and *reaction-formation* mentioned are themselves, of course, normal adjustive functions. Normally, repression is simply a physiological function, the forgetting of useless information. Sublimation we have regarded as only a normal function, the imperfect contact possible in the average situation. The interesting case is reaction formation. Normally, reaction-formation is the automatic emergency-response to a threat to the body: it is the class of such responses as playing dead, fainting, shock, panic, flight, etc. All these seem to imply an immediate, and therefore indiscriminate and total, interaction between the physiological signal and the ego-functions of caution, unmediated by the usual sequence of contacting. Normally, the emergency-response seems to meet a commensurate threat—though often a slight injury leads to shock. When the threat has to do with the anxiety resulting from releasing a chronic and forgotten inhibiting, we speak of reaction-formation.

Repression
Reaction-Formation
Sublimation

(The above scheme may be proliferated indefinitely by combinations of the classes with one another, as "confluence of introjects," "projection of retroflects," etc. Of these combinations we may perhaps mention the set of attitudes toward the introjects—the super-ego: (1) the confluence with one's introjects is guiltiness, (2) the projection of introjects is sinfulness, (3) the retroflection of introjects is rebelliousness, (4) the egotism of introjects is the ego-concept, (5) the spontaneous expression of introjects is the ego-ideal.)

The Above Is Not a Typology of Neurotic Persons

To repeat it, the above scheme is not a classification of neurotic persons, but a method of spelling out the structure of a *single* neurotic behavior.

This is obvious on the face of it, for every neurotic mechanism is a fixation and every mechanism contains a confluence, something unaware. Likewise every behavior is resigned to some false-identification, disowns an emotion, turns aggression against the self, and is conceited! What the scheme means to show is the *order* in which, against the background of a threatened repression, the fixation spreads throughout the entire process of contact, and the unawareness comes to meet it from the other direction.

That there must be a sequence of fixation in the actual experience is evident, if we consider that at a certain moment one is in fairly good contact, is exercising one's powers and adjusting to the situation, and yet a little later is paralyzed. The sequence may in fact be directly observed. The person walks in, smiles or frowns, says something, etc.: in so far he is vital, he has not lost his ego-functions and they are fully engaged. Then he becomes anxious—no matter what it is that is too exciting, it may be the other, a memory, the exercise, whatever. Instead then of proceeding to orient himself *further* (it is the furtherness, the on-goingness that is essential), he at once isolates himself and fixates the situation: he fixates the single achieved orientation. This is the "ego cut off from the self." But this "self-consciousness" at once makes him awkward; he upsets the ashtray. He becomes muscularly rigid (turns on himself), and then he thinks that the other must take him for a consummate ass. He adopts this standard for his own and is ashamed, and the next moment he is dizzy and paralyzed. Here we interpret the experience as created by the spreading of the fixation.

But of course it could be regarded in the opposite way, as the spreading of the confluence. At the anxious moment, he is out of contact with the ongoing situation—for whatever reason; he may want to be elsewhere, reject a hostile impulse against the other, etc. But it is his standard to be all there and attentive. What right do they have to judge him anyway! So he angrily upsets the ashtray on purpose. Next moment he excludes the environment altogether and is sufficient unto himself.

Regarding the experience as the spread of the unawareness, it would be hysteria; regarding it as the spread of the fixation, it would be compulsive. The hysteric has "too much spontaneity and too little control"; he says, "I cannot control the impulses that arise": the body looms in the foreground, he is swept by emotions, his ideas and inventions are capricious, everything is sexualized, etc. The compulsive overcontrols; there is no fantasy, warm feeling or sensation, action is strong but desire is weak, etc. Yet these two extremes come always to the same thing. It is just because there is too little self, too superficial desire and too little spontaneity, that the hysteric organizes the experience apparently desired: the feelings are not dominant enough to energize the functions of orientation and manipulation—and thus these are pointless and seem to be "too little." But conversely, it is because the functions of control, orientation, and manipulation are too fixated and inflexible that the compulsive is inadequate to cope with his exciting situations; therefore, he cannot control his impulses and turns against them, and then his feelings seem to be "too little." The split of self and ego is mutually disastrous.

This must be so, for neurosis is a condition of both chronic fear and chronic frustration. Because frustration is chronic, desire does not learn to activate important practical functions, for a man bound for disappointment and grief will not engage with the environment seriously. Nevertheless, the frustrated desire recurs and sets going fantasies and finally impulsive acts that are practically ineffective; and so he is again unsuccessful, hurt, and subject to chronic fear. On the other hand, a man who is chronically fearful controls himself and directly frustrates himself. Nevertheless, the drive is not annihilated, but it is merely isolated from the ego; it reappears as hysterical impulse. The frustration, the impulsiveness, the fear, and the self-control all aggravate one another.

In any single experience, all of the powers of the self are mobilized to complete the situation as well as possible, either in a final contact or a fixation. The accumulation of such experiences during a life-history results in well-marked personalities, characters, and types. But still in every single experience, regarded as the peculiar act of self, all the powers are mobilized. And since in therapy it is the self that must destroy and integrate the fixations, we must consider a "typology" not as a method of distinguishing among persons, but as a structure of the single neurotic experience.

Example of Reversing the Sequence of Fixations

Let us invent an example to illustrate a therapeutic sequence:

1. Fixation: The patient is "potent"; he can do the exercise to his own satisfaction. The bother is that when it comes to the finale, of getting something

out of it for himself, or thereby giving something to the therapist, he cannot let go. He becomes anxious. When his attention is called to the fact that he interrupts at this stage, he becomes aware of his conceit and exhibitionism.

2. Retroflection: He reproaches himself for his personal failings. He adduces examples to show how his love for himself and showing off have stood in his way. He has no one to blame but himself. The question is asked: "Instead of reproaching yourself, whom would you like to reproach?" Yes; he wants to tell the therapist a thing or two.

3. Projection: The sessions have been failing because the therapist does not really want to get on. He is using the patient; if the fee were higher, one would think his intention was to get money out of him. As it is, the situation is uncomfortable; no one likes to lie there and be stared at. Probably the orthodox method is better, when the therapist is out of the way. The question is asked, "What is your feeling when you are stared at?"

4. Introjection: He is embarrassed. The reason he shows off is that he wants the therapist to admire him; he considers him as a kind of ideal—in fact he had a fantasy about him (the opposite of the dream that was discussed). Question: "Am I really attractive to you?" No; but naturally one has to love, or at least be well-disposed to, a person who is trying to help you. This said with some anger.

5. Confluence: He is angry because the experiments . . . are boring, senseless, and sometimes painful, and he is tired of doing them; he is getting disgusted with the therapy. . . . At this he falls silent; he is not interested in making any further effort. The other must do it.

The therapist declines to cooperate and holds his peace. The patient suddenly feels that his rigid jaw is painful and he recalls, in the stillness, that his voice had come between his teeth. He closes his teeth.

Let us assume now that the energy bound in this confluent characteristic is available. During his silence he had been alternately guilty at not cooperating and resentful that the therapist did nothing to help him out (just like his wife). Now perhaps he sees that he has been imposing his own dependency unnecessarily; and he smiles at the picture it calls up. Nevertheless, the energy freed from the confluence will again be contacted and fixated according to the other characters. Thus:

Introjection: A man ought to be independent and do what he wants. Why shouldn't he look for other women? Question: "Is there anybody in particular you're interested in?"

Projection: He never had such thoughts before the therapy. He feels almost as though they were being put into his mind. "Really?"

Retroflection: It's the fault of his upbringing. He recognizes that censorious face on middle-class mothers, just like his own mother's. He embarks on a lengthy reminiscence. Question: "What about her now?"

Egotism: He understands everything perfectly. What people don't know won't hurt them. Just do it within the rules of the game. "Who's playing a game?"

Contacting the Situation: He'll try the experiment again now and see if he gets anything out of it.

Sense of Boundaries

The functioning of the ego, we have seen, can be described as a setting of boundaries of the self's interest, power, etc.; identifying with and alienating are the two sides of the boundary; and in any live contacting the boundary is definite but always shifting. Now in the therapeutic situation of deliberately contacting the character, what is the sense of the boundary?

Engaged in an interesting activity, the self contacts its lost ego-functions as blocks, resistances, sudden failures. One identifies with the interesting engagement, that is on one side of the boundary; but what is alienated is not—as in normal functioning—uninteresting and irrelevant, but precisely alien, oppressive, uncanny, immoral, numb; not a boundary, but a limitation. The sense is not indifference, but unpleasure. The boundary does not shift with will or need, as one tries to see, remember, move; but remains fixed.

Regarded topologically, as fixed boundaries in the shifting organism/environment field, the neurotic characters we have been describing are as follows:

Confluence: identity of organism and environment.

Introjection: something of the environment in the organism.

Projection: something of the organism in the environment.

Retroflection: part of the organism made the environment of another part of the organism.

Egotism: isolation from both id and environment, or: organism largely isolated from environment.

There is an exact opposition in the way these situations are sensed by the neurotic need of keeping them fixed and by the creative self concentrating on them:

In confluence, the neurotic is aware of nothing and has nothing to say. The concentrating self feels hemmed in by an oppressive darkness.

In introjection, the neurotic justifies as normal what the concentrating self feels as an alien body it wants to disgorge.

In projection, the neurotic is convinced as by sensory evidence, where the concentrating self feels a gap in experience.

In retroflection, the neurotic is busily engaged where the concentrating self feels left out, excluded from the environment.

In egotism, the neurotic is aware and has something to say about everything, but the concentrating self feels empty, without need or interest.

It can be seen from this that the treatments of an area of confluence and of an area of egotistic fixation present opposite difficulties. The confluent darkness is too embracing; the self is routine; no novel proposal is accepted as relevant—just as in the hysterical behavior anything is likely to be momentarily relevant (there is no dearth of symptoms for the therapist to interpret to his own satisfaction).

Now in the history of psychoanalysis the extreme opposite of this condition has been taken as the health of the self, namely the stage of all ego that feels a boundary of possible contact everywhere. The essential self is defined as the system of its ego-boundaries; it is not seen that this is an on-going stage of the self. The temptation to such a theoretical conception is irresistible because in therapy the awareness of boundaries dissolves the neurotic structures, and the physician defines according to what works in therapy; further, any particular "problem" that arises in therapy can finally be met and "solved" in egotism by compartmenting it and employing all the ego-functions within this safe framework, without engaging the feelings at all. This is a condition of too heightened consciousness, that will never have brilliant creative flashes, but is quite adequate for therapeutic sessions. To the self, everything is potentially relevant and novel—there is a boundary everywhere and no limit to action—but nothing is interesting. He is psychologically "emptied out." This is, as we have said, the "analysis-neurosis"; it is likely that *any* method of therapy continued too long must give this result, which in antiquity was praised as the Stoic apathy, and among the moderns is taken for a "free personality"—but such freedom of the individual, without animal or social nature, or in perfect hygienic and juridical control of the animal and social nature, such freedom is, as Kafka said, a lonely and senseless business.

Therapy of Boundaries

For a concentration-therapy, the problem of contacting the lost ego-functions is no different from any other problem of creative orientation and manipulation, for the unawareness, or the unsatisfactory kind of awareness, is felt simply as another obstacle in the organism/environment field. It is necessary to need, approach, destroy, in order to identify, contact, and assimilate. It is not a question of recovering something from the past nor of rescuing it from behind an armor, but of making a creative adjustment in the given present situation. To complete the gestalt in the present situation it is necessary to destroy and assimilate the unawareness as an obstacle. The therapeutic exercises consist of sharp delineation and precise verbal description of the felt block or void, and experiment on it to mobilize the fixed boundaries.

From this point of view there is no mystery in the psychoanalytical miracle, that simple awareness is somehow cathartic, for the effort of concentrated awareness and mobilizing of the block entails destroying, suffering, feeling, and excitement. (The therapist, correspondingly, is a vastly important part of the present situation, but it is not necessary to speak of "transference," the attachment of repressed Oedipal energies, for the actuality contains both the confluence of dependency and the rebellion against it.)

Let us return then to the question of the patient that we started with: "At what point do I begin not to solve the problem? How do I prevent myself?" And now let us lay the stress not on the moment of interruption, but on the *begin* and on the *how*. Let us contrast the nontherapeutic and the therapeutic situation. Ordinarily, the self, trying to contact some interesting present actuality, becomes aware of the boundaries of its lost functions—something of the environment or body is missing, there is not enough strength or clarity. It nevertheless presses on and tries to unify the foreground, even though the neurotic structure looms in the background as an unfinished situation, unknowable, a threat of confusion and a threat to the body. The mounting excitement is throttled, there is anxiety. Nevertheless, the self persists in the original task and allays the anxiety by further blotting out the background with reaction-formations and proceeding with less and less of its powers. In the therapy, on the contrary, it is just the point of the interruption that is now made the interesting problem, the object of concentration: the questions are: "What hinders? What does it look like? How do I feel it muscularly? Where is it in the environment? etc." The mounting anxiety is allayed by continuing the excitement in this new problem; what is felt is some quite different emotion, of grief, anger, disgust, fear, longing.

The Criterion

It is not the presence of "inner" obstacles that constitutes the neurosis: they are simply obstacles. To the extent that a situation is alive, when the obstacles to creativity appear, the excitement does not diminish, the gestalt does not stop forming, but spontaneously one feels new aggressive emotions and mobilizes new ego-functions of caution, deliberateness, paying attention, relevant to the obstacles. One does not lose the sense of oneself, of one's synthetic unity, but it continues to sharpen, to identify itself further and alienate what is not itself. In neurosis, on the contrary, at this point the excitement falters, the aggression is not felt, one loses the sense of the self, becomes confused, divided, insensitive.

This factual difference, of continuing creativity, is the crucial criterion of vitality and neurosis. It is an independent criterion, generally observable and also introspectable. It does not require norms of health for comparison. The test is given by the self.

The neurotic begins to lose contact with the actuality; he knows it but he does not have techniques for continuing the contact; he persists in a course that gets him further from the actuality, and he is lost. What he must learn is to recognize sharply when he is no longer in contact, how he is not, and where and what the actuality now is, so he can continue contacting it; an "inner" problem is now the actuality, or probably the relation of an "inner" problem to the previous experiencing. If he learns a technique of awareness, to follow up, to keep in contact with the shifting situation, so the interest, excitement, and growth continue, he is no longer neurotic, no matter whether his problems are "inner" or "outer." For the creative meaning of the situation is not what one thinks beforehand, but it emerges in bringing to the foreground the unfinished situations, whatever they are, and discovering-and-inventing their relevance to the apparent present lifeless situation. When in the emergency the self can keep in contact and keep going, the therapy is terminated.

In the emergency, the neurotic loses himself. To live on a little, with diminished self, he identifies with reactive feelings, a fixated interest, a fiction, a rationalization; but these in fact do not work, they do not alter the situation, release new energy and interest. He has lost something of actual life. But the patient comes to recognize that his own functioning is part of the actuality. If he has alienated some of his powers, he comes to identify with his own alienation of them as a deliberate act; he can say, "It is I who am doing this or preventing this." The final stage of experience, however, is not a subject of therapy: it is for a man to identify with his concern for the concernful and to be able to alienate what is unconcernful.

In its trials and conflicts, the self is coming to be in a way that did not exist before. In contactful experience the "I," alienating its safe structures, risks this leap and identifies with the growing self, gives it its services and knowledge, and at the moment of achievement stands out of the way.

17

CONSTRUCTIVE ALTERNATIVISM PSYCHOTHERAPY: PERSONAL CONSTRUCT PSYCHOLOGY

George A. Kelly

George A. Kelly was born in Perth, Kansas, on April 28, 1905. After spending 3 years at Friends University in Wichita, he left for Park College in Missouri, where he received a bachelor's degree in physics and mathematics in 1926. In 1928, he earned an M.A. in educational sociology at the University of Kansas. The following year was spent at the University of Edinburgh, where he received a B.Ed. in education and psychology. Then he earned a Ph.D. in psychology from the University of Iowa in 1931.

After his studies were completed, Kelly joined the faculty of Ft. Hays Kansas State College, where he stayed until 1943. The remainder of the war years were devoted to the Navy. After a year on the faculty of the University of Maryland, he left for Ohio State University in 1946. He relinquished his professorship at Ohio State for another at Brandeis University in 1965, a tenure that lasted until his death on March 6, 1967.

Among the several honors Kelly enjoyed were a symposium on his theories at the University of London (1964); presidency of the Consulting Division of the A.P.A. (1954–55); presidency of the American Board of Examiners in Professional Psychology (1951–53); chairmanship, Education and Training Board, A.P.A. (1954–56); presidency, Clinical Division, A.P.A. (1956–57); consultant in aviation psychology, The Surgeon General, U.S. Navy (1948–51).

Kelly's psychotherapy is based upon the premise of constructive alternativism —the belief that a variety of feasible choices are available by which to construct one's world. Thoughtful individuals are neither victimized by their personal history nor by their environment, but are motivated by their constructs. Certain constructs, such as anxiety, result from faulty or failing constructs. For example: *threat* results from disruption of one's core structure, *guilt* from separation from one's role, *hostility* from support of a discredited construct, and *aggression* from employment of a construct that may prove threatening to other persons. Psychotherapy is a matter of reconstruction, replacing ineffective constructs with suitable ones, replacing threatening constructs with compatible constructs.

New constructs are experimented with, utilized in the sense of playing a role. Thus personal construct psychotherapy is fundamentally role theory or role therapy. Only good diagnostic constructs should be implemented, such as, fertility, propositionality, dichotomy, permeability, definability, temporality, futurity, ability to generate testable hypotheses, ability to generate treatment hypotheses, and sociality. The underlying theory of constructive alternativism is that one's current interpretations of the world are always subject to revision and replacement, and the task of the psychotherapist is to assist in changing or uprooting undesirable old interpretations for suitable and wholesome new ones.

Kelly's principal writings are *The Psychology of Personal Constructs* (in two volumes, 1955) and the posthumously published *Selected Papers of George A. Kelly,* edited by Brendan A. Maher (1969). The latter work contains a number of previously unpublished papers, including: "The Personal Construct Theory and the Psychotherapeutic Interview," "Psychotherapy and the Nature of Man," "The Autobiography of a Theory," and "The Psychotherapeutic Relationship."

Other of Kelly's writings include:

"Man's Construction of His Alternatives," in *The Assessment of Human Motives,* ed. G. Lindzey (1958).
"Fixed Role Therapy," in *Handbook of Direct and Behavior Psychotherapies,* ed. R. M. Jurjevich.
"Innovations in Psychotherapy," a contribution to the Symposium on Innovations in Clinical Psychology at New York (1962).
"Personal Construct Theory as a Line of Inference," *Journal of Psychology* [Pakistan] 1 (1964): 80–93.
"Sin and Psychotherapy," in *Morality and Mental Health,* ed. O. H. Mowrer (1966).
"A Psychology of the Optimal Man," in *Goals of Psychotherapy,* ed. A. R. Mahrer (1966).
"Behavior Is an Experiment," an address before the Division of School Psychology, A.P.A. (1966).

Kelly compiled (in mimeographed form) a list of all of his writings, including unpublished ones, and a second bibliography containing published works of authors contributing to personal construct theory.

Psychology of Personal Constructs

The theory is based upon the philosophical position of constructive alternativism, the notion that there are many workable alternative ways for one to

Psychology of Personal Constructs, from George A. Kelly, *The Psychology of Personal Constructs,* vol. 2 (New York: Norton, 1955), pp. 560–65.

construe his world. The theory itself starts with the basic assumption, or postulate, that a person's processes are psychologically channelized by the ways in which he anticipates events. This is to say that human behavior may be viewed as basically anticipatory rather than reactive, and that new avenues of behavior open themselves to a person when he reconstrues the course of events surrounding him. Thus a thoughtful man is neither the prisoner of his environment nor the victim of his biography.

The patterns of man's construction are called *constructs;* and, since each person sets up his own network of pathways leading into the future, the concern of the psychologist is the study of personal constructs. Each personal construct is based upon the simultaneous perception of likeness and difference among the objects of its context. There is no such thing as a difference without a likeness being implied, and vice versa. Each construct is, therefore, dichotomous or bipolar in nature; and, in dealing with a client, the psychologist must frequently go off searching for the submerged poles in the client's thinking.

When a person finds his personal construction failing him, he suffers *anxiety.* When he faces an impending upheaval in his *core structure,* he experiences *threat.* A person who construes the construction system of another person sets the stage for playing a *role* in relation to that person. When he finds himself dislodged from his role, he experiences *guilt.* This has much to do with social organization. *Aggression* is merely the active pursuit of *constructive* experience, but it may be *threatening* to one's associates. *Hostility,* while not necessarily violent, is the continued attempt to extort *validational evidence* in support of a personal construction which has already discredited itself. ...

Fundamental Postulate and Corollaries

The theory of personality we have called the psychology of personal constructs starts with a basic assumption upon which all else hinges. It is called the *fundamental postulate.* This postulate is then elaborated by means of eleven corollaries. These, also, are assumptive in nature, and they lay the groundwork for most of what follows. While it may be difficult to see the implications of this series of assumptions from a bare recitation of them, it seems appropriate to give the reader an opportunity to see what the statements are. ...

Fundamental Postulate: A person's processes are psychologically channelized by the ways in which he anticipates events.

1. Construction Corollary: A person anticipates events by construing their replications.

2. Individuality Corollary: Persons differ from each other in their constructions of events.

3. Organization Corollary: Each person characteristically evolves, for his convenience in anticipating events, a construction system embracing ordinal relationships between constructs.

4. Dichotomy Corollary: A person's construction system is composed of a finite number of dichotomous constructs.

5. Choice Corollary: A person chooses for himself that alternative in a dichotomized construct through which he anticipates the greater possibility for extension and definition of his system.

6. Range Corollary: A construct is convenient for the anticipation of a finite range of events only.

7. Experience Corollary: A person's construction system varies as he successively construes the replications of events.

8. Modulation Corollary: The variation in a person's construction system is limited by the permeability of the constructs within whose ranges of convenience the variants lie.

9. Fragmentation Corollary: A person may successively employ a variety of construction subsystems which are inferentially incompatible with each other.

10. Commonality Corollary: To the extent that one person employs a construction of experience which is similar to that employed by another, his psychological processes are similar to those of the other person.

11. Sociality Corollary: To the extent that one person construes the construction processes of another he may play a role in a social process involving the other person.

Formal Aspects of Constructs

Range of Convenience. A construct's range of convenience comprises all those things to which the user would find its application useful.

Focus of Convenience. A construct's focus of convenience comprises those particular things to which the user would find its application maximally useful. These are the elements upon which the construct is likely to have been formed originally.

Elements. The things or events which are abstracted by a person's use of a construct are called elements. In some systems these are called objects.

Context. The context of a construct comprises those elements among which the user ordinarily discriminates by means of the construct. It is somewhat more restricted than the range of convenience, since it refers to the circumstances in which the construct emerges for practical use, and not necessarily to all the circumstances in which a person might eventually use the construct. It is somewhat more extensive than the focus of convenience, since the construct may often appear in circumstances where its application is not optimal.

Pole. Each construct discriminates between two poles, one at each end of its dichotomy. The elements abstracted are like each other at each pole with respect to the construct and are unlike the elements at the other pole.

Contrast. The relationship between the two poles of a construct is one of contrast.

Likeness End. When referring specifically to elements at one pole of a construct, one may use the term *likeness end* to designate that pole.

Contrast End. When referring specifically to elements at one pole of a construct, one may use the term *contrast end* to designate the opposite pole.

Emergence. The emergent pole of a construct is that one which embraces most of the immediately perceived context.

Implicitness. The implicit pole of a construct is that one which embraces contrasting context. It contrasts with the emergent pole. Frequently the person has no available symbol or name for it; it is symbolized only implicitly by the emergent term.

Symbol. An element in the context of a construct which represents not only itself but also the construct by which it is abstracted by the user is called the construct's symbol.

Permeability. A construct is permeable if it admits newly perceived elements to its context. It is impermeable if it rejects elements on the basis of their newness.

Constructs Classified According to the Nature of Their Control over Their Elements

Preemptive Construct. A construct which preempts its elements for membership in its own realm exclusively is called a preemptive construct. This is the "nothing but" type of construction—"If this is a ball it is nothing but a ball."

Constellatory Construct. A construct which fixes the other realm memberships of its elements is called a constellatory construct. This is stereotyped or typological thinking.

Propositional Construct. A construct which carries no implications regarding the other realm memberships of its elements is a propositional construct. This is uncontaminated construction.

General Diagnostic Constructs

Preverbal Constructs. A preverbal construct is one which continues to be used, even though it has no consistent word symbol. It may or may not have been devised before the client had command of speech symbolism.

Submergence. The submerged pole of a construct is the one which is less available for application to events.

Suspension. A suspended element is one which is omitted from the context of a construct as a result of revision of the client's construct system.

Level of Cognitive Awareness. The level of cognitive awareness ranges from high to low. A high-level construct is one which is readily expressed in socially effective symbols; whose alternatives are both readily accessible; which falls well within the range of convenience of the client's major constructions; and which is not suspended by its superordinating constructs.

Dilation. Dilation occurs when a person broadens his perceptual field in order to reorganize it on a more comprehensive level. It does not, in itself, include the comprehensive reconstruction of those elements.

Constriction. Constriction occurs when a person narrows his perceptual field in order to minimize apparent incompatibilities.

Comprehensive Constructs. A comprehensive construct is one which subsumes a wide variety of events.

Incidental Constructs. An incidental construct is one which subsumes a narrow variety of events.

Superordinate Constructs. A superordinate construct is one which includes another as one of the elements in its context.

Subordinate Constructs. A subordinate construct is one which is included as an element in the context of another.

Regnant Constructs. A regnant construct is a kind of superordinate construct which assigns each of its elements to a category on an all-or-none basis, as in classical logic. It tends to be nonabstractive.

Core Constructs. A core construct is one which governs the client's maintenance processes.

Peripheral Constructs. A peripheral construct is one which can be altered without serious modification of the core structure.

Tight Constructs. A tight construct is one which leads to unvarying predictions.

Loose Constructs. A loose construct is one leading to varying predictions, but which retains its identity.

Constructs Relating to Transition

Threat. Threat is the awareness of an imminent comprehensive change in one's core structures.

Fear. Fear is the awareness of an imminent incidental change in one's core structures.

Anxiety. Anxiety is the awareness that the events with which one is confronted lie mostly outside the range of convenience of his construct system.

Guilt. Guilt is the awareness of dislodgment of the self from one's core role structure.

Aggressiveness. Aggressiveness is the active elaboration of one's perceptual field.

Hostility. Hostility is the continued effort to extort validational evidence in favor of a type of social prediction which has already been recognized as a failure.

C-P-C Cycle. The C-P-C Cycle is a sequence of construction involving, in succession, circumspection, preemption, and control, and leading to a choice precipitating the person into a particular situation.

Impulsivity. Impulsivity is a characteristic foreshortening of the C-P-C Cycle.

Creativity Cycle. The Creativity Cycle is one which starts with loosened construction and terminates with tightened and validated construction.

Constructive Alternativism Psychotherapy

Psychotherapy as an Aid to Reconstruction

The psychology of personal constructs and the philosophy of constructive alternativism upon which it is based lead one to view psychotherapy as a reconstruing process. Within these two frameworks we see man not as the victim of his past, only the victim of his construction of it. To be sure, his past cannot be altered. Operationally speaking, its unalterability makes the past what it is, and its pliancy makes the future what it is. As for the present, man can divert some small part of the stream of events upon which he is borne. Moreover, he can navigate over broad latitudes if he has a mind to. Nature, inexorable as she is, is not half so intransigent as our thinking about her. And it is only a knuckle-headed outlook that makes the past seem to adults to be so implacable, the present so self-evident, and the future so fateful.

Our view, then, is that there is nothing in the world which is not subject to some form of reconstruction. This is the hope that *constructive alternativism* holds out to every man and it is the philosophical basis of the hope that a psychotherapist holds out to his client.

"Slot" Movement. In our chapter on the role of the psychotherapist we included a section on the clinician's conceptualization of his role. We pointed out that superficial movement could be produced by sliding the client back and forth in his construct slots. For example, a client who sees people as distinguished from each other principally in terms of "kindly" versus "hostile" may be encouraged to shift himself from "kindliness" to "hostility" or vice versa.

Constructive Alternativism Psychotherapy, from Kelly, *The Psychology of Personal Constructs,* vol. 2, pp. 937–41, 927–29.

This type of therapeutic movement amounts to no more than a shifting of one of the elements in the construct context—in this case himself—from one side of the construct dimension to the other. Sometimes this kind of superficial movement is worth seeking; but, as every clinician should know, it is all too likely to end up in seesaw behavior: the client is "kindly" as long as things are going well, then he turns to "hostility," then back again, ad infinitum. Let us call this type of reconstruction *contrast reconstruction.*

Controlled Elaboration.   The second type of reconstruction discussed in the section dealing with the clinician's conceptualization of his role was described as *controlled elaboration.* It is a way of bringing about reconstruction through clarification. This amounts to a reorganization of the hierarchical system of one's contructs, but not essential revision of the constructs themselves. The client is helped to work through his construct system experimentally by verbal as well as by other behavioral actions. He deals essentially with the subordination-superordination features of his system. He brings his constructs in line with his system as a whole. Essentially he works on the internal consistency of his system rather than attempting to make outright replacements of constructs. For example, the person who sees himself as "kindly" in a "kindly-hostile" dimensioned world may be helped to discover just what incidental constructs and behaviors are "kindly" and what ones are "hostile." Thus his system becomes clearly delineated whereas once it was sketchy, his superordinate constructs are tightened, and he becomes a person of greater integrity—though not necessarily a "better" man.

Formation of New Constructs.   The third and most basic type of reconstruction which may take place in psychotherapy is that which changes the reference axes against which the events of life are plotted. By judiciously introducing new elements into the client's field of experience, the therapist may so change the content of the construct contexts that the axes of the client's system are rotated. The same words may be used to symbolize the constructs, but the meanings may have been subtly changed in the course of psychotherapy. For example, the client who lumps humanity as either "kindly" or "hostile" may be brought to the point of seeing that some behavior which is constricting and repressive is the sort of thing he has been calling "kindly" and some elements which are straightforward and reliable are the sort of thing he has been calling "hostile." As this revision of contexts begins to take place, the "kindly-hostile" axis begins to rotate with respect to the rest of his system. As far as his own behavior is concerned, he sees himself confronted with alternatives which have somewhat different behavior implications. In a given situation to which the construct is applied, his *elaborative choice* will be affected. And once he has made his choice, the repertory of behaviors falling under that choice will, in turn, be revised.

The therapist may help the client accelerate the tempo of his experience. He may precipitate him into situations in which he can be expected to "mature." This is, of course, also a matter of adding new elements, but it is principally a matter of giving the client more new elements to deal with, rather than a matter of judiciously selecting new elements in order to rotate his axes or force him to contrive new constructs. For example, the client may be encouraged to take a job or enter a social situation in which the "nonkindly" people are not "hostile" but only disinterested and objective.

The therapist may help the client impose new constructs upon old elements. The new constructs may be tentatively originated as *incidental* constructs. But once formed, they can be made more permeable and their range of convenience gradually expanded until the client is able to use them to replace certain obsolete *core* constructs. For example, the therapist may help the client develop the notion that certain behaviors of people can be distinguished on the grounds of "objectivity vs. selfishness." At first this is no more than an *incidental* construct and can be used by the client to distinguish only between a few specific figures which seem relatively detached from himself. Later he may be able to apply it to more familiar figures; and, last of all, he may be able to apply the construct to his own behavior, past and present. At this stage of the game there is a reasonable chance that he can incorporate the new construct into his *core* system. Because it has proven to be a better basis for anticipating life than the old personal construct of "kindliness-hostility," he may begin to make his life's choices in terms of the alternatives the new construct provides instead of in terms of the old dichotomy.

Reduction of Constructs to Impermeability.   One of the most interesting approaches to construct revision is the reduction of obsolete constructs to a state of impermeability. As the writer sees it, this is essentially what the general semanticists propose as the basic approach to psychotherapy. Thinking is made more and more specific to its elements. Constructs are tightened and given sharply limited ranges of convenience. Our client who lumps his associates as either "kindly" or "hostile" may be urged to see only certain people as "kindly" or "hostile"—these and no more. Or better still, he might be urged to see only certain past behaviors of these people as "kindly" or "hostile"— these and no more. As far as other people and other behaviors of these same people are concerned he would be assisted in applying another construct, such as, for example, "objective-selfish."

Personal Construct Psychotherapy as Experimental

The psychotherapeutic approach of the psychology of personal constructs is experimental. The whole system is built upon the modern science model. Constructs are hypotheses. Prediction is the goal. Systematization extends the range of anticipation. Experiments are performed. They are carefully designed to yield definitive results. Only small samples are committed to experimentation at a time. Abortive undertakings are avoided. Hypotheses are revised on the basis of empirical evidence. Hostility is avoided, for the scientist seeks to learn from nature rather than extort from her a confirmation of his prejudices.

All of this is embodied in the approach of a psychotherapist to his client. The psychotherapist helps the client design and implement experiments. He pays attention to controls. He helps the client define the hypotheses. He helps the client avoid abortive undertakings. He uses the psychotherapy room as a laboratory. He does not extort results from his client to confirm his own systematic prejudices nor does he urge his client, in turn, to seek appeasement rather than knowledge. Finally, he recognizes that in the inevitable scheme of things he is himself a part of the validating evidence which the client must take into account in reckoning the outcome of his psychotherapeutic experiments. The client, in experimenting with the old "kindly-hostile" construct and the new "objective-selfish" construct, must see those bits of evidence which the therapist's own varying behaviors provide as fitting more neatly and meaningfully into the "objective-selfish" dichotomy.

In summary, we may say that psychotherapeutic movement may mean (1) that the client has reconstrued himself and certain other features of his world within his original system, (2) that he has organized his old system more precisely, or (3) that he has replaced some of the constructs in his old system with new ones. This last type of movement is likely to be the most significant, although the behavioral changes may not be as spectacular as in the first type. The second type of movement may be most impressive to those who always look to therapy to produce verbal consistency and "insight." . . .

Diagnostic Constructs and Control

We have defined control as an aspect of the relationship between a superordinate construct and the subordinate constructs which constitute its context. The way the subordinate constructs are subsumed determines the way in which they may operate, just as the way a person construes determines the way in which he behaves. In a sense, then, all disorders of construction are disorders which involve faulty control.

We have further described the Circumspection-Preemption-Control (C-P-C) Cycle, by means of which a person prepares himself to take definitive action in a given situation. We have pointed out that control involves the choice of an alternative and that the choice of the alternative is determined by that side of the construct which appears to provide a better opportunity for further elaboration (Choice Corollary).

Sometimes a clinician observes his client behaving in regularized ways which make it appear that there is *more* control operating than in the case of another client. This is misleading. From the standpoint of the psychology of personal constructs, all behavior may be seen as controlled, just as all behavior can be seen as natural and all nature seen as lawful. What makes one person's behavior seem more controlled than another is the way it is subsumed by overriding construction. The "controlled" person performs long-cycle experiments; the impulsive person indulges in short-range experimentation. Both must bow to the outcomes of their experiments sooner or later. Both control their behavior through superordinate construction systems.

Sometimes a person's behavior can be seen as regular, purposeful, and consistent and yet altogether so inimical to the welfare of others that it must be construed as pathological. The clinician must realize that in dealing with this type of case he is dealing with highly permeable superordinate constructions and with long-cycle prediction formulas. He cannot expect this type of client to be swayed by means of little ideas or simple interview-room experiments. The client may use anecdotes to illustrate his own constructions, but he will not be likely to change his control system as the result of having anecdotes cited by the therapist. He simply does not make such short-term wagers.

This type of client may be very baffling to the therapist, largely because the therapist never gets to see the faulty superordinate constructs laid on the line for examination and experimental test during the course of a single interview. Even if the person is not what one would ordinarily call "psychotic," he may be a very baffling person with whom to establish a role relationship. Perhaps his behavior is organized under a set of religious constructs which seem utterly primitive and magical to the therapist, and the person seems inaccessible to psychological treatment. The therapist is unable to think of any tests which will be sufficiently comprehensive to lead the person to reexamine his religious principles. Whatever new experience is introduced during the course of therapy is too readily subsumed and too easily brought under control of the superordinate construction causing all the difficulty.

The same difficulties are faced when nations try to work out role relations with each other. For example, little demonstrations of good will do not have much effect upon leaders basically indoctrinated with the 1955 political and social philosophy of the Soviet Union. Its leaders have so clear-cut a view of the course of events leading to the future that they cannot be swayed by border incidents or by sporadic demonstrations of determination on the part of those who differ with them. Like the systematized paranoid patients, such political zealots are not likely to shift from their pathological position until certain crucial experiments have been designed and executed. The hope of civilized mankind is that the experimentation will not include all-out war.

With those who are not so basically indoctrinated, however, a consistent policy of goodwill and liberal tolerance may serve to validate their more friendly interpretations of our motives. The task of the therapist (or the socially responsible nation) is to keep the client (or disturbed nation) actively experimenting with the relationship. He seeks to have the client put his superordinate construction to test, a test that will definitely yield results of one sort, if the construction is correct, or results of another sort, if the construction is in error. The therapist says, in effect, to the client, "This is what you have been assuming to be true; let us perform a reasonable experiment which will come out one way if it is true and another way if it is not."

As in all cases of psychotherapy, the therapist should be alert as to what alternatives will confront the client if his experiment turns up negative evidence. What alternative does the client have to his view of pervading hostility? What will there be to take the place of communism in the Soviet Union if the present regime is discredited? Will it be anything more than another kind of serfdom with only the manners and dress of the masters changed? In the client, whose interpretation of a hostile world is clearly invalidated, will there be any alternative left, save a chaos of anxiety or a schizophrenic fragmentation? It may be necessary to make sure that the client has certain role relationships and tentative structures to fall back upon as soon as the crucial experimentation is over. These stand-by structures may be of the dependency type, as we have suggested before; or they may be of the fixed-role type; or they may be of the occupational type. But whatever type they may be the therapist should always, before prodding his client to jump, make sure that there is something reasonably firm to land on, that there is a suitable basis for *control.*

In dealing with a disorder of control the therapist must, as in other problems, subsume the construction system which is faulty. If the control is of the long-cycle variety we have been describing, the therapist (or the socially responsible nation) must understand the personal construct system with which he is dealing. That means, of course, that he must understand it sympathetically and insightfully, not simply condemn it as something abhorrent and unthinkable. Rarely have therapists (or nations) exercised far-reaching influence over their clients (or fellow nations) by condemning them, instead of thoughtfully studying their beliefs and customs.

Fixed-Role Sketch Therapy

The panel . . . attempted to write a new personality sketch suitable for enactment by the client. This was then called a *role sketch,* although at that time it did not always meet the definition of *role* we have chosen to employ in the

Fixed-Role Sketch Therapy, from Kelly, *The Psychology of Personal Constructs,* vol. 1, pp. 369–73.

present writing. One written nowadays would be called a *fixed-role sketch* and it would come nearer meeting our criterion of role. Edwards then presented the fixed-role sketch to the client and asked him to act it out continuously over a period of several weeks. In later practice this period of enactment was reduced. . . .

Development of a Major Theme other than Correction of Minor Faults. The method of writing the fixed-role sketch has undergone some changes. In the beginning we took the view that, as much as possible, the person should be accepted in the way in which he already saw himself and that he should be asked to make minor readjustments only. Our thinking was that we would not devise the fixed-role sketch to correct all the client's faults; rather, we would attempt to mobilize his resources. We looked for features in his self-characterization sketch which might be generalized and put to good use. We then attempted to put them into the fixed-role sketch in their more permeable and useful form. Thus, even in our earlier efforts in connection with fixed-role therapy, we made an effort to recognize the uniqueness of the client, even if that meant an implicit approval of his imperfections. The object was not to make a model human being out of him or even to make him into an approximation of a model human being, but to accomplish realistic therapeutic ends with as little disturbance to the client's personality as possible.

The Use of Sharp Contrast. In the second place, it was not long before we began to realize that there is a kind of all-or-none characteristic in individuals' readjustments. It may be easier for a person to play up to what he believes to be the opposite of the way he perceives himself than it is to play *just a little less* in the way he perceives himself. We have attempted to embody this clinical observation into the psychology of personal constructs by using the notion of constructs as the basic units of adjustment rather than scales, dimensions, or axes. We recognize that this may at first seem archaic and not in line with modern quantitative thinking, and we have dealt with this issue elsewhere. Be that as it may, it is a common experience in therapy, when the client begins to report his first exploratory excursions into areas of behavior where he has not previously been free to adjust, to observe that his efforts are essentially jerky and crudely contrasting rather than modulated and consistent. Even his thinking tends to have an all-or-none "So it's black—no, it's white!" characteristic to it. Members of the client's family are likely to have an uncomfortable time of it during this "jerky" stage of psychotherapeutic readjustment. If what we have said about a scale's being a built-up hierarchy of dichotomous constructs is a meaningful notion in general, it makes sense that the client would tend first to move in an "either-or" manner among his constructs rather than in an "only-so-much" manner along a finely graduated scale.

Our experience indicated that clients tended to "forget" about minor differences between their own conception of themselves and the conceptualization proposed in the fixed-role sketch. To be sure, they protested less in the initial stage about the "a little less this way and a little more that way" readjustments which were proposed for enactment, but in the end *they did more* about the more shocking and sharply contrasting readjustments. There are limits, of course, to the contrasts which can be enacted by the client. These limits are not determined by the sharpness of the contrasts but by the constellatory nature of the constructs upon which the proposed movements are based. When a clinician proposes new behavior to a client and structures it along certain lines, he may not be aware of how much other behavior would, to the client's way of thinking, have to be swept along in its wake. Fortunately for the clinician, and for the client too, the client is likely to balk until he can differentiate the constructs in his constellation sufficiently clearly to be able to move in one respect without dislodging himself in all respects.

Soon we began to write fixed-role sketches which deliberately invited the client to explore certain sharply contrasting behavior. An effort was made to define this behavior so that its limits would be sharply perceived and the client would not shake down upon his head a whole closetful of carelessly stored ideas. The fact that the new sketch was to be played out behind the protective screen of make-believe tended to limit the constellatory implications of the constructs involved.

Setting Ongoing Processes in Motion Rather than Creating a New State. The third consideration in writing the fixed-role sketch was to set the stage for a resumption of growth rather than to accomplish a major psychotherapeutic relocation during the interview series. Just as the psychoanalytically oriented therapist has to spend considerable time setting the stage for psychotherapeutic activity by developing a particular kind of relationship between his client and himself, and by training the client in free association and in a self-controlled tightening and loosening of conceptualization, so any therapist needs to give careful consideration to the way in which he prepares his client for readjustment. The psychoanalyst may have to spend months in what should be called pretherapeutic training. In fixed-role therapy the clinician conceives his job as one of preparing the client to resume the natural developmental processes of which he is capable.

In writing the fixed-role sketch the clinician is particularly sensitive to the constructs in the self-characterization sketch which imply immobility—that is, the impermeable constructs in which the self is one of the elements. The new sketch is written and the interview series undertaken in order to shake the client loose from these constructs—in order to jounce him out of his rut. In terms of another figure an attempt is made to loose him from the semantic chains with which he has bound himself. This is done primarily not by the methods of particularization, as usually proposed by the general semanticists, but by the instigation of movement within constructural frames already erected and by the introduction of new and more permeable forms of conceptualization. Movement in oneself is subject to construction, and once a person can say, "Look, I have changed, haven't I?" he is more likely to be able to say, "I can change."

Testable Hypotheses for the Client.   The fourth consideration in writing the fixed-role sketch has been to introduce conceptualization which can be immediately and widely checked against reality. This is akin to saying that a new scientific theory should provide testable hypotheses. The new role should not be merely an "academic" one but should be freighted with implications for action and response. In other words, it should be a partial construction system by which a wide variety of the events of everyday life can be anticipated. Thus it becomes amenable to validation within the short span of time during which it is proposed that the client utilize it. Another way of saying the same thing is to describe the new role as being in fact exploratory and experimental.

Emphasis upon Role Perceptions.   The fifth consideration, and one which has developed more recently in our thinking about the writing of fixed-role sketches, is that it should provide a conceptual basis for a new role relationship with other people. This means that the new constructs proposed as a basis for enactment should be the kinds of constructs which enable one to subsume the construction systems of other people. There is now, therefore, much more emphasis upon the way in which other people are to be construed during the enactment period. It was, in fact, because of our clinical observations that this feature lent life to a new role that we came to adopt the particular definition of *role* which we have chosen to use consistently in this book. Fixed-role therapy is, therefore, more than the introduction of new patterns of behavior; it is a rationale of new patterns of behavior and, more particularly still, it is a way of introducing concepts enabling a person to subsume the rationales under which other people operate.

The Protective Mask.   The final consideration which is important to fixed-role therapy, though it bears only indirectly upon the actual writing of the fixed-role sketch, is that the client is to be given the full protection of "make-believe." As we have said before, this is probably man's oldest protective screen for reaching out into the unknown. The test tube and the scientific laboratory are outgrowths of this cautious approach to life. They enable man to explore his world without wholly and irrevocably committing himself. Fixed-role therapy is aligned with this ancient and respectable tradition. . . .

In summary, it should be said that the writing of the fixed-role sketch taxes the ingenuity and perceptive capacity of the therapist far more than does the conduct of the interviews. While there may be concretistic formulas for writing the fixed-role sketch, it has been impossible, so far, for the writer and his associates to discover them. Certainly it appears that there should be a kind of *acceptance* of the client running through the theme of the fixed-role sketch. *Acceptance* as it appears in most current psychological and psychiatric writings seems to be a pretty vague term. We have attempted to make it communicable by defining it as a willingness to see the world through the other person's eyes. It thus becomes a precondition for the intentional adoption of role relationships. Since the psychology of personal constructs lays great stress upon the interpretation of the regnancy of the constructs under which acts may be performed, rather than upon the mere acts themselves, and since it lays great stress upon *personal* constructs rather than *formalistic* constructs, it does demand of the psychologist that he have an acceptance of other persons. One might even say that the psychology of personal constructs is, among other things, a psychology of acceptance.

PART FOUR

Phenomenological and Existential Approaches

NONDIRECTIVE COUNSELING: CLIENT-CENTERED THERAPY

Carl R. Rogers

Carl R. Rogers, born on January 8, 1902, was educated at the University of Wisconsin, Union Theological Seminary, and Columbia University's Teachers College. From Wisconsin he earned his B.A. in 1924, and from Columbia the M.A. in 1928 and the Ph.D. in 1931. His career began as a fellow in psychology for the Institute for Child Guidance in New York City in 1927. The following year he left to assume a post as psychologist for the Child Study Department, S.P.C.C. in Rochester, New York, where he eventually became director. In 1939 he accepted a similar directorship with the Rochester Guidance Center for one year.

The year 1940 saw the opening of Rogers's teaching career, as professor of psychology at Ohio State University, a post he left in 1945 to accept an appointment with the University of Chicago as professor of psychology and executive secretary of its Counseling Center. Two years later he went to the University of Wisconsin as a professor in the Department of Psychology and Department of Psychiatry, and he remained there until 1963. He left to become resident fellow at the Western Behavioral Sciences Institute in California, a center for the study of interpersonal relations. Since 1968 he has been with the Center for the Studies of the Person at La Jolla, an institute he helped found.

Rogers's nondirective technique of psychotherapy is fundamentally client-centered. This nonauthoritarian approach, in which the patient is referred to as *client* (hence an equal) and the counseling session as an *interview,* places importance on the immediate situation, rather than on the client's past history. Accent is placed upon the subjective or phenomenological experiences of the client, and the interview is conducted from that orientation. The counselor's task is marked by permissiveness, for he neither interprets nor directs the client. He functions as a catalyst in assisting the client to achieve maturity through insight and self-scrutiny. In addition to acquiring a need for self-regard, the client possesses an actualizing tendency or self-actualizing tendency that aids in growth and mental health; hence counseling is essentially a process of change in which emotional blocks are removed, allowing for maturation, growth, and the assimilation of new experiences. As the forces of growth are released, the client, now capable of self-cure, assimilates new experiences, uproots emotional obstacles, releases expression, attains insight, and thus opens the road to growth and health. Interviews, occurring from several days to a week apart, may run from six to fifteen sessions, in contrast to the long, drawn-out ones of psychoanalysts, which often last for years.

Rogers, a prolific author, who has written more than 150 books and articles, is best known for three books: *Counseling and Psychotherapy: New Concepts in Practice* (1942); *Client-Centered Therapy: Its Current Practice, Implications, and Theory* (1951); and *On Becoming a Person: A Therapist's View of Psychotherapy* (1961), the latter work being a collection of his papers from 1951 to 1961. An excellent summary of his position is found in "A Theory of Therapy, Personality, and Interpersonal Relationships, as Developed in the Client-Centered Framework," in *Psychology: A Study of a Science,* vol. 3, ed. Sigmund Koch (1959).

Synopsis of Client-Centered Therapy

This theory is of the if-then variety. If certain conditions exist (independent variables), then a process (dependent variable) will occur which includes certain characteristic elements. If this process (now the independent variable) occurs, then certain personality and behavioral changes (dependent variables) will occur. This will be made specific. . . .

A. Conditions of the Therapeutic Process

For therapy to occur it is necessary that these conditions exist.

1. That two persons are in *contact.*

2. That the first person, whom we shall term the client, is in a state of *incongruence,* being *vulnerable,* or *anxious.*

3. That the second person, whom we shall term the therapist, is *congruent* in the *relationship.*

4. That the therapist is *experiencing unconditional positive regard* toward the client.

5. That the therapist is *experiencing* an *empathic* understanding of the client's *internal frame of reference.*

6. That the client *perceives,* at least to a minimal degree, conditions 4 and 5, the *unconditional positive regard* of the therapist for him, and the *empathic* understanding of the therapist.

Synopsis of Client-Centered Therapy, from Carl R. Rogers, "A Theory of Therapy, Personality, and Interpersonal Relationships, as Developed in the Client-Centered Framework," *Psychology: A Study of a Science,* vol. 3, ed. Sigmund Koch (New York: McGraw-Hill, 1959), pp. 212–21. Internal references have been deleted.

Comment.   These seem to be the necessary conditions of therapy, though other elements are often or usually present. The process is more likely to get under way if the client is anxious rather than merely vulnerable. Often it is necessary for the contact or relationship to be of some duration before the therapeutic process begins. Usually the empathic understanding is to some degree expressed verbally, as well as experienced. But the process often commences with only these minimal conditions, and it is hypothesized that it never commences *without* these conditions being met.

The point which is most likely to be misunderstood is the omission of any statement that the therapist *communicates* his empathic understanding and his unconditional positive regard to the client. Such a statement has been omitted only after much consideration, for these reasons. It is not enough for the therapist to communicate, since the communication must be received, as pointed out in condition 6, to be effective. It is not essential that the therapist *intend* such communication, since often it is by some casual remark, or involuntary facial expression, that the communication is actually achieved. However, if one wishes to stress the communicative aspect which is certainly a vital part of the living experience, then condition 6 might be worded in this fashion:

6. That the communication to the client of the therapist's empathic understanding and unconditional positive regard is, at least to a minimal degree, achieved.

The element which will be most surprising to conventional therapists is that the same conditions are regarded as sufficient for therapy, regardless of the particular characteristics of the client. It has been our experience to date that although the therapeutic relationship is used differently by different clients, it is not necessary nor helpful to manipulate the relationship in specific ways for specific kinds of clients. To do this damages, it seems to us, the most helpful and significant aspect of the experience, that it is a genuine relationship between two persons, each of whom is endeavoring, to the best of his ability, to be himself in the interaction.

The "growing edge" of this portion of the theory has to do with point 3, the congruence or genuineness of the therapist in the relationship. This means that the therapist's symbolization of his own experience in the relationship must be accurate, if therapy is to be most effective. Thus if he is experiencing threat and discomfort in the relationship, and is aware only of an acceptance and understanding, then he is not congruent in the relationship and therapy will suffer. It seems important that he should accurately "be himself" in the relationship, whatever the self of that moment may be.

Should he also express or communicate to the client the accurate symbolization of his own experience? The answer to this question is still in an uncertain state. At present we would say that such feelings should be expressed, if the therapist finds himself persistently focused on his own feelings rather than those of the client, thus greatly reducing or eliminating any experience of empathic understanding, or if he finds himself persistently experiencing some feeling other than unconditional positive regard. To know whether this answer is correct demands further testing of the hypothesis it contains, and this is not simple since the courage to do this is often lacking, even in experienced therapists. When the therapist's real feelings are of this order: "I find myself fearful that you are slipping into a psychosis," or "I find myself frightened because you are touching on feelings I have never been able to resolve," then it is difficult to test the hypothesis, for it is very difficult for the therapist to express such feelings.

Another question which arises is this: is it the congruence, the wholeness, the integration of the therapist in the relationship which is important, or are the specific attitudes of empathic understanding and unconditional positive regard vital? Again the final answer is unknown, but a conservative answer, the one we have embodied in the theory, is that for therapy to occur the wholeness of the therapist in the relationship is primary, but a part of the congruence of the therapist must be the experience of unconditional positive regard and the experience of empathic understanding.

Another point worth noting is that the stress is upon the experience *in the relationship.* It is not to be expected that the therapist is a completely congruent person at all times. Indeed if this were a necessary condition there would be no therapy. But it is enough if in this particular moment of this immediate relationship with this specific person he is completely and fully himself, with his experience of the moment being accurately symbolized and integrated into the picture he holds of himself. Thus it is that imperfect human beings can be of therapeutic assistance to other imperfect human beings.

The greatest flaw in the statement of these conditions is that they are stated as if they were all-or-none elements, whereas conditions 2 to 6 all exist on continua. At some later date we may be able to say that the therapist must be genuine or congruent to such and such a degree in the relationship, and similarly for the other items. At the present we can only point out that the more marked the presence of conditions 2 to 6, the more certain it is that the process of therapy will get under way, and the greater the degree of reorganization which will take place. This function can only be stated qualitatively at the present time. . . .

B. The Process of Therapy

When the preceding conditions exist and continue, a process is set in motion which has these characteristic directions:

1. The client is increasingly free in expressing his *feelings,* through verbal and/or motor channels.

2. His expressed feelings increasingly have reference to the *self,* rather than nonself.

3. He increasingly differentiates and discriminates the objects of his *feelings* and *perceptions*, including his environment, other persons, his *self*, his *experiences*, and the interrelationships of these. He becomes less *intensional* and more *extensional* in his *perceptions*, or to put it in other terms, his experiences are more *accurately symbolized*.

4. His expressed *feelings* increasingly have reference to the *incongruity* between certain of his *experiences* and his *concept of self*.

5. He comes to experience in awareness the threat of such *incongruence*.

    a. This *experience of threat* is possible only because of the continued *unconditional positive regard* of the therapist, which is extended to *incongruence* as much as to *congruence*, to *anxiety* as much as to absence of *anxiety*.

6. He *experiences* fully, in *awareness*, feelings which have in the past been *denied to awareness*, or *distorted in awareness*.

7. His *concept of self* becomes reorganized to assimilate and include these *experiences* which have previously been *distorted in* or *denied to awareness*.

8. As this reorganization of the *self-structure* continues, his *concept* of *self* becomes increasingly *congruent* with his *experience*, the *self* now including *experiences* which previously would have been too *threatening* to be in *awareness*.

    a. A corollary tendency is toward fewer perceptual *distortions in awareness*, or *denials to awareness*, since there are fewer *experiences* which can be *threatening*. In other words, *defensiveness* is decreased.

9. He becomes increasingly able to *experience*, without a feeling of *threat*, the therapist's *unconditional positive regard*.

10. He increasingly feels an *unconditional positive self-regard*.

11. He increasingly *experiences* himself as the *locus of evaluation*.

12. He reacts to *experience* less in terms of his *conditions of worth* and more in terms of an *organismic valuing process*.

Comment.   It cannot be stated with certainty that all of these are *necessary* elements of the process, though they are all characteristic. Both from the point of view of experience and the logic of the theory, 3, 6, 7, 8, 10, 12 are necessary elements in the process. Item 5a is not a logical step in the theory but is put in as an explanatory note.

The element which will doubtless be most puzzling to the reader is the absence of explanatory mechanisms. It may be well to restate our scientific purpose in terms of an example. *If* one strokes a piece of steel with a magnet, and *if* one places the piece of steel so that it can rotate freely, *then* it will point to the north. This statement of the if-then variety has been proved thousands of times. Why does it happen? There have been various theoretical answers, and one would hesitate to say, even now, that we know with certitude *why* this occurs.

In the same way I have been saying in regard to therapy, "If these conditions exist, *then* these subsequent events will occur." Of course we have speculations as to *why* this relationship appears to exist, and those speculations will be increasingly spelled out as the presentation continues. Nevertheless the most basic element of our theory is that if the described conditions exist, then the process of therapy occurs, and the events which are called outcomes will be observed. We may be quite wrong as to *why* this sequence occurs. I believe there is an increasing body of evidence to show that it *does* occur. . . .

C. Outcomes in Personality and Behavior

There is no clear distinction between process and outcome. Items of process are simply differentiated aspects of outcome. Hence the statements which follow could have been included under process. For reasons of convenience in understanding, there have been grouped here those changes which are customarily associated with the terms outcomes, or results, or are observed outside of the therapeutic relationship. These are the changes which are hypothesized as being relatively permanent:

1. The client is more *congruent,* more *open to his experience,* less *defensive.*

2. He is consequently more realistic, objective, *extensional* in his *perceptions.*

3. He is consequently more effective in problem solving.

4. His *psychological adjustment* is improved, being closer to the optimum.

    a. This is owing to, and is a continuation of, the changes in *self-structure* described in B7 and B8.

5. As a result of the increased *congruence* of *self* and *experience* (C4 above) his *vulnerability* to *threat* is reduced.

6. As a consequence of C2 above, his perception of his *ideal self* is more realistic, more achievable.

7. As a consequence of the changes in C4 and C5 his *self* is more *congruent* with his *ideal self.*

8. As a consequence of the increased *congruence* of *self* and *ideal self* (C6) and the greater *congruence* of *self* and *experience,* tension of all types is reduced—physiological tension, psychological tension, and the specific type of psychological tension defined as *anxiety.*

9. He has an increased degree of *positive self-regard.*

10. He *perceives* the *locus of evaluation* and the locus of choice as residing within himself.

    a. As a consequence of C9 and C10 he feels more confident and more self-directing.

    b. As a consequence of C1 and C10, his values are determined by an *organismic valuing process.*

11. As a consequence of C1 and C2, he *perceives* others more realistically and accurately.

12. He *experiences* more *acceptance* of others, as a consequence of less need for distortion of his perceptions of them.

13. His behavior changes in various ways.

    a. Since the proportion of *experience* assimilated into the *self-structure* is increased, the proportion of behaviors which can be "owned" as belonging to the *self* is increased.

    b. Conversely, the proportion of behaviors which are disowned as *self-experiences,* felt to be "not myself," is decreased.

    c. Hence his behavior is *perceived* as being more within his control.

14. His behavior is perceived by others as more socialized, more *mature.*

15. As a consequence of C1, 2, 3, his behavior is more creative, more uniquely adaptive to each new situation and each new problem, more fully expressive of his own purposes and values.

Comment.   The statement in part C which is essential is statement C1. Items 2 through 15 are actually a more explicit spelling out of the theoretical implications of statement 1. The only reason for including them is that though such implications follow readily enough from the logic of the theory, they are often not perceived unless they are pointed out. . . .

Comments on the Theory of Therapy

It is to be noted that this theory of therapy involves, basically, no intervening variables. The conditions of therapy, given in A, are all operationally definable, and some have already been given rather crude operational definitions in research already conducted. The theory states that if A exists, then B and C will follow. B and C are measurable events, predicted by A.

It should also be pointed out that the logic of the theory is such that: if A, then B; if A, then B and C; if A, then C (omitting consideration of B), if B, then C (omitting consideration of A).

Specification of Functional Relationships.   At this point, the functional relationships can only be stated in general and qualitative form. The greater the degree of the conditions specified in A, the more marked or more extensive will be the process changes in B, and the greater or more extensive the outcome changes specified in C. Putting this in more general terms, the greater the degree of anxiety in the client, congruence in the therapist in the relationship, acceptance and empathy experienced by the therapist, and recognition by the client of these elements, the deeper will be the process of therapy, and the greater the extent of personality and behavioral change. To revert now to the theoretical logic, all we can say at present is that

$$B = (f)A \quad C = (f)A \quad B + C = (f)A \quad C = (f)B$$

Obviously there are many functional interrelationships not yet specified by the theory. For example, if anxiety is high, is congruence on the part of the therapist less necessary? There is much work to be done in investigating the functional relationships more fully.

The Nature of Man

From the theory of therapy as stated above, certain conclusions are implicit regarding the nature of man. To make them explicit involves little more than looking at the same hypotheses from a somewhat different vantage point. It is well to state them explicitly, however, since they constitute an important explanatory link of a kind which gives this theory whatever uniqueness it may possess. They also constitute the impelling reason for developing a theory of personality. If the individual is what he is revealed to be in therapy, then what theory would account for such an individual?

We present these conclusions about the characteristics of the human organism:

1. The individual possesses the capacity *to experience in awareness* the factors in his *psychological maladjustment,* namely, the *incongruences* between his *self-concept* and the totality of his *experience.*

2. The individual possesses the capacity and has the tendency to reorganize his *self-concept* in such a way as to make it more *congruent* with the totality of his *experience,* thus moving himself away from a state of *psychological maladjustment* and toward a state of *psychological adjustment.*

3. These capacities and this tendency, when latent rather than evident, will be released in any interpersonal *relationship* in which the other person is *congruent* in the *relationship,* experiences *unconditional positive regard* toward, and *empathic* understanding of, the individual, and achieves some communication of these attitudes to the individual. . . .

It is this tendency which, in the following theory of personality, is elaborated into the tendency toward actualization.

I believe it is obvious that the basic capacity which is hypothesized is of very decided importance in its psychological and philosophical implications. It means that psychotherapy is the releasing of an already existing capacity in a potentially competent individual, not the expert manipulation of a more or less passive personality. Philosophically it means that the individual has the capacity to guide, regulate, and control himself, providing only that certain definable conditions exist. Only in the absence of these conditions, and not in any basic sense, is it necessary to provide external control and regulation of the individual. . . .

Perfect Adjustment: The Fully Functioning Person

Certain directional tendencies in the individual . . . and certain needs . . . have been explicitly postulated in the theory thus far presented. Since these tendencies operate more fully under certain defined conditions, there is already implicit in what has been given a concept of the ultimate in the actualization of the human organism. This ultimate hypothetical person would be synonymous with "the goal of social evolution," "the end point of optimal psychotherapy," etc. We have chosen to term this individual the fully functioning person. . . .

A.   The individual has an inherent tendency toward *actualizing* his organism.

B.   The individual has the capacity and tendency to *symbolize experiences* accurately in *awareness*.
   1. A corollary statement is that he has the capacity and tendency to keep his *self-concept* congruent with his *experience*.

C.   The individual has a *need for positive regard*.

D.   The individual has a *need for positive self-regard*.

E.   Tendencies *A* and *B* are most fully realized when needs *C* and *D* are met. More specifically, tendencies *A* and *B* tend to be most fully realized when
   1. The individual *experiences unconditional positive regard* from significant others.
   2. The pervasiveness of this *unconditional positive regard* is made evident through relationships marked by a complete and communicated *empathic* understanding of the individual's *frame of reference*.

F.   If the conditions under *E* are met to a maximum degree, the individual who experiences these conditions will be a fully functioning person. The fully functioning person will have at least these characteristics:
   1. He will be *open to his experience*.
      a. The corollary statement is that he will exhibit no *defensiveness*.
   2. Hence all *experiences* will be *available to awareness*.
   3. All *symbolizations* will be as accurate as the experiential data will permit.
   4. His *self-structure* will be congruent with his *experience*.
   5. His *self-structure* will be a fluid gestalt, changing flexibly in the process of assimilation of new *experience*.
   6. He will *experience* himself as the *locus of evaluation*.
      a. The *valuing process* will be a continuing *organismic* one.
   7. He will have no *conditions of worth*.
      a. The corollary statement is that he will *experience unconditional self-regard*.

Perfect Adjustment: The Fully Functioning Person, from Rogers, "A Theory of Therapy, Personality, and Interpersonal Relationships," pp. 234–35.

8. He will meet each situation with behavior which is a unique and creative adaptation to the newness of that moment.

9. He will find his *organismic valuing* a trustworthy guide to the most satisfying behaviors, because

    a. All available experiential data will be available to *awareness* and used.

    b. No datum of *experience* will be *distorted in,* or *denied to, awareness.*

    c. The outcomes of behavior in *experience* will be *available to awareness.*

    d. Hence any failure to achieve the maximum possible satisfaction, because of lack of data, will be corrected by this effective reality testing.

10. He will live with others in the maximum possible harmony, because of the rewarding character of reciprocal *positive regard.* . . .

Comment.   It should be evident that the term *the fully functioning person* is synonymous with optimal psychological adjustment, optimal psychological maturity, complete congruence, complete openness to experience, complete extensionality, as these terms have been defined.

Since some of these terms sound somewhat static, as though such a person "had arrived," it should be pointed out that all the characteristics of such a person are *process* characteristics. The fully functioning person would be a person-in-process, a person continually changing. Thus his specific behaviors cannot in any way be described in advance. The only statement which can be made is that the behaviors would be adequately adaptive to each new situation, and that the person would be continually in a process of further self-actualization. . . .

Nondirective Therapy

The Character of Client-Centered Therapy

This newer approach differs from the older one in that it has a genuinely different goal. It aims directly toward the greater independence and integration of the individual rather than hoping that such results will accrue if the counselor assists in solving the problem. The individual and not the problem is the focus. The aim is not to solve one particular problem, but to assist the individual to *grow,* so that he can cope with the present problem and with later

Nondirective Therapy, from Carl R. Rogers, *Counseling and Psychotherapy* (Boston: Houghton Mifflin, 1942), pp. 28–45.

problems in a better integrated fashion. If he can gain enough integration to handle one problem in more independent, more responsible, less confused, better organized ways, then he will also handle new problems in that manner.

If this seems a little vague, it may be made more specific by enumerating several of the ways in which this newer approach differs from the old. In the first place, it relies much more heavily on the individual drive toward growth, health, and adjustment. Therapy is not a matter of doing something *to* the individual or of inducing him to do something about himself. It is instead a matter of freeing him for normal growth and development, of removing obstacles so that he can again move forward.

In the second place, this newer therapy places greater stress upon the emotional elements, the feeling aspects of the situation, than upon the intellectual aspects. It is finally making effective the long-standing knowledge that most maladjustments are not failures in *knowing,* but that knowledge is ineffective because it is blocked by the emotional satisfactions which the individual achieves through his present maladjustments. The boy who steals knows that it is wrong and inadvisable. The parent who nags and condemns and rejects knows that such behavior is unfortunate in other parents. The student who cuts class is intellectually aware of the reasons against doing so. The student who gets low grades in spite of good ability frequently fails because of the emotional satisfactions of one sort and another which that failure brings to him. This newer therapy endeavors to work as directly as possible in the realm of feeling and emotion rather than attempting to achieve emotional reorganization through an intellectual approach.

In the third place, this newer therapy places greater stress upon the immediate situation than upon the individual's past. The significant emotional patterns of the individual, those which serve a purpose in his psychological economy, those which he needs to consider seriously, show up just as well in his present adjustment, and even in the counseling hour, as they do in his past history. For purposes of research, for understanding of the genetics of human behavior, past history is very important. For therapy to take place, it is not necessarily important. Consequently, there is much less stress on history for history's sake than formerly. Curiously enough, when there is no probing for the "facts" of the history, a better picture of the dynamic development of the individual often emerges through the therapeutic contacts.

One further general characteristic of this newer viewpoint should be mentioned. For the first time this approach lays stress upon the therapeutic relationship itself as a growth experience. In all the other approaches mentioned, the individual is expected to grow and change and make better decisions after he leaves the interview hour. In the newer practice, the therapeutic contact is itself a growth experience. Here the individual learns to understand himself, to make significant independent choices, to relate himself successfully to another person in a more adult fashion. In some respects this may be the most important aspect of the approach we shall describe. The discussion here is somewhat parallel to the discussion in education as to whether school work is a preparation for life, or whether it *is* life. Certainly this type of therapy is not a preparation for change, it *is* change.

Characteristic Steps in Nondirective Counseling

There is nothing so difficult to put into words as a point of view. If the foregoing seems vague and unsatisfactory, let us turn to the process of therapy itself. What happens? What goes on during a period of contacts? What does the counselor do? The client? The sections which follow attempt to state, briefly and in somewhat oversimplified form, the different steps in the process, as the writer has seen them occur many times, and to illustrate them with excerpts from clinical records. Although these different aspects of therapy are described separately and placed in a specific order, it should be emphasized that they are not discrete events. The processes mingle and shade into one another. They occur only approximately in the order given here.

I. The individual comes for help. Rightly recognized, this is one of the most significant steps in therapy. The individual has, as it were, taken himself in hand, and taken a responsible action of the first importance. He may wish to deny that this is an independent action. But if it is nurtured, it can lead directly toward therapy. It may as well be mentioned here that events insignificant in themselves often provide in therapy just as satisfactory a ground for self-understanding, for responsible action, as more important occasions. This may be made clear by an example from the record of Arthur, a boy who had been sent into a remedial course (Psychology 411) which automatically exposed him to counseling. Within the first three minutes of the first interview this exchange took place (phonographic recording):

> *C.* I don't think that I know very much how you happened to come in—I mean, I don't know whether someone suggested you come to see me or whether you had some things on your mind that you were disturbed about and wanted some help with.
> *S.* I talked with Miss G. at the Arts office and she suggested that I take the course. Then my instructor told me I would see you, so I came.
> *C.* That's how you came to take the course, because it was suggested to you.
> *S.* Mm-hm.
> *C.* So I suppose that's why you came in to see me, too. I mean that—
> *S.* Yeh.
> *C.* Well, now, one thing that I think I'd like to have straight at the outset is this; if there is anything that I can do to help you work through some of the things that may be bothering you, I'll be very glad to do so.

And on the other hand, I don't want you to think that you have to come to see me, or that it is part of what you must do for the course, or anything of that kind. Sometimes [students have] difficulty with their school work or sometimes with other things. They can work it through better if they talk it over with someone else and try to get at the bottom of it, but I think that should be up to them, and I just want to make it plain at the very start that if you wish to see me, perhaps I can save this time once a week and you can come in and talk things over—but you don't have to. Now I don't know—you might tell me a little bit more about how you happened to take 411—I believe because Miss G. suggested it to you.

S. Yes, Miss G. suggested it to me. She didn't think my study habits were good. If they were good, they didn't seem to be very beneficial on my grades and everything. So she thought that maybe if I'd get in this, I'd learn better study habits and make better use of time and concentration, and so forth.

C. So that—your purpose in taking it is to satisfy Miss G.

S. That's right. No, it isn't that. It's for my own improvement.

C. I see.

S. Dust off my study methods and habits and better use of time and how to concentrate.

C. Mm-hm.

S. I'm just taking————. She suggested it to me and I'm taking it for my own benefit.

C. I see. So that you got into it partly because she suggested it, but part of it was your own desire to get into something like that, is that it?

S. I thought I needed it, so I signed up. *(Laughs.)*

C. Well, now, I'm more interested in why you thought you needed it than why Miss G. thought you needed it. Why did *you* think you needed it?

Note in this opening of the first interview the complete dependence of the student in his initial statements. He takes no responsibility for taking the course or for coming to the counselor. When this attitude is recognized and clarified, he gradually veers over to a statement in which the responsibility is shared ("She suggested it to me and I'm taking it for my own benefit"), and finally takes full responsibility for his actions ("I thought I needed it, so I signed up"). It is difficult to overemphasize the difference this makes in counseling. If it is implicit that the counselor or some third person is responsible for the student's being present in the counseling situation, then suggestion or advice are almost the only avenues of approach open. If the client himself accepts responsibility for bringing himself, he also accepts the responsibility for working upon his problems.

II. The helping situation is usually defined. From the first the client is made aware of the fact that the counselor does not have the answers, but that the counseling situation does provide a place where the client can, with assistance, work out his own solutions to his problems. Sometimes this is done in rather general terms, while in other instances the situation is most plainly defined in terms of concrete issues, such as responsibility for appointments, or responsibility for steps to be taken and decisions to be made.

In the interview with Arthur, quoted above, we find an example of one way in which the situation is defined by the counselor, when it is explained that Arthur is under no compulsion, but may make use of the situation if he wishes. Obviously this type of intellectual explanation is not enough. The whole conduct of the interviews must reinforce this idea until the client feels that it is a situation in which he is free to work out the solutions that he needs.

Another example may be given from a first interview with a mother, Mrs. L. (from whose record there will be further quotations later on). This mother and her ten-year-old son had come to the clinic because of the mother's vehement complaints about the boy. After two diagnostic contacts the situation was put up to the mother as a difficulty in their relationships, and she was asked whether she and her boy would like to work through this problem. She had tentatively and somewhat fearfully agreed and she came in for the first contact with the psychologist who was to act as therapist. Here is the counselor's account (not phonographic) of a portion of this first treatment interview.

> As it was nearing the end of the hour, and I wanted to get something toward the settling up of the hour, I said, "How does your husband feel about your coming up here to work the problem through with us?" And she laughed slightly and said, "Well, he's sort of indifferent about it. But he did say something to the effect that he didn't want to be experimented on, or something—didn't want to be treated like white rats."
>
> And I said, "And you feel, too, perhaps, that is what will happen." "Well, I just don't know what will be done." And I assured her that she needn't feel that we were going to do anything at all strange or peculiar; that it would be a matter of her talking things through with me, and Jim with Mr. A., to see if we could think things through together to see how they both felt about the situation and to think out some of the relationships between them and other members of the family and get a view of the interrelationships within the family.
>
> At that she said, "Well, perhaps Marjorie too—maybe there is something a little funny about her. Maybe she is mixed up in it too."

Note that the counselor makes it plain that it is her task to provide a place and an atmosphere in which problems can be thought through and relationships recognized more clearly. She does not imply in any way that it is her responsibility to give the answers. The fact that this is understood by the mother is indicated by the fact that she then feels free to bring in a new aspect of the problem—the sister—and to suggest that she will wish to work on that, too.

Still another example may be given to illustrate how the situation is often defined in terms of actual responsibilities, no matter how minor they may be.

In a first counseling interview with a student, some verbal explanations of the situation were given early in the contact, but toward the end of the interview this exchange took place (phonographic recording):

> S. I think maybe the next time I come in to see you, it will be something different. Maybe I'll have a little bit better idea what to talk about by then.
> C. Would you like to come in next Friday at this time?
> S. Yes, it's all right with me.
> C. It's up to you.
> S. It's up to me?
> C. I'm here. I'd be glad to do anything I can do for you.
> S. All right, sir, I think I'll be there.
> C. All right.

In this brief excerpt, much has happened. The student makes a somewhat independent statement, showing that he plans at least to share the responsibility for the use of the next hour. The counselor encourages this by putting the decision about the appointment up to the student. The student feeling this is the usual meaningless gesture, leaves the responsibility with the counselor by saying, "Yes, it's all right with me." When the counselor shows that the counseling situation really belongs to the client, the student's surprise is clearly indicated in the phonographic record as he says, "It's up to *me?*" His whole tone changes as he then responds in a firm and decisive manner, "All right, sir, I think I'll be there"—genuinely accepting the responsibility for the first time.

Thus, through words, actions, or both, the client is helped to feel that the counseling hour is his—to use, to take responsibility for, an opportunity freely to be himself. With children words are of less use, and the situation must be defined almost entirely in terms of freedoms and responsibilities, but the underlying dynamics seem much the same.

III. The counselor encourages free expression of feelings in regard to the problem. To some extent this is brought about by the counselor's friendly, interested, receptive attitude. To some extent it is due to improved skill in treatment interviewing. Little by little we have learned to keep from blocking the flow of hostility and anxiety, the feelings of concern and the feelings of guilt, the ambivalences and the indecisions which come out freely if we have succeeded in making the client feel that the hour is truly his, to use as he wishes. I suppose that it is here that counselors have exercised the most imagination and have most rapidly improved their techniques of catharsis. This can be illustrated by brief excerpts from two contacts, one with the mother, Mrs. L., and one with her ten-year-old son, Jim. These are both from the first therapeutic contacts with mother and child.

During this first hour the mother spends a full half-hour telling with feeling example after example of Jim's bad behavior. She tells of his quarrels with his sister, of his refusal to dress, of his annoying manner of humming at the table, of his bad behavior in school, of his failure to help at home, and the like. Each of her comments has been highly critical of the boy. A brief segment toward the end of this tirade is given below (not phonographic).

> I said, "What things have you tried in helping him to do more as you would like?" "Well, last year," she said, "we put him in a special school, and I've tried rewarding him for things, and I've tried knocking off his allowance for things that he does that he shouldn't do, but by the time the day is over his allowance is practically all used up. I've put him in a room alone and I've ignored him until I've just felt frantic, nearly ready to scream." And I said, "Perhaps sometimes you do actually———." And she said (very quickly), "Yes, sometimes I do actually scream about it. I used to think I had a lot of patience with him, but I don't any more. The other day my sister-in-law came over for a meal and Jim was whistling during dinner. I told him not to, but he kept right on. Finally he did quit. Later my sister-in-law said she would have knocked him right off the chair if he had done that when she told him to quit. But I've found it just doesn't do any good to get after him that way." I said, "You feel that it wouldn't do any good to use as strong measures as she said."
>
> She replied, "No. And his table manners, that's another thing that's terrible. He eats most of the time with his fingers, even though he has a nice sterling silver knife, fork, and spoon of his own. And maybe he will pick up a piece of bread and eat a piece, eat a hole right out of the middle of it, or stick his finger clear down through the whole stack of slices of bread. And wouldn't you think a boy of his age would know better than to do that?" And I said, "That makes you both feel pretty terrible, you and your husband, too."
>
> She replied, "Yes, of course. And sometimes he can be just as good as gold. For instance, yesterday he was good all day, and in the evening he told his daddy that he had been a good boy."

Note the fact that the counselor's sole aim is not to impede this flow of hostile and critical feeling. There is no attempt to persuade the mother that her boy is bright, essentially normal, pathetically eager for affection, though all of that is true. The counselor's whole function at this stage is to encourage free expression.

What this means in terms of a child is best shown by listening in on a portion of Jim's contact with a second psychologist during that same hour. This is Jim's first play-therapy contact. He indulges in some preliminary play and then makes a clay image which he identifies as his father. A great deal of dramatic play with this figure goes on, most of it centered around the struggle of Jim in getting his father out of bed and the father's resistance to this (the reverse of the home situation, as might be guessed). Jim played both parts in different voices and the following is from the phonographic recording, with *F.* and *J.* inserted to indicate which voice is being used.

F. "I want you to stay and help me." *J.* "I ain't goin' to. I want to make somethin' of it." *F.* "Oh, ya do, do you?" *J.* "Yeah, I want to make somethin' of it!" *F.* "O.K., come on, make somethin' of it!" *J.* "All right you! (*Striking him and knocking head off.*) He won't get back on in a hurry. Huh, I'll take a piece of ya off, that'll fix him. There. I'll make you weak, that'll fix him. Now don't you go to sleep on me again! (*Very short pause.*) Oh, say, what did you do, go to sleep? Hah, hah!" *F.* "I didn't go to sleep." *J.* "Well, you must have done *somethin'!* I'm gettin' tired of your impudence. Get up, get up, get up (*shouting*), come on, dad, get up."

A few moments later he pretends that someone is holding his father up in the air to torture him. His play follows:

J. "Let's git that guy for making his kid hold him all day. (*Short pause.*) They got 'im." *F.* "Hey, let me down." *J.* "Not till you promise to let your boy go for all day." *F.* "No, I won't." *J.* "All right, then, you're going to have to balance up high, see, and you are going to like it, and you'll do it." *F.* "Help, you guys, I'm fallin'. Help!!" (*Short pause as he drops clay and crushes it.*) *J.* "That's all, folks. (*Pause.*) He ain't there. He fell off a cliff in a car."

These two excerpts may make plain how deep and how violent are the feelings spontaneously expressed if the counselor does not block them. The counselor has more than a negative function in this process, perhaps best described as a separate aspect of therapy.

IV. The counselor accepts, recognizes, and clarifies these negative feelings. Here is a subtle point which seems to be very difficult for students to grasp. If the counselor is to accept these feelings, he must be prepared to respond, not to the intellectual content of what the person is saying, but to the feeling which underlies it. Sometimes the feelings are deep ambivalences, sometimes they are feelings of hostility, sometimes they are feelings of inadequacy. Whatever they are, the counselor endeavors, by what he says and by what he does, to create an atmosphere in which the client can come to recognize that he has these negative feelings and can accept them as a part of himself, instead of projecting them on others or hiding them behind defense mechanisms. Frequently the counselor verbally clarifies these feelings, not trying to interpret their cause or argue in regard to their utility—simply recognizing that they exist, and that he accepts them. Thus, such phrases as "You feel pretty bitter about this," "You want to correct this fault, but still you don't want to," "What you are saying sounds as though you feel pretty guilty," seem to crop out rather frequently in this type of therapy, and nearly always, if they are accurate portrayals of feeling, allow the individual to go forward in a freer fashion.

Sufficient examples of this type of help have already been given. In the excerpt from the case of Arthur (page 393), almost every statement of the counselor, with the exception of the long explanation, is an attempt to verbalize and clarify the feeling the student has been expressing about coming in. In the first fragment from the case of Mrs. L. (page 395), the counselor makes no attempt to combat the mother's implied fear of being treated "like white rats"; she merely recognizes and accepts that fear. In the second excerpt from this case (page 397), there are further examples of this aspect of therapy. The counselor accepts the mother's frantic feeling, her hopelessness, her annoyance, and her despair without criticism, without argument, without undue sympathy, accepting these feelings merely as a fact, and verbalizing them in somewhat clearer form than the mother has put them. The counselor is, it will be noted, alert to the feeling, not the content, of the mother's complaints. Thus, when the mother wails about Jim's table manners, there is no attempt to respond in terms of table etiquette, but in terms of the mother's obvious feeling about it. Note, however, that the counselor does not go beyond what the mother has already expressed. This is highly important, since real damage can be done by going too far and too fast, and verbalizing attitudes of which the client is not yet conscious. The aim is to accept completely and to recognize those feelings which the client has been able to express.

V. When the individual's negative feelings have been quite fully expressed, they are followed by the faint and tentative expressions of the positive impulses which make for growth. There is nothing which gives more surprise to the student who is learning this type of therapy for the first time than to find that this positive expression is one of the most certain and predictable aspects of the whole process. The more violent and deep the negative expressions (provided they are accepted and recognized), the more certain are the positive expressions of love, of social impulses, of fundamental self-respect, of desire to be mature.

This is plainly shown in the interview with Mrs. L. (page 397) to which reference has just been made. After all her antagonistic feeling has been fully accepted, it is inevitable that she should slowly work through to the positive feeling which comes out so suddenly in her statement, "And sometimes he can be just as good as gold."

With Jim, her son, it is a longer time before the positive feelings break through. For three contacts (spaced a week apart) he keeps up his aggressive play, torturing, beating, and killing father images and Satan images (sometimes called "Dad"). During the latter part of the third hour his dramatic play continues and becomes a dream, then not a dream.

> "No, it wasn't any dream. I meant it. Now that will be a warning to you (*beating the clay image*). Now that will teach you not to be funny with your kids! Then the guy wakes up and finds it is all a dream, and he says, 'It's about time I got out of these dreams.' " Then Jim ceased playing with the clay, and wandered around the room a bit. He took a newspaper clipping out of his pocket, showing a picture to the psychologist and saying, "Chamberlain looked like such a nice man, so I cut out his picture and carried it with me."

This was his first statement of positive feeling toward anyone. Following it there was never more than a mild expression of hostility, and the change in the therapeutic situation was roughly paralleled by the change in the home.

VI. The counselor accepts and recognizes the positive feelings which are expressed, in the same manner in which he has accepted and recognized the negative feeling. These positive feelings are not accepted with approbation or praise. Moralistic values do not enter into this type of therapy. The positive feelings are accepted as no more and no less a part of the personality than the negative feelings. It is this acceptance of both the mature and the immature impulses, of the aggressive and the social attitudes, of the guilt feelings and the positive expressions, which gives the individual an opportunity for the first time in his life to understand himself as he is. He has no need to be defensive about his negative feelings. He is given no opportunity to overvalue his positive feelings. And in this type of situation, insight and self-understanding come bubbling through spontaneously. Unless one has thus watched insight develop, it is difficult to believe that individuals can recognize themselves and their patterns so effectively.

VII. This insight, this understanding of the self and acceptance of the self, is the next important aspect of the whole process. It provides the basis on which the individual can go ahead to new levels of integration. One graduate student says with genuine feeling: "I'm really just a spoiled brat, but I do want to be normal. I wouldn't let anyone else say that of me, but it's true." A husband says: "I know now why I feel mean toward my wife when she's sick, even though I don't want to feel that way. It's because my mother predicted when I married her that I'd always be saddled with a sick wife." A student says, "I see now why I hated that prof—he criticized me just like my dad did." Mrs. L., the mother whose remarks have already been quoted, makes this surprising statement about her relationship with her boy, after she has worked through most of her hostile feelings and some positive feelings during a number of therapeutic contacts. This is the counselor's account:

> One of the things that she brought up was that he seems to want attention, but that the methods he uses get negative attention. After we had talked a little bit about that she said, "Perhaps what would do him most good would be for him to have some affection and love and consideration entirely apart from any correcting. Now, I guess that we've been so busy correcting him that we haven't had time to do anything else." Her expression of that indicated that she really felt that a change of program might do some good. And I said, "That is a very good observation on your part and nobody needs to tell you that that is what you feel really has happened." She said, "No, I know that's what has happened."

VIII. Intermingled with this process of insight—and it should again be emphasized that the steps outlined are not mutually exclusive, nor do they proceed in a rigid order—is a process of clarification of possible decisions, possible courses of action. Often this is infused with a somewhat hopeless attitude. Essentially the individual seems to be saying: "This is what I am, and I see that much more clearly. But how can I reorganize myself in any different fashion?" The counselor's function here is to help clarify the different choices which might be made, and to recognize the feeling of fear and the lack of courage to go ahead which the individual is experiencing. It is not his function to urge a certain course of action or to give advice.

IX. Then comes one of the fascinating aspects of such therapy, the initiation of minute, but highly significant, positive actions. An extremely withdrawn high-school boy, who has expressed his fear and hatred of others and has also come to recognize his deeply buried desire to have friends, spends a whole hour giving all the reasons why he would be too terrified to accept a social invitation he has had. He even leaves the office saying he will probably not go. He is not urged. It is sympathetically recognized that such action would take a great deal of courage, and that while he wishes he had such fortitude, he may not be able to take such a step. He goes to the party and is enormously helped in his self-confidence.

To give still another illustration from the record of Mrs. L., the following positive forward step followed immediately the outstanding statement of insight quoted above. Again this is the psychologist's account:

> I said, "Then giving him attention and affection when he is not demanding it in any way would perhaps do him a lot of good." Then she said, "Now you may not believe this, but as old as he is he still believes in Santa Claus, at least he did last year. Of course he may be trying to pull the wool over my eyes, but I don't think so. Last year he was away taller than any of the other kids who went up to talk to Santa in the stores. Now this year I've just *got* to tell him the truth. But I'm so afraid he will tell Marjorie. I was wondering if maybe I could tell him about it and it would be our secret between us. I would let him know that he is a big boy now and mustn't tell Marjorie. That it's *our* secret and he's a big boy and he can help me keep things. And also, if I can get her to go to bed early enough —she's such a little wiggle worm, but if I can get her to go to bed—perhaps he can help me with some of the Christmas things. And then on Christmas Eve—that's when we have our Christmas—I'll send the other children over to grandmother's house while we get ready and Jim can stay at the house and help me to get the things ready." The way she spoke it seemed that she felt it would be quite a pleasure to have Jim help. (She seemed really more enthusiastic about it than about anything so far.) So I said, "It will be quite a bit of pleasure, won't it, to think that you have a ten-year-old boy who can help with the Christmas work." With a sparkle in her eyes she replied that it would be fun for him to be able to help her, and that she felt it would do him a lot of good. I replied that I thought so too and that it would certainly be something to try.

One can only comment here that once insight is achieved the actions that are taken are likely to be admirably suited to the new insight. Thus, having achieved better emotional understanding of the relationship between herself and her boy, Mrs. L. translates that insight into action which shows how much she has gained. Her plan gives Jim her special affection in a very adroit way, helps him to be more mature, avoids making the younger sister jealous—in short, it shows that she can now carry out with genuine motivation the type of behavior which will solve her problem. If such behavior had been suggested to her after the diagnosis of the case, she would almost certainly have rejected the suggestion or carried it out in such a way as to cause it to be a failure. When it grows out of her own insightful drive to be a better, more mature mother, it will be successful.

X. The remaining steps need not hold us long. Once the individual has achieved considerable insight and has fearfully and tentatively attempted some positive actions, the remaining aspects are elements of further growth. There is, first of all, a development of further insight—more complete and accurate self-understanding as the individual gains courage to see more deeply into his own actions.

XI. There is increasingly integrated positive action on the part of the client. There is less fear about making choices, and more confidence in self-directed action. The counselor and client are now working together in a new sense. The personal relationship between them is at its strongest. Very often the client wants for the first time to know something of the clinician as a person and expresses a friendly and genuine interest which is very distinctive. Actions are brought into the discussion for consideration, but there is no longer the dependence and fear which were noticeable earlier. As an example, this excerpt is taken from the record of one of the closing interviews with a mother who has successfully gained insight:

> Mrs. J. says, "I don't know what you have done to us, to Patty and me, but everything's all right. I couldn't have wanted a nicer little girl, I should say for the past three weeks. Oh, yesterday she had sort of an off day. She didn't want to come when I'd call her, that is, not right away. She was a little bit down, but she wasn't ugly. I don't know if I can make you see what I mean, but there's a difference in her naughtiness. It's not as if she, well, is ugly, especially to me." C. responded, "I know what you mean, I think. It is that she doesn't refuse just to hurt you." Mrs. J. nodded and said, "That's it. It's a more natural sort of thing."

As is often true in this type of therapy, certain of the behavior symptoms remain, but the mother has a totally different feeling about them and about her ability to handle them.

XII. There is a feeling of decreasing need for help, and a recognition on the part of the client that the relationship must end. Often there are apologies for having taken so much of the counselor's time. The counselor helps to clarify this feeling as he has done before, by accepting and recognizing the fact that the client is now handling his situation with increased assurance and that he will not wish to continue the contacts much longer. As at the first, there is neither compulsion on the client to leave, nor attempt on the part of the counselor to hold the client.

During this aspect of therapy there are likely to be expressions of personal feeling. Often the client makes some such statement as "I shall miss coming; I have enjoyed these contacts so much." The counselor can reciprocate these feelings. There is no doubt that we do become emotionally involved, to a certain healthy extent, when personal growth takes place under our very eyes. A time limit is set for the contacts, and they are brought to a reluctant but healthy close. Sometimes, in the last contact, the client brings up a number of old problems or new ones, as though in a gesture to retain the relationship, but the atmosphere is very different from that in the first contacts, when those problems were real.

These seem to be the essential elements of the therapeutic process as it is being carried on in a variety of organizations and with a variety of problems —with parents and their children, even very young children; in situations demanding marital counseling; in situations of maladjustment and neurotic behavior among students; in situations of difficult vocational choice; in short, in most instances where the individual finds himself facing a serious problem of adjustment.

It will be readily recognized that the analysis given above might be differently organized. In a process with so many subtleties, any attempt to break it down into steps or elements contains much that is subjective and approximate, rather than objective and exact. Yet as a whole the therapy that has been described is an orderly, consistent process—even a predictable process in its major outlines. It is very different from an approach which is diffuse, opportunistic, stressing the notion that "every case is different." It is a process which has sufficient unity to provide suitable hypotheses for experimental tests. . . .

When Counseling Is Indicated

Having discussed the various elements and questions which the counselor should consider in his first contacts with the client, we may attempt to make them more definite and precise by casting them in the form of criteria. In the three sections which follow, an effort has been made to state the criteria which indicate that direct counseling and psychotherapy is, or is not, advisable as a focus of treatment in a particular case. It should be stressed that these are

---

When Counseling Is Indicated, from Rogers, *Counseling and Psychotherapy*, pp. 76–77.

tentative criteria, and that one of the reasons for stating them in as definite a manner as possible is to encourage their modification or verification through an experimental approach.

Conditions Indicating Counseling or Psychotherapy.   From the material given in the previous portions of this chapter, it would seem that direct counseling treatment of the individual, involving planned and continued contacts, is advisable provided all of the following conditions exist:

1. The individual is under a degree of tension arising from incompatible personal desires or from the conflict of social and environmental demands with individual needs. The tension and stress so created are greater than the stress involved in expressing his feelings about his problems.

2. The individual has some capacity to cope with life. He possesses adequate ability and stability to exercise some control over the elements of his situation. The circumstances with which he is faced are not so adverse or so unchangeable as to make it impossible for him to control or alter them.

3. There is an opportunity for the individual to express his conflicting tensions in planned contacts with the counselor.

4. He is able to express these tensions and conflicts either verbally or through other media. A conscious desire for help is advantageous, but not entirely necessary.

5. He is reasonably independent, either emotionally or spatially, of close family control.

6. He is reasonably free from excessive instabilities, particularly of an organic nature.

7. He possesses adequate intelligence for coping with his life situation, with an intelligence rating of dull-normal or above.

8. He is of suitable age—old enough to deal somewhat independently with life, young enough to retain some elasticity of adjustment. In terms of chronological age this might mean roughly from ten to sixty. . . .

The Therapeutic Relationship

There would seem to be at least four definite qualities which characterize the most helpful counseling atmosphere. We shall describe these in terms of the situation which the counselor endeavors to create.

First is a warmth and responsiveness on the part of the counselor which makes rapport possible, and which gradually develops into a deeper emotional

---

The Therapeutic Relationship, from Rogers, *Counseling and Psychotherapy,* pp. 87–90, 95–96, 113–14.

relationship. From the counselor's point of view, however, this is a definitely controlled relationship, an affectional bond with defined limits. It expresses itself in a genuine interest in the client and an acceptance of him as a person. The counselor frankly recognizes that he becomes to some extent emotionally involved in this relationship. He does not pretend to be superhuman and above the possibility of such involvement. . . .

The second quality of the counseling relationship is its permissiveness in regard to expression of feeling. By the counselor's acceptance of his statements, by the complete lack of any moralistic or judgmental attitude, by the understanding attitude which pervades the counseling interview, the client comes to recognize that all feelings and attitudes may be expressed. No attitude is too aggressive, no feeling too guilty or shameful, to bring into the relationship. Hatred for a father, feelings of conflict over sexual urges, remorse over past acts, dislike of coming for help, antagonism and resentment toward the therapist, all may be expressed. In this respect the therapeutic relationship differs markedly from the other relationships of ordinary life. It offers a place where the client may bring into the situation, as rapidly as his inhibitions will allow him, all the forbidden impulses and unspoken attitudes which complicate his life.

While there is this complete freedom to express feelings, there are definite limits to action in the therapeutic interview, helping to give it a structure which the client can use in gaining insight into himself. These therapeutic limits are a third and an important aspect of the counseling situation. Take, for example, the matter of time. The client is free to keep an appointment or to break it, to come on time or to come late, to use the hour in idle talk in order to avoid his real problems, or to use it constructively. There is the limitation, however, that he is not free to control the counselor and gain more time, no matter by what subterfuge. Not infrequently the counselee waits until the last moments of the counseling hour to bring up some matter of vital importance, thus implicitly demanding more time. The small child is more direct about it and announces that he will stay two hours instead of one. The counselor is most wise, however, who holds to the essential time limits that have been set. The client can make much more effective use of a well-structured situation. There are also other limits. With the small child in the play-therapy situation, there is complete freedom to express any type of feeling, but certain broad limits to action. He may smash clay figures, break dolls, shout, spill water, but he may not throw blocks through the window, nor carry his destructive activities out into the hall or into other offices. He may tear to pieces an image of the therapist, but he may not attack the therapist personally. In short, the most complete freedom is given for the person to express his feelings and to face himself. There is not, however, freedom to harm others by carrying all his impulses into action. It is often fascinating to see the child exploring all the aspects of the therapeutic situation, to find where the limits are. We make a great mistake if we suppose that the limits are a hindrance to therapy. They are, with both adult and child, one of the vital elements which make the therapeutic situation a microcosm in which the client can meet all the basic aspects which characterize life as a whole, face them openly, and adapt himself to them.

A fourth characteristic of the counseling relationship is its freedom from any type of pressure or coercion. The skillful counselor refrains from intruding his own wishes, his own reactions or biases, into the therapeutic situations. The hour is the client's hour, not the counselor's. Advice, suggestion, pressure to follow one course of action rather than another—these are out of place in therapy. As we shall see in our further discussion of the therapeutic process, this is not a mere negative restraint, a wooden refusal to influence the client. It is the positive ground for personality growth and development, for conscious choice, and for self-directed integration. It is in this type of soil that growth can take place. No doubt it is in this fourth characteristic that the therapeutic relationship differs most sharply from the usual relationships of everyday life in the family, the school, and the working world. ...

Limits to the Therapeutic Relationship

It may seem to some that the notion of setting certain definite limits to the therapeutic situation is an artificial or unnecessary procedure. Nothing could be farther from the truth. Every counseling situation has some sort of limit, as many an amateur therapist has discovered to his sorrow. He wishes to be of help to the child in a counseling situation, wishes to make plain his interest in the youngster. If the child asks for gifts, shall he give them to him? At what point shall he stop? If the child seeks physical affection, shall he give it? Indefinitely? If the child wishes the counselor to intercede for him with parent or school, shall he do it? How many times? One maladjusted youngster wished to observe the counselor at the toilet. Should it be permitted? In short, in any therapeutic situation, whether with child or adult, demands are made, desires expressed, toward which the counselor must take some attitude. The amateur or untrained counselor, bolstered by good intentions, anxious not to hurt the client, has a tendency to accede to these requests, to do almost anything which the client feels will help, until the demands upon time or affection or responsibility grow too great for the counselor to bear. Then his affection and desire to help turn to avoidance and dislike. He blames the client and rejects him. The net result is that the client feels that one more person has betrayed him, that one more person who claimed to wish to help has actually failed in time of stress. He may be definitely and sometimes permanently hurt by this bungled attempt at counseling.

Every counseling situation has, then, its limits. The only question is whether these limits are clearly defined, understood, and helpfully used, or whether the client, in a moment of great need, suddenly finds limits erected as barriers against him. It should be obvious that the former is the preferable procedure. . . .

The Uniqueness of the Therapeutic Relationship

The counseling relationship is one in which warmth of acceptance and absence of any coercion or personal pressure on the part of the counselor permits the maximum expression of feelings, attitudes, and problems by the counselee. The relationship is a well-structured one, with limits of time, of dependence, and of aggressive action which apply particularly to the client, and limits of responsibility and of affection which the counselor imposes on himself. In this unique experience of complete emotional freedom within a well-defined framework, the client is free to recognize and understand his impulses and patterns, positive and negative, as in no other relationship. . . .

The Superiority of Nondirective over Directive Therapy

The first basic difference in purpose centers around the question of who is to choose the client's goals. The directive group assumes that the counselor selects the desirable and the socially approved goal which the client is to attain, and then directs his efforts toward helping the subject to attain it. An unstated implication is that the counselor is superior to the client, since the latter is assumed to be incapable of accepting full responsibility for choosing his own goal. Nondirective counseling is based on the assumption that the client has the right to select his own life goals, even though these may be at variance with the goals that the counselor might choose for him. There is also the belief that if the individual has a modicum of insight into himself and his problems, he will be likely to make his choice wisely. . . .

The nondirective viewpoint places a high value on the right of every individual to be psychologically independent and to maintain his psychological integrity. The directive viewpoint places a high value upon social conformity and the right of the more able to direct the less able. These viewpoints have a significant relationship to social and political philosophy as well as to techniques of therapy.

As a consequence of this difference in value judgments, we find that the directive group tends to focus its efforts upon the problem which the client presents. If the problem is solved in a manner which can be approved by the

---

The Superiority of Nondirective over Directive Therapy, from Rogers, *Counseling and Psychotherapy,* pp. 126–28.

counselor, if the symptoms are removed, the counseling is considered success-ful. The nondirective group places its emphasis upon the client himself, not upon the problem. If the client achieves through the counseling experience sufficient insight to understand his relation to the reality situation, he can choose the method of adapting to reality which has the highest value for him. He will also be much more capable of coping with future problems that arise, because of his increased insight and his increased experience in independent solution of his problems.

It will be evident that the approach of the nondirective group applies to the overwhelming majority of clients who have the capacity to achieve reason-ably adequate solutions for their problems. Counseling, from this viewpoint, cannot be the only method for dealing with that small group—the psychotic, the defective, and perhaps some others—who have not the capacity to solve their own difficulties, even with help. Neither does it apply to children or adults who are faced with impossible demands from their environments. For the great bulk of maladjusted individuals, however—children, young people, or adults —some reasonable adjustment between the individual and his social environ-ment is possible. For this group a therapeutic approach which encourages growth and responsible maturity has much to offer. . . .

Releasing Expression

The Client the Best Guide.   The surest route to the issues which have importance, to the conflicts which are painful, to the areas with which counsel-ing may constructively deal, is to follow the pattern of the client's feeling as it is freely expressed. As a person talks about himself and his problems, particularly in the counseling relationship, where there is no necessity of defending himself, the real issues become more and more evident to the obser-vant listener. It is to some extent true that the same issues may be uncovered by patient questioning in all of the areas in which the client may be experienc-ing concern. As we shall see, however, this is likely to be a costly process in terms of time, and the difficulties which are uncovered may turn out to be difficulties of the counselor rather than of the client. Consequently, the best techniques for interviewing are those which encourage the client to express himself as freely as possible, with the counselor consciously endeavoring to refrain from any activity or any response which would guide the direction of the interview or the content brought forth.

Releasing Expression, from Rogers, *Counseling and Psychotherapy,* pp. 131–33, 138, 141, 143–44, 148–49, 152, 173.

The reasons for this approach are not far to seek. Few problems are solely intellectual in nature, and when they are intellectual only, counseling is not called for. If the student's only problem is that he cannot comprehend a binomial equation or does not understand how to score a psychological test or is puzzled as to the difference between a cretin and a mongoloid, additional information of an intellectual sort is obviously called for. Such problems are solved in the realm of the intellect. But problems of adjustment are rarely of this type. The intellectual factors in adjustment difficulties are often childishly simple. It is the unrecognized emotional factors which are usually basic. These emotional factors are most quickly understood by the client and the counselor if the counseling recognizes and follows the pattern of the client's feeling. Thus, a perplexed student tells of his difficulty in choosing between two vocations. He describes them in terms which give to each occupation scrupulously equal advantages, so far as his own future is concerned. They seem to be mathematically equivalent in value to him, and hence his dilemma appears insoluble. It is only as he talks further, revealing that his choice of college was nicely balanced between two institutions and solved only by the intervention of a friend, and that he frequently cannot choose which movie to attend, but follows the lead of a companion, that the true configuration of his problem begins to appear in terms of its emotional elements. The fact that indecision has a value to him comes gradually to light. The client is the only one who can guide us to such facts, and we may rest assured that the patterns which are sufficiently important to cause difficulties in life adjustment will crop up again and again in conversation about himself, provided that conversation is free from restriction and inhibition. . . .

Response to Feeling versus Response to Content. Probably the most difficult skill to acquire in counseling is the art of being alert to and responding to the feeling which is being expressed, rather than giving sole attention to the intellectual content. . . .

In other words, when the counselor is alertly responsive to the client's expressed attitudes and recognizes and clarifies these feelings, the interview is client-centered, and the material which comes forth is the material which is emotionally relevant to the client's problem. On the other hand, when the counselor responds to the intellectual content, the direction of the interview follows the pattern of the counselor's interest, and only very slowly and with much winnowing and sifting do the essential problems of the client become evident. At its worst, this process leads to a blocking of the client's expression of his own problems and follows only the pattern set by the counselor. . . .

When the counselor responds on an intellectual basis to the ideas which the client expresses, he diverts expression into intellectual channels of his own choosing, he blocks the expression of emotionalized attitudes, and he tends wastefully to define and solve the problems in his own terms, which are often not the true terms for the client. On the other hand, when the counselor continually keeps himself alert not only to the content which is being stated, but to the feelings which are being expressed, and responds primarily in terms of the latter element, it gives the client the satisfaction of feeling deeply understood, it enables him to express further feeling, and it leads most efficiently and most directly to the emotional roots of his adjustment problem. ...

Responding to Negative Feelings. As has already been mentioned, although the pattern of the client's feeling constitutes the most efficient road to a mutual understanding on the part of client and counselor of the basic problems to be dealt with, it is by no means an easy road to perceive. The counselor needs to develop a fresh mind-set, different from his mind-set in reading a book, carrying on a social conversation, or hearing a lecture. He needs to learn to pay attention to the feeling tone of what is being said, as well as to its superficial content. In following this aim there are several problems which occur with sufficient frequency to deserve special comment.

It is generally not too difficult for the counselor to recognize and help to bring to conscious expression hostile attitudes which are directed toward others—toward employers, parents, and teachers, or toward rivals and enemies. When the negative attitudes being expressed are directed toward the client himself, or toward the counselor, then too often we find ourselves springing to the defense of the client out of our sympathy for him, or rising to our own defense as counselors. It should be recognized that in these areas, also, the counselor is most effective when he aids in bringing the feeling consciously into the picture without taking sides. Here it is especially important that he should recognize his function as that of a mirror which shows the client his real self and enables him, aided by this new perception, to reorganize himself.

When the client is thoroughly discouraged, when he feels that he is "no good," when his fears are overwhelming, when he hints that he has thought of suicide, when he pictures himself as completely unstable, completely dependent, entirely inadequate, unworthy of love—in short, when he is expressing any type of negative feeling toward himself, the natural tendency on the part of the inexperienced counselor is to try to convince him that he is exaggerating the situation. This is probably true, and the counselor's argument is intellectually logical, but it is not therapeutic. The client feels worthless, no matter how many good qualities may be objectively pointed out to him. He knows that he has contemplated suicide, no matter how many reasons may be pointed out for not doing so. He knows that he has worried about going insane, no matter how unlikely that possibility may be made to appear. The counselor is giving more genuine help if he assists the client to face these feelings openly, recognize them for what they are, and admit that he has them. Then, if he no longer has to prove that he is worthless or abnormal, he can, and does, consider himself more comfortably and find in himself more positive qualities. . . .

It need not disturb the counselor that feelings which are expressed may be in direct contradiction to one another. Often it is these contradictory feelings that constitute the most significant ambivalences which are serving as sources of conflict. Thus, a student talks in the bitterest of terms in regard to his father. He dislikes his father. He has always been ashamed of his father. It was his father's unreasonably harsh and contemptuous criticisms which were responsible for the attitudes of inadequacy which have crippled his life. Yet after several interviews of this type, he slowly recognizes that he admired his father's scientific interests, admired his father's disregard for convention, looked up to his father for his independence of the maternal control which the boy was experiencing. These attitudes are contradictory, but not in the sense that one is true and one false. They are both true feelings, the hostile attitude conscious, the attitude of admiration never before having been recognized openly by the student. As they are both brought openly into the counseling situation, the client is able to reach a much more realistic emotional evaluation of his relationship to his father, and finds himself free of conflicts which previously he has been unable to understand.

If, as feelings are expressed, the counselor refrains from a too sympathetic identification with and approval of the attitude, and likewise from a critical and disapproving response, the client will be free to bring out other and contradictory feelings which may be hampering him in any clear-cut approach to his problems of adjustment.

Attitudes Toward the Counselor.   In any counseling which is more than superficial, the client is likely to indicate, by one mode of expression or another, either positive or negative feelings toward the counselor and the counseling situation. The counselor will be likely to handle these more effectively if he can genuinely recognize and accept the fact that these expressions are directed not toward him as a person, but toward the counseling experience, in terms of the pain or satisfaction which it is at that moment giving to the client.

With most of the positive attitudes expressed, there is probably little that the counselor needs to do beyond accepting them as a casual part of the situation. . . .

The Recognition of Unexpressed Feeling.   The point of view has been stressed that the counselor must be alert indeed to be responsive to the client's feeling. It should also be emphasized that only these feelings should be verbally recognized which have been expressed. Often the client has attitudes which are implied in what he says, or which the counselor through shrewd observation judges him to have. Recognition of such attitudes which have not yet appeared in the client's conversation may, if the attitudes are not too deeply repressed, hasten the progress of therapy. If, however, they are repressed attitudes, their recognition by the counselor may seem to be very much of a threat to the client, may create resentment and resistance, and in some instances may break off the counseling contacts. . . .

The Free Release of Feeling

In effective counseling and psychotherapy one of the major purposes of the counselor is to help the client to express freely the emotionalized attitudes which are basic to his adjustment problems and conflicts. In carrying out this purpose, the counselor adopts various methods which enable the client to release his feelings without inhibition. Primarily the counselor endeavors to respond to, and verbally recognize, the feeling content, rather than the intellectual content, of the client's expression. This principle holds, no matter what the type of emotionalized attitude—negative attitudes of hostility, discouragement, and fear, positive attitudes of affection and courage and self-confidence, or ambivalent and contradictory attitudes. This approach is sound whether the client's feelings are directed toward himself, toward others, or toward the counselor and the counseling situation. In each case, the counselor aims to recognize and respond to the feeling expressed, openly accepting it as an element in the problem and in the counseling relationship. He avoids the verbal recognition of repressed attitudes which the client has not yet been able to express.

In this process the client finds emotional release from feelings heretofore repressed, increasing awareness of the basic elements in his own situation, and an increased ability to recognize his own feelings openly and without fear. He also finds his situation clarified by this process of exploration and begins to see relationships between his various reactions. This is the beginning of and the basis for insight, which we shall now consider. . . .

The Achievement of Insight

The free release of the client's feelings and emotionalized attitudes in an accepting type of counseling relationship leads inevitably to insight. This development of insight comes for the most part spontaneously, though cautious and intelligent use of interpretive techniques can increase the scope and the clarity of such self-understanding.

The Achievement of Insight, from Rogers, *Counseling and Psychotherapy.* p. 216.

The client's insight tends to develop gradually, and proceeds in general from less to more significant understandings. It involves the new perception of relationships previously unrecognized, a willingness to accept all aspects of the self, and a choice of goals, now clearly perceived for the first time.

Following these new perceptions of self, and this new choice of goals, come self-initiated actions which move toward achieving the new goals. These steps are of the most significant sort for growth, though they may relate only to minor issues. They create new confidence and independence in the client, and thus reinforce the new orientation which has come about through increased insight. . . .

The Closing Phases of Therapy

As the client develops in his insight and self-understanding and selects new goals around which he reorients his life, counseling enters its closing phase, which has certain distinctive characteristics. The client gains in self-confidence as he gains fresh insight and as he takes an increased number of positive actions directed toward his goal. In his confidence he desires to be finished with counseling, yet at the same time he fears to leave its support. Recognition by the counselor of this ambivalence enables the client to see clearly the choice ahead of him and to develop the assurance that he is capable of handling his problems independently. The counselor aids by helping the client to feel entirely free to end the relationship as soon as he is ready. Ordinarily the counseling ends with a sense of loss on both sides, but with a mutual recognition that independence is another healthy step toward growth. Even when counseling has not been successful, it may often be closed in a constructive fashion.

The length of the therapeutic process is as much dependent on the skill of the counselor in keeping the contacts client-centered as it is upon the severity of the maladjustment or upon any other factor.

Not infrequently it is plain in these closing contacts that the client has clearly perceived the unusual structure of the counseling situation and realizes how he has used it for his own growth. The spontaneous statements of clients lend weight to the thesis of this article, that a client-centered counseling relationship releases dynamic forces in a manner achieved by no other relationship. . . .

The Closing Phases of Therapy, from Rogers, *Counseling and Psychotherapy,* pp. 237–38.

Personality Theory

In endeavoring to order our perceptions of the individual as he appears in therapy, a theory of the development of personality, and of the dynamics of behavior, has been constructed. It may be well to repeat the warning previously given, and to note that the initial propositions of this theory are those which are furthest from the matrix of our experience and hence are most suspect. As one reads on, the propositions become steadily closer to the experience of therapy. . . .

A. Postulated Characteristics of the Human Infant

It is postulated that the individual, during the period of infancy, has at least these attributes.
   1. He perceives his *experience* as reality. His *experience* is his reality.
      a. As a consequence he has greater potential *awareness* of what reality is for him than does anyone else, since no one else can completely assume his *internal frame of reference.*
   2. He has an inherent tendency toward *actualizing* his organism.
   3. He interacts with his reality in terms of his basic *actualizing* tendency. Thus his behavior is the goal-directed attempt of the organism to satisfy the experienced needs for *actualization* in the reality as *perceived.*
   4. In this interaction he behaves as an organized whole, as a gestalt.
   5. He engages in an *organismic valuing process,* valuing *experience* with reference to the *actualizing tendency* as a criterion. *Experiences* which are *perceived* as maintaining or enhancing the organism are valued positively. Those which are *perceived* as negating such maintenance or enhancement are valued negatively.
   6. He behaves with adience toward positively valued *experiences* and with avoidance toward those negatively valued.

   Comment.   In this view as formally stated, the human infant is seen as having an inherent motivational system (which he shares in common with all living things) and a regulatory system (the valuing process) which by its "feedback" keeps the organism "on the beam" of satisfying his motivational needs. He lives in an environment which, for theoretical purposes, may be said to exist only in him, or to be of his own creation.
   This last point seems difficult for some people to comprehend. It is the perception of the environment which constitutes the environment, regardless as to how this relates to some "real" reality which we may philosophically

Personality Theory, from Rogers, "A Theory of Therapy, Personality, and Interpersonal Relationships," pp. 221–29.

postulate. The infant may be picked up by a friendly, affectionate person. If his perception of the situation is that this is a strange and frightening experience, it is this perception, not the "reality" or the "stimulus" which will regulate his behavior. To be sure, the relationship with the environment is a transactional one, and if his continuing experience contradicts his initial perception, then in time his perception will change. But the effective reality which influences behavior is at all times the perceived reality. We can operate theoretically from this base without having to resolve the difficult question of what "really" constitutes reality.

Another comment which may be in order is that no attempt has been made to supply a complete catalogue of the equipment with which the infant faces the world. Whether he possesses instincts, or an innate sucking reflex, or an innate need for affection, are interesting questions to pursue, but the answers seem peripheral rather than essential to a theory of personality.

B. The Development of the Self

1. In line with the tendency toward differentiation which is a part of the *actualizing tendency,* a portion of the individual's *experience* becomes differentiated and *symbolized* in an *awareness* of being, *awareness* of functioning. Such awareness may be described as *self-experience.*

2. This representation in *awareness* of being and functioning becomes elaborated, through interaction with the environment, particularly the environment composed of significant others, into a *concept of self,* a perceptual object in his *experiential field.*

Comment. These are the logical first steps in the development of the self. It is by no means the way the construct developed in our own thinking, as has been indicated in the section of definitions.

C. The Need for Positive Regard

1. As the awareness of self emerges, the individual develops a *need for positive regard.* This need is universal in human beings, and, in the individual, is pervasive and persistent. Whether it is an inherent or learned need is irrelevant to the theory. Standal . . . who formulated the concept, regards it as the latter.

    a. The satisfaction of this need is necessarily based upon inferences regarding the experiential field of another.

        (1) Consequently it is often ambiguous.

    b. It is associated with a very wide range of the individual's *experiences.*

    c. It is reciprocal, in that when an individual discriminates himself as satisfying another's need for *positive regard,* he necessarily experiences satisfaction of his own need for *positive regard.*

       (1) Hence it is rewarding both to satisfy this need in another, and to experience the satisfaction of one's own need by another.

    d. It is potent, in that the *positive regard* of any social other is communicated to the total *regard complex* which the individual associates with that social other.

       (1) Consequently the expression of positive regard by a significant social other can become more compelling than the *organismic valuing process,* and the individual becomes more adient to the *positive regard* of such others than toward *experiences* which are of positive value in *actualizing* the organism.

D. The Development of the Need for Self-Regard

1. The positive regard satisfactions or frustrations associated with any particular *self-experience* or group of *self-experiences* come to be *experienced* by the individual independently of *positive regard* transactions with social others. *Positive regard experienced* in this fashion is termed *self-regard.*

2. A *need for self-regard* develops as a learned need developing out of the association of *self-experiences* with the satisfaction or frustration of the *need for positive regard.*

3. The individual thus comes to *experience positive regard* or loss of *positive regard* independently of transactions with any social other. He becomes in a sense his own significant social other.

4. Like *positive regard, self-regard,* which is *experienced* in relation to any particular *self-experience* or group of *self-experiences,* is communicated to the total *self-regard complex.*

E. The Development of Conditions of Worth

1. When *self-experiences* of the individual are discriminated by significant others as being more or less worthy of *positive regard,* then *self-regard* becomes similarly selective.

2. When a *self-experience* is avoided (or sought) solely because it is less (or more) worthy of *self-regard,* the individual is said to have acquired a *condition of worth.*

3. If an individual should *experience* only *unconditional positive regard,* then no *conditions of worth* would develop, *self-regard* would be unconditional, the needs for *positive regard* and *self-regard* would never be at variance with *organismic evaluation,* and the individual would continue to be *psychologically adjusted,* and would be fully functioning. This chain of events is hypo-

thetically possible, and hence important theoretically, though it does not appear to occur in actuality.

Comment. This is an important sequence in personality development, stated more fully by Standal. ... It may help to restate the sequence in informal, illustrative, and much less exact terms.

The infant learns to need love. Love is very satisfying, but to know whether he is receiving it or not he must observe his mother's face, gestures, and other ambiguous signs. He develops a total gestalt as to the way he is regarded by his mother, and each new experience of love or rejection tends to alter the whole gestalt. Consequently each behavior on his mother's part such as a specific disapproval of a specific behavior tends to be experienced as disapproval in general. So important is this to the infant that he comes to be guided in his behavior not by the degree to which an experience maintains or enhances the organism, but by the likelihood of receiving maternal love.

Soon he learns to view himself in much the same way, liking or disliking himself as a total configuration. He tends, quite independently of his mother or others, to view himself and his behavior in the same way they have. This means that some behaviors are regarded positively which are not actually experienced organismically as satisfying. Other behaviors are regarded negatively which are not actually experienced as unsatisfying. It is when he behaves in accordance with these introjected values that he may be said to have acquired conditions of worth. He cannot regard himself positively, as having worth, unless he lives in terms of these conditions. He now reacts with adience or avoidance toward certain behaviors solely because of these introjected conditions of self-regard, quite without reference to the organismic consequences of these behaviors. This is what is meant by living in terms of introjected values ... or conditions of worth.

It is not theoretically necessary that such a sequence develop. If the infant always felt prized, if his own feelings were always accepted even though some behaviors were inhibited, then no conditions of worth would develop. This could at least theoretically be achieved if the parental attitude was genuinely of this sort: "I can understand how satisfying it feels to you to hit your baby brother (or to defecate when and where you please, or to destroy things) and I love you and am quite willing for you to have those feelings. But I am quite willing for me to have my feelings, too, and I feel very distressed when your brother is hurt (or annoyed or sad at other behaviors), and so I do not let you hit him. Both your feelings and my feelings are important, and each of us can freely have his own." If the child were thus able to retain his own organismic evaluation of each experience, then his life would become a balancing of these satisfactions. Schematically he might feel, "I enjoy hitting baby brother. It feels good. I do not enjoy mother's distress. That feels dissatisfying to me. I enjoy pleasing her." Thus his behavior would sometimes involve the satisfaction of hitting his brother, sometimes the satisfaction of pleasing mother. But he would never have to disown the feelings of satisfaction or dissatisfaction which he experienced in this differential way.

F. The Development of Incongruence Between Self and Experience

1. Because of the need for *self-regard,* the individual *perceives* his *experience* selectively, in terms of the *conditions of worth* which have come to exist in him.
   a. Experiences which are in accord with his *conditions of worth* are *perceived* and *symbolized* accurately in *awareness.*
   b. Experiences which run contrary to the *conditions of worth* are *perceived* selectively and distortedly as if in accord with the *conditions of worth,* or are in part or whole, *denied to awareness.*
2. Consequently some experiences now occur in the organism which are not recognized as *self-experiences,* are not accurately *symbolized,* and are not organized into the *self-structure* in *accurately symbolized* form.
3. Thus from the time of the first selective *perception* in terms of *conditions of worth,* the states of *incongruence between self and experience,* of *psychological maladjustment* and of *vulnerability,* exist to some degree.

Comment.   It is thus because of the distorted perceptions arising from the conditions of worth that the individual departs from the integration which characterizes his infant state. From this point on his concept of self includes distorted perceptions which do not accurately represent his experience, and his experience includes elements which are not included in the picture he has of himself. Thus he can no longer live as a unified whole person, but various part functions now become characteristic. Certain experiences tend to threaten the self. To maintain the self-structure defensive reactions are necessary. Behavior is regulated at times by the self and at times by those aspects of the organism's experience which are not included in the self. The personality is henceforth divided, with the tensions and inadequate functioning which accompany such lack of unity.

This, as we see it, is the basic estrangement in man. He has not been true to himself, to his own natural organismic valuing of experience, but for the sake of preserving the positive regard of others has now come to falsify some of the values he experiences and to perceive them only in terms based upon their value to others. Yet this has not been a conscious choice, but a natural —and tragic—development in infancy. The path of development toward psychological maturity, the path of therapy, is the undoing of this estrangement in man's functioning, the dissolving of conditions of worth, the achievement of a self which is congruent with experience, and the restoration of a unified organismic valuing process as the regulator of behavior.

G. The Development of Discrepancies in Behavior

1. As a consequence of the incongruence between self and experience described in F, a similar incongruence arises in the behavior of the individual.
   a. Some behaviors are consistent with the *self-concept* and maintain and actualize and enhance it.
      (1) Such behaviors are *accurately symbolized* in *awareness.*
   b. Some behaviors maintain, enhance, and actualize those aspects of the experience of the organism which are not assimilated into the *self-structure.*
      (1) These behaviors are either unrecognized as *self-experiences* or *perceived* in distorted or selective fashion in such a way as to be *congruent* with the *self.*

H. The Experience of Threat and the Process of Defense

1. As the organism continues to *experience,* an *experience* which is incongruent with the self-structure (and its incorporated *conditions of worth*) is *subceived* as *threatening.*
2. The essential nature of the *threat* is that if the *experience* were *accurately symbolized* in *awareness,* the *self-concept* would no longer be a consistent gestalt, the *conditions of worth* would be violated, and the *need for self-regard* would be frustrated. A state of *anxiety* would exist.
3. The process of *defense* is the reaction which prevents these events from occurring.
   a. This process consists of the selective *perception* or *distortion* of the *experience* and/or the *denial to awareness* of the *experience* or some portion thereof, thus keeping the total *perception* of the *experience* consistent with the individual's *self-structure,* and consistent with his *conditions of worth.*
4. The general consequences of the process of *defense,* aside from its preservation of the above consistencies, are a rigidity of *perception,* due to the necessity of distorting *perceptions,* an inaccurate *perception* of reality, due to distortion and omission of data, and *intensionality.*

Comment. Section G describes the psychological basis for what are usually thought of as neurotic behaviors, and section H describes the mechanisms of these behaviors. From our point of view it appears more fundamental to think of defensive behaviors (described in these two sections) and disorganized behaviors (described below). Thus the defensive behaviors include not only the behaviors customarily regarded as neurotic—rationalization, compensation, fantasy, projection, compulsions, phobias, and the like—but also some of the behaviors customarily regarded as psychotic, notably paranoid behaviors and perhaps catatonic states. The disorganized category includes many of the "irrational" and "acute" psychotic behaviors, as will be explained below. This seems to be a more fundamental classification than those usually employed, and perhaps more fruitful in considering treatment. It also avoids any concept of neurosis and psychosis as entities in themselves, which we believe has been an unfortunate and misleading conception.

Let us consider for a moment the general range of the defensive behaviors from the simplest variety, common to all of us, to the more extreme and crippling varieties. Take first of all, rationalization. ("I didn't really make that mistake. It was this way. . . .") Such excuses involve a perception of behavior distorted in such a way as to make it congruent with our concept of self (as a person who doesn't make mistakes). Fantasy is another example. ("I am a beautiful princess, and all the men adore me.") Because the actual experience is threatening to the concept of self (as an adequate person, in this example), this experience is denied, and a new symbolic world is created which enhances the self but completely avoids any recognition of the actual experience. Where the incongruent experience is a strong need, the organism actualizes itself by finding a way of expressing this need, but it is perceived in a way which is consistent with the self. Thus an individual whose self-concept involves no "bad" sexual thoughts may feel or express the thought, "I am pure, but you are trying to make me think filthy thoughts." This would be thought of as projection or as a paranoid idea. It involves the expression of the organism's need for sexual satisfactions, but it is expressed in such a fashion that this need may be denied to awareness and the behavior perceived as consistent with the self. Such examples could be continued, but perhaps the point is clear that the incongruence between self and experience is handled by the distorted perception of experience or behavior, or by the denial of experience in awareness (behavior is rarely denied, though this is possible), or by some combination of distortion and denial.

I. The Process of Breakdown and Disorganization

Up to this point the theory of personality which has been formulated applies to every individual in a lesser or greater degree. In this and the following section certain processes are described which occur only when certain specified conditions are present.

1. If the individual has a large or significant degree of *incongruence between self and experience* and if a significant experience demonstrating *incongruence* occurs suddenly, or with a high degree of obviousness, then the organism's process of *defense* is unable to operate successfully.

2. As a result *anxiety* is *experienced* as the *incongruence* is subceived. The degree of *anxiety* is dependent upon the extent of the *self-structure* which is *threatened*.

3. The process of *defense* being unsuccessful, the *experience* is *accurately symbolized* in *awareness,* and the gestalt of the *self-structure* is broken by this *experience* of the *incongruence* in *awareness.* A state of disorganization results.

4. In such a state of disorganization the organism behaves at times in ways which are openly consistent with experiences which have hitherto been distorted or denied to awareness. At other times the self may temporarily regain regnancy, and the organism may behave in ways consistent with it. Thus in such a state of disorganization, the tension between the concept of self (with its included distorted perceptions) and the experiences which are not accurately symbolized or included in the concept of self, is expressed in a confused regnancy, first one and then the other supplying the "feedback" by which the organism regulates behavior.

Comment. This section, as will be evident from its less exact formulation, is new, tentative, and needs much more consideration. Its meaning can be illuminated by various examples.

Statements 1 and 2 above may be illustrated by anxiety-producing experiences in therapy, or by acute psychotic breakdowns. In the freedom of therapy, as the individual expresses more and more of himself, he finds himself on the verge of voicing a feeling which is obviously and undeniably true, but which is flatly contradictory to the conception of himself which he has held. Anxiety results, and if the situation is appropriate (as described under J) this anxiety is moderate, and the result is constructive. But if, through overzealous and effective interpretation by the therapist, or through some other means, the individual is brought face to face with more of his denied experiences than he can handle, disorganization ensues and a psychotic break occurs, as described in statement 3. We have known this to happen when an individual has sought "therapy" from several different sources simultaneously. It has also been illustrated by some of the early experience with sodium pentathol therapy. Under the drug the individual revealed many of the experiences which hitherto he had denied to himself and which accounted for the incomprehensible elements in his behavior. Unwisely faced with the material in his normal state he could not deny its authenticity, his defensive processes could not deny or distort the experience, and hence the self-structure was broken, and a psychotic break occurred. . . .

J. The Process of Reintegration

. . . A process of reintegration is possible, a process which moves in the direction of increasing the *congruence* between *self* and *experience.* This may be described as follows:

1. In order for the process of *defense* to be reversed—for a customarily *threatening experience* to be *accurately symbolized* in *awareness* and assimilated into the *self-structure,* certain conditions must exist.

    a. There must be a decrease in the *conditions of worth.*

    b. There must be an increase in *unconditional self-regard.*

2. The communicated *unconditional positive regard* of a significant other is one way of achieving these conditions.

    a. In order for the *unconditional positive regard* to be communicated, it must exist in a context of *empathic* understanding.

    b. When the individual *perceives* such *unconditional positive regard,* existing *conditions of worth* are weakened or dissolved.

    c. Another consequence is the increase in his own *unconditional positive self-regard.*

    d. Conditions 2a and 2b above thus being met, *threat* is reduced, the process of *defense is reversed,* and *experiences* customarily *threatening* are *accurately symbolized* and integrated into the *self-concept.*

3. The consequences of 1 and 2 above are that the individual is less likely to encounter *threatening experiences,* the process of *defense* is less frequent and its consequences reduced, *self* and *experience* are more *congruent, self-regard* is increased, *positive regard* for others is increased, *psychological adjustment* is increased, the *organismic valuing process* becomes increasingly the basis of regulating behavior, the individual becomes nearly fully functioning.

19

EXISTENTIAL PSYCHOTHERAPY AND DASEIN ANALYSIS

Rollo May

Ludwig Binswanger

Henri F. Ellenberger

Rollo May, born in Ada, Ohio, on April 21, 1909, was educated at Oberlin College (A.B., 1930), Union Theological Seminary (B.D., 1939), and Columbia University (Ph.D., 1949). In 1930 he began his teaching career at the American College in Saloníki, Greece, where he taught for three years. From 1934 to 1936 he was counselor to male students at Michigan State College, and held a similar position at the College of the City of New York during the 1943–44 school season. While in private practice as a psychoanalyst he served on a number of faculties: the William Alanson White Institute of Psychiatry, Psychology, and Psychoanalysis (from 1948 to 1955 and again in 1958 to the present); the New School of Social Research (1955 to 1960); New York University (1960 to the present); Harvard University (summer of 1964); and Princeton University (1966 to 1967). He is also a fellow of Branford College, Yale University.

May's professional associations include past president of the New York State Psychological Association, cochairman of the Conference on Psychotherapy and Counseling of the New York Academy of Sciences, member of the board of trustees of the American Foundation for Mental Health, member of the board of directors of the Manhattan Society for Mental Health, fellow of the American Psychological Association, president of the William Alanson White Psychoanalytic Society, and fellow of the National Council of Religion in Higher Education. In addition to many scientific papers, his publications include the following books in the field of psychology: *The Art of Counseling* (1939), *The Meaning of Anxiety* (1950), *Man's Search for Himself* (1953), *Psychology and the Human Dilemma* (1967), *Love and Will* (1967), *Existence: A New Dimension in Psychiatry and Psychology* (1958) (of which he was coeditor), *Power and Innocence* (1972), and *The Courage to Create* (1975).

Ludwig Binswanger, a Swiss psychiatrist born in Kreuzlingen on April 13, 1881, was the son of a psychiatrist and the grandson of the founder of Sanatorium Bellevue. After a classical gymnasium education at Konstanz and Shaffhouse, he attended the universities of Lausanne, Heidelberg, and Zurich from 1900 to 1906. He began his career as a medical assistant at Burghölzli (Zurich) in 1906. He then spent a year under Eugen Bleuler at the Psychiatric University Clinic in Jena, and in 1910 left for a permanent post as medical superintendent at Sanatorium Bellevue at Kreuzlingen. Binswanger, the leading force in existential psychiatry, died in 1966.

Among Binswanger's many honors are doctorates from the University of Basel (1941) and the University of Freiburg (1955); honorary memberships in *Verein f. Medizinische Psychologie* (1950), *Österreichische Allg. Arztegesellschaft f. Psychotherapie* (1951), *Société med.-psychologie* (1952), and *Ges. deutscher Neurologen und Psychiater* (1953).

His many books in German are being translated into English. His first collection of important writings published in English is *Being-in-the-World* (1963). A second is *Ideas of the Dream from the Greeks to the Present.* Another rich source of his thought is found in *Existence: A New Dimension in Psychiatry and Psychology* (1958), the book coedited by May, Angel, and Ellenberger. His articles are also appearing in translation, two of which offer fine insights into his Dasein analysis: "Existential Analysis and Psychotherapy," in *Progress in Psychotherapy,* ed. F. Fromm-Reichmann and J. L. Moreno (1956); and "Existential Analysis, Psychiatry, Schizophrenia" (*Journal of Existential Psychiatry,* 1960).

The Swiss Protestant, Henri Frédéric Ellenberger, born on November 6, 1905, in North Rhodesia, South Africa, was educated at the University of Paris, where he received his doctorate in medicine in 1934. For a number of years he served at hospitals in Paris, including the Ste. Anne Psychiatric Hospital. His war years were spent as a neuropsychiatrist at the Swiss Military Hospital. After teaching for a school season at the Volks Universität of Zurich during 1951–52, he came to the Menninger School of Psychiatry, Kansas, in 1953, as a professor of psychiatry, a tenure which lasted until 1958. The following year he left for Canada to accept a position as assistant professor in the department of psychiatry at McGill University, a post he relinquished in 1965 to assume his present appointment as a professor on the faculty of social sciences at the University of Montreal. An international figure, Ellenberger is a member of a number of professional societies throughout North America and Europe, and since 1964 he has held the title of consultant for the Institute Philippe Pinel. Ellenberger published *Discovery of the Unconscious* in 1970.

Existential psychotherapy, emanating from the philosophy of Heidegger and Kierkegaard, views humanity as *Dasein,* a special quality of existence peculiar to humans alone. The analysis or structure of Dasein reveals humans to be existential beings, constantly in a state of process, i.e., of development of countless possibilities. Through freedom and choice, individuals can choose themselves, that is, make their personalities; accordingly, people are responsible for the personality that they have decided to become. This exercise of freedom and choice renders a person authentic, while those who follow the crowd lose selfhood, thus becoming anonymities, impersonal beings. Fatalism is repudiated inasmuch as one can and does transcend oneself. Through choice, and the awareness of accepting responsibility for one's decisions, a person transcends himself, chooses the personality that he wants to become, and gains authentic selfhood.

The psychotherapist's task in existential therapy is not that of making choices for the patients, but of seeing that the patients make their own responsible choices and make themselves the beings they decide to become by transcending themselves. The individual who has lost life's meaning is a victim of an existential neurosis. Therapy's aim is that the patient experience existence as real. The psychotherapeutic "encounter" of patient and therapist aids in bringing about a decisive inner experience for the patient to gain a new *Weltanschauung* on life, and to reconstruct the personality. The moment of decision, of *kairos,* is the critical turning point. The therapist must not treat the patient as a thing, a mere object, but become immersed in the therapist-patient encounter as an "I-thou" relationship, as an interpersonal experience that both undergo, a genuine human "presence." Since no two patients undergo the same malady, each patient must be treated as an individually unique case. It is important to understand the subjective world of each patient.

Existential Analysis

The reconstruction of the inner world of the patient may be an aim in itself for the phenomenologist, but if he is an existential analyst, it is a part of a broader task to which we are coming now. It is necessary at this point, however, to clarify the distinction between *existentialist philosophy, existentialist psychotherapy,* and Binswanger's *existential analysis,* since there is so much confusion concerning these three areas.

Existential Philosophy

Existentialism is the philosophical trend of thought which takes as its focus of interest the consideration of man's most immediate experience, his own existence. Existentialist thinking has been implicit from time immemorial in many religions and philosophical systems. Kierkegaard was the first to make explicit its basic assumptions. In our time these concepts have been elabo-

Existential Analysis, from Henri F. Ellenberger, "A Clinical Introduction to Psychiatric Phenomenology and Existential Analysis," in *Existence: A New Dimension in Psychiatry and Psychology,* ed. Rollo May, Ernest Angel, and Henri F. Ellenberger (New York: Basic Books, 1958), pp. 117–22.

rated by Jaspers, Heidegger, Sartre, and the religious existentialists (Marcel, Berdyaev, Tillich). The main influence upon psychiatry came from Heidegger.

In Heidegger's thought we can distinguish three main sources:

1. Starting point was the old problem of being versus existence. Ancient philosophers contrasted "essence" and "existence." The abstract concept and knowledge of a triangle reveals to us the "essence" of the triangle; an actually drawn triangle demonstrates its "existence." Plato's essentialist philosophy contended that everything that exists is the reflection of an essence (or "idea"). Modern philosophers, notably Dilthey, focused the problem on the fact that the concept of existence must be very different for an inanimate object and for human beings. Heidegger's philosophy is based on the contrast between existence as *Vorhandensein* (characteristic of things) and as *Dasein* (for human beings). The untranslatable word *Dasein* designates the mode of existence peculiar to human beings. Thus Heidegger's philosophy is a *Daseinsanalytik* (analysis of the structure of *Dasein*).

2. Some of the main features of the structure of human existence had already been outlined by Kierkegaard. Man is not a ready-made being; man will become what he makes of himself and nothing more. Man constructs himself through his choices, because he has the freedom to make vital choices, above all the freedom to choose between an *inauthentic* and an *authentic* modality of existence. Inauthentic existence is the modality of the man who lives under the tyranny of the *plebs* (the crowd, i.e., the anonymous collectivity). Authentic existence is the modality in which a man assumes the responsibility of his own existence. In order to pass from inauthentic to authentic existence, a man has to suffer the ordeal of despair and "existential anxiety," i.e., the anxiety of a man facing the limits of his existence with its fullest implications: death, nothingness. This is what Kierkegaard calls "the sickness unto death."

3. Heidegger was a pupil of Husserl and took over from his master the principles of phenomenology. Heidegger's philosophy is, in the main, a phenomenology of human *Dasein*.[1] It is an analysis of unparalleled subtlety and profundity and one of the greatest philosophical achievements of all times.

This philosophical system influenced psychiatry in three ways: (1) It stimulated the development of an *existentialist psychotherapy*. (2) It exerted an influence on such psychiatrists as Alfred Storch and Hans Kunz.[2] (3) It inspired the elaboration of a new psychiatric system, Ludwig Binswanger's *Daseinsanalyse* (existential analysis).

---

[1] Martin Heidegger, *Sein und Zeit* (Halle: Niemeyer, 1926).

[2] Alfred Storch, "Die Welt der beginnenden Schizophrenie," *Zeitschrift für die gesammte Neurologie und Psychiatrie,* vol. 127, 1930, pp. 799–810; Hans Kunz, "Die Grenze der psychopathologischen Wahninterpretationen," *Zeitschrift für die gesammte Neurologie und Psychiatrie,* vol. 135, 1931, pp. 671–715.

Existentialist Psychotherapy

Existentialist psychotherapy is simply the application of certain existentialist concepts to psychotherapy, without regard to phenomenology and psychoanalysis. It should not be confused with Binswanger's existential analysis. There is no standard system or method of existentialist psychotherapy, but three of its concepts are especially worthy of attention.

1. The concept of *existential neurosis,* i.e., illnesses arising not so much from repressed traumata, a weak ego, or life-stress, but rather from the individual's inability to see meaning in life, so that he lives an inauthentic existential modality. The problem for him is to find meaning in life and to pass to an authentic modality of existence.[3]

2. Existentialist psychotherapy prefers, to the use of psychoanalytic transference, the use of another interpersonal experience, *encounter.* Encounter is, in general, not so much the fortuitous meeting and first acquaintance of two individuals, but rather the decisive inner experience resulting from it for one (sometimes for both) of the two individuals.[4] Something totally new is revealed, new horizons open, one's *Weltanschauung* is revised, and sometimes the whole personality is restructured. Such encounters are manifold, perhaps with a philosopher who reveals a new way of thinking or with a man of great life experience, of practical understanding of human nature, of heroic achievements, of independent personality. An encounter can bring a sudden liberation from ignorance or illusion, enlarge the spiritual horizon, and give a new meaning to life.

It is obvious that *encounter* has nothing in common with *transference* in the stricter meaning given to this word by Freud. Far from being a revival of an ancient interpersonal relationship, encounter works through the very fact of its novelty. On the other hand, it is not to be confounded with *identification.* If the personality of the subject is changed, it means not that he copies a model but that the model serves as a catalyst in whose presence he comes to realize his latent and best abilities and to shape his own self (in Jung's terminology, to accomplish a progress in his *individuation*).

3. Some psychotherapists make use of another existentialist concept, *kairos.* This Greek word meant, in Hippocratic medicine, the typical moment when an acute disease was expected to change its course for better or worse; "critical" symptoms would appear at this point for a short time, indicating the new direction; and the proficient physician would prove his capacity by his way of handling the situation. This long forgotten concept was revived in the

---

[3]Viktor Frankl, *Theorie und Therapie der Neurosen* (Wien: Urban und Schwarzenberg, 1956).

[4]See, about the *encounter,* F. J. Buytendijk, "Zur Phänomenologie der Begegnung," *Eranos-Jahrbuch,* vol. 19, 1950, pp. 431–86—about the psychotherapeutic implications, Hans Trüb, *Heilung aus der Begegnung* (*Healing Through Encounter*) (Stuttgart: Klett, 1951).

theological field by Paul Tillich and introduced in psychotherapy by Arthur Kielholz.[5]

Good psychotherapists have always known that there are specific times when a certain patient is inwardly ready for a certain kind of intervention and that the intervention is likely to be fully successful at such times, whereas it would be premature before and without prospects later. Agents of temperance societies have often demonstrated their ability to choose such a time for an interview with an alcoholic. They try to choose the moment when the drinker is close to despair, realizing that he is falling into the abyss and aware of his incapacity to help himself, yet has not completely given up any wish of salvation. According to Kielholz, similar instances of a critical, decisive point—of *kairos*—are not rare among neurotic, psychopathic, or even psychotic individuals. Unfortunately, the concept of a psychotherapeutic treatment is often associated with the idea of a standard course of development involving a slow elaboration and resolution of transference, without much concern for moments when time suddenly acquires a qualitatively different value. Such critical points, when adequately handled, enable a skillful psychotherapist to obtain a surprisingly rapid cure of cases which were considered severe, if not desperate.

Binswanger's Existential Analysis

What Binswanger termed *Daseinsanalyse* (existential analysis) represents a synthesis of psychoanalysis, phenomenology, and existentialist concepts modified by original new insights. It is a reconstruction of the inner world of experience of psychiatric patients with the help of a conceptual framework inspired by Heidegger's studies on the structure of human existence.

Binswanger, a psychiatrist of the school of Eugen Bleuler, was one of the first Swiss followers of Freud. Then, in the early 1920s, he became, with Eugene Minkowski, one of the first proponents of psychiatric phenomenology. With his paper "Dream and Existence" (1930) and his studies on mania (1931–1932), he shifted toward existential analysis. His system was expounded in 1942 in his major work[6] and later illustrated in a number of clinical cases, the first of which [is] "Ellen West.". . .

Binswanger was also influenced by Martin Buber's book *I and Thou.*[7] Buber described in poetic style how the pronoun *I* has two very different meanings, depending upon its relation to a "thou" or a "him." In the sphere of the I-Thou, *I* is expressed with one's whole being and expects reciprocity;

[5]Paul Tillich, *Kairos* (Darmstadt: Reichl, 1926); A. Kielholz, "Vom Kairos," *Schweizerische Medizinische Wochenschrift,* vol. 86, 1956, pp. 982–84.

[6]L. Binswanger, *Grundformen und Erkenntnis menschlichen Daseins* (Zurich: Max Niehans, 1942).

[7]Martin Buber, *Ich und Du* (Leipzig: Inselverlag, 1923).

it is the sphere of the *encounter,* of the primary human relationships, and of the Spirit. In the sphere of I-Him, *I* is expressed with a part of one's being; it is the sphere of utilitarian relationships. Binswanger developed these ideas, with his descriptions of the "dual" and the "plural" modes of existence, to which he added a "singular" and an "anonymous" mode.

There are a few differences between phenomenology and existential analysis:

1. Existential analysis does not restrict itself to the investigation of states of *consciousness,* but takes into account the entire structure of *existence* of the individual.

2. Whereas phenomenology had emphasized the unity of the individual's inner world of experience, existential analysis emphasizes that one individual may live in two or more sometimes conflicting "worlds."

3. Phenomenology takes into account only immediate subjective worlds of experience. Existential analysis strives to reconstruct the development and transformations of the individual's "world" or conflicting "worlds." Binswanger stressed the fact that this study implies a biographic investigation conducted according to psychoanalytic methods.

Thus, existential analysis differs from phenomenology in that it operates within a larger frame of reference.

In his first existential analytic studies, Binswanger organized his descriptions around the distinction of the *Umwelt, Mitwelt,* and *Eigenwelt* of his subjects. Later he organized his analyses around a still larger frame of reference: the distinction of the "existential modes."

The "existential mode" is the dimension of *Dasein* in regard to the *Mitwelt* (fellow men). In contradistinction to classical psychology, which assumes continuity and sameness in the subject, existential analysis takes into account the fact that the "self" changes according to the various forms of "dual," "plural," "singular," and "anonymous" existential modes.

The *dual existential mode* corresponds very roughly to the current concept of "intimacy" and is an extension of Buber's views of the I-Thou relationship. There are several varieties of dual mode, such as the relationships of mother-child, brother-sister, lover-beloved, and even (according to Buber) of the faithful and God. Binswanger gave an extensive analysis of two of these relationships, the dual modes of love and friendship.[8] In the dual mode of love, Binswanger says, space presents the paradox of being simultaneously infinite and all-near; distance and proximity are transcended by a particular spatial mode which bears the same relation to space that eternity does to time. The dual mode of love is also made manifest by an exigency of eternity, not only future but retrospective; the moment coincides with eternity by excluding transient duration. This *Heimat* (inner home of love), which transcends space

---

[8]Binswanger, *Grundformen und Erkenntnis menschlichen Daseins,* pp. 23–265.

and in which the moment and eternity fuse, forms the core of the normal existential experience, according to Binswanger.

Many problems have been considered by existential analysts in the light of the dual existential mode. Boss analyzed the aspects of marriage: whereas normal marriage should imply the dual mode, there are "degraded forms of marriage," in which the partners live in the plural or in the singular existential modes.[9]

The *plural mode* corresponds roughly to the area of formal relationships, competition, and struggle. Here, the intimacy of "Thou and I" yields to the coexistence of "one and the other," or of two beings who are "grappling" with each other. Binswanger describes at length the various ways of "seizing" and "yielding to" one's fellow man, through sensitivity, passions, morality, reputation, etc. Many psychopathological problems are thus viewed in a new light.

The *singular mode* includes the relationships of a man with himself (including his body). Psychoanalysis knows of narcissism, self-punitive, and self-destructive behavior. Binswanger's concept is much broader and includes a wide range of intrapsychic relationships, which he analyzes in an extremely subtle way. These studies also cast a new light on certain problems; for instance, inner conflict is viewed as a variety of singular mode patterned on the model of the plural mode; autism is not only the lack of relations to one's fellow men but also a specific mode of relationship to oneself.

The *anonymous mode* was briefly sketched by Binswanger and its description developed after him by Kuhn in his study of the interpretation of masks in the Rorschach test.[10] It is the mode of the individual living and acting in an anonymous collectivity, such as the dancer in a masked ball or the soldier who kills and is killed by individuals whom he does not know. Certain individuals seek refuge in this mode as a means of escaping or fighting their fellow men; the latter is the case with the authors of anonymous letters, as Binder shows.[11]

Existential Psychotherapy

Implications of Existential Analysis for Psychotherapy

In regard to the implications of existential analysis for psychotherapy, several points must be distinguished.

[9]Medard Boss, *Die Gestalt der Ehe und ihre Zerfallsformen* (Bern: Huber, 1944).

[10]R. Kuhn, *Ueber Maskendeutungen im Rorschachschen Versuch* (Basel: S. Karger, 1944).

[11]Hans Binder, "Das anonyme Briefschreiben," *Schweizer Archiv für Neurologie und Psychiatrie*, 1948, vol. 61, pp. 41–134, vol. 62, pp. 11–56.

Existential Psychotherapy, from Ellenberger, "A Clinical Introduction to Psychiatric Phenomenology and Existential Analysis," pp. 123–24.

1. It should be understood that the activity of an existential analyst does not usually differ *seemingly* from what the ordinary psychiatrist or psychoanalyst does. He studies the patient's behavior, speech, writings, dreams, and free associations and reconstructs his biography. While doing this, however, he observes in a somewhat different way and classifies his observations within the framework of existential analytic concepts. This often makes possible a much deeper understanding and, consequently, may furnish new approaches for psychotherapy. In his interpersonal relationship to his patients, he will also be aware of the phenomenon of "encounter" and distinguish it from transference and countertransference reactions (in the stricter original sense of these words).

2. Phenomenology opens the path to a new type of psychotherapy which is still in its early stages of development. Every individual has his own subjective "world." Research in the field of perception, e.g., by Gardner Murphy, demonstrates correlations between an individual's personality and his way of perceiving the sensory world; Murphy's research also shows that errors in perception can be corrected and the perceiver reeducated. This applies also to phenomenology in general. An individual's approach to temporality, spatiality, and the like can be reconsidered and readjusted—this, of course, independent of other methods, which keep their value. Take a case of agoraphobia. Psychoanalytic investigation will unravel the psychogenesis of the symptoms and treat them causally. Phenomenology will demonstrate subjective disturbances in the experience of spatiality, which could be treated in their own right concurrently to the analytic approach. Kuhn, in an above-mentioned article, relates how he treated a girl afflicted with anorexia nervosa, using the phenomenological concept of "distance" as a means of approach; his patient was cured. This is not to say that she could not have been cured with an analytically oriented psychotherapy or with both approaches simultaneously. In fact, it is surprising how accessible uneducated or very sick patients are to phenomenological considerations. Here lies a wide open field for research and discoveries.

3. Reconstruction of the subjective world of a patient is more than an academic exercise. Patients are not inert material; they react in one way or another to any kind of approach. Take a severe regressed schizophrenic who would be the object of an existential analytic investigation. If the psychiatrist is merely concerned with an intellectual, one-sided scientific study, the patient will feel that his personality is being disregarded; such an investigation could do considerable harm. On the other hand, if it is done with genuine interest in the patient himself, the patient feels understood. He will be like the miner imprisoned under earth after an explosion, hearing the signals of the rescuers; he does not know when they will arrive or whether they will be able to save him, but he knows that they are at work, doing their best, and he feels reassured. . . .

Binswanger's Existential Psychotherapy

The Patient's Life History as a Being-in-the-World

A psychotherapy on existential-analytic bases investigates the life-history of the patient to be treated, just as any other psychotherapeutic method, albeit in its own fashion. It does not explain this life history and its pathologic idiosyncrasies according to the teachings of any school of psychotherapy or by means of its preferred categories. Instead, it *understands* this life history as modifications of the total structure of the patient's being-in-the-world, as I have shown in my studies "On Flight of Ideas" (*Über Ideenflucht*), in my studies of schizophrenia, and most recently in the case of "Suzanne Urban."

The Experience of the Fullness of One's Humanity

A psychotherapy on existential-analytic bases thus proceeds *not* merely by showing the patient where, when, and to what extent he has failed to realize the fullness of his humanity, but it tries to make him *experience* this as radically as possible—how, like Ibsen's master-builder, Solness, he has lost his way and footing in "airy heights" or "ethereal worlds of fantasy." In this case the psychotherapist could be compared to someone who is informed, e.g., a mountain guide, familiar with the particular terrain, who attempts the trip back to the valley with the unpracticed tourist who no longer dares either to proceed or to return. And inversely, the existential-analytically oriented therapist seeks to enable the depressed patient to get out of his cavernous subterranean world, and to gain footing "upon the ground" once more, by revealing it to him as being the only mode of existence in which the fullness of human possibilities can be realized. And further, the existential-analytically oriented therapist will lead the twisted schizophrenic out of the autistic world of distortion and askewness in which he lives and acts, into the shared worlds, the *koinos kosmos* of Heraclitus; or he will strive to help a patient who, in her own words, lives "in two speeds" to "synchronize" these (again using her own expression). Yet, another time the therapist will see (as happened in one of Roland Kuhn's cases of anorexia mentalis) that the goal may be reached much more rapidly if one explores not the temporal but the spatial structures of a particular patient's world. It came as a surprise to us to find how easily some otherwise not particularly intelligent or educated patients proved accessible to an existential-analytic kind of exploration, and how thoroughly they felt un-

Binswanger's Existential Psychotherapy, from Ludwig Binswanger, "Existential Analysis and Psychotherapy," *Progress in Psychotherapy,* vol. 1, ed. Frieda Fromm-Reichmann and J. L. Moreno (New York: Grune & Stratton, 1956), pp. 145–48.

derstood by it in their singularity. This is, after all, an altogether indispensable prerequisite for any kind of psychotherapeutic success.

The Plane of Common Existence

Regardless of whether the existential analyst is predominantly psychoanalytic or predominantly Jungian in orientation, he will always stand on the same plane with his patients—the plane of common existence. He will therefore not degrade the patient to an object toward which he is subject, but he will see in him an existential partner. He will therefore not consider the bond between the two partners to be as that of two electric batteries—a "psychic contact" —but as an *encounter* on what Martin Buber calls the "sharp edge of existence," an existence which *essentially* "is in the world," not merely as a self but also as a being-together with one another—relatedness and love. Also what has, since Freud, been called transference is, in the existential-analytic sense, a kind of encounter. For encounter is a being-with-others in *genuine presence,* that is to say, in the present which is altogether continuous with the *past* and bears within it the possibilities of a *future.*

Dreams as a Specific Way of Existing

Perhaps you will also be interested in hearing what is the position of existential analysis toward the *dream,* and this again particularly with regard to psychotherapy. Here again it is removed from any theoretic "explanation" of the dream, especially from the purely sexual exegesis of dream contents in psychoanalysis; rather, it understands the dream, as I emphasized a long time ago, as a specific way of being-in-the-world, in other words, as a specific world and a specific way of existing. This amounts to saying that in the dream we see the whole man, the *entirety* of his problems, in a different existential modality than in waking, but against the background and with the structure of the a priori articulation of existence, and therefore the dream is also of paramount therapeutic importance for the existential analyst. For precisely by means of the structure of dreams he is enabled first of all to show the patient the structure of his being-in-the-world in an over-all manner, and secondly, he can, on the basis of this, free him for the *totality* of existential possibilities of being, in other words, for open resoluteness (*Entschlossenheit*); he can, to use Heidegger's expression "retrieve" (*zurückholen*) existence from a dream existence to a genuine capacity for being itself. For the time being, I will refer you to Roland Kuhn's paper, "On the Existential Structure of a Neurosis" in Gebsattel's *Jahrbuch für Psychologie und Psychotherapie.* I only ask of you not to imagine existential structure as something static, but as something undergoing constant change. Similarly, what we call neurosis represents a changed existential *pro-*

cess, as compared with the healthy. Thus, existential analysis understands the task of psychotherapy to be the opening up of new structural possibilities to such altered existential processes.

As you see, existential analysis, instead of speaking in theoretic concepts, such as "pleasure principle" and "reality principle," investigates and treats the mentally ill person with regard to the structures, structural articulations and structural alterations of his existence. Hence, it has not, by any means, consciousness as its sole object, as has been erroneously stated, but rather the whole man, prior to any distinction between conscious and unconscious, or even between body and soul; for the existential structures and their alterations permeate man's entire being. Obviously, the existential analyst, insofar as he is a therapist, will not, at least in the beginning of his treatment, be able to dispense with the distinction between conscious and unconscious, deriving from the psychology of consciousness and bound up with its merits and its drawbacks.

Existential Therapy as the Understanding of the Structure of Human Existence

Taking stock of the relationship between existential analysis and psychotherapy, it can be said that existential analysis cannot, over long stretches, dispense with the traditional psychotherapeutic methods; that, however, it can, as such, be therapeutically effective only insofar as it succeeds in opening up to the sick fellow man an understanding of the structure of human existence and allows him to find his way back from his neurotic or psychotic, lost, erring, perforated, or twisted mode of existence and world, into the freedom of being able to utilize his own capacities for existence. This presupposes that the existential analyst, insofar as he is a psychotherapist, not only is in possession of existential-analytic and psychotherapeutic competence, but that he must dare to risk committing his own existence in the struggle for the freedom of his partner's. . . .

Rollo May's Existential Psychotherapy

Existential analysis is a way of understanding human existence, and its representatives believe that one of the chief (if not *the* chief) blocks to the understanding of human beings in Western culture is precisely the overemphasis on

---

Rollo May's Existential Psychotherapy, from Rollo May, "Contributions of Existential Psychotherapy," *Existence: A New Dimension in Psychiatry and Psychology,* pp. 76–91.

technique, an overemphasis which goes along with the tendency to see the human being as an object to be calculated, managed, "analyzed."[12] Our Western tendency has been to believe that *understanding follows technique;* if we get the right technique, then we can penetrate the riddle of the patient, or, as said popularly with amazing perspicacity, we can "get the other person's number." The existential approach holds the exact opposite; namely, that *technique follows understanding.* The central task and responsibility of the therapist is to seek to understand the patient as a being and as being-in-his-world. All technical problems are subordinate to this understanding. Without this understanding, technical facility is at best irrelevant, at worst a method of "structuralizing" the neurosis. With it, the groundwork is laid for the therapist's being able to help the patient recognize and experience his own existence, and this is the central process of therapy. This does not derogate disciplined technique; it rather puts it into perspective.

When editing this volume, therefore, we had difficulty piecing together information about what an existential therapist would actually *do* in given situations in therapy, but we kept asking the question, for we knew American readers would be particularly concerned with this area. It is clear at the outset that what distinguishes existential therapy is not what the therapist would specifically do, say, in meeting anxiety or confronting resistance or getting the life history and so forth, but rather the *context* of his therapy. How an existential therapist might interpret a given dream, or an outburst of temper on the patient's part, might not differ from what a classical psychoanalyst might say, if each were taken in isolated fashion. But the context of existential therapy would be very distinct; it would always focus on the questions of how this dream throws light on this particular patient's existence in his world, what it says about *where* he is at the moment and what he is moving toward, and so forth. The context is the patient not as a set of psychic dynamisms or mechanisms but as a human being who is choosing, committing, and pointing himself toward something right now; the context is dynamic, immediately real, and present.

I shall try to block out some implications concerning therapeutic technique from my knowledge of the works of the existential therapists and from my own experience of how their emphases have contributed to me, a therapist trained in psychoanalysis in its broad sense. Making a systematic summary

---

[12]The term *analyzed* itself reflects this problem, and patients may be doing more than using a semantic difficulty as a way of expressing resistance when they aver that the idea of "being analyzed" makes them objects being "worked upon." The term is carried over into the phrase *existential analysis* partly because it has become standard for deep psychotherapy since the advent of psychoanalysis and partly because existential thought itself (following Heidegger) is an "analysis of reality." This term is of course a reflection of the tendency in our whole culture, called "The Age of Analysis" in the title of a recent survey of modern Western thought. Though I am not happy about the term, I have used the identification *existential analyst* for the writers in this book because it is too clumsy to say "phenomenological and existential psychiatrists and psychologists."

would be presumptuous to try and impossible to accomplish, but I hope the following points will at least suggest some of the important therapeutic implications. It should be clear at every point, however, that the really important contributions of this approach are its deepened understanding of human existence, and one gets no place talking about isolated techniques of therapy unless the understanding we have sought to give in the earlier portions of these chapters is presupposed at every point.

The *first* implication is the variability of techniques among the existential therapists. Boss, for example, uses couch and free association in traditional Freudian manner and permits a good deal of acting out of transference. Others would vary as much as the different schools vary anyway. But the critical point is that the existential therapists have a definite reason for using any given technique with a given patient. They sharply question the use of techniques simply because of rote, custom, or tradition. Their approach also does not at all settle for the air of vagueness and unreality that surrounds many therapeutic sessions, particularly in the eclectic schools which allegedly have freed themselves from bondage to a traditional technique and select from all schools as though the presuppositions of these approaches did not matter. Existential therapy is distinguished by a sense of reality and concreteness.

I would phrase the above point positively as follows: Existential technique should have flexibility and versatility, varying from patient to patient and from one phase to another in treatment with the same patient. The specific technique to be used at a given point should be decided on the basis of these questions: What will best reveal the existence of this particular patient at this moment in his history? What will best illuminate his being-in-the-world? Never merely "eclectic," this flexibility always involves a clear understanding of the underlying assumptions of any method. Let us say a Kinseyite, for example, a traditional Freudian, and an existential analyst are dealing with an instance of sexual repression. The Kinseyite would speak of it in terms of finding a sexual object, in which case he is not talking about sex in human beings. The traditional Freudian would see its psychological implications but would look primarily for causes in the past and might well ask himself how this instance of sexual repression *qua* repression can be overcome. The existential therapist would view the sexual repression as a holding back of *potentia* of the existence of this person, and though he might or might not, depending on the circumstances, deal immediately with the sex problem as such, it would always be seen not as a mechanism of repression as such but as a limitation of this person's being-in-his-world.

The *second* implication is that psychological dynamisms always take their meaning from the existential situation of the patient's own, immediate life. The writings of Medard Boss, whose small book on existential psychotherapy and psychoanalysis was published just as this article went to press, are very pertinent at this point. Boss holds that Freud's practice was right but his theories explaining his practice were wrong. Freudian in technique, Boss places the theories and concepts of traditional psychoanalysis on a fundamental existential basis. Take *transference,* for example, a discovery which Boss greatly values. What really happens is not that the neurotic patient "transfers" feelings he had toward mother or father to wife or therapist. Rather, the neurotic is one who in certain areas never developed beyond the limited and restricted forms of experience characteristic of the infant. Hence in later years he perceives wife or therapist through the same restricted, distorted "spectacles" as he perceived father or mother. The problem is to be understood in terms of perception and relatedness to the world. This makes unnecessary the concept of transference in the sense of a displacement of detachable feelings from one object to another. The new basis of this concept frees psychoanalysis from the burden of a number of insoluble problems.

Take, also, the ways of behaving known as *repression* and *resistance.* Freud saw repression as related to bourgeois morality, specifically, as the patient's need to preserve an acceptable picture of himself and therefore to hold back thoughts, desires, and so forth which are unacceptable according to bourgeois moral codes. Rather, says Boss, the conflict must be seen more basically in the area of the patient's acceptance or rejection of his own potentialities. We need to keep in mind the question—What keeps the patient from accepting in freedom his potentialities? This may involve bourgeois morality, but it also involves a lot more: it leads immediately to the existential question of the person's freedom. Before repression is possible or conceivable, the person must have some possibility of accepting or rejecting—that is, some margin of freedom. Whether the person is aware of this freedom or can articulate it is another question; he does not need to be. To repress is precisely to make one's self unaware of freedom; this is the nature of the dynamism. Thus, to repress or deny this freedom already presupposes it as a possibility. Boss then points out that psychic determinism is always a secondary phenomenon and works only in a limited area. The primary question is how the person relates to his freedom to express potentialities in the first place, repression being one way of so relating.

With respect to *resistance,* Boss again asks the question: What makes such a phenomenon possible? He answers that it is an outworking of the tendency of the patient to become absorbed in the *Mitwelt,* to slip back into *das Man,* the anonymous mass, and to renounce the particular unique and original potentiality which is his. Thus, "social conformity" is a general form of resistance in life; and even the patient's acceptance of the doctrines and interpretations of the therapist may itself be an expression of resistance.

We do not wish here to go into the question of what underlies these phenomena. We want only to demonstrate that at each point in considering these dynamisms of transference, resistance, and repression Boss does something critically important for the existential approach. *He places each dynamism on an ontological basis.* Each way of behaving is seen and understood in the light of the existence of the patient as a human being. This is shown, too, in his conceiving of drives, libido, and so forth always in terms of *potentialities* for existence. Thus he proposes "to throw overboard the painful intellectual acrobatic of the old psychoanalytic theory which sought to derive the phenomena from the interplay of some forces or drives behind them." He does not deny forces as such but holds that they cannot be understood as "energy transformation" or on any other such natural science model but only as the person's *potentia* of existence. "This freeing from unnecessary constructions facilitates the understanding between patient and doctor. Also it makes the pseudo-resistances disappear which were a justified defense of the analysands against a violation of their essence." Boss holds that he thus can follow the "basic rule" in analysis—the one condition Freud set for analysis, namely, that the patient give forth in complete honesty whatever was going on in his mind—more effectively than in traditional psychoanalysis, for he listens with respect and takes seriously and without reserve the contents of the patient's communication rather than sieving it through prejudgments or destroying it by special interpretations. Boss holds himself to be entirely loyal to Freud in all of this and to be simply engaged in bringing out the underlying meaning of Freud's discoveries and placing them on their necessary comprehensive foundation. Believing that Freud's discoveries have to be understood below their faulty formulation, he points out that Freud himself was not merely a passive "mirror" for the patient in analysis, as traditionally urged in psychoanalysis, but was "translucent," a vehicle and medium through which the patient saw himself.

Presence

The *third* implication in existential therapy is the emphasis on *presence.* By this we mean that the relationship of the therapist and patient is taken as a real one, the therapist being not merely a shadowy reflector but an alive human being who happens, at that hour, to be concerned not with his own problems but with understanding and experiencing so far as possible the being of the patient. The way was prepared for this emphasis on presence by our discussion above of the fundamental existential idea of truth-in-relationship. It was there pointed out that existentially truth always involves the relation of the person to something or someone and that the therapist is part of the patient's relationship "field." We indicated, too, that this was not only the therapist's best avenue to understanding the patient but that he cannot really *see* the patient unless he participates in the field.

Several quotations will make clearer what this presence means. Karl Jaspers has remarked, "What we are missing! What opportunities of understanding we let pass by because at a single decisive moment we were, with all our knowledge, lacking in the simple virtue of a *full human presence!*"[13] In similar vein, but greater detail, Binswanger writes as follows, in his paper on psychotherapy, concerning the significance of the therapist's role of the relationship:

> If such a (psychoanalytic) treatment fails, the analyst inclines to assume that the patient is not capable of overcoming his resistance to the physician, for example, as a "father image." Whether an analysis can have success or not is often, however, not decided by whether a patient is capable *at all* of overcoming such a transferred father image but by the opportunity *this particular physician* accords him to do so; it may, in other words, be the rejection of the therapist as a person, the impossibility of entering into a genuine communicative rapport with him, that may form the obstacle against breaking through the "eternal" repetition of the father resistance. Caught in the "mechanism" and thus in what inheres in it, *mechanical repetition,* the psychoanalytic doctrine, as we know, is altogether strangely blind toward the entire category of the *new,* the properly *creative* in the life of the psyche everywhere. Certainly it not always is true to the facts if one attributes the failure of treatment only to the patient; the question always to be asked first by the physician is whether the fault may not be his. What is meant here is not any technical fault but the far more fundamental failure that consists of an impotence to wake or rekindle that divine "spark" in the patient which only true communication from existence to existence can bring forth and which alone possesses, with its light and warmth, also the fundamental power that makes any therapy work—the power to liberate a person from the blind isolation, the *idios kosmos* of Heraclitus, from a mere vegetating in his body, his dreams, his private wishes, his conceit, and his presumptions, and to ready him for a life of *koinonia,* of genuine community.[14]

Presence is not to be confused with a sentimental attitude toward the patient but depends firmly and consistently on how the therapist conceives of human beings. It is found in therapists of various schools and differing beliefs —differing, that is, on anything except one central issue—their assumptions about whether the human being is an object to be analyzed or a being to be understood. Any therapist is existential to the extent that, with all this techni-

---

[13]Ulrich Sonnemann, in *Existence and Therapy* (New York: Grune & Stratton, 1954), p. 343, quoted from Kolle. Sonnemann's book, we may add, was the first in English to deal directly with existential theory and therapy and contains useful and relevant material.

[14]Quoted by Sonnemann, *Existence and Therapy,* p. 255, from L. Binswanger, "Uber Psychotherapie," in *Ausgewählte Vorträge und Aufsätze,* pp. 142–43.

cal training and his knowledge of transference and dynamisms, he is still able to relate to the patient as "one existence communicating with another," to use Binswanger's phrase. In my own experience, Frieda Fromm-Reichmann particularly had this power in a given therapeutic hour; she used to say, "The patient needs an experience, not an explanation." . . .

Before leaving the topic of *presence,* we need to make three caveats. One is that this emphasis on relationship is in no way an oversimplification or short cut; it is not a substitute for discipline or thoroughness of training. It rather puts these things in their context—namely, discipline and thoroughness of training directed to understanding human beings as human. The therapist is assumedly an expert; but, if he is not first of all a human being, his expertness will be irrelevant and quite possibly harmful. The distinctive character of the existential approach is that understanding *being human* is no longer just a "gift," an intuition, or something left to chance; it is the "proper study of man," in Alexander Pope's phrase, and becomes the center of a thorough and scientific concern in the broad sense. The existential analysts do the same thing with the structure of human existence that Freud did with the structure of the unconscious—namely, take it out of the realm of the hit-and-miss gift of special intuitive individuals, accept it as the area of exploration and understanding, and make it to some extent teachable.

Another caveat is that the emphasis on the reality of presence does not obviate the exceedingly significant truths in Freud's concept of transference, rightly understood. It is demonstrable every day in the week that patients, and all of us to some extent, behave toward therapist or wife or husband as though they were father or mother or someone else, and the working through of this is of crucial importance. But in existential therapy "transference" gets placed in the new context of *an event occurring in a real relationship between two people.* Almost everything the patient does vis-à-vis the therapist in a given hour has an element of transference in it. But nothing is ever "just transference," to be explained to the patient as one would an arithmetic problem. The concept of "transference" as such has often been used as a convenient protective screen behind which both therapist and patient hide in order to avoid the more anxiety-creating situation of direct confrontation. For me to tell myself, say when especially fatigued, that the patient-is-so-demanding-because-she-wants-to-prove-she-can-make-her-father-love-her may be a relief and may also be in fact true. But the real point is that she is doing this to me in this given moment, and the reasons it occurs at this instant of intersection of her existence and mine are not exhausted by what she did with her father. Beyond all considerations of unconscious determinism—which are true in their partial context—she is at some point choosing to do this at this specific moment. Furthermore, the only thing that will grasp the patient, and in the long run make it possible for her to change, is to experience fully and deeply that she is doing precisely this to a real person, myself, in this real moment.[15] Part of the *sense of timing* in therapy—which ... has received special development among the existential therapists—consists of letting the patient experience what he or she is doing until the experience really grasps him.[16] Then and only then will an explanation of *why* help. For the patient referred to above to become aware that she is demanding this particular unconditioned love from this real person in this immediate hour may indeed shock her, and thereafter —or possibly only hours later—she should become aware of the early childhood antecedents. She may well explore and reexperience then how she smoldered with anger as a child because she couldn't make her father notice her. But if she is simply told this is a transference phenomenon, she may have learned an interesting intellectual fact which does not existentially grasp her at all.

Another caveat is that *presence* in a session does not at all mean the therapist imposes himself or his ideas or feelings on the patient. It is a highly interesting proof of our point that Rogers ... is precisely the psychologist who has most unqualifiedly insisted that the therapist not project himself but at every point follow the affect and leads of the patient. Being alive in the relationship does not at all mean the therapist will chatter along with the patient; he will know that patients have an infinite number of ways of trying to become involved with the therapist in order to avoid their own problems. And he, the therapist, may well be silent, aware that to be a projective screen is one aspect of his part of the relationship. The therapist is what Socrates

---

[15]This is a point the phenomenologists make consistently, namely, that to know fully *what* we are doing, to feel it, to experience it all through our being, is much more important than to know *why*. For, they hold, if we fully know the *what*, the *why* will come along by itself. One sees this demonstrated very frequently in psychotherapy: the patient may have only a vague and intellectual idea of the "cause" of this or that pattern in his behavior, but as he explores and experiences more and more the different aspects and phases of this pattern, the cause may suddenly become real to him not as an abstracted formulation but as one real, integral aspect of the total understanding of what he is doing. This approach also has an important cultural significance: is not the *why* asked so much in our culture precisely as a way of detaching ourselves, a way of avoiding the more disturbing and anxiety-creating alternative of sticking to the end with the *what*? That is to say, the excessive preoccupation with causality and function that characterizes modern Western society may well serve, much more widely than realized, the need to abstract ourselves from the reality of the given experience. Asking *why* is generally in the service of a need to get power *over* the phenomenon, in line with Bacon's dictum, "knowledge is power" and, specifically, knowledge of nature is power over nature. Asking the question of *what*, on the other hand, is a way of *participating* in the phenomenon.

[16]This could well be defined as "existential time"—*the time it takes for something to become real.* It may occur instantaneously, or it may require an hour of talk or some time of silence. In any case, the sense of timing the therapist uses in pondering when to interpret will not be based only on the negative criterion—How much can the patient take? It will involve a positive criterion —Has this become real to the patient? As in the example above, has what she is doing in the present to the therapist been sharply and vividly enough experienced so that an exploration of the past will have dynamic reality and thus give the power for change?

named the *midwife*—completely real in "being there," but being there with the specific purpose of helping the other person to bring to birth something from within himself.

The *fourth* implication for technique in existential analysis follows immediately from our discussion of presence: therapy will attempt to "analyze out" the ways of behaving which destroy presence. The therapist, on his part, will need to be aware of whatever in him blocks full presence. I do not know the context of Freud's remark that he preferred that patients lie on the couch because he could not stand to be stared at for nine hours a day. But it is obviously true that any therapist—whose task is arduous and taxing at best —is tempted at many points to evade the anxiety and potential discomfort of confrontation by various devices. We have earlier described the fact that real confrontation between two people can be profoundly anxiety-creating. Thus it is not surprising that it is much more comfortable to protect ourselves by thinking of the other only as a "patient" or focusing only on certain mechanisms of behavior. The *technical* view of the other person is perhaps the therapist's most handy anxiety-reducing device. This has its legitimate place. The therapist is presumably an expert. But technique must not be used as a way of blocking presence. Whenever the therapist finds himself reacting in a rigid or preformulated way, he had obviously best ask himself whether he is not trying to avoid some anxiety and as a result is losing something existentially real in the relationship. The therapist's situation is like that of the artist who has spent many years of disciplined study learning technique; but he knows that if specific thoughts of technique preoccupy him when he actually is in the process of painting, he has at that moment lost his vision; the creative process, which should absorb him, transcending the subject-object split, has become temporarily broken; he is now dealing with objects and himself as a manipulator of objects.

The Aim of Therapy: The Patient's Experience of his Existence (Dasein) as Real

The *fifth* implication has to do with the goal of the therapeutic process. The aim of therapy is that the patient *experience his existence as real.* The purpose is that he become aware of his existence fully, which includes becoming aware of his potentialities and becoming able to act on the basis of them. The characteristic of the neurotic is that his existence has become "darkened," as the existential analysts put it, blurred, easily threatened and clouded over, and gives no sanction to his acts; the task of therapy is to illuminate the existence. The neurotic is overconcerned about the *Umwelt,* and underconcerned about *Eigenwelt.* [17] As the *Eigenwelt* becomes real to him in therapy, the patient tends

---

[17] The point in this and the rest of the sentences in this paragraph is Binswanger's, interpreted by Dr. Hoffman.

to experience the *Eigenwelt* of the therapist as stronger than his own. Binswanger points out that the tendency to take over the therapist's *Eigenwelt* must be guarded against, and therapy must not become a power struggle between the two *Eigenwelten*. The therapist's function is to *be there* (with all of the connotation of *Dasein*), present in the relationship, while the patient finds and learns to live out his own *Eigenwelt*.[18]

An experience of my own may serve to illustrate one way of taking the patient existentially. I often have found myself having the impulse to ask, when the patient comes in and sits down, not "*How* are you?" but "*Where* are you?" The contrast of these questions—neither of which would I probably actually ask aloud—highlights what is sought. I want to know, as I experience him in this hour, not just how he feels, but rather *where he is,* the "where" including his feelings but also a lot more—whether he is detached or fully present, whether his direction is toward me and toward his problems or away from both, whether he is running from anxiety, whether this special courtesy when he came in or appearance of eagerness to reveal things is really inviting me to overlook some evasion he is about to make, where he is in relation to the girl friend he talked about yesterday, and so on. I became aware of this asking "where" the patient was several years ago, before I specifically knew the work of the existential therapists; it illustrates a spontaneous existential attitude.

It follows that when mechanisms or dynamisms are interpreted, as they will be in existential therapy as in any other, it will always be in the context of this person's becoming aware of his existence. This is the only way the dynamism will have reality for him, will affect him; otherwise he might as well —as indeed most patients do these days—read about the mechanism in a book. This point is of special importance because precisely the problem of many patients is that they think and talk about themselves in terms of mechanisms; it is their way, as well-taught citizens of twentieth-century Western culture, to avoid confronting their own existence, their method of repressing ontological awareness. This is done, to be sure, under the rubric of being "objective" about one's self; but is it not, in therapy as well as in life, often a systematized, culturally acceptable way of rationalizing detachment from one's self? Even the motive for coming for therapy may be just that, to find an acceptable system by which one can continue to think of himself as a mechanism, to run himself as he would his motor car, only now to do it successfully. If we assume, as we have reason for doing, that the fundamental neurotic process in our day is the repression of the ontological sense—the loss of the sense of being, together with the truncation of awareness and the locking up of the potentialities which are the manifestations of this being—then we are playing directly

---

[18] *Umwelt* is the world of man in relation to his biological environment; *Mitwelt* is man's world in reference to interpersonal relations, relations with his fellow men; while *Eigenwelt* is the sphere of man in relation to himself.

into the patient's neurosis to the extent that we teach him new ways of thinking of himself as a mechanism. This is one illustration of how psychotherapy can reflect the fragmentation of the culture, structuralizing neurosis rather than curing it. Trying to help the patient on a sexual problem by explaining it merely as a mechanism is like teaching a farmer irrigation while damming up his stream.

This raises some penetrating questions about the nature of "cure" in psychotherapy. It implies that it is not the therapist's function to "cure" the patients' neurotic symptoms, though this is the motive for which most people come for therapy. Indeed, the fact that this is their motive reflects their problem. Therapy is concerned with something more fundamental, namely, helping the person experience his existence; and any cure of symptoms which will last must be a by-product of that. The general ideas of "cure"—namely, to live as long as possible and as satisfactorily adjusted as possible—are themselves a denial of *Dasein,* of this particular patient's being. The kind of cure that consists of adjustment, becoming able to fit the culture, can be obtained by technical emphases in therapy, for it is precisely the central theme of the culture that one live in a calculated, controlled, technically well-managed way. Then the patient accepts a confined world without conflict, for now his world is identical with the culture. And since anxiety comes only with freedom, the patient naturally gets over his anxiety; he is relieved from his symptoms because he surrenders the possibilities which caused his anxiety. This is the way of being "cured" by giving up being, giving up existence, by constricting, hedging in existence. In this respect, psychotherapists become the agents of the culture whose particular task it is to adjust people to it; psychotherapy becomes an expression of the fragmentation of the period rather than an enterprise for overcoming it. As we have indicated above, there are clear historical indications that this is occurring in the different psychotherapeutic schools, and the historical probability is that it will increase. There is certainly a question how far this gaining of release from conflict by giving up being can proceed without generating in individuals and groups a submerged despair, a resentment which will later burst out in self-destructiveness, for history proclaims again and again that sooner or later man's need to be free will out. But the complicating factor in our immediate historical situation is that the culture itself is built around this ideal of technical adjustment and carries so many built-in devices for narcotizing the despair that comes from using one's self as a machine that the damaging effects may remain submerged for some time.

On the other hand, the term *cure* can be given a deeper and truer meaning, namely, becoming oriented toward the fulfillment of one's existence. This may include, as a by-product, the cure of symptoms—obviously a desideratum, even if we have stated decisively that it is not the chief goal of therapy. The important thing is that the person discovers his being, his *Dasein.*

Commitment

The *sixth* implication which distinguishes the process of existential therapy is the importance of *commitment.* The basis for this was prepared at numerous points in our previous sections, particularly in our discussion of Kierkegaard's idea that "truth exists only as the individual himself produces it in action." The significance of commitment is not that it is simply a vaguely good thing or ethically to be advised. It is a necessary prerequisite, rather, for seeing truth. This involves a crucial point which has never to my knowledge been fully taken into account in writings on psychotherapy, namely, that *decision precedes knowledge.* We have worked normally on the assumption that, as the patient gets more and more knowledge and insight about himself, he will make the appropriate decisions. This is a half truth. The second half of the truth is generally overlooked, namely, that *the patient cannot permit himself to get insight or knowledge until he is ready to decide, takes a decisive orientation to life, and has made the preliminary decisions along the way.*

We mean "decision" here not in the sense of a *be-all-and-end-all* jump, say, to get married or to join the foreign legion. The possibility or readiness to take such "leaps" is a necessary condition for the decisive orientation, but the big leap itself is sound only so far as it is based upon the minute decisions along the way. Otherwise the sudden decision is the product of unconscious processes, proceeding compulsively in unawareness to the point where they erupt, for example, in a "conversion." We use the term *decision* as meaning a "decisive attitude toward existence," an attitude of commitment. In this respect, *knowledge and insight follow decision rather than vice versa.* Everyone knows of the incidents in which a patient becomes aware in a dream that a certain boss is exploiting him and the next day decides to quit his job. But just as significant, though not generally taken into account because they go against our usual ideas of causality, are the incidents when the patient cannot have the dream *until* he makes the decision. He makes the jump to quit his job, for example, and then he can permit himself to see in dreams that his boss was exploiting him all along.

One interesting corollary of this point is seen when we note that a patient cannot recall what was vital and significant in his past until he is ready to make a decision with regard to the future. Memory works not on a basis simply of what is there imprinted; it works rather on the basis of one's decisions in the present and future. It has often been said that one's past determines one's present and future. Let it be underlined that one's present and future—how he commits himself to existence at the moment—also determines his past. That is, it determines what he can recall of his past, what portions of his past he selects (consciously but also unconsciously) to influence him now, and therefore the particular gestalt his past will assume.

This commitment is, furthermore, not a purely conscious or voluntaristic phenomenon. It is also present on so-called "unconscious" levels. When a person lacks commitment, for example, his dreams may be staid, flat, impoverished; but when he does assume a decisive orientation toward himself and his life, his dreams often take over the creative process of exploring, molding, forming himself in relation to his future or—what is the same thing from the neurotic viewpoint—the dreams struggle to evade, substitute, cover up. The important point is that either way the issue has been joined.

With respect to helping the patient develop the orientation of commitment, we should first emphasize that the existential therapists do not at all mean activism. This is no "decision as a short cut," no matter of premature jumping because to act may be easier and may quiet anxiety more quickly than the slow, arduous, long-time process of self-exploration. They mean rather the attitude of *Dasein,* the self-aware being taking his own existence seriously. The points of commitment and decision are those where the dichotomy between being subject and object is overcome in the unity of readiness for action. When a patient discusses intellectually *ad interminum* a given topic without its ever shaking him or becoming real to him, the therapist asks what is he doing existentially by means of this talk? The talk itself, obviously, is in the service of covering up reality, rationalized generally under the idea of unprejudiced inquiry into the data. It is customarily said that the patient will break through such talk when some experience of anxiety, some inner suffering or outer threat, shocks him into committing himself really to getting help and gives him the incentive necessary for the painful process of uncovering illusions, of inner change and growth. True, this of course does occur from time to time. And the existential therapist can aid the patient in absorbing the real impact of such experiences by helping him develop the capacity for silence (which is another form of communication) and thus avoid using chatter to break the shocking power of the encounter with the insight.

But in principle I do not think the conclusion that we must wait around until anxiety is aroused is adequate. If we assume that the patient's commitment depends upon being pushed by external or internal pain, we are in several difficult dilemmas. Either the therapy "marks time" until anxiety or pain occurs, or we arouse anxiety ourselves (which is a questionable procedure). And the very reassurance and quieting of anxiety the patient receives in therapy may work against his commitment to further help and may make for postponement and procrastination.

Commitment must be on a more positive basis. The question we need to ask is: What is going on that the patient has not found some point in his own existence to which he can commit himself unconditionally? In the earlier discussion of nonbeing and death, it was pointed out that everyone constantly faces the threat of nonbeing if he lets himself recognize the fact. Central here is the symbol of death, but such threat of destruction of being is present in a thousand and one other guises as well. The therapist is doing the patient a disservice if he takes away from him the realization that it is entirely within the realm of possibility that he forfeit or lose his existence and that may well be precisely what he is doing at this very moment. This point is especially important because patients tend to carry a never-quite-articulated belief, no doubt connected with childhood omnipotent beliefs associated with parents, that somehow the therapist will see that nothing harmful happens to them, and therefore they don't need to take their own existence seriously. The tendency prevails in much therapy to water down anxiety, despair, and the tragic aspects of life. Is it not true as a general principle that we need to engender anxiety only to the extent that we already have watered it down? Life itself produces enough, and the only real, crises; and it is very much to the credit of the existential emphasis in therapy that it confronts these tragic realities directly. The patient can indeed destroy himself if he so chooses. The therapist may not say this: it is simply a reflection of fact, and the important point is that it not be sloughed over. The symbol of suicide as a possibility has a far-reaching positive value; Nietzsche once remarked that the thought of suicide has saved many lives. I am doubtful whether anyone takes his life with full seriousness until he realizes that it is entirely within his power to commit suicide.[19]

Death in any of its aspects is the fact which makes of the present hour something of absolute value. One student put it, "I know only two things— one, that I will be dead someday; two, that I am not dead now. The only question is what shall I do between those two points." We cannot go into this matter in further detail, but we only wish to emphasize that the core of the existential approach is the taking of existence seriously.

We conclude with two final caveats. One is a danger that lies in the existential approach, the danger of *generality*. It would indeed be a pity if the existential concepts were tossed around among therapists without regard for their concrete, real meaning. For it must be admitted that there is temptation to become lost in words in these complex areas with which existential analysis deals. One can certainly become philosophically detached in the same way as one can be technically detached. The temptation to use existential concepts in the service of intellectualizing tendencies is especially to be guarded against, since, because they refer to things that have to do with the center of personal reality, these concepts can the more seductively give the illusion of dealing with reality. It must be confessed that some of the writers in the papers in this volume may not have fully resisted this temptation, and some readers may feel that I myself have not. I could plead the necessity of having to explain a great

---

[19]We are of course not speaking here of the practical question of what to do when patients actually threaten suicide; this introduces many other elements and is a quite different question. The conscious awareness we are speaking of is a different thing from the overwhelming and persistent depression, with the self-destructive impulse unbroken by self-conscious awareness, which seems to obtain in actual suicides.

deal within a short compass; but extenuating circumstances are not the point. The point is that to the extent that the existential movement in psychotherapy becomes influential in this country—a desideratum which we believe would be very beneficial—the adherents will have to be on guard against the use of the concepts in the service of intellectual detachment. It is, of course, precisely for the reasons that the existential therapists pay much attention to making clear the verbal utterances of the patient, and they also continually make certain that the necessary interrelation of verbalizing and acting is never overlooked. The "logos must be made flesh." The important thing is *to be* existential.

The other caveat has to do with the existential attitude toward the *unconscious*. In principle most existential analysts deny this concept. They point out all the logical as well as psychological difficulties with the doctrine of the unconscious, and they stand against splitting the being into parts. What is called unconscious, they hold, is still part of this given person; *being,* in any living sense, is at its core indivisible. Now it must be admitted that the doctrine of the unconscious has played most notoriously into the contemporary tendencies to rationalize behavior, to avoid the reality of one's own existence, to act as though one were not himself doing the living. (The man in the street who has picked up the lingo says, "My unconscious did it.") The existential analysts are correct, in my judgment, in their criticism of the doctrine of the unconscious as a convenient blank check on which any causal explanation can be written or as a reservoir from which any deterministic theory can be drawn. But this is the "cellar" view of the unconscious, and objections to it should not be permitted to cancel out the great contribution that the historical meaning of the unconscious had in Freud's terms. Freud's great discovery and his perdurable contribution was to enlarge the sphere of the human personality beyond the immediate voluntarism and rationalism of Victorian man, to include in this enlarged sphere the "depths," that is, the irrational, the so-called repressed, hostile, and unacceptable urges, the forgotten aspects of experience, *ad infinitum.* The symbol for this vast enlarging of the domain of the personality was "the unconscious."

I do not wish to enter into the complex discussion of this concept itself; I wish only to suggest a position. It is right that the blank check, deteriorated, cellar form of this concept should be rejected. But the far-reaching enlargement of personality, which is its real meaning, should not be lost. Binswanger remarks that, for the time being, the existential therapists will not be able to dispense with the concept of the unconscious. I would propose, rather, to agree that being is at some point indivisible, that unconsciousness is part of any given being, that the cellar theory of the unconscious is logically wrong and practically unconstructive; but the meaning of the discovery, namely, the radical enlargement of being, is one of the great contributions of our day and must be retained.

20

EXPERIENTIAL OR NONRATIONAL PSYCHOTHERAPY

Carl A. Whitaker

Thomas P. Malone

Carl A. Whitaker, born in Raymondville, New York, on February 20, 1912, was educated at Syracuse University, where he received his M.D. in 1936 and his M.A. in 1941. After interning at New York City Hospital from 1936 to 1938, he served as a psychiatric resident at Syracuse University Psychopathic Hospital for the next two years. Then he served one year at the Child Guidance Fellowship in Louisville, Kentucky, before entering private practice. From the close of World War II until 1955 he served as a consultant psychiatrist at the Veterans Administration Hospital in Atlanta, Georgia, and acted as consultant for the mental hygiene division of the State Mental Department in Atlanta from 1950 to 1954.

After a year's appointment at Emory University as assistant professor of psychiatry in 1946, he was promoted to full professor and chairman of the department in 1947, a post he held until 1955, when he left for duties at the Atlanta Psychiatric Clinic. Subsequently he was appointed professor of psychiatry at the University of Wisconsin, a position that he presently occupies.

Thomas P. Malone, long-time associate of Whitaker, was born on October 1, 1919, in Mahoney City, Pennsylvania. Educated at Duke, Maryland, and Emory universities, he earned the A.B. (1939) and Ph.D. (1947) from Duke, the M.A. (1940) from Maryland, and the M.D. (1953) from Emory. The highlights of his professional career consisted of an assistant professorship from 1945 to 1947 at Duke University in the Department of Psychology, and in 1947 an appointment as director of research in the Department of Psychiatry at Emory University's School of Medicine. Since 1958 he has been at the Atlanta Psychiatric Clinic.

Whitaker and Malone refer to their system of psychotherapy as "experiential" and "nonrational," experiential because of a feeling experience involving a person-to-person relationship transpiring in therapy (both on the conscious and unconscious level), and nonrational because it lays stress upon the feeling experience rather than the patient's intellect. This system of therapy takes cognizance of the naturalness of the unconscious and concludes that certain aspects of the human personality are able to function properly when responding on an unconscious level. Thus, psychotherapy is never complete when it neglects to re-repress elements of a patient's personality that were initially intended by nature to function unconsciously. Personal growth, of paramount importance in this system, is the outcome of successful therapy, and it is characterized by spontaneous, autonomous choice, freely and unconsciously made by the patient without the necessity of calculated cerebration. Psychotherapy, a person-to-person (I-we-I) relationship, enables the patients to choose their own scale of values by increasing their ability to relate with more of the self, gradually to diminish experiences of anxiety, to increase their integrity or internal consistency, and to exercise a greater freedom of choice.

As coauthors, Whitaker and Malone have written a considerable number of works, their most important being *The Roots of Psychotherapy* (1953). In 1958, Whitaker published *Psychotherapy of Chronic Schizophrenia*. Other joint efforts related to their psychotherapeutic technique are:

"Restatement of the Problems of Psychotherapy" (*Orthopsychiatry*, 1950).

"Multiple Therapy and Psychotherapy," in *Progress in Psychotherapy*, ed. F. Fromm-Reichmann and J. L. Moreno (1956).

"Social Origins of Delusions" (*Southern Medical Journal*, 1959).

"The Involvement of the Professional Therapist," in *Case Studies of Counseling and Psychotherapy*, ed. A. Burton (1959).

"Organic Psychosis as Picked Up in Psychiatric Examination" (*Journal of the Medical Association of Georgia*, 1960).

"Rational and Nonrational Psychotherapy" (*American Journal of Psychotherapy*, 1961).

"First Stage Techniques in the Experiential Psychotherapy," in *The Training of Psychotherapists*, ed. N. P. Dellis and H. K. Stone (1961).

"The Usefulness of Craziness" (*Medical Times*, 1961).

"Experiential Psychotherapy: Evaluation of Relatedness" (*Journal of Existential Psychiatry*, 1963).

"The Psychotherapy of the Acting-Out Schizophrenic" (*American Journal of Psychotherapy*, 1963).

Family Treatment of Schizophrenia (with others, 1965).

"The Community of Psychotherapists" (*International Journal of Group Psychotherapy*, 1965).

Experiential Nonrational Psychotherapy

The therapist who conceives of man as primarily an intelligent being will deal differently with the patient than the psychotherapist who sees man as primarily a feeling person, with the intellect as a controlling mechanism. In recent years, the various schools of psychotherapy appear to gravitate into either one or the other of these opposing ideologies. We identify an *emphasis* on the patient's intellect as *rational psychotherapy,* whereas we identify an *emphasis* on the feeling experience of the patient as experiential psychotherapy. We consider this an ideological rather than a technical difference.

We do not presume to define *rational psychotherapy* in detail. We see the following as a broad definition of an experiential psychotherapeutic process. It is a person-to-person relationship. To this relationship the patient brings his total person, expressing as openly and directly as possible all of his anxieties about himself. The patient does this in an admittedly dependent way. The therapist also brings his total person, including his constructive responses to the patient's anxiety and wellness. The therapist accepts his own dominant role and his medical responsibility, which means that he will set aside his personal anxieties and share only those related to the patient and the interview. Obviously the conscious skills and professional adequacies of the therapist are part of the therapeutic process. In addition, we believe that the preconscious and unconscious responses of the therapist to that patient are essential elements in the curative process and the facilitation of the therapeutic movement. These preconscious and unconscious responses determine the failures in movement as well as the distortions of the therapeutic process. The total person of the therapist is an essential ingredient in psychotherapy.

Such a person-to-person relationship involves some dynamics of which neither participant is consciously aware while they are going on. These cannot be dealt with in a calculated manner. Some areas of the therapeutic experience are known consciously to the patient and even larger areas are understood by the trained psychotherapist. The "consciously known" areas can be dealt with rationally. One effort in psychotherapy is to increase the areas of conscious awareness. However, another important aspect of treatment is to make the patient less conscious of some of his experience, that is, to develop his spontaneity and sincerity. We describe this entire therapeutic process, including both rational and feeling components, as experiential psychotherapy.

The philosophy of experiential psychotherapy includes certain basic assumptions concerning human nature and certain objectives in treatment. Of fundamental importance in the ideology of the experiential psychotherapist is his concept of personal growth. He sees the sickness not as an inherent disease

Experiential Nonrational Psychotherapy, from Thomas P. Malone, Carl A. Whitaker, et al., "Rational and Nonrational Psychotherapy," *American Journal of Psychotherapy,* 15 (1961): 213–19.

but as dynamic pressure. Such pressures are minimal during long impasses in personal growth. When hope emerges, onward pressure increases. The patient becomes caught up in personal growth, even if he decompensates. The experiential psychotherapist assumes that wellness (continued personal growth) emerges except as it is interfered with. Wellness is perceived as fundamentally the increasing capacity to choose. Shorn of all of its frills, sickness is perceived as any hindrance to free choice. Choice is seen as more than a conscious intellectual exercise. The well person chooses correctly without thinking. This is the essence of what the Buddhist refers to as the hallmark of the mature person in their concept of *Mushin* (without thought), and what in our Western culture we mean by a *sincere* person (literally without cerebration, without calculation, without maneuvering). Experiential psychotherapy aims at providing a relationship within which the patient increases his capacity to so choose without a dominant influence dictating in any way the ultimate choice (democracy vs. communism).

The therapeutic relationship involves dependent-dominant vectors. It resembles the child-parent relationship. However, treating a patient differs significantly from rearing a child. The patient is not a child but a responding adult for whom the therapist has a very sharply circumscribed responsibility which is much less than the responsibility of the parent for his child. Because of these differences the interaction between the patient and therapist, despite the dependent-dominant vector, is reciprocal, but only within the specific delimited areas described above. The experiential psychotherapist does not assume the responsibility of educating the patient in the same way that the parent and society are responsible for educating the child. Psychotherapy is seen as providing a relationship which enables the patient to extend his interpersonal horizons as well as his intrapersonal experience. The therapist contributes a dynamic ingredient to the patient's growth effort but only as an ancillary participant. In contrast, the real parents inevitably dominate the growth of their child.

What are the limitations of personal growth? More specifically, what are the limitations of psychotherapy's contribution to personal growth? Psychotherapy can be useful to any person to increase his capacity to relate to, and with, more of his self. People continue to mature and grow throughout life, and psychotherapy can contribute to this at any period. The most profound aspects of character, as well as personality, can be altered. Experiences in the adult can be as significant in forming both character and personality as childhood experiences. Psychotherapy *can* provide such total and significant experiences. Practically speaking, we know that it often does not. To be effective in providing total experience significant enough to alter basic elements in character, psychotherapy must involve primary processes similar to those which were initially involved in character formation. These were beyond the rational control of the original parent. In one respect the professional therapist has an advantage over the parents. He has some awareness of the primary process interchange. The fundamental dynamics in each instance are operative with minimal conscious intent.

The experiential psychotherapist assumes that growth is inexorable in every person. This growth can be distorted. Furthermore, the growing process may remain ineffective in the absence of access to therapeutic persons in the world surrounding the patient. There are, however, limitations to the therapist's participation in psychotherapy. Unlike the parent, he should be unwilling to risk his life for a patient. Nor should he be willing to jeopardize any significant segment of his real life experience for the patient. The therapist as well as the parents are part of a culture and society, with needs apart from their responsibility for the patient or child. Just as the therapist has a certain limited parent-like function with the patient, so he also has a limited society-like function with the patient. . . .

Since the individual person is basically dependent on society, he is inevitably hostile to it. Conformity then is always ambivalent. The ambivalence is lessened to the extent to which the person increases the area of choice in his acceptance and denial of conforming patterns. Happily, most customs and conventions of society seem designed wisely for the growth and satisfaction of the individual. Thus, though the psychotherapist actively participates in increasing the area of choice, he is not unaware that most social values embody good choices. He simply helps the patient to discover this for himself.

The psychotherapist actively participates in helping the patient increase the area of choice. The new choices are among those which were already offered by society. Most patients leave psychotherapy with value systems similar to the ones they had at the beginning of therapy. But these are now *chosen* values. This is a critical difference.

A patient comes to psychotherapy because of his anxiety. This may be open or bound in a variety of psychiatric symptoms. Anxieties, and therefore symptoms, are resolved as transferences develop and countertransferences emerge. These create new anxieties which are in turn resolved in the relationship with transference-countertransference dynamics. The *natural* aim of the transferences, however, is to provide a responsiveness and counterresponsiveness which can gradually become experiential and existential. This emerges slowly and in accumulative bits of experience. The end point is the replacement of the transferential with an existential relationship. This provides the patient with an ongoing basis for continued experience and growth and gives him access to the community and cultural resources. The relationship ends when it is less satisfying and growth provoking than his community interaction. Psychotherapy has, therefore, both transferential and existential dimensions. The transferential aspects are predominant in the initial phases of psychotherapy but are gradually replaced by existential relationships. The transference relationships can be dealt with to some extent rationally, realizing that the necessary counterresponses (countertransferences) are nonrational. Of course we differentiate *nonrational,* for example, countertransference, from *irrational,* for example, transference. The existential relationship is not rational but personal and involves the total responsiveness of the person of the therapist to the person of the patient in the current living situation. The totality of both transferential and existential relationships we call the *experiential relationship.* As is true of any responding human being, it involves both rational and feeling (nonrational) components. Although emphasizing relational factors, the intrapersonal experiences of both therapist and patient function as reciprocals primarily through nonverbal communication. It is an "I-we-I" rather than an "I-I" or a "we" system. . . .

What then are the objectives of experiential psychotherapy? Obviously symptom relief, social adjustment, productive work, and employment are important. However, we see these as by-products of more major objectives. Certainly these results can be achieved independently of psychotherapy. For example, symptoms are often relieved by chemotherapy.

Experiential psychotherapy hopes for more than symptom relief. From psychotherapy we expect patients to develop an increased integrity. By integrity we mean an increase in their individual internal consistency, greater congruence between the inner aspects of their person and their manifestations in thought, words, and behavior. We expect a patient to achieve a greater freedom of choice. This means a capacity to choose conformity or not, that is, a freedom from compulsive rebellion or compulsive conformity. It means a freedom to construct one's own ethical and moral values within the framework of the social format without mimicking the social structure. In fact, the patient may have the identical moral values that he learned from his parents or had before psychotherapy, but after therapy they are more meaningful and useful to the patient because he has chosen these from among other choices. The therapist does not *deliberately* educate the patient to any moral or ethical values or systems. The patient may leave psychotherapy with stated values which constructively differ from those of the therapist.

Another objective of psychotherapy is the resolution of the dependent relationship of the patient on the therapist. This becomes difficult when the therapist assumes the grandiose role of educating the patient rationally to a given set of values (the Communist philosophy).

Psychotherapy aims at specific growth changes, including characterological changes. It seeks specific alterations in the persistent motivations which identify the person. It further seeks the unification and integration of these changes within the person. This develops out of a breakup in the repetition compulsions. The dependence on parental figures (including the therapist) then resolves with a resultant release from impassed living. It includes the objective helping the patient expand his experience to provide more material growth, both within the self and with others. This means an expansion of the limits of the self. This includes, among other things, an increased feeling repertoire and increasing creativity. Ideally we expect the ending patient to be creative, spontaneous, productive in his work and his community, loving and lovable, capable of gaining satisfaction from intimate and casual personal relationships, increasing in wisdom, tolerant, genuinely concerned with other human beings, rational and coherent, democratic, sensitive, practical, appropriate, and responsible.

We do not consider that the psychotherapy achieving this is irrational. It certainly includes the rational (thought) and the nonrational (feeling). We designate it as *experiential.*

Explicit Psychotherapy

Psychotherapy occurs in many different relationships and under many different guises. Such psychotherapy is *implicit. Explicit* psychotherapy, or the science of psychotherapy, has but recently emerged. It has been accompanied by labor pains similar to those which characterized the birth of other medical therapeutics. The relationship of these implicit forms of therapy to the present day explicit science is still unclear. The art of medicine as practiced by the country physician resembles the esoteric work of the psychiatrist. It is difficult to make explicit what has helped the patient emotionally in either instance. The experientially developed capacity of the professional psychiatrist was presumed to be related to both his knowledge of psychodynamics and psychopathology, and his appreciation of the relationship of the individual to the culture. The intuitive, clinically developed capacity of the general practitioner was assumed to come from his long and intimate contact with patients. Ideally, treatment by the professional psychiatrist is *explicit* psychotherapy, in contrast to the implicit methods of the physician. In either instance, however, psychotherapy may occur and is *an interpersonal operation in which the total organismic adaptation of one individual is catalyzed by another individual in such a way that the patient's level of adaptive capacity is increased. . . .*

In contrast, many dynamic psychiatrists generally consider the aim of therapy to be the extension of ego control over unconscious impulses. To the extent that unconscious material is made conscious, the patient is thought to be well. This is the fundamental basis of so-called insight therapy. This approach grossly underrates the adaptative and growth capacities of the unconscious and its usefulness biologically. The more unconscious the responses or

Explicit Psychotherapy, from Carl A. Whitaker and Thomas P. Malone, *The Roots of Psychotherapy* (New York: Blakiston, 1953), pp. 48–56.

the greater the participation of the unconscious in his total functioning, the more likely is the individual to function personally and socially on an adequate and gratifying level. Biologically, life is fundamentally an unconscious process, and in the degree to which internal stimuli must be handled on a conscious level, consciousness is under stress and, therefore, less able to perform its limited but appropriate function of reality testing. In a very real sense, the individual becomes "self-conscious." Intelligence itself is something to be used by the deeper core levels of the personality, i.e., those levels that have to do with the gratification of the more fundamental and unconscious needs of the individual.

In this sense, one of the primary aims of psychotherapy would be to restore to unconsciousness functions which seem to work best when the person is unaware of them. An example in physiology might clarify the issue. In many ways, cardiac action is less adequate to the extent that it is conscious. Frequent, continued and prolonged treatment, if it makes the patient more acutely aware of his heart action, may leave him with greater disability and sometimes precipitate final physical failure. . . .

The schizophrenic individual has more of his unconscious made conscious and sums up in his sickness precisely the principle illustrated. In this respect, he resembles the pseudoanalyzed patient who is aware of all of the symbolic implications of his simplest natural behavior. Finally, it is paradoxical that while in psychiatry one leads the neurotic to express the kind of unconscious material which the psychotic individual has readily available, nevertheless, psychiatry often hesitates to treat the psychotic patient. The problem in treating the psychotic is considered to be one of increasing the reality component of the patient, in contrast to the effort to force the neurotic individual to express his fantastic component.

Patients in psychotherapy reflect a deep need to restore to the unconscious those capacities freed during therapy. The neurotic needs to "re-repress" the symbolic material which was so readily available during the process of therapy itself. Re-repression seems to be inherent in the ending process. Thus, after a very deep fantasy relationship, the patient in the final interview may react to any fantastic orientation with a starkness which is chilling. In essence, the patient completely denies any fantastic involvement in the relationship. He may subsequently greet the therapist impersonally, leaving him with the feeling that, if nothing else, the patient is certainly ungrateful. This may not be far different from the need of the analyzed patient to deny the analysis. For instance, one patient visited a chiropractor after two years of analysis, got one treatment, and came back to the analyst saying, "Look here, you have spent two years with me and haven't helped me at all. I went down to the chiropractor for one treatment and I feel much better." The analyst has traditionally assumed that this was an effort on the part of the patient to handle his guilt about the transference relationship. It may partially be his need to reestablish the integrity of the unconscious through re-repression. This re-repression is, in some very fundamental respects, far different from repression as we ordinarily use the concept. Repression involves fear, guilt, shame, or anxiety. It represents one of the most pervasive unconscious dynamics for the resolution of conscious conflicts. Re-repression has more positive aspects. The relegation of a function to the unconscious, in this instance, does not stem from fear or guilt but more from the biological fact that some functions operate with maximum integrative effect when they operate unconsciously. . . .

Nongenetic Psychotherapy

Therapy aims at a reorganization and different integration of areas of the personality in a total sense. This has two dimensions: (1) the genetic has to do with past experience as it determines present experience; (2) the nongenetic, or what we prefer to call the dimension of experience, has to do with the present experience as it determines the relationship of other current experiences to each other and to past experiences, and summatively integrates current experiences and their projection into the future. In the case of the genetic dimension, one looks at current experience from the point of view of its past determinants. In the case of the nongenetic, one looks at current experiences as emergent determinants in themselves.

Therapeutic movement, then, can theoretically result from a "working through" or reexperiencing of past experiences that have determined present pathology. This therapeutic approach deals at length with the longitudinal dimension and takes up intensively the genetic causal interrelationship. Such a therapeutic procedure is properly called analytical therapy. The quality of consciousness, particularly ego function through insight, assumes considerable importance in this process. This results from the fact that one integrates retrospectively in order to extend the control of conscious ego over the unconscious. In contrast, therapeutic change can also result from certain current experiences which, because of their pervasiveness, change the relationship of other current experiences to each other and somehow mitigate the pathological effect of past experience on the organization of one's current living. This therapy could properly be called experiential. It is essentially a nonhistorical, atemporal one and uses, primarily, the current interpersonal experience in all of its facets, and depth as the means of altering personality.

Nongenetic Psychotherapy, from Whitaker and Malone, *The Roots of Psychotherapy,* pp. 62–66.

Assuming that this distinction can be made, therapy in the first instance has to do with how deep the analytical process penetrates in terms of reworking various genetic experiences. In the second case, the depth of psychotherapy has to do with how pervasive and integrative the experiential process is in terms of the two individuals involved at the time. Presumably, the same depth may result from either approach. Superficiality in analytical therapy is considered by some as "working through" the less significant genetic experiences. Superficiality in brief therapy would have to do with a limited personal involvement on the part of both individuals in the current therapeutic experience. Depth therapy through either approach involves mainly unconscious experiences. In the case of analysis, these are presented, worked through, and analyzed away. As such, the conscious-ego segment of the patient becomes more immediately involved. In experiential therapy, unconscious dynamics are again most significant. Comparison of depth in analytical therapy and experiential therapy can be justified only if the experiential in some way reverberates to the genetic and, conversely, if the genetic working through has resonance in the current experience. That some relationship exists between the genetic and the experiential may be assumed on the basis of our present knowledge of brain function which, though timeless, has at the same time adequate genetic representations. Furthermore, the fact that memory—and certainly every memory involved in current experience—can be changed by an alteration in the total experiential *gestalt,* substantiates the relationship between the genetic and the experiential. The unconscious itself seems to be atemporal in its function, and certainly its reflections in experience as, for example, in dreams, are nontemporal. . . .

Psychiatry needs a denominator which is common not only to the schools of therapy, but to the functions of individuals in the therapeutic process. The authors are trying to describe those aspects of the therapeutic process which are implicit in all successful therapy. It can probably be said with equal validity that psychoanalysis, to the degree to which it is successful, is implicitly experiential, and that experiential therapy reinforces the concepts of psychoanalysis. In the search for a common denominator in the therapeutic process as such, one must disregard a great part of the explicit formulation of what all therapists (including the authors) think happens in the therapeutic process. The common denominator is the interpersonal relationship, an interpersonal relationship fundamentally subjective in character. The relationship of the unconscious of the therapist to the unconscious of the patient underlies any therapy. This provides the ultimate in depth, the ultimate in experience, and as such, must be both quantitatively and qualitatively the common denominator of therapy. . . .

From this point of view, psychotherapy becomes not so much a social as a biological process. Being biological, it has a certain unity which centers around the integrative effect of certain current experiences in the growth of the total person. We have spoken of this orientation in psychotherapy as being experiential, involving, as we have pointed out, emphasis on the ahistorical, the atemporal, and the unconscious processes. This contrasts with the historical, analytical therapy, with its emphasis on insight and consciousness. The three central comparisons involve experience as against insight, unconscious as against conscious, integration and synthesis as against analysis. The willingness to involve one's self totally with the patient, and the recognition of the patient's fitness to judge more adequately than the therapist the process of therapy and its objectives, is based on an acceptance of the principle of homeostasis, as it operates psychologically. The patient can quite adequately maintain and protect himself within the therapeutic relationship. The recognition of his ability to do so is of critical importance in the effectiveness with which the therapy is achieved.

The concept of the synthetic grows out of this orientation. Unfortunately, the word has many connotations related to the artificial. Perhaps it would be better to speak of an emphasis on synthesis and integration as against analysis and insight. The therapist's or patient's understanding of the genetic panorama of his current inadequacies assumes less significance than the development of the patient's capacity to function as a person integrated within himself and with the surrounding culture. This synthesis can be achieved by experience and seldom simply by understanding. It may or may not be pertinent for a patient to understand that his inability to be aggressive toward a parental figure is due to certain infantile fears and guilt. In contrast, the experience of being aggressive toward a parental figure, even if he does not understand what occurs, will be helpful if the patient finds that after such expressed aggression he does not suffer and is not rejected. This is the precise difference between synthesis and analysis, between experience and insight. . . .

The Process of Psychotherapy

Although the process is an integral whole, still three general segments can be distinguished within the overall process. These are the Pre-Interview Segment, the Interview Segment, and the Post-Interview Segment.

In order to simplify the presentation of a process which has so many variables, we first have to present, in gross outline, the framework within which the total process falls. This, in turn, necessitates some discussion of the relationship of the process of psychotherapy to the culture, i.e., the manner in

---

The Process of Psychotherapy, from Whitaker and Malone, *The Roots of Psychotherapy,* pp. 82–117.

FIGURE 20.1 Movement in the psychotherapeutic process

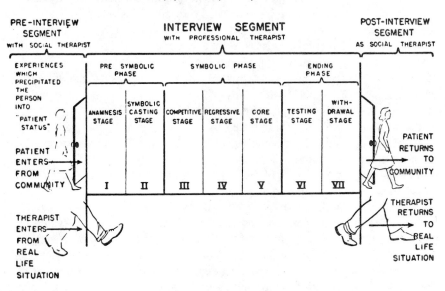

which the patient comes to the interview, and the ways in which the previous experiences of the patient reflect themselves in the interview. This is called the Pre-Interview Segment of the process, and it antedates the first interview with the professional therapist. It has no discernible stages within it. . . .

The Interview Segment follows. This empirically involves only the contacts the patient has with the professional therapist. This segment seems to fall into three general phases: the pre-symbolic, the symbolic, and the post-symbolic (ending) phases.

The pre-symbolic phase involves the early interviews with the patient where the primary problem seems to be the transition of the patient into deep therapy. It includes two stages, the Anamnestic and Casting Stages.

The symbolic phase of therapy follows this. Its central problem is the resolution of symbolic or transference needs of the patient and, thus, it comprises the essence of the process of therapy. It appears to follow a rather definitive pattern which is designated in sequence as the Competitive, the Regressive, and the Core Stages.

The concluding phase is termed the post-symbolic (ending) phase and involves primarily the transition of the patient out of therapy into the culture. This subsumes two stages, Testing and Withdrawal.

After the interviews are completed, the patient still has the problem of integrating the gains of therapy into his real life function within the culture. This occurs in the Post-Interview Segment, which seems to endure for only a definitive time, and the patient reaches a point at which we can say the process of therapy has been completed. . . .

The Symbolic and the Real in Psychotherapy

The Interview Segment develops only after both participants accept the preeminent importance of symbolism in their relationship. This phase brings into focus again the relationship of this symbolic involvement to the realities of both patient and therapist. Some systems of energy develop around the individual's pragmatic relationship with external realities; other systems of energy are linked with his relationship to himself and his inner experiences. These latter are defined as symbolic. In this sense, even though quantities of energy may flow from one system to another, the living function has two general facets, one of which is realistic, while the other is essentially fantastic and symbolic. The energy systems in therapy are primarily those which are fantastic and symbolic. . . .

FIGURE 20.2   Degree of fantasy involvement of therapist and patient at successive stages of the interview segment in the therapeutic process

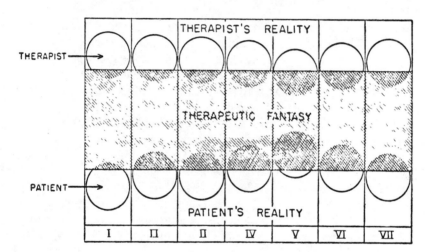

The process now looks fairly simple. We have two individuals, each responding to the other within a relationship, isolated from the real worlds of both. One of these persons has greater capacity for symbolic experience and unconscious functioning than the other. He is the therapist. The patient, even though he, too, has a large area of symbolic functioning, is not quite able to share with another the experience of these symbolic relationships. In general, the energies which impel his symbolic experiences are fettered by his inability to live them through to a different outcome, i.e., one which would free him as a person. By contrast, the energies of the therapist are free even in this symbolic experience, and the therapist differs, also, since he can better utilize these energies in his functioning as a real person. . . .

The Loci of the Process

The therapeutic process is, thus, intrapsychic in both the therapist and the patient, and only becomes possible through the interrelation between the two. This is not another way of saying that the therapeutic process resides in the interpersonal relationship. Therapy is possible only when such a relationship exists, but it specifically involves the unconscious dynamics of each of the participants. The really essential aspect of the relationship is simply the accessibility of the unconscious dynamics of both participants, each to the other. The therapy which occurs intrapsychically almost seems to be made possible by some special mode of communication. For example, the therapeutic impasse seems related to a modification of the communication in such a manner that the participants no longer have access to the intrapsychic dynamics of each other.

Intrapsychic dynamics mean, of course, essentially unconscious dynamics. Therapy involves an increasing accessibility of each participant's unconscious dynamics to the other. More specifically, the intrapsychic dynamics of the therapist involve his unconscious reactions to the patient as a projection of himself. The intrapsychic dynamics of the therapist demand, primarily, the integration of his current feelings into his total self (body-image problem) as these are specifically stimulated by the projected feelings of the patient. Together these force the therapist to precipitate himself into residues of his own transference feelings. In short, the therapist experiences both the dynamics of his own body-image integration, and the vestiges of his infantile familial experience as these continue to be present in residual as his "intrapsychic family." The intra-psychic dynamics of the patient involve, primarily, his reaction to the therapist as the latter provokes feelings specific to the functioning of the patient's transference needs where these have been previously internalized as his own intrapsychic family. The patient, in short, has an intrapsychic experience in which the therapist participates to a greater or lesser extent. In contrast, the therapist has an essentially nonfamilial and, primarily, personal experience which deals with the relationship of his various "parts" to his integrated wholeness. . . .

Disequilibrium Dynamics

Unfortunately, the process of therapy is not quite so simple as the therapist responding to obtunded areas in the patient. Some areas and energy systems within the professional therapist resemble those of the patient. Further, the patient also has systems of energy which can express themselves freely, and which are not bound. In other words, each individual participating in this realtionship includes both a *patient vector* and a *therapist vector*. This duality of function prevents the establishment of any static equilibrium in the relationship. Whatever the specific process, the chief characteristic of therapy is its constant disequilibrium. The process of therapy itself involves successive, and perhaps sequential, resolutions of deeper and more pervasive states of disequilibrium. This formulation may seem to suggest that the locus of the process of therapy lies in the interpersonal relationship. Yet that is not the case.

What are the general dynamics of "movement" in the therapeutic process? Therapy "moves" whenever the character of the emotional relationship between the patient and therapist changes in some manner. An impasse in therapy exists whenever the emotional relationship becomes fixed, e.g., the therapist is unable to alter a transference projection of the patient. The various ways in which these transference projections emerge and then are altered can be spoken of as "disequilibrium dynamics." Through these the infantile transferences are upset, or "disequilibriated." Utilizing the kind of communication spoken of above, these dynamics involve affective stimuli from one person which bring about changes in the intrapsychic experience of the other person. When integrated, these subsequently serve as stimuli which reciprocally provoke additional changes in the first person. This is a constant process. The stimuli may be minute or massive and may be reacted to either with significant or with minute intrapsychic changes in the other person. . . .

Anxiety specifically expresses a breakdown in the relational communicability. When either of the participants becomes inaccessible to the other on an unconscious level, there results what amounts to a primitive form of separation. The separation engenders a specific type of anxiety. In this sense, all disequilibrium dynamics are motivated initially by anxiety. In other words, anxiety makes up the "stuff" which moves the process of therapy toward its completion. . . .

FIGURE 20.3   Relative patient vector and therapist vector that each participant brings to the relationship at successive stages of the interview segment in the therapeutic process

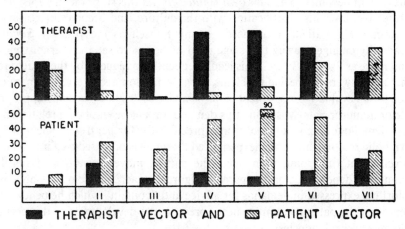

Stages of the Interview Segment

Anamnestic Stage (I).   In the anamnestic stage (I) which is pre-symbolic, the therapist sees himself as a professional person endowed with certain functional potentialities and responsibilities. He tends to regard himself as a function, that is, as the *Therapist,* although he also retains his concept of himself as a person. In this initial period—which endures not a minute nor an interview but an indefinite period of time—the therapist sees the patient as an *Adult,* and shortly thereafter as a *Pseudo-Adult.* This latter term serves to indicate the adult who obviously lives behind a façade, e.g., the neurotic. . . .

Casting Stage (II).   With the development of early fantasy and bilateral intrapsychic representations, the therapeutic process emerges into what is called the symbolic casting stage (II). The therapist moves ahead of the patient, in that he pushes the patient toward the core of the therapeutic process. Strange as it may seem, this does not have any particular relationship to the intrapsychic representation in the developing process itself. Even though the patient holds back and resists the movement in the process, he is the one whose symbolization changes. The therapist in the second stage still sees himself in his professional functioning, as *Therapist,* although he becomes distinctly more of a person to himself and becomes more free to relate in his own unique way. He may now see the patient intrapsychically not just as *Pseudo-Adult,* but as *Adolescent.* . . .

Competitive Stage (III).   In the Competitive Stage (III), the therapist sees himself as *Parent-Person,* and his perception of himself as a unique individual becomes less pervasive than it was before. He takes on, by means of this intrapsychic representation of himself, an unconscious parental responsibility for the patient. His representation of the patient within himself changes so that the patient becomes to him his own *Child-Self.* At this stage the therapist feels protective, loses his identification with the culture, and becomes increasingly "warm." The patient, though still seeing himself as the younger *Sibling,* gradually changes during this stage until he begins to see the therapist more and more as *Parent-Person.* This leads frequently to requests by the patient for factual answers to specific problems, for information about psychodynamics, and for an evaluative assessment of his behavior as "right or wrong," appropriate or inappropriate. Mistaking this demand for a close emotional relationship as a demand for content response may preclude the further development of the symbolic relationship. The inexperienced therapist is often seduced into reality precisely at this point, even while the patient moves toward an infantile, emotional dependence on the parental figure. An acceptance of this abortive effort (as expressed in demands for advice and "content" which he believes to represent the patient's ultimate need) prevents the development of this deeper parent-child relationship. . . .

FIGURE 20.4 Symbolic representation

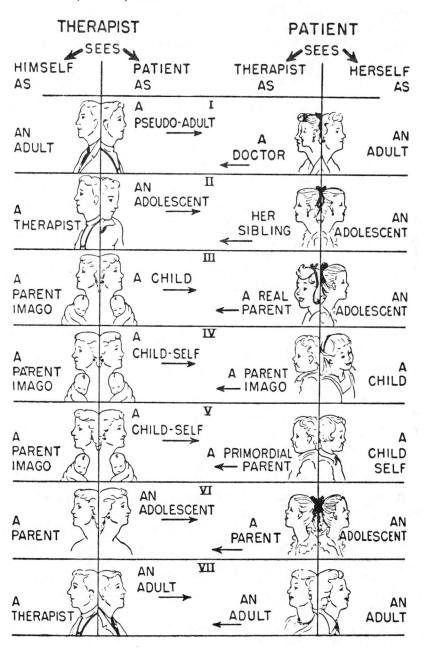

THERAPIST   PATIENT

SEES   SEES

| HIMSELF AS | PATIENT AS | THERAPIST AS | HERSELF AS |

I
A PSEUDO-ADULT →

AN ADULT   ← A DOCTOR   AN ADULT

II
AN ADOLESCENT →

A THERAPIST   HER SIBLING ←   AN ADOLESCENT

III
A CHILD →

A PARENT IMAGO   A REAL PARENT ←   AN ADOLESCENT

IV
A CHILD-SELF →

A PARENT IMAGO   A PARENT IMAGO ←   A CHILD

V
A CHILD-SELF →

A PARENT IMAGO   A PRIMORDIAL PARENT ← A CHILD SELF

VI
AN ADOLESCENT →

A PARENT   A PARENT ←   AN ADOLESCENT

VII
AN ADULT →

A THERAPIST   AN ADULT ←   AN ADULT

Regressive Stage (IV). As the therapeutic process approaches the Core Stage, the patient, secure in the therapist, conceives of himself as a *Child* and of the therapist as the *Primordial-Parent.* The therapist, in accepting this and in seeing himself as the *Primordial-Parent,* goes further in the denial of himself as a professional person, and sees the patient more completely as his own *Child-Self.* The manifestations of this phase are usually very overt and specific. The patient says, "I feel like a little baby," and most often the experienced therapist responds to this remark nonverbally by means of the most pervasive acceptance possible to him.

Core Stage (V). In the Core Stage (V), both the therapist and the patient see themselves in their true therapeutic roles—the therapist as *Parent* and the patient as *Child-Self.* Each of them introjects the other and regards the other as his whole intrapsychic "society." In this area the greatest therapeutic depth accrues. Only at this level do the bilateral symbolic relationships converge fully. The relationship involves only two symbolic roles, even though each is unique to the intrapsychic "society" of the participants. This symbolic synchronization and complementary articulation increases the depth and extent of the symbolic participation because of the singleness of the vector, and because each sees himself in the very role in which he is seen by the other. Once such a symbolic relationship has been established, the patient has the capacity to develop other such relationships as a pattern through which segmental problems or conflicts can be worked out. The aim of Stage IV is the attainment of Stage V. The aim of V, however, is not VI. The Core Stage aims at an indefinite continuation of itself. It is the essential therapeutic relationship of and in itself. It is the relationship which, throughout the rest of therapy, and even subsequent to interview therapy, can be used by the patient in the attempt to work through his residual transference problems, and the problems of his emotional growth in general.

Testing Stage (VI). The Testing Stage (VI) does not necessarily evolve spontaneously from the use of the core experience. The symbolic emergence from Stages II or III to V is unitary; it is an emergent whole, the implicit aim of each level being the attainment of the succeeding level. If the process begins, and no new pathological factors intervene, it will naturally gravitate toward the Core Stage. This is apparently a primary quality of the symbolic relationship—it seems to seek the most primitive symbolism. The emergence, therefore, of Stages II to V is a by-product of the "symbolic need." In contrast, the movement of therapy from Stage V is a by-product not of symbolic need, but of reality and of social pressure, and presupposes a certain security gained from the experience of the core relationship. The breakout of the Core Stage into the Testing Stage resembles the battle for status between the mature adolescent and the parent.

The Testing Stage marks the beginning of new patterns of intrapsychic representation both on the part of the therapist and of the patient. The therapist still functions as a *Parent-Person,* but in a somewhat different sense, for out of the synchronous fantasy of Stage V has come an increasing awareness of his own separateness from the patient. Although still a parent, he is also more of a person. He now sees the patient as a real person, whose immaturities are fading away, i.e., he sees him as a potential adult.

Typical of this phase is the therapist's delight in the story of how the patient "told off" the man next door. The patient conceives of himself as an *Adolescent* much as the therapist sees him, but with the added sense of power so typical of the adolescent. This also entails an incipient awareness of the therapist's inadequacies. The patient's concept of the therapist now becomes much less specifically parental and comes closer to the benign tolerance which the maturing adolescent shows toward his "aging" parent. It recapitulates the adolescent's belief that his parents belong to a different and passing generation, which has very little appreciation of the realities of his own life experience and which, in a sense, is doomed to be left behind, alone with its memories of the earlier family life.

Thus, this stage reveals the growing rejection of the therapist as a symbolic parent, and the development of the patient's concept of himself as an adult. He has increasing sureness that adulthood is possible for him, too, and that he can bring it into being.

Withdrawal Stage (VII).   The mechanism of the growth process appears in the Withdrawal Stage, with the patient beginning to see his *Child-Self* in the therapist, and to obtain a glimpse of the first realities of his own integrated adulthood. The therapist now loses his pervasive parental quality. He becomes just a professional means wherewith the patient can round out his own capacity to carry on therapy as an intrapsychic process, and without direct participation by a professional therapist. The finald ending occurs when the therapist loses his intrapsychic representation of the patient as his own *Adult-Self.* The patient sees himself now as real and *Adult,* with a growing perception of his uniqueness as a person. He even begins to see the therapist as a *Pseudo-Adult,* in much the same way in which the therapist had previously seen the patient. Stage VII parallels the manner in which, in real life, the young man resolves his relationship to his parent. It involves a rejection of the parent in his symbolic role, and an acceptance, on the part of both, of the autonomous adult status of himself and of the other. . . .

Termination of Therapy

There seem to be three general types of endings. First is the so-called positive ending, in which both the therapist and the patient have emotionally accepted the termination of the relationship and their capacity to live separately. Each implicitly recognizes the contribution of the other to his own living, and separation feelings on both sides are, therefore, minimal. This ending parallels the going away to college of a boy who thereby becomes independent of the family; yet both he and the family have accepted the right to separateness. There is, of course, always a minimal bilateral feeling of rejection. Coincidentally with this, the boy accepts the fact that he has gotten all the parents have to give him and has given to the parents all that he is capable of giving. The parents accept the fact that the boy's leaving will not be too grievous a loss to them, and that what residual needs they have will have to be satisfied in other ways.

Second is the negative ending. It may be as clear-cut as the positive one, with the patient leaving the therapist aggressively or defiantly, and with the therapist nurturing minor feelings of rejection. . . .

The third and most unsatisfactory of all endings seems to us to be the most common ending in contemporary psychiatry. The therapist compromises the ending phase, and this results in a dependency relationship of the patient to himself, so that the therapist never has to face directly the fact of his rejection by the patient. . . .

The Post-Interview

The process of therapy does not terminate with the Interview Segment. On the contrary, from the point of view of time, most of the realistic therapeutic gain occurs in the Post-Interview Segment. An adequate ending of the relationship does not completely resolve the transference neurosis but, rather, provides the impetus which begins the resolution of this neurosis. The final resolution of the transference needs occurs in the Post-Interview Segment of therapy. This segment involves, primarily, an increase in the importance of the patient's real needs, and in his capacity to gratify them as they become fused with his fantasy needs, which he is able now to gratify outside of his relationship to the therapist. The fantasy-reality ratio swings toward the real. The patient leaves, not free of intrapsychic obligations, but now confronted with the introject of the therapist, as it has come to replace the "intrapsychic family" during the process of therapy. Patients frequently refer to the fact that after the interviews have ended, they carry the therapist around within them for some time as a dynamic part of their functioning in their social and real relationships. . . .

Much as the process of therapy, once begun, has an inherent movement of its own which carries it to termination, so the Post-Interview phase of transference-neurosis resolution has an inherent movement, and seems to "carry itself" to a successful termination, although different patients require different periods of time for this and work it through differently.

An attempt by the therapist to intrude himself into the Post-Interview phase may contaminate this on a personal level, thereby upsetting the ratio between the real and the fantastic by an intensification of the importance of the fantastic relationship. This difficulty arises invariably when the therapist and the patient have not only a professional relationship, but also a social relationship. One sees this most vividly when one attempts therapy with colleagues or close friends.

The patient makes these transitions in the Post-Interview Segment better if social therapists, external to the interview situation, are readily available. The patient uses these individuals in this phase with about equal emphasis on the real and on the symbolic. In the relationship with the social therapist, fantasy needs do not overwhelm the patient as readily, and he expands the real areas of his living in a relationship with persons who have some awareness of his fantasy need. There seems to be a point at which the patient finally extrudes the therapist, and a more gratifying balance between real and fantastic satisfaction obtains.

This point is usually followed by a new swing in the patient toward his fantasy gratifications. He is no longer afraid of his fantasy experiences and, therefore, no longer has as deep a need for "flight into reality." The patient obtains greater real satisfactions and also shows a capacity for more fantasy satisfactions, with a fusion between the two which represents the most functional balance possible for that particular patient. This continues as a process of growth.

The Function of Re-repression

The successful termination of therapy, as described above, involves extensive repression. It has always seemed paradoxical that the psychiatrist deliberately breaks through repressions in the neurotic person to bring to consciousness unconscious fantasies, while he, at the same time, diagnoses as refractory or incurable those individuals who have almost all of their unconscious available to awareness and expression, that is, the schizophrenic. It is not far wrong to say that many of the individuals who have had extensive, but incomplete, psychiatric treatment have, in a sense, been made somewhat "schizophrenic." At any rate, the community consistently expresses such an idea in characterizing the post-depth therapy patient as one who never simply eats food without, at the same time, being conscious of his introjective dynamics and the cannibalistic implications of the simple process of eating.

A person concerned with the mechanisms of breathing and of heart action is less apt to breathe well and more apt to have cardiac difficulties. Like those primitive biological systems with diencephalic representations, the unconscious functions best when we are unaware of its functioning. The restoration of this unawareness subsequent to the interview phase occurs during the

Post-Interview phase of therapy, sic, re-repression. The dynamics of this type of re-repression are so radically different from those of the original repressions that perhaps even the use of the term *re-repression* is ill-advised. The re-repression discussed here occurs not out of guilt or fear but, rather, in order to raise the level of homeostatic functioning in the individual. In this sense, it may be likened to one facet of the original repression, i.e., that facet which involves repression not from guilt or shame (interpersonal factors), but for the sake of personal well-being. Whatever the dynamics of the re-repression, fundamentally, it occurs simply because this constitutes the best way for the organism to function.

As a therapist, one does not aim at creating a cult of therapeutized persons who are different from, and can expect to be isolated within, our total culture. On the contrary, the individual should be better able to return to his culture, to become part of it, to contribute to it, and to obtain maximum gratification within it. This involves a certain submission to the cultural structure for the economy of the culture as a whole. . . .

Definition of Psychotherapeutic Technique

. . . Since much of the basic operation of therapy might be considered technical, the need for a specific definition of technique is apparent.

A technique is an *interpersonal operation deliberately used by the therapist, the function of which is to transpose social, latent affect in both participants into deeper, manifest affect in order to catalyze the affective and symbolic process of psychotherapy.* Technique so defined implies an underlying unconscious set (disposition to feel) on the part of the therapist; and further, it suggests that the affect he has at that point is less deep than what is implied by his behavior. The basic dynamics involved in a technique are similar to those in dream work, i.e., condensation, undoing, dramatization, and symbolization. Unlike dream work, the major transposition here is not of content, but rather of affect, although some psychotherapists continue to approach the patient through content. A technique is effective if it induces personal and deep feeling in the relationship, producing relatedness which is no longer deliberate and conscious, but spontaneous and integrated.

Definition of Psychotherapeutic Technique, from Whitaker and Malone, *The Roots of Psychotherapy,* pp. 195–96.

Group Psychotherapy

TRANSACTIONAL ANALYSIS
PSYCHOTHERAPY

Eric Berne

A naturalized American, Eric Lennard Berne was born in Montreal in 1910. He studied there at McGill University, where he earned his M.D. in 1931 and his C.M. in 1935. Berne took up permanent residence in the United States during World War II. The early 1940s found him at New York City Psychoanalytic Institute, and for a decade (1947–56) at the San Francisco Psychoanalytic Institute. In seminars starting in 1958, the International Transactional Analysis Association was incorporated in 1965. In 1971, the organ of this school, the *Transactional Analysis Journal,* made its initial appearance. His private practice of transactional analysis continued until the remainder of his life in San Francisco, and in Carmel, California, where he made his home. He died in a Monterey, California hospital of a heart attack on July 15, 1970, at the age of sixty. While he spent his weekends at Carmel, Berne travelled seventy miles from there to San Francisco every Tuesday morning by driving or flying, returning Thursday evenings.

Berne's method of transactional analysis was stimulated in the mid-1950s from a patient's insight. The patient, a lawyer, commented in a psychotherapeutic session that he was just a little boy rather than a mature lawyer. This perceptiveness led to structural analysis and ego states (child and adult mental states).

Transactional analysis (a term used both to identify Berne's entire psychotherapeutic system as well as a stage of pysochotherapeutic analysis) proceeds to take the patient through the following progressive stages: (1) structural analysis, (2) transactional analysis proper, (3) game analysis, (4) script analysis, and finally (5) social control.

The patient begins with the stage of *structural analysis,* becoming aware of ego states that structure and govern the personality phenomenologically. The three ego states include: (1) *parent,* or states resembling parental figures, i.e., identificatory behavior acquired from one's parents; (2) *adult,* those mature states in which a person faces and appraises reality autonomously or deals with the world as it really is, i.e., data processing; and (3) *child,* those states resembling the fixations or residues of one's early childhood that are still active as archaic relics within the personality of grown-ups. Compare these three ego states with Freud's structure of the personality (superego, ego, and id respectively). The adult state, comparable to Freud's potent ego, is the preferred state and an indication of mental health.

The stage of *transactional analysis proper* deals with a unit of social intercourse termed a *transaction,* resulting from the encounter of two or more individuals. The first person to speak creates a *transactional stimulus;* the one responding produces a *transactional response.* Transactions are *complementary* when the respondent reacts appropriately as expected, thus allowing social intercourse to proceed smoothly. Otherwise it is a *crossed transaction* or disrupted communication, such as those transactions contributing to divorce.

Berne defined the stage of *games* as "an ongoing series of complementary ulterior transactions progressing to a well-defined, predictable outcome."[1] Berne classified games as segments of scripts. A game is an unconscious maneuver to govern relationships in dealing with other people in order to manipulate them. Impatient with losers, Berne saw them as wasting time explaining why they lost, and spending "their lives thinking about what they're going to do. They rarely enjoy doing what they're doing." Parent, adult, and child, as pieces utilized in games, are manifestations of universal states of mind. *Pastimes,* defined as straightforward interpersonal transactions, are games without dissimulation of maneuvering and manipulating other people.

While structural analysis is a prerequisite for transactional analysis proper, the stage of transactional analysis is followed by game analysis, which is succeeded by script analysis. Comparable to theatrical scripts, scripts in transactional analysis are those of a person's entire lifetime-drama, e.g., the tragic script of a woman whose compelling fantasy motivates her to marry alcoholic after alcoholic. Progressing through each state of structural analysis, the patient seeks ultimately to attain social control.

Whereas the public knows Berne best for his *Games People Play: The Psychology of Human Relationships* (1964), his psychotherapeutic system is less popularly and more concisely explicated in his *Transactional Analysis in Psychotherapy: A Systematic Individual and Social Psychiatry* (1961). Berne introduced his new psychotherapy in "Transactional Analysis: A New and Effective Method of Group Therapy" in the *American Journal of Psychotherapy* (1958).

---

[1]Eric Berne, *Games People Play: The Psychology of Human Relationships* (Grove, 1964), p. 48.

Synopsis of Transactional Analysis Psychotherapy

In both individual and group work, this method proceeds in stages which can be clearly defined, and which schematically at least succeed one another, so that both the therapist and the patient can at any given moment state the therapeutic position with some precision; that is, what they have been accomplished so far, and what the next step is likely to be.

Procedure

Structural analysis, which must precede transactional analysis, is concerned with the segregation and analysis of ego states. The goal of this procedure is to establish the predominance of reality-testing ego states and free them from contamination by archaic and foreign elements. When this has been accomplished, the patient can proceed to *transactional analysis:* first, the analysis of simple transactions, then the analysis of stereotyped series of transactions, and finally the analysis of long complex operations often involving several people and usually based on rather elaborate fantasies. An example of the last is the rescue fantasy of the woman who marries one alcoholic after another. The goal of this phase is *social control:* that is, control of the individual's own tendency to manipulate other people in destructive or wasteful ways and of his tendency to respond without insight or option to the manipulations of others.

In the course of these therapeutic operations, traumatically fixated archaic ego states have been segregated, but not resolved. At the end of this program, the individual is in a particularly favorable position, because of the predominance of reality-testing, to attempt the resolution of the archaic conflicts and distortions. Experience has shown that such a sequel is not essential to the therapeutic success of the method, and the decision as to whether or not it is undertaken becomes a problem of clinical judgment and situational freedom.

Language.   While the theoretical exposition is more complex, the application of structural and transactional analysis requires an esoteric vocabulary of only six words. *Exteropsyche, neopsyche,* and *archaeopsyche* are regarded as psychic *organs,* which manifest themselves phenomenologically as exteropsychic (e.g., identificatory), neopsychic (e.g., data-processing), and archaeopsychic (e.g., regressive) *ego states.* Colloquially, these types of ego states are referred to as *Parent, Adult,* and *Child,* respectively. These three substantives form the terminology of structural analysis. The methodological problems involved in moving from organs to phenomena to substantives are not relevant to the practical applications.

Pastimes, Games, and Scripts. Certain repetitive sets of social maneuvers appear to combine both defensive and gratificatory functions. Such maneuvers are colloquially called *pastimes* and *games.* Some of them, which readily yield both primary and secondary gains, tend to become commonplace; the game of "PTA" for example is prevalent in this country wherever parents come together in parties or groups. More complex operations are based on an extensive unconscious life plan which is called a *script,* after the theatrical scripts which are intuitive derivatives of these psychological dramas. These three terms, *pastime, game,* and *script,* form the vocabulary of transactional analysis.

It will be demonstrated that Parent, Adult, and Child are not concepts, like Superego, Ego, and Id, or the Jungian constructs, but phenomenological realities; while pastimes, games, and scripts are not abstractions, but operational social realities. Once he has a firm grasp of the psychological, social, and clinical meanings of these six terms, the transactional analyst, whether physician, psychologist, social scientist, or social worker, is in a position to use them as therapeutic, research, or case-work tools according to his or her opportunities and qualifications.

Introduction

An ego state may be described phenomenologically as a coherent system of feelings related to a given subject, and operationally as a set of coherent behavior patterns; or pragmatically, as a system of feelings which motivates a related set of behavior patterns. . . .

Complete Diagnosis

There are three types of ego states: Parent, Adult, and Child, which reside in or are manifestations of the corresponding psychic organs: exteropsyche, neopsyche, and archaeopsyche. The significant properties of these organs are as follows:

1. Executive power. Each gives rise to its own idiosyncratic patterns of organized behavior. This brings them within the purview of psychophysiology and psychopathology, and ultimately of neurophysiology.

Introduction and Complete Diagnosis, from Berne, *Transactional Analysis in Psychotherapy,* pp. 17, 75–79, 90.

2. Adaptability. Each is capable of adapting its behavioral responses to the immediate social situation in which the individual finds himself. This brings them into the realm of the "social" sciences.

3. Biological fluidity, in the sense that responses are modified as a result of natural growth and previous experiences. This raises historical questions which are the concern of psychoanalysis.

4. Mentality, in that they mediate the phenomena of experience and hence are the concern of psychology, particularly of introspective, phenomenological, structural, and existential psychologies.

The complete diagnosis of an ego state requires that all four of these aspects be available for consideration, and the final validity of such a diagnosis is not established until all four have been correlated. The diagnosis tends to proceed clinically in the order given.

A. A Parental ego state is a set of feelings, attitudes, and behavior patterns which resemble those of a parental figure. The diagnosis is first usually made on the basis of clinical experience with demeanors, gestures, voices, vocabularies, and other characteristics. This is the *behavioral* diagnosis. The diagnosis is corroborated if the particular set of patterns is especially apt to be elicited in response to childlike behavior on the part of someone else in the environment. This is the *social* or *operational* diagnosis. It is further corroborated if the individual can eventually state exactly which parental figure offered the prototype for the behavior. This is the *historical* diagnosis. The diagnosis is validated if the individual can finally re-experience in full intensity, with little weathering, the moment or epoch when he assimilated the parental ego state. This is the *phenomenological* diagnosis.

The Parent is typically exhibited in one of two forms. The *prejudicial* Parent is manifested as a set of seemingly arbitrary nonrational attitudes or parameters, usually prohibitive in nature, which may be either syntonic or dystonic with the local culture. If they are culturally syntonic, there is a tendency to accept them without adequate skepticism as rational or at least justifiable. The *nurturing* Parent is often manifested as *sympathy for* another individual, which again may be either culturally syntonic or culturally dystonic.

The Parental ego state must be distinguished from the Parental *influence*. Such an influence can be inferred when the individual manifests an attitude of childlike compliance. The *function* of the Parent is to conserve energy and diminish anxiety by making certain decisions "automatic" and relatively unshakable. This is particularly effective if the decisions tend to be syntonic with the local culture.

B. The Adult ego state is characterized by an autonomous set of feelings, attitudes, and behavior patterns which are adapted to the current reality. Since the Adult is still the least well understood of the three types of ego states, it is best characterized in clinical practice as the residual state left after the segregation of all detectable Parent and Child elements. Or it may be more formally considered as the derivative of a model of the neopsyche. Such a model may be briefly specified as follows:

The neopsyche is a partially self-programing probability computer designed to control the effectors in dealing with the external environment. It has the special characteristic that its energy state at each epoch is determined by how closely the computed probabilities correspond with the actual results. This energy state is signaled as discharge or overload. (E.g., a green light, experienced as pleasure, satisfaction, or admiration; or a red light, experienced as "frustration," disappointment, or indignation.) This characteristic, under various conditions of probability, accounts descriptively for the "instinct of mastery" and for the admiration of the striving toward such qualities as responsibility, reliability, sincerity, and courage. Interestingly enough, each of these four qualities can be reduced to a simple probability statement.

In accordance with the four diagnostic levels, the Adult is noted to be organized, adaptable, and intelligent, and is experienced as an objective relationship with the external environment based on autonomous reality-testing. In each individual case, due allowances must be made for past learning opportunities. The Adult of a very young person or of a peasant may make very different judgments from that of a professionally trained worker. The criterion is not the accuracy of the judgments, nor the acceptability of the reactions (which depends on the local culture of the observer), but on the quality of the data processing and the use made of the data available to that particular individual.

C. The Child ego state is a set of feelings, attitudes, and behavior patterns which are relics of the individual's own childhood. Again, the behavioral diagnosis is usually made first on the basis of clinical experience. The social diagnosis emerges if that particular set of patterns is most likely to be elicited by someone who behaves parentally. If the diagnosis is correct, it will be corroborated historically by memories of similar feelings and behavior in early childhood. The decisive phenomenological validation only occurs, however, if the individual can re-experience the whole ego state in full intensity with little weathering. This occurs most effectively and dramatically if he can, in the waking state, relive a traumatic moment or epoch of fixation, and this will best bring about the feeling of conviction on the part of both the therapist and the patient which is one critical step in the therapeutic process.

The Child is exhibited in one of two forms. The *adapted* Child is manifested by behavior which is inferentially under the dominance of the Parental influence, such as compliance or withdrawal. The *natural* Child is manifested by autonomous forms of behavior such as rebelliousness or self-indulgence. It is differentiated from the autonomous Adult by the ascendancy of archaic mental processes and the different kind of reality-testing. It is the proper function of the "healthy" Child to motivate the data processing and programing of the Adult so as to obtain the greatest amount of gratification for itself. . . .

Structural analysis proper deals with the mastery (but not necessarily the resolution) of internal conflicts through diagnosis of ego states, decontamination, boundary work, and stabilization, so that the Adult can maintain control of the personality in stressful situations. After maximum therapeutic benefit has been obtained through structural analysis alone, there are three choices open: trial or permanent termination, psychoanalysis, or transactional analysis. . . . Psychoanalysis, in structural terms, consists of deconfusing the Child and resolving the conflicts between the Child and the Parent.

Analysis of Transactions

The aim of transactional analysis is *social control,* in which the Adult retains the executive in dealings with other people who may be consciously or unconsciously attempting to activate the patient's Child or Parent. This does not mean that the Adult alone is active in social situations, but it is the Adult who decides when to release the Child or Parent, and when to resume the executive. Thus one patient might think: "At this party, in contrast to last night's formal dinner, I can afford to take a few drinks and have some fun." Later he might think: "Now I'm beginning to get sloppy, so I'd better stop drinking and simmer down, even though they're all trying to encourage my clowning."

Transactional analysis is best done in therapy groups; or conversely, it may be said that the natural function of therapy groups is transactional analysis. Structural analysis, which is a prerequisite for transactional analysis, may also be learned in the group instead of in individual therapy. It is usually advisable, however, to have two or three preliminary individual sessions. The function of individual sessions prior to group therapy, aside from routine matters such as history taking, is to introduce the patient to structural analysis.

Transactional analysis proper is followed by game analysis and that in turn by script analysis. The first is a prerequisite for the other two; otherwise they may degenerate into a kind of pastime instead of being used as rational therapeutic procedures. Game analysis is necessary in order to attain social control. Script analysis, whose aim might be called "life-plan control," is so complex that this stage may never be reached in many therapy groups, but ordinary social control is possible without it. In special situations, such as social counseling and marital group therapy, a special procedure called "relationship analysis" may be indicated. Ordinarily formal relationship analysis may be omitted, but every group therapist, in order to be able to do his best,

Analysis of Transactions, from Berne, *Transactional Analysis in Psychotherapy,* pp. 90–96.

should have a clear understanding of this procedure and some experience in carrying it through.

Transactional Analysis

At this point we may consider a group of housewives between thirty and forty years of age, each with one or more children, who met weekly for an hour and a half at the office of their psychiatrist, Dr. Q. At the end of eighteen months, Daphne, Lily, and Rosita, who had attended from the beginning, were the most sophisticated members; Hyacinth, Holly, Camellia, and Cicely, who joined later in that order, were less so. A common *seating diagram* and the *schedule* for this group is shown in figure 21.1.

One day Camellia, following a previous train of thought, announced that she had told her husband she was not going to have intercourse with him any more and that he could go and find himself some other woman. Rosita asked curiously: "Why did you do that?" Whereupon Camellia burst into tears and replied: "I try so hard and then you criticize me."

There were two transactions here, which may be represented by the diagrams in figures 21.2(a) and (b). These were drawn and analyzed before the

FIGURE 21.1 Seating diagram

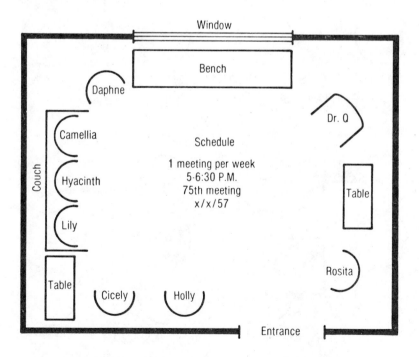

group. The personalities of the two women are represented structurally as comprising Parent, Adult, and Child. The first transactional stimulus is Camellia's statement about what she told her husband. She related this in her Adult ego state, with which the group was familiar. It was received in turn by an Adult Rosita, who in her response ("Why did you do that?") exhibited a mature, reasonable interest in the story. As shown in figure 21.2(a), the transactional stimulus was Adult to Adult, and so was the transactional response. If things had continued at this level, the conversation might have proceeded smoothly,

Rosita's question ("Why did you do that?") now constituted a new transactional stimulus and was intended as one adult speaking to another. Camel-

FIGURE 21.2

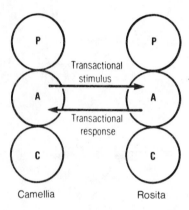

(a) Complementary transaction — Type I

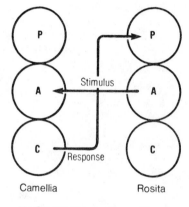

(b) Crossed transaction — Type I

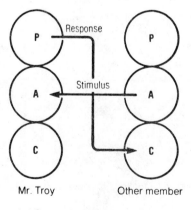

(c) Crossed transaction — Type II

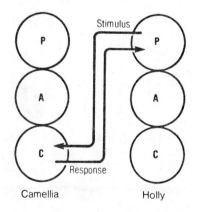

(d) Complementary transaction — Type II

lia's response, however, was not that of one adult to another, but that of a child answering a critical parent. Camellia's misperception of Rosita's ego state, and the shift in her own ego state, resulted in a *crossed transation* and broke up the conversation, which now had to take another turn. This is represented in figure 21.2(b).

This particular type of crossed transaction, in which the stimulus is directed to the Adult while the response originates from the Child, is probably the most frequent cause of misunderstandings in marriage and work situations, as well as in social life. Clinically, it is typified by the classical transference reaction. In fact this species of crossed transaction may be said to be the chief problem of psychoanalytic technique.

The reciprocal of this occurs when a stimulus is directed to the Adult and it is the Parent who responds. Thus anyone who asked Mr. Troy a rational question, expecting a judicious answer, might be disconcerted to find himself being treated to a set of dogmatic, ill-considered prejudices, as though he were a backward child in need of correction. This situation is represented in figure 21.2(c). (The same diagram may be used, *mutatis mutandis,* to represent a countertransference reaction.)

It will be noted that in this scheme, as long as the vectors are not crossed, the conversation proceeds smoothly as a series of *complementary transactions.* As soon as there is a crossed transaction, someone is disconcerted, and the *complementary relationship* terminates. In the case of Camellia and Rosita, for example, Rosita said nothing after Camellia burst into tears. Holly, however, immediately began to comfort Camellia and apologize for Rosita, just as she might talk to a hurt child. A free version of her remarks would read: "Don't cry, honey, everything will be all right, we all love you and that stupid lady didn't intend to be mean." Camellia responded with grateful "self-pity." These transactions are represented in figure 22.2(d). Since Camellia's Child is now trying to get a Parental response, and that is just what Holly gives her, Rosita's eventual cynical comment: "This love-making could go on forever!" is technically correct. These mutual Parent-Child transactions would go on, if not interrupted from outside, until either Holly or Camellia grew tired of them and changed her ego state, whereupon there would be another crossed transaction and the complementary relationship would terminate.

As it was, it was terminated by Rosita's intervention, which caused the collapse of Holly's Parent and the activation of her hurt and frightened Child. In this state, she was of no more use to Camellia, who then withdrew into a sullen silence. Now it was the therapist's turn to intervene. He gauged the situation carefully and was able to switch everyone back to an Adult level so that he could proceed with the analysis mentioned above. During this phase, his own transactions with the group reverted back to the original level represented in figure 21.2(a).

Dr. Q's intervention was motivated by the ultimate aim of establishing social control. Rosita, the most sophisticated of the three members concerned, had already acquired this to a large degree, as demonstrated by her silence when Camellia began to protest and weep; while Holly, being a novice, immediately responded to the overtures of Camellia's Child. Rosita had a clear, rational understanding of the purpose of the group as a learning experience. She knew that Camellia would learn nothing from being comforted, and that Holly would learn nothing from comforting her. Similarly, the other sophisticated members, Daphne and Lily, remained silent because they knew that was the only thing to do; while the other two novices, Hyacinth and Cicely, had kept quiet because they didn't know anything else to do.

The point was that this sort of thing happened regularly to Camellia. As she saw it, people were always misunderstanding her and criticizing her. In reality, it was she who made a practice of misunderstanding people and criticizing them. Rosita perceived correctly that she herself hadn't criticized Camellia and that, on the contrary, Camellia had implicitly criticized her by weeping. She retained Adult control of the situation by not allowing herself to be drawn unfairly into the parental role of comforting and apologizing to Camellia. Her Adult was reinforced by the knowledge that to succumb would be to defeat the stated therapeutic object of the meetings. Camellia had demonstrated more than once that she was adroit in eliciting pity and apologies. The educated members were now becoming aware that they were being manipulated into giving her something she did not deserve, and the purpose of this segment of the group at that moment was to make Camellia aware of what she was doing. The most effective way to do this was by withholding what she demanded.

They were also becoming aware of how eagerly Holly sought opportunities to be parental. Thus Camellia and Holly complemented each other in certain tendencies, tendencies which in each case promoted marital discord. Holly was about to get a divorce because her husband was exploiting her, and Camellia was having trouble because her husband misunderstood and criticized her. Dr. Q's transactional analysis of this episode, therefore, was pertinent. In the course of repeated analyses of similar situations these two women became more and more aware of what they were up to, and more and more able to control these tendencies both in the group and at home, with corresponding benefits in their marital situations. At the same time, the analyses became increasingly instructive and convincing to the other novices, while the sophisticated members were gaining further understanding and experience in social control, each experience serving to strengthen the Adult. Thus, transactional analysis of the relationship between two members benefited everyone in the group, and these benefits accrued long before any of them was ready to attempt a deconfusion of the Child or a resolution of underlying conflicts.

Analysis of Games

Pastimes

The great bulk of social intercourse is made up of engagements. This is particularly true of psychotherapy groups, where both activity and intimacy are prohibited or inhibited. Engagements are of two types: pastimes and games. A pastime is defined as an engagement in which the transactions are straightforward. When dissimulation enters the situation, the pastime becomes a game. With happy or well-organized people whose capacity for enjoyment is unimpaired, a social pastime may be indulged in for its own sake and bring its own satisfactions. With others, particularly neurotics, it is just what its name implies, a way of passing (i.e., structuring) the time: until one gets to know people better, until this hour has been sweated out, and on a larger scale, until bedtime, until vacation-time, until school starts, until the cure is forthcoming, until some form of charism, rescue, or death arrives. Existentially, a pastime is a way of warding off guilt, despair, or intimacy, a device provided by nature or culture to ease the quiet desperation. More optimistically, at best it is something enjoyed for its own sake and at least it serves as a means of getting acquainted in the hope of achieving the longed-for crasis with another human being. In any case, each participants uses it in an opportunistic way to get whatever primary and secondary gains he can from it.

The pastimes in psychotherapy groups are generally Parental or Adult, since their function is to evade the issue, which revolves around the Child. The two commonest pastimes in such groups are variations of "PTA" and "Psychiatry." The projective form of "PTA" is a Parental pastime. Its subject is delinquency in the general meaning of the word, and it may deal with delinquent juveniles, delinquent husbands, delinquent wives, delinquent tradesmen, delinquent authorities, or delinquent celebrities. Introjective "PTA" is Adult and deals with one's own socially acceptable delinquencies: "Why can't I be a good mother, father, employer, worker, fellow, hostess?" The motto of the projective form is "Isn't It Awful?"; that of the introjective form is "Me Too!"

"Psychiatry" is an Adult, or at least pseudo-Adult, pastime. In its projective form it is known colloquially as "Here's What You're Doing," and its introjective form is called "Why Do I Do This?" In transactional analysis groups, intellectualizers may play "What Part Of Me Said That?" but a sophisticated group will soon call this off if it is evident that it is being prolonged into a diversionary pastime after the learning phase of structural analysis is past.

Analysis of Games, from Berne, *Transactional Analysis in Psychotherapy,* pp. 98–99, 112–13.

Games People Play

Games specifically mentioned, "Uproar," with its loud voices and slamming doors, is classically a defense against sexual threats, between father and daughter or husband and wife, for example. It is often the terminal phase of the provocation-rejection-projection game of "Frigid Woman" ("All You Think About Is Sex"). "Ain't It Awful?" is played most grimly and poignantly by lonely surgery addicts. "You Got Me Into This" is a two-handed game of money, sex, or crime, played between a gullible one (You) and the one who is "it" (Me); in this game the one who gets caught is the winner. Its inverse is "There I Go Again"; here the gullible one (I) is "it," and the ostensible winner is the *agent provocateur*. In the first, "Me" is typically a man, and in the second "I" is typically a woman. "Let's You And Him Fight" is an essentially feminine opening to a game which may be played with any degree of seriousness from cocktail banter to homicide.

It is evident that games can be classified in various ways. Nosologically, "Schlemiel" is obsessional, "You Got Me Into This" is paranoid, and "There I Go Again" is depressive. Zonally, "Alcoholic" is oral, "Schlemiel" is anal, and "Let's You And Him Fight" is generally phallic. They can also be classified according to the principal defenses used, the number of players, or the "counters." Just as a pack of cards or a pair of dice or a ball can each be used for a number of different games, so can time, money, words, jokes, parts of the body, and other "counters."

Games must be distinguished from operations, which belong to the sphere of intimacy. A game, by definition, must involve a snare or "gimmick" through an ulterior transaction. An operation is a direct transaction, simply something that somebody does socially, such as asking for reassurance and getting it. This only becomes a game if the individual presents himself as doing something else, but is really asking for reassurance, or asks for reassurance and then rejects it in order to make the other person feel uncomfortable in some way.

Game analysis not only has its rational function, but also lends a lively interest to the serious proceedings of individual or group psychotherapy. While it should be corrupted to hedonistic purposes, and must be handled with the utmost correctness, the evident pleasure that it gives to many of the participants is a bonus which the conscientious therapist should be grateful for, and is not something to become querulous about.

Analysis of Scripts

Games appear to be segments of larger, more complex sets of transactions called *scripts*. Scripts belong in the realm of transference phenomena, that is,

---

Analysis of Scripts, from Berne, *Transactional Analysis in Psychotherapy. pp. 116–17.*

they are derivatives, or more precisely, adaptations, of infantile reactions and experiences. But a script does not deal with a mere transference reaction or transference situation; it is an attempt to repeat in derivative form a whole transference drama, often split up into acts, exactly like the theatrical scripts which are intuitive artistic derivatives of these primal dramas of childhood. Operationally, a script is a complex set of transactions, by nature recurrent, but not necessarily recurring, since a complete performance may require a whole lifetime.

A common tragic script is that based on the rescue fantasy of a woman who marries one alcoholic after another. The disruption of such a script, like the disruption of a game, leads to despair. Since the script calls for a magical cure of the alcoholic husband, and this is not forthcoming, a divorce results and the woman tries again. Many such women were raised by alcoholic fathers, so that the infantile origins of the script are not far to seek.

A practical and constructive script, on the other hand, may lead to great happiness if the others in the cast are well chosen and play their parts satisfactorily.

In the practice of script analysis, transactional (intragroup) and social (extragroup) material is collected until the nature of his script becomes clear to the patient. Neurotic, psychotic, and psychopathic scripts are almost always tragic, and they follow the Aristotelian principles of dramaturgy with remarkable fidelity: there is prologue, climax, and catastrophe, with real or symbolic pathos and despair giving rise to real threnody. The current life-drama must then be related to its historical origins so that control of the individual's destiny can be shifted from the Child to the Adult, from archaeopsychic unconsciousness to neopsychic awareness. In the group the patient can soon be observed feeling out through games and pastimes the potentialities of the other members to play their parts in his script, so that at first he acts as a casting director and then as protagonist.

22

GROUP PSYCHOTHERAPY AND PSYCHODRAMA

J. L. Moreno

Jacob Levy Moreno, born in Bucharest, Romania, on May 20, 1892, was a student of philosophy and later of medicine at the University of Vienna, receiving his M.D. in 1917. In 1918 he was appointed superintendent of Mitterndorf State Hospital in the vicinity of Vienna, and from 1919 to 1925 he was a health officer at Vöslau, Austria. During the same period he was engaged in private psychiatric practice. He founded the Spontaneity Theatre in 1921, remaining with it until 1925, and in 1923 he originated the first "living newspaper" and psychodrama.

After migrating to the United States in 1927 (he obtained his citizenship in 1935), Moreno practiced psychiatry in New York City. He undertook psychodrama with children at the Plymouth Institute in Brooklyn, and introduced the "spontaneity test" at Mt. Sinai Hospital in New York City in 1928. His work in psychodrama continued at Grosvenor Neighborhood House and at Hunter College. In 1929 he founded the Impromptu Theatre and two years later he started the *Impromptu Magazine*. He established the Moreno Sanitarium in Beacon, New York, in 1936 and founded the Therapeutic Theatre, the first theater of psychodrama. The following year Moreno began publication of *Sociometry: A Journal of Interpersonal Relations*. Credited to him also is the founding of the Moreno Institute, an institution for sociometry and psychodrama.

Moreno has been accorded a number of honors, including honorary president of the first and second International Congress of Psychodrama, fellow of the American Medical Association, and president of the American Sociometric Association (1945). He also has allocated time to academic pursuits. From 1951 until his death in 1974, Moreno was an adjunct professor of sociology at the New York University's graduate school and has lectured at the New School for Social Research and Teachers College Columbia University.

Spontaneity and creativity are of major importance in the psychotherapy of Moreno. Anxiety concomitantly functions with spontaneity, for with an increase of spontaneity, anxiety diminishes. In a "spontaneity theatre," participants are encouraged to enact scenes elicited by their own private worlds of experience, thereby evoking an emotional catharsis. This is of great value to a patient who is unable to establish a transference toward the therapist. In psychodrama, an individual expresses a real past experience or a fanciful one, involving real persons or imaginary ones. "Auxiliary egos," assistants who participate in the patient's drama, aid in a number of capacities, e.g., as a "double" (playing the role of the patient along with the patient), or a variation of a double, termed the *mirror technique* (playing the role of the patient while the patient observes). Psychodrama, a form of social psychotherapy, makes for community feeling, a greater intensity of catharsis (for acting can be superior to a talking cure), is a better vehicle for purging the patient's emotions, and keeps the patient more attune with society.

Moreno's influence is widespread. He has published a considerable number of works, many of which have been translated into several languages. His most influential books in the field of psychotherapy are the following: *Sociometry: Experimental Method and the Science of Society* (1951), *Who Shall Survive: Foundations of Sociometry, Group Psychotherapy and Sociodrama* (1934, rev. ed., 1953), *Sociometry and the Science of Man* (1956), *Psychodrama* (vol. 1, 1946; vol. 2, 1959), and *International Handbook of Group Psychotherapy* (1966).

Spontaneity-Creativity

The cornerstones of sociometric conceptualization are the universal concepts of spontaneity and creativity. Sociometry has taken these concepts from the metaphysical and philosophical level and brought them to empirical test by means of sociometric method. A presentation of these concepts is the first step within the sociometric system. Spontaneity and creativity are not identical or similar processes. They are different categories, although strategically linked. In the case of man his s may be diametrically opposite to his c; an individual may have a high degree of spontaneity but be entirely uncreative, a spontaneous idiot. Another individual may have a high degree of creativity but be entirely without spontaneity, a creator "without arms." . . . At least, in the world of our experience we may never encounter pure spontaneity or pure cultural conserves, they are functions of one another.

The universe is infinite creativity. The visible definition of creativity is the "child." Spontaneity by itself can never produce a child but it can help enormously in its delivery. The universe is filled with the products of spontaneity-creativity interaction, as (1) the effort which goes into the birth and rearing

---

Spontaneity-Creativity, from J. L. Moreno, *Who Shall Survive: Foundations of Sociometry, Group Psychotherapy and Sociodrama* (Beacon, N.Y.: Beacon House, 1953), pp. 39–48.

of new babies; (2) the effort which goes into the creation of new works of art, "cultural conserves," of new social institutions, social conserves and stereotypes, of technological inventions, robots and machines; and (3) the effort which goes into the creation of new social orders. Spontaneity can enter the creatively endowed individual and evoke a response. There were many more Michelangelos born than the one who painted the great paintings, many more Beethovens born than the one who wrote the great symphonies, and many more Christs born than the one who became Jesus of Nazareth. What they have in common are creativity and the creative ideas. What separates them is the spontaneity which, in the successful cases, enables the carrier to take full command of his resources, whereas the failures are at a loss with all their treasures; they suffer from deficiencies in their warming-up process. Creativity without spontaneity becomes lifeless; its living intensity increases and decreases in proportion to the amount of spontaneity in which is partakes. Spontaneity without creativity is empty and runs abortive. *Spontaneity and creativity are thus categories of a different order; creativity belongs to the categories of substance—it is the arch substance—spontaneity to the categories of catalyzer—it is the arch catalyzer.*

The fate of a culture is decided by the creativity of its carriers. But creativity as a scientific frame of reference has never been established and so a basis for a critique of deviations has been missing. If a disease of the creative functions has afflicted the primary group, the creative men of the human race, then it is of supreme importance that the principle of creativity be redefined and that its perverted forms be compared with creativity in its original states. . . .

Spontaneity operates in the present, now and here; it propels the individual towards an adequate response to a new situation or a new response to an old situation. It is strategically linked in two opposite directions, to automatism and reflexivity, as well as to productivity and creativity. It is, in its evolution, older than libido, memory, or intelligence. Although the most universal and evolutionarily the oldest, it is the least developed among the factors operating in man's world; it is most frequently discouraged and restrained by cultural devices. A great deal of man's psycho- and sociopathology can be ascribed to the insufficient development of spontaneity. Spontaneity "training" is therefore the most auspicious skill to be taught to therapists in all our institutions of learning and it is his task to teach his clients how to be more spontaneous without becoming excessive. There is ample evidence that the spontaneity of the infant has "something to do" with his arrival in this world. During pregnancy he warms up to the act of birth. The length of gestation is largely determined by the genotype of the foetus and not by the dam of the carrying individual. The infant wants to be born. Birth is a primary and creative process. It is positive before it is negative, it is healthy before it is pathological, it is a victory before it is a trauma. Anxiety results from "loss" of spontaneity. . . .

Spontaneity, Anxiety, and the Moment

But what is spontaneity and creativity? And *what are the instruments which can be used to bring about a new cultural order?*

Spontaneity can be defined as the adequate response to a new situation, or the novel response to an old situation. Without creativity the spontaneity of a universe would run empty and end abortive; without spontaneity the creativity of a universe would become perfectionism and lifeless. *Some of the instruments are spontaneity and role-playing tests, psychodrama, sociodrama and axiodrama:* there are many more to be invented.

Anxiety is a function of spontaneity. Spontaneity is, as defined, the adequate response to a present situation. If the response to the present situation is adequate—"fullness" of spontaneity—anxiety diminishes and disappears. *With decrease of spontaneity anxiety increases. With entire loss of spontaneity anxiety reaches its maximum, the point of panic.* In the "warm-up" of an actor to a present situation anxiety may move into two opposite directions; it may start with his striving to move out of an old situation without having enough spontaneity available to do so; or, the anxiety may set in as soon as some "external" force pushes him out of the old situation and leaves him hanging in the air. *The terrifying thing for an actor is this wavering between a situation which he has just abandoned and to which he cannot return and a situation which he must attain in order to get back into balance and feel secure.* The infant, immediately after birth, is the illustration par excellence for this phenomenon. He cannot return to the womb, he has to stay within this new world, but he may not have enough spontaneity to cope with its demands. In such moments of complete abandonment it is imperative that he draws upon all his resources or that someone comes to his aid, an auxiliary ego. Another illustration is a soldier who is suddenly attacked by an overwhelming number of enemies, or the protagonist of the psychodramatic situation facing a group of unbelievers, a man in a frenzy, who acts to save his life.

Thinking through this process it is dialectically faulty to start with the negative, with anxiety. The problem is to name the dynamic factor provoking anxiety to emerge. *Anxiety sets in because there is spontaneity missing, not because "there is anxiety," and spontaneity dwindles because anxiety rises. . . .*

Spontaneity and Libido Theory Contrasted

Spontaneity propels a variable degree of satisfactory response which an individual manifests in a situation of variable degree of novelty. The warming-up process is the *operational* expression of spontaneity. Spontaneity and warming-up processes operate on all levels of human relations, eating, walking, sleeping,

---

Spontaneity, Anxiety, and the Moment, from Moreno, *Who Shall Survive,* pp. 336–37.

sexual intercourse, social communication, creativity, in religious self-realiza
tion, and asceticism.

The place of the *s* factor in a universal theory of spontaneity is an
important theoretical question. Does the *s* factor emerge only in the human
group or can the *s* hypothesis be extended within certain limits to nonhuman
groups and to the lower animals and plants? How can the existence of the *s*
factor be reconciled with the idea of a mechanical, law-abiding universe, as,
for instance, with the law of the conservation of energy? *The idea of the
conservation of energy has been the "unconscious" model of many social and
psychological theories,* as the psychoanalytic theory of the libido. In accordance with this theory Freud thought that, if the sexual impulse does not find
satisfaction in its direct aim, it must displace its unapplied energy elsewhere.
It must, he thought, attach itself to a pathological locus or find a way out in
sublimation. He could not conceive of this unapplied effect vanishing because
he was biased by the physical idea of the conservation of energy. If we, too,
were to follow here this precept of the energy pattern, and would neglect the
perennial inconsistencies in the development of physical and mental phenomena, we would have to consider spontaneity as a psychological energy—a
quantity distributing itself within a field—which, if it cannot find actualization
in one direction, would flow in another direction in order to maintain its
volume and attain equilibrium. We should have to assume that an individual
has a certain amount of spontaneity stored up to which he adds and which he
spends as he goes on living. As he lives he draws from this reservoir. He may
use it all or even overdraw. Such an interpretation is, however, unsatisfactory
according to spontaneity research, at least on the level of human creativity.
The following theory is offered.

The individual is not endowed with a reservoir of spontaneity, in the sense
of a given, stable volume or quantity. Spontaneity is (or is not) available in
varying degrees of readiness, from zero to maximum, operating like a catalyzer. Thus he has, when faced with a novel situation, no alternative but to
use the *s* factor as a guide or searchlight, prompting him as to which emotions,
thoughts, and actions are most appropriate. At times he has to invoke more
spontaneity and at other times less, in accord with the requirements of the
situation or task. He should be careful not to produce less than the exact
amount of spontaneity needed—for if this were to happen he would need a
"reservoir" from which to draw. Likewise he should be careful not to produce
more than the situation calls for because the surplus might tempt him to store
it, to establish a reservoir, conserving it for future tasks as if it were energy,
thus completing a vicious circle which ends in the deterioration of spontaneity
and the development of cultural conserves. Spontaneity functions only in the
moment of its emergence just as, metaphorically speaking, light is turned on
in a room, and all parts of it become distinct. When the light is turned off in
a room, the basic structure remains the same, but a fundamental quality has
disappeared. . . .

Spontaneity-Creativity as the Essence of Personality

The principle which set sociometry into motion is the twin concept of spontaneity and creativity, not as abstractions but as a function in actual human beings and in their relationships. Applied to social phenomena, it made clear that human beings do not behave like dolls but are endowed in various degrees with initiative and spontaneity. The so-called social structure resulting from the interaction of two and a half thousand million individuals is not open to perception. It is not "given" like an immense visual configuration—for example, like the geographical configuration of the globe, but it is every *moment* submerged and changed by interindividual and collective factors. If there is any primary principle in the mental and social universe, it is found in this twin concept which has its most tangible reality in the interplay between person and person, between person and things, between person and work, between society and society, between society and the whole of mankind.

The fact that spontaneity and creativity can operate in our mental universe and evoke levels of organized expression which are not fully traceable to preceding determinants causes us to recommend *the abandonment or reformulation of all current psychological and sociological theories, openly or tacitly based upon psychoanalytic doctrine, for example, the theories of frustration, projection, substitution, and sublimation. These theories have to be rewritten, retested, and based on spontaneity-creativity formulation.*

In spontaneity theory energy as an organized system of psychological forces is not entirely given up. It reappears in the form of the cultural conserve. But instead of being the fountainhead, at the beginning of every process such as libido, it is at the end of a process, an end product. It is evaluated in the relativity, not as an ultimate form but as an *intermediate* product from time to time rearranged, reshaped, or entirely broken up by new spontaneity factors acting upon them. It is in the interaction between spontaneity-creativity and the cultural conserve that the existence of the s factor can be somewhat reconciled with the idea of a law-abiding universe, as for instance with the law of the conservation of energy.

The canon of creativity has four phases: creativity, spontaneity, warming-up process, and conserve. (See figure 22.1.) Spontaneity is the catalyzer. Creativity is the elementary X, it is without any specialized connotation, the X which may be recognized by its acts. In order to become effective, it (the sleeping beauty) needs a catalyzer—spontaneity. The operational manifestation of the interacting spontaneity-creativity is the warming-up process. As far as is known the only products of such interactions are the conserves. . . .

There is apparently little spontaneity in the universe, or, at least, if there is any abundance of it only a small particle is available to man, hardly enough to keep him surviving. In the past he has done everything to discourage its development. He could not rely upon the instability and insecurity of the moment with an organism which was not ready to deal with it adequately; he

FIGURE 22.1 Canon of creativity: spontaneity–creativity–conserve

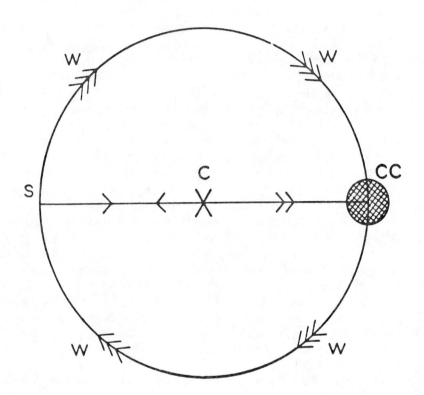

Field of Rotating Operations Between Spontaneity–Creativity–Cultural Conserve (S-C-CC)

S–Spontaneity, C–Creativity, CC–Cultural (or any) Conserve (for instance, a biological conserve, i.e., an animal organism, or a cultural conserve, i.e., a book, a motion picture, or a robot, i.e., a calculating machine); W–Warming-up is the "operational" expression of spontaneity. The circle represents the field of operations between S, C, and CC.

Operation I: Spontaneity arouses Creativity, C. S ⟶ C.
Operation II: Creativity is receptive to Spontaneity. S ⟵ C.
Operation III: From their interaction Cultural Conserves, CC, result. S ⟶ C ⟶⟩ CC.
Operation IV: Conserves (CC) would accumulate indefinitely and remain "in cold storage." They need
                  to be reborn, the catalyzer Spontaneity revitalizes them. CC ⟶⟩⟩ S ⟶⟩⟩ CC.
S does not operate in a vacuum; it moves either towards Creativity or towards Conserves.

Total Operation

Spontaneity–creativity–warming-up-act $<{{\rm actor}\atop{\rm conserve}}$

encouraged the development of devices as intelligence, memory, social and cultural conserves, which would give him the needed support with the result that he gradually became the slave of his own crutches. If there is a neurological localization of the spontaneity-creativity process it is the least developed function of man's nervous system. The difficulty is that one cannot store spontaneity, one either is spontaneous at a given moment or one is not. If spontaneity is such an important factor for man's world why is it so little developed? The answer is: man *fears* spontaneity, just like his ancestor in the jungle feared fire; he feared fire until he learned how to make it. Man will fear spontaneity until he will learn how to train it.

When the nineteenth century came to an end and the final accounting was made, what emerged as its greatest contribution to the mental and social sciences was to many minds the idea of the unconscious and its cathexes. When the twentieth century will close its doors that which I believe will come out as the greatest achievement is the idea of spontaneity and creativity, and the significant, indelible link between them. It may be said that the efforts of the two centuries complement one another. *If the nineteenth century looked for the "lowest" common denominator of mankind, the unconscious, the twentieth century discovered, or rediscovered its "highest" common denominator—spontaneity and creativity. . . .*

Psychodrama

Drama is a transliteration of the Greek $\delta\rho\acute{a}\mu\alpha$ which means action, or a thing done. Psychodrama can be defined, therefore, as the science which explores the "truth" by dramatic methods. It deals with interpersonal relations and private worlds.

The psychodramatic method uses mainly five instruments—the stage, the subject or actor, the director, the staff of therapeutic aides or auxiliary egos, and the audience. The first instrument is the stage. Why a stage? It provides the actor with a living space which is multidimensional and flexible to the maximum. The living space of reality is often narrow and restraining, he may easily lose his equilibrium. On the stage he may find it again due to its methodology of freedom—freedom from unbearable stress and freedom for experience and expression. The stage space is an extension of life beyond the reality test of life itself. Reality and fantasy are not in conflict, but both are functions within a wider sphere—the psychodramatic world of objects, persons, and events. In its logic the ghost of Hamlet's father is just as real and

---

Psychodrama, from Moreno, *Who Shall Survive,* pp. 81–87.

permitted to exist as Hamlet himself. Delusions and hallucinations are given flesh—embodiment on the stage—and an equality of status with normal sensory perceptions. The architectural design of the stage is made in accord with operational requirements. Its circular forms and levels of the stage, levels of aspiration, pointing out the vertical dimension, stimulate relief from tensions and permit mobility and flexibility of action. The locus of a psychodrama, if necessary, may be designated everywhere, wherever the subjects are, the field of battle, the classroom, or the private home. The ultimate resolution of deep mental conflicts requires an objective setting, the psychodramatic theater.

The second instrument is the subject or actor. He is asked to be himself on the stage, to portray his own private world. He is told to be himself, not an actor, as the actor is compelled to sacrifice his own private self to the role imposed upon him by a playwright. Once he is warmed up to the task it is comparatively easy for the subject to give an account of his daily life in action, as no one is as much of an authority on himself as himself. He has to act freely, as things rise up in his mind; that is why he has to be given freedom of expression, spontaneity. Next in importance to spontaneity comes the process of enactment. The verbal level is transcended and included in the level of action. There are several forms of enactment, pretending to be in a role, reenactment or acting out a past scene, living out a problem presently pressing, creating life on the stage or testing oneself for the future. Further comes the principle of involvement. We have been brought up with the idea that, in test as well as in treatment situations, a minimum of involvement with other persons and objects is a most desirable thing for the subject. In the psychodramatic situation all degrees of involvement take place, from a minimum to a maximum. In addition comes the principle of realization. The subject is enabled not only to meet parts of himself, but the other persons who partake in his mental conflicts. These persons may be real or illusions. The reality test which is a mere word in other methods is thus actually made true on the stage. The warming-up process of the subject to psychodramatic portrayal is stimulated by numerous techniques, only a few of which are mentioned here: self-presentation, soliloquy, projection, interpolation of resistance, reversal of roles, double ego, mirror techniques, auxiliary world, realization, and psychochemical techniques. The aim of these sundry techniques is not to turn the subjects into actors, but rather to stir them up to be on the stage what they *are,* more deeply and explicitly than they appear to be in life reality. The patient has as dramatis personae either the real people of his private world, his wife, his father, his child, etc., or actors portraying them, auxiliary egos.

The third instrument is the director. He has three functions: producer, counsellor, and analyst. As producer he has to be on the alert to turn every clue which the subject offers into dramatic action, to make the line of production one with the life line of the subject, and never to let the production lose rapport with the audience. As director, attacking and shocking the subject is at times just as permissible as laughing and joking with him; at times he may become indirect and passive and for all practical purposes the session seems to be run by the subject. As analyst he may complement his own interpretation by responses coming from informants in the audience, husband, parents, children, friends, or neighbors.

The fourth instrument is a staff of auxiliary egos. These auxiliary egos or participant actors have a double significance. They are extensions of the director, exploratory and guiding, but they are also extensions of the subject, portraying the actual or imagined personae of their life drama. The functions of the auxiliary ego are threefold: the function of the actor, portraying roles required by the subject's world; the function of the counsellor, guiding the subject; and the function of the social investigator.

The fifth instrument is the audience. The audience itself has a double purpose. It may serve to help the subject or, being itself helped by the subject on the stage, the audience becomes the problem. In helping the subject it is a sounding board of public opinion. Its responses and comments are as extemporaneous as those of the subject, they may vary from laughter to violent protest. The more isolated the subject is, for instance, because his drama on the stage is shaped by delusions and hallucinations, the more important becomes, to him, the presence of an audience which is willing to accept and understand him. When the audience is helped by the subject, thus becoming the subject itself, the situation is reversed. The audience sees itself, that is, one of its collective syndromes portrayed on the stage.

In any discussion of psychodrama the important dynamics which operate should be considered. In the first phase of psychodramatic process the director may meet with some resistance from the subject. In most cases the resistance against being psychodramatized is small or nil. Once a subject understands the degree to which the production is of his own making he will cooperate. The fight between director and subject is in the psychodramatic situation extremely real; to an extent they have to assess each other like two battlers, facing each other in a situation of great stress and challenge. Each of them has to draw spontaneity and cunning from his resources. Positive factors which shape the relationship and interaction in the reality of life itself exist: spontaneity, productivity, the warming-up process, tele and role processes.

The psychodramatist, after having made so much ado to get the subject started, recedes from the scene; frequently he does not take any part in it; at times he is not even present. From the subject's point of view his object of transference, the director, is pushed out of the situation. The retreat of the director gives the subject the feeling that he is the winner. Actually it is nothing but the preliminary warm-up before the big bout. To the satisfaction of the subject, other persons enter into the situation, persons who are nearer to him, like his delusions and hallucinations. He knows them so much better than this stranger, the director. The more they are in the picture the more he forgets him and the director wants to be forgotten, at least for the time being. The dynamics of this forgetting can be easily explained. Not only does the director leave the scene of operation, the auxiliary egos step in and it is between them that his share of *tele,* transference, and empathy is divided. In the course of the production it becomes clear that *transference is nothing by itself, but the pathological portion of a universal factor, tele,* operating in the shaping and balancing of all interpersonal relations. As the subject takes part in the production and warms up to the figures and figureheads of his own private world, he attains tremendous satisfactions which take him far beyond anything he has ever experienced; he has invested so much of his own limited energy in the images of his perceptions of father, mother, wife, children, as well as in certain images which live a foreign existence within him, delusions and hallucinations of all sorts, that he has lost a great deal of spontaneity, productivity, and power for himself. They have taken his riches away and he has become poor, weak, and sick. The psychodrama gives back to him all the investments he had made in the extraneous adventures of his mind. He takes his father, mother, sweethearts, delusions, and hallucinations unto himself and the energies which he has invested in them, they return by actually living through the role of his father or his employer, his friends or his enemies; by reversing the roles with them he is already learning many things about them which life does not provide him. When he can be the persons he hallucinates, not only do they lose their power and magic spell over him but he gains their power for himself. His own self has an opportunity to find and reorganize itself, to put the elements together which may have been kept apart by insidious forces, to integrate them and to attain a sense of power and of relief, a "catharsis of integration" (in difference from a catharsis of abreaction). It can well be said that the psychodrama provides the subject with a new and more extensive experience of reality, a *"surplus" reality,* a gain which at least in part justifies the sacrifice he made by working through a psychodramatic production.

The next phase in psychodrama comes into play when the audience drama takes the place of the production. The director vanished from the scene at the end of the first phase; now the production itself vanishes and with it the auxiliary egos, the good helpers and genii who have aided him so much in gaining a new sense of power and clarity. The subject is now divided in his reactions; on one hand he is sorry that it is all gone, on the other he feels cheated and mad for having made a sacrifice whose justification he does not see completely. The subject becomes dynamically aware of the presence of the audience. In the beginning of the session he was angrily or happily aware of it. In the warming up of the production he became oblivious of its existence, but now he sees it again, one by one, strangers and friends. His feelings of shame and guilt reach their climax. However, as he was warming up to the production the audience before him was warming up too. But when he came to an end they were just beginning. The *tele*-empathy-transference complex undergoes a third realignment of forces; it moves from the stage to the audience, initiating among the audio-egos intensive relations. As the strangers from the group begin to rise and relate their feelings as to what they have learned from the production, he gains a new sense of catharsis, a group catharsis; *he has given love and now they are giving love back to him.* Whatever his psyche is now, it was molded originally by the group; by means of psychodrama it returns to the group; and now the members of the audience are sharing their experiences with him as he has shared his with them.

The description would not be complete if we would not discuss briefly the role which the director and the egos play in the warm-up of the session. The theoretical principle of psychodrama is that the director acts directly upon the level of the subject's spontaneity—obviously it makes little difference to the operation whether one calls the subject's spontaneity his *unconscious*—that the subject enters actually the areas of objects and persons, however confused and fragmented, to which is spontaneous energy is related. He is not satisfied, like the analyst, to observe the subject and translate symbolic behavior into understandable, scientific language; he enters as a participant-actor, armed with as many hypothetic insights as possible, into the spontaneous activities of the subject, to talk to him in the spontaneous languages of signs and gestures, words and actions which the subject has developed. Psychodrama does not require a theatrical setting, a frequent misunderstanding; it is done *in situ*—that is, wherever the subject is found. According to psychodramatic theory a considerable part of the psyche is not language-ridden, it is not infiltrated by the ordinary, significant language symbols. Therefore, bodily contact with subjects, if it can be established, touch, caress, embrace, hand-shake, sharing in silent activities, eating, walking or other activities, are an important preliminary to psychodramatic work itself. Bodily contact, body therapy, and body training continue to operate in the psychodramatic situation. An elaborate system of production techniques has been developed by means of which the director and his auxiliary egos push themselves into the subject's world, populating it with figures extremely familiar to him, with the advantage, however, that they are not delusionary but half imaginary, half real. Like good and bad genii they shock and upset him at times, at other times they surprise and comfort him. He finds himself, as if trapped, in a near-real world. *He sees himself acting, he hears himself speaking, but his actions and thoughts, his feelings and perceptions do not come from him, they come, strangely enough, from another person, the psychodramatist, and from other persons, the auxiliary egos, the doubles and mirrors of his mind.*

Sociodrama

Sociodrama has been defined as a deep action method dealing with intergroup relations and collective ideologies.

Sociodrama, from Moreno, *Who Shall Survive,* pp. 87–89.

The procedure in the development of a sociodrama differs in many ways from the procedure which I have described as psychodramatic. In a psychodramatic session, the attention of the director and his staff are centered upon the individual and his private problems. As these are unfolded before a group, the spectators are affected by the psychodramatic acts in proportion to the affinities existing between their own context of roles, and the role context of the central subject. Even the so-called group approach in psychodrama is in the deeper sense individual-centered. The audience is organized in accord with a mental syndrome which all participating individuals have in common, and the aim of the director is to reach every individual in his own sphere, separated from the other. He is using the group approach only to reach actively more than one individual in the same session. The group approach in psychodrama is concerned with a group of *private* individuals, which makes the group itself, in a sense, private. Careful planning and organizing the audience is here indispensable because there is no outward sign indicating which individual suffers from the same mental syndrome and can share the same treatment situation.

The true subject of a sociodrama is the *group*. It is not limited by a special number of individuals, it can consist of as many persons as there are human beings living anywhere, or at least of as many as belong to the same culture. Sociodrama is based upon the tacit assumption that the group formed by the audience is already organized by the social and cultural roles which, in some degree, all the carriers of the culture share. It is therefore incidental who the individuals are, or of whom the group is composed, or how large their number is. It is the group as a whole which has to be put upon the stage to work out its problem, because the group in sociodrama corresponds to the individual in psychodrama. Sociodrama, therefore, in order to become effective, has to assay the difficult task of developing deep action methods, in which the working tools are representative types within a given culture and not private individuals. Catharsis in the sociodrama differs from catharsis in the psychodrama. The psychodramatic approach deals with personal problems principally and aims at personal catharsis; the sociodramatic approach deals with social problems and aims at social catharsis.

The concept underlying this approach is the recognition that *man is a role-player*, that every individual is characterized by a certain range of roles which dominate his behavior, and that every culture is characterized by a certain set of roles which it imposes with a varying degree of success upon its membership.

The problem is how to bring a cultural order to view by dramatic methods. Even if full information could be attained by observation and analysis, it has become certain that observation and analysis are inadequate tools for exploring the more sophisticated aspects of intercultural relations, and that deep action methods are indispensable. Moreover, the latter have proven to be of indisputable value and unreplaceable because they can, in the form of the sociodrama, *explore as well as treat in one stroke* the conflicts which have arisen between two separate cultural orders, and at the same time, by the same action, undertaking to change the attitude of the members of one culture versus the members of the other. Furthermore, it can reach large groups of people, and by using radio or television it can affect millions of local groups and neighborhoods in which intercultural conflicts and tensions are dormant or in the initial phases of open warfare. Therefore, the potentialities of drama research and role research for giving clues to methods by which public opinion and attitudes can be influenced or changed are still unrecognized and unresolved.

Role Test and Role-Playing

The role test measures the role behavior of an individual; it reveals thereby the *degree* of differentiation which a specific culture has attained within an individual, and his interpretation of this culture. The role range of an individual stands for the inflection of a given culture into the personalities belonging to it. As the intelligence test measures the mental age of an individual, the role test can measure his *cultural* age. The ratio between the chronological age and the cultural age of an individual may then be called his cultural quotient.

The set of roles used for the test may vary from one community to another, and more drastically, from one culture to another. The selection of the roles to be tested is of crucial importance, because if the roles of which the set consists are only incidental to the life of that particular community, no true picture of the individual's role behavior and potentialities can be attained. Therefore, the point is to select such roles which are truly representative and operative in the community in which the testees live.

Group Psychotherapy

The late arrival of group psychotherapy has a plausible explanation when we consider the development of modern psychiatry out of somatic medicine. The premise of scientific medicine has been since its origin that the *locus of physical*

Role Test and Role-Playing, from Moreno, *Who Shall Survive*, p. 89.
Group Psychotherapy, from Moreno, *Who Shall Survive*, pp. 89–91.

ailment is within an individual organism. Therefore, treatment is applied to the locus of the ailment as designated by diagnosis. The physical disease with which an individual A is afflicted does not require the collateral treatment of A's wife, his children, and friends. If A suffers from an appendicitis and an appendectomy is indicated, only the appendix of A is removed; no one thinks of the removal of the appendix of A's wife and children too. When in budding psychiatry scientific methods began to be used, axioms gained from physical diagnosis and treatment were *automatically* applied to mental disorders as well. The premise prevailed that there is no locus of ailment beyond the individual, that there is, for instance, no group situation which requires special diagnosis and treatment.

Although, during the first quarter of our century, there was occasional disapproval of this exclusive, individualistic point of view, it was more silent than vocal, coming from anthropologists and sociologists particularly. The decisive turn came with the development of sociometric and psychodramatic methodology.

When the locus of therapy changes from the individual to the group, the group becomes the new subject (first step). When the group is broken up into its individual little therapists and they become the agents of therapy, the chief therapist becomes a part of the group (second step) and finally, the medium of therapy is separated from the healer as well as the group therapeutic agents (third step). Due to the transition from individual psychotherapy to group psychotherapy, group psychotherapy includes individual psychotherapy.

The three principles, *subject, agent,* and *medium* of therapy, can be used as points of reference for constructing a table of polar categories of group psychotherapies. In table 22.1 are eight pairs of categories: amorphous vs. structured, *loco nascendi* vs. secondary situations, causal vs. symptomatic, therapist vs. group-centered, spontaneous vs. rehearsed, lectural vs. dramatic, conserved vs. creative, and face-to-face vs. from-a-distance. With these eight sets of pairs, a classification of every type of group psychotherapy can be made.

Construction of the Sociometric Test

The problem was to construct the test in such manner that it is itself a motive, an incentive, a purpose, primarily for the *subject* instead of for the tester. If the test procedure is identical with a life-goal of the subject he can never feel himself to have been victimized or abused. Yet the same series of acts performed of the subject's own volition may be a "test" in the mind of the tester. We have developed two tests in which the subject is in action for his own ends.

Construction of the Sociometric Test, from Moreno, *Who Shall Survive,* pp. 105–6.

TABLE 22.1 Basic categories of group psychotherapy

Subject of Therapy

1. As to *Constitution* of the Group

Amorphous	vs.	Structured (organized) Group
Without considering the organization of the group in the prescription of therapy.		Determining the dynamic organization of the group and prescribing therapy upon diagnosis.

2. As to *Locus* of Treatment

Treatment of Group in *Loco Nascendi, In Situ*	vs.	Treatment Deferred to Secondary Situations
Situational, for instance within the home itself, the workshop itself, etc.		Derivative, for instance in especially arranged situations, in clinics, etc.

3. As to *Aim* of Treatment

Causal	vs.	Symptomatic
Going back to the situations and individuals associated with the syndrome and including them *in vivo* in the treatment situation.		Treating each individual as a separate unit. Treatment may be deep, in the psychoanalytic sense, individually, but it may not be deep groupally.

Agent of Therapy

1. As to *Source* or *Transfer* of Influence

Therapist-Centered	vs.	Group-Centered Methods
Either chief therapist alone or chief therapist aided by a few auxiliary therapists. Therapist treating every member of the group individually or together, but the patients themselves are not used systematically to help one another.		Every member of the group is a therapeutic agent to one or another member, one patient helping the other. The group is treated as an interactional whole.

2. As to *Form* of Influence

Spontaneous and Free	vs.	Rehearsed and Prepared Form
Freedom of experience and expression. Therapist or speaker (from inside the group) is extemporaneous, the audience unrestrained.		Suppressed experience and expression. Therapist memorizes lecture or rehearses production. The audience is prepared and governed by fixed rules.

Medium of Therapy

1. As to *Mode* of Influence

Lecture or Verbal	vs.	Dramatic or Action Methods
Lectures, interviews, discussion, reading, reciting.		Dance, music, drama, motion pictures.

2. As to *Type* of Medium

Conserved, Mechanical, or Unspontaneous	vs.	Creative Media
Motion pictures, rehearsed doll drama, rehearsed dance step, conserved music, rehearsed drama.		Therapeutic motion pictures as preparatory steps for an actual group session, extemporaneous doll drama with the aid of auxiliary egos behind each doll, psychomusic, psychodrama, and sociodrama.

3. As to *Origin* of Medium

Face-to-Face	vs.	From-a-Distance Presentations
Any drama, lecture, discussion, etc.		Radio and television.

One is the sociometric test. From the point of view of the subject it is not a test at all and this is as it should be. It is merely an opportunity for him to become an active agent in matters concerning his life situation. But to the sociometric tester it reveals his actual position in the community in relation to the actual position of others. The second test meeting this demand is the spontaneity and role-playing test. Here is a standard life situation which the subject improvises to his own satisfaction. But to the tester it releases a source of information in respect to the character, intelligence, conduct, and social relations of the subject.

Psychometric tests and psychoanalysis of the child and of the adolescent, however contrasting in procedure, have one thing in common. They throw the subject into a passive state, the subject being in a role of submission. The situation is not motivated for him. This tends to produce an attitude of suspicion and tension on the part of the subject towards the tester and to attribute to him ulterior motives in inducing the subject to submit to the test. This *situational* fact has to be considered irrelevant to how valuable and significant the revelations may be which come from psychometric testing and from psychoanalysis. This aspect of the testing becomes especially conspicuous if the findings are used for the purpose of determining some change in the life situation of the subject, as, for instance, his transfer to an institution for the feeble-minded. Through the sociometric, spontaneity, and role-playing tests the artificial setting of the psychoanalytic situation and of the Binet intelligence tests can be substituted by natural or life settings.

Directions for Sociometric Testing

A point which deserves emphasis is the *accurate giving* of the sociometric test. Only such a test can be correctly called *sociometric* which attempts to determine the *feelings* of individuals towards each other and, second, to determine these in respect to the *same criterion*. For instance, if we demand from the inhabitants of a given community to choose the individuals with whom they want to live together in the same house and to motivate these choices, this is a sociometric procedure. Or, if we determine through such procedure to whom the individuals are sexually attracted or with whom they want to study together in the same classroom. In each of these cases a definite criterion is given, living in proximity, working in proximity, or sexual proximity. Further, a sociometric test to be accurate has *not* to gain the necessary information through observation of these individuals only, how they appear to behave in

Directions for Sociometric Testing, from Moreno, *Who Shall Survive,* pp. 106–7.

their home groups, work groups, or whatever, to one another and to construct, through these observations, the position they possibly have in their groups. But it is necessary that the subjects themselves be taken into partnership, that they become sufficiently interested in the test, that they transfer to the tester their spontaneous attitudes, thoughts, and motivations in respect to the individuals concerned in the same criterion. Whatever additional material is gained by other methods to support the essential information, this is not able to substitute the two requirements mentioned above. If, therefore, the inhabitants of a community are asked whom they like or dislike in their community irrespective of any criterion this should be called near-sociometric. These likes and dislikes being unrelated to a criterion are not analytically differentiated. They may relate to sexual liking, to the liking of working together, or whatever. Secondly, the individuals have no interest to express their likes and dislikes truthfully as no practical consequences for themselves are derivable from these. Similarly, if children in a classroom are asked whom they like or dislike among their classmates irrespective of any criterion and without immediate purpose for them. Even if such a form of inquiry may at some age level produce similar results as the results gained through our procedure, it should not be called sociometric testing. It does not provide a systematic basis for sociometric research.

The Sociometrist

The problem of investigating a social situation has two fundamental aspects, the *first* of which is the question of how to achieve a close and accurate approach to the social process to be investigated so that the truly real and valid facts are harvested and not, perhaps, illusionary and unreliable ones. Sociometry in communities and the psychodrama in experimental situations make a deliberate attempt to bring the subjects into an experimental state which will make them sensitive to the realization of their own experiences and action-patterns. In this "spontaneity state" they are able to contribute revealing material concerning the web of social networks in which they move and the life situations through which they pass. This conditioning of the subjects for a more total knowledge of the social situation in which they are is accomplished by means of processes of warming-up and by learning to summon the degree of spontaneity necessary for a given situation.

The second fundamental aspect of the problem concerns the investigator himself. In the social sciences, the problem of the investigator and the situation

---

The Sociometrist, from Moreno, *Who Shall Survive*, pp. 107–10.

in which the experiment or study is to be carried out have been of the gravest concern. However, the methods for dealing with this fundamental difficulty have been most unsatisfactory to date.

The participant observer, in the course of his exploration, enters into contact with various individuals and situations, but he, himself—with his biases and prejudices, his personality equation and his own position in the group—remains unexamined and therefore, himself, an unmeasured quantity. The displacement in the situation to be investigated which is partly produced by his own social pattern does not appear as an integral part of the findings. Indeed, we have to take the inviolability of his own judgments and opinions for granted and *the "uninvestigated investigator" constitutes, so to speak, an ever-present error.* This is, of course, only true for social studies in which the investigators are, as individuals, essential parts of the investigation. It is different in social studies which investigate finished products—processes which have become stereotyped and stationary, lending themselves to actuarial study and the development of scales. Social measurements of such processes are, of course, a part of sociometry in its broader sense, but they have a limited practical meaning without the frontal approach—the direct measurement of interpersonal phenomena.

In order to overcome the grave errors which may arise in and from the investigator himself, we resort to a sociometric approach which is especially adapted to the microscopic study of social phenomena. The participant observer—in one particular form of this work—does not remain "objective" or at a distance from the persons to be studied; he becomes their friend. He identifies himself with their own situations; he becomes an extension of their own egos. In other words, the "objective" participant becomes a "subjective" one. As a *subjective participant* he can enter successively or simultaneously into the lives of several individuals, and then function as a medium of equilibration between them. This is the first step.

If we consider the investigator who gives out questionnaires as being in a situation of maximum *formal* objectivity, then the investigator who identifies himself successively with every individual participating in the situation approaches a *maximum of subjectivity.* A professional worker acting in this fashion produces excellent therapeutic effects, but the method does not improve upon the intended objectification of the investigator, himself.

A step beyond this is *the psychodramatic method, a situation which provides an experimental and a therapeutic setting simultaneously.* Here, the director of the theatre is present, but outside the exploratory situation itself. The investigators to be tested are placed in life situations and roles which may occur in the community or in their own private lives until their ranges of roles and their patterns of behavior in these life situations have been adequately gauged. This procedure is carried on until every one of the investigators is thoroughly objectified. Retests are made from time to time in order to keep pace with any changes which may have taken place in their various behavior-patterns.

In the course of such work, the range of roles and the range of expansiveness of each investigator become clearly defined and the stimulus which he may be to the subjects of his investigations has become a known quantity. Thus, the psychodramatic procedure provides a yardstick by which we can measure and evaluate an indefinitely large number of subjects in specific life situations and in specific roles. The paradox is that the investigator, although he has become objectified by this process—a "controlled participant observer," so to speak—still continues to be what he originally started out to be: a subjective participant.

The process of objectifying the investigator takes many forms in accord with the situation which he is to explore and it has, also, many degrees of perfection. An ideal situation of this kind is obtained with a psychodramatic group in the experimental setting of the therapeutic theatre. For the members of a psychodramatic group, a range of spontaneity is permitted in roles and situations which far surpasses that of any actual community and yet may include all the roles and situations which exist there. At the same time, the behavior of every member of the community—however spontaneous it may be —is recorded in addition to the interaction between the members of the group both on the stage and off it. Thus, the ideal background is constructed for the task assigned to testers within the psychodramatic group itself.

When the investigator has been tested in this manner, we are able to use him as a tool for testing any group of subjects in typical situations, as described above. In addition to this, he can be used for the treatment of subjects in his new qualification as a subjective participant who is objectified to a point where he can be considered a known quantity in the procedure. He has become an auxiliary ego whose behavior in the process of guidance on the psychodramatic stage is within some degree of control.

This method can be used to advantage as an improvement upon the participant-observer technique of investigation. As a result of careful gauging of the personalities of the investigators who are to be employed as sociometrists or observers in the community at large, a frame of reference is established at the research center to which the investigators return with their data and findings. The use of this frame of reference provides a more objective basis than has heretofore existed for evaluating the reflection of the investigators' own behavior-characteristics upon their findings in the community. *The social investigation of any community when based upon sociometric principles is equipped with two complementary frames of reference. The one is the objectified investigator so prepared and evaluated that his own personality is no longer an unknown factor in the findings. The other frame of reference consists of the*

*members of the community who are brought to a high degree of spontaneous
participation in the investigation by means of sociometric methods, and therefore
contribute genuine and reliable data.* Thus, the social structures which actually
exist in the community at the moment of investigation are brought to our
knowledge with a minimum of error on the part of both the investigators and
the investigated.

Psychodrama versus Psychoanalysis

Model

Psychoanalysis was constructed to permit words and their associations, then
to analyze and estimate indirectly the behavior which may underlie them.
Psychodrama was constructed to permit action and production so as to study
behavior in its concrete form. In a broad sense, it is total production versus
total analysis.

Objectivity and Neutrality of the Therapist

The range of direct observation of the patient's behavior is restricted in psychoanalysis; in psychodrama it is immeasurably greater. The psychoanalytic therapist has to "interpret" because he has no other alternative; it depends upon
his intuition to interpret correctly what is going on in the patient. In the
psychodrama the behavior and the acting of the patient interprets for the
therapist in the here and now; the therapist's interpretation is reduced to a
minimum.

  In classic psychodrama, similar to classic psychoanalysis, the chief therapist does not take part in the production itself. He is like a conductor in an
orchestra; he does not play an instrument himself, but supervises, directs, and
observes. He keeps a certain distance from the patient. In the psychoanalytic
situation of two the therapist may be tempted to develop an illegitimate private
relationship to the patient, although not necessarily called for by the therapeutic situation. At certain times, however, the needs of the patient may challenge
the analyst to step out and play a specific role towards the patient, but the
psychoanalytic rule does not permit such action. The psychodramatic rule
permits the therapist to take open and direct action.

Psychodrama versus Psychoanalysis, from J. L. Moreno in collaboration with Z. T. Moreno,
Psychodrama: Foundations of Psychotherapy, vol. 2 (Beacon, N.Y.: Beacon House, 1959), pp.
231–33.

The Auxiliary Ego

When in psychodrama the chief therapist feels a need to play a specific role towards a patient, for instance, the role of a father or of an employer, there is an alternative: he may use another person as a helper to fulfill this task, an auxiliary ego. There are four reasons why the auxiliary ego was introduced into psychodramatic therapy. One was an *economic reason:* it was because the physical distance made it impossible to bring people who live far away to the scene. Two, a *sociological reason:* the individuals who populate the private world of the patient are prevented from participating by social obligations of their own. Three, a *psychological reason:* it helped the therapist not to get involved—to maintain his objectivity and neutrality. The auxiliary ego removes the therapist from the obligation to play a part towards the patient. The chief therapist can afford to be neutral and objective and it helps the patient to maintain a reasonable psychological distance from him. Four, a *therapeutic reason:* it is often preferable not to have the other *real* person present.

The auxiliary ego needs training very different from that of the chief therapist. His function is primarily that of a participant actor, not of an observer or analyst. *His* neutrality would defeat the purpose of therapy. He has to play the role required of him in the full sense of the word. He has to learn how to play the game of the patient and still not be carried away by it. But if the role requires him to get involved with the patient as it is in life itself, he should carry out the prescription. It should also be remembered that in contrast to psychoanalysis in the psychodramatic situation the therapist is not alone with the patient. There are other individuals present; therefore, the neutrality and objectivity of the therapist is better safeguarded.

Psychodrama à Deux

The psychodrama à deux, a parallel to the psychoanalytic situation on the couch, has been tried from time to time, but it is interesting to point out that the psychodramatist in private practice frequently prefers to employ his nurse as an auxiliary ego to maintain his own identity as director unimpaired.

Ferenczi and Freud

The famous conflict between Freud and Ferenczi touches on this fundamental question. It is a good illustration of the differences between the psychoanalytic and the psychodramatic techniques. In the years of 1930 to 1931 Ferenczi had been changing his technique towards patients by acting the part of a loving parent. When Freud heard of it, he wrote Ferenczi in a letter of December

13th, 1931, "You have not made a secret of the fact that you kiss your patients and let them kiss you. ... We have hitherto in our technique held to the conclusion that patients are to be refused erotic gratifications."[1] Freud had no alternative to offer his old friend and former analysand. Had he been acquainted with the psychodramatic method which was used in the Viennese Stegreiftheater since 1923, he would have had an alternative to offer. He might have written him, "If you believe that your patient needs love, the affection of a genuine father or mother, let *another* person who is especially trained and equipped for this task take the part and act it out with the patient under your supervision. *But you yourself keep out of it.* You will then prevent the accusation of getting some sexual gratification under the cloak of professional service, and of permitting the patient to attain sexual gratification from you." But Freud never wrote such a letter to his friend.

Ferenczi struck, however, on a basic problem when he had the urge to make love to his patients. He may have been mentally sick at that time but that did not change the logic of his problem. If the patient needs "love" for his well-being and mental progress, the technique has to be changed. But the technology of psychoanalysis remained unchanged until psychodrama entered the scene. By employing another therapist, a helper, to assume the part the patient needed, the dilemma was overcome, but not entirely. If the auxiliary ego were instructed to act for him in the role of a loving parent or wife, the helper might easily have turned into an erotic actor and Ferenczi into something which tickled his senses, a "voyeur."

It is typical that the new generation of psychoanalysts, the "psychoanalytic intelligentsia," criticize Freud on most of the theoretical issues, libido, transference, countertransference, etc., but they have no alternative technologies to offer. They still place the patient on a couch or if they are more radical they permit the patient to sit on a chair facing the therapist.

The Problem of Control

The problem of "uncontrolled" involvement of the chief therapist is also one confronted frequently in psychodramatic work. We have had directors who, not satisfied with "passing the buck" so to speak to auxiliary egos, are often displeased with the intensity of the ongoing process and step into the situation themselves, doubling, reversing, mirroring, soliloquizing, etc. But it rarely happens that the chief therapist will push the auxiliary ego out of the scene and assume the entire role for himself. The general rule is that the chief therapist is the conductor and does not assume the role of an auxiliary ego, unless required by an emergency.

---

[1]Ernest Jones, *Biography of Freud,* vol. 3.

Glossary of Technical Terms

Sociometric Test (of a group): measures the *conflict* between the actual structure of a group which the members maintain at the time when the test is given against the structure of the group as revealed by their choices.

Sociometric Test (of an individual): measures the *conflict* between the actual position an individual maintains within a group against the position revealed by his choices.

Sociometric Questionnaire: requires an individual to choose his associates for any group of which he is or might become a member.

Sociogram: depicts by means of a set of symbols the two-way or interpersonal relations which exist between members of a group. If A chooses B this is only one-half of a two-way relation. In order that the relationship should become sociometrically meaningful the other half must be added. It may be that B chooses A or that he rejects A or that he is indifferent towards A.

As the sociogram can be read by everyone who knows the symbols it can be considered as a *sociological alphabet.*

Isolate: not choosing and being unchosen on any criterion. He does not send out or receive any negative choices. His sociometric score is zero.

Reciprocated Choice: choosing and being chosen on the same criterion, a pair.

Pair: choosing and being chosen on the same criterion, a reciprocated choice.

Triangle: three individuals choosing each other on the same criterion.

Chain: an open series of mutual choices on any criterion—A chooses B, B chooses A, B chooses C, C chooses B, C chooses D, D chooses C, etc.

Star: an individual who receives the expected number or more than the expected number of choices on the same criterion. (Note the difference between star and popular leader.)

Sociometric Status (operational definition): the number of times an individual has been chosen by other individuals as a preferred associate for all activities in which they are engaged at the time of the test. It is obtained by adding the number of choices each individual receives on each criterion.

Sociometric Score: the number of different persons who have chosen an individual on all criteria used.

Score of Emotional Expansiveness: the number of different persons whom an individual chooses or to whom he is attracted on any criterion.

Choices: Choices are fundamental facts in all ongoing human relations, choices of people and choices of things. It is immaterial whether the motiva-

---

Glossary of Technical Terms, from Moreno, *Who Shall Survive,* pp. 719–23.

tions are known to the chooser or not; they are significant only as clues to his cultural and ethical index. It is immaterial whether they are inarticulate or highly expressive, whether irrational or rational. They do not require any special justification as long as they are spontaneous and true to the self of the chooser. They are facts of the first existential order.

Intensity of Choice: This is measured by the amount of time actually spent with the individuals chosen against the amount of time one wants to spend with them. . . .

Social Atom (operational definition): Plot all the individuals a person chooses and those who choose him, all the individuals a person rejects and those who reject him; all the individuals who do not reciprocate either choices or rejections. This is the "raw" material of a person's social atom; conceptual definition: the smallest unit of the sociometric matrix.

Sociometric Leader: (1) popular leader, (2) powerful leader, and (3) isolated leader. *The popular leader* receives more than the number of expected choices on *all* criteria in which he and the choosers are mutually involved; the choosers have themselves a *low* sociometric status. *The powerful leader* receives more than the number of expected choices on all criteria in which he and the choosers are mutually involved; the choosers have themselves a *high* sociometric status. Through the chain relations which they provide he can exercise a far-reaching influence. *The isolated leader* receives less than the number of expected choices or, in an extreme case, not more than a single mutual first choice. This choice comes from a powerful leader who is himself the recipient of a large number of choices coming from a number of individuals who enjoy high sociometric status. The isolated leader individual may operate like an invisible ruler, the power behind the throne, exercising indirectly a wide influence throughout sociometric networks.

These are by definition sociometric leader types and should not be confused with what is called a *leader* in folk usage, magic or charysmatic. Many other factors enter into their development, especially the phenomenon of the role, but however complex a leadership process may appear *in situ,* its sociometric base is an indispensable clue for its deeper understanding; it should not be bypassed.

Sociometric Cleavage: two groups of individuals in which self-preference —that is preference for members of own group—rules out other-preference, that is, preference for members of outgroups. It is the dynamic reason for the tendency of a group to break up into subgroups.

The Saturation Point: is the point of maximum absorption of a population in power for a minority group, the point which a population cannot exceed if it is to prevent a break-out of frictions and various disturbances. A given population may be saturated with a certain minority group at a given time. If an excess of members of the minority group move into the community from the outside in numbers exceeding this point, the delicate balance begins to break. In the case of a chemical solution, its point of saturation for a certain substance may change, for instance, with the rise or fall of temperature. In the case of social groups, the point of saturation may change with the organization of the interrelated groups.

Sociodynamic Law: holds that the distribution of sociometric scores is positively skewed. The tendency in any particular group for more choices to go to few members is the sociodynamic effect. "This tendency is related to the development of.the value system of the group. Values develop by becoming more precisely embodied in the persons of fewer members of the group." . . .

Spontaneity: is the variable degree of adequate response to a situation of a variable degree of novelty. Novelty of behavior by itself is not the measure of spontaneity. Novelty has to be qualified against its adequacy *in situ.* Adequacy of behavior by itself is also not the measure of spontaneity. Adequacy has to be qualified against its novelty. The novelty, for instance, of extreme psychotic behavior may be to such a degree incoherent that the actor is unable to solve any concrete problem, to plan an act of suicide, to cut a piece of bread, or to solve a thought problem. (We speak here of pathological spontaneity.) The adequacy of behavior may be unnovel to a degree which results in strict rigid or automatic conformity to a cultural conserve. Such adherence may gradually obliterate the ability of the organism and the talent of the actor to change.

Spontaneity can be conceived as the *arch catalyser;* metaphorically speaking it has a procreative function. Creativity can be conceived as the *archsubstance;* metaphorically speaking it has a maternal function.

Role-taking: is "being" in a role in life itself, within its relatively coercive and imperative contexts, for instance, being a mother, a father, a policeman, etc. The roles are social conserves; they have, or at least pretend to have, a finished form.

Role-playing: is "playing" a role, by choice, in a chosen setting, for the purpose of exploring, experimenting, developing, training or changing a role. Playing a role can take the form of a test or is an episode in the course of a psychodrama or sociodrama.

Technique of Self-Presentation: The subject acts in his own roles and portrays the figures which fill his own private world. Psychodrama is here a form of individual psychotherapy. He is his own auxiliary ego, the physician may be the other. One of the first uses of the psychodramatic technique was in this individual form. It was and is an improvement upon psychoanalysis as a patient-physician relationship. Erroneously, psychodrama is thought of only in its group form.

Technique of Role-Reversal: Its shortest definition is that the person A becomes the person B and that the person B becomes the person A. On the psychodramatic stage this reversal is meant as an actuality because for certain mental patients it is an actuality. It is not fiction or "as if." It illustrates the revolutionary aspect of psychodramatic logic. An abbreviated form of this technique is if A takes one of the "roles" of B and B takes one of the "roles" of A.

The Mirror Technique: The subject or patient is represented by an auxiliary ego who portrays him: how he acts in the various situations of his life, how he really is as others see him. The spectators in the audience react towards him and discuss him as if he would be the real person. The real person sits in the audience and is often taken unawares. "He is physically present but not psychologically" (Ray Corsini), at least that is what is pretended. The real purpose of the technique is to let the patient see himself "as in a mirror," provoke him, and shock him into action.

The Technique of the Double: The shortest definition is that two persons, A and B, are one and the same person. This is another illustration of the psychodramatic logic. B acts as the double of A and is accepted by A as such. The degree of nonacceptance and the conflict derived from it between the individual and his double is an important phase in double catharsis.

23

ANALYTIC GROUP PSYCHOTHERAPY

S. R. Slavson

Samuel Richard Slavson, born in Russia on Christmas Day, 1890, immigrated to the United States in 1903 and became a citizen in 1913. After receiving his B. S. from Cooper Union, he attended graduate school at the College of the City of New York, Columbia College, and the Teachers College at Columbia University. He pursued a varied career in education, social group work, and research in child psychology in schools and community centers in the United States and in England before entering the field of mental hygiene and psychotherapy. He first introduced activity group therapy with children in latency in 1934 and later expanded it to include eleven techniques of group psychotherapy. Slavson's career included director of research in child psychology at the Malting House School in Cambridge, England; providing youth consultation service at Hudson Guild Counseling Service in New York: Northshore Youth Consultation Service in New York; and Community Service Society of New York. He was also a consultant for staff development at the Brooklyn State Hospital and New York State Division for Youth and director of Group Psychotherapy at the Jewish Board of Guardians in New York from 1934 to 1956. Slavson lectured at New York University and Yeshiva University.

Among the honors accorded Slavson are the Adolf Meyer Award in Mental Health (1956), the Wilfred C. Hulse Award (1964), copresidency of the International Congress on Group Psychotherapy (1957 and 1964), presidency of the Group Psychotherapy Institute, and president emeritus of the American Group Psychotherapy Association.

Slavson is the founder and was editor-in-chief (1951–60) of the *International Journal of Group Psychotherapy,* the organ of the American Group Psychotherapy Association. He is also contributing editor of the second edition of the *Psychiatric Dictionary.*

Slavson's group psychotherapies are of several types: (1) *play group psychotherapy,* primarily for children of preschool age; (2) *activity group therapy,* for children eight to twelve years of age; (3) *activity-interview group psychotherapy,* for children and those in their latency period who are more seriously disturbed than those in the original activity therapy groups; (4) *para-analytic group psychotherapy,* for adolescents and certain adults, (5) *analytic group psychotherapy,* a variety of counseling and guidance groups to meet the needs of adults; and (6) *transitional and interactional groups,* for children and adolescents.

Among his publications are *Science in the New Education* (1934), *Creative Education* (1937), *Character Education in a Democracy* (1939), *Introduction to Group Therapy* (1942), *Recreation and the Total Personality* (1946), *The Practice of Group Therapy* (1947), *Analytic Group Psychotherapy* (1950), *Child Psychotherapy* (1952), *Re-Educating the Delinquent* (1954), *The Fields of Group Psychotherapy* (1956), *Child-Centered Group Guidance of Parents* (1958), *A Textbook in Analytic Group Psychotherapy* (1964), *Reclaiming the Delinquent through Para-Analytic Group Psychotherapy and the Inversion Technique* (1965), and *Because I Live Here, Vita-Erg Ward Therapy with Psychotic Women* (1970).

Group Psychotherapy

Group psychotherapy with prepubertal children as practiced at the present time falls into four different categories: (1) activity group psychotherapy, (2) transitional groups, (3) play group psychotherapy, and (4) activity-interview group psychotherapy. ... Interview (analytic) groups ... are designed for postpubertal patients.

Activity Group Psychotherapy

The general pattern of activity group therapy for small groups of no more than eight children, is free acting out in a specially designed physical setting and carefully planned group milieu. The setting must be simple so that the children can feel free to display their aggressions against the physical environment, and the group must be so planned that they are equally free to behave in a like manner toward each other. The only person the young patients are not permitted directly to harass or attack is the therapist, nor can they invade his personality in any other manner. Hostility and aggression that children inevitably feel toward him as a substitute for parents and teachers may be displaced upon the materials, the walls, and the furniture of the treatment room and upon each other. The therapist is aware of the true intent of such behavior,

---

S. R. Slavson, *Child Psychotherapy* (New York: Columbia University Press, 1952), pp. 280–96. An internal reference has been deleted.

but he does not call attention to it, nor does he react to it in any way. The therapist plays a *neutral role.* By this is meant that he does not assume any specific characteristics or set criteria for behavior. Unilateral transference, that is, transference from the patient to the therapist only, is necessary in this type of therapy for a number of reasons. Chief among them are the presence of more than one patient and the fact that interpretation is not employed. Each child assigns a role to the therapist most appropriate to his particular emotional state or stage of development, and he can act out his feelings in the group setting.

In order to maintain a neutral role, the therapist is as passive as the children will allow. This predominantly passive role is confined to both his physical and his emotional activity, which leaves the children free to utilize him in whatever capacity they desire at a given time. Children whose basic attitudes are hostile may act them out; those who need a good and indulgent parent substitute may find one in him; while those who need restraint and control may expect that at appropriate times he will exert them if the other group members fail to do so. This variety of roles can be assumed by an adult only when he remains neutral so that he can meet the unconscious needs of each. Because of this role, the therapist can be always positive and encouraging. He neither criticizes, prohibits, nor in any way expresses disapproval, but his failure to respond serves as action interpretation.

The free atmosphere in the groups and the interactions of the children automatically places them in specific, though fluid, relations to each other. Some become the dominant individuals; others the submissive. There are some whose contributions to the group are almost nil; the group is not affected by either their presence or their absence. There are those who by various and devious means isolate themselves from relations with others. They are similar to spectators. In order to describe the various roles assumed by different children, we have designated them respectively as instigators, neutralizers, social neuters, and isolates.

The *instigators* are rather important in all forms of group psychotherapy, because they set up the emotional and social dynamics essential for the creation of situations similar to those in the outer social reality. When there are no instigators present to activate the others either emotionally or in physical activity, the groups stagnate and have very little therapeutic effect, for in these groups the therapy results from the active contacts of the individuals in them. The action level must be rather high at the early stages of treatment, but should subside when personality integration is attained and the ego of each is strengthened by freeing impulses from repression or bringing them under control when necessary. However, when the instigators are weak and infantile, the hyperactivity they arouse in the group may become too uncontrollable for the group to tolerate. The aggression tolerance of any given group has definite limits, and when they are exceeded, disorganization is likely to follow, accompanied by anxiety in the individual members. Children who are selected for the role of instigator in groups must possess at least a minimal degree of ego and superego development. If they are lacking, the therapeutic effect of the group on all who are involved in it is negligible.

The *neutralizers* are the more integrated individuals whose superego development is on a higher level and whose ego strengths are sufficient to keep impulses in check and to regulate behavior. Therefore, they possess the strength to influence other children and the course of the members' behavior and acts. Thus, when a stage of excessive hilarity is reached, the neutralizer can reduce the high level of hyperactivity and inaugurate a state of comparative quiet. This transition is essential, for the actual improvement in the young patients occurs at the point of transition from the high peak of hyperactivity, which we term *nodal behavior,* to the low level of activity, or *anti-nodal behavior.* It is during this transition, when the individuals in the group bring themselves under control, that the regulative forces of the personality are brought to the fore and are developed and strengthened.

The *social neuters,* as the name implies, are the ineffectual persons who do not influence the atmosphere or the behavior of the group by themselves and fall in with the current activities, games, and play instigated by stronger group members. As treatment proceeds, however, they often blossom out into leaders and even instigators.

The *isolates* are the individuals who because of specific personality difficulties, such as neurotic anxieties and fears or other constrictions of character, are actually afraid of close association and direct contacts. They must have an opportunity to overcome their emotional encapsulation by slow stages and therefore should at first be allowed to remain by themselves until they gather enough security to join the group.

Despite the definiteness of these characterizations of the patients in groups, actually the roles of the children are fluid and changeable. Often an isolate ultimately becomes an active participant in the group. He may even assume the part of an instigator, while an instigator, on the other hand, may level off and become a neutralizer. The reversibility of roles and relations is one of the major aspects of the therapeutic dynamics in activity group therapy and is made possible only by the fact that the group has no specific plan of organization, no program or objectives and that the therapist is nondirective and neutral. The absence of these external rigidities makes it possible for the children to work out their inner difficulties and social barriers so that they can alter their roles in relation to one another and to the group as a whole. This fluidity in groups I term *group motility,* in contrast to the structure of ordinary clubs or recreational groups, which are planned so that each has a specific function or part in them. This pattern I have described as *group fixity,* which is inevitable and desirable in working with persons for whom the aim is not therapy.

The arts and crafts materials and tools supplied to such groups have a unique place in the therapeutic process, which is quite different from their function in an educational setting, such as arts and crafts, shopwork, or in a special-interest group. The materials are used here to direct the children's libido and attendant aggressions from their companions and onto inanimate objects. Because the personality problems of children accepted for group therapy are such that the children are unable to utilize personal relations constructively and are not mature enough or resourceful enough to create for themselves a meaningful environment, idleness could lead only to extreme disorganization, hilarity, and uncontrolled aggression.

The function of the materials and tools is to fix the libido—in this case the nonsexual, but sometimes the sexual libido as well—upon the materials first. This is intended to be only a temporary step. The underlying intention is that activities and interests which are at first directed toward objects will eventually be transferred to the other members of the group and the therapist and that the materials will be gradually relegated to the background. This happens in all groups. One of the reasons for this, in addition to personality growth and increased security, is the fact that the materials and the tools are always the same. No matter how long the group may meet, the equipment is not changed. This is intended to invoke the law of diminishing returns through monotony and the loss of interest and the transfer of interest by the group members to each other. Additional materials and tools and greater opportunities for creative work would isolate them from each other and prevent emotional interaction. Constancy and the uniformity of the physical environment accelerate social contacts in each in accordance with his state of readiness.

An important part of the therapy sessions is the refreshment period. Sharing a simple repast in an atmosphere different in every respect from that to which the children have been accustomed in their homes in the company of an understanding and tolerant adult in an experience that leaves indelible memories. The standard of conduct here, as in other respects at the "meetings," is left entirely to the participants. They can either eat the food, throw it at each other, stuff it in their pockets, give it away, or take it home. No one except, perhaps, one of their own number, expects them to behave well or to display any decorum. Only the therapist displays perfect table manners and retains his equanimity, no matter how intense is the hilarity or annoying the provocation. . . .

Therapy groups provide for the child tangible social reality, and the conditions under which they are conducted help to improve the self-image and strengthen the ego. Because the therapist always praises appropriately, encourages, and helps, attaining one's ends serves these and other aims of psychotherapy. The therapist's calm, tolerant, and kindly behavior makes him a suitable object of identification, and the children unconsciously assume his manners and attitudes. The therapist, however, is not the sole object of identification, for other children, as well, serve in the same capacity, and because of this it is essential that children who would have a too negative influence on their fellow members shall not be included in these groups. Corrective identifications, the therapist's action interpretation, and restraint by fellow members cause each to regulate and to restrain himself in return for group acceptance. Continuous exposure to the need for such adaptation and the repetition of self-control and selective judgment result in a strengthened ego. The reader has probably already become aware of the fact that activity group therapy is predominantly an ego therapy, and children who have suffered intensive libido distortion and disorganization cannot be helped by activity group therapy exclusively. In many instances it is employed as supplementary to individual treatment. . . .

The immature child may attach himself briefly to another on whom he leans for support in his upward climb, and having received this sustenance, he may soon begin to work and act on his own more appropriately. This is the phenomenon of the *supportive ego.* . . .

Activity group therapy is suitable only for children during the latency period, especially between the ages of eight and twelve. In this period the sexual libido remains in a stage of comparative dormancy, and ego development attains its maximum acceleration; also centripetal interests and identifications are at their height. Group associations are, therefore, most important and most meaningful at this stage in the child's development. At the height of genital development or during the first and second Oedipal periods, activity therapy groups alone cannot be considered adequate, because they inherently deal with libido redistribution problems only indirectly. . . .

Transitional Groups

Transitional groups are so termed because they serve as a bridge between therapy groups or individual psychotherapy, whence patients are chosen, and the social realities of their world. Children who are not ready to take part in group activities or regular social clubs need a more protected social environment and are assigned to such groups. Their members are carefully selected, and the "leader" is a trained psychotherapist. These groups, unlike therapy groups, follow a program of organized activities and have a plan. The group elects officers, keeps minutes of proceedings, and has a treasuer. Various facilities, such as tools, materials, food, and a field for uninhibited acting out, are not provided here. Under the leadership and stimulation of the "leader," the members censor, punish, and control the acts of their fellow members, and the group as a whole planfully takes action and makes decisions on all matters relating to its work and plans.

The difference between these groups and ordinary clubs lies in the fact that their members are selected because, though almost ready for realistic social participation, they are as yet unable to enter into the competitive relations and high social pressures of the latter. Another difference is that the leader, who is really a therapist, is aware of the needs of the members as individuals, which is not always the case in social clubs. He prevents conflicts and dissensions that may prove too difficult for the members to resolve. Also, participation in intergroup activities is carefully graded, even though transitional groups meet in a neighborhood center or a settlement house. Transitional groups also provide an attenuated reality, but here the social demands are much greater than in therapy groups. Programing, planning, and carrying out projects make demands upon the members which are strictly avoided in the latter. But caution is exercised that too great responsibilities are not thrust upon the children or demands made upon them for which they may not be ready.

Instead of a specially designed setting and an isolated environment, the transitional groups meet in ordinary meeting rooms in a neighborhood center at the same time that other groups meet. The members are, therefore, exposed to contact with other children in the community. The leader makes a conscious, though cautious, effort to bring them into contact with the other members of the center and to involve them in its activities. This is done by visiting clubs, special activity rooms, gymnasiums, and different parts of the building. The children meet staff members and are encouraged to join the various activities of the center. Some of the members of the transitional groups may be interested in art, some in athletics, others in dramatics, still others in music, science, or arts and crafts shops. Gradually the programing and planning of the group is directed toward the general activities in the building, which may include individuals outside the group itself and other clubs. These widened social contacts bring in their wake real and increased demands, which must occur with graded intensity. Each child needs to be helped to fit into them. Usually the transitional groups finally pattern themselves after other clubs in the center, join them in their activities, and are included in the roster of the regular clubs under the direction of a regular leader. Our experience shows that these clubs do not survive long because of the absence of a true social and interest homogeneity. They always disband, each member joining a group best suited to his needs and special interests.

Play Group Psychotherapy

Play group psychotherapy is employed for children of preschool age whose maladjustments are severe and who suffer from deep psychoneuroses as well as behavior disorders. The conduct of these groups conforms in every respect to the same principles and techniques as are used in individual play therapy, except that when three to five children are present they interact with one another and activate each other's catharsis. The meaning and significance of the play is greatly enhanced when it occurs in the presence of other children and is stimulated and shared by them. The materials employed are the same as those used in individual play therapy. Their basic characteristics are that they are *libido-revealing* and *libido-activating,* in contrast to those recommended for activity groups, where the materials are rather *libido-fixating.* Activation of the libido is necessary in treating children chosen for these groups, since it is in this area that their difficulties usually lie. Therefore, they have to act out their oral, anal, urethral, and sexual phantasies and preoccupations in play, as well as their hostilities and resentments. They must have opportunities to abreact to and to reenact traumatic and disturbing situations in their homes, rid themselves of the emotional pressures, and attain insight into their feelings and actions on their own level through interpretation by the other patients and by the psychotherapist.

The materials must, therefore, be adjusted to meet these needs. Water, clay, plasticene, watercolor paints, a doll's house, with toy figures of males, females, and children, bedroom furnishings, bathroom equipment, rubber tubing, sponges, toy guns, soldiers, animals, masks, dolls of various kinds with which the children can identify and play out their fantasies. Refreshments are served in play psychotherapy groups, where the therapist reenacts the maternal role as she does in activity groups and where the children can behave as they do at home. The children are permitted to act out freely their aggressions and to abreact to frustrations and hostilities and recreate situations that disturb them. The therapist in these groups should be preferably a woman.

In play group psychotherapy the therapist is active. As in individual play therapy, she participates with the children, interprets behavior both to individual children and to the group as a whole, encourages their attempts to uncover the motivating feelings behind action, and relates current feelings to the trauma to which the children attempt vaguely to react. Background facts and events are elicited from the young patients in so far as they are capable of supplying and understanding them. Thus, this therapy proceeds in precisely the same manner as does individual psychotherapy. Libido distribution and the changing of the self-image as much as is possible for little children are its goals. The children in these groups (unlike those in the activity groups) are allowed to attack the therapist physically, and the reasons are interpreted to them. Because of the youth of the children and their limited ego development and controls, hyperactivity is regulated by the psychotherapist, for she uses both passive and active restraint. The passive restraint is practiced, as it is in activity group therapy, by the physical setting and action interpretation. Direct restraint is exercised when the therapist feels that the anxiety generated by the behavior may disturb the young patients or lead to intense disorganization of the group.

The children chosen for these groups may include serious cases of psychoneurosis, primary behavior disorders, and character disorders, as well as schizoid personalities who would not be frightened by the other children. For these groups selection need not be as rigid as for activity group therapy. However, children who disturb the group climate seriously enough to arouse anxiety in fellow members are eliminated here as well. Transference in these groups is bilateral; the therapist is active and utilizes the transference in a therapeutic process as in interpretation. The age range of children in these groups should not be more than six months, in contrast to two years in activity groups.

Activity-Interview Group Psychotherapy

In activity-interview group psychotherapy we also treat children in the latency period, but this procedure differs from activity group therapy in the choice of patients and in the function of the therapist. Activity-interview group psychotherapy is actually a combination of activity group therapy and individual interview psychotherapy and has many elements in common with both as well as with play group psychotherapy. The term has been chosen because of the commonness of these elements.

The setting in activity-interview therapy is the same as that in activity group therapy, with the addition of some of the libido activating materials, as in play group psychotherapy, but suitable for older children. The catharsis is both active and verbal. The children are free to act out, as in activity groups, but their acts are interpreted by the therapist, who also encourages the young patients to communicate to each other and to the therapist their problems, difficulties, preoccupations, fears, and anxieties. These are openly discussed, either with one child or with the group as a whole, depending upon the situation and the need. The aims here are libido distribution, ego-strengthening, and changing the self-image. Severely psychoneurotic children may therefore be included in these groups. The function of the therapist is the same as it is in individual psychotherapy, but instead of working with one patient, in these groups he may work sometimes with one, at other times with several children, and, again, with the whole group. The similarity between play group psychotherapy and activity-interview psychotherapy is apparent. The difference is that the latter has a wider scope of activities and there is less control over the behavior of the children. The benefits to the child from this treatment are the same as listed under activity group psychotherapy, because both are of the same age. To these must be added the correction in libido distribution, reduction of traumatic foci, and acquisition of insight. . . .

Analytic Group Psychotherapy

In analytic group psychotherapy, as in all analytically oriented psychotherapies, the aims are: redistribution of the libido where it is excessively cathexed either on oneself or on an object; strengthening of the ego so that it may deal with inner and outer demands and pressures and regulate the impingement (or lack of it) emanating from the superego; and correction of the self-image.

The *aim* of true group psychotherapy is the achieving of a relatively permanent intrapsychic change, rather than the alleviating of symptoms or behavior improvement only. The next consideration is the *process*. Neither "relationships," "understanding," nor "reenactment" (action) are adequate procedures for achieving "cures" or lasting changes in emotionally disturbed patients. Explanation is not interpretation, and understanding is not insight. Action as a form of therapy may be adequate for some highly selected, mild behavior and character disorders in children, if it is carried on in a specially designed environment and in a group (not individual) setting. The more disturbed, even among children, and all adult nonpsychotic patients cannot be therapeutically affected by abreaction, acting out, or reenactment alone. In true psychotherapy, action and reflection go hand in hand, and the latter (reflection) can stand alone, but not the former (action). Nor is it enough for the ends of real psychotherapy with adult patients to foster relationships. There is no proof that a better adjustment to a therapy group, and more friendly and tolerant relations among its members, results in lasting inner changes in the individual patient that carry over to other areas of his life. Improvement in behavior and attitude nearly always results from any type of friendly and constructive individual and group associations, but no one who really understands the structure and dynamics of character and of neuroses can confidently claim that they can be changed or dissolved by such superficial means as "relationships in a group."

Analytic group psychotherapy, with nonpsychotic adolescent and adult patients, relies on free associative verbal communication by each individual, interpretation of individual and group resistances, interpretation of the individual, multiple, and collective (group) transferences, and the attainment of

---

The remainder of this chapter is from S. R. Slavson, *A Textbook in Analytic Group Psychotherapy* (New York: International Universities Press, 1964), pp. 90–93, 116–19, 128, 176, 177.

insight by *each* of the participating group members *as individuals.* True psychotherapy can hardly be expected to occur if the sexual and nonsexual libido are not involved and primary and secondary hostilities and aggressions are not worked through.

Such "working through" cannot be achieved in guidance and counseling or in the so-called psychotherapies that rely on artifices for behavioral change. Working through can be achieved only through regressive infantile memories and feelings in a transference relation to a parent surrogate. This process is especially indispensable in the treatment of real psychoneuroses.

Action without reflection is insufficient. "Role taking," which is sometimes suggested as the sole therapeutic tool, cannot affect the personality structure so profoundly as to alter it. What is necessary to reconstructive psychotherapy is not reenactment, but rather the reliving of past affect-laden traumatic events with all the accompanying distortions and fantasies. But this must occur in a setting devoid of the original threats and anxiety-inducing reactions and situations. In addition to freeing ego energies consumed in dealing with these unconscious pressures, the deeply affecting emotional experiences are here relived in the light of new and more mature attitudes, with the help of the therapist and fellow patients. Thus, the second requisite of true group psychotherapy with nonpsychotic patients is free verbal catharsis that leads to early memories of traumata with the associative anxieties (though it may also involve regressive acting out).

The third requirement for real group psychotherapy is *free and spontaneous* participation and response from *all* members of the group, as feelings, memories, and ideas are stirred up (catalyzed) by fellow patients. Any technique that does not permit this is invalid. The concatenation set up in the unconscious of individuals (and sometimes in the group as a whole) must be permitted free flow. It is through this freedom (which the neurotic was not permitted in his past history) that the noxious elements in the psyche are thrown off.

From this point of view, techniques such as psychodrama, didactic therapies, and role-playing in a *structured* situation or pseudorelations do not conform with sound group psychotherapy or, for that matter, any kind of psychotherapy. It is the free flow of stored-up memories and feelings that lead the patient to the core of his problem, help him unburden himself of his psychic tensions and anxieties, and allow him to acquire insight into his mechanisms and reactions.

Devices and artifices often play into the resistances that patients inevitably present. These resistances are part and parcel of sound psychotherapy. However, where there is no free cathartic flow in the interviews, patients can be activated to communicate, but this communication is not therapeutically meaningful. Such devices as "forced," "contractual," "transactional," or "imposed communication" have no therapeutic validity. . . . Verbalization, in all psychotherapy, is effective when it releases associated and bound-up affect and anxiety stored in the unconscious, and occurs most tellingly by overcoming censors and resistances. Facilitated statements do not place the individual in a position to encounter himself and his unconscious and, therefore, do not constitute a true therapeutic experience.

The fourth requirement for effective group psychotherapy is correct selection and grouping of patients. Initially, diagnoses must be established for each patient and his suitability for one of many types of treatment determined.

A fifth requirement of a therapy group is that it meet the corrective needs of each patient according to his unique personality structure and clinical indications.

A sixth and important requirement of a true therapy group is that it remain small (not exceeding eight persons), so that interpersonal reactions and interactions can take place. But in a group that is too small, say less than five, prolonged relations would tend to reinforce the patients' problems and play into each person's neuroses without interactions, neutralization, cathartic elaborations, and other corrective dynamics. Mutual induction occurs in inverse geometric ratio to the size of the group, since the neutralizing and diluting elements stem from the variations in personality and ego-functioning between the group members.

The small group provides a narrower field for emotional operation and, therefore, greater concentration of affect. It prevents a loss of self-identity and pits individuals against each other more poignantly and more directly than is possible in larger groups. A small group is more likely to reactivate and reawaken the hostilities and discomforts experienced by the patient in his natural family. Since, aside from constitutional predispositions, psychic distortions predominantly stem from relations with members of one's own family, the duplication of these relations in a therapeutic setting and the process of working them through are the key to psychic reintegration. This can be achieved in a small group in a face-to-face relation, in intimate and affect-laden interpenetration.

We can therefore say, with justification, that *group psychotherapy had its beginnings with the introduction of the small group.* It is only in a small group that free-associative catharsis can occur, that valid interpretation can be given, and that telling insights are acquired. . . .

Para-Analytic Group Psychotherapy

We employ the term *para-analytic group psychotherapy* to designate a type of therapy which, though having the same base and orientation as analytic therapy, is lesser in depth. While the problems of some patients may still stem from the unconscious, the process of their therapy cannot, for a variety of reasons, proceed along conventional analytic lines and is modified accordingly. Instead of employing free association and predominant therapist passivity, the prevailing subjects of the interviews may be top realities and their content drawn from the conscious and the preconscious, rather than regressive memories and feelings and recall from the unconscious as is the case in psychoanalytic therapy.

There are individual patients and categories of patients for whom a lesser depth of uncovering is indicated, but for whom counseling and guidance would be inadequate, because their superficial nature would not solve the patients' problems. There are also patients whose difficulties require intellectual clarity or change in attitude, which they cannot achieve without first dissolving some rigidities and resistances. However, despite this need, the patients' egos could not withstand the assailment and stress of a fully uncovering, analytic therapy, and a less stressful procedure has to be employed.

We shall describe at some length, later in this volume, the precautionary measures necessary in the treatment of latent and borderline schizophrenic patients, but at this juncture it can be said that though an analytically oriented therapy can be employed with some of them, it must be of a low degree of uncovering and exploration. When concepts of a depth nature are employed, great care must be exercised against causing disturbance or agitation in such patients.

Another category of patients for whom lesser depth therapy is indicated is adolescents. The state of maturity and life experiences of adolescents makes them unfit for introspective plumbing of the unconscious. The surface nature of their incestuous and libidinal urges and their transferential antagonism to adults (and, therefore, the therapist) militate against their entering into a relation and into their own psyche, as required by a true analytic therapy. . . . On the other hand, adolescents whose inner stress brings them to therapy cannot be helped by counseling or guidance alone. Consequently, another approach is needed—*para-analytic group psychotherapy,* the treatment of choice for most adolescents.

Para-analytic group psychotherapy is also most suitable for the aged (not the senile), whose descending libidinal quantum and ascending egotistic drives engender a radical reorganization of their psychic structure. In the treatment of patients in this category, limits to self-confrontation and the unraveling of unconscious strivings have to be tightly drawn, partly because of diminishing inner resources and partly because of the automatic and largely unconscious disengagement process that goes on in all elderly and aging persons.

The comparative dynamics of para-analytic psychotherapy are as follows: transference is of the same level of intensity as in analytic groups; catharsis is considerably less regressive than in the latter; the same levels of insight cannot be reached in para-analytic, as in analytic, therapy (though they are much higher than in guidance); and reality testing and sublimations are more or less of the same nature. The greatest difference, and the most telling one, is the activity of the therapist. In para-analytic group psychotherapy, the therapist is much more active in leading and also, at times, directing the interviews. He offers explanations and interpretations, suggests ideas, principles, philosophies, and guides for conduct and living, and he may assume the role of a discussion leader at certain points. However, as in analytic psychotherapy, he follows the leads and cues from the group and is careful to relate comments and questions to the subjective meanings and unconscious strivings of the patients, although universalizing them more often than personalizing them.

In para-analytic group therapy, dreams are employed just as they are in analytic groups and unconscious material is allowed to come through and is utilized to advance interviews whenever indicated, or avoided when it is not to therapeutic advantage. Actually, para-analytic maneuvers and levels are employed in *all* types of individual and group psychotherapy, as they are needed, except that they are of transitory duration and short lived, while with patients requiring therapy of lesser intensity, para-analytic procedures form the major pattern of the treatment.

The general rules for the application of para-analytic psychotherapy are as follows: the therapist must not press for regression in his patients to deep levels of the unconsious; the interviews consist predominantly of top realities dealing with current problems and preoccupations; only a minimal level of anxiety is permissible; rise of the anxiety level has to be prevented, allayed, or diverted; introspective or uncovering therapy, if used at all, needs to follow the acquisition of "psychologic literacy" which involves conceptual understanding (as differentiated from emotional insight); free association is not demanded or expected; rather, associated thinking is prevalent, that is, horizontal association of ideas, thoughts, feelings, and events (as differentiated from vertical, regressive, free association); the therapist is much more active than in analytic psychotherapy; and by and large, the therapist addresses himself to behavioral patterns of the patients and their ego functioning and is less concerned with the libido and superego than he would be in analytic therapy.

[EDITOR'S NOTE: Also see figure 23.1 on page 527, and the table on pages 528–29 that presents Differential Dynamics in Group Therapies.]

FIGURE 23.1   Types of therapy groups

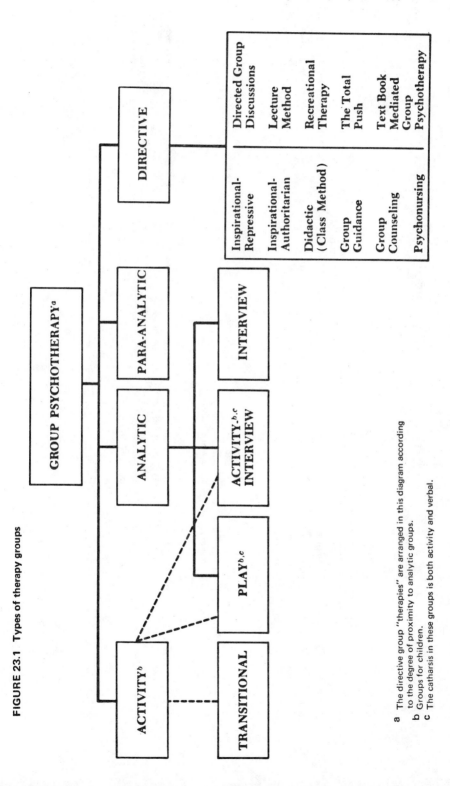

a The directive group "therapies" are arranged in this diagram according
   to the degree of proximity to analytic groups.
b Groups for children.
c The catharsis in these groups is both activity and verbal.

TABLE 23.1 Differential dynamics in group therapies

Type of Group	Transference	Catharsis	Insight	Reality Testing	Sublimation	Resistance
Activity (Children)	Sibling Identification Multilateral Unilateral Group	Activity Induced Vicarious	Derivative	*In Situ*	*In Situ*	Absenteeism Lateness Passivity
Play (Children)	Libidinal Sibling Identification Multilateral Group	Activity Verbal Activity-Verbal Free Association Induced Vicarious	Direct Derivative	*In Situ*	*In Situ* *Ex Situ*	Irrelevancy Silence Passivity
Activity-Interview (Children)	Libidinal Sibling Indentification Multilateral Group	Associative Free Association Activity Verbal Activity-Verbal Induced Vicarious	Direct Derivative	*In Situ*	*In Situ* *Ex Situ*	Irrelevancy Silence Lateness Absenteeism Passivity

TABLE 23.1 (Continued)

Type of Group	Transference	Catharsis	Insight	Reality Testing	Sublimation	Resistance
Analytic (Adults)	Libidinal Sibling Identification Multilateral Group	Associative Free Association Verbal Directed Induced Vicarious	Direct Derivative	Ex Situ In Situ	Ex Situ	Displacement Deflection Distraction Abruptness Planned Communication Associative Thinking Irrelevancy Silence Absenteeism Lateness Acting Out
Para-Analytic (Adolescents)	Libidinal Sibling Identification Multilateral Group	Associative Free Association Verbal Directed Induced Vicarious	Direct Derivative	Ex Situ In Situ		(as above)

24

MILIEU THERAPY: THE THERAPEUTIC COMMUNITY

Maxwell Jones

Robert N. Rapoport

Maxwell Jones, born in 1907 of British parents in Queenstown, South Africa, was educated at the University of Edinburgh, where he received his M.B. and Ch.B. in 1931, his M.R.C.P. in 1935, and his M.D. (which earned him a Gold Medal Thesis) in 1947. The University of London awarded him the D.P.M. in 1934. After serving as senior house surgeon at the Deaconess Hospital in Edinburgh from 1932, he became senior assistant at the Royal Edinburgh Hospital from 1934 to 1936 and at the same time held the positions of lecturer in psychiatry at the University of Edinburgh and physician-in-charge at the Jordanburn Nerve Hospital. He spent the next two years in the United States at the University of Pennsylvania and Columbia University. In 1938, he went to Maudsley Hospital in London. The years 1939 to 1945 were spent as a psychiatric specialist at Mill Hill Emergency Hospital, and the following two years as psychiatrist-in-charge at the P.O.W. Neurosis Unit at Southern Hospital, Dartford, Kent.

In 1947 Jones lectured on mental health at the London School of Economics. From 1948 to 1952 he held the positions of consultant psychiatrist at the British Post Graduate Medical School in Hammersmith and the Post Graduate Medical School of London. From 1947 to 1959, he acted as director of the Belmont Hospital Social Rehabilitation Unit, Sutton, England, and in 1951 he was a consultant in mental health for the World Health Organization. Then his career brought him again to the United States, where he was visiting professor of psychiatry at Stanford University (1959–60), clinical professor of psychiatry at the University of Oregon Medical School (1961–62), and director of educational research at Oregon State Hospital in Salem. His latest position has been physician superintendent, Dingleton Hospital, Melrose, Roxburghshire, Scotland.

The best known of Jones's works is *The Therapeutic Community: A New Treatment Method in Psychiatry,* which was first published in England as *Social Psychiatry.* In 1953 he published *Psychiatric Rehabilitation,* and in 1962, *Social Psychiatry: In the Community, in Hospitals and in Prisons.* In addition, Jones has published articles in a number of journals in the United States and Great Britain, many of them in collaboration with Robert Rapoport.

Robert N. Rapoport, born in Brockton, Massachusetts, on the first of November 1924, received an M.A. degree in anthropology at the University of Chicago in 1949 and a Ph.D. in social anthropology from Harvard in 1951. From 1950 to 1953 he was an assistant professor in the Department of Sociology and Anthropology at Cornell University. In connection with this post, he was social science field director for the Stirling County Study in Canada. He then left for England, where he accepted an appointment as social science research director at Belmont Hospital Social Rehabilitation Unit, Sutton, England.

From 1957 to 1962 Rapoport taught social anthropology at Harvard University's Department of Social Relations, while heading the Department of Social Science at McLean Hospital in Belmont, Massachusetts. From 1963 to 1965 he was research professor of sociology and anthropology at Northeastern University, while directing the Institute of Human Sciences at Boston College. From 1962 to 1965 Rapoport was a member of the editorial board of *Human Organization,* the journal of the Society for Applied Anthropology. Currently, he is senior social scientist at the Tavistock Institute of Human Relations in London.

Rapoport collaborated with Maxwell Jones on a number of papers in the field of milieu therapy. These papers included "Social and Administrative Psychiatry" (*The Lancet,* 1955); "Psychiatric Rehabilitation" (*Yearbook of Education,* 1955); "The Absorption of New Doctors in a Therapeutic Community" (*Behavioral Science,* 1957); "Toward the Definition of the 'Therapeutic Community'" (*Report on Social Psychiatry,* Research Report NM 73 03 00.01 Naval Medical Research Institute, Bethesda, Maryland, 1958). Rapoport summarizes milieu therapy in "The Therapeutic Community" (*International Encyclopedia of the Social Sciences,* 1967) and in "Principles for Developing a Therapeutic Community" (in J. Masserman [ed.], *Current Psychiatric Therapies, 1963). Rapoport's most comprehensive work, Community as Doctor: New Perspectives on a Therapeutic Community* (1960), is a thorough and systematic presentation of the system of milieu therapy developed by Maxwell Jones.

Milieu psychotherapy, a form of group therapy, is a mental hospital community so structured that it possesses psychotherapeutic value; the social climate of the community provides healing qualities. Viewed as the third revolution in psychiatry, milieu psychotherapy is based on a wholesome psychological atmosphere created by all of the participants or members of a hospital community, not merely the doctors and the patients. Its scope is broad, and successful treatment entails adherence to an ideology, the organization of staff and patient roles, and the proper recruitment of staff suitable to the objectives of a therapeutic community. In milieu therapy, a high premium is placed upon a sense of permissiveness, a feeling of communalism, and a democratic atmosphere, i.e., an atmosphere highlighted by free and open communication. The therapeutic community extends beyond the grounds of the mental institution, for it encompasses the family/social unit and society at large as well.

The Community as Doctor

At the present we are in the throes, many observers maintain, of a third "revolution" in psychiatry, one that is signalized by the use of group methods, milieu therapy, and administrative psychiatry. In general, *social* psychiatric approaches in therapy stress multi-person involvement in contrast to approaches aimed at affecting only one individual through the efforts of one other individual.

One of the brightest stars in the social psychiatric firmament is the "therapeutic community" idea. According to this approach, the hospital is seen not as a place where patients are classified and stored, nor a place where one group of individuals (the medical staff) gives treatment to another group of individuals (the patients) according to the model of general medical hospitals; but as a place which is organized as a community in which everyone is expected to make some contribution towards the shared goals of creating a social organization that will have healing properties. "The therapeutic community views treatment as located not in the application by specialists of certain shocks, drugs, or interpretations, but in the normal interactions of healthy community life."[1]

The present book is an attempt to describe and analyze some of the characteristics of one of the earliest and most vigorous pioneering attempts at the construction of a therapeutic community—the Social Rehabilitation Unit of Belmont Hospital in England—from a social science viewpoint. This is a 100-bed unit within a neurosis center that serves the United Kingdom under the National Health Service and gears its program to the treatment of patients with long-standing personality disorders. . . .

The Social Rehabilitation Unit at Belmont Hospital is an experiment in milieu therapy. Its work is part of the larger movement sometimes termed the

The Community as Doctor, from Robert N. Rapoport, *Community as Doctor: New Perspectives on a Therapeutic Community* (London: Tavistock Publications, 1967; and Springfield, Ill.: Charles C. Thomas, 1960), pp. 9–10, 268–69.

[1]Maxwell Jones, et al., *The Therapeutic Community: A New Treatment Method in Psychiatry* (New York: Basic Books, 1953), p. vii.

third revolution in psychiatry. The Unit developed in response to the convergence of a number of favorable forces during and after the Second World War in England. These included the increasing awareness of the inadequacies of the conventional "custodial" system of hospital care for the psychically ill, the growth of a national sense of responsibility for dealing with pervasive health problems, and the influence of psychoanalytic and social scientific ideas in psychiatry generally.

Experimentation with therapeutic milieux has taken different forms, the particular form in each hospital being governed by the type of patient being treated, the position of the hospital or unit in the larger psychiatric context, the orientation of the staff, and the personality of the director. It has been pointed out that innovating directors tend to have certain personal qualities in common—their dedication, optimism, and enthusiasm in keynoting conspicuous change. Now that the therapeutic milieu approach is more widely acknowleged as relevant to the general treatment of psychiatric patients and an interest in its principles is becoming increasingly modish, it is perceived as germane to the work of a wider range of psychiatrists.

In this chapter we shall examine the implications of the Unit study for "live" and controversial issues in the contemporary field of milieu therapy. We use our Belmont observations in this chapter to derive general principles for the development of therapeutic milieux in other contexts.

We shall divide our discussion of issues into five categories that reflect problems in the field of milieu therapy generally. In each case we shall discuss the general problem and principles involved, state the Unit's position, and indicate the implications of the United study for the development of a milieu therapy program. The problems are concerned with: (1) the formation of a treatment ideology, (2) the organization of staff roles, (3) the organization of the patient role, (4) the involvement of individuals external to the hospital in treatment, and (5) the conceptualization of treatment and rehabilitation as goals. . . .

The Formation of a Treatment Ideology

Ideologies are formal systems of ideas or beliefs that are held with great tenacity and emotional investment, that have self-confirming features, and that are resistant to change from objective rational reappraisal. Ideaologues not only perceive and interpret the world around them in terms of the precepts of

---

The Formation of a Treatment Ideology, from Rapoport, *Community as Doctor,* pp. 269–75. An internal reference has been deleted.

their own system of beliefs, but they tend to be especially convinced of the moral worth and special importance of their own particular orientations. Ideology welds observable aspects of the environment into a kind of unit by filling in gaps in knowledge with various projections that ultimately supply a coherent belief system on which action can be based and justified.

The beliefs of the Unit staff showed many features characteristic of ideology. The staff have taken ideas from a variety of sources and added some of their own to integrate a nominally logical system for the active treatment of problems about which there was incomplete knowledge, considerable professional controversy, and few precedents or technical skills. After a formative period, their system of belief and action was presented as a unified group product shared by all members of the Unit and as an effective approach to the problems at hand.

The fundamental position on which the Unit treatment ideology is based is that socioenvironmental influences are themselves capable of effectively changing individual patterns of social behavior. Etiologically, patients with no clear organic defect are seen as having personalities malformed by pathogenic social influences in their early lives. The Unit staff conceptualize this malformation of personality in terms of anomalous ego growth. These abnormal ego-structures are presumably manifested in defective performance of social roles. The Unit holds that faulty performance in social roles is a reliable index of psychiatric disorder, particularly for patients diagnosed as personality disorders. But the staff consider that therapeutic socioenvironmental influences can be mobilized to reduce or modify the effects of harmful early experience. The most effective harnessing of socioenvironmental forces for this purpose is the creation of a therapeutic community.

The deliberate choice of milieu therapy is thus *focal* within the Unit. This is in contrast to some other hospitals, where it may be ancillary, perhaps supplementing other forms of treatment which are considered the principal therapeutic agents—e.g., chemotherapy or individual psychotherapy. In the Unit, the use of milieu influences is not only focal but is also *total.* This means that every aspect of hospital life is regarded as relevant and potentially therapeutic. Hence the term *therapeutic community* is used to denote the total hospital (Unit) involvement in the treatment enterprise.

As with many innovations, the Unit's ideas are based in large part on a reaction against the "evils" of custodial hospital and punitive prison regimes. Many of the staff's ideas are derived from attempts to avoid some of the problems of the conventional mental hospital system. We have abstracted four major themes as comprising the core of the Unit ideology—rehabilitation through reality confrontation, democratization, permissiveness, and communalism. Each of these themes embodied a protest against perceived shortcomings of the conventional hospital system.

Patients in conventional mental hospitals were seen as becoming "institutionalized" through adaptation to the special conditions of a closed, impersonal, controlled, and bureaucratic social system. Rehabilitation ideals were initiated to counteract the effects of a prisonlike environment. In the Unit, the theme of "rehabilitation through reality confrontation" is intended to make the hospital as much like the ordinary world as possible, and the adjustment of patients to this microcosm is assumed to prepare them to adjust to society outside.

The Unit staff saw many characteristics of conventional mental hospitals as inimical to the goals of rehabilitation. Patients were handled in custodial hospitals in an impersonal, standardized way. This tended to reduce their participation in, and ultimately their capacity for, forming ordinary social relationships; and it encouraged a passive, dependent relationship to the hospital authorities.

The Unit staff consider this process to be perpetuated in the training of individuals for conventional psychiatric hospital roles. In consequence, they emphasize the value of "untrained," "natural" persons, particularly in nursing roles, to form personal relationships with patients. Thereby they hope to eliminate impersonal, bureaucratic hierarchies, and to replace "bad" relationships in patients' significant interaction networks with "ordinary," "good" relationships.

Under the conventional hospital system there was not only a chronic shortage of trained personnel, but presumably the definition of roles within the hospital system did not allow for the most effective use of what talent did exist. This was largely attributed to the medical staff's narrow conception of what therapy comprised and who was qualified to administer it. Conventionally, only physicians were authorized to give therapy, and therapy was considered to cover a limited range of transactions between the physician and the patient. The theme of *democratization* in the Unit aims at increasing patients' authority and participation in the therapeutic process. The Unit's position holds that everyone should be involved in both clinical administration of the hospital and in the administration of therapy; that *each member of the Unit* should have an equal voice in conducting these affairs; and that every experience is potentially therapeutic and every relationship potentially a channel of therapeutic influence.

The suppressive regime in the old-fashioned mental hospitals and prisons tended, it was felt, to reinforce patients' resentment of and anger against the established authorities. This is considered especially true of patients with "psychopathic" personality disorders. Disciplinary situations induce in these patients either rebellious withdrawal or other forms of expressing negative attitudes towards authority, all of which are unfavorable for psychotherapy. The Unit theme of *permissiveness* is intended to foster a more positive attitude towards authorities and to permit freer behavior that could be studied by staff and patients in order to help offenders to improve their social adjustment. The Unit theme of *communalism*—according to which a quasi-familistic environment relatedly provides patients with a supportive group acceptance—was developed to prevent the bureaucratic hospital's depersonalization and isolation of its patients.

The development of these ideological themes within the Unit serves several valuable functions. For one thing, a collection of staff and patients with diverse social and cultural backgrounds can be integrated into an organization about a minimum set of shared values and beliefs. Furthermore, the ideology helps members of the Unit to choose among alternative courses of action in complex problematic situations, thus improving morale, flexibility, and effectiveness. The ideology can also be seen as a loose body of theory whose development aids the quest for scientific psychiatric and sociological knowledge.

There is a tendency for the Unit staff to state its tenets in absolute terms (such as "free all communications") which may raise problems. Such slogans are rooted in opposition to features of the old-fashioned mental hospital system. Slogans may lend a clarity and cogency that qualified statements would vitiate. For example, the *ex cathedra* simplicity of the slogan, "We favor free communications," gains neither clarity nor elegance with the added proviso that "We favor more open communication, particularly in authorized groups or with members of the staff." Similarly, a psychiatrist and a hardened psychopath might agree that, "Most doctors don't know enough about the emotional problems of working-class people," and still establish a relationship. But if all the implicit qualifications of this statement were immediately made explicit, they might not be able to find a basis for even beginning the relationship. Thus, to leave many qualifications implicit allows for increased consensus when there are possible grounds for dissensus and where solidarity is necessary to achieve the group's goals.

However, if taken literally, slogans are not fully attainable. It is neither possible, nor in practice always desirable for communication, for example, to be absolutely free or for any staff member to be completely permissive. Ideological tenets are ideals which function with numerous implicit qualifications. Taken too literally they suffer from the discrepancy between ideal policies and real necessities, imposing a sense of "contradiction" or inconsistency, as when a staff member behaves nonpermissively because of incompatible or conflicting pressures in the situation.

One factor tending to keep qualifications implicit is the great gap in level of abstraction between the statement of ideals and the concrete situations to which they nominally refer. Everyone is willing to agree that permissiveness is a desirable thing. But the therapeutic value of permissiveness in a particular situation depends on the careful assessment of motivation and subjective and objective consequences of behavior for the patient and for others. The decision may rest on the relative importance assigned in the circumstances to permissiveness, communalism, or reality confrontation. The principles themselves furnish no *a priori* basis of judgment. Particular acts are capable of being rationalized in terms of different ideals, and often it is not clear how any particular deal is to be implemented in a complex 'reality' situation.

Another factor is that specific ideological tenets tend to be held with fervor and conviction for somewhat autonomous reasons. A danger that this poses is that they may become goals in themselves. Being "democratic" or "permissive" comes to be the *summum bonum,* and the more fundamental question of how such behavior contributes to any patient's therapy may be lost sight of. This tendency is enhanced, in the Unit, because of the separate formulation of each idea as an independent, absolute principle—with no statement of their interrelationship as a guide in the resolution of any conflict between them. There tends to be an assumption that each is a "good," worthy end in itself, more or less regardless of context.

While the humanistic-sounding goals described are now rather generally accepted in psychiatry, some psychiatrists advocate different degrees of firmness and control (even punishment) as therapeutic necessities for certain cases. Even where there is general agreement on broad orientation—e.g., democratization—there are differences in the type and degree of democratization considered therapeutic under different conditions. In some forms of "patient government," the patients' participation in decision-making is restricted to a well-defined and comparatively narrow range of administrative problems. In other forms, the patients' role is limited to the formulation of opinions, which are then referred for decision to the staff who make no pretense of delegating their authority to patients.

Aside from the overall means-ends problems, there are also problems of internal organization of ideological tenets which flow from their heterodox origin. Unlike more evolved systems of belief, the ideology as it stands does not contain a set of principles for hierarchizing these values at points in which they conflict with one another. Thereby, any member of the Unit who is faced with a situation, for example, in which it is "unrealistic" to be "permissive" must resolve the dilemma adventitiously or expediently. Thus, the ideology functions adequately in very simple situations, but furnishes fewer guiding principles as the complexity of situations increases.

As an experimental psychiatric treatment center the Unit is not only dedicated to goals of therapy (to which the ideology is directed), but also to goals of scientific knowledge (which may conflict with therapeutic goals). We have observed that some of the qualities that have helped to make Unit ideology therapeutically effective—the staff's deep sense of conviction and emotional commitment—are precisely those that transform treatment means into entrenched ends in themselves, with consequent resistance to objective appraisal and to changes in the system.

In this section we have examined some points intrinsic to the treatment ideology. On the basis of our observations of unit ideology in action, it seems possible to state several implications that might be helpful as general postulates for guiding the organization of a therapeutic milieu.

Postulate 1.   It is important to make explicit the ideas that are held by members of the group about how the milieu should be developed and used.

Postulate 2.   A higher degree of consensus than is necessary in most hospitals is desirable among practitioners of milieu therapy.

Postulate 3.   The principles developed should be explicitly related to therapeutic goals and recognized as means towards the achievement of these goals. There are dangers in regarding ideological principles as ends in themselves which may frequently serve to contravene the larger goals.

Postulate 4.   In order to avoid confusion and maintain consensus the staff should continuously try to clarify how abstract principles are to be related to concrete behavior in specific situations.

Postulate 5.   It is important that the ideology itself constitute a coherent, logical system so that confusion in conflict situations may be minimized. Continuous work on internal organization of the ideology should assist people in the system in choosing from among alternative courses of action in an acceptable way. Techniques must be developed for hierachizing values in action situations.

Postulate 6.   There is an advantage in developing a shorthand concise and simplified way of expressing the ideas about which consensus is sought. These concise, sloganish statements should be presented with enthusiam and a sense of positive commitment.

Postulate 7.   Dilemmas and conflicts, however, can be avoided if the staff remains aware of the implicit qualifications accompanying the shorthand statement of ideological tenets.

Postulate 8.   The enthusiasm and positive endorsement of ideology must not close the minds of the practitioners to the necessity for continuous scrutiny, evaluation, and revision. These measures are required if the clinicians are to use their ideas for the development of a scientific treatment theory, as well as for achieving social integration in the particular therapy context.

Ideology itself only *partly* determines the staff's treatment, which in turn only partly affects the actual outcome for particular patients. We shall examine some of the other determinates of social processes and therapeutic outcomes for the light that they cast on larger issues in the field.

The Organization of Staff Roles

In psychiatric hospitals there is a great deal of experimentation with redefinition of staff roles. Dissatisfaction with the rigid hierarchies and with the classic restriction of therapy to a narrow range of role relationships is growing. The type and degree of change, however, varies greatly. In some hospitals therapies are being developed in a wider variety of professional roles than heretofore. Group therapy may be conducted in a single hospital by doctors, nurses, social workers, or psychologists, and patients may be assigned to any of the groups on a random basis. Each group therapist can, and sometimes does, interchange his role with the others. Other hospitals do not display this interchangeability of function among staff, but have increased the joint participation of people from several roles in activities formerly considered the exclusive province of only one. Thus, a doctor may not yield his therapeutic group leadership to a nurse, but he may have nurses participate as coleaders of groups that he formerly conducted himself. The emphasis given to any particular method varies from hospital to hospital, as does the degree of jointness or interchangeability of functions among personnel. But the overall trend is towards the overlapping of functions which previously were sharply differentiated by role.

The Unit advocates an extensive interchangeability and jointness of functions among staff members. Specialized role prescriptions are deemphasized and blurred as much as possible so as to stimulate an equalitarian community with a great deal of joint participation of staff and patients in both therapeutic and administration affairs. In addition to the elimination of bureaucratic formalities, the Unit seeks through the flattening of the power hierarchy to maximize the use of whatever skills and talents are present in the staff, regardless of anybody's formal position in the authority structure.

What are some of the difficulties observed in this revision of the conventional staff roles and what generalizations and implications may be derived from these observations?

The Organization of Staff Roles, from Rapoport, *Community as Doctor,* pp. 275–79.

First, we have noted discrepancies between the informal role conceptions promulgated by the Unit staff and those formally laid down in tradition and statute within the profession and the hospital structure. While the Unit wants its staff to be equalitarian and to have interchangeable functions, the hospital system prescribes a hierarchical and specialized organization of roles. In other words, a system of broadly diffused authority and responsibility is posed against formal requirements of highly differentiated authority and responsibility. The "built-in" contradictions between these two sets of role conceptions and their associated expectations give rise to patterned dilemmas for the staff. These dilemmas vary according to specific role. Doctors, for example, tend to experience more acute dilemmas in the area of responsibility and authority, while nurses encounter conflicts in the area of affectual involvement with patients. All roles, however, have many common elements. People must work out for themselves ways of resolving the dilemmas of any particular position. Their modes of resolution vary somewhat by role according to such factors as transiency, formal authority, and the number of persons in the role. The choice of resolution also depends on the personality of the incumbent. Thus, an obsessional doctor on the permanent staff, one of the few people close to the pinnacle of the formal authority structure, may resolve strains by becoming unusually restrictive. He might rationalize this in terms of medical responsibility and reality pressures. Another doctor in the same position might tend to withdraw from the Unit and to spend time drinking in local bars with patients, rationalizing this on the grounds of permissiveness and communalism.

In general, it may be observed that where deviating innovations occur within an established system which retains jurisdiction over the innovating subsystem, personnel will experience endemic strains. Conflict may develop in external relations; conflicts may arise between staff members who are more exposed to external controls (e.g., the director) and subordinates who are less exposed (e.g., a staff physician with tenure who does not immediately account for his activities to higher authorities outside the Unit); or personal strains may develop which reflect the chronic conflict between two incompatible sets of role obligations.

In the Unit, the staff's ideal role conceptions, which blur specialized skills and attributes, are not fully accepted by patients. There is a systematic tendency for patients to defer to doctors and other staff in accordance with the prevailing cultural definitions of hierarchical role authority. Indeed, it would seem that such differential deference may indicate good "reality testing" and mental health as reflected in the superior improvement of those patients who act as if staff authority cohered with conventional patterns.

The deemphasis of formal differences between staff positions is reflected in the conception that *untrained* personnel are best in the social therapist role. The social therapists are transient and drawn from the general population outside the hospital. They do not systematically return to any specific professional positions, though many of them do go into some form of social work. The use of untrained nurses avoids the difficulties of *inappropriately* trained staff and has some additional positive functions (e.g., creating a group of personnel comparable to the patients in transiency, but made up of healthy individuals). However, it does not develop a stable corps of competent, *appropriately* trained specialists within the Unit or for the profession at large. Conceivably the continuous recruitment of these "healthy" transients represents the most satisfactory way to create and maintain therapeutic milieux, although there is little evidence for this assumption. It seems more likely that this approach was effective in the transitional period when the new concepts of milieu therapy were being implemented.

The stimuli towards change, to which the social therapist role was one response, are generally being met in milieu therapy in at least two different ways. One approach is by modification of psychiatric nurses' training and practice. With increased professionalization of nursing has come a trend towards their more active participation in medical treatment and rehabilitation. This experimentation in the changing nurses' role includes their conduct of therapeutic groups, formerly the prerogative of doctors and/or clinical psychologists. The second new approach that parallels the Unit's conception of social therapists makes greater use of volunteers and untrained people in involving mental hospital patients in a normal-like round of activities. A good deal of experimentation is under way on the efforts of such people, under various conditions, upon the rehabilitation of patients.

From observations of the Unit's organization of staff roles, it seems possible to derive some implications that might be valuable as general postulates of staff organization in therapeutic communities.

Postulate 9.   Role conflicts can be reduced by minimizing discrepant directives impinging on staff members. Among innovating institutions there is frequently a discrepancy between ideologically prescribed behavior and role behavior prescribed in the conventional system. The first step in minimizing contratherapeutic potentials engendered by these discrepancies is to make them explicit.

Postulate 10.   Where there is a radical discrepancy between formally prescribed conventional role obligations and informally prescribed ideological norms, which cannot be handled informally, a structural change in the social system may be required. Relevant structural changes might be a change in the formal requirements, a change in the ideological requirements, or a change in the relation between the two by disengaging the innovating system from the jurisdiction of the discrepant formal system (e.g., by establishing an autonomous institution).

Postulate 11. Where harmonization, neutralization, or disengagement of discrepant role directives are not possible, it is advisable to make explicit the effective limitations of the ideological prescriptions in the particular context. Where this is not done, role-incumbents may feel and unnecessary sense of failure or it may encourage the extensive use of denial. Both reactions tend to be antithetical to the goals of therapy.

Postulate 12. Continuous turnover of staff is a short-term expedient for abolishing tradition-bound rigidities and introducing therapeutic "naturalness" and "spontaneity." However, the haphazard training and the flow of transient trainees to work outside the profession is inimical to the consolidation of milieu therapy methods in an experienced corps of practitioners. The development of professional practitioners with the new skills of milieu therapy will depend in part on systematic training and institutionalization of the therapeutic roles.

The Organization of Patient Activities

The organization of patient roles will vary within the capacities of different groups of patients. Psychiatrists generally agree that those with the greatest personality resources are easiest to work with, can accept the greatest responsibilities, and do best therapeutically. Other things being equal, younger individuals, with comparatively strong egos, generally respond more favorably and with longer effects than do the older entrenched and deteriorated cases. These differences will affect institutional policy in defining the role of the patient.

One point emphasized by the Unit staff in structuring the role of patient is the importance of peer-group relationships. They feel that this is effective not only because psychopathic patients tend to resist the influence of staff authority figures, but also because of cultural gaps that exist between the majority of physicians and the majority of patients. Middle-class physicians must bridge subcultural differences in treating working-class patients. One way to improve patient-staff communications across this gap is to channel it through patient intermediaries. Thereby, possible barriers of class norms and language with individual patients may be hopefully moderated by translations of other more perceptive patients.

In the larger field, milieu therapists differ in the way they allow patients to participate in therapy. In some instances it is considered useful for patients

The Organization of Patient Activities, from Rapoport, *Community as Doctor,* pp. 279–88.

to increase their interaction and "socializing" without discussion of one another's psychological problems or motives; in other instances they are encouraged to comment on social consequences of one another's behavior but not on motivation; in only a few instances outside of formal group therapy are patients encouraged to analyze one another's motivations. The only element apparently common to all approaches in psychiatry is the feeling that some degree of professional supervision is necessary.

Our findings indicate that collateral influences are indeed important, but as supportive factors rather than as major mechanisms of therapeutic change. Patients who improved tended to relate to their peers in a comparatively friendly and intimate way, but they were also the same patients who formed positive cathexes with staff figures. That is, they showed a higher *generalized* capacity to identify with and relate to others, and consequently they received therapeutic influence directly from staff members as well as from their peers.

The benefits of a levelled hierarchy, patient participation, and collateral relationships are most effectively experienced by patients who can also identify with senior staff members. The latter presumably provide exemplars and ego ideal models. Fellow patients, on the other hand, afford group support during the period of disturbance sometimes entailed in psychotherapeutic confrontations. They also provide opportunities to work through problems specifically involving peer relationships. All would seem to be valuable, complementary elements of therapy.

A second point concerns the staff's view that the dominant culture of the Unit should be geared to the working-class norms to which patients must ultimately return. The actual culture of the patients tends to be a *tertium quid*, different from the staff culture or the culture of the working class outside. This was symbolically expressed by the patient who, after striking one of his fellows, said: "I'm only trying to therapeut this bloke," illustrating the blend of staff language and Cockney modes of interaction. Many patients show an even clearer misuse than this of psychiatric technique. For example, some patients carry over the therapeutic techniques to their family settings after discharge and apply them inappropriately to family problems. Other patients introduce the technique of the therapist destructively to their intimate relationships, as in imputing certain distorted drives to the motivation of their spouses, and cite their Unit experience to legitimize the procedure. Whatever the merits of presenting therapeutic procedures in the idiom of the patients' subcultural groups, there can be no question of matching posthospital modes of interaction in the milieu therapy situation. The latter is novel to most patients and will remain extraneous to the others in the patients' posthospital life.

Another issue in the definition of the patient role is the extent to which "antisocial" behavior ought to be allowed. The Unit ideology stresses the importance of a permissive policy for diagnostic and therapeutic purposes. Our data partially bear out the value of this position, indicating that patients who show a *moderate* amount of destructiveness and nonconformity are considered more improved at discharge than those who were either inordinately rebellious or impeccably compliant. Strong conformists and "actors-out," those who most intensely accept and reject Unit values, experience the greatest difficulties in making the transition to life outside the hospital. The former never effectively enter treatment; the latter use the Unit way to satisfy their immediate needs, but not as a means to learning how to fit them into a more ordinary social environment. The special tolerance of deviant behavior within the therapeutic community does not correspond to the attitudes outside the Unit; similarly, the high value placed on expressiveness and discussion of "problems" and motives has few counterparts in ordinary life, and communication in such terms often arouses antagonism. The type and degree of interest given to individuals in the Unit by idealized authority figures, likewise, is often lacking in the world outside. Though the Unit seeks to simulate the world of ordinary life (and approximates to it more than do the conventional mental hospitals), there is a profound discontinuity between the patients' roles during and after treatment which must be transcended if they are to adjust successfully in the outside world.

This suggests a more complex set of questions about the prediction of treatment results. What kind of patients does a therapeutic milieu actually help? The Unit claims that its method is the best for patients with personality disorders, but that it is also suitable for other kinds of patients. Data indicate that patients respond in a complex pattern to the treatment given. They tend to do so in proportion to their "ego-strength." The strong-ego patients presumably had fewer initial difficulties in role performance than those with weaker egos. It could be argued that because they had "less room for improvement," one might, therefore, expect them to show less improvement. In fact, they are more frequently seen as "better" at the end of treatment. This may reflect their greater resources in the therapeutic situation, or even the staff's satisfaction at their superior role performance in comparison with other patients. With level of ego strength held constant, the factor that is most related to improvement is the duration of treatment. Patients who stay more than six months get better much more frequently than those who stay less than six months. This raises the question whether the Unit should concentrate on fewer patients for longer periods rather than on many more who do not benefit from briefer treatment. Such a course would require instruments to predict the types of patients to be kept who would accept the necessary course of therapy. Such instruments, however, are notoriously difficult to develop because of the multiplicity of factors involved.

A further problem in defining the patient role inheres in patients' conceptions about the organization of a treatment institution. The Unit staff consider their values to be representative of "normal" society and patient deviation from them to be evidence of personal pathology. Our data indicate that Unit values differ markedly from those of people outside. We have shown that new patients have a range of values vis-à-vis the Unit's treatment ideology, and these cannot be simply attributed to their psychopathology or even their background. New patients whose values resemble those of the Unit or who subsequently adopt them tend to adjust better in the hospital and are considered more improved on discharge than those with discrepant views. While congruent values were found to be predictors of success *within* the Unit, they are notably less successful predictors of good adjustment after discharge. Patients whose values came to resemble those of the Unit showed steady improvement in their posthospital adjustment, while those with pro-U value shifts showed declining rates of improvement afterwards. The latter group apparently experienced a greater discontinuity in their transition to the world outside than did the former.

In any given hospital the administrative policies and milieu will interact with the personal proclivities of the patient to create unique patterns of response.

The organization of group activities as well as their composition and intended purposes affect the way they function and consequently their impact on participating individuals. The Unit's structure—i.e., the pattern of continuous reshuffling of groups with interlocking memberships—fosters both the desired high level of intergroup communication and also the less explicitly sought phenomena of emotional contagion. The latter, particularly in the context of a permissive staff policy and a patient population with predispositions to behave disruptively, contributes to frequent and great periodic surges between states of relatively good social organization and relative disorganization.

We have noted that the Unit is subject to variations that are oscillatory or cyclical. These affect the degree and type of patient participation, the staff 's practices, and therapeutic results. Some concomitants of the oscillatory process seem to support the generally held notion that "collective disturbances" in psychiatric hospitals are antitherapeutic—e.g., premature discharges increase in number, patients change their orientation to one another and their leaders to more negative ones. On the other hand, some aspects of the oscillatory process seem therapeutic for individual patients—e.g., the reparative drives, the affective involvements stimulated by mounting crises.

It must be recognized that permissive and dynamic institutions provide different kinds of stimuli for patients at different times. When things are functioning smoothly, the organization may be able to assimilate patients with acting-out symptoms without much trouble. On the other hand, when disorganization is at its height, the institution cannot absorb too disruptive, acting-out patients and will tend to transfer or discharge them. This implies that a given individual might experience a different therapeutic fate if he were present at one stage rather than another. The Unit's arrangement entails the loss of patients who might otherwise be helped. Such transfers and discharges tend not to be easily readmitted, despite the formal policy favoring it. In some cases the patient's own attitudes constitute the barrier, particularly if he feels that he has been rejected; in other cases he may have developed a reputation that makes the organization reluctant to accept him back from a mental hospital or elsewhere.

Thus, the issue of patient participation in treatment and administration becomes more complex than the Unit staff suppose. We have already indicated that patients actually define doctors in their formal authority roles, however democratic and benign their manner. We have also noted that doctors in fact retain control over important decisions, and this control is actively exercised in times of crisis and disorganization. On the other hand, it has also been noted that active patient participation in treatment may contribute to the Unit's therapeutic effect. It would seem that something between the Unit's ideal position and its more drastic expedients based on the conventional medical authority pattern might ultimately prove most effective with nonpsychotic patients. In order to implement this modified approach, the staff would have to clarify the limits of and conditions under which democratic participation may apply, avoiding both the total commitment implied in current unit ideology and the inconsequential commitment implied in some superficial efforts at "patient government."

Democratization, like other aspects of the patients' ideological role pre-scriptions, has the dual purpose of creating a milieu favorable for changing the patient's personality on the one hand and helping him learn to participate constructively in ordinary life, following discharge from the hospital, on the other. As we shall indicate again in a later section, these purposes do not always coincide. It cannot be said, therefore, that as patients improve they should be granted increasingly great participation in administrative and thera-peutic decision-making. As the degree of such participation in the Unit is abnormally higher, this would only unfit patients for participation in their normal roles outside the hospital. It would seem that some plan of graduated involvement followed by progressive disengagement from participation in Unit modes of group interaction would be best.

Another issue is the choice between segregated groups of similar patients and mixed groups of heterogeneous patients. Some hospitals favor the sorting of patients into relatively homogeneous groups according to their behavioral capacities and tendencies. The advantage of this, aside from ease of administra-tion, is in focusing of specific treatment efforts. The Unit's mixed group plan rests on the assumption that patients will benefit more from a broad diversity of stimuli and behavior than from a fairly uniform group. The mixed group also shows symbiotic elements suggestive of a "balanced aquarium." Patients in such groups somehow complement one another's needs in a fashion beneficial to individuals and to the group as a whole. Since the strengths and weaknesses vary widely from one person to another, the group has a range of resources, flexibility, and capacity for group support beyond that of homogeneous groups.

Mixed and homogeneous groups are not necessarily mutually exclusive alternatives. It seems possible to exploit the advantages of the "balanced aquarium" while also providing more specialized experiences for those who need them. Specially sheltered structures might be developed for people who temporarily cannot function in the larger institution. When they achieve the capacity or when disturbances in the system subside so that they can be accommodated, they can then return to the larger group. Such group supports need not be left to chance nor to the spontaneous formation of informal groups. These informal groups do not necessarily arise when they are needed nor are they always therapeutic. It cannot be assumed that the mere existence of a spontaneous peer group is "good" or that its possible harmful effects can safely be ignored. Systematic efforts should be made not only to provide opportunities for such grouping to emerge but to guide their activities in therapeutic directions. As knowledge develops about the peculiar needs of patients at different junctures in therapy, special roles can be devised to enable patients to advance from one stage of treatment to the next.

The Unit established an unstructured system in which each patient was expected to "find his own" pattern in a universal round of communal activities. However, there seems to be a need to restore more explicit expectations and clearer structure. Patients' individual resources and needs require differential handling which the ideology of democratization and communalism tends to obscure. The implication of equal opportunity for treatment by the community as a whole is that any individual who cannot seize the opportunity tends to be discarded as "too sick for the Unit method of treatment," "not really wanting treatment," and so on. Although patients are *defined* as a mixed group, they are *handled* as a homogeneous group, or at least as one where deficient participation is regarded as pathological and deviant. Another approach would carefully assess individual needs and resources, fitting individuals to suitable social roles in the Unit—roles that are carefully prescribed for their therapeutic appropriateness to the individual patient. Under the present system, the Unit staff have developed roles which are blurred but still fundamentally differentiated. An important component, for example, in the way any staff member's participation is evaluated by others in the Unit is in reference to the formal role of which he is a member (e.g., social worker, psychologist, nurse, physician). Amongst the patients there are relatively few such roles, (reception committee member, entertainment committee chairman, etc.), and of these there is little systematic assignment with therapeutic rationality. In some cases patients are elected, in others they may volunteer, in others they are assigned. The ideology of democratization and permissiveness taken too uncritically here allows any of these procedures to be rationalized as therapeutic. The path to rational use of milieu therapy would seem to require more critical specification of patient roles within the overall structure than is at present possible or in practice.

On the basis of our observations of the patient role as it is developed in the Unit it seems possible to state some general postulates about the role of patients in therapeutic communities.

Postulate 13.   The maximum therapeutic benefit to be derived from patients' participation in hospital life seems to depend on the provision of a variety of relationships. Effective influence in any given situation may flow from a patient's relationships with peers or seniors, with members of his own sex or of the opposite sex, or from some combination of these.

Postulate 14.   Patients' administration of therapy to one another is fraught with hazards. Its success depends on the careful selection of patients, the close supervision, and their careful indoctrination in the dangers of indiscriminate, irresponsible "therapizing," especially in their personal relations outside.

Postulate 15.   Rigid coercion and conformity do not seem conducive to therapeutic reorientations, but this does not imply that complete permissiveness is. Permissiveness is not in and of itself an effective therapeutic policy, nor is it an adequate way of defining patients' role prescriptions. A modification of permissiveness, designed on explicit principles to suit the therapeutic requirements of particular situations, would seem most profitable.

Postulate 16.   A hospital milieu that is inordinately permissive poses different but comparably great problems for posthospital adjustment as compared to a milieu that is extremely repressive. Neither prepares the patient for coping with the learning potential engendered by having the permissiveness policies operate within explicit limits; it would seem that a more moderate course during treatment would facilitate the transition between hospital and ordinary life.

Postulate 17.   To the extent that a therapeutic institution engenders in its patients values that are at variance with those of the outside social world, patients who have successfully adapted to treatment must be "resocialized" prior to their discharge. The very experience of socializing patients to the institution may entail important therapeutic gains, but these may be lost in the posthospital period if the norms adopted for treatment are not appropriately revised in preparation for the world outside.

Postulate 18. Psychiatric hospitals with permissive policies can expect an unusually high level of periodic interpersonal disturbances. These disturbances will be greater to the extent that the social structure is a segmentary one, reshuffling its participants into groups with interlocking membership, and fostering great internal communication.

Postulate 19. Collective disturbances among patients are neither intrinsically desirable nor undesirable.

Postulate 19a. Collective disturbances contain social forces which can be potent therapeutic influences. One example would be the mobilization of individuals' tendencies to participate in a process of social reconstruction.

Postulate 19b. Collective disturbances may have harmful as well as beneficial effects on individuals. Patients may become personally disturbed, or the staff may feel that conditions favorable for some patients' therapy require the removal of other patients from the Unit. But patient casualties are not the inevitable price of the survival and stability of a therapeutic community. Steps can be taken to diminish casualty rates by postponing admissions and by removing, sheltering, or otherwise protecting particularly vulnerable patients until such time as they can be absorbed into the community.

Postulate 20. While democratic procedures may be valuable therapeutically, a completely democratic system is neither possible within the framework of psychiatric medicine nor directly applicable to the goals of rehabilitation. Where democratic measures are used in modified form, it would seem valuable to arrange patient participation to take into explicit account both considerations—i.e., the real structure of formal authority and discrete requirements of treatment and rehabilitation.

Postulate 21. Each patient's treatment and rehabilitation plan should be made individually. Emphasis on shared community life does not necessarily imply that all patients must be uniformly exposed to all aspects of the therapeutic community. Thus, for example, patients, at different times in their therapeutic careers, could be assigned to different role relationships, different group activities, and different degrees of responsibility.

Postulate 21a. Where the therapeutic community constitutes only one phase of a therapeutic plan (other phases of which might be external to the facility in which the therapeutic community method is employed) overall perspective should be maintained so that whatever the therapeutic community has available can be used to fit with other efforts to fulfill the individual patient's long-term needs.

The Involvement of Individuals Outside the Hospital in Treatment

Like any psychiatric center, the Unit has external relationships that affect its internal functioning. We have at different places in this [chapter] considered some of these relationships—those governing the referral of patients, those governing the recruitment of staff, those governing the Unit's relations with its larger authority structure, and the family relations of patients.

The Unit maintains a flow of patients through its professional referral sources, which in turn makes use of the Unit for different purposes. Interest in the Unit among leading psychiatric institutions grew in response to reports of its novel and experimental method. In time, the bulk of professional use of the Unit has shifted to more peripheral agencies. This may be due in part to the fact that leadership institutions which tried the Unit wanted more rigorous evaluation of treatment results than were forthcoming. The failure to produce satisfactory evaluative data probably accounts for some of the decline in use of the Unit by major institutions. In addition, despite the lack of precise evaluative evidence, the Unit's methods are spreading to many modern psychiatric centers, and are thereby losing their uniqueness. This makes it less necessary for the other hospitals to refer as many patients away for milieu therapy. The Unit itself has also in recent years solicited and drawn an increasing proportion of its patients from the courts. This reflects not only the general trend in penal reform but also the Unit's own special interest in treating sociopathic individuals.

The necessity of recruiting certain categories of transient staff further involves the Unit staff in external relations. Aside from the social therapist discussed previously, the other major staff role involving transient personnel is the junior psychiatrist. Unlike the social therapists, doctors are recruited from a formally defined, qualified, and organized professional group. Doctors present themselves as applicants for National Health Service posts in the Unit, typically selecting these posts because of their special interests in milieu therapy. In contrast to the social therapists, who typically come for the purpose of getting valuable life-experience, junior doctors come to the Unit for the purpose of learning a technical skill. When they leave the Unit, doctors, in contrast to the social therapists, characteristically remain part of the same professional community, and several of them have sought to apply therapeutic milieu methods to other settings.

The problem of what kind of a relationship an innovating therapeutic community should have to its larger authority external structure is a complex one. All innovating institutions face problems of opposition and resistance to some degree, no matter how sound their support in the formal structure within

---

The Involvement of Individuals Outside the Hospital in Treatment, from Rapoport, *Community as Doctor,* pp. 288–96.

which they take form. Different types of innovations arouse different types of reaction, and for any particular innovation different strategies may be found to offset the disturbing effects of such reaction. Among experimental therapeutic communities external authority relationships have been handled in various ways. Some innovators, as in the Unit's case, form a subunit within a larger hospital. It seems to hold generally that such units tend to be "snobbish," "odd," "cliquey" on the one hand, and on the other hand to consider the more conventional part of the hospital as "reactionary," "authoritarian," or "rigid." It has been noted that under some circumstances the sharing of antipathies may help to promote group cohesiveness, and that this may have a therapeutic affect. However, our data indicate that such a strategy may have anti-therapeutic consequences as well. Many patients have a tendency to project negative feelings onto the established authorities; where this tendency is reinforced rather than counteracted in a hospital environment, the consequences are not therapeutically so desirable. In some innovating experiments, the innovation comes from the top of the authority structure. This pattern seems to entail other problems—factionalism, splitting of authority figures, critical areas of inertia within the system, etc. To some extent the type of problems experienced will also vary with whether or not the innovator is attempting to change an established hospital or set up a new one. In general, each innovating strategy seems to have certain advantages and a certain cost. The nuances of each innovating procedure must receive considerable systematic study before we shall be able to state the conditions under which one or another procedure will produce the greatest gains with the smallest cost.

Perhaps the most important external relations for workaday therapy are those that the patients have with persons significant to them, mainly their family members. The Unit staff believe that these relationships contain not only the roots and manifestations of the patient's pathology but also vital therapeutic forces which might be harnessed to contribute to the patient's ultimate recovery.

Within the Unit "bringing the family into treatment" has become an ideological imperative comparable to the directives about democratization or permissiveness. Our analysis has brought out some of the complexities of involving patients' families in the treatment situation.

Psychiatric findings about the effects of family relations on patients are ambiguous. On the one hand, family members are sometimes represented as pathogenic forces to be excluded from the therapeutic enterprise, or at best neutralized. On the other hand, they are sometimes seen as persons relatively disengaged from the patient's pathogenesis who might be either irrelevant to therapy or potential allies of the therapist.

The traditional psychoanalytical position has been to strengthen the relationship between therapist and individual patient and keep the family out. To the extent that therapy is effective for the patient, it is assumed that he will successfully work out his problems with other people. The therapist does not hold himself responsible for the functioning of a family but only of an individual patient.

The Unit's position seems to be somewhere between this view and the increasingly fashionable opinion that the family should be treated as a unit. The Unit seems to use information and efforts from family members. Yet the primary focus is on the individual patient who was referred for treatment, and comparatively minor attention is given to others in his family.

When families visit the Unit some judgment is made about what assets and liabilities they contain relevant to the patient's therapy, and whether the family members are therapeutic resources or "in need of treatment" themselves, or neither. Consequently, a policy crystallizes on whether relatives should be objects of treatment, sources of information, or cotherapists. This decision is made without explicit criteria or systematic procedures, and is quite inconsistently observed.

When patients' families do become involved in the treatment situation, particularly by being taken into the Unit as full-time patients themselves, they tend to be handled as individuals with their own problems, rather than as members of a family in treatment. Indeed, the Unit separates spouses, assigning them to male and female wards. Further, there are no situations comparable to the home itself in which family members work out a domestic division of labor and pattern of interaction. In fact, family members might have some of their centrifugal tendencies strengthened in the Unit. In some cases, the arrangements may even strengthen any incipient tendencies toward involvements outside the family. This may help some inwardly turned families to function more satisfactorily, but it may serve to disintegrate other families. We have few data, however, to specify the probable outcome in any given situation.

The norms of Unit practice do not distinguish treatment goals and procedures which are appropriate for different family types. This parallels the failure to clarify differential needs of individual patients. The blurring of individual requirements under uniform treatment techniques misses the opportunity provided by having several members of a family in therapy together. The Unit staff's differentiation of family types and their needs is usually implicit and ambiguous. This makes for erratic operation and the neglect of theoretical and applied problems of family treatment.

Despite the fact that patients with stronger egos are more likely than those with weaker egos to marry and to improve during and after treatment, marital responsibility itself may be related to therapeutic outcome. We found empirically that married patients do better than the unmarried. Married patients, for example, recover in greater numbers than unmarried patients from the postdischarge setback that is generally experienced. But for many, particularly among the unmarried patients, family relationships serve not as a stimulus for responsible role performance, but as a buffer against the demands of the world. Then the Unit and the family pressures operate at cross-purposes, one towards the patient's adult role performance and the other towards his continued dependency and passivity. Where these counter-pressures exist, the Unit experience may not alter the patient's condition in the face of the family organization. This is less likely to occur in the case of married patients who are typically not insulated from adult role responsibility and who may be more influential in changing their overall family structure. It is also among the married patients that there is a greater tendency for the Unit and the family pressures to reinforce one another.

If the Unit were to treat whole families, it would have to conceptualize how its therapy contributes to the family's superior functioning. This cannot simply be inferred from the patient's effects upon the functioning of the Unit. Furthermore, the Unit would have to consider the family as a self-contained system of interacting members rather than as the social background for a patient who is kept in the foreground. The appropriate variables in this approach would emphasize the fit of personality, norms, and emotional reaction patterns in role relationships, as discussed earlier, rather than individual characteristics. These changes require a great deal of thought and exploration on the frontiers of psychiatry and a redefinition of the physician's role which expands his treatment focus from an individual to a group.

For all patients, whether they live with families or not, there exists the problem of how they are to articulate with their network of social relationships after discharge from the hospital. Our follow-up studies indicate that the therapeutic community approach, however closely it is geared ideally to being in continuous experience with ordinary life, presents characteristic problems of posthospital rehabilitation for its patients. While these problems may differ in substance from the problems faced by patients discharged from other kinds of hospitals, they are similar in general type. Patients must revise the ways they learned to relate to others in the Unit in favor of modes more adaptive in the outside world. This usually entails an immediate postdischarge setback, particularly for those who had adapted themselves to the Unit's special conditions and showed improvement therein.

Just as patients show a diverse pattern of improvement under therapy, they show a diverse pattern of posthospital recovery. Given the limitations of some patients' regenerative capacities and psychiatrists' current methods, there is a sizeable group of patients who cannot sustain any enduring improvement, or who retain serious residual incapacities, regardless of how well they may have performed in the therapeutic community. For such patients the increasing tendency among psychiatrists is to attempt to work out some way of maintaining them in the community rather than in institutions. This means that both the individual and those who relate to him must adjust to some level of chronic incapacity in the expatient. Where the acceptance of chronicity is the most realistic goal, it need not be adopted by default or with a sense of failure. This form of ultimate adjustment where collaboratively worked out as an explicit goal by staff, patient, and significant others, is more likely to be a viable one for all concerned. It is an area that especially needs development of therapeutic techniques for following on through the handling of problems arising after discharge. It would be expected that sociological perspectives would be useful in restructuring family and other role relationships to accommodate an individual from whom only deviant forms of participation can ever be expected.

On the basis of our observations of the Unit's external relations as they effect the internal functioning of the therapeutic community, it is possible to state some further postulates.

Postulate 22.   A number of pitfalls are attendant on the innovating character of most contemporary therapeutic communities. Innovators tend to arouse opposition in the more established segments of their network of external relationships. While this opposition may have some therapeutic value in promoting internal cohesion, it may also have some therapeutic dysfunctions.

Postulate 22a.   One of the therapeutic dysfunctions, short of the termination of the experiment by authoritative action by opposing external authorities, is to foster in the patients stereotyped negative attidutes towards authority figures. One of the aims of therapy is to modify precisely such attitudes in patients.

Postulate 22b.   Another more indirect dysfunction is to block the flow of communications and personnel from the experimental unit to the larger system which it perceives as embodying structured defects needing remedy. To the extent that the experiment thus fails to contribute to the remedy, it deals inadequately with some of its goals.

Postulate 22c.   At some points in the development of an innovating unit, the best consensus with its external authority system may be to disagree and to arrange an insulated form of functioning. This mode is usually not, however, the best permanent arrangement, and it tends not only to foster the pitfalls noted above, but to allow the innovators to beg many questions that more active professional interchanges would stimulate.

Postulate 23.   Family members of patients often act as significant forces in their lives. If one wishes to understand a patient either to return him to functioning in his family context or to society generally, it is necessary to assess these forces and to plan therapy to take them into account.

Postulate 24. The goals may vary with any particular patient from treating his family as a whole system to treating him in isolation from his family.

Postulate 24a. One factor that affects the scope of the goal is the responsibility assumed by the therapist. Where responsibility is felt only for the individual patient, other members of the family tend to be seen as sources of information and possibly assistance, but not as objects of therapy. To the extent that responsibility towards the family as a whole is to be assumed, changes in the conventional medical way of defining therapeutic obligations will have to be developed.

Postulate 24b. Another factor affecting the involvement of other family members in the definition of therapeutic goals is the sociological status of the patient. With single patients of good prognosis, for example, the generally held goals of increasing mature independence seem to work against pressing for greater involvement of their (parental) families. With married patients of similarly good prognosis, the usual goal is towards improving family integration, and thus towards the attempt to include other family members in the definition of social dimensions of therapeutic goals.

Postulate 25. In addition to setting goals, an assessment of the actual situation will affect the planning for family involvement in any particular case.

Postulate 25a. In some cases the family members or the patient may not wish to have anyone besides the patient involved, or the others may be unable to become involved.

Postulate 25b. Where the family members are accessible, their participation in therapy may still be contraindicated. The therapist may assess them as providing such negative or inflexible stimuli as best to be kept out of the therapeutic situation.

Postulate 26. Where participation of family members is possible and indicated, the development of an explicit though flexible therapeutic strategy is advisable. In formulating therapeutic strategies for whole families, it will be useful to assess how individuals "fit" with one another as well as attempting to understand each individual as a psychodynamic entity. By understanding how the patient "fits" with his family members—in terms of personality, norms, and emotional toning in the relationships—one can assess how family elements constitute assets or liabilities with reference to the therapeutic goals.

Postulate 26a.   One of the first tasks of the therapist is to work toward consensus among the perspectives—his own, the patient's, the family members who become involved—as to the goals of therapy and how particular aspects of the family network of relationships constitute assets or liabilities in relation to these goals.

Postulate 26b.   Changes in the asset-liability balance can be achieved by shifts in personality or norms of the patient or his family members, or by changes or emotional toning in the problematic areas of their interpersonal relationships.

Postulate 27.   The problem of choice of techniques for dealing with families is to be considered independently of setting the goals and of assessing the family situation. Even with the choice of the goal of treating the family as a whole and with the assessment of their value and amenability for such treatment, there is no necessary implication that all the members of the family need be dealt with directly or simultaneously.

Postulate 27a.   It may be judged that the healthy functioning of the family would be improved by dealing, at some stages at least, with only the patient; or with the patient and his family members separately; or only with the members of the family who were not initially referred to the hospital. To some extent these choices are functions of the therapists' styles of treatment, but circumstances may favor one or another approach. It is not necessary to consider that these segmental techniques imply an abandonment of the goals of family treatment.

Postulate 27b.   If treatment is to take place in an institution rather than at home, it is valuable, diagnostically and therapeutically, to provide situations that replicate those the family members must deal with in their ordinary setting.

Postulate 27c.   If treatment is to take place in an institution, follow-through techniques are important to assist with the transitions from performance in sheltered, somewhat unusual social role situations to performance in those of ordinary life. Help is needed for the transfer of learning and the "working through" of emotional and interpersonal upheaval often consequent on therapy.

Postulate 27d.   To the extent that consideration of the healthy functioning of whole families becomes a paramount therapeutic goal, the efficiency of transplanting the family into the hospital becomes increasingly questionable. Techniques for conducting therapy in the family's natural habitat will probably be preferable for this purpose wherever possible.

The Conceptualization of Treatment and Rehabilitation

Some problems about the way therapeutic goals are conceptualized in the Unit have been discussed. The Unit staff state that they aim at the simultaneous maximization of treatment (reorganization of individual psychodynamics) and rehabilitation (the adjustment of the individual to his social roles). Our analysis indicates that this ideal of *simultaneously* implementing these goals is not always possible, though sometimes the same activities may be used to implement either goal.

We have provided data that indicate the advisability of distinguishing conceptually between activities oriented to treatment aims and activities oriented to rehabilitation aims. For example, we have shown how the special conditions of permissiveness, communalism, and democracy, which characterize the milieu of the Unit (and have a putative treatment value) may pose problems for the patient after his discharge because of the discontinuity between the Unit way and the way of the outside world. Thus, to the extent that the Unit provides a special treatment milieu, it may not be able simultaneously to provide a microcosm of the "real" world. Another example was seen in the role of social therapist. The social therapists experience a number of dilemmas due to the potential conflict in the two sets of role directives; to the extent that a therapist is "natural" and "herself," she may not be able to maintain at the same time an impersonal distance that is prescribed for the detection and handling of transference phenomena. To be simply "oneself" may not coincide with being "therapeutic," and the reconciliation of these directives constitutes a fundamental and recurrent problem for social therapists.

Thus, current therapeutic strategies in the Unit, by emphasizing simultaneous implementation of both sets of goals, tend to obscure the numerous and important situations in which it would be advantageous to see them as conceptually distinct.

In formulating the kinds of refinements that may be made on the basis of our observations, we take as our point of departure the central cluster of assumptions made by the Unit staff—i.e., that treatment and rehabilitation goals can be pursued simultaneously by one set of activities directed uniformly towards all patients (who are conceived as having essentially a single type of nuclear personality problem). In actual fact, therapeutic outcomes are linked to personality proclivities of individual patients; different kinds of activities are sometimes rationalized by staff as required for treatment goals as contrasted with rehabilitation goals; and finally the actual characteristics of therapy vary with the state of the Unit and the particular network of relationships which the patient generates in it—so that different patients get different treatment, but not through design of the staff.

The Conceptualization of Treatment and Rehabilitation, from Rapoport, *Community as Doctor,* pp. 296–303.

In part, the different needs of patients because of their differences in fundamental personality structure and/or their differences in capacity to participate in treatment at various points in time could be recognized by instituting phases in the treatment regimen. All patients have problems that are in some ways similar, requiring assistance at predeterminable points in the treatment career—e.g., at points of entry and exit—but it would be helpful also to recognize their differences. Some patients come with greater ego-strengths than others, and can participate more rapidly in the whole range of Unit activities. Other patients might require considerable attention in preparatory stages before they can tolerate the levels of expressiveness and confrontations in treatment groups as they function in the Unit. For these patients, more sheltered phases could be used as anticipatory to the entry into the more advanced stages of therapy. The degree to which preparatory phases would be necessary before entering the more rigorous phases of therapy and the speed with which progression through the phases would be accomplished would depend on the particular patient's capacities.

While mental hospitals have always had different wards that partly reflect the patients' capacities and prospects for "normal" behavior, they have been essentially different from the phase concept advanced here. The phases would be part of a regular program of expectations put forth for each patient to accomplish at his own speed. Great attention would be given to how supportive and rewarding incentives might be provided for each patient to advance through the system. The emphasis in providing these rewards might initially be on things not ordinarily available to the patient outside the hospital, but on the special conditions of communal life that a therapeutic community could offer. Then, when patients reach a suitable point of personality strength, emphasis might be placed on using the hospital for rehearsing ways of getting greater rewards from generally available life opportunities, as in friendships, social activities, or work.

Throughout the progression, the patient need not be transferred from one organized group or ward to another. Rather his changing therapy regimen might comprise changing his activities and changing his network of role relationships. Thus, neither the composition nor the timing of the phases need be standardized, but might vary according to the individual patient's needs. While the Unit ideology emphasizes the dual utility of all its activities—for treatment and rehabilitation—it is recognized informally that some activities and some relationships are closely geared to the goals of personality reorganization (e.g., the doctor-patient relationship in doctors' groups) while others are more closely geared to goals of social adjustment (e.g., the instructor-patient relationship in workshops). The failure to give these distinctions explicit recognition leads to certain limitations. For example, the view that treatment and rehabilitation should be simultaneously implemented makes the staff tend to take a position about workshops such that a choice is posed between a "realistic" industrial type of workshop on the one hand, and "diversionary" occupational therapy program on the other. When the choice is made in favor of the industrial workshops, with the implication that these are better for treatment and rehabilitation than the other, opportunities are lost to use occupational therapy programs for purposes to which they are especially adapted. For example, occupational therapy could be used to provide treatment channels for very disorganized personalities, allowing the rehabilitation goals to be pursued at a more advanced therapy stage through the later assignment of patients to industrial type workshops if appropriate. If each individual's therapy is to have a "tailored" character, geared to his individual rehabilitative needs, it might be that in some cases both kinds of therapy—occupational and work—would be necessary, in other cases only one, and in some cases neither. The range of types of occupational and work therapy provided would be used, ideally not as a blanket and randomly assigned regimen, but provided as appropriate to the treatment and rehabilitation needs of each individual patient.

A similar redeployment of the use of staff in therapy can be visualized. In blurring the role prescriptions within the Unit the staff effectively did away with many of the attributes of conventional roles that were undesirable in a therapeutic milieu. It is apparent, however, in the emergent pattern of role performances under the joint impact of conventional definitions and Unit ideology that a new kind of role differentiation has come into existence. Basically within the Unit there are two kinds of attributes in staff members that have proved useful corresponding to the requirements of treatment on the one hand, and rehabilitation on the other. The physicians and experienced permanent staff, whatever their "human" qualities or their acquaintance with the patients' subcultures, have a degree of training and skill in understanding psychodynamics that is not found reliably associated with other roles. Those who use the Unit successfully recognize this fact. The workshop instructors and D.R.O.s, whatever else they might have by way of therapeutic gifts, function reliably to present the patients with a realistic picture of the requirements of the outside industrial situation. The social therapists, representing an intermediate position, seem to function on the one hand as "natural," "good" female figures, and on the other hand they act as extensions of the physicians, serving as figures onto whom transferences of prior female relationships and fantasies are projected for psychodynamic interpretation. It seems clear that the physician's role is primarily a treatment role, that of the workshop instructors is primarily a rehabilitation role, and the social therapists have aspects of each.

The patients' involvement in treatment-rehabilitation seems also to have a mixed quality. Patients do seem to influence one another in ways that lead to personality change (as when, under supervision, they serve as channels for "beaming" the doctors' view onto their peers). But on the other hand, another use of patients for therapy in the Unit is to gain information on the nature of one another's normal social network outside the hospital and to provide characteristic interaction patterns for rehearsing typical role relationships.

It would seem that there are two reasons for clarifying the definition of role obligations so as to distinguish between treatment and rehabilitation. First, incumbents in any given role would experience less conflict about what they should be doing if their primary commitment were clearer. Second, with a clearer concept of the responsibilities and capacities associated with any given role, it might be possible to use the different roles more strategically in planning each individual patient's therapy. Thus, rather than having a blanket prescription that each patient must have a doctor, a workshop instructor, etc., it might be possible to construct a "tailored" social network of role relationships as each individual required it. For example, in the early stages it might be that one patient would only be exposed to a relationship with a physician and then only later with others who became concerned with his social behavior as well as his intrapsychic state, while another patient might be assigned to a peer group and perhaps a social therapist before exposing him to the interpretations of a psychiatrist.

The notion of phases, then, needed not involve the movement of patients from one totally organized set of groupings to another (as prevails in custodial mental hospital wards, or in movement from one institution to another). The phases might be conceptually distinguished by those administering therapy, but integration might be maintained by retaining the mixed group concept in the overall community life. Thus, a patient, once he had received his introductory communication (anticipatory socialization) and been absorbed into the Unit through the admission procedures, might live in the wards and participate in the informal and formal social activities of the Unit, but not be assigned to other therapy groups until it was felt that he was ready for them. Then assignments of groups and role relationships could be made for each individual as his therapy requires it—in no fixed sequence, speed, or composition of phases. In general, a paradigm of the following kind might be used as an overall guiding plan, but the specifications of its use for each patient would be different.

anticipatory socialization (preentry phase) —e.g., letters, visits, information via referring person

entry— (e.g., new-patient groups, orientation, diagnosis)

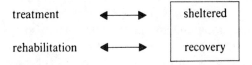

resettlement—(postdischarge)—(e.g., home visits, expatient clubs)

When the patient is perceived to be ready to be "in treatment" assignments of groups and role relationships could be made that would serve treatment goals. There would be no necessary effort to rationalize resemblance between the milieu influences exerted here and those of ordinary life outside. They would be self-consciously geared to personality reorganization, regardless of their resemblance to other kinds of activities and relationships. If conflicts were to arise in this phase, they would be resolved in favor of treatment goals. The phase of rehabilitation, on the other hand, some elements of which might begin concurrently with the treatment phase, would be designed to fit patients into "ordinary" networks or social relationships. The subphases of rehabilitation that occur within the Unit would be oriented to creating as much of a microcosm of the patients' probable outside environment as possible for the purpose of rehearsing appropriate social behavior in a sheltered milieu. In the later subphases, stretching over into the resettlement (postdischarge) phase, efforts would be made to adapt the patient's behavior to the *specific* social network in which he is to live. Increasingly, real role relationships would replace role surrogates, and therapists gradually withdraw, but not precipitously at discharge.

In some hospitals the social behavioral dimensions of treatment are distinguished from the intrapsychic ones through recognizing the difference between the role of administrator and that of therapist. We have learned from studies of this type of system that its good functioning depends, in part, on the coordination of the activities of the individuals in these two roles. A similar point might be made about sequential as well as synchronic relationships to which a patient is exposed in the course of his therapy. Coordination of the activities of those engaged in treatment and those in rehabilitation of each patient should be dealt with by constant recognition of the essential interrelationship of these tasks. Treatment goals can most effectively be served by incorporating a planned dimension of rehabilitation in the overall therapy program and vice versa.

Considering the factors that we have indicated to be linked to therapeutic success, we would propose the following postulates:

Postulate 28. The distinction between goals of social adaptation (rehabilitation) and goals of personality change (treatment) helps to clarify changing requirements of patients at different therapeutic stages. This lays the basis for more systematic, less intuitive judgments about therapeutic strategies.

Postulate 29. One way in which the distinction between treatment and rehabilitation can be institutionalized would be by planning the therapeutic program in terms of stages which are conceptualized as pathways towards the goals of therapy. Recognition could thus be given to the different requirements of patients at different phases of treatment and resettlement.

Postulate 29a. A relevant distinction in differentiating aspects of the therapy program would be between groups or activities that are primarily oriented to treatment goals and groups that are primarily oriented to rehabilitation goals. Patients could then be assigned to groups according to their particular therapeutic needs at any given time. Within groups having mixed aims, conflicts could be resolved in terms of the goals of particular patients within the groups.

Postulate 29b. Another way of building more rational therapeutic strategies based on the distinction between treatment and rehabilitation would be to distinguish between roles primarily geared to one set of goals and roles primarily geared to the other. Formal recognition of this distinction would imply that some are authorized and expected to assume responsibility for treatment-oriented activities and others for rehabilitative activities.

Postulate 30. All the distinctions recommended can lead to a harmful fragmentation of therapeutic efforts unless integrative activities give recognition to their essential interdependence.

The Therapeutic Community

Our findings appear to justify the conclusion that it is possible to change social attitudes in relatively desocialized patients with severe character disorders, provided they are treated together in a therapeutic community. Our results show that six months after leaving the hospital, two-thirds of the patients followed up had made a fair adjustment or better, and one-third were rated poor or very poor adjustments; just over one-half had worked the full time since leaving the hospital. We believe (but cannot prove) that the results described could not have been achieved by individual psychotherapy and hospitalization alone.

From the follow-up results there would appear to be a tendency for the patients to make either good or bad adjustments. This tendency is demonstrated by the shape of the distribution of adjustment scores. . . .

It would appear that our patient population is composed of two main types, those who derive much benefit from treatment and those who improve but little; there are relatively few patients who fall between these two groups (only 18 percent of our patients have adjustment scores in the range 2 to 7).

The Therapeutic Community, from Maxwell Jones, et al., *The Therapeutic Community: A New Treatment Method in Psychiatry* (New York: Basic Books, 1953), pp. 156–61. Published in England under the title of *Social Psychiatry* (London: Routledge & Kegan Paul, 1952).

Those patients who showed clinical improvement in the hospital, irrespective of the severity of their illness on admission, do significantly better as a group than those who show no comparable improvement in the hospital. Thus a very ill patient who improves considerably in the hospital has a tendency to a better prognosis than a mildly ill patient who shows relatively slight improvement. This may imply much more than symptomatic improvement. It usually went with change in social adjustment, attitude to work, etc. It is worth stressing that it is the capacity of the individual for change, rather than the severity of his illness, which is the important factor in estimating the prognosis. This may possibly modify current concepts regarding the assessment in the initial interviews of the outcome of treatment.

Dr. Sandler's work on vocational guidance with our type of patient suggests that too much emphasis has in the past been placed on the patient's abilities and aptitudes as measured by psychological tests. Attention should rather be directed to an assessment of the patient's "general employability" ... which determines the patient's attitude to work as such. A high general employability implies that the patient will have had little difficulty in adjusting to whatever work is available to him. Conversely, a person with a low general employability will not succeed in keeping a job no matter how favorable the initial prospects may have seemed.

There are many people who doubt the value of in-patient treatment of the neuroses; what appears to us to be important is the organization of the hospital community. Clearly every general hospital, mental hospital, or neurosis center has some form of social structure, but all too frequently this has been established on intuitive, empirical, or dictatorial grounds. Too little attention has been paid to the effect of the hospital community on the individual patient. Even less has any serious attempt been made to use the hospital community as an active force in treatment. (The Cassel Hospital near London is one exception to this.) We have tried to build up a therapeutic community where each member of the staff has a clear concept of his or her role. By frequent (daily) meetings of the staff, these roles have been elaborated and clarified and the interpersonal relationships developed by discussion and by resolution of tensions where possible. The social structure of the Unit has become a relatively integrated one and has stood firm in the face of serious threats to its existence from both inside and outside the Unit. The traditions and culture of the staff group have become more sharply defined in relation to the treatment needs of the patients. The Unit culture is more clearly seen and understood in the staff group, but the majority of patients are influenced by it to a considerable extent. The patients come to us as social casualties; they are mainly people who have no real place in society coming as they do from broken homes and being unemployed. We attempt to absorb them into a hospital group where everything is done to find them social and vocational roles. As far as possible the workshops simulate normal factory conditions where the tensions associated with work roles can be worked out while still in the hospital. In this sense the

Unit is a transitional community. The nurses play an important role being accepted by both staff and patient groups—more than any other members of the staff they can be said to transmit the culture of the Unit to the patients.

A nurse trained in general nursing or in a mental hospital has in addition to her various skills come to accept certain traditions regarding, say, the nurse-patient relationship, the nurse-doctor relationship, and so on. It is probable that most of these traditions have never been subjected to close scrutiny; hospitals in Britain have in general remained peculiarly ignorant of developments in the sociological field. On the Unit we have tried to be as objective as possible in developing our therapeutic community and to become conscious of our motives when establishing a pattern of behavior expected from the staff or patients. Along with this we have paid special attention to communications throughout the entire Unit population, together with free discussion of any problem affecting the community. This has meant a considerable distribution of responsibility, e.g., at a staff meeting a nurse may describe one of her disturbed patients whom she considers to be unsuitable for nursing in an open ward. Her previous training in a general or mental hospital has led her to expect that the doctor will "do something," which in this case would probably mean removing the patient to a closed ward (usually a mental hospital). In the staff meeting the nurse finds herself playing an entirely different role. She is expected to consider the problem as one which, if possible, we should resolve within the Unit; certainly the doctor is not prepared to solve it for her on his own. He wants to know what, in her opinion, has contributed to the exacerbation of symptoms (if that has occurred), while he on his side will discuss any factors which in his opinion have contributed to the disturbed state of the patient. Other nurses who have been looking after the patient may express divergent views and the meeting may become aware that considerable tension exists between the several nurses handling the patient. The workshop instructor may tell the group that the patient has become increasingly more hostile towards the other patients and along with this has sought more and more attention and praise from the instructor. The charge nurse too may have noticed that he has been in her office more often than previously, and frequently with quite trivial requests. The social worker may describe the patient's appalling home conditions and the complete indifference of his parents to his condition—no help can be expected from this direction. At this point the nurse who originally raised the problem may feel that the tension is unbearable and may interject angrily, "Why don't you *do* something about it instead of all this talking? In my last hospital Dr. Smith would have acted immediately." Such action if taken would not necessarily resolve the nurse's anxiety. There might be an immediate feeling of relief for the nurse but all too frequently the guilt engendered by such actions appears later in critical remarks by the nurse about the doctor, who is accused of showing no real interest in his patients and so on. Our aim is to achieve a communal responsibility in relation to all our Unit problems whether they relate to patients or staff. This distribution of responsibility, while frequently increasing the tensions, particularly of the less trained and more dependent members of the staff, leads to a far more realistic attitude towards treatment.

We have come to feel that it is high time that hospital communities throughout the country became more conscious of their treatment roles. All too often established practice bears no relationship to the treatment needs of the patient. In many instances they appear to be an elaborate defense protecting the staff against such needs. Take any acute surgical ward with, say, several recent amputees; the staff are gay and inconsequential and expect an appropriate response from the patients. It is not until the patients have returned home that they can talk about the very real problems that now face them. The staff have protected themselves from facing responsibilities that they shrink from, and moreover this is part of the established tradition of "good nursing"; but one of the major aspects of treatment, the patient's own emotional problems, has been ignored. We believe that the application of some of the principles of sociology, such as we have described, would favorably alter the existing social structure of hospital communities with considerable benefit to the patient.

In many psychiatric hospitals which I have visited in the U.S.A. and Europe while acting as consultant in mental health to the World Health Organization, I have seen what appears to be a most sincere attempt to give the patient the best possible treatment, spoiled by a failure to distinguish between a hospital role and a normal community role. In these hospitals everything possible was done to make the patient's stay pleasant and interesting; even when the patient was nearing discharge, the planned day was designed to please him rather than to prepare him for his outside role. The result of this was that frequently the patient was unable to settle down when discharged to his home, and he soon found his way back to the hospital. On the Unit we have tried to avoid this error and have stressed the ultimate job goal from the time of the patient's admission. The cultural pressure of the Unit community is directed towards his acceptance of a more useful social role, which may then appear desirable because of his growing identification with the group. This insistence on a work goal is much more unpleasant for both patients and staff than the most usual type of hospital environment, but it is more realistic, and probably yields better results in the long run.

We believe that too little use is made of educational methods in psychiatric hospitals. Our use of daily discussion groups with the entire patient population, documentary films, psychodramas, etc., represent an attempt to develop such methods; the main principle involved is that social problems and real life situations are either raised in discussion or acted out in psychodrama. The whole group attempts to arrive at a constructive attitude in relation to the problem raised. The degree of participation by the doctor taking the meeting varies with the situation and the personality of the doctor, but in his summing up he has an opportunity to present an informed and comprehensive point of view. To take the patient population repeatedly through this type of discussion or acting out of real life situations does possibly give them a new perception of such situations and so may alter behavior patterns; this new awareness may prove helpful in dealing with the patient's own problems. The awareness may not amount to actual insight, but the very process of acting out or verbalization of feelings and attitudes gives definition to them, and in so doing modifies them. However, in our educational procedure individual responses cannot be separated from the group climate. What appears to matter most is the degree of "group learning"—the extent to which the community accepts an idea which then becomes an integral part of the group culture. Patients seem to accept new ideas much more readily when these have behind them the weight of group acceptance. This attempt to achieve a change in the attitude of a group was discussed earlier in relation to cardiac neurosis. Cases of efforts syndrome (neurocirculatory asthenia) were treated in a group and fed with information of an anatomical and physiological kind, sufficient to give them a mechanistic understanding of the nature of their symptoms. The group ingested the information and in time the attitude of the group changed significantly. Originally every man had thought of his symptoms as a demonstration of severe heart disease; but this attitude slowly changed and was replaced by a more mechanistic view which disallowed the possibility of heart disease. The symptoms might persist but their significance was now completely altered. New patients rapidly came to accept this orientation which had become part of the culture of the group, and was discussed by the patients at the daily community meetings, and in this way was perpetuated. This process of acculturation seems to be an essential part of our social therapy techniques. We realize only too well the limitations of such treatment procedures. There are probably some patients who remain unaffected by the group meetings. Moreover there must be other patients who are unlikely to be helped by anything but uncovering types of psychotherapy. It must be borne in mind, however, that we are dealing with severe character disorders with poor personalities, who would in most cases be quite unsuitable for analytic types of treatment.

At the present time we believe it is necessary to get the severe character disorder, of the type discussed in this book, into a therapeutic community in order to effect some degree of resocialization; however, we have been impressed by Miss Tuxford's experiences in doing the home visits for the follow-up study; these led her to the conclusion that the cause of much of the desocialization which we see in hospitals is due to the absence of any real family life. It may be that we would be able to do more useful work if we were keeping the patient at home and attempting treatment within the home environment as is being done by the psychiatrists and social workers in the Amsterdam Municipal Health Service and in other Dutch cities. Moreover we have so far failed to bring the patients' families into our community treatment, mainly because we get patients from all over the United Kingdom. We believe that our experiment might yield more valuable information if we were serving only the local community. Whatever the advantages of working within the family environment may be, however, we feel certain that there is ample therapeutic justification for bringing patients into a therapeutic community until other and better methods of treatment are known. There is no reason to think that the changes in social attitude which the patient follow-up inquiry demonstrated, and the striking differences in this sphere between the treated and untreated groups, were temporary phenomena.

25

THE ENCOUNTER GROUP

Carl R. Rogers

For an introduction to Rogers, the reader is referred to chapter 18, which gives Rogers's biography and discusses his therapeutic system.

The Group Process

As I consider the terribly complex interactions which arise during twenty, forty, sixty, or more hours of intensive sessions, I believe that I see some threads which weave in and out of the pattern. Some of these trends or tendencies are likely to appear early and some later in the group sessions, but there is no clear-cut sequence in which one ends and another begins. The interaction is best thought of, I believe, as a varied tapestry, differing from group to group, yet with certain kinds of trends evident in most of these intensive encounters and with certain patterns tending to precede and others to follow. Here are some of the process patterns which I see developing, briefly described in simple terms, illustrated from tape recordings and personal reports, and presented in roughly sequential order. I am not aiming at a high-level theory of group process but rather at a naturalistic observaton out of which, I hope, true theory can be built.

Milling Around

As the leader or facilitator makes clear at the outset that this is a group with unusual freedom, that it is not one for which he will take directional responsibility, there tends to develop a period of initial confusion, awkward silence, polite surface interaction, "cocktail-party talk," frustration, and great lack of

Carl R. Rogers, "The Process of the Basic Encounter Group," in *Challenges of Humanistic Psychology*, ed. James F. Bugental (New York: McGraw-Hill, 1967), pp. 263–72.

continuity. The individuals come face-to-face with the fact that "there is no structure here except what we provide. We do not know our purposes; we do not even know one another, and we are committed to remain together over a considerable period of time." In this situation, confusion and frustration are natural. Particularly striking to the observer is the lack of continuity between personal expressions. Individual A will present some proposal or concern, clearly looking for a response from the group. Individual B has obviously been waiting for his turn and starts off on some completely different tangent as though he had never heard A. One member makes a simple suggestion such as, "I think we should introduce ourselves," and this may lead to several hours of highly involved discussion in which the underlying issues appear to be, "Who is the leader?" "Who is responsible for us?" "Who is a member of the group?" "What is the purpose of the group?"

Resistance to Personal Expression or Exploration

During the milling period, some individuals are likely to reveal some rather personal attitudes. This tends to foster a very ambivalent reaction among other members of the group. One member, writing of his experience, says:

> There is a self which I present to the world and another one which I know more intimately. With others I try to appear able, knowing, unruffled, problem-free. To substantiate this image I will act in a way which at the time or later seems false or artificial or "not the real me." Or I will keep to myself thoughts which if expressed would reveal an imperfect me.
>
> My inner self, by contrast with the image I present to the world, is characterized by many doubts. The worth I attach to this inner self is subject to much fluctuation and is very dependent on how others are reacting to me. At times this private self can feel worthless.

It is the public self which members tend to reveal to one another, and only gradually, fearfully, and ambivalently do they take steps to reveal something of their inner world.

Early in one intensive workshop, the members were asked to write anonymously a statement of some feeling or feelings which they had which they were not willing to tell in the group. One man wrote:

> I don't relate easily to people. I have an almost impenetrable facade. Nothing gets in to hurt me, but nothing gets out. I have repressed so many emotions that I am close to emotional sterility. This situation doesn't make me happy, but I don't know what to do about it.

This individual is clearly living inside a private dungeon, but he does not even dare, except in this disguised fashion, to send out a call for help.

In a recent workshop when one man started to express the concern he felt about an impasse he was experiencing with his wife, another member stopped him, saying essentially:

Are you sure you want to go on with this, or are you being seduced by the group into going further than you want to go? How do you know the group can be trusted? How will you feel about it when you go home and tell your wife what you have revealed, or when you decide to keep it from her? It just isn't safe to go further.

It seemed quite clear that in his warning, this second member was also expressing his own fear of revealing *himself* and *his* lack of trust in the group.

Description of Past Feelings

In spite of ambivalence about the trustworthiness of the group and the risk of exposing oneself, expression of feelings does begin to assume a larger proportion of the discussion. The executive tells how frustrated he feels by certain situations in his industry, or the housewife relates problems she has experienced with her children. A tape-recorded exchange involving a Roman Catholic nun occurs early in a one-week workshop, when the discussion has turned to a rather intellectualized consideration of anger:

Bill: What happens when you get mad, Sister, or don't you?

Sister: Yes, I do—yes I do. And I find when I get mad, I, I almost get, well, the kind of person that antagonizes me is the person who seems so unfeeling toward people—now I take our dean as a person in point because she is a very aggressive woman and has certain ideas about what the various rules in a college should be; and this woman can just send me into high "G"; in an angry mood. *I mean this.* But then I find, I. . . .

Facil.: But what, what do you do?

Sister: I find that when I'm in a situation like this, that I strike out in a very sharp, uh, *tone,* or else I just refuse to respond—"All right, this happens to be her way"—I don't think I've ever gone into a tantrum.

Joe: You just withdraw—no use to fight it.

Facil.: You say you use a sharp tone. To *her,* or to other people you're dealing with?

Sister: Oh, no. To *her.*

This is a typical example of a *description* of feelings which are obviously current in her in a sense but which she is placing in the past and which she describes as being outside the group in time and place. It is an example of feelings existing "there and then."

Expression of Negative Feelings

Curiously enough, the first expression of genuinely significant "here-and-now" feeling is apt to come out in negative attitudes toward other group members or toward the group leader. In one group in which members introduced themselves at some length, one woman refused, saying that she preferred to be known for what she was in the group and not in terms of her status outside. Very shortly after this, one of the men in the group attacked her vigorously and angrily for this stand, accusing her of failing to cooperate, of keeping herself aloof from the group, and so forth. It was the first *personal current feeling* which had been brought into the open in the group.

Frequently the leader is attacked for his failure to give proper guidance to the group. One vivid example of this comes from a recorded account of an early session with a group of delinquents, where one membr shouts at the leader:

> You will be licked if you don't control us right at the start. You have to keep order here because you are older than us. That's what a teacher is supposed to do. If he doesn't do it we will cause a lot of trouble and won't get anything done. [Then, referring to two boys in the group who were scuffling, he continues.] Throw'em out, throw'em out! You've just *got* to make us behave![1]

An adult expresses his disgust at the people who talk too much, but points his irritation at the leader:

> It is just that I don't understand why someone doesn't shut them up. I would have taken Gerald and shoved him out the window. I'm an authoritarian. I would have told him he was talking too much and he had to leave the room. I think the group discussion ought to be led by a person who simply will not recognize these people after they have interrupted about eight times.[2]

Why are negatively toned expressions the first current feelings to be expressed? Some speculative answers might be the following: This is one of the best ways to test the freedom and trustworthiness of the group. "Is it really a place where I can be and express myself positively and negatively? Is this really a safe place, or will I be punished?" Another quite different reason is that deeply positive feelings are much more difficult and dangerous to express than negative ones. "If I say, 'I love you,' I am vulnerable and open to the most awful rejection. If I say, 'I hate you,' I am at best liable to attack, against which I can defend." Whatever the reasons, such negatively toned feelings tend to be the first here-and-now material to appear.

Expression and Exploration of Personally Meaningful Material

It may seem puzzling that following such negative experiences as the initial confusion, the resistance to personal expression, the focus on outside events, and the voicing of critical or angry feelings, the event most likely to occur next is for an individual to reveal himself to the group in a significant way. The

---

[1]T. Gordon, *Group-Centered Leadership* (Boston: Houghton Mifflin, 1955), p. 214.
[2]Gordon, *Group-Centered Leadership,* p. 210.

reason for this no doubt is that the individual member has come to realize that this is in part *his group*. He can help to make of it what he wishes. He has also experienced the fact that negative feelings have been expressed and have usually been accepted or assimilated without any catastrophic results. He realizes there is freedom here, albeit a risky freedom. A climate of trust is beginning to develop.[3] So he begins to take the chance and the gamble of letting the group know some deeper facet of himself. One man tells of the trap in which he finds himself, feeling that communication between himself and his wife is hopeless. A priest tells of the anger which he has bottled up because of unreasonable treatment by one of his superiors. What should he have done? What might he do now? A scientist at the head of a large research department finds the courage to speak of his painful isolation, to tell the group that he has never had a single friend in his life. By the time he finishes telling of his situation, he is letting loose some of the tears of sorrow for himself which I am sure he has held in for many years. A psychiatrist tells of the guilt he feels because of the suicide of one of his patients. A woman of forty tells of her absolute inability to free herself from the grip of her controlling mother. A process which one workshop member has called a "journey to the center of self," often a very painful process, has begun.

Such exploration is not always an easy process, nor is the whole group always receptive to such self-revelation. In a group of institutionalized adolescents, all of whom had been in difficulty of one sort or another, one boy revealed an important fact about himself and immediately received both acceptance and sharp nonacceptance from members of the group:

> George: This is the thing. I've got too many problems at home—uhm, I think some of you know why I'm here, what I was charged with.
>
> Mary: I don't.
>
> Facil.: Do you want to tell us?
>
> George: Well, uh, it's sort of embarrassing.
>
> Carol: Come on, it won't be so bad.
>
> George: Well, I raped my sister. That's the only problem I have at home, and I've overcome that, I think. (*Rather long pause.*)
>
> Freda: Oooh, that's *weird!*
>
> Mary: People have problems, Freda, I mean ya know. . . .
>
> Freda: Yeah, I know, but *yeOUW!!!*
>
> Facil. (*to Freda*): You know about these problems, but they still are weird to you.
>
> George: You see what I mean; it's embarrassing to talk about it.
>
> Mary: Yeah, but it's O.K.
>
> George: It *hurts* to talk about it, but I know I've got to so I won't be guilt-ridden for the rest of my life.

---

[3] J. R. Gibb, "Climate for Trust Formation," in *T-Group Theory and Laboratory Method*, eds. L. Bradford, J. R. Gibb, and K. D. Benne (New York: Wiley, 1964).

Clearly Freda is completely shutting him out psychologically, while Mary in particular is showing a deep acceptance.

The Expression of Immediate Interpersonal Feelings in the Group

Entering into the process sometimes earlier, sometimes later, is the explicit bringing into the open of the feelings experienced in the immediate moment by one member about another. These are sometimes positive and sometimes negative. Examples would be: "I feel threatened by your silence." "You remind me of my mother, with whom I had a tough time." "I took an instant dislike to you the first moment I saw you." "To me you're like a breath of fresh air in the group." "I like your warmth and your smile." "I dislike you more every time you speak up." Each of these attitudes can be, and usually is, explored in the increasing climate of trust.

The Development of a Healing Capacity in the Group

One of the most fascinating aspects of any intensive group experience is the manner in which a number of the group members show a natural and spontaneous capacity for dealing in a helpful, facilitative, and therapeutic fashion with the pain and suffering of others. As one rather extreme example of this, I think of a man in charge of maintenance in a large plant who was one of the low-status members of an industrial executive group. As he informed us, he had not been "contaminated by education." In the initial phases the group tended to look down on him. As members delved more deeply into themselves and began to express their own attitudes more fully, this man came forth as, without doubt, the most sensitivie member of the group. He knew intuitively how to be understanding and acceptant. He was alert to things which had not yet been expressed but which were just below the surface. When the rest of us were paying attention to a member who was speaking, he would frequently spot another individual who was suffering silently and in need of help. He had a deeply perceptive and facilitating attitude. This kind of ability shows up so commonly in groups that it has led me to feel that the ability to be healing or therapeutic is far more common in human life than we might suppose. Often it needs only the permission granted by a freely flowing group experience to become evident.

In a characteristic instance, the leader and several group members were trying to be of help to Joe, who was telling of the almost complete lack of communication between himself and his wife. In varied ways members endeavored to give help. John kept putting before Joe the feelings Joe's wife was almost certainly experiencing. The facilitator kept challenging Joe's facade of "carefulness." Marie tried to help him discover what he was feeling at the moment. Fred showed him the choice he had of alternative behaviors. All this was clearly done in a spirit of caring, as is even more evident in the recording itself. No miracles were achieved, but toward the end Joe did come to the realization that the only thing that might help would be to express his real feelings to his wife.

Self-Acceptance and the Beginning of Change

Many people feel that self-acceptance must stand in the way of change. Actually, in these group experiences, as in psychotherapy, it is the *beginning* of change. Some examples of the kind of attitudes expressed would be these: "I *am* a dominating person who likes to control others. I do want to mold these individuals into the proper shape." Another person says, "I really have a hurt and overburdened little boy inside of me who feels very sorry for himself. I *am* that little boy, in addition to being a competent and responsible manager."

I think of one governmental executive in a group in which I participated, a man with high responsibility and excellent technical training as an engineer. At the first meeting of the group he impressed me, and I think others, as being cold, aloof, somewhat bitter, resentful, and cynical. When he spoke of how he ran his office it appeared that he administered it "by the book," without any warmth or human feeling entering in. In one of the early sessions, when he spoke of his wife, a group member asked him, "Do you love your wife?" He paused for a long time, and the questioner said, "OK, that's answer enough." The executive said, "No. Wait a minute. The reason I didn't respond was that I was wondering if I ever loved anyone. I don't think I *ever* really *loved* anyone." It seemed quite dramatically clear to those of us in the group that he had come to accept himself as an unloving person.

A few days later he listened with great intensity as one member of the group expressed profound personal feelings of isolation, loneliness, and pain, revealing the extent to which he had been living behind a mask, a facade. The next morning the engineer said, "Last night I thought and thought about what Bill told us. I even wept quite a bit by myself. I can't remember how long it has been since I have cried, and I really *felt* something. I think perhaps what I felt was love."

It is not surprising that before the week was over, he had thought through new ways of handling his growing son, on whom he had been placing extremely rigorous demands. He had also begun genuinely to appreciate the love which his wife had extended to him and which he now felt he could in some measure reciprocate.

In another group one man kept a diary of his reactions. Here is his account of an experience in which he came really to accept his almost abject desire for love, a self-acceptance which marked the beginning of a very significant experience of change. He says:

During the break between the third and fourth sessions, I felt very droopy and tired. I had it in mind to take a nap, but instead I was almost compulsively going around to people starting a conversation. I had a begging kind of feeling, like a very cowed little puppy hoping that he'll be patted but half afraid he'll be kicked. Finally, back in my room I lay down and began to know that I was sad. Several times I found myself wishing my roommate would come in and talk to me. Or, whenever someone walked by the door, I would come to attention inside, the way a dog pricks up his ears; and I would feel an immediate wish for that person to come in and talk to me. I realized my raw wish to receive kindness.[4]

Another recorded excerpt, from an adolescent group, shows a combination of self-acceptance and self-exploration. Art had been talking about his "shell," and here he is beginning to work with the problem of accepting himself, and also the facade he ordinarily exhibits:

Art: I'm so darn used to living with the shell; it doesn't even bother me. I don't even know the real me. I think I've uh, well, I've pushed the shell more away here. When I'm out of my shell—only twice—once just a few minutes ago—I'm really me, I guess. But then I just sort of pull in the [latch] cord after me when I'm in my shell, and that's almost all the time. And I leave the [false] front standing outside when I'm back in the shell.

Facil.: And nobody's back in there with you?

Art (*crying*): Nobody else is in there with me, just me. I just pull everything into the shell and roll the shell up and shove it in my pocket. I take the shell, and the real me, and put it in my pocket where it's safe. I guess that's really the way I do it—I go into my shell and turn off the real world. And here: that's what I want to do here in this group, ya know, come out of my shell and actually throw it away.

Lois: You're making progress already. At least you can talk about it.

Facil.: Yeah. The thing that's going to be hardest is to stay out of the shell.

Art (*still crying*): Well, yeah, if I can keep talking about it, I can come out and stay out, but I'm gonna have to, ya know, protect me. It hurts; it's actually hurting to talk about it.

Still another person reporting shortly after his workshop experience said, "I came away from the workshop feeling much more deeply that 'It is all right to be me with all my strengths and weaknesses.' My wife has told me that I appear to be more authentic, more real, more genuine."

This feeling of greater realness and authenticity is a very common experience. It would appear that the individual is learning to accept and to *be* himself, and this is laying the foundation for change. He is closer to his own

---

[4]G. F. Hall, "A Participant's Experience in a Basic Encounter Group," mimeographed (Western Behavioral Sciences Institute, 1965).

feelings, and hence they are no longer so rigidly organized and are more open to change.

The Cracking of Facades

As the sessions continue, so many things tend to occur together that it is difficult to know which to describe first. It should again be stressed that these different threads and stages interweave and overlap. One of these threads is the increasing impatience with defenses. As time goes on, the group finds it unbearable that any member should live behind a mask or a front. The polite words, the intellectual understanding of one another and of relationships, the smooth coin of tact and cover-up—amply satisfactory for interactions outside —are just not good enough. The expression of self by some members of the group has made it very clear that a deeper and more basic encounter is *possible,* and the group appears to strive, intuitively and unconsciously, toward this goal. Gently at times, almost savagely at others, the group *demands* that the individual be himself, that his current feelings not be hidden, that he remove the mask of ordinary social intercourse. In one group there was a highly intelligent and quite academic man who had been rather perceptive in his understanding of others but who had not revealed himself at all. The attitude of the group was finally expressed sharply by one member when he said, "Come out from behind that lectern, Doc. Stop giving us speeches. Take off your dark glasses. We want to know *you.*"

In Synanon, the fascinating group so successfully involved in making persons out of drug addicts, this ripping away of facades is often very drastic. An excerpt from one of the "synanons," or group sessions, makes this clear:

> Joe (*speaking to Gina*): I wonder when you're going to stop sounding so good in synanons. Every synanon that I'm in with you, someone asks you a question, and you've got a beautiful book written. All made out about what went down and how you were wrong and how you realized you were wrong and all that kind of bullshit. When are you going to stop doing that? How do you feel about Art?
>
> Gina: I have nothing against Art.
>
> Will: You're a nut. Art hasn't got any damn sense. He's been in there, yelling at you and Moe, and you've got everything so cool.
>
> Gina: No, I feel he's very insecure in a lot of ways but that has nothing to do with me. . . .
>
> Joe: You act like you're so goddamn understanding.
>
> Gina: I was *told* to act as if I understand.
>
> Joe: Well, you're in a synanon now. You're not supposed to be acting like you're such a goddamn healthy person. Are you so well?
>
> Gina: No.
>
> Joe: Well why the hell don't you quit acting as if you were.[5]

---

[5]D. Casbriel, *So Fair a House* (Englewood Cliffs, N.J.: Prentice-Hall, 1963), p. 81.

If am I indicating that the group at times is quite violent in tearing down a facade or a defense, this would be accurate. On the other hand, it can also be sensitive and gentle. The man who was accused of hiding behind a lectern was deeply hurt by this attack, and over the lunch hour looked very troubled, as though he might break into tears at any moment. When the group reconvened, the members sensed this and treated him very gently, enabling him to tell us his own tragic personal story, which accounted for his aloofness and his intellectual and academic approach to life.

The Individual Receives Feedback

In the process of this freely expressive interaction, the individual rapidly acquires a great deal of data as to how he appears to others. The "hail-fellow-well-met" discovers that others resent his exaggerated friendliness. The executive who weighs his words carefully and speaks with heavy precision may find that others regard him as stuffy. A woman who shows a somewhat excessive desire to be of help to others is told in no uncertain terms that some group members do not want her for a mother. All this can be decidedly upsetting, but as long as these various bits of information are fed back in the context of caring which is developing in the group, they seem highly constructive.

Feedback can at times be very warm and positive, as the following recorded excerpt indicates:

> Leo *(very softly and gently):* I've been struck with this ever since she talked about her waking in the night, that she has a very delicate sensitivity. *(Turning to Mary and speaking almost caressingly.)* And somehow I perceive—even looking at you or in your eyes—a very— almost like a gentle touch and from this gentle touch you can tell many—things—you sense in—this manner.
>
> Fred: Leo, when you said that, that she has this kind of delicate sensitivity, I just felt, *Lord yes!* Look at her eyes.
>
> Leo: M-hm.

A much more extended instance of negative and positive feedback, triggering a significant new experience of self-understanding and encounter with the group, is taken from the diary of the young man mentioned before. He had been telling the group that he had no feeling for them, and felt they had no feeling for him:

> Then, a girl lost patience with me and said she didn't feel she could give any more. She said I looked like a bottomless well, and she wondered how many times I had to be told that I *was* cared for. By this time I was feeling panicky, and I was saying to myself, "My God, can it be true that I can't be satisfied and that I'm somehow compelled to pester people for attention until I drive them away!"

At this point while I was really worried, a nun in the group spoke up. She said that I had not alienated her with some negative things I had said to her. She said she liked me, and she couldn't understand why I couldn't see that. She said she felt concerned for me and wanted to help me. With that, something began to really dawn on me, and I voiced it somewhat like the following. "You mean you are all sitting there, feeling for me what I say I want you to feel, and that somewhere down inside me I'm stopping it from touching me?" I relaxed appreciably and began really to wonder why I had shut their caring out so much. I couldn't find the answer, and one woman said: "It looks like you are trying to stay continuously as deep in your feelings as you were this afternoon. It would make sense to me for you to draw back and assimilate it. Maybe if you don't push so hard, you can rest awhile and then move back into your feelings more naturally."

Her making the last suggestion really took effect. I saw the sense in it, and almost immediately I settled back very relaxed with something of a feeling of a bright, warm day dawning inside me. In addition to taking the pressure off of myself, however, I was for the first time really warmed by the friendly feelings which I felt they had for me. It is difficult to say why I felt liked only just then, but, as opposed to the earlier sessions, I really *believed* they cared for me. I never have fully understood why I stood their affection off for so long, but at that point I almost abruptly began to trust that they did care. The measure of the effectiveness of this change lies in what I said next. I said, "Well, that really takes care of me. I'm really ready to listen to someone else now." I *meant* that, too.[6]

Confrontation

There are times when the term *feedback* is far too mild to describe the interactions which take place, when it is better said that one individual *confronts* another, directly "leveling" with him. Such confrontations can be positive, but frequently they are decidedly negative, as the following example will make abundantly clear. In one of the last sessions of a group, Alice had made some quite vulgar and contemptuous remarks to John, who was entering religious work. The next morning, Norma, who had been a very quiet person in the group, took the floor:

Norma *(loud sigh):* Well, I don't have *any* respect for you, Alice. *None!* *(Pause.)* There's about a hundred things going through my mind I want to say to you, and by God I hope I get through 'em all! First of all, if you wanted us to respect you, then why couldn't you respect *John's* feelings last night? Why have you been on him today? Hmm? Last night—couldn't you—couldn't you accept—*couldn't you* comprehend in any way at all that—that *he felt* his unworthiness in the service of God? Couldn't you accept this, or did you have to dig into it today to find something *else there?*

---

[6]Hall, "A Participant's Experience in a Basic Encounter Group."

And his respect for womanhood—he *loves* women—yes, he does, because he's a real person, but you—you're not a real woman—to me—and thank God, you're not my mother!!!! I want to come over and beat the hell out of you!!! I want to slap you across the mouth so hard and—oh, and you're so, you're many years above me—and I respect age, and I respect people who are older than me, *but I don't respect you, Alice. At all!* And I was so *hurt* and *confused* because you were making someone else feel *hurt* and *confused*. . . .

It may relieve the reader to know that these two women came to accept each other, not completely, but much more understandingly, before the end of the session. But this *was* a confrontation!

The Helping Relationship Outside the Group Sessions

No account of the group process would, in my experience, be adequate if it did not make mention of the many ways in which group members are of assistance to one another. Not infrequently, one member of a group will spend hours listening and talking to another member who is undergoing a painful new perception of himself. Sometimes it is merely the offering of help which is therapeutic. I think of one man who was going through a very depressed period after having told us of the many tragedies in his life. He seemed quite clearly, from his remarks, to be contemplating suicide. I jotted down my room number (we were staying at a hotel) and told him to put it in his pocket and to call me anytime of day or night if he felt that it would help. He never called, but six months after the workshop was over he wrote to me telling me how much that act had meant to him and that he still had the slip of paper to remind him of it.

Let me give an example of the healing effect of the attitudes of group members both outside and inside the group meetings. This is taken from a letter written by a workshop member to the group one month after the group sessions. He speaks of the difficulties and depressing circumstances he has encountered during that month and adds:

I have come to the conclusion that my experiences with you have profoundly affected me. I am truly grateful. This is different than personal therapy. None of you *had* to care about me. None of you had to seek me out and let me know of things you thought would help me. None of you had to let me know I was of help to you. Yet you did, and as a result it has far more meaning than anything I have so far experienced. When I feel the need to hold back and not live spontaneously, for whatever reasons, I remember that twelve persons, just like those before me now, said to let go and be congruent, to be myself, and, of all unbelievable things, they even loved me more for it. This has given me the *courage* to come out of myself many times since then. Often it seems my very doing of this helps the others to experience similar freedom.

The Basic Encounter

Running through some of the trends I have just been describing is the fact that individuals come into much closer and more direct contact with one another than is customary in ordinary life. This appears to be one of the most central, intense, and change-producing aspects of such a group experience. To illustrate what I mean, I would like to draw an example from a recent workshop group. A man tells, through his tears, of the very tragic loss of his child, a grief which he is experiencing *fully*, for the first time, not holding back his feelings in any way. Another says to him, also with tears in his eyes, "I've never felt so close to another human being. I've never before felt a real physical hurt in me from the pain of another. I feel *completely* with you." This is a basic encounter.

Such I-Thou relationships (to use Buber's term) occur with some frequency in these group sessions and nearly always bring a moistness to the eyes of the participants.

One member, trying to sort out his experiences immediately after a workshop, speaks of the "commitment to relationship" which often developed on the part of two individuals, not necessarily individuals who had liked each other initially. He goes on to say:

> The incredible fact experienced over and over by members of the group was that when a negative feeling was fully expressed to another, the relationship grew and the negative feeling was replaced by a deep acceptance for the other. . . . Thus real change seemed to occur when feelings were experienced and expressed in the context of the relationship. "I can't *stand* the way you talk!" turned into a real understanding and affection for you the *way* you talk.

This statement seems to capture some of the more complex meanings of the term *basic encounter*.

The Expression of Positive Feelings and Closeness

As indicated in the last section, an inevitable part of the group process seems to be that when feelings are expressed and can be accepted in a relationship, a great deal of closeness and positive feelings result. Thus as the sessions proceed, there is an increasing feeling of warmth and group spirit and trust built, not out of positive attitudes only, but out of a realness which includes both positive and negative feeling. One member tried to capture this in writing very shortly after the workshop by saying that if he were trying to sum it up, ". . . it would have to do with what I call confirmation—a kind of confirmation of myself, of the uniqueness and universal qualities of men, a confirmation that when we can be human together something positive can emerge."

A particularly poignant expression of these positive attitudes was shown in the group where Norma confronted Alice with her bitterly angry feelings. Joan, the facilitator, was deeply upset and began to weep. The positive and healing attitudes of the group, for their own *leader*, are an unusual example of the closeness and personal quality of the relationships.

> Joan *(crying):* I somehow feel that it's so *damned* easy for me to—to put myself *inside* of another person and I just guess I can feel that—for John and Alice and for you, Norma.
>
> Alice: And it's *you* that's hurt.
>
> Joan: Maybe I am taking some of that hurt. I guess I am. *(crying.)*
>
> Alice: That's a wonderful gift. I wish I had it.
>
> Joan: You have a lot of it.
>
> Peter: In a way you bear the—I guess in a special way, because you're the —facilitator, an, you've probably borne, an, an extra heavy burden for all of us—and the burden that you, perhaps, you bear the heaviest is—we ask you—we ask one another; we grope to try to accept one another as we are, and—for each of us in various ways I guess we reach things and we say, *please* accept me. . . .

Some may be very critical of a "leader" so involved and so sensitive that she weeps at the tensions in the group which she has taken into herself. For me, it is simply another evidence that when people are real with each other, they have an astonishing ability to heal a person with a real and understanding love, whether that person is "participant" or "leader."

Behavior Changes in the Group

It would seem from observation that many changes in behavior occur in the group itself. Gestures change. The tone of voice changes, becoming sometimes stronger, sometimes softer, usually more spontaneous, less artificial, more feelingful. Individuals show an astonishing amount of thoughtfulness and helpfulness toward one another.

Our major concern, however, is with the behavior changes which occur following the group experience. It is this which constitutes the most significant question and on which we need much more study and research. One person gives a catalog of the changes which he sees in himself which may seem too "pat" but which is echoed in many other statements:

> I am more open, spontaneous. I express myself more freely. I am more sympathetic, empathic, and tolerant. I am more confident. I am more religious in my own way. My relations with my family, friends, and coworkers are more honest, and I express my likes and dislikes and true feelings more openly. I admit ignorance more readily. I am more cheerful. I want to help others more.

Another says:

> Since the workshop there has been a new relationship with my parents. It has been trying and hard. However, I have found a greater freedom in talking with them, especially my father. Steps have been made toward being closer to my mother than I have ever been in the last five years.

Another says:

> It helped clarify my feelings about my work, gave me more enthusiasm for it, and made me more honest and cheerful with my coworkers and also more open when I was hostile. It made my relationship with my wife more open, deeper. We felt freer to talk about anything, and we felt confident that anything we talked about we could work through.

Sometimes the changes which are described are very subtle. "The primary change is the more positive view of my ability to allow myself to *hear,* and to become involved with someone else's 'silent scream.' "

At the risk of making the outcomes sound too good, I will add one more statement written shortly after a workshop by a mother. She says:

> The immediate impact on my children was of interest to both me and my husband. I feel that having been so accepted and loved by a group of strangers was so supportive that when I returned home my love for the people closest to me was much more spontaneous. Also, the practice I had in accepting and loving others during the workshop was evident in my relationships with my close friends.

Thus far one might think that every aspect of the group process was positive. As far as the evidence at hand indicates, it appears that it nearly always is a positive process for a majority of the participants. There are, nevertheless, failures which result. Let me try to describe briefly some of the negative aspects of the group process as they sometimes occur.

The most obvious deficiency of the intensive group experience is that frequently the behavior changes, if any, which occur, are not lasting. This is often recognized by the participants. One says, "I wish I had the ability to hold permanently the 'openness' I left the conference with." Another says, "I experienced a lot of acceptance, warmth, and love at the workshop. I find it hard to carry the ability to share this in the same way with people outside the workshop. I find it easier to slip back into my old unemotional role than to do the work necessary to open relationships."

Sometimes group members experience this phenomenon of "relapse" quite philosophically:

> The group experience is not a way of life but a reference point. My images of our group, even though I am unsure of some of their meanings, give me a comforting and useful perspective on my normal routine. They are like a mountain which I have climbed and enjoyed and to which I hope occasionally to return.

CONJOINT FAMILY THERAPY

Virginia Satir

Born in Neillsville, Wisconsin, Virginia Satir received her M.A. in psychiatric social work from the University of Chicago in 1948. In the 1940s she served as social work supervisor for the Chicago Home for Girls and as a social worker for the Mary Bartelme Club. Her work in the 1950s carried her into family counseling, when she served as supervisor and counselor for the Association for Family Living in Chicago and instructor in family dynamics at the Illinois State Psychiatric Institute in Chicago. A founder of the Mental Research Institute in Palo Alto, California, Satir became director of training for its family project in 1959. She then took a position as associate in residence at the Esalen Institute at Big Sur, California, where she is still working.

Satir's ideas for conjoint family therapy were jelling in the mid-fifties, when she was an instructor in the Family Dynamics Residency Training Program of the Illinois State Psychiatric Institute in Chicago. In 1959 she became associated with Don D. Jackson and Jules Riskin (both doctors) to form the staff of the newly established Mental Research Institute in Palo Alto, California, an institute structured for the investigation of family interaction and its relationship to illness and health. She pioneered the development of family therapy since 1951.

Concerned with interpersonal relationships that inhibit growth and development, Satir formulated what she termed *conjoint family therapy*. Viewing the family as a therapeutic unit, she attributes behavior to more than intrapsychic forces; it stems from interactional experiences. The family's attitude toward the "patient" is significant, for the relatives themselves become an integral part of the problem. Critical relationships exist between patients and their family members, so much so that a person's behavior may be regarded as conscious and unconscious responses to a "complex set of regular and predictable 'rules' governing his family group."[1]

She became widely known for her book, *Conjoint Family Therapy* (1964). Her other publications comprise a number of journal articles and the books *People Making* (1972) and *Self: Esteem: A Declaration* (1975).

---

[1]Virginia Satir, *Conjoint Family Therapy,* rev. ed. (Palo Alto, Calif.: Science and Behavior Books, 1967), p. x.

Family Theory

1. Family therapists deal with family pain.
   a. When one person in a family (the patient) has pain which shows up in symptoms, all family members are feeling this pain in some way.
   b. Many therapists have found it useful to call the member who carries the symptoms the "Identified Patient," or "I.P.," rather than to join the family in calling him "the sick one," or "the different one," or "the one who is to blame."
   c. This is because the therapist sees the Identified Patient's symptoms as serving a family function as well as an individual function.

2. Numerous studies have shown that the family behaves as if it were a unit. In 1954 Jackson introduced the term "family homeostasis" to refer to this behavior.
   a. According to the concept of family homeostasis, the family acts so as to achieve a balance in relationships.
   b. Members help to maintain this balance overtly and covertly.
   c. The family's repetitious, circular, predictable communication patterns reveal this balance.
   d. When the family homeostasis is precarious, members exert much effort to maintain it.

3. The marital relationship influences the character of family homeostasis.
   a. The marital relationship is the axis around which all other family relationships are formed. The mates are the "architects" of the family.
   b. A pained marital relationship tends to produce dysfunctional parenting.

4. The Identified Patient is the family member who is most obviously affected by the pained marital relationship and most subjected to dysfunctional parenting.
   a. His symptoms are an "SOS" about his parents' pain and the resulting family imbalance.
   b. His symptoms are a message that he is distorting his own growth as a result of trying to alleviate and absorb his parents' pain.

5. Many treatment approaches are called *family therapy* but differ from the definition which will be presented here, since they are oriented primarily to family members as individuals rather than to the family as a unit as well. For example:

Family Theory, from Virginia Satir, *Conjoint Family Therapy*, rev. ed. (Palo Alto, Calif.: Science and Behavior Books, 1970), pp. 1–7.

a. Each family member may have his own therapist.

b. Or family members may share the same therapist, but the therapist sees each member separately.

c. Or the patient may have a therapist who occasionally sees other family members "for the sake of" the patient.

6. A growing body of clinical observation has pointed to the conclusion that family therapy must be oriented to the family as a whole. This conviction was initially supported by observations showing how family members respond to the individual treatment of a family member labeled as "schizophrenic." But further studies showed that families with a delinquent member respond in similar ways to the individual treatment of this member. In both cases it was found that:

a. Other family members interfered with, tried to become part of, or sabotaged the individual treatment of the "sick" member, as though the family had a stake in his sickness.

b. The hospitalized or incarcerated patient often got worse or regressed after a visit from family members, as though family interaction had a direct bearing on his symptoms.

c. Other family members got worse as the patient got better, as though sickness in one of the family members were essential to the family's way of operating.

7. These observations led many individually oriented psychiatrists and researchers to reevaluate and question certain assumptions.

a. They noted that when the patient was seen as the victim of his family, it was easy to overidentify with and overprotect him, overlooking the fact that:

—Patients are equally adept at victimizing other family members in return.

—Patients help to perpetuate their role as the sick, different, or blamed one.

b. They noted how heavily transference was relied on in order to produce change.

—Yet perhaps much of the patient's so-called transference was really an appropriate reaction to the therapist's behavior in the unreal, noninteractive, therapeutic situation.

—In addition, there was a greater chance that the therapeutic situation would perpetuate pathology, instead of presenting a new state of affairs which would introduce doubts about the old perceptions.

—If some of the patient's behavior did represent transference (that is, his characteristic way of relating to his mother and father), why shouldn't the therapist help the patient deal with the family more directly by seeing both the patient and his family together?

c. They noted that the therapist tended to be more interested in the patient's fantasy life than in his real life. But even if they were interested in the patient's real life, as long as they saw just the patient in therapy, they had to rely on his version of that life or try and guess what was going on in it.

d. They noted that in trying to change one family member's way of operating they were, in effect, trying to change the whole family's way of operating.

—This put the burden of family change-agent on the patient all by himself rather than on all family members.

—The patient was already the family member who was trying to change the family's way of operating, so when he was urged to increase his efforts, he only received a more intense criticism from the family. This also led him to feel even more burdened and less able.

8. Aside from all these observations, once therapists started to see the whole family together, other aspects of family life which produced symptoms were revealed, aspects which had been largely overlooked. Other investigators of family interaction were making similar discoveries. As Warren Brodey sees it, the mates act differently with the normal sibling than they do with the symptomatic sibling:

> . . . the parents in the presence of the "normal" sibling are able to relate with a freedom, flexibility, and breadth of awareness that one finds hard to believe, considering the limitations that exist in the relationship between the parents when involved with the symptomatic sibling. The pathological ways of relating seem to be focused within the relationship with the symptomatic member. One wonders how this has come about.[2]

9. But those psychiatrists who became increasingly devoted to family therapy were not the first to recognize the interpersonal nature of mental illness. Sullivan and Fromm-Reichmann, along with many other psychiatrists, psychologists, and social workers, were pioneers in this area of discovery. The Child Guidance movement was another important development which helped break the tradition of singling out just one family member for treatment.

a. Child Guidance therapists included both mother and child in treatment, even though they still tended to see mother and child in separate treatment sessions.

b. They also increasingly recognized the importance of including the father in therapy, though they found him hard to reach and generally failed to engage him in the therapy process.

---

[2]M. Bowen, "A Family Concept of Schizophrenia," in *The Etiology of Schizophrenia,* ed. Don D. Jackson (New York: Basic, 1960), p. 370.

—Therapists reported that the father felt parenting was his wife's job more than his; if the child acted disturbed, his wife was the one who should be seen.

—The Child Guidance therapists, being mother-child oriented anyway, tended to agreed with the father's reasoning, so they could not easily convince him that his role in the family was important to the health of his child.

—Child Guidance clinics remained primarily focused on "mothering," even though they increasingly recognized the importance of "fathering." And whether or not they included the father in their thinking, they continued to focus on the husband and wife as parents of the child rather than as mates to each other. Yet it has been repeatedly noted how critically the marital relationship affects parenting. Murry Bowen writes, for example:

> The striking observation was that when the parents were emotionally close, more invested in each other than either was in the patient, the patient improved. When *either* parent became more emotionally invested in the patient than in the other parent, the patient immediately and automatically regressed. When the parents were emotionally close, they could do no wrong in their "management" of the patient. The patient responded well to firmness, permissiveness, punishment, "talking it out," or any other management approach. When the parents were "emotionally divorced," any and all "management approaches" were equally unsuccessful.[3]

10. Family therapists have found it easier to interest the husband in family therapy than in individual therapy. This is because the family therapist is himself convinced that both architects of the family must be present.
    a. Once the therapist convinces the husband that he is essential to the therapy process, and that no one else can speak for him or take his place in therapy or in family life, he readily enters in.
    b. The wife (in her role as mother) may initiate family therapy, but once therapy is under way, the husband becomes as involved as she does.
    c. Family therapy seems to make sense to the whole family. Husband and wife say: "Now, at last, we are together and can get to the bottom of this."

11. Right from the first contact, family therapists operate from certain assumptions about why a family member has sought therapeutic help.
    a. Usually the first contact is made because someone outside the family has labeled Johnny as disturbed. This first contact will probably

[3]W. M. Brodey, "Some Family Operations of Schizophrenia: A Study of Five Hospitalized Families each with a Schizophrenic Member," *Archives of General Psychiatry* 1 (1959):391.

be made by an anxious wife (we will call her Mary Jones), acting in her role as mother of a disturbed child, Johnny. The child is disturbed, so she, the mother, must be to blame.

b. But Johnny was probably exhibiting disturbed behavior long before he became labeled disturbed by someone outside the family.

c. Until the outsider (often a teacher) labeled Johnny as disturbed, members of the Jones family probably acted as though they did not notice Johnny's behavior; his behavior was appropriate because it served a family function.

d. Usually some event has occurred which has precipitated symptoms in Johnny, symptoms which make the fact that he is disturbed obvious to outsiders. These events are:

—Changes from outside the nuclear family: war, depression, etc.

—Changes in the two families of origin: sickness of a grandmother, financial distress of a grandfather, etc.

—Someone enters or leaves the nuclear family: grandmother comes to live with the family, the family takes on a boarder, the family adds to its membership with the birth of another child, a daughter gets married.

—Biological changes: a child reaches adolescence, mother reaches menopause, father is hospitalized.

—Major social changes: a child leaves home to attend school, the family moves to a new neighborhood, father gets a job promotion, son goes to college.

e. These events can precipitate symptoms because they require the mates to integrate the changes. This requirement puts an extra strain on the marital relationship because it calls for a redefinition of family relationships and thus affects family balance.

f. The family homeostasis can be functional (or "fitting") for members at some periods of family life and not at other periods, so events affect members differently at different times.

g. But if one member is affected by an event, all are to some degree.

12. After the first contact with Mary Jones, the therapist may speculate about the relationship between Mary and her husband, whom we will call Joe. If it is correct to assume that a dysfunctional marital relationship is the main contributor to symptoms in a child, the relationship between the mates will be the therapist's first concern.

a. What kind of people are Mary and Joe? What kind of families did they come from?

—Once they were two separate people who came from different family environments.

—Now they are the architects of a new family of their own.

b. Why, out of all the people in the world, did they choose each other as mates?
    —How they chose each other gives clues to why they may now be disappointed with each other.
    —How they express their disappointment with each other gives clues to why Johnny needs to have symptoms in order to hold the Jones family together.

Theory and Practice of Conjoint Family Therapy

13. This brings us to a discussion of the role of the therapist. How will he act? What picture will he have of himself?
    a. Perhaps the best way that he can see himself is as a *resource person.* He is not omnipotent. He is not God, parent, or judge. The knotty question for all therapists is how to be an expert without appearing to the patient to be all-powerful, omniscient, or presuming to know always what is right and wrong.
    b. The therapist does have a special advantage in being able to study the patient's family situation as an experienced observer, while remaining outside it, above the power struggle, so to speak. Like a camera with the wide-angle lens, he can see things from the position of each person present and act as a representative of each. He sees transactions, as well as the individuals involved, and thus has a unique viewpoint.
    c. Because of this, the family can place their trust in him as an "official observer," one who can report impartially on what he sees and hears. Above all, he can report on what the family cannot see and cannot report on.
14. The therapist must also see himself as a *model of communication.*
    a. First of all, he must take care to be aware of his own prejudices and unconscious assumptions so as not to fall into the trap he warns others about, that of suiting reality to himself. His lack of fear in revealing himself may be the first experience the family has had with clear communication.
    b. In addition, the way he interprets and structures the action of therapy from the start is the first step in introducing the family to new techniques in communication.

Theory and Practice of Conjoint Family Therapy, from Satir, *Conjoint Family Therapy,* pp. 97–105.

c. Here is an example of how the therapist clarifies the process of interaction for a family:

Th *(to husband):* I notice your brow is wrinkled, Ralph. Does that mean you are angry at this moment?

H: I did not know that my brow was wrinkled.

Th: Sometimes a person looks or sounds in a way of which he is not aware. As far as you can tell, what were you thinking and feeling just now?

H: I was thinking over what she (his wife) said.

Th: What thing that she said were you thinking about?

H: When she said that when she was talking so loud, she wished I would tell her.

Th: What were you thinking about that?

H: I never thought about telling her. I thought she would get mad.

Th: Ah, then maybe that wrinkle meant you were puzzled because your wife was hoping you would do something, and you did not know she had this hope. Do you suppose that by your wrinkled brow you were signalling that you were puzzled?

H: Yeh, I guess so.

Th: As far as you know, have you ever been in that same spot before, that is, where you were puzzled by something Alice said or did?

H: Hell, yes, lots of times.

Th: Have you ever told Alice you were puzzled when you were?

W: He never says anything.

Th *(smiling, to Alice):* Just a minute, Alice, let me hear what Ralph's idea is of what he does. Ralph, how do you think you have let Alice know when you are puzzled?

H: I think she knows.

Th: Well, let's see. Suppose you ask Alice if she knows.

H: This is silly.

Th *(smiling):* I suppose it might seem so in this situation, because Alice is right here and certainly has heard what your question is. She knows what it is. I have the suspicion, though, that neither you nor Alice is very sure about what the other expects, and I think you have not developed ways to find out. Alice, let's go back to when I commented on Ralph's wrinkled brow. Did you happen to notice it, too?

W *(complaining):* Yes, he always looks like that.

Th: What kind of a message did you get from that wrinkled brow?

W: He don't want to be here. He don't care. He never talks. Just looks at television or he isn't home.

Th: I'm curious. Do you mean that when Ralph has a wrinkled brow that you take this as Ralph's way of saying, "I don't love you, Alice. I don't care about you, Alice."?

W *(exasperated and tearfully):* I don't know.

Th: Well, maybe the two of you have not yet worked out crystal-clear ways of giving your love and value messages to each other. Everyone needs crystal-clear ways of giving their value messages. (*to son*) What do you know, Jim, about how you give your value messages to your parents?

S: I don't know what you mean.

Th: Well, how do you let your mother, for instance, know that you like her when you are feeling that way. Everyone feels different ways at different times. When you are feeling glad your mother is around, how do you let her know?

S: I do what she tells me to do. Work and stuff.

Th: I see, so when you do your work at home, you mean this for a message to your mother that you're glad she is around.

S: Not exactly.

Th: You mean you are giving a different message then. Well, Alice, did you take this message from Jim to be a love message? (*to Jim*) What do you do to give your father a message that you like him?

S (*after a pause*): I can't think of nothin'.

Th: Let me put it another way. What do you know crystal-clear that you could do that would bring a smile to your father's face?

S: I could get better grades in school.

Th: Let's check this out and see if you are perceiving clearly. Do you, Alice, get a love message from Jim when he works around the house?

W: I s'pose—he doesn't do very much.

Th: So from where you sit, Alice, you don't get many love messages from Jim. Tell me, Alice, does Jim have any other ways that he might not now be thinking about that he has that say to you that he is glad you are around?

W (*softly*): The other day he told me I looked nice.

Th: What about you, Ralph, does Jim perceive correctly that if he got better grades you would smile?

H: I don't imagine I will be smiling for some time.

Th: I hear that you don't think he is getting good grades, but would you smile if he did?

H: Sure, hell, I would be glad.

Th: As you think about it, how do you suppose you would show it?

W: You never know if you ever please him.

Th: We have already discovered that you and Ralph have not yet developed crystal-clear ways of showing value feelings toward one another. Maybe you, Alice, are now observing this between Jim and Ralph. What do think, Ralph? Do you suppose it would be hard for Jim to find out when he has pleased you?

15. The therapist will not only exemplify what he means by clear communication, but he will teach his patients how to achieve it themselves.

    a. He will spell out the rules of communication accurately. In particular, he will emphasize the necessity for checking out meaning *given* with meaning *received*. He will see that the patient keeps in mind the following complicated set of mirror images:

—Self's idea (how I see me).

—Self's idea of other (how I see you).

—Self's idea of other's idea of self (how I see you seeing me).

—Self's idea of other's idea of self's idea of other (how I see you seeing me seeing you).

Only if a person is able to check back and forth across the lines of communication can he be sure that he has completed a clear exchange.

b. The therapist will help the patient to be aware of messages that are incongruent, confused, or covert.

c. At the same time, the therapist will show the patient how to check on invalid assumptions that are used as fact. He knows that members of dysfunctional families are afraid to question each other to find out what each really means. They seem to say to each other: "I can't let you know what I see and hear and think and feel or you will drop dead, attack, or desert me." As a result, each operates from his assumptions, which he takes from the other person's manifestations and thereupon treats as fact. The therapist uses various questions to ferret out these invalid assumptions, such as:

"What did you say? What did you hear me say?"

"What did you see or hear that led you to make that conclusion?"

"What message did you intend to get across?"

"If I had been there, what would I have seen or heard?"

"How do you know? How can you find out?"

"You look calm, but how do you feel in the stomach?"

d. Like any good teacher, the therapist will try to be crystal-clear.

—He will repeat, restate, and emphasize his own observations, sometimes to the point of seeming repetitious and simple. He will do the same with observations made by members of the family.

—He will also be careful to give his reasons for arriving at any conclusion. If the patient is baffled by some statement of the therapist's and does not know the reasoning behind it, this will only increase his feelings of powerlessness.

16. The therapist will be aware of the many possibilities of interaction in therapy.

a. In the therapeutic situation, the presence of the therapist adds as many dyads (two-person systems) as there are people in the family, since he relates to each member. The therapist, like the other people present, operates as a member of various dyads but also as the observer of other dyads. These shifts of position could be confusing to him and to the family. If, for example, he has taken someone's part, he should clearly state he is doing so.

b. The therapist clarifies the nature of interchanges made during therapy, but he has to select those that are representative since he can't possibly keep up with everything that is said. Luckily, family sequences are apt to be redundant, so one clarification may serve a number of exchanges.

c. Here is an illustration of the way the therapist isolates and underlines each exchange.

When the therapist states, "When you, Ralph, said you were angry, I noticed that you, Alice, had a frown on your face," this is an example of the therapist reporting himself as a monad ("I *see* you, Alice; I *hear* you, Ralph,"), and reporting to Ralph and Alice as monads (the use of the word *you,* followed by the specific name). Then, by the therapist's use of the word *when,* he establishes that there is a connection between the husband's report and the wife's report, thus validating the presence of an interaction.

If the therapist then turns to the oldest son, Jim, and says, "What do you, Jim, make of what just happened between your mother and father?" the therapist is establishing Jim as an observer, since family members may forget that they monitor each other's behavior.

When Jim answers, everyone knows what his perception is. If it turns out that Jim's report does not fit what either Alice or Ralph intended, then there is an opportunity to find out what was intended, what was picked up by Jim, and why he interpreted it that way.

17. Labeling an illness is a part of therapy that a therapist must approach with particular care.

a. A therapist, when he deals with a patient, is confronting a person who has been labeled by others or by himself as having emotional, physical, or social disorders. To the nontherapeutic observer, the behavior which signals the presence of a disorder is usually labeled "stupid," "crazy," "sick," or "bad."

b. The therapist will use other labels, like "mentally defective," "underachieving," "schizophrenic," "manic-depressive," "psychosomatic," "sociopathic." These are labels used by clinicians to describe behavior which is seen to be deviant: deviant from the rest of the person's character, deviant from the expectation of others, and deviant from the context in which the person finds himself.

c. The observations made by clinicians over the years have been brought together under a standardized labeling system called the *psychiatric nomenclature.* It is a method of shorthand used by clinicians to describe deviant behavior.

d. These labels often presuppose an exact duplication of all the individuals so labeled. Over the years, each of the labels has been given an identity, with prognosis and treatment implications based on the dimensions of that identity.

e. If a therapist has labeled a person "schizophrenic," for instance, he may have based his prognosis of that person on his ideas about schizophrenia, rather than on an observation of a person who, among other labels like "human being," "Jim," "husband," "father," "chemist," has the label "schizophrenic."

f. But neither the clinician nor any other person has the right to treat him only in terms of the label "schizophrenic" while losing sight of him as a total human being. No label is infallible because no diagnosis is, but by identifying the person with the label, the therapist shuts his mind to the possibility of different interpretations which different evidence might point to.

g. The therapist must say to his patient, in effect: You are behaving now with behavior which I, as a clinician, label "schizophrenia." But this label only applies *at this time, in this place,* and *in this context.* Future times, places, and contexts may show something quite different.

18. Let us close this discussion of the role of the therapist with a look at some of the specific advantages family therapy will have compared to individual or group therapy.

a. In family therapy, the therapist will have a greater opportunity to observe objectively. In individual therapy, since there are only two people, the therapist is part of the interaction. It is hard for him to be impartial. In addition, he must sift out the patient's own reactions and feelings from those which might be a response to clues from the therapist himself.

b. The family therapist will be able to get firsthand knowledge of the patient in two important areas.
—By observing the individual in his family, the therapist can see where he is in terms of his present level of growth.
—By observing a child in the family group, the therapist can find out how his functioning came to be handicapped. He can see for himself how the husband and wife relate to each other and how they relate to the child.
—This kind of firsthand knowledge is not possible in individual therapy, or even in group therapy, where the individual is with

members of his peer group and the kind of interaction that can be studied is limited to this single aspect.

19. As a therapist, I have found certain concepts useful, somewhat like measuring tools, in determining the nature and extent of dysfunction in a family.

a. I make an analysis of the techniques used by each member of the family for *handling the presence of differentness.* A person's reaction to differentness is an index of his ability to adapt to growth and change. It also indicates what attitudes he will have toward other members of his family, and whether he will be able to express these attitudes directly or not.

—The members of any family need to have ways to find out about and make room for their differentness. This requires that each can report directly what he perceives about himself and the other, to himself and to the other.

—Example: Janet misses her hatpin. She must say, "I need my hatpin (clear), which I am telling you, Betty, about, (direct), and it is the hatpin that I use for the only black hat I have (specific). Not: "Why don't you leave my hat alone?" or "Isn't there something you want to tell me?" or going into Betty's room and turning things upside-down (unclear, indirect, and unspecific).

—As I have said before, when one of the partners in a marriage is confronted with a differentness in the other that he did not expect, or that he did not know about, it is important that he treat this as an opportunity to explore and to understand rather than as a signal for war.

—If the techniques for handling differentness are based on determining who is right (war), or pretending that the differentness does not exist (denial), then there is a potential for pathological behavior on the part of any member of the family, but particularly the children.

b. I make what I call a *role function analysis* to find out whether the members of a family are covertly playing roles different from those which their position in the family demands that they play.

—If two people have entered a marriage with the hope of extending the self, each is in effect put in charge of the other, thus creating a kind of mutual parasitic relationship.

—This relationship will eventually be translated into something that looks like a parent-child relationship. The adults, labeled "husband" and "wife," may in reality be functioning as mother and son, father and daughter, or as siblings, to the confusion of the rest of the family and, ultimately, themselves.

—Here is an oversimplified example of the way things might go in such a family:

Suppose Mary takes over the role of sole parent, with Joe acting the part of her child. Joe then takes the part of a brother to their two children, John and Patty, and becomes a rival with them for their mother's affections. To handle his rivalry and prove his place, he may start drinking excessively, or he may bury himself in his work in order to avoid coming home. Mary, deserted, may turn to John in such a way as to make him feel he must take his father's place. Wishing to do so but in reality unable to, John may become delinquent, turning against his mother and choosing someone on the outside. Or he may accept his mother's invitation, which would be to give up being male and become homosexual. Patty may regress or remain infantile to keep her place. Joe may get ulcers. Mary may become psychotic.

—These are only some of the possibilities for disturbance in a family that has become dislocated by incongruent role-playing.

c. I make a *self-manifestation analysis* for each member of a family. If what a person says does not fit with the way he looks, sounds, and acts, or if he reports his wishes and feelings as belonging to someone else or as coming from somewhere else, I know that he will not be able to produce reliable clues for any other person interacting with him. When such behavior, which I call *manifesting incongruency,* is present in the members of a family to any large degree, there will be a potential for development of pathology.

d. In order to find out how the early life of each member of a family has affected his present ways of behaving, I make what I call a *model analysis.*

—This means that I try to discover who the models were (or are) that influenced each family member in his early life; who gave him messages about the presence and desirability of growth; who gave him the blueprint from which he learned to evaluate and act on new experience; who showed him how to become close to others.

—Because these messages have survival significance, the ways in which they are given will automatically determine the way the individual interprets later messages from other adults, who may not be survival-connected but who may be invested with survival significance, like spouses, in-laws, or bosses.

PART SIX

Counseling Psychology:
Educational and Guidance
Counseling

27

Counseling Psychology

C. H. Patterson

Cecil Holden Patterson was born in Lynn, Massachusetts, in 1912 and received his Ph.D. from the University of Minnesota in 1955. He began his career as a research assistant and instructor at Antioch College in Ohio. His interest in counseling psychology intensified during the 1940s, when he served as a counseling psychologist at veteran administration hospitals in New York state and in St. Paul, Minnesota. After a decade and a half at these hospitals, he left for the University of Illinois (Urbana) in 1960, where, at its College of Education, he continued his profession as a counseling psychologist. Since 1963 he has been professor of educational psychology. Among his works are *Theories of Counseling and Psychotherapy* (2nd ed., 1973); *An Introduction to Counseling in the School* (1971), which includes portions of his earlier work, *Counseling and Guidance in Schools: A First Course; Rehabilitation Counseling* (1969); *Relationship Counseling and Psychotherapy* (1974); and *Counseling and Psychology in Elementary Schools* (with H. Kaczkowski, 1975).

Patterson, who structured his counseling psychology along the lines of client-centered therapy, sees the quintescence of counseling as a "kind of relationship." The counseling relationship, therefore, has priority over the knowledge and technique of the counselor. Counseling, primarily involved with voluntary behavior change, entails influencing by utilizing goals and methods. Voluntary change is facilitated through counseling. Through counseling, limits determined by the goals of counseling are imposed on the client. The counselor's values and philosophy determine the goals, which in turn have a decided influence on the counselor's methods and technique.

Counseling Psychology Defined

1. In contrast to the attempt to create a new and different profession, this point of view attempts to prevent divisiveness among counselors simply' because they work in different settings and with different kinds of clients. Counseling is counseling, wherever and with whomever it is performed. The generic aspects of counseling are emphasized, and the common identity of counselors as members of a single profession is made central.

2. The major function of a counselor is counseling, whether in the elementary school, the secondary school, or the college or university. The recognition of counseling as the major function assures that counseling will be provided for elementary school children. It will not be sacrificed for consultation nor will it be pushed out by numerous other duties and activities. The counselor trained in counseling can also consult, but the consultant with no preparation in counseling cannot counsel.

3. The fact that the major function of the counselor is counseling does not mean that the counselor will not consult with teachers, administrators, and parents. It does mean that the counselor is a counselor and will be justified in retaining this designation or title.

4. The consultant who does not have direct relations with children *as a counselor* loses his effectiveness as a consultant. Contacts with children for the purpose of obtaining data as a basis for consultation are not sufficient. The consultant thus becomes no closer to children than the teacher, who also observes from an external point of view. His observations are evaluative, and he becomes remote from the children in terms of understanding their perceptions and feelings. His data are incomplete, inadequate, and one-sided, and leave out the important area of the perceptions, thoughts, feelings, and attitudes of the child. As time goes on his observations of individual children become more limited. The consultant becomes an expert on children, not on a particular child. Soon it may be felt unnecessary to have a counselor for every 300 or 400 or even 500 children. Since the consultant deals with children in general, he can be expected to give quick and easy consultation and advice and serve a thousand or more children. He will become like the school psychologist, with the eventual recognition and complaint—now universally heard about the psychologist—that his recommendations are too general, not useful, not practical, that he does not understand the specific child with whom the teacher is concerned, or the uniqueness of the problem.

The contention is often made that the counselor as a specialist in counseling is outside the school program, the mainstream of the school. However, the counselor who spends the major part of his time with children is not outside but as close to inside as it is possible to get, since the children share their perceptions and feelings with him. He is in an excellent position to know, and

C. H. Patterson, *An Introduction to Counseling in the School* (New York: Harper & Row, 1971), pp. 74–75, 109–12, 115, 129, 139–40, 143, 185–86.

to make recommendations about, the psychological climate (not only the learning climate) of the school. It is the consultant who is outside. This is the common meaning of the word—a consultant is not a participant, but someone from outside.

5. The counselor in the elementary school will certainly need to be well-grounded in the behavioral sciences or human behavior, particularly child development and child psychology. He will have a broader picture of developmental psychology throughout the life span—he must have this if he is to work with teachers, administrators, and parents. He will also be adequately trained in counseling, including play therapy, but with background in counseling both adolescents and adults. . . .

Characteristics of Counseling

What, then, is counseling? Is it concerned with influencing and changing behavior? Certainly it is. If this were not the case there would be little point to counseling. Counselors are interested in changing the client's behavior, but counseling is a particular kind of influencing, with particular methods and goals. First of all, counseling is concerned with voluntary behavior change. That is, the client wants to change and seeks the help of the counselor in making the change.

Second, the purpose of counseling is to provide the conditions which facilitate such voluntary change. These conditions respect the right of the individual to make his own choices. He is treated as an independent, responsible individual capable of making his own choices under appropriate conditions.

Third, as in any sphere of life, there are limits which are imposed on the individual. These limits are determined by the goals of counseling as accepted by the counselor.

All counselors have goals determined by their values or philosophy, which influence techniques and methods of counseling. Goals among counselors apparently vary, and although some counselors claim that their goal is only to help the client achieve his goals, they still do not accept all the goals of all their clients. Moreover, such a goal is sometimes a very narrow one, and one which is still determined by the counselor and imposed on the client. A goal accepted by many counselors, and one which appears to be consistent with the goals of society and a democratic philosophy, is the development of responsible independence. This is a goal which, while determined by the counselor and imposed upon the client, maximizes the client's freedom in making specific choices. Thus, counseling is concerned with changing behavior by providing a situation in which the client who desires to change can become more responsible, more independent, more in control of himself and his behavior.

How is this achieved? What are the common aspects or methods of counseling? What are the conditions under which such behavior change occurs? A common aspect of counseling is the interview, but, as already mentioned, not all interviewing is counseling. There are also those who feel the interview is no longer necessary. The application of conditioning in the changing of behavior is having a revival, and conditioning is being used in the interview to condition the verbal behavior of clients. This approach is called behavioral counseling, and it is suggested by some that the interview is not necessary for changing behavior by conditioning. However, there seems to be a confusion here between behavior change and counseling or therapy. Not all behavior change is counseling, and while conditioning is a method of behavior change, it is not counseling. Thus, while not all interviewing is counseling, counseling always involves interviewing.

The same might also be said of another common aspect of counseling—listening. All counselors listen to their clients, at least some of the time. But not all listening is counseling. Many other people listen to others at times. To be sure, the counselor listens in a special kind of way, but so do some other people some of the time.

The counselor understands his client. But again, so do others understand people, although again the counselor usually understands better and in a different sort of way. But the difference is quantitative rather than qualitative, so that we cannot say that understanding alone differentiates counseling from other situations.

Counseling is conducted in private, and the discussion is confidential. But there are other private and confidential interviews, such as those between the doctor and lawyer and their patients and clients, and the priest and parishioner in the confessional.

None of these characteristics alone constitutes counseling or differentiates it from all other interviews or interpersonal relationships. Counseling involves an interview, in which the counselor listens and attempts to understand the client, or counselee, in private and with an understanding that what the client says will be held in confidence. It is expected that there will be a change in the client's behavior, in some way or ways which he himself chooses or decides, within limits. This seems like an acceptable definition of counseling. But is it adequate? Not if, as has been indicated, it does not distinguish counseling from other relationships. Even the presence of all these factors does not differentiate between counseling and some other kinds of relationship which we would not consider counseling. What is there, then, about counseling which is different?

There are two other characteristics necessary for a counseling relationship. One is that one of the participants, the client, has a problem—specifically, a psychological problem. Second, and following from the first, the counselor is someone who is skilled in working with clients with psychological problems. This obviously requires some specialized training or preparation beyond that which the usual person has and different from that which other professional people have. This preparation and training is psychological in nature. . . .

The Counseling Relationship

The unique aspect of counseling is that it is a relationship between a client with a psychological problem and a counselor who is trained to help clients with such problems. This relationship shares many of the characteristics of other relationships, including relationships between other professional persons and their clients. It also has the characteristics of all good human relationships. Fiedler, in a study of the ideal therapeutic relationship, found that therapists of different views agreed in their descriptions of this relationship. Moreover, nontherapists described the ideal therapeutic relationship in the same manner as therapists, leading Fiedler to conclude that "the therapeutic relationship may therefore be but a variation of good interpersonal relationships in general."[1] These relationships include acceptance of and respect for others, understanding, mutual confidence and trust, genuineness, sincerity, openness, honesty, and integrity. . . .

However, if counseling is nothing more than the practicing of good human relationships, why is it so difficult to become a counselor—why shouldn't everyone be a counselor? To some extent, everyone who practices good human relationships is, at times, a counselor with some people, but there are certain characteristics of counseling which set it aside as a specific kind of relationship.

In the first place, the principles of good human relationships, though many of them are known, are not obvious, nor necessarily natural, nor easily practiced. The understanding of the nature of good human relationships is something that must be learned.

Second, the practice of these principles requires training and experience. The ability to apply the principles is related to the psychological characteristics, or mental health, of the individual applying them. It is not a matter of information or knowledge; it is a matter of attitudes.

Third, the implementation of these principles in a counseling relationship differs somewhat from their practice in everyday relationships. The counseling relationship is a special kind of relationship; it is a formal relationship between two persons who may, and perhaps preferably, have no other relationship. The counseling relationship is for the sole purpose of improving or restoring the mental health, adjustment, or functioning of one of the participants. The counselor consciously and purposefully practices the principles of good human relations for the benefit of the counselee. Whereas the application of the principles of good human relationships in general is for the purpose of maintaining good mental health among normal individuals, their application in counseling is to restore or improve the mental health of disturbed persons.

Fourth, the relationship is usually established between a trained individual and another individual who is in need of help or assistance by reason of

---

[1]F. E. Fiedler, "The Concept of an Ideal Therapeutic Relationship," *Journal of Counsel. Psychology,* 14 (1950):239–245.

being disturbed, unhappy, or in conflict because of an unsolved problem or another condition resulting in dissatisfaction with himself, or lack of self-respect or self-esteem.

Fifth, the relationship is established at the request or desire of the disturbed individual, is continued at his wish, and is characterized by certain conditions—privacy, confidentiality, set time limits, and regularity, on an appointment basis.

Sixth, the counseling relationship, even though it is a formal relationship and may be very limited in terms of time relative to the life of the individual (seldom more than an hour a day, more often an hour a week), is a closer, more intense, and deeper relationship than any ordinary social relationship. This is due to its purpose and to the application of the principles of good human relations in their purest form, divested of the formalities of the usual social relationships.

The basic approach to the counseling relationship, the philosophy of client-centered counseling, is simple and may be summarized in three beliefs, assumptions, or attitudes:

1. Each individual is a person of worth in himself and is therefore to be respected and valued as such.

2. Each individual is capable of assuming responsibility for himself. He can, and will under appropriate conditions, become a responsible, independent, self-actualizing person. Jersild suggests that " . . . human beings, from an early age, have more capacity for learning to face and to understand and to deal with the realities of life than we hitherto assumed in our psychological theories and in our educational practices."[2]

3. Each individual has the *right* to self-direction, to choose or select his own values and goals, to make his own decisions.

The counselor thus recognizes and respects the client as a unique, autonomous individual, worthy of acceptance as a human being, a person. His right to freedom of choice, to self-determination of his behavior, to live his own life, is recognized and respected. Moreover, it is recognized that coercion and pressure are detrimental to the client's taking responsibility for himself and reaching adequate decisions. . . .

The Counselor's Function

Our emphasis has been on the attitudes of the counselor in forming an atmosphere in which the client can achieve a feeling of security and self-esteem. But

---

[2]A. T. Jersild, "Self-Understanding in Childhood and Adolescence," *American Psychologist* 6 (1951):122–26.

what does the counselor do; how does he act; what does he say? How does he express these attitudes; how does he understand the client and convey this understanding to him? While the attitudes of the counselor are of first importance, their implementation must also be considered. Their expression in a therapeutic manner is not usually natural or automatic, and while it is true that their expression must become natural so that the counselor may be himself, genuine and not playing a role, it is also true that he must be his counseling or therapeutic self, not his social, or even teaching, self.

The objectives of the counselor are to show his genuine interest in the client, to show that he accepts the client as someone worthy of respect and esteem, and to understand the client and communicate this understanding to him. How can the counselor do this, while at the same time allowing the client to be responsible for himself, for his behavior and decisions, including his communications to the counselor, from the beginning of the counseling process?

The methods or techniques by which this can be accomplished appear to be simple, yet they are often difficult to practice. The basic activity of the counselor is listening, and this is often a difficult thing for a counselor to learn. It is difficult to listen to another because one is thinking about what one wants to say, but this kind of listening is not what is meant by listening in counseling. Listening is not, on the other hand, passive, but an active following of what the client is saying, or trying to say. It is listening without interference by one's own personal reactions and associations. The counselor's attention and interest are concentrated upon the client's communication, and the client is free to express himself as he desires, to tell his own story in his own way, without interruption, without questioning, without probing, without judgments. Remember that the counselor is trying to see things as the client sees them; he is not concerned with obtaining an ordered, complete life history, to be recorded and filed away, but with helping the client express his attitudes, feelings, concerns, and perceptions of himself and the world. . . .

Vocational Counseling

It thus becomes apparent that vocational counseling is more than the matching of aptitudes, abilities, and interests with job demands and job requirements. A definition of counseling as assisting the person to develop an understanding of himself and his environment and to integrate the two so that he can resolve problems, make choices, and develop and carry out plans is perhaps still adequate. However, this requires more than the use and interpretation of tests and the providing of occupational information. Super prefers a revised definition: "Vocational guidance is the process of helping a person to develop and accept an integrated and adequate picture of himself and of his role in the world of work, to test this concept against reality, and to convert it into reality, with satisfaction to himself and benefit to society."[3] ...

Testing in Vocational Counseling

Uses of Tests

Tests may be and are used in schools for a variety of purposes. The most common uses may be grouped under three headings: for administrative purposes, for classroom purposes, and for counseling purposes. These can be outlined as follows:

Administrative Purposes:
  Determining emphasis to be given different areas of instruction.
  Measuring the progress (or changes) in the school from year to year.
  Identifying the changing character of the student body.
  Determining the appropriateness of the school curricula for students of differing characteristics or ability levels.
  Determining how well students are attaining educational goals.
  Evaluating curricular experimentation.
  Evaluating the school as a unit.
  Providing evidence for improvement of public relations.
  Providing information for outside agencies.
  Providing basis for student placement and the formation of classroom groups or curriculum tracks.
  Providing basis for pupil promotion or retardation.

Classroom Purposes:
  Grouping pupils for instruction within a class.
  Determining reasonable level of classroom achievement for each pupil.
  Identifying pupils who need special diagnostic study and remedial instruction.
  Measuring class progress over a period of time.
  Appraising relative achievement within a class.
  Assigning course grades.

---

[3]D. E. Super, *The Psychology of Careers* (New York: Harper & Row, 1957), p. 197.

Counseling Purposes:
   Building realistic self-pictures on the part of pupils.
   Helping pupils to set education and vocational goals.
   Helping pupils choose an occupation or plan for further education.
   Discovering interests of which the pupil may not be aware.
   Improving counselor, teacher, and parent understanding of problem
      cases.
   Helping pupils select suitable courses of study.
   Predicting success in future educational work.
   Identifying superior or gifted students for scholarship purposes.[4] ...

The Purpose of Tests in Guidance Counseling

What, then, is the purpose of tests in client-centered counseling? The answer should be clear. *Tests are used to assist the client in evaluating himself.* It is the client who evaluates, not the counselor. The ultimate purpose of the tests —indeed the purpose of counseling—is not to help the counselor understand the client (though they may do this, and understanding of the client by the counselor is necessary) but to help the client understand himself. This confusion about the ultimate goal of counseling, the failure to recognize that this goal is not simply knowledge about or understanding of the client by the counselor, has led to a misunderstanding of the place of data and information about the client in counseling. The result has been an overemphasis upon the collection of data, including test data, by the counselor. It is not what the counselor knows about the client, but what the client knows about himself, which is important. The client must make his own decisions; therefore, he must make the evaluations. ...

Group Counseling and Individual Counseling

There are many basic similarities between individual and group counseling. The goal is the same—the development of self-actualizing behavior. The essential conditions are the same, with the counselor providing empathic understanding, respect and warmth, and genuineness. The counselor functions in

---

[4]Adapted from H. H. Remmers, N. L. Gage, & J. F. Rummel, *A Practical Introduction to Measurement and Evaluation* (New York: Harper & Row, 1960), pp. 80–81.

much the same way—understanding the communications of individuals and facilitating communication. In the group the counselor must be alert to the interrelationships among group members as well as the relationships between himself and the individual members.

The interrelationships among the group members is perhaps the major difference between individual and group counseling. For the counselor, this is more a quantitative than a qualitative difference. For the participants, however, it introduces a number of elements not present in individual counseling.

The presence of other individuals in the counseling relationship makes it possible for each client to have experiences which are not possible in individual counseling. In individual counseling, there is usually concern with the interpersonal relationships of the client. He discusses these relationships with the counselor, and he may engage in efforts to change his interpersonal behavior and report these experiences to the counselor. The counselor also can develop some understanding of the client's ways of relating to others by the way the client relates to him. This, however, may not be typical of his relationships with other persons in his environment. The counselor is a special person, with special training and experience that leads the client to view him as an authority, at least as a professional authority. In the case of school counseling, the counselor is older and is identified often with the authority aspects of the teaching situation and administration. The client may relate quite differently to his peers and to his subordinates or to younger people.

In the group situation the client demonstrates the nature of his relationships with others, and this becomes one of the major concerns of the group. The client can thus develop a direct understanding of his effects on others and their perceptions of him on the basis of immediate feedback. Moreover, he can experiment with changing his interpersonal behavior and obtain immediate knowledge of the results.

On the other hand, in the group the client, in addition to learning about his impact on others, can experience the impact of others on him in a situation where he can become more aware of this and can communicate it to others. This two-way communication of perceptions and experiences provides practice in human interpersonal relationships in a situation which is optimal for learning. Individual counseling does not provide this direct learning experience in interpersonal relationships.

This experience involves learning to listen to, accept, and understand others—in effect learning the principles of good human relationships. This amounts to training in human relationships through experience rather than instruction. This is the basis for the description of T-groups as laboratory groups in human relations.

This learning is the basis for the observation that in group counseling the participants become, in a sense and to some extent, cotherapists, because the characteristics of a good human relationship are those of the counseling or therapy relationship. Thus, participants in group counseling gain experience in helping others, with its resulting satisfactions.

There are some other aspects of group counseling which are not necessarily beneficial and can be harmful. Group dynamics are powerful and thus have the potential for harm as well as good. The characteristics of group cohesion and group identification are significant in this regard. Most group leaders desire, and foster, group cohesion and the identification of individuals with the group. The productivity of the group may be increased as these characteristics develop. This may be a desirable outcome for a task-oriented group, but in a counseling group too great a level of group cohesion and group identification may not be desirable. Two dangers arise. First, the individuals may become so closely identified with the group that their relationships outside the group suffer. They may become overdependent on the group, so that the counseling group becomes an in-group, leading to conflict with out-groups. A second danger lies in the power of the group to lead to conforming behavior. Acceptance in the group requires a certain amount of conformity. Overemphasis on group cohesion may result in excessive demands for conformity. There is some evidence that school counselors view group counseling as a means to "shape up" or bring into line nonconforming students. Group pressures are powerful, and the use of group pressure to manipulate the behavior of students is unprofessional, if not unethical.

Group counseling, finally, may have an advantage over individual counseling in that some individuals find it easier to express and discuss their problems in a group than with the counselor alone. The example of other clients, the recognition that others have similar, or equally or more serious, problems, may make it easier for a particular group member to bring out his problem. The acceptance and support of the group is also a facilitating factor.

28

COUNSELING PSYCHOLOGY AND THE COUNSELING RELATIONSHIP

Edward S. Bordin

Born in Philadelphia in 1913, Edward S. Bordin was educated at Temple University and Ohio State University, receiving his Ph.D. from the latter institution in 1942. Upon completion of his studies, Bordin was affiliated with the University of Minnesota's counseling bureau. In 1946 he left to accept a position at Washington State University, where he remained two years. His long association with the University of Michigan began in 1948 as chief of the Counseling Division of the Bureau of Psychological Services.

Virtually Bordin's entire career encompasses an interest in counseling in an educational atmosphere. His early interest in counseling is evidenced by the publication of "Diagnosis in Counseling and Psychotherapy" (1946), followed by his book, *Training of Psychological Counselors* (1950). He is best known for *Psychological Counseling* (1955), which was revised in 1968. His *Research Strategies in Psychotherapy* appeared in 1974.

Regarding counseling as aiding persons whose discomforts are of insufficient severity to seek psychotherapy or who face a critical stage of development in their lives, Bordin defined counseling and psychotherapy as "terms which have been used to apply to interactions where one person, referred to as the counselor or the therapist, has taken the responsibility for making his role in the interaction process contribute positively to the other person's personality development."[1] The primary goal of the counselor is that of understanding the obstacles to furthering the growth and development of personality—obstacles typical of the individual's specific and temporarily limited difficulty. The crux of the counseling process is "the ability to be sensitive in the fullest possible way to the reactions of clients and to one's own reactions to them."[2] Counseling, like psychotherapy, is concerned with affect, motivation, and personality but differs from dynamic psychotherapy in its cognitive orientation, that is, in its rational approach of engaging in a problem-

---

[1]Edward S. Bordin, *Psychological Counseling,* 2nd ed. (New York: Appelton-Century-Crofts, 1968), p. 10.

[2]Bordin, *Psychological Counseling,* p. 105.

solving process. The counseling relationship includes three dimensions: (1) the ambiguous, (2) the cognitive-conative, and (3) the personal. Acceptance, understanding, and interpretation are three principal techniques of the counselor, as well as the use of tests, which are especially helpful with educational and vocational counseling.

The Counseling Relationship in Counseling Psychology

Counseling Defined

Our developmental orientation poses the question of what distinguishes the counseling experience from the many others which shape the individual's personality. In the course of living, many kinds of interpersonal experiences further personality growth. When one person interacts with another, the experience may either go according to plan or inadvertently play a role in the growth process. *Counseling, as well as psychotherapy, are terms which have been used to apply to interactions where one person, referred to as the counselor or the therapist, has taken the responsibility for making his role in the interaction process contribute positively to the other person's personality development. . . .*

We have already remarked that personality deficits become apparent when people face situations which bring their personal inadequacies to the fore, and that at such times the average person is most amenable to the kinds of therapeutic influence which lead to further emotional integration. It follows, then, that counseling can be most effective when a person seeks help in dealing with a specific personal problem. This means that the counseling service must be perceived by clients as a place where a person experiencing some situational difficulty may profitably seek help. . . .

The Goal of Psychological Counseling

We have discussed counseling in the context of personality development and disturbance. We shall see that this kind of personal service has its roots in the activities designed to help persons with the specific difficulties they face without very much involvement with the long-term implications of the aid. The implications of this later concern with personality development reach much

Edward S. Bordin, *Psychological Counseling,* 2nd ed. (New York: Appleton-Century-Crofts, 1968), pp. 10, 11, 12, 13, 221–31, 429–32.

farther than is at first evident. They mean, for one thing, that when a troubled person comes to the psychological counselor, as he often does, with concrete decisions to be made, specific problems to be solved, or particular situations to be clarified, the counselor's *primary* goal is not to contribute to the resolution of these immediate situations. That major goal lies farther ahead. The primary goal requires understanding of the obstacles to further personality growth and development that are typified by this person's rather specific and temporarily limited difficulty. The counselor aims to contribute to the removal of these deeper lying personal obstacles and to bring about the reactivation of the psychological growth processes in that person. . . .

The Counselor's Initial Orientation

As the counselor sits down to talk with a new client one of his most definite feelings is the need to begin to understand this client. He wants to be able to see the client's needs so he can meet them in a helpful way. The inexperienced counselor is often impatient with the necessarily slow process of accumulating understanding by constantly attentive listening and observing. Sometimes he foolishly rushes ahead, assuming he can more efficiently extract the information he wants through direct questioning or by indirectly (or "subtly" as he hopes) guiding the conversation. The inexperienced counselor may overvalue the neatly concise outline of the client's past history and be relatively insensitive to the cues the client communicates by his tone of voice, his pace and his interruptions of the level on which talk is proceeding, his changes in bodily position and facial expression, and all the other signs not found in the mere words.

   Too often, in reviewing therapeutic situations the student concentrates on only one person—the client. The counselor seems to be merely an impersonal equation; he may act according to one formula or another which will have the expected effect upon the client. But of course the fact is that the counselor is also a person, and human. He has other goals than simply being an effective mechanism at the service of the client, even though that role may be consistent with his other goals. The counselor wants to be an adequate person, but his adequacy is only partially defined in terms of his counseling role. He wants clients to have confidence in him, and he wants to feel likeable and respected. As we have reiterated, the counseling situation is so very frequently one in which a client presents his problems as pretty much outside of himself. To the degree that the counselor sees himself as providing mental health service, he is likely to experience considerable pressure to have his client move from this impersonal to a more personal plane of discussion. Adequacy or inadequacy in the counselor, professionally judged, often becomes closely tied to this criterion. For the beginning counselor the issue of adequacy is likely to be even more intense, since he has less experience and less competence in meeting such interpersonal responsibilities.

Clarifying the Goal

In our earlier discussions of the interpretive process we mentioned briefly the importance of the client's strong conviction that he needs therapy. Let us now consider this a little more fully, particularly as it bears upon initiating therapeutic relationships. Before the counselor's interpretations can help the client deal more freely and more fully with his own feelings, the client must have reached an understanding that the complicated maze of his own feelings has been an important factor in bringing about whatever dissatisfying situation he finds himself in. He must have been presented with a reasonably clear statement of what the therapeutic task is and must have accepted his share of the commitment to it. Counselors' interpretations are likely to call attention to ways in which a client seems to be now either attempting to deny his initial acceptance of the fact of his own involvement in his difficulties or trying to avoid the therapeutic task of communicating his feelings. It is the client's clear recognition that he needs help and that he is a prime source of his own difficulties which helps him to use the counselor's interpretation as a means of reexamining himself from a new point of view. Without these initial commitments the interpretive process is relatively meaningless.

In their eagerness to have the client move from looking outside to looking inside himself, counselors will knowingly or unknowingly make efforts to entice the client into a more personal relationship. They will encourage the client to become more personal by showing an interest in his feelings and by taking advantage of whatever specific signs he shows of needing to express his feelings. Thus, the client may have shifted from matter-of-fact and relatively uninvolved talking about his problem and the possible conclusions or decisions he might make into a much more personal and direct outpouring of his own feelings, without at the same time having arrived at any particular acknowledgment, either explicitly or implicitly, that these feelings are a critical part of the problem he faces.

Discussions at this more affective level may continue beyond the first interview, with the counselor already congratulating himself on having been so successful in involving the client in a therapeutic process. However, the counselor is often astonished at the consequences of his failure to help the client arrive at a redefinition of his goal and task. Suddenly the client will pull up short and say something like, "Well, this has been very interesting; now I guess we'd better get down to business and talk about my specific decision." Then he proceeds to return to a very matter-of-fact, externally oriented discussion of his problem in which the feelings discussed earlier are pretty much disregarded. At other times, the client may suddenly terminate the interviews with a remark like, "Well, I guess this is as much of your time as I ought to take. It has been very worthwhile talking to you, and I would be tempted to continue but I don't think I have any right to."

What has appeared to the counselor as a revision in the client's conception of his problem and of the uses to which counseling can be put has all the while seemed to the client an irrelevant interlude. Where the shift to a more personal relationship has been induced by efforts to seek gratification for some deep-lying impulses through the relationship with the counselor, it may even be associated with considerable guilt. Often these guilt feelings are used by the client in partial defense against getting more deeply involved in the therapeutic process. Many times the break will occur at some point where his discussions with the counselor were approaching especially sensitive and firmly defended areas of his emotional life.

Clarifying the Task

All therapists, whether they strive for comprehensive personality change, as is the case in psychotherapy, or for relatively restricted change, such as characterizes counseling, plan to draw the client into a relationship which they can then use as the vehicle for achieving therapeutic goals. To establish this relationship, the therapist must give the client a task which will facilitate its forward movement. That task is, naturally, revealing himself to the therapist. Since counseling has been initiated by the client, it is natural for him to start by telling why he came. And since he is usually unknown to the counselor, he begins by telling the counselor something about himself and his general situation. The early phases of the task of communicating are accomplished with relatively little defining from the counselor. Many times he need only pause expectantly after he and the client are seated, and the client will take the cue to explain why he is there. A certain proportion of fearful and passive clients will want the counselor to take the initiative and set even this first task more overtly. This the counselor can accomplish with some simple direct question like, "Would you like to tell me what brings you to see me?"

It is beyond the point where the client tells why he wants counseling and has reached the boundary of his initial free communications about himself that some of the important clarifying problems appear. First of all, the counselor must decide how close to free association he wants to come in the task he imposes. .... We must emphasize the fact that the definition of the task is communicated only partially by explicit statements such as these:

1. This is a situation which is different from the usual social situation. In the usual social situation you have certain thoughts or feelings which it would be considered a social mistake to express. They may be critical thoughts about the other person. They may be certain kinds of admiring thoughts. They may be thoughts which are far away from the particular people and the particular topics being discussed. In this situation you are expected to give expression to all thoughts, no matter how inappropriate or how irrelevant they seem to be.

2. Almost anything you think of to tell me about this problem will probably be useful to talk about.

3. Whatever you want to tell me will probably be useful.

4. We find that when people try to think through these questions out loud with us it can help them to see their problems in a new light.

The definition of the task is conveyed not only by such statements but also by indirect verbal and nonverbal cues. For example, as the counselor responds to the client's recital of his problem or his general circumstances either by questioning him or by indicating that he understands, the counselor inevitably, through the selective character of his responses, lets the client see in part what aspects of his communications he considers most important. The fact that the counselor asks questions about or otherwise responds to the client's attitudes indicates his special interest in them. If, for example, he responds to the clients attitudes toward and relationships with parents, he is signifying his special interest in that set of feelings and relationships. But of course he can do this in other ways than by direct reference to them. He can show it by his posture, whether relaxed or leaning forward as though to catch every word, or by cues to the amount of his involvement and interest in what is being communicated. He can show by the loudness and tone of voice that he is reacting differently to different things the client is talking about. The client, who feels uncomfortable in this situation and feels unfamiliar with its demands, and who is consequently looking for any sign that he is meeting the demands of the situation positively and constructively, seizes upon and reacts to every cue the counselor gives him.

As we suggested ..., in most of the short-term contacts that arise in counseling, the client comes to the counselor without feeling any need to admit a pronounced inability to handle his problems and certainly with no salient expectation of becoming personal or giving up responsibility for himself, even momentarily. Thus, the typical counseling client is not prepared to accept a task which is pure free association. This client will be given simply the task of telling about feelings which seem to have a bearing on his problem. He will naturally be expected to go beyond reporting on mere matters of fact. He must be willing to come out with his feelings. It is not unusual for a counseling relationship to proceed stepwise from the client's initial task of describing his problems to the free communication of his thoughts and feelings without taking any responsibility for their relevance.

Meeting the Client's Initial Needs

This topic, already touched upon in the discussion of variation in intake procedures and of the types of tasks defined for the client, must be treated more directly.

We go back again to the very beginning of the counseling relationship. At this point many counselors are moved to establish rapport by such devices as talking about the weather, trying to find something out about his client's antecedents or whom he knows. All this is in order to get on common ground with him. In most instances this turns out to be a relatively artificial process. We note that the client is so preoccupied with an explanation for soliciting counsel that he is unresponsive to the counselor's chattiness. Since he has thought enough about his difficulties to come to someone for help, he is anxious to begin "really" talking. Time and again in these cases it is apparent that he is wondering why the counselor is wasting his time with small talk. Fortunately, the counselor has a ready-made relationship to the client, established by his purpose in coming, so he can get going quickly. However, we do not want to suggest that the counselor should be a lifeless machine or a cold fish. If the weather does in fact seem to be extraordinary, a remark about it certainly would not be out of place, since most people who meet casually mention it to each other. But this should come as a spontaneous reaction—this day the weather *is* something to remark about—rather than out of a false heartiness of the Babbitt variety.

As the client begins to describe his problem, he may convey a sense of particular urgency about one aspect of it. Perhaps he is a student who must complete registration that week and feels helpless in the face of the big or little decisions this involves, or the father of a family who must meet an immediate financial obligation, or an unmarried pregnant girl who must make some kind of arrangements for the period immediately before and after delivery. The urgency of these needs will vary. If they exceed the client's present capacity to meet them, the counselor cannot remain detached, doggedly adhering to the role of an uninvolved sounding board for the client's feelings. It is out of the question for him to ask the client to postpone facing such needs until perchance he has somehow acquired the capacity for meeting them without aid. The client must be freed of the relatively disorganizing pressures and helped to avoid the panic that comes from facing overwhelming tasks without prospect of succor. At the same time, the counselor must beware of underestimating the client's resources so that he helps the client beyond what is necessary. The more the client is able to contribute to the solution of his own problem, the less he will suffer from having had to be dependent upon someone else. The fact that the solution is not all the counselor's doing, but the client's also, can be a source of encouragement to the client that he can take over full responsibility for himself in the near future.

Many times meeting the client's immediate needs is not so much a matter of helping the client take care of some pressing demand as it is the much more subtle and prolonged process of adapting one's relationship with the client to his present capacity for interacting, all for the purpose of ultimately closing in on the client's difficulties. In addition to gauging the client's readiness for a relatively ambiguous task, the counselor must be able to recognize when he is going to be threatened by any appreciable decrease in distance between him and the counselor. A counselor's efforts to establish the kind of friendly atmosphere that prevails among social associates may foster unnecessary defensive reactions. Conversely, the counselor who maintains his impersonal remoteness may repel many clients, particularly those who are very dependent. Similarly, the time when and the degree to which a counselor encourages objective analysis will be related to the particular client and his state. With some clients the counselor may have to interpret early, to foster their recognition that helping them control their feelings will also be part of the process.

The Diagnostic Potentialities of Initial Interviews

Since we advocate that counseling start with the very first interview rather than allotting time in first contacts to diagnostic testing, we must underline the need for exploring the diagnostic potentialities of the early meetings. The unusual diagnostic possibilities offered by the first contact have been emphasized by Voiland, who writes of them:

> To view the client's reaction as he presents his problem for the first time has a diagnostic advantage which is invaluable and which seldom presents itself at a later time in the same dynamic way, for as the contact develops, the material becomes more detailed and consequently more difficult to sift in terms of significant trends. For this reason it is highly important that the worker develop real sensitivity to the client's problem which can be utilized to the fullest at the first points of contact.[3]

---

[3]A. L. Voiland, M. L. Grundelach, and M. Corner, *Developing Insight in Initial Interviews* (New York: Family Service Association, 1947), pp. 6–7.

Many other students of counseling and psychotherapy have written in the same vein, stressing the usefulness of going back to the first interview as a means of regaining perspective on the client's problems. They believe the first interview frequently contains the clearest representation of the core problem. The client's first efforts to verbalize his problem and the feelings he experiences as he sets about sharing it with another person are likely to lead him to express his major conflicts unconsciously, thus providing a basis for understanding all of his other ambivalent feelings. It seems probable that if the initial interview or interviews are to have this potential significance, certain requisite conditions must be met. In the kind of first interview that has the characteristics mentioned above, a client, approaching the therapeutic situation for the first time, has already reached the stage of feeling that his difficulties are to some extent of his own making. He has already decided that he needs to understand himself, his emotions, impulses, and feelings. Because he has reached this decision, he will be predisposed to reveal his inner life as fully as he can comfortably. In these circumstances there is an opportunity to observe in what terms he chooses to begin talking about these issues, how he tries to describe himself and his feelings, and at what point and in what ways he has to defend himself against too-free expression of affect.

A certain number of clients will come to the counseling situation with this kind of readiness. In such instances it should be possible to obtain considerable understanding of each of them and their present ways of operating. Many clients will not have reached this stage of thinking. Their first interview will reflect how they are defining their problem and how they define their relationship to the counselor but may not reveal a great deal about their personality structure. This is not surprising. Virtually the same phenomenon is encountered in diagnostic projective testing when the subject has not been adequately prepared for the confidential relationship. He is likely to give only a barren, rigidly controlled record, reflecting his condition with his defenses up. Very perceptive observation can sometimes enable one to make use of the slight variability in behavior which appears in even this type of interview; for example, attention to points where the client seems to approach the threshold of involvement and how he tries to withdraw from such involvement may provide important cues.

The function of ambiguous characteristics in the therapist and the therapeutic task in understanding the patient has already been discussed. The freedom with which the client responds to this ambiguous situation can be an index of his overall flexibility and spontaneity. The particular aspects of his problem which he chooses to take up and their order of appearance, along with the accompanying affect, can all be meaningful. One of the important diagnostic sets of the counselor will be the amount of attention he gives to understanding the sequence of the client's communications and his surmises concerning what has accounted for this sequence. He must be able to pick out what parts of the continuity have been fostered by his own defining behavior and what parts of the continuity reflect the motivational sets of the client. To take an example, the client starts talking about his inability to control his anger. He would like to be able to keep his temper better. He is afraid that he will do something that he will regret. Under the influence of anger he fears he might actually do serious harm to someone else. Then he begins to talk about how his father seems to be able to control his own anger and how his father has given him suggestions for improving his self-control. He speaks of his admiration for his father and how much he desires to be like him. Then he begins to talk about teachers he has admired and how often he has become disappointed with them and how many times his admiration has turned to dislike. He talks about how he often loses his temper with teachers and how guilty he feels afterward.

Already the emerging pattern and continuity are easy to see. This client's communications and his feelings are flowing quite freely. It is true that he has defenses against his feelings. He is not expressing them in their most direct form. At the same time, he is moving toward direct expression with relatively little anxiety and relatively little holding back. Other clients might be evolving the same pattern but with greater anxiety and therefore with a more subtle continuity, a continuity which taxes the sensitivity of the counselor. Each time the client introduces a new topic the counselor must ask himself, "How did he get from the previous topic to this one? What is the connection between them?" In some instances the counselor will become aware that the client, in going to the new topic, was reacting to something that he, the counselor, had said earlier. Or he may note that one thing the two topics have in common is that they deal with the same affect, whatever it is. The counselor will need to seek connections between the persons the client mentions under each succeeding topic. He must try to understand their functional psychological relationship. In this example, the first topic deals with the client's father; the topic which follows deals with teachers. In some way, teachers are a lot like fathers. They are older. They have authority. They are also looked up to and emulated.

If we examine the above communication with the assumption that fathers and teachers are in some respects equivalent, still further impressions emerge. Father was talked about directly when his helpful and admirable qualities were being emphasized. But when the client discusses feelings of disappointment, anger, and dislike, teachers are cited as the objects. When we examine the beginning of the client's message, its total import is revealed. It seems reasonable to say the client started with concern about his anger and feared that he would yield to aggressive impulses. His association to hurting someone is to talk about his father. Can his father be the object of his anger and does he fear for his father's safety? The tenor of his remarks seems to deny this. Can this be their purpose? The shift to teachers, the implication that they may be the objects of his aggressive impulses, and his concern that this is so seem to give affirmative answers to our questions. We may want to test our impressions with data obtained from his subsequent communications before we give them more than hypothetical status, but we will have made an important start toward understanding the conflicting feelings which beset this young man. Continued alert listening to the sequences of his verbal behavior will insure the richness of the diagnostic yield.

In most cases, initial contacts will offer the counselor similar opportunities to acquire important diagnostic insights that help him make the decisions necessary at this point. He will be able to judge the level of disclosure on which the client is approaching his problem, the salient features of his motivation and his conflicts, and his methods of defending against the latter. In a small proportion of cases, the counselor will feel he has not been able to establish contact with the client. He may observe enough to feel sure the client's difficulties are profound. When such problems face the counselor in the initial meeting, he will need to proceed with caution, avoiding any definite therapeutic move until there has been an opportunity for more thorough diagnostic analysis, including the administration of psychological tests. . . .

Process Issues in the Developmental Model

When a client seeks counseling at a transition point in his vocational career, the counselor must decide how to go about facilitating an optimal self-confrontation under conditions of minimal anxiety. We see three stages in this process: an exploratory, contract-setting stage, a stage of critical decision, which often blends almost imperceptibly into the third stage, working through problems indigenous to that stage of his development or, where present, dealing with long-standing chronic problems. The major problem is to avoid either overly superficial abortive self-examination or seduction into an equally abortive psychotherapy. As a vehicle for illustrating how one treads this fine line, we will use the case of Kenneth, who was seen for twelve interviews. Kenneth was a moderately obsessive character whose chronic difficulties may ultimately force him into intensive psychotherapy. He asked for counseling near the end of his freshman year saying that he was not certain of his vocational preference and expected to be helped by interviews and tests. Kenneth was casually but neatly dressed, held himself rather stiffly, and betrayed his initial anxiety by the tightness with which he kept his hands clasped. His speech, simultaneously rapid, tense, and halting, betrayed little of his early years in England other than his pronounciation of "dog" as "dahg." With respect to his long-standing character problem and his initial anxiety Kenneth was not a typical vocational counseling client. At the same time he was oriented to deal with a circumscribed problem—vocational choice—rather than with any sensed feeling of personal inadequacy.

Exploration and Contract Setting

At the outset the vocational counselor must tread a fine line between two major pitfalls. On the one hand, the client may have a very restricting set toward what is relevant to his choice. He may see counseling as no more than obtaining the results of tests and examining their implications in terms of possible occupations. He sees all of the impact coming from outside, supplied by the counselor. His, the client's, role is a passive and compliant one. Looking inward is not part of his task. The other pitfall of inappropriately offering or demanding a therapeutic effort flows from the counselor's efforts to counteract this restricting set. Somehow he must strive to disclose to his client that the question of his vocational choice deserves a closer, more painstaking look at the kind of person he is, his ways of seeking gratification and protecting himself from anxiety, and the images of self that go along with it. But this effort must not become an ultimatum to acknowledge personal inadequacy and to commit oneself to unlimited confiding that a long-term psychotherapeutic effort implies. Unless the latter pitfall is avoided, clients with little anxiety are likely to leave counseling rather than comply and those with more than developmental problems may be seduced into a therapeutic effort without the necessary commitment.

How can the counselor facilitate a meaningful self-confrontation without forcing a therapeutic contract to confide without limitations? He does this, we believe, by staying with the client's focus on the issue of vocational choice. Our view of the personal issues involved in the choice of vocation raises questions bearing on the individual's doubts and hesitations, which disclose to him the relevance of coming to grips with himself rather than confining his efforts to an examination of the externals of a vocation. Almost everyone has thoughts and feelings about occupations which are intimately related to his reactions to and observations of himself. Even if these reactions are not on the surface, they are usually readily available and reflected indirectly in comments about the occupations he has considered, how he came to be interested, and the hesitations he may feel about choosing any one of them. Eliciting such reactions and probing for the kind of future he imagines for himself in an occupation often serves as a means of establishing communication regarding the individual's desires, his needs, and his anxieties about fulfilling them. To be able to sense the self-struggle that lies behind a client's talk about the occupations he has considered and to make contact with these struggles within the occupational context, the counselor must become thoroughly immersed in the above described way of viewing occupations. He must, in addition, have given thought to the developmentally based conflicts that might be provoked by particular vocations. . . . An overly stern father, one who is unable to balance his demanding and controlling ways with warm friendliness and willingness to share his interests and enthusiasms with his son, can induce a strong but highly fearful identification. Such a son will fear the task of following in his father's footsteps, yet be reluctant to reject father's demand that he emulate him. Deans of engineering schools are familiar with the timid, reluctant boys dragged into their offices by domineering, unrealistic fathers. Sometimes anger and rebellion, covertly expressed, is the son's response. He may be capable of functioning as an engineer and under freer circumstances would have chosen the profession of his own accord, but finds that the only way he can express his rebellion against his father is by failing out of the training program. With this general framework in mind the counselor will be able to react similarly to occupations not yet the objects of formal investigation.

PART SEVEN

*Hypnotic Technique in
Psychotherapy*

29

HYPNOTHERAPY

Lewis R. Wolberg

Lewis Robert Wolberg, born in Russia on July 4, 1905, was educated at the University of Rochester (A.B., 1926) and Tufts College Medical School (M.D., 1930). After interning at Vassar Brothers Hospital in 1931 and at Los Angeles General Hospital in 1932, he spent his residency at Boston Psychopathic Hospital as assistant executive officer and then served as senior supervising psychiatrist at Kings Park State Hospital from 1933 to 1945.

His teaching career began at the New York Medical College, a post he assumed in 1946. From 1946 to 1970, he was on the faculty of the Psychoanalytic Division of New York Medical College, where he is presently dean and medical director at the Postgraduate Center for Mental Health. Since 1970, Wolberg has been clinical professor of psychiatry at New York University Medical School and attending psychiatrist at the Medical Center. His professional associations include life fellow of the American Psychiatric Association and fellow of the Academy of Psychoanalysis.

Wolberg believes that, theoretically, everyone can be hypnotized, although, in actual practice, only 90 percent can be. There is a correlation between one's suggestibility and the ease with which one can be hypnotized. Hypnotic therapy must proceed gradually from the early sessions, which are used to establish confidence in the therapist and intensification of the trance depth. In anxiety neurosis the objective is the alleviation of anxiety by fortifying ego defenses against danger, but if anxiety is related to personality structure then hypnoanalysis is indicated. Conversion hysteria is most responsive to hypnotherapy, but prolonged psychotherapy is required to delve into the personality problem causing the condition. Like obsessional neurosis, anxiety hysteria characterized by phobias responds poorly to hypnosis, hence requires indirect and devious means of approach and therapy. By way of contrast, hypnosis is dramatically effective therapy for the traumatic neuroses and is almost as effective in psychosomatic disorders. Character disorders, however, are as resistant to hypnosis as they are to ordinary methods of psychotherapy; and in respect to psychoses, it is at best merely an adjunct. Intensification of the patient's suggestibility, thereby facilitating the elimination of repressions by psychotherapy, is an important value of hypnosis.

A prolific writer, Wolberg's papers include over fifty publications plus twenty chapters in a variety of books. Among his more important books are *The Psy-*

chology of Eating (1936); *Medical Hypnosis* (two volumes, 1948); *The Technique of Psychotherapy* (1954; 2nd ed., 1967); *Hypnoanalysis* (1945; 2nd ed., 1964); *Short-Term Psychotherapy* (1965), of which he was the editor; and *Psychotherapy and the Behavioral Sciences* (1966).

The Technic of Hypnosis

Susceptibility to Hypnosis

Hypnotizability is a normal trait, and theoretically at least, every person can be hypnotized. In actual practice, however, only approximately 90 percent can be inducted into a trance state. What determines the resistance to hypnosis in those persons who are not amenable to induction is not entirely clear. No correlation has been found between hypnosis and body build, extroversion, introversion, race, sex, or social position. On the other hand, age apparently plays some part in susceptibility, children being slightly more amenable and older people slightly less amenable to hypnotic suggestion than young adults.

Many efforts have been made to establish a correlation between mental traits and susceptibility to hypnosis. Findings have been contradictory and hence are not reliable. . . .

Suggestibility Tests

A correlation exists between some forms of suggestibility and susceptibility to hypnosis. In therapeutic hypnosis, suggestibility tests may be utilized as a preparatory stage to trance induction. They often get a patient into a suitable frame of mind, developing in him confidence in his ability to respond to suggestions that will lead to a trance. There are many kinds of suggestibility tests, the most common being the postural-sway test, hand levitation, hand clasp, and the pendulum test. . . .

The Depth of Trance

A number of attempts have been made to classify the symptoms of hypnosis into stages of varying depth.[1] These attempts have not proven themselves to

---

Susceptibility to Hypnosis, from Lewis R. Wolberg, *The Principles of Hypnotherapy,* MEDICAL HYPNOSIS, vol. 1, (New York: Grune, 1948), p. 98.

Suggestibility Tests, from Wolberg, *The Principles of Hypnotherapy,* pp. 102–3.

The Depth of Trance, from Wolberg, *The Principles of Hypnotherapy,* p. 105.

[1] C. L. Hull, *Hypnosis and Suggestibility: An Experimental Approach* (New York: Appleton-Century-Crofts, 1933).

be completely satisfactory because of the extreme variability of the responses among different patients and even in the same patient on different induction days.

There is some objection to classifying hypnotic "stages." All phenomena are due to implied or direct suggestion. Subjects vary in their ideas as to what constitutes the hypnotic state. Some persons are unable to develop posthypnotic amnesia even after attaining a somnambulistic stage. Others may respond to suggestions to dream or to write automatically in merely a light state of hypnosis. There is never in any subject a steady progression of all hypnotic phenomena. As a matter of fact the level of consciousness constantly shifts in the trance state. . . .

The First Hypnotic Session

At the first hypnotic session the aim is to give the patient confidence in his ability to enter the trance state. To achieve this aim the physician may execute the following steps in order: (1) encourage motivations that will lead to hypnosis; (2) remove as fully as possible misconceptions, fears, and resistances that oppose hypnosis; (3) give the patient a suggestibility test to demonstrate that he can follow suggestions; (4) encourage relaxation by a suggestive preparatory talk; (5) induce a trance; (6) deepen the trance; (7) awaken the patient; (8) discuss with him his reaction to hypnosis.

The Second Hypnotic Session

The management of the second hypnotic session will depend on the depth of the first trance and the patient's emotional response to it. The induction of hypnosis cannot help but mobilize feelings which in part are a reflection of the individual's basic problems in interpersonal relationships. The activity of the physician inherent in hypnosis, and the feelings of closeness that develop in the patient toward the physician during the trance, bring out in sharp focus the patient's fears, demands, expectations, and conflicts. Success in hypnotherapy will depend upon the correct evaluation and proper handling of these reactions. . . .

The First Hypnotic Session, from Wolberg, *The Principles of Hypnotherapy*, p. 111.
The Second Hypnotic Session, from Wolberg, *The Principles of Hypnotherapy*, pp. 138–52.

The patient should therefore be questioned about his reaction to the last session and particularly about subsequent dreams. His dreams, interpreted correctly, frequently reveal not only his immediate emotional attitude toward the physician, but also may contain the essence of his neurotic problem. It may be necessary to postpone further hypnotic sessions until his fears have been clarified, or suggestions can be made in the second trance which take into account his reactions.

If the patient resisted entering the first trance, his subsequent waking productions and his dreams will often yield clues to his resistance. Such clues utilized adroitly may make the second induction attempt a success.

Trance Management in Resistive Patients

Should the patient have failed to enter a trance state in the previous session, a modification of technic will be necessary in order to overcome his resistance. Among the more common resistances are defiance of the authority of the hypnotist, a fear of yielding one's will or independence, a need to prove oneself superior, or a fear of failure.

Where the nature of the resistance is known it may in some cases be circumvented. For example, where the patient spontaneously admits that he fears giving up his independence, the physician may assure him that no suggestion will be made without first gaining his consent. It may be stressed that it is impossible to obtain any effect that he, himself, is unwilling to produce. During hypnosis the patient is repeatedly assured on this score, and, as he consents to deeper and deeper states, he may finally become a very apt hypnotic subject.

Where the patient defies the authority of the physician, he may sometimes admit that hostile, challenging, and depreciatory impulses, or strivings to be negativistic invade his mind during the attempted induction process. The ventilation of these feelings may possibly make him more susceptible. . . .

Mechanical Devices. Hypnosis may be resisted on the basis of a conscious or unconscious fear of the physician. This occurs mostly in detached people who have built a shell around themselves, and who attempt to ward off contacts of an interpersonal nature. When the physician approaches the patient, terror may become so extreme that hypnosis is impossible. To obviate this a mechanical contrivance may be utilized. Mechanical devices are also helpful in impressionable people who expect the mysterious in hypnosis. They are furthermore successful in distractible persons who are unable to concentrate their attention on words.

Listening to a monotonous auditory stimulation may be successful where other methods fail. The beat of a metronome or a clock may be utilized as a fixation stimulus, the suggestion being given the patient that he will get sleepier and sleepier as he listens to the rhythmic beat. If he is unable to concentrate on the idea of sleep, it may be possible for him to visualize in his mind a very peaceful scene, or a monotonous drowsy mental picture. If musical, he may mentally reproduce a musical composition. . . .

Hypnotic Drugs (Narcosynthesis).   In some instances, a resistant subject may be hypnotized successfully after taking a hypnotic drug. The patient may be given six to nine grains of sodium amytal one-half hour prior to hypnosis, or he may get one to two drams of paraldehyde five to ten minutes before hypnosis is attempted. Where the patient has tremors, spasms, hiccups, or other symptoms which make it impossible for him to relax sufficiently to concentrate his attention, a hypnotic is indispensable.

When other methods fail, the intravenous injection of a solution of hypnotic drug may be used. This method, which has been called narcosynthesis or narcoanalysis, produces in itself a hypnoticlike state which resembles, but is not similar to, hypnosis.

Increasing Trance Depth

Once the patient is brought to a point in the trance where he experiences a disturbance in cutaneous sensibility, he may proceed to the next phase in the training process. In nonresistive patients, the second trance session may proceed from this point on. Where the patient prefers it, he may lie on a couch rather than sit up in a chair. Many patients prefer the couch position because it allows them to relax better.

The patient first is inducted into a trance and rapidly carried through limb and lid catalepsy, inhibition of voluntary movements, automatic movements and disturbances in cutaneous sensibility. Then he is given the following suggestions, successful execution of which indicate greater trance depth.

Ability to Talk in the Trance Without Awakening.   It is desirable to get the patient to a point in hypnosis where he is able to carry on a conversation without arousing from the trance. In a number of cases this ability can be developed in the subject through training, even though he may not have the aptitude of developing analgesia. Suggestions such as these may be used: "Even though you are asleep, you will be able to hear my voice very distinctly and to talk to me without awakening. You will talk back just like a person in his sleep. You will be able to answer my questions without awakening and without difficulty." . . .

Hallucinatory Suggestions.   To produce hallucinations by suggestion the patient may be trained as follows: "As you sit there I'm going to suggest to you that you imagine yourself and myself walking out of the door together. We approach a churchyard. We walk into the churchyard and as we look directly overhead, we notice the church steeple. I want you to picture this in your mind and as soon as you see the church, indicate it to me by your left hand rising about six inches off your thigh." ...

Fantasy and Dream Induction.   These are extremely valuable technics which permit the physician to work much more dynamically with the patient's problems. Instructions such as follow are given the patient: "Now as you sit there, I'm going to ask you to visualize yourself inside a theater. You are sitting in a seat in the second or third row. You are observing the stage. You notice that the curtains are drawn together. Raise your hand about six inches when you visualize this." When the patient raises his hand, suggestions continue. "You are curious as to what is going on behind the curtain. Then you notice a man *(or a woman if the patient is a woman)* standing in the stage at the far end of the curtain. He has an expression of extreme fear and horror on his face as if he is observing behind the curtain the most frightening and horrible thing imaginable. You wonder what this may be, and you seem to absorb this man's *(or woman's)* fear. In a moment the curtain will open suddenly and you will see what frightens the person. As soon as you do tell me about it without waking up. As soon as you see action on the stage, tell me exactly what you see." ...

Psychotherapeutic Suggestions.   Before the second trance session, the physician will probably have made an appraisal of the patient's problem, and in consideration of such factors as the time available for therapy, the depth of personality modifications desired, the motivations of the patient, and his ego strength, an estimate will have been made of the therapeutic goal. Depending upon the goal, suggestions may be made during the second trance session toward symptom removal, guidance, reassurance, persuasion, desensitization, reeducation, reconditioning, or towards an analytic understanding of the dynamic sources of the patient's difficulty.

Once the therapeutic objective has been determined, the physician must work in the trance toward establishing the type of relationship which will permit the achievement of this objective. For instance, if symptom removal through prestige suggestion is the goal, and no structural changes in the personality are planned, strong directiveness and authoritarianism will have to be maintained in the trance. If, on the other hand, deep changes are desired in the personality structure, a cooperative, nondirective type of relationship will probably be necessary, and the conduct of the trance session must be of a type where the patient participates actively.

Posthypnotic Suggestions.   Where the patient has been told, prior to the induction of hypnosis, that he will remember all events that have occurred, specific directions to forget the events during hypnosis should not be given him. Despite the statement that he remember, if he has developed a somnambulistic trance, a partial or complete amnesia will probably exist. A very simple way of determining the presence of amnesia is to have the patient repeat a six digit series without instructing him to remember this. In recounting his trance experiences the patient, in failing to recall the numbers, may give indication as to the presence of amnesia.

There are two posthypnotic suggestions which are more or less easily produced. The first involves posthypnotic dreaming, the second, posthypnotic blinking.

Posthypnotic suggestions to dream may be phrased as follows: "After you go to bed tonight, you will have a dream which you will probably remember. You will also probably dream on other evenings after tonight. I want you to remember the dreams, if possible, and bring them to me when you come here next time. Do you understand?"

In giving the patient suggestions for posthypnotic blinking, he is told: "I am going to awaken you soon by counting slowly from one to five. At the count of five, open your eyes and look at me. You will notice that your eyes will begin blinking spasmodically, and that no matter how hard you try to control blinking, it will be impossible to prevent your eyes from blinking as you look at me. I will then ask you to close your eyes, and I will count from one to three. At the court of three I want you to open your eyes, and this time it will be possible for you to look at me steadily without blinking. Now start waking up slowly. One, two, three, four, five."

Awakening the Patient

The regular counting suggestions for awakening the patient are then given to him, and, if the suggestion for posthypnotic blinking has been made, this suggestion is repeated immediately prior to the completion of the count. After the patient awakens, he may be asked what he remembers of the trance and his reaction to it. In many instances the patient will express a fear that he is not responding to suggestions or that he has not been asleep. He should be quickly reassured, and told that he is responding quite satisfactorily, and that he will become more and more convinced of this as time goes on.

Subsequent Hypnotic Sessions

Subsequent hypnotic sessions are concerned with the following: (1) continued training in trance depth to the limit of the patient's capacities, (2) teaching the

---

Subsequent Hypnotic Sessions, from Wolberg, *The Principles of Hypnotherapy*, pp. 153–66.

patient to enter a trance state rapidly at a given signal, (3) administration of therapeutic suggestions, (4) training in hypnoanalytic procedures in cases where a modified analytic approach is indicated.

Continued Training in Trance Depth

While the great majority of patients will not require more than a light or medium trance for hypnotherapy, a somnambulistic state is necessary in some forms of symptom removal: in reconditioning, in the induction of experimental conflicts, and in such hypnoanalytic technics as regression and revivification, play therapy, dramatics, automatic drawing, and mirror gazing. . . .

Conditioning the Trance to a Given Signal

As a general rule successive inductions are associated with an ability on the part of the patient to sink into a trance more and more easily. It is usually best at the second or third session to condition the patient to enter a trance upon a given signal. The nature of this signal can vary. It may be a certain word or sentence, or an auditory stimulus such as a bell or buzzing sound, or a visual stimulus like a blinking electric light. The patient is given a suggestion, such as follows, while he is in a trance:

"You are deeply asleep at the present time. Now listen to me carefully. From now on it will not be necessary to go through the process of hypnotizing you each time you come here. When I give you a certain signal like tapping on the desk *(any other signal may be introduced here if desired),* you will very easily and immediately enter into a state of sleep as deep as the one you are in now."

Administration of Therapeutic Suggestions

The point in the induction process where therapeutic suggestions are introduced will vary with the patient's problems, his aptitude for hypnosis, and his personality makeup. In some cases of symptom removal it may be expedient to confine therapy to a prolonged single session, slowly and progressively inducting the patient into a very deep trance prior to the termination of which therapeutic suggestions are introduced. In other cases a half dozen sessions may pass before therapy is started. As a general rule therapeutic suggestions should be made when the patient has achieved his maximum in trance depth.

Because of the heightened suggestibility in the trance, psychotherapeutic efforts are usually responded to more readily than in the waking state. The close relationship to the physician which is a product of hypnosis carries over into waking life, and the patient will continue to respond better to therapy even when hypnosis is discontinued. . . .

Hypnoanalytic Procedures

Where the patient's problem is such that it requires analytic probing, and where his motivations and ego strength will allow of such an approach, he may be trained in the various hypnoanalytic procedures.

The technics of free association, of fantasy and dream induction, will require no more than a light or medium trance. The specific directions for these technics have already been discussed, and more complete details on the latter procedures, as well as on the other hypnoanalytic methods to be outlined, may be obtained elsewhere.[2]

The technics of automatic writing, hypnotic drawing, play therapy during hypnosis, dramatics under hypnosis, regression and revivification, crystal and mirror gazing, and the induction of experimental conflicts will require a deep if not somnambulistic trance.

The patient may be trained in automatic writing by being told during a trance that it will be possible for him to write without being completely aware of what his hand is doing. A suggestion such as the following may be made:

"I'm going to stroke your hand, and you will begin to experience the feeling as if it is detached from your body. I will place a pencil in your hand and then put the pencil on a pad of paper. Your hand will begin moving along, writing on the paper, as if an outside force were pushing it along. Your hand will continue to move even though you concentrate your attention on something entirely apart from the writing."

Because the productions in automatic writing are fragmentary and cryptic, it will be essential to train the patient to translate what he has written. This can be done by giving him a suggestion that he will be able to open his eyes without awakening, and that he will be able to translate the meaning of what his hand has written. Posthypnotic suggestions may be given the patient that it will be possible for him to write automatically in the waking state, that he may do this while engaged in another activity, such as reading a book. What he has written during the waking state may, of course, require translation under hypnosis. . . .

Self-Hypnosis and Group Hypnosis

An effective psychotherapeutic plan may consider the following four stages in succession: (1) inducting the patient into as deep a trance as possible; (2) utilizing the trance to expedite the type of psychotherapy most suitable for the

---

[2]L. R. Wolberg, *Hypnoanalysis* (New York: Grune, 1945).

Self-Hypnosis and Group Hypnosis, from Wolberg, *The Principles of Hypnotherapy*, pp. 169–79.

patient; (3) teaching the patient, once the cure, improvement, or symptom relief is obtained, that he can bring about the same effects through his own efforts; (4) demonstrating to him, as soon as the latter is achieved, that therapeutic results can be maintained without need for further recourse to hypnosis.

One means by which the patient is taught that he can duplicate therapeutic effects through his own efforts is by the technic of self-hypnosis. Self-hypnosis, as the term is employed here, means an actual trance induced by the patient as a result of posthypnotic suggestions given him by the physician.

The aim of self-hypnosis is to convince the patient that there is nothing magical about hypnosis, and that he can obtain benefits of suggestion through his own efforts. In this way he conceives of himself as capable of functioning without the need for a dependent relationship on the physician. Self-hypnosis is a means of reinforcing indefinitely hypnotic suggestions. Eventually it is a way of proving to the patient that the trance is no longer necessary for permanent improvement.

The capacity to induce a trance through self-suggestions and to experience certain phenomena in the trance has, in itself, little effect on the patient's neurosis, on his esteem, or the strengthening of the ego. However, where the individual is capable of mastering his symptoms through psychotherapy aided by hypnosis, the conviction that he can produce the same effects without the agency of another person can contribute to his self-confidence. The influence it exerts on the ego is wholly dependent on the effect it has on the patient's sense of self-mastery.

Various technics may be used to produce self-hypnosis. While in a trance the patient is given the suggestion that he will, by repeating a signal, be able to go into a deep hypnotic sleep, during which he is conscious of everything. He may then give himself whatever therapeutic suggestions are prescribed, and thereafter awaken himself by another signal. . . .

Hypnosis in Anxiety Neurosis

Where the patient's character defenses are more or less adequate, emphasis may be placed upon submerging anxiety through the fortification of those defenses that had previously protected the ego against danger. Hypnosis with reassurance, guidance, externalization of interests, socialization, occupational therapy, persuasion, and reeducation may be utilized in fulfillment of this goal.

Where anxiety attacks are related to deep-seated conflicts in the personality structure, which have little relationship to inimical environmental difficulties, hypnoanalytic approach is indicated. Here an attempt is made to discover

---

Hypnosis in Anxiety Neurosis, from Wolberg, *The Principles of Hypnotherapy*, pp. 218–19.

the sources of anxiety, their meaning, and historical origin. The duration of therapy will be dependent upon the rigidity of personality and the extent to which the neurosis has been structuralized. The individual must be shown how his present-day attitudes are distorted by anxieties which are rooted in past misconceptions and in unconscious conflict, and a reintegration to life and to people must be effected in the light of his new understanding. ...

Hypnosis in Conversion Hysteria

Conversion hysteria is a neurosis which classically responds rapidly to hypnotherapy. While hysterical symptoms can often be removed dramatically in relatively few hypnotic sessions, the personality constellation associated with this condition will require more prolonged psychotherapy along the lines indicated in the chapter on character disorders.

The conversion syndrome is found in persons who have an infantile attitude toward life, who are explosive in their reactions to stress and frustration, and who tend to act out their personal conflicts and demands. The world for the hysteric is a theater in which he dramatizes himself for the benefit of those around him whom he considers his audience. The histrionic performances are ingenious and utilize for their content prevailing attitudes and customs. It is for this reason that the forms of hysterical behavior of different epochs, though seemingly dissimilar, are actually of one fabric. Thus the religious dramatizations of the medieval hysteric, the prudish overacting of the Victorian, and the present-day hysterical concern with health and hygiene are different only in so far as they utilize divergent symbols. The motivations underlying the behavior distortions are the same. Essentially there is a need to display oneself and to gain recognition and sympathy from people, particularly authority.

The relationship the hysterical individual establishes with authority is aimed toward winning praise and admiration, and in this effort the person will press into service a host of technics and devices. The superego of the hysteric, though enlarged and punitive, prohibiting the expression of inner needs and strivings, is remarkably plastic. The person, consequently, is extraordinarily suggestible, and when he establishes faith in an authoritative individual, he generally abides by the latter's mandates, even to the abandonment of symptoms which have served a defensive purpose. This explains why the hysterical patient is so susceptible to hypnotherapy. The hypnotist in the mind of the

Hypnosis in Conversion Hysteria, from Wolberg, *The Principles of Hypnotherapy,* pp. 220–21.

patient becomes a sort of deity, the embodiment of power and omniscience. The yielding of a symptom upon command is apparently motivated by a desire to derive security gratifications through compliance. The basic motif of life then is dependency with a need to gain security through the agency of a more powerful individual. . . .

Hypnosis in Anxiety Hysteria

Anxiety hysteria is a syndrome characterized chiefly by the development of phobias. It is allied to obsessional states in compulsion neurosis and to conversion hysteria. For clinicial rather than pathologic reasons, it is treated as a distinct entity.

Unlike conversion hysteria, anxiety hysteria is usually unresponsive to symptom removal by hypnotic command. The psychopathology of the condition apparently does not lend itself to this form of approach.

Anxiety is the central problem in anxiety hysteria. Instead of being free-floating as in anxiety neurosis, the anxiety is controlled by the formation of phobic defenses. Phobia formation is a technic by which anxiety is objectified as an external danger, the individual adapting himself to this danger through avoidance and inhibition of function. Exposure to the situation which is being avoided creates anxiety. The patient usually realizes that his fear is groundless or ridiculous, but he cannot seem to do anything about it. . . .

It is to be expected, therefore, that phobic removal by hypnotic suggestion, as well as the mastery of fearsome situations through hypnotically reinforced willpower, will result in limited success.

Hypnosis with psychobiologic therapy is nevertheless sometimes successful in anxiety hysteria, particularly with technics of persuasion, reconditioning, desensitization, and reeducation. . . .

Associated with persuasive technics, technics of self-mastery through the medium of self-hypnosis may be utilized. Here the individual fortifies himself to face a phobic situation by minimizing its fearful aspects, and by concentrating on the pleasure values incidental to the phobic pursuit. Persistent suggestions to gather courage and to master his fears may inspire sufficient fortitude to pull the person successfully through a situation he ordinarily would be unable to face. Needless to say this technic is palliative and results are temporary at best. . . .

Another means of treating phobias is by desensitization. Under hypnosis the patient is given suggestions to expose himself gradually to the terrifying situation. The aim in desensitization is to get the patient to master his fears by actually facing them. It is essential for the individual to force himself again and again into the phobic situation, in order that he may finally learn to control it. For example, if a person fears open spaces, or going outdoors, he can, on the first day, walk several steps from his house, and then return. On the second day he may increase the distance between himself and his house, and similarly on each following day until he is able to walk a considerable distance from his home. The hope is that the conquering of graduated doses of his fear will desensitize him to its influence.

Reeducational methods, utilizing psychobiologic or psychoanalytic approaches along with hypnosis, are far more rational than the aforegoing technics, since they deal with the causes of the phobia. The object is to understand the function of the phobia, and then to readjust the individual to its dynamic source.

Hypnoanalysis is often eminently successful in tracing the origin of a phobia. Where a fear has been produced by an incident so terror-inspiring that it has been repressed, it may be possible to get the person to recall the original emotional experience under hypnosis and then to reevaluate the situation in terms of his present-day understanding. A helpful technic is to regress the person to a period prior to the development of the phobia, and then gradually to reorient him in his age level to later and later periods of life, until the original situation associated with the development of the phobia has been uncovered. Where the phobia is the product of character patterns that have originated early in life, it will be necessary to produce a more or less drastic reorganization of the personality through further therapy after the phobia has been analyzed and its sources determined. . . .

Hypnosis in Compulsion Neurosis

The therapy of compulsion neurosis or compulsive-obsessive personality disorders must take into account the patient's dependency, the profoundly hostile impulses he has toward people, his need for detachment, the tendency to "isolate" intellect from feeling, and the magical frame of reference in which his ideas operate.

Among the most important tasks to be achieved in the therapy of this condition are demonstrating to the patient that his symptoms have a definite cause and that they stem from no magical source; that aggression is a nor-

Hypnosis in Compulsion Neurosis, from Wolberg, *The Principles of Hypnotherapy,* pp. 248–50.

mal impulse originating in hostile attitudes; that he can express a certain amount of hostility without destroying other people or injuring himself; that he can relate to a person without needing to make himself dependent or compliant.

Hypnosis is often valuable in achieving these objectives. Because the framework of compulsive thinking is magical, the compulsion neurotic very often is motivated towards receiving hypnotherapy. Secretly he hopes that hypnosis can, in some magical way, neutralize his obsessional concern with injury, with killing, with death, and with sexuality. Where this is the sole motivation, hypnosis is bound to fail, since hypnosis will not effect a magical neutralization of impulses. Another motive the compulsion neurotic has for hypnosis is that the hypnotist reinforce his waning repressive powers. Inasmuch as his inner impulses and demands make him desire to break down his controls, he may feel that his willpower, unless buttressed, will not keep in check the tumultuous emotions within. As a consequence, he will want the hypnotist to play a parental role giving him orders to lead a restrictive, rigid life. Under these circumstances, too, hypnosis is apt to fail. The individual, though he asks for this type of handling, will actually resist the hypnotic process, or hypnotic suggestions, or he will develop intense hostility towards the physician.

In the induction of hypnosis, certain problems occur in the obsessive-compulsive that are not encountered in other neuroses. The individual may be obstinate, so insistent upon exercising his will, and so resistive to accepting suggestions that he will be unable to enter a trance state. One means of circumventing this is to couch suggestions in such a way that the patient himself feels that he is in control of the hypnotic process. Many patients will spontaneously ask that this be done; as a matter of fact, some compulsion neurotics come to therapy for the sole purpose of learning self-hypnosis. There is an attempt here to reinforce a waning superego, to get strength from some outside agency which will enable them to control their inner conflicts and drives. Once the initial resistances which militate against assuming a trance state are overcome, the individual usually makes an excellent subject.

The patient thus may be quite resistive to hypnosis at the start, and one may gain the impression that it is impossible to hypnotize him; however, with properly phrased suggestions directed at making the patient believe he is in control of his own processes, he will eventually be able to enter a hypnotic state. Very often it is essential to spend a great deal of time in the first induction process to break through resistances. It is usually best to induct a compulsion neurotic as deeply as possible at the first trance. He will be caught off guard the first time but thereafter will know what to expect and will mobilize his defenses better. A slow induction brought to a depth where the patient will be able to follow certain suggestions posthypnotically convinces the patient that he has been in a trance and that he can follow suggestions effectively.

The particular type of therapy to be employed with hypnosis is determined by the patient's motivations and inner resources, and by the therapeutic goal. In my experience, a combination of psychobiologic and psychoanalytic technics is most effective. This involves a directive reeducational approach along psychoanalytic lines, avoiding a neurotic transference, and utilizing guidance, persuasion, and reassurance whenever necessary. . . .

Hypnosis in Traumatic Neurosis

Hypnosis is one of the most effective agents in the therapy of the traumatic neuroses. During the last war it was utilized with great success in many of the acute combat reactions.[3] The psychopathology of traumatic neurosis apparently makes it remarkably susceptible to the hypnotic method.

Traumatic neurosis is due to a violent episode of a physical or emotional nature obtruding itself in the life of the person. Under civilian conditions the usual causes are transportation and industrial accidents. In military life the causes are contingent on the stresses of war.

As a general rule the traumatic stimulus acts on an individual whose adaptive resources are being taxed to an extreme. He is then unable to cope with the added stress imposed on him by the inimical event. Traumatic neurosis, thus, is not the result of a single catastrophic circumstance but rather is the end product of a number of harsh situations to which the individual has reacted adversely.

Everyone has his breaking point and may be overwhelmed by a disastrous situation with which he is powerless to cope. Customary controls and defenses being ineffectual, these may be abandoned for regressive modes of adaptation which are, of course, inadequate to deal with the situation. However, in the average individual, recovery takes place shortly after the traumatic stimulus ceases. . . .

Where the patient had a well-defined traumatic neurosis, hypnotherapy was often remarkably effective. Hypnosis was utilized for the purposes of symptom removal and as a means of controlling insomnia and tension along the lines detailed in volume 2. Though palliative, these measures often reassured the patient and restored to him a sense of control and mastery.

Under hypnosis it is possible to intensify, to diminish, or to remove a symptom, to transfer it to another part of the body, and, finally, to demonstrate

---

Hypnosis in Traumatic Neurosis, from Wolberg, *The Principles of Hypnotherapy.* pp. 260–70.

[3]E. Slater and W. Sargent, "Acute War Neuroses," *Lancet* 2 (1940):1; A. Kardiner and H. Spiegel, *War Stress and Neurotic Illness* (New York: Paul B. Hoeber, 1947).

to the patient that he can do the same things through his own suggestions. This frequently removes feelings of helplessness. Kardiner and Spiegel illustrate this method, as used in war, with excellent case material.[4]

In instances where anxiety is extreme one may utilize an "uncovering" type of technic. Here hypnosis and narcosynthesis are of signal help. The recovery of amnesias and the reliving of the traumatic scene in action or verbalization have markedly ameliorative or curative effects on acute traumatic neuroses.

While hypnosis and narcosynthesis accomplish approximately the same results, the emotions accompanying hypnotherapy are much more vivid, and the cathartic effect consequently greater, than with narcosynthesis. There are other advantages to hypnosis. The induction of a trancelike state, once the patient has been hypnotized, is brought about easily without the complication of injections and without posttherapeutic somnolence. Additionally, hypnotic suggestions are capable of demonstrating to the patient his ability to gain mastery of his functions. . . .

Where it is essential to remove an amnesia, the patient is encouraged under hypnosis or narcosynthesis to talk about the events immediately preceding the traumatic episode, and to lead into the episode slowly, reliving the scene as if it were happening again. Frequently the patient will approach the scene and then block, or he may actually awaken. Repeated trance inductions often break through this resistance. Also it will be noted that the abreactive effect will increase as the patient describes the episode repeatedly. Apparently the powerful emotions which are bound down are subject to greater repression than the actual memories of the event.

In the treating of postwar neuroses of traumatic origin Hadfield's original technic is still useful.[5] The patient is hypnotized and instructed that when the physician places his fingers on the patient's forehead, the latter will picture before him the experiences that caused his breakdown. This usually produces a vivid recollection of the traumatic event with emotions of fear, rage, despair, and helplessness. The patient often spontaneously relives the traumatic scene with a tremendous cathartic effect. If he hesitates, he must be encouraged to describe the scenes before him in detail. This is the first step in therapy and must be repeated for a number of sessions until the restored memory is complete. The second step is the utilization of hypnosis to readjust the patient to the traumatic experience. The experience must be worked through, over and over again, until the patient accepts it during hypnosis and remembers it upon awakening. Persuasive suggestions are furthermore given him, directed at increasing assurance and self-confidence. After this the emotional relationship to the physician is analyzed at a conscious level to prevent continuance of the dependency tie.

[4]Kardiner and Spiegel, *War Stress.*
[5]J. A. Hadfield, in *Functional Nerve Disease,* ed. Chrichton-Miller (London, 1920).

Horsley mentions that where the ordinary injunctions to recall a traumatic scene fail, several reinforcing methods can be tried.[6] The first has to do with commanding the patient to remember, insisting that he will not leave the room until his memory is complete. The second method is that of soothing, coaxing, and encouraging the patient, telling him he is about to remember battle scenes that will remind him of his experiences. The patient may, if this is unsuccessful, be told that although he does not remember the experience during hypnosis, he will remember it upon awakening. He may also be instructed to recall it in a dream the next day.

Various hypnoanalytic procedures, such as dramatization, regression and revivification, play therapy, automatic writing, and mirror gazing may be utilized to recover an obstinate amnesia. The reaction of patients to the recall of repressed experiences varies. Some patients act out the traumatic scene, getting out of bed, charging about the room, ducking to avoid mortar shells and approaching tanks. Other patients live through the traumatic episode without getting out of bed. Some individuals collapse with anxiety, and they should be reassured and encouraged to go on. Where the patient voices hostility, he should be given an opportunity to express his grievances and dislikes, and clarification of his feelings of injustice may afford him considerable relief. . . .

Hypnosis in Psychosomatic Conditions

Hypnosis lends itself admirably to the treatment of many forms of psychosomatic disorder. Where somatic symptoms have a symbolic meaning, simple symptom removal by authoritative suggestion is often remarkably successful. This is especially the case in an individual with a hysterical makeup, in whom the symptom serves a symbolic function as well as a means of pleading for help, love, and reassurance. The hypnotic situation here seems to fulfill an important need in the patient, and compliance with the physician's command to abandon a symptom is often automatic. There are many limitations to this type of therapy, since effects are treated rather than causes. Character disturbances are influenced minimally even though an abatement of symptoms has been brought about.

Simple symptom removal is usually ineffective where the psychosomatic disorder is the consequence of a diffuse autonomic drainage of tension, anxiety,

---

[6]J. S. Horsley, *Narco-Analyses* (London: Oxford University Press, 1943), p. 12.

Hypnosis in Psychosomatic Conditions, from Wolberg, *The Principles of Hypnotherapy*, pp. 279–82.

and hostility. Furthermore, where the symptom represents an important defense against anxiety, simple suggestions are insufficient. For instance, where impotency or frigidity represent a defense against acknowledging one's sexual needs, or reflect a fear of relating oneself intimately to another person, the removal of the symptom may be interpreted by the patient as potentially dangerous. He will consequently resist suggestions along lines of symptom removal.

Hypnosis, utilized as a means of persuasion and guidance, may permit the patient to organize his life around his defects and liabilities, to avoid situations that arouse conflict and hostility, and to attain, at least in part, a sublimation of his basic needs. This approach is, of course, more scientific than simple symptom removal because it deals with the causative emotions themselves, attempting to control their severity. The object here is to build up ego strength to a point where it can handle damaging emotions more rationally, as well as to improve interpersonal relationships so that hostility and other disturbing emotions are not constantly being generated. In many instances, hypnosis used with such psychobiologic therapies liberates the individual from the vicious cycle of his neurosis, facilitates externalization of interest, increases self-confidence, and provides a means of discharging emotions by way of motor channels instead of internalizing them with drainage through the autonomic system.

Another approach to the problem of psychosomatic illness is desensitizing the patient to the effects of his emotions by exposing him under hypnosis to situations in which he can tolerate graduated doses of anxiety and hostility. Dramatic technics in which scenes are reenacted that provoke the patient's psychosomatic symptoms teach the patient the dynamics of his illness and permit him to master provocative emotions. For instance, if symptoms of gastric distress have been found to be associated with hostility stirred up by a competitive relationship, demonstrations to the patient, by means of an experimental neurosis, may show him how he develops and represses hostility. During hypnosis dramatized scenes may also be suggested in which the patient is capable of expressing hostility without fear of counteraggression.

Hypnosis with confession and ventilation may be useful in certain types of psychosomatic illness. Where a patient represses certain impulses on the basis of a fear of estrangement from an authoritative person on whom he is dependent, a somatization response may result. French believes that psychogenic asthma is brought about by this mechanism.[7] In asthma, when confession of impulses to the mother or mother substitute occurs, with reassurance on her part to the effect that the person will not be rejected, considerable relief is consequent. Hypnosis may aid in uncovering forbidden impulses, as well as

---

[7]T. M. French, "Brief Psychotherapy in Bronchial Asthma," *Psychosomatic Medicine* (January 1944).

in facilitating their expression. The physician encourages the patient to talk, and then reassures him that there will be no retaliatory rejection.

Determining the meaning of the patient's psychosomatic illness in terms of its historical development is successful in removing some symptoms, particularly of a hysterical character. Recall in the hypnotic state, either at adult or regressed levels, may result in the recovery of traumatic memories and experiences associated with the original development of the illness. It is essential to remember that while a symptom may be relieved, the basic personality structure is not influenced by this technic.

Where the character structure is very neurotic, an analysis of the individual's interpersonal relationships in operation may be the only way of removing his physical illness. Here a hypnoanalytic approach may be used, with analysis of the transference or reeducation utilizing analytic insight. The discovery by the patient of his unconscious compulsive drives, the uncovering of the genetic origins of these drives, the inevitable liberation of submerged anxiety and hostility lead to a new phase of independence and to bettered relationships with people. The changing of the patient's sense of values, and the ability to pursue biologic and social goals previously repressed, serve to remove sources of tension. The uncovering of anxieties rooted in unconscious conflict helps reintegrate the patient to a present shorn of the fears related to his past. . . .

Hypnosis in Character Disorders

The treatment of character disorders by hypnosis is no less difficult than by traditional methods of psychotherapy. Time itself is an element in the treatment, since the disturbance is deeply structuralized and involves extensive areas of the personality. It is doubtful whether hypnosis is capable of reducing the time element required to reorganize the obdurate habit and behavior patterns that are present in most forms of this condition. Hypnosis, nevertheless, can help in the management of some types of character disorders, and may bring success where otherwise failure might have resulted. . . .

Hypnosis in Alcoholism

In the event the patient is deeply hypnotizable—as are many alcoholics—he is, in the trace state, reminded that alcohol is a poison and that it will ulti-

---

Hypnosis in Character Disorders, in Wolberg. *The Principles of Hypnotherapy*, p. 293.
Hypnosis in Alcoholism, from Wolberg, *The Principles of Hypnotherapy*, 331–32.

mately damage him. He can get "on the wagon" if he so desires, and he can learn how to be happy and adjusted without needing to drink. As soon as the patient verbalizes a desire to give up alcohol, he is told that strong suggestions will fortify his ability to abandon the drinking urge.

When the patient is able to follow posthypnotic suggestions, conditioned reflex therapy is started. The first suggestion deals with substituting some oral satisfaction for the alcoholic craving. He may be told: "When you awaken, you will have an uncontrollable desire to drink. You will find that all your thoughts are concerned with wanting to drink. At the same time you will realize that drink is like poison, that it will destroy your health and your mind. In spite of this realization, the craving for a drink will be strong. You will notice on the desk near you a bottle of malted milk tablets. You will reach for a tablet and put it in your mouth. As soon as you do this, the craving for drink will immediately leave you. You will be filled with a sense of pleasure and relaxation. You may have no recollection of the suggestions I have just given you, but you will follow them nevertheless."

Should the patient be unable to stop drinking, hypnosis is often quite effective as a support. No more than a light trance is required in which strong suggestions are given him emphasizing the destructive effects of alcohol, the distaste that he will have for all forms of drink, his ability to control his craving, and the need to substitute food, hobbies, sports, and social activities for liquor. If nothing seems capable of controlling alcoholic indulgence, conditioned reflex therapy may be started, utilizing hypnosis or emetine hydrochloride.

An important phase of therapy is encouraging the patient to make social contacts and to affiliate himself with groups. If a branch of "Alcoholics Anonymous" exists in the community, the patient will find that he can make many friends there, and that he can involve himself in numerous constructive activities that will engage his energies and consolidate the gains he has made in therapy. . . .

Hypnosis in Psychosis

Hypnosis has, for obvious reasons, a limited utility in the psychoses. It may, however, occasionally be employed as an adjunct to other treatment procedures.

A psychosis represents a total collapse of the resources of the ego when the individual is no longer capable of adjusting to external pressures and internal demands. It follows failure of the customary defenses of the person

---

Hypnosis in Psychosis, from Wolberg, *The Principles of Hypnotherapy,* pp. 343–45.

to handle anxiety and to restore psychobiologic equilibrium. A combination of adverse constitutional and environmental factors renders the ego of the psychotic person incapable of adapting him on a realistic level of integration when he is exposed to conditions of extreme stress. . . .

Hypnosis can sometimes be utilized to consolidate the interpersonal relationship once contact has been established with the patient. Trance induction is not as difficult as might be imagined provided the patient's attention can be maintained. Sedatives are helpful in getting the patient to relax to a point where he is accessible. As the patient gains confidence in the physician, he will become more susceptible to suggestions. Hypnoanalytic probing should at first be assiduously avoided, since the emotions released cannot be handled by an already overburdened ego. Treatment efforts during an acute psychosis are in line with repressing rather than expressing the unconscious content. Where the ego has been sufficiently strengthened to repress anxiety, and where reality testing is restored, the cautious use of a hypnoanalytic approach may then be attempted. . . .

Hypnosis in Miscellaneous Conditions

A variety of habit disturbances and symptoms are amenable to hypnotic therapy. However, the extent to which they can be influenced, and the permanency of the improvement, will vary with the existing dynamics.

Such problems as overeating, insomnia, excessive smoking, nail-biting, drug addictions, enuresis, "stage fright" and stuttering, though appearing as isolated symptoms, are merely surface disturbances of much deeper emotional processes which affect vast areas of the individual's functioning. The patient may actually be unaware of the significance of his symptom in terms of broader personality implications. He will, therefore, resist any interference with his customary patterns of living, even though these are manifestly neurotic, and, without question, underlie his difficulties.

In treating any complaint by means of symptom removal, and by the various psychobiologic therapies, an effort must always be made to create in the patient a motivation to explore the sources of his problem. Unless some fundamental change develops in the patient's life patterns through a real alteration in the personality structure, amelioration or removal of a symptom may prove ineffective or temporary.

Hypnosis in Miscellaneous Conditions, from Wolberg, *The Principles of Hypnotherapy,* p. 386.

NAME INDEX

Abarbanel, A., 273
Abe, T., 318
Adler, A., 43–79, 115, 285, 288, 289, 291, 297, 298, 300
Adler, C., 228
Adler, G., 81, 82
Adler, R., 43
Alexander, F., 148
Allport, G. W., 291
Anrep, G. V., 216
Ansbacher, H. L., 291, 300
Ansbacher, R. R., 291
Ard, B., 284
Argabrite, A. H., 285
Aristotle, 348
Armstrong, T., 284
Ayllon, T., 217

Bachrach, A. J., 217
Bandura, A., 206–12
Bartlett, 213
Becker, G., 267
Benne, K. D., 572
Berdyaev, N., 426
Berenberg, A. N., 319
Bergson, H., 213
Berkowitz, L., 285
Berne, E., 472–85
Binder, H., 430
Binswanger, L., 266, 298, 304, 423–48
Bleuler, E., 2, 80, 92, 428
Bordin, E. S., 609–21
Boss, M., 298, 430, 435–37
Bowen, M., 586, 587
Brandsma, J. M., 284
Brodey, W., 586, 587
Brücke, E. W., 2
Budzinski, T., 228
Burnhead, D. E., 284
Burton, A., 284, 450
Buytendijk, F. J., 427

Callahan, R., 284
Caudill, W., 315
Carlson, A., 285
Casbriel, D., 576
Clark, D. E., 223
Condrau, G., 298
Conklin, R. C., 285
Cook, S. W., 285
Corner, M., 616
Corsini, R., 328, 512
Crumbaugh, J. C., 260, 261

Davies, R. L., 285
Davis, J. W., 285
Davison, G. C., 217
Dellis, N. P., 450
Deloreto, A., 284
Dennerll, D., 284
Devos, G. A., 322
Diamond, L., 284
Doi, L. T., 320
Doi, T., 306
Dollard, J., 168–205
Drovota, S., 223
Dubois, P., 269, 304

Ellenberger, H. F., 423–48
Ellis, A., 272–85
Epictetus, 287, 291
Epicurus, 287
Erwin, W. J., 217
Eysenck, H. J., 217, 283

Feather, B. W., 223
Fenichel, O., 147
Ferenczi, S., 508
Fiedler, F. E., 602
Fordham, M., 81, 82
Frank, P. R., 285
Frankl, V. E., 250–71, 292, 293, 299, 321, 427
French, T. M., 641

Freud, S., 2–42, 44, 52, 80, 86, 104, 105, 115, 142, 143, 144, 145, 146, 147, 149, 168, 213, 250, 252, 285, 291, 427, 428, 433, 436–37, 440, 473, 508
Fried, R., 224
Fromm, E., 142, 305
Fromm-Reichmann, F., 424, 432, 440, 450, 586
Fujita, B., 318

Gage, N. L., 606
Ganes, R. G., 284
Garrett, H. E., 331
Gebsattel, V. E. von, 251
Geis, H. J., 285
Gibb, J. R., 572
Glicken, M. D., 284
Goldstein, K., 330
Goodman, P., 330–63
Gordon, T., 571
Greenberg, I., 284
Grinker, R., 184
Grossack, M., 284
Grundelach, M. L., 616
Gullo, J. M., 284
Gutheil, E. A., 263

Hadfield, J. A., 639
Hall, G. F., 575, 578
Harper, R. A., 273, 283, 285
Harrington, G. L., 324
Harris, R. E., 285
Hartman, B. J., 285
Hauck, P. A., 284
Hauckel, P., 284
Hefferline, R. F., 330–63
Heidegger, M., 266, 298, 300, 424, 426, 434
Heimann, R. A., 284
Hein, P. L., 223
Heraclitus, 432
Horney, K., 141–65, 305, 320
Horsley, J. S., 640
Hull, C. L., 168, 214, 218, 625
Hull, R. F. C., 82
Hume, D., 213
Husserl, E., 426

Ikeda, K., 314

Jackson, D. D., 583, 586
Jacobson, A., 319
Jacobson, E., 223, 228
James, W., 287
Janet, P., 92
Jaspers, K., 56, 258, 426, 439
Jersild, A. T., 603
Jones, E., 508

Jones, H. G., 217
Jones, M., 530–67, 588
Jones, R. G., 285
Jung, C. G., 2, 80–114, 427

Kaczkowski, H., 598
Kakeda, K., 321
Kant, I., 213
Kardiner, A., 638
Karst, T. O., 284
Kataguchi, Y., 317
Kato, M., 320
Kawai, H., 318
Kelly, G. A., 364–79
Kelman, H., 305
Kielholz, A., 428
Kierkegaard, S., 298, 299, 300, 424, 426, 433
Kobayashi, J., 319
Koch, S., 292, 383
Kocourek, K., 266
Kondo, A., 320
Konitz, H. M., 284
Kora, T., 305, 306, 309, 321
Korzbyski, A., 284
Kotchen, T. A., 257
Kraepelin, E., 303, 304
Krasner, L., 217
Kratochvil, S., 260
Kraus, W., 285
Krippner, S., 284
Kuhn, R., 430, 433
Kumano, A., 316
Kumasaka, Y., 321
Kure, S., 304

Lafferty, J. C., 284
Lazarus, A. A., 215, 283
Lazarus, R., 285
Lebensohn, Z., 321
Lemere, F., 233
Lepinsky, J. P., 285
Levy, N. J., 322
Levy, O., 299
Lindsley, O. R., 217
Lindzey, G., 365
Linton, J., 48
Lovibond, S. H., 217
Lussiev, G., 284

MacDonald, A. P., 284
Maddi, S. R., 298
Maes, W. R., 284
Maher, B. A., 365
Maholick, L. T., 260, 261
Mahrer, A. R., 365
Malinowski, B., 213
Malone, T. P., 449–70

Marcel, G., 426
Marui, S., 319
Maslow, A. H., 263
Masserman, H., 252
Maultsby, M., 283, 284
May, R., 298, 423–48
Menoeceus, 287
Meyer, A., 142
Michenbaum, D. H., 284
Miller, N. E., 168–205, 285
Millner, M. A., 213
Minkowski, E., 428
Mitchell, W., 304
Mohr, J. P., 217
Moore, G. E., 213
Moreno, J. L., 252, 424, 432, 450, 486–512
Moreno, Z. T., 505
Morita, S., 303–23
Morns, K. T., 284
Moseley, S., 283
Mowrer, O. H., 285, 365
Muira, M., 304
Müller-Hegemann, D., 262
Murphy, G., 431

Nakae, S., 317
Nidorf, L. J., 285
Niebauer, E., 267
Nietzsche, F., 115, 258, 288, 299, 447
Nomura, A., 305, 321

O'Connell, D. N., 232
Okuda, Y., 318
Osgood, C. E., 216
Otto, H. A., 331

Patterson, C. H., 285, 598–608
Paul, G. L., 223
Pavlov, I. P., 168, 213, 216
Peirce, C. S., 289, 300
Perls, F. S., 330–63
Perls, L. P., 330
Phillips, E. L., 234–47
Pinel, P., 424
Plant, J. S., 142
Plato, 426
Pope, A., 440
Pottash, R. R., 283

Rank, O., 115–22, 345
Rapoport, R. N., 530–67
Rauschenbach, E., 80
Read, H., 81, 82
Remmers, H. H., 606
Renya, L. J., 215
Rettich, P., 284
Riskin, J., 583

Rogers, C. R., 285, 292, 298 382–422 441,
    568–82
Rom, P., 300
Rorschach, H., 317, 318, 430
Rummel, J. F., 606
Russell, B., 213
Russell, P. L., 284

Sagarin, E., 273
Sahakian, W. S., 286–302
Salter, A., 215
Sargent, W., 638
Sartre, J.-P., 298, 300, 426
Satir, V., 583–96
Sato, K., 305, 319
Schacter, S., 285
Scheler, M., 298
Schilder, P., 330
Schopenhauer, A., 258, 288
Schultz, J. H., 251, 263
Schwab, E. A., 285
Schweitzer, A., 149
Seneca, 297
Sharma, K. L., 284
Shimoda, M., 305
Simpson, H. N., 297
Singer, J. E., 285
Skinner, B. F., 206, 217
Slater, E., 638
Slavson, S. R., 513–29
Socrates, 155, 441–42
Sonnemann, U., 439
Spiegel, H., 184, 638
Stern, A., 298
Stone, H. K., 450
Storch, A., 426
Stoyva, J., 228
Strachey, J., 5
Straus, E. W., 252
Sullivan, H. S., 123–40, 142, 285, 321, 486
Super, D. E., 605
Suzuki, C., 316
Suzuki, D. T., 305
Suzuki, T., 317

Taft, G. L., 285
Taft, J., 116
Takahashi, Y., 318
Takano, K., 318
Takeyama, T., 309
Taylor, J. E., 283
Taylor, J. G., 214
Teplov, B. M., 216
Thorndike, E. L., 168
Thorne, F. C., 298
Tillich, P., 426, 428
Travers, R. M. W., 285

Trexler, L. D., 284
Trotsky, L., 43
Tursky, B., 232

Ullman, L., 217
Usa, G., 305, 307, 318, 322
Usa, S., 304, 318

Vaihinger, H., 57, 288
Valins, S., 285
Van Egeren, L. F., 223, 224
Vaughan, R., 48
Velten, E., 285
Voegtlin, W. L., 233
Voiland, A. L., 616

Wagner, E. E., 284
Waldman, R. D., 298

Watson, P. D., 232
Weisskopf-Joelson, E., 268
Wendt, Y., 305, 322
Wertheimer, M., 262
West, E., 428
Whitaker, C. A., 449–70
White, W. A., 123
Whitehead, A. N., 213
Wiener, D. W., 240, 243, 245
Wolberg, L. R., 624–44
Wolfe, J. L., 283
Wolpe, J., 213–33

Yamamoto, S., 318
Yokoyama, K., 323

Zingle, H. W., 284
Zunin, L. M., 328

SUBJECT INDEX

abaissement, 92–95
abnormal psychology
  defined, 333
abreaction, 3, 5–7, 105–7
abyss-experience, 263
achievement
  of insight, 412–13
activities
  patient, 542–49
activity group psychotherapy, 513, 514–18,
  520–21
adjustment, 387, 389
adult therapy
  questionnaire, 79
aggression, 364
agoraphobia, 262
alcoholism
  hypnosis in, 642–43
alienation, 160–61
  of self, 160–61
amplification, 81
analysis, 472–85
  and synthesis, 158–61
  character, 141–65
  Freudian, 2–42
  game, 472
  Jungian, 80–114
  of neurosis, 352–53
  script, 472
  structural, 472–73
  transactional, 472
analytical psychotherapy, 80–114
analytic group psychotherapy, 522–24
anamnesis, 3
anima, 81
animus, 81
anticipatory response, 175
anxiety, 124–30, 154–55, 264, 283, 383, 386,
  387, 396, 420, 486–87, 633–34
  and relaxation, 230–32
  anticipatory, 262
  counteracting, 230–32

desensitization, 230–32
  hierarchies, 228–30
  induction of, 127
  manifest, 141
  neurosis, 308, 633–34
  scale, 229–30
anxiety hysteria
  hypnosis in, 635–36
anxiety neurosis, 308, 633–34
  hypnosis in, 633–34
approval, 199–200
archetypes, 81
art, 342–43
arugamama, 303
assertions, 235–43
  defined, 236
assertion-structured psychotherapy, 234–47
  and learning theory, 243–44
  characteristics of, 241
  nature of, 235–41
  precepts of, 241–43
assertive training, 218–21
atom
  social, 510
attentional processes, 209
attitude, 86
  change, 268
  toward counselor, 411
authenticity, 301–2
autism, 210–11
aversion therapy, 232–33
  through drugs, 233
awareness, 420–21

bed-rest therapy, 303
behavior
  antinodal, 516
  change, 581–82
  discrepancies in, 419
  modification, 297–98
  nodal, 516
  rehearsal, 220–21

behavioristic technique, 277–78
being-of-the-future, 301
beliefs
    irrational, 274–77
    rational, 274–77
birth trauma, 115
boundaries
    psychological, 360–62
    therapy of, 361–62

case study, 237–41, 294–97, 301–2
catharsis, 5–7, 487
character analysis, 141–65
    compared with psychoanalysis, 144–48
    obstructive forces in, 154–55
    therapy, 141–65
character disorder
    hypnosis in, 642
choice, 301–2
claustrophobia, 262
client
    as guide, 408–9
    initial needs of, 615–16
client-centered therapy, 382–422
    characteristics of, 391–92
    synopsis of, 383–89
collective unconscious, 81, 97
communalism, 536
community
    as doctor, 532–33
complimentary types, 120–21
compulsion-neurosis, 70
    hypnosis in, 636–38
conflict, 160–61, 170–72, 181–82
confrontation, 578–79
congruence, 387, 420–21, 422
conjoint family therapy, 583–96
    theory of, 584–96
conscience, 39–40
consciousness, 89
consequences
    inappropriate, 275–77
    irrational, 275–77
construct
    diagnostic, 368–69, 373
    formation of, 371–72
    impermeable, 372
constructive alternativism therapy, 364–69
    as experimental, 372–73
    diagnostic constructs of, 368–69
    fixed-role sketch, 375–79
    formal aspects of, 367–68
    postulates, 366–67
    transitional constructs of, 369–70
consultation periods, 114
    analytical psychology, 114

contextual method, 341–42
    applied to psychotherapy, 342
contradiction of theory, 310–11
control, 508
conversion hysteria
    hypnosis in, 634–35
counseling, 598–621
    characteristics of, 600–601
    defined, 598–600
    educational, 598–621
    goal of, 610–11
    guidance, 598–621
    indication of, 403–4
    relationship, 602–3, 609–21
    vocational, 604–5
counseling goal, 610–11
    clarification of, 612–13
counseling psychology
    characteristics of, 600–1
    defined, 598–600
    goal of, 610–11
    group, 606–8
    individual, 606–8
    vocational, 604–5
counseling task
    clarification of, 613–15
counselor
    function of, 603–4
    goal, 610–13
    initial orientation, 611–12
counterconditioning, 215–18
countertransference, 105
creative adjustment, 342, 343, 344
creativity, 354–55, 486, 487–93
cue, 172, 184
    as stimulus, 172
    distinctiveness of, 174
    producing responses, 178–79
cue-producing response
    role of, 179

Dasein, 426–30
    analysis, 423–48
    as real, 442–44
decision, 301–2
    defined, 445
defense mechanisms, 354–60, 419–21
    confluence, 356–59
    egotism, 356
    introjection, 356, 359
    projection, 105, 356, 359
    reaction formation, 357
    repression, 357
    retroflection, 356, 359
    sublimation, 357
defensiveness, 152–54

democratization, 535
denial, 118–19
dereflection, 260–62, 269
desensitization, 222–32
  basis of, 222–23
  paradigm, 223–32
  systematic, 222–23
  technique of, 224–32
development, 35–37
diagnosis, 475–76, 616–19
  operational, 476
  phenomenological, 476
  social, 476
dialectical method, 111–14
disapproval, 199–200
disconfirmation, 239
discrimination, 174
  new, 196
disinhibitory effect, 208
displacement, 184
double technique, 512
dream, 71–72, 95–101, 433–34
  analysis, 32–35
  forms, 99–101
  induction, 629
  interpretation, 32–35
  therapeutic value of, 95–101
drive, 172, 184
drug therapy, 233
dynamics, 462–63
dynamism, 139

educational counseling, 598–621
ego, 37–38, 81–82, 347–49, 487, 507
  auxiliary, 81–82
  functions, 349–55
  ideal, 116, 145
ego state
  adult, 473, 474–78
  child, 473, 474–78
  parent, 473, 474–78
Eigenwelt, 429, 442–44
electrical stimulation, 232
empathy, 124, 383
encounter, 427
  basic, 580
encounter group, 568–82
  confrontation, 578–79
  feedback, 577–78
  feelings in, 570, 580–81
  healing capacity, 573–74
  personal expression, 569–73
  process, 568
energy transformation, 128
environment, 332–34
eros, 36–37

euphoria, 124, 126
existence
  as real, 442–44
  authentic, 426
  common, 433
  inauthentic, 426
  mode of, 433–34
existential
  analysis, 428–31
  and noology, 254–56
  frustration, 252, 258–60
  guilt, 271
  philosophy, 425–26
  relationship, 454
  vacuum, 252–54, 258, 264
existential analysis
  Binswanger's, 428–30
existential psychotherapy, 297–302, 423–48
  and existential analysis, 428–31
  characteristics of, 299–301
  Binswanger's, 432–34
  May's, 434–48
  nature of, 297–302
  objective of, 298–99
experience
  of threat, 419–20
experiential
  psychotherapy, 449–70
  relationship, 454
experimental extinction, 218
explicit psychotherapy, 455–57
expression
  releasing, 408–12
extinction, 173
  of fear, 177
  rate of, 173
  vicarious, 211

facades
  cracking of, 576–77
facing reality, 325
factors in psychotherapy, 188–90
faiblesse de la volonté, 92
family therapy, 583–96
  theory of, 584–96
fantasies, 86, 629
fate, 120
fear, 125, 310
  and reassurance, 200–201
  as cue, 178
  as learned, 178
  extinction of, 177
  function of, 178
  innate factors of, 176
  reinforcement of, 176–77
  responses inhibiting, 177–78

feedback, 577–78
feelings
  negative, 410–11
  release of, 412
  unexpressed, 411–12
fictional finalism, 54–59
field theory, 128
figure/ground, 334–35, 349–52
  in neurosis, 349–52
fixation, 15–16, 358
fixed-role sketch, 375–79
forces, 158–61
  constructive, 158–61
foresight, 129
free association, 8–12, 191
frustration, 18–20, 139–40
  existential, 258–59
functional relationships, 388

game, 472, 483–84
  analysis, 472, 483–84
  defined, 473
games people play, 484
generalization, 170, 173–74
gestalt
  analysis, 334–35
  concepts, 339–41
gestalt psychotherapy, 330–65
  principles of, 337–47
goals, 157–58
group
  analytic, 522–24
  fixity, 516
  hypnosis, 632–33
  motility, 516
  para-analytic, 524–29
  play, 519–21
  psychotherapy, 472–596
  transitional, 518–19
group psychotherapy, 472–596
  analytic, 513–29
  conjoint family, 583–96
  encounter, 568–82
  family, 583–96
  milieu, 530–67
  psychodrama, 486–512
  transactional analysis, 472–85
guidance counseling, 598–601
  group, 606–8
  individual, 606–8
  tests in, 606
  vocational, 604–6
guilt, 364
  existential, 271

hallucination, 185, 628–29
here-and-around-us reality, 331

hermeneutics, 87
higher mental processes, 178–80
  cue-producing responses in, 179
  gains from, 196–97
  restoring, 196–97
  social training of, 179–80
hostility, 364
humanity
  fullness of, 432–33
human relations, 142–43
hyperintention, 261–62
hyperreflection, 261–62
hyperthyroidism, 262
hypnosis, 29
  depth of, 625–26
  devices in, 627–28
  susceptibility to, 625
  technique of, 625
hypnotherapy, 624–44
hypnotic
  drugs, 628
  sessions, 626–27
hysteria, 6, 184

id, 36–37, 347–49
ideal self, 387
identification, 427
incentive, 210
individuality, 83
individuation, 427
  process, 81, 113–14
inhibition, 177–78, 188, 213–33
  increased, 198–99
  of fear, 177–78
insight
  achievement of, 412–13
instincts, 36–37
intentionality, 419
interference theory of psychotherapy,
    234–47
interpersonal
  psychotherapy, 123–40
  situations, 139
  theory, 125–33
interview, 382
  stages of, 464–67
intrapsychic processes, 142–43

labeling, 193–94
language, 474–75
law
  of movement, 74–75
  sociodynamic, 511
learning, 169–75
  approaches to psychotherapy, 168–247
  fundamentals of, 172–75
  in assertion structural therapy, 243–47

no trial, 208–9
  observational, 208
  of fear, 178
  theory, 215–18, 243–47
  vicarious, 212
libidinal bond, 116
libido, 29–32, 81, 520
life
  history, 432
  style, 74–75
logotherapy, 250–71
  characteristics of, 252–57
  meaning of, 252–57
love, 119–20, 341

manifest-anxiety, 141
maternal function, 72–74
mechanisms, 354–59
  confluence, 356, 359
  egotism, 356
  introjection, 356, 359
  projection, 105, 356, 359
  reaction-formation, 357
  repression, 357
  retroflection, 356, 359
  sublimation, 357
memory, 71–72
mental
  disorder, 82, 86–89
  freedom, 201–2
method
  dialectical, 111–14
  word association, 81, 107–11
milieu therapy, 530–67
  activities, 542–49
  postulates of, 538–62
  treatment, 557–62
mirror technique, 512
Mitwelt, 429, 437
modeling, 206–12
  effects, 207–8
  influences, 207–8
  patterns, 209–10
Morita therapy, 303–23
  criticism of, 319–23
  development of, 304–6
  origin of, 304–6
  practice of, 312–17
  principles of, 312–17
  recovery through, 317–19
motivation, 303–23

narcosynthesis, 628
nature
  human, 389
need
  to be cared for, 325–26

to be loved, 326
  to love, 326
negative feelings, 410–11
nervosity, 303, 306–8, 310
  classification of, 307–8
neurasthenia, 308
neurosis, 120–21, 169–75, 357–58, 362–63
  analysis of, 352–53
  and learning theory, 169–78
  anxiety, 308, 633–34
  as ego-function loss, 349–52
  as learned, 181–88
  compulsion, 636–38
  conversion, 634–35
  cultural basis of, 142–43
  existential, 429
  factors in, 187
  gestalt therapy of, 427
  Horney's theory of, 142–58
  noogenic, 255
  obsessive-compulsive, 263
  paroxysmal, 308
  social conditions of, 181–82
  theory of, 142–58
  traumatic, 638–40
neurotic
  conflict, 171–72
  misery, 172
  needs, 154–55
  self-idealization, 148–49
  striving, 54–59
  symptoms, 171–72
neutralizer, 516
nondirective counseling, 382–422
  characteristics of, 391–92
  synopsis of, 391–92
nondirective psychotherapy, 391–422
  characteristics of, 391–92
nongenetic psychotherapy, 457–59
nonrational psychotherapy, 256–57
noogenic neurosis, 255–60, 264
noology, 254–56
no-trial learning therapy, 208–9

obedience to nature, 311–12
object-cathexis, 3
object-imago, 82
observational learning, 208
obsession, 308
obsessive-compulsive neurosis, 263
Oedipus complex, 3, 35–37, 147
organ inferiority, 60–62
organism, 332–34
organism-as-a-whole, 331
organism/environment field, 334
outcome patterns, 139–40
overcompensation, 62–64
over restraint, 188

paradoxical intention, 260, 262, 264–71
parataxic distortion, 135–36
pastimes, 473, 483
patient, 103–5
patterns of modeling, 209–10
peak-experience, 263
penis-envy complex, 145
perception, 419
    distortion of, 419
permissiveness, 200, 535–37
persona, 82–83
personal construct psychology, 364–69
    diagnostic constructs, 368–69, 373
    formal aspects of, 367–69
    postulates, 366–67
    transitional constructs, 369–70
personality, 347–49
    development, 35–37, 332–33
    gestalt, 332–33
    theory, 35–42, 82–83, 127–28, 414–22
personal unconscious, 97
phenomenological psychotherapy, 250–71,
        382–470
phenomenology, 431
philosophical psychotherapy, 286–302
    character of, 290–92
    defined, 288–89
    effectiveness of, 291–92
    existential, 297–302
    technique of, 292–97
phobia, 308
play, 342–43
positive
    outlook, 202
    regard, 383, 386, 391, 415–16, 422
presence, 438–42
pride system, 143–44, 157–58
process
    attentional, 209
    higher mental, 178–79
    loci of, 462
    motivational, 210
    of psychotherapy, 459–70
    primary, 36–37
    retention, 209
    vicarious, 206–12
projection, 105, 185–186
psyche, 82
    collective, 82–84
psychiatric interview, 132–35
    defined, 134
    interruption of, 137
    stages of, 136–38
    termination of, 137
psychiatrist
    as participant observer, 135

psychiatry, 128–35
psychoanalysis, 2–42
psychodrama, 486–512
    à deux, 507
    and psychoanalysis, 506–8
    defined, 493
    glossary of, 509–12
psychogenesis
    of schizophrenia, 91–95
psychological types, 81
psychonoetic antagonism, 271
psychosis, 40–42, 95–96
    hypnosis in, 643–44
psychotherapist
    prerequisites of, 201–2
psychotherapy
    activity, 513, 524–29
    activity-interview, 513
    agent, 121–22
    aim of, 442–44
    analytical, 80–114
    as aid to reconstruction, 370–73
    as a vicarious process, 206–12
    as a maternal function, 72–74
    as modeling, 206–12
    assertion-structured, 234–47
    aversion, 232–33
    behavior, 206–33
    by behavior modification, 207–33
    by reciprocal inhibition, 213–33
    client-centered, 382–422
    closing phases of, 413
    cognitive, 250–379
    constructive alternativism, 303–323
    counseling, 50–54
    dynamic, 2–165
    end phase, 121–22
    existential, 297–302, 382–470, 423–48
    experiential, 449–70
    explicit, 455–57
    factors in, 188–90
    failure in, 203–5
    fixed-role, 375–79
    Freudian, 2–42
    gestalt, 330–63
    group, 472–596
    hypnotic, 624–44
    individual, 43–79
    interference, 234–47
    interpersonal, 123–40
    Jungian, 80–114
    logotherapy, 250–71
    Morita, 303–23
    motivation in, 201
    nondirective, 382–422
    nongenetic, 457–59
    nonrational, 449–70

no-trial learning, 208–9
 of adults, 79
 of children, 74–78
 of compulsion neurosis, 70
 of neurosis, 66–70
 para-analytic, 513
 personal construct, 364–79
 phenomenological, 250–71, 382–470
 philosophical, 286–302
 practice of, 82
 process of, 459–70
 psychoanalytic, 2–165
 Rankian, 115–22
 rational-emotive, 272–83
 reality, 324–29
 self-knowledge, 155–57
 stoical, 286–97
 Sullivanian, 123–40
 supportive, 199
 technique, 47–54, 470
 termination of, 467–68
 through social usefulness, 73
 through understanding, 73–74
 Washington school of, 123–40
 will therapy, 115–22
 work, 313–14
 writing, 245–47
 Zen Buddhistic, 303–23
psychotherapy stages
 anamnestic, 464
 casting, 464
 competitive, 464–65
 core, 466
 post-interview, 468–69
 regressive, 466
 termination, 467–68
 testing, 466
 withdrawal, 467
punishment, 199–200

questionnaire
 individual psychology, 75–79

Rankian therapy, 115–22
 basis of, 117–18
rational-emotive psychotherapy, 272–83
 application to education, 281
 characteristics of, 282–83
 cognitive aspect of, 274–77
 defined, 273
 validation of, 280–81
rationalization, 184
rational psychotherapy, 451
reality principle, 37–38
reality therapy, 324–29
 characteristics of, 327–28
 procedure of, 327

 summarized, 324
 synopsis of, 328–29
realization, 311
reassurance, 200–201
 in reducing fear, 200
reciprocal emotion, 138
reciprocal inhibition, 213–33
 defined, 216
 principle of, 215–16
 psychotherapy, 213–33
reconditioning, 217
recovery, 173
 spontaneous, 173
redundancy, 239
regard
 positive, 391
regression, 16–18, 184
rehearsal, 195–96
 behavior, 220–21
 of verbal units, 195
 operations, 209
 reward for, 195–96
reinforcement, 172
 as reward, 172
 gradient in effects of, 174–75
 of fear, 176–77
 of symptoms, 190–91
 principle of, 170
 theory, 170
reintegration, 339
 process, 421–22
relationship
 therapeutic, 404–7
relaxation, 230–32
 training, 224–28
releasing expression, 408–12
repression, 8–14, 16–18, 170, 186–88
 and suppression, 186
 as learned, 186–88
 defined, 186
 increased, 198–99
re-repression, 469–70
 function of, 469–70
resistance, 8–12, 152–54
 defined, 152
response, 172
 anticipatory, 175
 as act, 172
 as thought, 172
 cue-producing, 178–79
 defined, 176
 incompatible, 197–98
 new, 210
 patterns, 210
 verbal, 194–96
response facilitation effect, 208
responsibility, 326

restraint, 202
retention processes, 209
reward, 191, 199–201, 204
    for rehearsal, 195–96
    in therapy, 199–201
role
    neutral, 515
    player, 489
    playing, 499, 511
    reversal, 511–12
    taking, 511
    test, 499
role-reversal
    technique of, 511–12

satisfaction, 129, 138
    of needs, 138
satori, 303
script analysis, 472, 484–85
self, 81, 144, 347–49, 418, 421
    development of, 415–16, 418
    ideal, 144, 387
    real, 144
self-acceptance, 119–20, 574–76
self-accusation, 271
self-actualization, 148–49, 349, 390
self-alienation, 160–61
self-concept, 389–90
self-consciousness, 303
self-determinism, 120
self-experience, 388
self-hypnosis, 632–33
self-idealization, 143–44, 148–49, 162–65
    neurotic, 148–49
self-knowledge therapy, 155–57
self-presentation, 511
    technique of, 511
self-realization, 162–65
self-regard, 386, 390, 416, 422
self-regulation, 343–44
self-structure, 390, 420
self-system, 131
self-transcendence, 256–57
shadow, 81
shinkeishitsu, 303, 306–8
    classification of, 307–8
social
    atom, 510
    control, 474
    interest, 43
    learning, 191
    neuter, 516
    training, 179–80
sociodynamic law, 511
sociogram, 509
sociometric test, 500–503, 509
    cleavage, 510

directions for, 502–3
    leader, 510
    questionnaire, 509
    score, 509
    status, 509
sociometrist, 503–6
spontaneity, 486, 487–93
    contrasted with libido, 489–90
    defined, 511
    theatre, 486
spontaneous recovery, 173
status quo, 152–54
stimulation
    electrical, 232
stimulus
    and cue, 172
    defined, 176
stoical psychotherapy, 286–97
structural analysis, 472–73
    procedure, 474–75
style of life, 74–75
suggestibility tests, 625
suggestion, 87
    posthypnotic, 629–30
    psychotherapeutic, 629–31
Sullivanian psychotherapy, 123–40
superego, 39–40
superiority
    complex, 54–59
    lust for, 62–64
supportive therapy, 199
    effects of, 199
suppression, 186
symbolic representation, 209
symbolism, 461
symbolization, 390, 418
sympathy, 200
symptom, 4, 171–72
    as learned, 182–88
    displacement, 184
    eradication of, 197–99
    hallucination, 185
    hysteria, 184
    phobia, 182–84
    projection, 185–86
    rationalization, 184
    regression, 184
    reinforcement of, 190–91
    repression, 186–88
synthesis, 158–61
symptom-dissolution, 29–32
symptom-formation, 14–15, 18
syzygy, 81

technique
    double, 512
    mirror, 512

psychotherapy, 470, 487
self-presentation, 511
tension, 124, 126, 128, 239
hunger, 129
increase of, 139–40
patterns of, 128
test
sociometric, 500–503
suggestibility, 625
thanatos, 36–37
therapeutic
agent, 121–22
attitude, 344–47
community, 530–67
experience, 116–17
postulates, 538–62
process, 150–51
rehabilitation, 557–62
relationship, 404
situation, 116
therapeutic community, 530–67
activities of, 542–49
postulates, 538–62
rehabilitation, 557–62
therapeutic intervention, 199–201
techniques of, 199–201
therapeutic process, 150–51
patient's standpoint of, 150–51
therapeutic relationship, 404
limits of, 406–7
uniqueness of, 407
therapeutics, 71–72
therapist, 120–21
neutrality of, 506
objectivity of, 506
therapy
dynamics of, 20–29
through self-knowledge, 155–57
toraware, 303, 306
training
assertive, 218–21
relaxation, 224–28
trance, 627–30
conditioning, 631
transactional
analysis, 472–85
response, 473
stimulus, 473
transactional analysis psychotherapy, 472–85
synopsis of, 474–78
transcendent function, 88–91
transference, 3, 24–29, 90–91, 104–5, 116,
192–93, 427, 453
as generalized response, 192–93
behavior, 192
neurosis, 104
transformation symbols, 81

traumatic neurosis
hypnosis in, 638–40
treatment, 83–88
ideology, 533
stages of, 101–4
types, 81
complementary, 120–21
typology, 357–58

Umwelt, 429, 442–44
unconscious, 4, 82, 338–39, 341, 448
archetypes, 81
collective, 81–84
impersonal, 82
individual, 83
mind, 81
personal, 97
understanding, 118–19

value, 157–58
therapeutic, 158
valuing process, 386–87
vector
patient, 462–63
therapist, 462–63
verbal
novelties, 194
responses, 194–96
verbalizing, 118–19
vicarious
extinction, 211
learning, 212
processes, 206–12
vocational counseling, 604–6
testing in, 605–6

Washington school, 123–40
Weltanschauung, 427
will, 120
will therapy, 115–22
basis of, 117–18
will-to-health, 118
will-to-meaning, 250, 257–58
will-to-power, 250
withdrawal, 460
word association, 81
method, 107–11
work therapy, 313–14
worth
conditions of, 390, 416–18, 421
writing therapy, 245–47

Zen Buddhistic therapy, 303–23
criticism of, 319–23
practice of, 312–17
principles of, 310–12
recovery through, 317–19